POLYBIUS

V

LCL 160

POLYBIUS

THE HISTORIES

BOOKS 16–27

TRANSLATED BY

W. R. PATON

REVISED BY

FRANK W. WALBANK

AND

CHRISTIAN HABICHT

HARVARD UNIVERSITY PRESS

CAMBRIDGE, MASSACHUSETTS

LONDON, ENGLAND

2012

Library of Congress Control Number 2009937799
CIP data available from the Library of Congress

ISBN 978-0-674-99660-1

*Composed in ZephGreek and ZephText by
Technologies 'N Typography, Merrimac, Massachusetts.
Printed on acid-free paper and bound by
The Maple-Vail Book Manufacturing Group*

CONTENTS

THE HISTORIES OF POLYBIUS

ΠΟΛΥΒΙΟΥ
FRAGMENTA LIBRI XVI

I. RES MACEDONIAE

1. Ὅτι Φίλιππος ὁ βασιλεὺς παραγενόμενος εἰς τὸ
Πέργαμον καὶ νομίζων οἷον αὐτόχειρ Ἀττάλου γενέ-
2 σθαι πᾶσαν αἰκίαν ἐναπεδείκνυτο. χαριζόμενος γὰρ
οἷον εἰ λυττῶντι τῷ θυμῷ, τὸ πλεῖον τῆς ὀργῆς οὐκ εἰς
3 τοὺς ἀνθρώπους, ἀλλ᾽ εἰς τοὺς θεοὺς διετίθετο. κατὰ
μὲν γὰρ τοὺς ἀκροβολισμοὺς εὐχερῶς αὐτὸν ἀπήρυκον
διὰ τὰς τῶν τόπων ὀχυρότητας οἱ τὸ Πέργαμον παρα-
φυλάττοντες. ἀπὸ δὲ τῆς χώρας οὐδὲν ὠφελεῖτο τῷ
4 προνενοῆσθαι τὸν Ἄτταλον ὑπὲρ τούτων ἐπιμελῶς. λοι-

---

[1] In chapters 1–12 P. discusses Philip's campaign in Asia Minor in 201. The events include the sea battles at Chius and at
Lade, Philip's attack on Pergamum (the order of these events is
hotly debated), and finally his invasion of the Rhodian Peraea
in Caria. As Chius was Attalus' first engagement against Philip,
prompted by the Rhodian admiral (9.4), and as Attalus did not
take part in the battle at Lade (10.1), it follows that Lade preceded Chius. After Philip had taken Cius the previous year, the
Rhodians considered him an enemy (15.23.10). Philip's attack on

FRAGMENTS OF BOOK XVI[1]

I. AFFAIRS OF MACEDONIA

Philip's Operations in Asia Minor

1. King Philip, on reaching Pergamon[2] and thinking he had almost given a deathblow to Attalus, showed himself capable of every kind of outrage. For yielding to anger little less than insane he spent most of his fury not on men but on the gods.[3] In the skirmishes which took place the garrison of Pergamon easily kept him at a distance owing to the strength of the town. But as he got little booty from the country owing to the care Attalus had taken to prevent

202–201 B.C.

Pergamum and his irrational anger there suggest that it was in retaliation for Attalus making war on him. This leads to the sequence Lade – Chius – Pergamum. So now also, changing his former view, F. W. Walbank, *Gnomon* 76 (2004) 77–78. There is a good map in WC 2.498. See R. M. Errington, *CAH*[2] 8 (1989), 252–254 with bibliography, and H.-U. Wiemer, *EA* 33 (2001), 1–14.

[2] For the capital of the Attalids, see W. Radt, *Pergamon. Geschichte und Bauten einer antiken Metropole* (Darmstadt 1999).

[3] As he had done at Thermum (5.11.4) and as Prusias II later did, likewise at Pergamum (32.15.3–14). For similar acts of Philip's army in Attica a year later, see Livy 31.26.9–13, with H. A. Thompson, *Hesp.* 50 (1981), 352–354.

πὸν εἰς τὰ τῶν θεῶν ἔδη καὶ τεμένη διετίθετο τὴν
ὀργήν, ὑβρίζων οὐκ Ἄτταλον, ὥς γ᾽ ἐμοὶ δοκεῖ, πολὺ
5 δὲ μᾶλλον ἑαυτόν. οὐ γὰρ μόνον ἐνεπίμπρα καὶ κατα-
σπῶν ἔρριπτε τοὺς νεὼς καὶ τοὺς βωμούς, ἀλλὰ καὶ
τοὺς λίθους ἔθραυε πρὸς τὸ μηδὲ πάλιν ἀνασταθῆναι
6 μηδὲν τῶν κατεφθαρμένων. ἐπεὶ δὲ τὸ Νικηφόριον
ἐλυμήνατο τὸ μὲν ἄλσος ἐκτεμών, τὸν δὲ περίβολον
διαρρύψας, τούς τε ναοὺς ἐκ θεμελίων ἀνέσκαψε, πολ-
7 λοὺς καὶ πολυτελεῖς ὑπάρχοντας, ὥρμησε τὰς μὲν
ἀρχὰς ἐπὶ Θυατείρων· ἐκεῖθεν δὲ ποιησάμενος τὴν
ἀναζυγὴν εἰς τὸ Θήβης πεδίον εἰσέβαλε, νομίζων εὐ-
πορήσειν λείας μάλιστα περὶ τούτους τοὺς τόπους.
8 ἀποπεσὼν δὲ καὶ ταύτης τῆς ἐλπίδος, καὶ παραγενόμενος εἰς Ἱερὰν κώμην, διεπέμπετο πρὸς Ζεῦξιν, παρακαλῶν αὐτὸν σῖτον χορηγῆσαι καὶ τὰ λοιπὰ συμ-
9 πράττειν κατὰ τὰς συνθήκας. ὁ δὲ Ζεῦξις ὑπεκρίνετο
μὲν ποιεῖν τὰ κατὰ τὰς συνθήκας, οὐκ ἐβούλετο δὲ
σωματοποιεῖν ἀληθινῶς τὸν Φίλιππον.

2. Ὁ δὲ Φίλιππος, τῶν μὲν κατὰ τὴν πολιορκίαν
ἀντιπιπτόντων αὐτῷ, τῶν δὲ πολεμίων ἐφορμούντων

---

4 The sanctuary of Athena Nicephorus; Radt (1.1), 242–243.
A new location, on the Acropolis, has now been proposed by M.
Kohl, *Rev. Arch.* 34 (2002), 227–253.

5 In northwest Lydia. See the full account in *TAM* V, pp. 306–
418 (P. Herrmann).

6 Village, later a city under the name of Hierocaesarea, between Thyatira and the Hermus River. *TAM* V, pp. 444–462 (P.
Herrmann). There was a famous sanctuary of the "Persian God-

this, he henceforth wreaked his fury on the statues and sanctuaries of the gods, outraging, in my opinion, not Attalus but rather himself. For he not only burnt and pulled down temples and altars, but even broke up the stones so that none of the things he destroyed could ever be repaired. After he had laid waste the Nicephorium[4] where he cut down the holy grove, pulled down the wall enclosing it and dug up the temples, which were numerous and splendid, from their foundations, he first proceeded to Thyatira,[5] and upon leaving that city invaded the plain of Thebe, thinking that that district would afford him plenty of booty. When he was foiled in this expectation also and reached Hiera Come,[6] he sent a message to Zeuxis,[7] begging him to supply him with corn and to support him according to the terms of the agreement. Zeuxis pretended to do this, but had no intention of giving Philip any real and substantial support of the kind.

Battle of Chios

2. Philip, as his siege[8] proved unsuccessful and as the enemy were blockading him with a considerable number

dess" (Anahita, identified by the Greeks as Artemis). L. Robert, *Hellenica* 6 (1948), 27–33.

[7] Last mentioned in 5.60.4. He was chancellor of Antiochus III and in charge of Asia Minor. Documents mentioning him were collected in 1972 in *RE* Zeuxis 381–385 by E. Olshausen and have since multiplied, with at least fourteen new documents, all from Asia Minor and dating from 213 to at least 193. They are reprinted in J. Ma, *Antiochus III and the Cities of Western Asia Minor* (Oxford 1999), 284–372.   [8] Of the city of Chius.

THE HISTORIES OF POLYBIUS

πλείοσι καταφράκτοις *ναυσίν*, ἠπορεῖτο καὶ δυσχρή-
2 στως διέκειτο περὶ τοῦ μέλλοντος. οὐκ ἐπιδεχομένων
δὲ τῶν παρόντων αἵρεσιν, ἀνήχθη παρὰ τὴν τῶν πο-
3 λεμίων προσδοκίαν· ἔτι γὰρ αὐτὸν ἤλπιζον οἱ περὶ
τὸν Ἄτταλον προσκαρτερήσειν τῇ τῶν μετάλλων
4 κατασκευῇ. μάλιστα δ' ἐσπούδαζε ποιήσασθαι τὸν
ἀνάπλουν αἰφνίδιον, πεπεισμένος καταταχήσειν καὶ
τὸ λοιπὸν ἀσφαλῶς ἤδη κομισθήσεσθαι παρὰ τὴν
5 γῆν εἰς τὴν Σάμον. διεψεύσθη δὲ παρὰ πολὺ τοῖς λο-
γισμοῖς· οἱ γὰρ περὶ τὸν Ἄτταλον καὶ Θεοφιλίσκον,
ἅμα τῷ συνιδεῖν αὐτὸν ἀναγόμενον, εἴχοντο τῶν προ-
6 κειμένων εὐθέως. συνέβη δὲ τὸν ἀνάπλουν αὐτῶν γενέσθαι διαλελυμένον, ἅτε πεπεισμένων τὸν Φίλιππον,
7 καθάπερ εἶπον, ἔτι μένειν ἐπὶ τῶν ὑποκειμένων. οὐ μὴν
ἀλλὰ χρησάμενοι ταῖς εἰρεσίαις ἐνεργῶς προσέβαλ-
λον, Ἄτταλος μὲν τῷ δεξιῷ καὶ καθηγουμένῳ τῶν πο-
8 λεμίων, Θεοφιλίσκος δὲ τοῖς εὐωνύμοις. Φίλιππος δὲ
περικαταλαμβανόμενος τοῖς καιροῖς, δοὺς τὸ σύνθημα
τοῖς ἐπὶ τοῦ δεξιοῦ καὶ παραγγείλας ἀντιπρώρρους
ποιεῖν τὰς ναῦς καὶ συμπλέκεσθαι τοῖς πολεμίοις ἐρρωμένως, αὐτὸς ὑπὸ τὰς νησίδας ἀναχωρήσας μετά
τινων λέμβων, τὰς μεταξὺ τοῦ πόρου κειμένας, ἀπ-
9 εκαραδόκει τὸν κίνδυνον. ἦν δὲ τῶν μὲν τοῦ Φιλίππου
νεῶν τὸ πλῆθος τὸ συγκαταστὰν εἰς τὸν ἀγῶνα κατάφρακτοι τρεῖς καὶ πεντήκοντα, σὺν δὲ τούτοις ἄφρα-
κτα ... λέμβοι δὲ σὺν ταῖς πρίστεσιν ἑκατὸν καὶ πεν-
τήκοντα· τὰς γὰρ ἐν τῇ Σάμῳ ναῦς οὐκ ἠδυνήθη
10 καταρτίσαι πάσας. τὰ δὲ τῶν πολεμίων σκάφη κατά-

6

of warships, found difficulty in deciding what to do. But as the situation did not admit of much choice, he put to sea contrary to the expectation of his adversaries; for Attalus[9] had expected that he would continue his mining operations. His great object was to get out to sea suddenly as he believed he would be able to outstrip the enemy and afterward proceed in safety along the coast to Samos.[10] But his calculations proved entirely fallacious. For Attalus and Theophiliscus,[11] as soon as they saw him putting to sea, at once took the requisite steps. They were sailing in loose order, since they believed, as I said, that Philip still adhered to his original intention, but nevertheless they attacked him, rowing their hardest, Attalus engaging the right and leading wing of the enemy's fleet and Theophiliscus his left. Philip, thus anticipated, after signaling to those on his right orders to turn their ships directly toward the enemy and engage him vigorously, retired himself with a few light vessels to the islands in the middle of the strait and awaited the result of the battle. Philip's fleet which took part in the battle consisted of fifty-three decked warships, . . . undecked ones, and a hundred and fifty galleys and beaked ships, for he had not been able to fit out all the ships which were at Samos. The enemy had sixty-five

[9] The king of Pergamum, last mentioned 11.7.1.

[10] Philip had conquered the island from the Ptolemies in 201. A few years later, they reconquered it, as *IG* XII 6.12 has shown.

[11] *RE* Theophiliscus 2134–2135 (F. Geyer).

φρακτα μὲν ἦν ἑξήκοντα καὶ πέντε σὺν τοῖς τῶν Βυζαντίων, μετὰ δὲ τούτων ἐννέα τριημιολίαι καὶ τριή-
ρεις τρεῖς ὑπῆρχον.

3. Λαβούσης δὲ τὴν καταρχὴν τῆς ναυμαχίας ἐκ
τῆς Ἀττάλου νεώς, εὐθέως πάντες οἱ σύνεγγυς ἀπαραγ-
2 γέλτως συνέβαλον ἀλλήλοις. Ἄτταλος μὲν οὖν συμπεσὼν ὀκτήρει, καὶ προεμβαλὼν ταύτῃ καιρίαν καὶ ὕφα-
λον πληγήν, ἐπὶ πολὺ τῶν ἐπὶ τοῦ καταστρώματος
3 ἀγωνισαμένων τέλος ἐβύθισε τὴν ναῦν. ἡ δὲ τοῦ Φιλίππου δεκήρης, ναυαρχὶς οὖσα, παραλόγως ἐγένετο
4 τοῖς ἐχθροῖς ὑποχείριος. ὑποπεσούσης γὰρ αὐτῇ τρι-
ημιολίας, ταύτῃ δοῦσα πληγὴν βιαίαν κατὰ μέσον τὸ
κύτος ὑπὸ τὸν θρανίτην σκαλμὸν ἐδέθη, τοῦ κυβερνή-
του τὴν ὁρμὴν τῆς νεὼς οὐκέτι δυνηθέντος ἀναλαβεῖν·
5 διὸ καὶ προσκρεμαμένου τοῦ πλοίου τοῖς ὅλοις ἐδυσ-
6 χρηστεῖτο καὶ δυσκίνητος ἦν πρὸς πᾶν. ἐν ᾧ καιρῷ
δύο πεντήρεις προσπεσοῦσαι, καὶ τρώσασαι τὴν ναῦν
ἐξ ἀμφοῖν τοῖν μεροῖν, καὶ τὸ σκάφος καὶ τοὺς ἐπιβάτας τοὺς ἐν αὐτῷ διέφθειραν, ἐν οἷς ἦν καὶ Δημο-
7 κράτης ὁ τοῦ Φιλίππου ναύαρχος. κατὰ δὲ τὸν αὐτὸν
καιρὸν Διονυσόδωρος καὶ Δεινοκράτης, ὄντες ἀδελφοὶ
καὶ ναυαρχοῦντες παρ' Ἀττάλῳ, συμπεσόντες ὁ μὲν
ἐπῄρει τῶν πολεμίων, ὁ δ' ὀκτήρει, παραβόλως ἐχρή-
8 σαντο τῇ ναυμαχίᾳ. Δεινοκράτης μὲν πρὸς ὀκτήρη

---

[12] Light, undecked warships; see L. Robert, *Rev. Phil.* 18
(1944), 11–17; *Hellenica* 2 (1946), 123–126.

decked warships, including those of the Byzantines, nine trihemioliae,[12] and three triremes.

3. The ship of Attalus began the battle, and all those near it at once charged without orders. Attalus engaged an "eight"[13] and ramming her first and inflicting on her a fatal blow under water, after considerable resistance on the part of the troops on her deck finally sank the ship. Philip's galley, a "ten," which was the flagship, fell by a strange chance into the hands of the enemy. Charging a trihemiolia which was in her path and ramming her with great force in the middle of her hull she stuck fast under the enemy's top bench of oars, the captain being unable to arrest the way she had on her. So that as the ship was thus hanging on to the trihemiolia she was in a most difficult position and entirely incapable of moving. Two triremes seized the opportunity to attack her, and striking her on both sides destroyed the ship and all the men on board her, among whom was Democrates,[14] Philip's admiral. Just at the same time Dionysodorus[15] and Deinocrates, who were brothers and both of them admirals of Attalus, met with equally strange experiences in the battle in engaging, one a "seven" and the other an "eight." Deinocrates engaged an "eight"

[13] Probably a large decked ship with eight men to an oar; similarly in the following: a "ten," etc.

[14] Mentioned nowhere else.

[15] He and his brother Deinocrates were citizens of Sicyon in Achaea. Dionysodorus represented King Attalus in the fall of 198 in negotiations with King Philip (18.1.3). Much earlier at Pergamum he had dedicated a statue of a dancing satyr, the work of Thoinias of Sicyon, to Dionysus and Attalus I (*SEG* 39, 1334 and much later bibliography).

συμπεσὼν αὐτὸς μὲν ἔξαλον ἔλαβε τὴν πληγήν, ἀνα-
στείρου τῆς νεὼς οὔσης, τὴν δὲ τῶν πολεμίων τρώσας
ναῦν ὑπὸ τὰ . . . βίαχα τὸ μὲν πρῶτον οὐκ ἐδύνατο
χωρισθῆναι, καίπερ πολλάκις ἐπιβαλόμενος πρύμναν
9   κρούειν· διὸ καὶ τῶν Μακεδόνων εὐψύχως ἀγωνιζομένων
10 εἰς τὸν ἔσχατον παρεγένετο κίνδυνον. Ἀττάλου δ᾽ ἐπιβοηθήσαντος αὐτῷ καὶ διὰ τῆς εἰς τὴν πολεμίαν ναῦν
ἐμβολῆς λύσαντος τὴν συμπλοκὴν τῶν σκαφῶν, ὁ
11 μὲν Δεινοκράτης ἀπελύθη παραδόξως, οἱ δὲ τῆς πολεμίας νεὼς ἐπιβάται πάντες εὐψύχως διαγωνισάμενοι
διεφθάρησαν, τὸ δὲ σκάφος ἔρημον ἀπολειφθὲν ὑπο-
12 χείριον ἐγένετο τοῖς περὶ τὸν Ἄτταλον. ὁ δὲ Διονυσόδωρος μετὰ βίας ἐπιφερόμενος εἰς ἐμβολὴν αὐτὸς μὲν
ἥμαρτε τοῦ τρῶσαι, παραπεσὼν δὲ τοῖς πολεμίοις
ἀπέβαλε τὸν δεξιὸν ταρσὸν τῆς νεώς, ὁμοῦ συρραγέν-
13 των καὶ τῶν πυργούχων. οὗ γενομένου περιέστησαν
14 αὐτὸν πανταχόθεν οἱ πολέμιοι. κραυγῆς δὲ καὶ θορύ-
βου γενομένου τὸ μὲν λοιπὸν πλῆθος τῶν ἐπιβατῶν
ἅμα τῷ σκάφει διεφθάρη, τρίτος δ᾽ αὐτὸς ὁ Διονυσόδωρος ἀπενήξατο πρὸς τὴν ἐπιβοηθοῦσαν αὐτῷ τρι-
ημιολίαν.

4. Τῶν δὲ λοιπῶν νεῶν τοῦ πλήθους ὁ κίνδυνος
2   ἐφάμιλλος ἦν· καθ᾽ ὅσον γὰρ ἐπλεόναζον οἱ παρὰ τοῦ
Φιλίππου λέμβοι, κατὰ τοσοῦτον διέφερον οἱ περὶ τὸν
3   Ἄτταλον τῷ τῶν καταφράκτων νεῶν πλήθει. καὶ τὰ
μὲν περὶ τὸ δεξιὸν κέρας τοῦ Φιλίππου τοιαύτην εἶχε
τὴν διάθεσιν ὥστ᾽ ἀκμὴν ἄκριτα μένειν τὰ ὅλα, πολὺ
δὲ τοὺς περὶ τὸν Ἄτταλον ἐπικυδεστέρας ἔχειν τὰς

and himself received his adversary's blow above water, as she was very high in the prow, but striking the enemy under ⟨the water level⟩ . . . could not at first get free of her although he repeatedly tried to back out. So that, as the Macedonians also displayed gallantry, he was in the utmost peril. But when Attalus came up to rescue him and by ramming the enemy set the two ships free, Deinocrates was unexpectedly saved, and when the troops on the enemy's ship after a gallant resistance had all perished, she herself with no one left on board was captured by Attalus. Dionysodorus charging a ship at full speed, missed her, but in passing close alongside her, lost all his right banks of oars, his turrets also being carried away. Upon this the enemy completely surrounded him, and amidst loud and excited cheers, the rest of the crew and the ship itself were destroyed, but Dionysodorus and two others swam away to a trihemiolia which was coming up to help him.

4. Among the other ordinary ships of the fleet the contest was equal; for the advantage that Philip had in the number of his galleys was balanced by Attalus' superiority in decked ships. The position of affairs on Philip's right wing was such that the result was still doubtful; but Attalus

4 ἐλπίδας. οἱ δὲ Ῥόδιοι κατὰ μὲν τὰς ἀρχὰς εὐθέως ἐκ
τῆς ἀναγωγῆς ἀπεσπάσθησαν τῶν πολεμίων, καθάπερ ἀρτίως εἶπα, τῷ δὲ ταχυναυτεῖν παρὰ πολὺ δια-
φέροντες τῶν ἐναντίων συνῆψαν τοῖς ἐπὶ τῆς οὐραγίας
5 Μακεδόσι. καὶ τὸ μὲν πρῶτον ὑποχωροῦσι τοῖς σκάφεσι κατὰ πρύμναν ἐπιφερόμενοι τοὺς ταρσοὺς παρέ-
6 λυον· ὡς δ' οἱ μὲν παρὰ τοῦ Φιλίππου συνεπιστρέφειν
ἤρξαντο παραβοηθοῦντες τοῖς κινδυνεύουσι, τῶν δὲ
Ῥοδίων οἱ καθυστεροῦντες ἐκ τῆς ἀναγωγῆς συνῆψαν
7 τοῖς περὶ τὸν Θεοφιλίσκον, τότε κατὰ πρόσωπον ἀντιπρώρρους τάξαντες τὰς ναῦς ἀμφότεροι συνέβαλον
εὐψύχως, ὁμοῦ ταῖς σάλπιγξι καὶ τῇ κραυγῇ παρακα-
8 λοῦντες ἀλλήλους. εἰ μὲν οὖν μὴ μεταξὺ τῶν καταφράκτων νεῶν ἔταξαν οἱ Μακεδόνες τοὺς λέμβους,
ῥᾳδίαν ἂν καὶ σύντομον ἔλαβε κρίσιν ἡ ναυμαχία·
νῦν δὲ ταῦτ' ἐμπόδια πρὸς τὴν χρείαν τοῖς Ῥοδίοις
9 ἐγίνετο κατὰ πολλοὺς τρόπους. μετὰ γὰρ τὸ κινηθῆναι
τὴν ἐξ ἀρχῆς τάξιν ἐκ τῆς πρώτης συμβολῆς πάντες
10 ἦσαν ἀναμὶξ ἀλλήλοις, ὅθεν οὔτε διεκπλεῖν εὐχερῶς
οὔτε στρέφειν ἐδύναντο τὰς ναῦς οὔτε καθόλου χρῆσθαι τοῖς ἰδίοις προτερήμασιν, ἐμπιπτόντων αὐτοῖς
τῶν λέμβων ποτὲ μὲν εἰς τοὺς ταρσούς, ὥστε δυσχρηστεῖν ταῖς εἰρεσίαις, ποτὲ δὲ πάλιν εἰς τὰς πρώρρας, ἔστι δ' ὅτε κατὰ πρύμναν, ὥστε παραποδίζεσθαι
καὶ τὴν τῶν κυβερνητῶν καὶ τὴν τῶν ἐρετῶν χρείαν.
11 κατὰ δὲ τὰς ἀντιπρώρρους συμπτώσεις ἐποίουν τι τε-
12 χνικόν· αὐτοὶ μὲν γὰρ ἔμπρωρα τὰ σκάφη ποιοῦντες
ἐξάλους ἐλάμβανον τὰς πληγάς, τοῖς δὲ πολεμίοις

12

was by far the most sanguine of success. The Rhodians, as I just said,[16] were at first from the moment that they put out to sea very widely separated from the enemy, but as they sailed a great deal faster they caught up the rear of the Macedonian fleet. At first they attacked the ships which were retreating before them from the stern, breaking their banks of oars. But as soon as the rest of Philip's fleet began to put about and come to the assistance of their comrades in peril and those of the Rhodians who had been the last to put to sea joined Theophiliscus, then both fleets directing their prows against each other engaged gallantly, cheering each other on with loud cries and the peal of trumpets. Now had not the Macedonians interspersed their galleys among their decked ships the battle would have been quickly and easily decided, but as it was these galleys impeded the action of the Rhodian ships in many ways. For, once the original order of battle had been disturbed in their first charge, they were utterly mixed up, so that they could not readily sail through the enemy's line nor turn their ships round, in fact could not employ at all the tactics in which they excelled, as the galleys were either falling foul of their oars and making it difficult for them to row, or else attacking them in the prow and sometimes in the stern, so that neither the pilots nor the oarsmen could serve efficiently. But in the direct charges prow to prow they employed a certain artifice. For depressing[17] the ships toward the prow themselves they received the enemy's blow above water, but piercing him below water

[16] In a lost passage preceding 2.1.

[17] The technique is not known and the passage may be corrupt.

ὕφαλα τὰ τραύματα διδόντες ἀβοηθήτους ἐσκεύαζον
13 τὰς πληγάς. σπανίως δ' εἰς τοῦτο συγκατέβαινον·
καθόλου γὰρ ἐξέκλινον τὰς συμπλοκὰς διὰ τὸ γενναίως ἀμύνεσθαι τοὺς Μακεδόνας ἀπὸ τῶν κατα-
14 στρωμάτων ἐν ταῖς συστάδην γινομέναις μάχαις. τὸ
δὲ πολὺ κατὰ μὲν τοὺς διέκπλους παρασύροντες τῶν
πολεμίων νεῶν τοὺς ταρσοὺς ἠχρείουν· μετὰ δὲ ταῦτα
πάλιν ἐκπεριπλέοντες, καὶ τοῖς μὲν κατὰ πρύμναν
ἐμβάλλοντες, τοῖς δὲ πλαγίοις καὶ στρεφομένοις
ἀκμὴν προσπίπτοντες οὓς μὲν ἐτίτρωσκον, οἷς δὲ παρ-
15 έλυον ἀεί τι τῶν πρὸς τὴν χρείαν ἀναγκαίων. καὶ δὴ
τῷ τοιούτῳ τρόπῳ μαχόμενοι παμπληθεῖς τῶν πολεμίων ναῦς διέφθειραν.

5. Ἐπιφανέστατα δ' ἐκινδύνευσαν τρεῖς πεντήρεις
τῶν Ῥοδίων, ἥ τε ναυαρχίς, ἐφ' ἧς ἔπλει Θεοφιλίσκος,
μετὰ δὲ ταύτην ἧς ἐτριηράρχει Φιλόστρατος, τρίτη δ'
ἦν ἐκυβέρνα μὲν Αὐτόλυκος, ἐπέπλει δὲ Νικόστρατος.
2 ταύτης γὰρ ἐμβαλούσης εἰς πολεμίαν ναῦν καὶ κατα-
λιπούσης ἐν τῷ σκάφει τὸν ἔμβολον, συνέβη δὴ τὴν
μὲν πληγεῖσαν αὔτανδρον καταδῦναι, τοὺς δὲ περὶ τὸν
Αὐτόλυκον, εἰσρεούσης εἰς τὴν ναῦν τῆς θαλάττης
διὰ τῆς πρώρρας, κυκλωθέντας ὑπὸ τῶν πολεμίων τὰς
μὲν ἀρχὰς ἀγωνίζεσθαι γενναίως, τέλος δὲ τὸν μὲν
Αὐτόλυκον ἐκπεσεῖν τρωθέντα μετὰ τῶν ὅπλων εἰς
3 τὴν θάλατταν, τοὺς δὲ λοιποὺς ἐπιβάτας ἀποθανεῖν
4 μαχομένους γενναίως. ἐν ᾧ καιρῷ Θεοφιλίσκος, βοη-

---

[18] The familiarity with Rhodian individuals below the rank of

produced breaches which could not be repaired. It was but seldom, however, that they resorted to this mode of attack; for as a rule they avoided closing with the enemy, as the Macedonian soldiers offered a valiant resistance from the deck in such close combats. For the most part they cut the enemy's line and put his banks of oars out of action, afterward turning and sailing round again and charging him sometimes in the stern and sometimes in flank while he was still turning; thus they made breaches in some of the ships and in others damaged some part of the necessary gear. Indeed by this mode of fighting they destroyed quite a number of the enemy's ships.

5. The most brilliant part in the battle was taken by three Rhodian quinqueremes, the flagship on board of which was Theophiliscus, that commanded by Philostratus,[18] and lastly that of which Autolycus was pilot, but on board of it was Nicostratus.[19] The latter had charged an enemy ship and left her ram in it: the ship that had been struck sank with all on board, while Autolycus and his men, the sea now pouring into the ship from the prow, were surrounded by the enemy and at first fought bravely, but finally Autolycus himself was wounded and fell into the sea in his armor, and the rest of the soldiers perished after a gallant struggle. At this moment Theophiliscus

admirals suggests a Rhodian source, Zenon, as is usually assumed; see H.-U. Wiemer, *Rhodische Traditionen in der hellenistischen Historiographie* (Frankfurt/M. 2001), 95–97.

[19] Not (*pace* WC 2.508) the Nicostratus of the Coan decree *SIG* 568. 4 (see the more complete edition *Chiron* 28 [1998], 116–121, no. 12, line 24, and the comments pp. 120–121), who is not a Rhodian, but in fact a well-known citizen of Cos.

θήσας μετὰ τριῶν πεντήρων, τὴν μὲν ναῦν οὐκ ἠδυνήθη σῶσαι διὰ τὸ πλήρη θαλάττης εἶναι, δύο δὲ ναῦς
5 πολεμίας τρώσας τοὺς ἐπιβάτας ἐξέβαλε. ταχὺ δὲ
περιχυθέντων αὐτῷ λέμβων πλειόνων καὶ καταφράκτων νεῶν, τοὺς μὲν πλείστους ἀπέβαλε τῶν ἐπιβατῶν
6 ἐπιφανῶς ἀγωνισαμένους, αὐτὸς δὲ τρία τραύματα
λαβὼν καὶ παραβόλως τῇ τόλμῃ κινδυνεύσας μόλις
ἐξέσωσε τὴν ἰδίαν ναῦν ἐπιβοηθήσαντος αὐτῷ Φιλο-
στράτου καὶ συναναδεξαμένου τὸν ἐνεστῶτα κίνδυνον
7 εὐψύχως. συνάψας δὲ τοῖς αὐτοῦ σκάφεσι πάλιν ἐξ
ἄλλης ὁρμῆς συνεπλέκετο τοῖς πολεμίοις, τῇ μὲν
σωματικῇ δυνάμει παραλυόμενος ὑπὸ τῶν τραυμάτων, τῇ δὲ τῆς ψυχῆς γενναιότητι λαμπρότερος ὢν καὶ
8 παραστατικώτερος ἢ πρόσθεν. συνέβη δὲ δύο γενέσθαι ναυμαχίας πολὺ διεστώσας ἀλλήλων· τὸ μὲν
γὰρ δεξιὸν κέρας τοῦ Φιλίππου κατὰ τὴν ἐξ ἀρχῆς
πρόθεσιν ἀεὶ τῆς γῆς ὀρεγόμενον οὐ μακρὰν ἀπεῖχε
9 τῆς Ἀσίας, τὸ δ᾽ εὐώνυμον διὰ τὸ παραβοηθῆσαι τοῖς
ἐπὶ τῆς οὐραγίας ἐξ ὑποστροφῆς οὐ πολὺ τῆς Χίας
ἀπέχον ἐναυμάχει τοῖς Ῥοδίοις.

6. Οὐ μὴν ἀλλὰ παρὰ πολὺ τοῦ δεξιοῦ κέρατος
κατακρατούντων τῶν περὶ τὸν Ἄτταλον, καὶ συνεγγι-
ζόντων ἤδη πρὸς τὰς νησίδας ὑφ᾽ αἷς ὁ Φίλιππος
2 ὥρμει καραδοκῶν τὸ συμβησόμενον, συνιδὼν Ἄτταλος
μίαν πεντήρη τῶν ἰδίων ἐκτὸς τοῦ κινδύνου τετρωμένην καὶ βαπτιζομένην ὑπὸ νεὼς πολεμίας, ὥρμησε
3 παραβοηθήσων ταύτῃ μετὰ δύο τετρήρων. τοῦ δὲ πο-
λεμίου σκάφους ἐγκλίναντος καὶ ποιουμένου τὴν ἀπο-

16

came up to help with three quinqueremes, and though he could not save the ship as she was full of water, rammed two of the enemy's ships and forced the troops on board to take to the water. He was rapidly surrounded by a number of galleys and decked ships, and after losing most of his soldiers, who fought splendidly, and receiving himself three wounds and displaying extraordinary courage, just managed to save his own ship, Philostratus coming up to his succor and taking a gallant part in the struggle. Theophiliscus now joined his other ships and again fell upon the enemy, weak in body from his wounds, but more magnificent and desperate than ever in bravery of spirit. There were now two distinct battles in progress at a considerable distance from each other. For Philip's right wing, following out his original plan, continued to make for the shore and were not far away from the continent, while his left as it had put about to assist the rear was fighting with the Rhodians at a short distance from the island of Chios.

6. Attalus, however, by this time had a distinct advantage over the Macedonian right wing and had approached the islands under which Philip lay awaiting the result of the battle. He had observed one of his own quinqueremes rammed by an enemy ship and lying in a sinking condition out of the general action, and he hastened to her assistance with two quadriremes. When the enemy vessel gave way and retired toward the land he followed her up with more

χώρησιν ὡς πρὸς τὴν γῆν, ἐπέκειτο φιλοτιμότερον,

4 ἐγκρατὴς γενέσθαι σπουδάζων τῆς νεώς. ὁ δὲ Φίλιππος, συνθεασάμενος ἀπεσπασμένον πολὺ τὸν Ἄτταλον
ἀπὸ τῶν ἰδίων, παραλαβὼν τέτταρας πεντήρεις καὶ
τρεῖς ἡμιολίας, ἔτι δὲ τῶν λέμβων τοὺς ἐγγὺς ὄντας,
ὥρμησε, καὶ διακλείσας τὸν Ἄτταλον ἀπὸ τῶν οἰκείων
νεῶν ἠνάγκασε μετὰ μεγάλης ἀγωνίας εἰς τὴν γῆν

5 ἐκβαλεῖν τὰ σκάφη. τούτου δὲ συμβάντος αὐτὸς μὲν
ὁ βασιλεὺς μετὰ τῶν πληρωμάτων εἰς τὰς Ἐρυθρὰς
ἀπεχώρησε, τῶν δὲ πλοίων καὶ τῆς βασιλικῆς κατα-

6 σκευῆς ἐγκρατὴς ὁ Φίλιππος ἐγένετο. καὶ γὰρ ἐποίη-
σάν τι τεχνικὸν ἐν τούτοις τοῖς καιροῖς οἱ περὶ τὸν
Ἄτταλον· τὰ γὰρ ἐπιφανέστατα τῆς βασιλικῆς κατα-

7 σκευῆς ἐπὶ τὸ κατάστρωμα τῆς νεὼς ἐξέβαλον. ὅθεν
οἱ πρῶτοι τῶν Μακεδόνων, συνάψαντες ἐν τοῖς λέμ-
βοις, συνθεασάμενοι ποτηρίων πλῆθος καὶ πορφυρῶν
ἱματίων καὶ τῶν τούτοις παρεπομένων σκευῶν, ἀφέμε-
νοι τοῦ διώκειν ἀπένευσαν ἐπὶ τὴν τούτων ἁρπαγήν.

8 διὸ συνέβη τὸν Ἄτταλον ἀσφαλῆ ποιήσασθαι τὴν

9 ἀποχώρησιν εἰς τὰς Ἐρυθράς. Φίλιππος δὲ τοῖς μὲν
ὅλοις ἡλαττωμένος παρὰ πολὺ τὴν ναυμαχίαν, τῇ δὲ
περιπετείᾳ τῇ κατὰ τὸν Ἄτταλον ἐπαρθείς, ἐπανέπλει,
καὶ πολὺς ἦν συναθροίζων τὰς σφετέρας ναῦς καὶ
παρακαλῶν τοὺς ἄνδρας εὐθαρσεῖς εἶναι, διότι νικῶσι

10 τῇ ναυμαχίᾳ· καὶ γὰρ ὑπέδραμέ τις ἔννοια καὶ πιθα-
νότης τοῖς ἀνθρώποις ὡς ἀπολωλότος τοῦ <βασιλέως>
Ἀττάλου διὰ τὸ κατάγειν τοὺς περὶ τὸν Φίλιππον

11 ἀναδεδεμένους τὴν βασιλικὴν ναῦν. ὁ δὲ Διονυσόδω-

energy, hoping to capture her. Philip now, seeing that Attalus was widely separated from his own fleet, took four quinqueremes and three hemioliae and such galleys as were near him and, intercepting the return of Attalus to his own fleet, compelled him in great disquietude to run his ships ashore. After this the king and the crews escaped to Erythrae,[20] but Philip gained possession of the ships and the royal furniture. Attalus indeed resorted to an artifice on this occasion by causing the most splendid articles of his royal furniture to be exposed on the deck of his ship, so that the Macedonians who were the first to reach it in their galleys, when they saw such a quantity of cups, purple cloaks, and other objects to match, instead of continuing the pursuit turned aside to secure this booty, so that Attalus made good his retreat to Erythrae. Philip had been on the whole decidedly worsted[21] in the battle, but elated by the misfortune that had befallen Attalus, he put to sea again and set busily about collecting his ships and bade his men be of good cheer as the victory was theirs. In fact a sort of notion or half belief spread among them that Attalus had perished, as Philip was returning with the royal ship in tow. Dionysodorus, however, guessing what had

[20] On the mainland opposite Chius.
[21] An exaggeration.

ρος ὑπονοήσας τὸ περὶ τὸν αὑτοῦ βασιλέα γεγονός,
ἤθροιζε τὰς οἰκείας ναῦς ἐξαίρων σύνθημα· ταχὺ δὲ
συλλεχθεισῶν πρὸς αὐτὸν ἀπέπλει μετ᾽ ἀσφαλείας
12 εἰς τοὺς κατὰ τὴν Ἀσίαν ὅρμους. κατὰ δὲ τὸν αὐτὸν
καιρὸν οἱ πρὸς τοὺς Ῥοδίους ἀγωνιζόμενοι τῶν Μακεδόνων, πάλαι κακῶς πάσχοντες, ἐξέλυον αὑτοὺς ἐκ
τοῦ κινδύνου μετὰ προφάσεως κατὰ μέρη ποιούμενοι
τὴν ἀποχώρησιν, ὡς ταῖς οἰκείαις σπεύδοντες ἐπικου-
13 ρῆσαι ναυσίν. οἱ δὲ Ῥόδιοι, τὰς μὲν ἀναδησάμενοι
τῶν νεῶν, τὰς δὲ προδιαφθείραντες ταῖς ἐμβολαῖς, ἀπέπλευσαν εἰς τὴν Χίον.

7. Ἐφθάρησαν δὲ τοῦ μὲν Φιλίππου ναῦς ἐν μὲν
τῇ πρὸς Ἄτταλον ναυμαχίᾳ δεκήρης, ἐννήρης, ἑπτή-
ρης, ἑξήρης, τῶν δὲ λοιπῶν κατάφρακτοι μὲν δέκα καὶ
τριημιολίαι τρεῖς, λέμβοι δὲ πέντε καὶ εἴκοσι καὶ τὰ
2 τούτων πληρώματα· ἐν δὲ τῇ πρὸς Ῥοδίους διεφθάρησαν κατάφρακτοι μὲν δέκα, λέμβοι δὲ περὶ τετταράκοντα τὸν ἀριθμόν· ἥλωσαν δὲ δύο τετρήρεις καὶ λέμ-
3 βοι σὺν τοῖς πληρώμασιν ἑπτά. τῶν δὲ παρ᾽ Ἀττάλου
κατέδυσαν μὲν τριημιολία μία καὶ δύο πεντήρεις,
⟨ἥλωσαν δὲ δύο τετρήρεις⟩ καὶ τὸ τοῦ βασιλέως σκά-
4 φος. τῶν δὲ Ῥοδίων διεφθάρησαν μὲν δύο πεντήρεις
5 καὶ τριήρης, ἥλω δ᾽ οὐδέν. ἄνδρες δὲ τῶν μὲν Ῥοδίων
ἀπέθανον εἰς ἑξήκοντα, τῶν δὲ παρ᾽ Ἀττάλου πρὸς
ἑβδομήκοντα, τῶν δὲ τοῦ Φιλίππου Μακεδόνες μὲν εἰς
τρισχιλίους, τῶν δὲ πληρωμάτων εἰς ἑξακισχιλίους.
6 ἑάλωσαν δὲ ζωγρίᾳ τῶν μὲν συμμάχων καὶ Μακεδόνων εἰς δισχιλίους, τῶν δ᾽ Αἰγυπτίων εἰς ἑπτακο-
σίους.

20

happened to his sovereign, began to collect his own vessels by hoisting a signal, and when they had rapidly assembled round him sailed safely away to the harbor on the mainland. At the same time the Macedonians, who were engaged with the Rhodians and had long been in distress, abandoned the scene of battle, retreating in groups on the pretense that they were hastening to the assistance of their own ships. The Rhodians, taking some of the enemy's ships in tow and sinking others with their rams before their departure, sailed off to Chios.

7. Of Philip's ships there were sunk[22] in the battle with Attalus one "ten," one "nine," one "seven," and one "six," and of the rest of his fleet ten decked ships, three trihemioliae, and twenty-five galleys with their crews. In his battle with the Rhodians he lost ten decked ships and about forty galleys sunk and two quadriremes and seven galleys with their crews captured. Out of Attalus' fleet one trihemiolia and two quinqueremes were sunk, two quadriremes and the royal ship were taken. Of the Rhodian fleet two quinqueremes and a trireme were sunk, but not a single ship captured. The loss of life among the Rhodians amounted to about sixty men and in Attalus' fleet to about seventy, while Philip lost about three thousand Macedonian soldiers and six thousand sailors. About two thousand of the allies and Macedonians and about seven hundred Egyptian crew members[23] were taken prisoners.

---

[22] On the losses on both sides, see WC 2.509–510; the Rhodian source gives too small figures for the allies.

[23] That is, crewmembers of the Ptolemaic navy captured and integrated into his own forces by Philip when he took Samos.

8. Καὶ τὸ μὲν τέλος τῆς περὶ Χίον ναυμαχίας τοι-
2 οῦτον συνέβη γενέσθαι, τῆς δὲ νίκης ὁ Φίλιππος
ἀντεποιεῖτο κατὰ δύο προφάσεις, κατὰ μίαν μέν, ᾗ τὸν
Ἄτταλον εἰς τὴν γῆν ἐκβαλὼν ἐγκρατὴς τῆς νεὼς ἐγεγόνει, καθ᾽ ἑτέραν δ᾽, ᾗ καθορμισθεὶς ἐπὶ τὸ καλούμενον Ἄργεννον ἐδόκει πεποιῆσθαι τὸν ὅρμον ἐπὶ τῶν
3 ναυαγίων. ἀκόλουθα δὲ τούτοις ἔπραττε καὶ κατὰ τὴν
ἑξῆς ἡμέραν συνάγων τὰ ναυάγια καὶ τῶν νεκρῶν
ποιούμενος ἀναίρεσιν τῶν ἐπιγινωσκομένων, χάριν
4 τοῦ συναύξειν τὴν προειρημένην φαντασίαν. ὅτι γὰρ
οὐδ᾽ αὐτὸς ἐπέπειστο νικᾶν, ἐξήλεγξαν αὐτὸν οἵ τε
5 Ῥόδιοι καὶ Διονυσόδωρος μετ᾽ ὀλίγον· κατὰ γὰρ τὴν
ἐπιοῦσαν ἡμέραν ἔτι περὶ ταῦτα γινομένου τοῦ βασιλέως διαπεμψάμενοι πρὸς ἀλλήλους ἐπέπλευσαν
αὐτῷ, καὶ στήσαντες ἐν μετώπῳ τὰς ναῦς, οὐδενὸς ἐπ᾽
αὐτοὺς ἀνταναγομένου πάλιν ἀπέπλευσαν εἰς τὴν
6 Χίον. ὁ δὲ Φίλιππος, οὐδέποτε τοσούτους ἄνδρας ἀπο-
λωλεκὼς οὔτε κατὰ ⟨γῆν οὔτε κατὰ⟩ θάλατταν ἑνὶ
καιρῷ, βαρέως μὲν ἔφερε τὸ γεγονὸς καὶ τὸ πολὺ τῆς
7 ὁρμῆς αὐτοῦ παρῄρητο, πρὸς μέντοι γε τοὺς ἐκτὸς
ἐπειρᾶτο κατὰ πάντα τρόπον ἐπικρύπτεσθαι τὴν αὐτοῦ διάληψιν, καίπερ οὐκ ἐώντων αὐτῶν τῶν πραγμά-
8 των. χωρὶς γὰρ τῶν ἄλλων καὶ τὰ μετὰ τὴν μάχην
9 συμβαίνοντα πάντας ἐξέπληττε τοὺς θεωμένους· γενομένης γὰρ τοσαύτης φθορᾶς ἀνθρώπων, παρ᾽ αὐτὸν
μὲν τὸν καιρὸν πᾶς ὁ πόρος ἐπληρώθη νεκρῶν, αἵ-
ματος, ὅπλων, ναυαγίων, ταῖς δ᾽ ἑξῆς ἡμέραις τοὺς
αἰγιαλοὺς ἦν ἰδεῖν φύρδην σεσωρευμένους ἀναμὶξ

8. Such was the result of the battle of Chios. Philip claimed the victory on two pretenses, the first being that he had driven Attalus ashore and captured his ship, and the second that by anchoring off the place called Argennum[24] he had to all appearance anchored among the wreckage. Next day also he pursued the same line of conduct, collecting the wreckage and picking up the dead bodies that were recognizable,[25] in order to give force to his imaginary claim; but that he did not himself believe in his victory was clearly proved by the Rhodians and Dionysodorus in a very short time. For on the following day, while the king was still thus occupied, they communicated with one another and sailing against him drew up their ships facing him, and upon no one responding to their challenge, sailed back again to Chios. Philip, who had never lost so many men in a single battle by land or by sea, felt the loss deeply, and his inclination for the war was much diminished, but he did his best to conceal his view of the situation from others, although the facts themselves did not admit of this. For, other things apart, the state of things after the battle could not fail to strike all who witnessed it with horror. There had been such a destruction of life that during the actual battle the whole strait was filled with corpses, blood, arms, and wreckage, and on the days which followed quantities of all were to be seen lying in confused

[24] Modern Asprokavo at the southwestern promontory of the Erythrean peninsula.

[25] As being from his forces, not the enemy's.

10 πάντων τῶν προειρημένων. ἐξ ὧν οὐ μόνον αὐτός,
ἀλλὰ καὶ πάντες οἱ Μακεδόνες εἰς διατροπὴν ἐνέπιπτον
οὐ τὴν τυχοῦσαν.

9. Θεοφιλίσκος δὲ μίαν ἡμέραν ἐπιβιώσας, καὶ τῇ
πατρίδι γράψας ὑπὲρ τῶν κατὰ τὴν ναυμαχίαν, καὶ
Κλεωναῖον ἡγεμόνα συστήσας ἀνθ᾽ ἑαυτοῦ ταῖς δυ-
2 νάμεσι, μετήλλαξε τὸν βίον ἐκ τῶν τραυμάτων, ἀνὴρ
καὶ κατὰ τὸν κίνδυνον ἀγαθὸς γενόμενος καὶ κατὰ
3 τὴν προαίρεσιν μνήμης ἄξιος. μὴ γὰρ ἐκείνου τολμή-
σαντος προεπιβαλεῖν τῷ Φιλίππῳ τὰς χεῖρας πάντες
ἂν καταπροεῖντο τοὺς καιρούς, δεδιότες τὴν τοῦ Φι-
4 λίππου τόλμαν. νῦν δ᾽ ἐκεῖνος ἀρχὴν πολέμου ποιήσας ἠνάγκασε μὲν τὴν αὐτοῦ πατρίδα συνεξαναστῆναι
τοῖς καιροῖς, ἠνάγκασε δὲ τὸν Ἄτταλον μὴ μέλλειν
καὶ παρασκευάζεσθαι τὰ πρὸς τὸν πόλεμον, ἀλλὰ
5 πολεμεῖν ἐρρωμένως καὶ κινδυνεύειν. τοιγαροῦν εἰκότως αὐτὸν οἱ Ῥόδιοι καὶ μεταλλάξαντα τοιαύταις ἐτί-
μησαν τιμαῖς δι᾽ ὧν οὐ μόνον τοὺς ζῶντας, ἀλλὰ καὶ
τοὺς ἐπιγενομένους ἐξεκαλέσαντο πρὸς τοὺς ὑπὲρ τῆς
πατρίδος καιρούς.

(1a) 10. Ὅτι μετὰ τὸ συντελεσθῆναι τὴν περὶ τὴν Λάδην
ναυμαχίαν καὶ τοὺς μὲν Ῥοδίους ἐκποδὼν γενέσθαι,
τὸν δ᾽ Ἄτταλον μηδέπω συμμεμιχέναι, δῆλον ὡς ἐξῆν
γε τελεῖν τῷ Φιλίππῳ τὸν εἰς τὴν Ἀλεξάνδρειαν
πλοῦν. ἐξ οὗ δὴ καὶ μάλιστ᾽ ἄν τις καταμάθοι τὸ μα-
νιώδη γενόμενον Φίλιππον τοῦτο πρᾶξαι.

24

heaps on the neighboring beaches. This created a spirit of no ordinary dejection not only in Philip, but in all the Macedonians.

9. Theophiliscus survived for one day, and after writing a dispatch to his country about the battle and appointing Cleonaeus[26] to replace him in command, died of his wounds. He had proved himself a man of great bravery in the fight and a man worthy of remembrance for his resolution. For had he not ventured to assail Philip in time all the others would have thrown the opportunity away, intimidated by that king's audacity. But as it was, Theophiliscus by beginning hostilities obliged his own countrymen to rise to the occasion and obliged Attalus not to delay until he had made preparations for war, but to make war vigorously and give battle. Therefore very justly the Rhodians paid such honors to him after his death as served to arouse not only in those then alive but in their posterity a spirit of devotion to their country's interests.

10. After the sea fight at Lade[27] was over, the Rhodians being out of the way and Attalus having not yet joined, it was evidently quite possible for Philip to sail to Alexandria. This is the best proof that Philip had become like a madman when he acted thus.

[26] Remembered in a later inscription (*SIG* 673, 12) as the admiral at this time.   [27] Small island off the coast of Miletus, the site of another sea battle three hundred years earlier (Hdt. 6.7–17). In 201 Philip had obviously the upper hand, as the result opened the way to Alexandria for him. The remark proves the MS reading in 3.2.8 to be correct: P. was convinced that Philip's goal was to conquer Egypt. Chapter 15 confirms that Philip had won the engagement.

2 Τί οὖν ἦν τὸ τῆς ὁρμῆς ἐπιλαβόμενον; οὐδὲν ἕτερον
3 ἀλλ' ἡ φύσις τῶν πραγμάτων. ἐκ πολλοῦ μὲν γὰρ
ἐνίοτε πολλοὶ τῶν ἀδυνάτων ἐφίενται διὰ τὸ μέγεθος
τῶν προφαινομένων ἐλπίδων, κρατούσης τῆς ἐπιθυμίας
4 τῶν ἑκάστου λογισμῶν· ὅταν δ' ἐγγίσωσι τοῖς ἔργοις,
οὐδενὶ λόγῳ πάλιν ἀφίστανται τῶν προθέσεων, ἐπι-
σκοτούμενοι καὶ παραλογιζόμενοι τοῖς λογισμοῖς διὰ
τὴν ἀμηχανίαν καὶ τὴν δυσχρηστίαν τῶν ἀπαντω-
μένων.

11. Μετὰ ταῦτα δὲ ποιησάμενος ὁ Φίλιππός τινας
ἀπράκτους προσβολὰς διὰ τὴν ὀχυρότητα τοῦ πολί-
σματος αὖθις ἀπεχώρει, πορθῶν τὰ φρούρια καὶ τὰς
2 κατὰ τὴν χώραν συνοικίας. ὅθεν ἀπαλλαττόμενος
προσεστρατοπέδευσε τῇ Πρινασσῷ. ταχὺ δὲ γέρρα
καὶ τὴν τοιαύτην ἑτοιμάσας παρασκευὴν ἤρξατο πο-
3 λιορκεῖν διὰ τῶν μετάλλων. οὔσης δ' ἀπράκτου τῆς
ἐπιβολῆς αὐτῷ διὰ τὸ πετρῶδη τὸν τόπον ὑπάρχειν
4 ἐπινοεῖ τι τοιοῦτον. τὰς μὲν ἡμέρας ψόφον ἐποίει κατὰ
γῆς, ὡς ἐνεργουμένων τῶν μετάλλων, τὰς δὲ νύκτας
ἔξωθεν ἔφερε χοῦν καὶ παρέβαλλε παρὰ τὰ στόμια
τῶν ὀρυγμάτων, ὥστε διὰ τοῦ πλήθους τῆς σωρευομέ-
νης γῆς στοχαζομένους καταπλαγεῖς γενέσθαι τοὺς
5 ἐν τῇ πόλει. τὰς μὲν οὖν ἀρχὰς ὑπέμενον οἱ Πρινασσεῖς
εὐγενῶς· ἐπεὶ δὲ προσπέμψας ὁ Φίλιππος ἐνεφάνιζε
διότι πρὸς δύο πλέθρα τοῦ τείχους αὐτοῖς ἐξήρεισται,
καὶ προσεπυνθάνετο πότερα βούλονται λαβόντες τὴν
ἀσφάλειαν ἐκχωρεῖν ἢ μετὰ τῆς πόλεως συναπολέ-

What was it then that arrested his impulse? Simply the nature of things. For at a distance many men at times strive after impossibilities owing to the magnitude of the hopes before their eyes, their desires getting the better of their reason: but when the hour of action approaches they abandon their projects again without any exercise of reason, their faculty of thought being confused and upset by the insuperable difficulties they encounter.

Capture of Prinassus

11. After this Philip, having delivered several assaults which proved futile owing to the strength of the place, again withdrew, sacking the small forts and country residences, and when he had desisted from this, sat down before Prinassus.[28] Having soon prepared penthouses and other materials he began to besiege it by mining. But when this project proved impracticable owing to the rocky nature of the ground he hit on the following device. During the day he produced a noise underground as if the mines were going ahead, and at night he brought soil from elsewhere and heaped it round the mouths of the excavations, so that those in the town judging from the quantity of soil piled up might be alarmed. At first the Prinassians held out valiantly, but when Philip sent to inform them that about two hundred feet of their wall had been underpinned and inquired whether they wished to withdraw under promise of safety or to perish all of them with their

[28] Small city in the (subject: see n. on 18.2.3) Peraea of Rhodes. The site has not been identified.

6 σθαι πανδημεί, τῶν ἐρεισμάτων ἐμπρησθέντων, τηνικάδε πιστεύσαντες τοῖς λεγομένοις παρέδοσαν τὴν
πόλιν.

12. Ἡ δὲ τῶν Ἰασέων πόλις κεῖται μὲν ἐπὶ τῆς
Ἀσίας ἐν τῷ κόλπῳ τῷ μεταξὺ κειμένῳ τοῦ τῆς Μι-
λησίας Ποσειδίου καὶ τῆς Μυνδίων πόλεως, προσαγο-
ρευομένῳ . . ., παρὰ δὲ τοῖς πλείστοις Βαργυλιητικῷ
συνωνύμως ταῖς περὶ τὸν μυχὸν αὐτοῦ πόλεσιν ἐκ-
2 τισμέναις. εὔχονται δὲ τὸ μὲν ἀνέκαθεν Ἀργείων ἄποι-
κοι γεγονέναι, μετὰ δὲ ταῦτα Μιλησίων, ἐπαγαγομένων
τῶν προγόνων τὸν Νηλέως υἱὸν τοῦ κτίσαντος Μίλη-
τον διὰ τὴν ἐν τῷ Καρικῷ πολέμῳ γενομένην φθορὰν
αὐτῶν. τὸ δὲ μέγεθος τῆς πόλεώς ἐστι δέκα στάδια.
3 καταπεφήμισται δὲ καὶ πεπίστευται παρὰ μὲν τοῖς
Βαργυλιήταις διότι τὸ τῆς Κινδυάδος Ἀρτέμιδος
ἄγαλμα, καίπερ ὂν ὑπαίθριον, οὔτε νίφεται τὸ παρά-
4 παν οὔτε βρέχεται, παρὰ δὲ τοῖς Ἰασεῦσι τὸ τῆς
Ἀστιάδος· καὶ ταῦτά τινες εἰρήκασι καὶ τῶν συγγρα-
5 φέων. ἐγὼ δὲ πρὸς τὰς τοιαύτας ἀποφάσεις τῶν ἱστο-
ριογράφων οὐκ οἶδ᾽ ὅπως παρ᾽ ὅλην τὴν πραγματείαν
6 ἐναντιούμενος καὶ δυσανασχετῶν διατελῶ. δοκεῖ γάρ
μοι τὰ τοιαῦτα παντάπασι παιδικῆς εὐηθείας ὅσα μὴ
μόνον τῆς τῶν εὐλόγων ἐκτὸς πίπτει θεωρίας, ἀλλὰ
7 καὶ τῆς τοῦ δυνατοῦ. τὸ γὰρ φάσκειν ἔνια τῶν σωμάτων ἐν φωτὶ τιθέμενα μὴ ποιεῖν σκιὰν ἀπηλγηκυίας
ἐστὶ ψυχῆς· ὃ πεποίηκε Θεόπομπος, φήσας τοὺς εἰς τὸ

town after the underpinning had been fired, they believed what he said and surrendered the town.

12. The city of Iasus lies on the coast of Asia on the gulf situated between the Milesian Poseidion and Myndus, called by some the gulf of Iasus,[29] but usually known as the gulf of Bargylia after the names of the cities at the head of it. It claims to have been originally a colony of Argos recolonized from Miletus, the son of Neleus the founder of Miletus having been invited there by the ancient inhabitants owing to the losses they had suffered in their war with the Carians. The town has a circumference of ten stades. It is reported and believed that at Bargylia no snow nor rain ever falls on the statue of Artemis Kindyas,[30] although it stands in the open air, and the same story is told of that of Artemis Astias at Iasus.[31] This statement has even been made by some authors. But I myself throughout my whole work have consistently viewed such statements by historians with a certain opposition and repugnance. For I think that to believe things which are not only beyond the limits of probability but beyond those of possibility shows quite a childish simplicity. For instance it is a sign of a blunted intelligence to say that some solid bodies when placed in the light cast no shadow, as Theopompus

[29] On the gulf of Bargylia, west of Mylasa; see the two volumes of *I. Iasos*. Philip must have taken the city, since the Rhodians claimed it from him in 198 (18.2.3; 8.9), but both sides witnessed its falling to Antiochus in 197 (*I. Iasos,* ed. W. Blümel, 2 vols. [Cologne 1985], 4–5).   [30] The main goddess of Bargylia. The walls of her temple recently yielded several sacred laws: W. Blümel, *EA* 32 (2000), 89ff.   [31] The main goddess of Iasus; see *I. Iasos* [12. 1], vol. 2, Index, p. 230.

τοῦ Διὸς ἄβατον ἐμβάντας κατ' Ἀρκαδίαν ἀσκίους
8 γίνεσθαι. τούτῳ δὲ παραπλήσιόν ἐστι καὶ τὸ νυνὶ λε-
9 γόμενον. ὅσα μὲν οὖν συντείνει πρὸς τὸ διασῴζειν
τὴν τοῦ πλήθους εὐσέβειαν πρὸς τὸ θεῖον, δοτέον ἐστὶ
συγγνώμην ἐνίοις τῶν συγγραφέων τερατευομένοις
καὶ λογοποιοῦσι περὶ τὰ τοιαῦτα· τὸ δ' ὑπεραῖρον οὐ
10 συγχωρητέον. τάχα μὲν οὖν ἐν παντὶ δυσπαράγραφός
11 ἐστιν ἡ ποσότης, οὐ μὴν ἀπαράγραφός γε. διὸ καὶ
παρὰ βραχὺ μὲν εἰ καὶ ἀγνοεῖται καὶ ψευδοδοξεῖται,
δεδόσθω συγγνώμη, τὸ δ' ὑπεραῖρον ἀθετείσθω κατά
γε τὴν ἐμὴν δόξαν.

II. RES GRAECIAE

13. Ὅτι κατὰ τὴν Πελοπόννησον τίνα μὲν ἐξ ἀρχῆς
προαίρεσιν ἐνεστήσατο Νάβις ὁ τῶν Λακεδαιμονίων
τύραννος, καὶ πῶς ἐκβαλὼν τοὺς πολίτας ἠλευθέρωσε
τοὺς δούλους καὶ συνῴκισε ταῖς τῶν δεσποτῶν γυναιξὶ
2 καὶ θυγατράσιν, ὁμοίως δὲ καὶ τίνα τρόπον ἀναδείξας
τὴν ἑαυτοῦ δύναμιν οἷον ἄσυλον ἱερὸν τοῖς ἢ δι'
ἀσέβειαν ἢ πονηρίαν φεύγουσι τὰς ἑαυτῶν πατρίδας
ἤθροισε πλῆθος ἀνθρώπων ἀνοσίων εἰς τὴν Σπάρτην,
3 ἐν τοῖς πρὸ τούτων δεδηλώκαμεν. πῶς δὲ καὶ τίνα τρόπον κατὰ τοὺς προειρημένους καιροὺς σύμμαχος
ὑπάρχων Αἰτωλοῖς, Ἠλείοις, Μεσσηνίοις, καὶ πᾶσι

---

[32] The same story, with more detail, in Paus. 8.38.6; see *RE*
Lykaios 2244–2246 (gr. Kruse).

does when he tells us that those who enter the holy of holies of Zeus in Arcadia become shadowless.[32] The statement about these statues is very much of the same nature. In cases indeed where such statements contribute to maintain a feeling of piety to the gods among the common people we must excuse certain writers for reporting marvels and tales of the kind, but we should not tolerate what goes too far. Perhaps in all matters it is difficult to draw a limit, but a limit must be drawn. Therefore, in my opinion at least, while we should pardon slight errors and slight falsity of opinion, every statement that shows excess in this respect should be uncompromisingly rejected.

II. AFFAIRS OF GREECE

Attempt of Nabis on Messene

13. I have already narrated what was the policy initiated in the Peloponnese by Nabis the tyrant of Sparta,[33] how he sent the citizens into exile and freeing the slaves married them to their masters' wives and daughters, how again by advertising his powerful own protection as a kind of inviolable sanctuary to those who had been forced to quit their own countries owing to their impiety and wickedness he gathered round him at Sparta a host of infamous men. I will now describe how being at the time I mention the ally[34] of the Aetolians, Eleans, and Messenians, bound

[33] See 13.6–8 and nn. on 4.81.13 and 13.6.1.

[34] The alliance, dominated by the Aetolians, continued from the First Macedonian War. For Nabis' attack on Messene in 201, see *Messenien* (*RE*-Suppl. 15), 273–274 (E. Meyer). The story is continued in chapter 16.

THE HISTORIES OF POLYBIUS

τούτοις ὀφείλων καὶ κατὰ τοὺς ὅρκους καὶ κατὰ τὰς
συνθήκας βοηθεῖν, εἴ τις ἐπ᾽ αὐτοὺς ἴοι, παρ᾽ οὐδὲν
ποιησάμενος τὰς προειρημένας πίστεις ἐπεβάλετο
παρασπονδῆσαι τὴν τῶν Μεσσηνίων πόλιν, νῦν ἐροῦ-
μεν.

14. Ὅτι φησὶ Πολύβιος ἐπεὶ δέ τινες τῶν τὰς κατὰ
μέρος γραφόντων πράξεις γεγράφασι καὶ περὶ τούτων τῶν καιρῶν, ἐν οἷς τά τε κατὰ Μεσσηνίους καὶ τὰ
κατὰ τὰς προειρημένας ναυμαχίας συνετελέσθη, βού-
2 λομαι βραχέα περὶ αὐτῶν διαλεχθῆναι. ποιήσομαι δ᾽
οὐ πρὸς ἅπαντας, ἀλλ᾽ ὅσους ὑπολαμβάνω μνήμης
ἀξίους εἶναι καὶ διαστολῆς· εἰσὶ δ᾽ οὗτοι Ζήνων καὶ
3 Ἀντισθένης οἱ Ῥόδιοι. τούτους δ᾽ ἀξίους εἶναι κρίνω
διὰ πλείους αἰτίας. καὶ γὰρ κατὰ τοὺς καιροὺς γεγόνασι καὶ προσέτι πεπολίτευνται καὶ καθόλου πεποίηνται τὴν πραγματείαν οὐκ ὠφελείας χάριν, ἀλλὰ δόξης
4 καὶ τοῦ καθήκοντος ἀνδράσι πολιτικοῖς. τῷ δὲ τὰς
αὐτὰς γράφειν ἡμῖν πράξεις ἀναγκαῖόν ἐστι μὴ παρα-
σιωπᾶν, ἵνα μὴ τῷ τῆς πατρίδος ὀνόματι καὶ τῷ
δοκεῖν οἰκειοτάτας εἶναι Ῥοδίοις τὰς κατὰ θάλατταν
πράξεις, ἡμῶν ἀντιδοξούντων πρὸς αὐτοὺς ἐνίοτε,
μᾶλλον ἐπακολουθήσωσιν ἐκείνοις ἤπερ ἡμῖν οἱ φιλο-
5 μαθοῦντες. οὗτοι τοιγαροῦν ἀμφότεροι πρῶτον μὲν
τὴν περὶ Λάδην ναυμαχίαν οὐχ ἧττω τῆς περὶ Χίον,
ἀλλ᾽ ἐνεργεστέραν καὶ παραβολωτέραν ἀποφαίνουσι
καὶ τῇ κατὰ μέρος τοῦ κινδύνου χρείᾳ καὶ συντελείᾳ

by oath and treaty to come to the help of them if they were attacked, he paid no respect to these solemn obligations, but attempted to betray Messene.

Criticism of the Historians Zeno and Antisthenes

14. Since some authors of special histories have dealt with this period comprising the attempt on Messene and the sea battles I have described, I should like to offer a brief criticism of them. I shall not criticize the whole class, but those only whom I regard as worthy of mention and detailed examination. These are Zeno[35] and Antisthenes[36] of Rhodes, whom for several reasons I consider worthy of notice. For not only were they contemporary with the events they described, but they also took part in politics, and generally speaking they did not compose their works for the sake of gain but to win fame and do their duty as statesmen. Since they treated of the same events as I myself I must not pass them over in silence, lest owing to their being Rhodians and to the reputation the Rhodians have for great familiarity with naval matters, in cases where I differ from them students may be inclined to follow them rather than myself. Both of them, then, declare that the battle of Lade was not less important than that of Chios, but more severe and terrible, and that both as regards the issue of the separate contests that occurred in the fight and

---

[35] *FGrH* 523 and Wiemer (5.1), 19–27: "Polybios über Zenon." [36] *FGrH* 508. A base with his name calling him "historian" was found at Rhodes in 1960. It is of imperial date and probably comes from a bust; see V. Kontorini, Ἀνέκδοτες Ἐπιγραφὲς Ῥόδου, II (Athens 1989), 59–63 and pl. VIII b.

καὶ καθόλου φασὶ τὸ νίκημα γεγονέναι κατὰ τοὺς
6 Ῥοδίους. ἐγὼ δὲ διότι μὲν δεῖ ῥοπὰς διδόναι ταῖς
αὐτῶν πατρίσι τοὺς συγγραφέας, συγχωρήσαιμ᾽ ἄν,
οὐ μὴν τὰς ἐναντίας τοῖς συμβεβηκόσιν ἀποφάσεις
7 ποιεῖσθαι περὶ αὐτῶν. ἱκανὰ γὰρ τὰ κατ᾽ ἄγνοιαν γι-
νόμενα τοῖς γράφουσιν, ἃ διαφυγεῖν ἄνθρωπον δυσ-
8 χερές· ἐὰν δὲ κατὰ προαίρεσιν ψευδογραφῶμεν ἢ πατρίδος ἕνεκεν ἢ φίλων ἢ χάριτος, τί διοίσομεν τῶν
9 ἀπὸ τούτου τὸν βίον ποριζομένων; ὥσπερ γὰρ ἐκεῖνοι
τῷ λυσιτελεῖ μετροῦντες ἀδοκίμους ποιοῦσι τὰς αὐτῶν
συντάξεις, οὕτως οἱ πολιτικοὶ τῷ μισεῖν ἢ τῷ φιλεῖν
ἑλκόμενοι πολλάκις εἰς ταὐτὸ τέλος ἐμπίπτουσι τοῖς
10 προειρημένοις. διὸ δεῖ καὶ τοῦτο τὸ μέρος ἐπιμελῶς
τοὺς μὲν ἀναγινώσκοντας παρατηρεῖν, τοὺς δὲ γρά-
φοντας αὐτοὺς παραφυλάττεσθαι.

15. Δῆλον δ᾽ ἔστι τὸ λεγόμενον ἐκ τῶν ἐνεστώτων.
ὁμολογοῦντες γὰρ οἱ προειρημένοι διὰ τῶν κατὰ μέρος ἐν τῇ περὶ Λάδην ναυμαχίᾳ δύο μὲν αὐτάνδρους
πεντήρεις τῶν Ῥοδίων ὑποχειρίους γενέσθαι τοῖς πο-
2 λεμίοις, ἐκ δὲ τοῦ κινδύνου μιᾶς νηὸς ἐπαραμένης τὸν
δόλωνα διὰ τὸ τετρωμένην αὐτὴν θαλαττοῦσθαι, πολλοὺς καὶ τῶν ἐγγὺς τὸ παραπλήσιον ποιοῦντας ἀπο-
3 χωρεῖν πρὸς τὸ πέλαγος, τέλος δὲ μετ᾽ ὀλίγων κατα-
λειφθέντα τὸν ναύαρχον ἀναγκασθῆναι ταὐτὸ τοῖς
4 προειρημένοις πράττειν, καὶ τότε μὲν εἰς τὴν Μυνδίαν

---

37 This is hard to reconcile with 10.1.
38 P., while criticizing this in others, is not entirely free of it

its general result the victory lay with the Rhodians.[37] Now I would admit that authors should have a partiality for their own country but they should not make statements about it that are contrary to facts. Surely the mistakes of which we writers are guilty and which it is difficult for us, being but human, to avoid are quite sufficient; but if we make deliberate misstatements in the interest of our country or of friends or for favor, what difference is there between us and those who gain their living by their pens? For just as the latter, weighing everything by the standard of profit, make their works unreliable, so politicians, biased by their dislikes and affections, often achieve the same result. Therefore I would add that readers should carefully look out for this fault[38] and authors themselves be on their guard against it.

15. What I say will be made clear by the present case. The above authors confess that among the results of the separate actions in the battle of Lade were the following. Two Rhodian quinqueremes with their complements fell into the hands of the enemy, and when one ship after the battle raised her jury mast[39] as she had been rammed and was going down, many of those near her followed her example and retreated to the open sea, upon which the admiral, now left with only a few ships, was compelled to do likewise. The fleet reached the coast of Myndus[40] and,

himself; see, for instance, the n. on 5.106.6 and WC 2.292 (on 11.16.4): "here writes the Achaean." In general see G. A. Lehmann, *Untersuchungen zur historischen Glaubwürdigkeit des Polybios* (Münster 1967).   [39] A nautical term for flight from a battle.   [40] City on the Halicarnassian peninsula. *RE* Myndos 1075–1079 (W. Ruge).

ἀπουρώσαντας καθορμισθῆναι, τῇ δ' ἐπαύριον ἀνα-
5 χθέντας εἰς Κῶ διᾶραι, τοὺς δὲ πολεμίους τὰς πεντήρεις ἐνάψασθαι καὶ καθορμισθέντας ἐπὶ τὴν Λάδην
ἐπὶ τῇ 'κείνων στρατοπεδείᾳ ποιήσασθαι τὴν ἔπαυλιν,
6 ἔτι δὲ τοὺς Μιλησίους, καταπλαγέντας τὸ γεγονός, οὐ
μόνον τὸν Φίλιππον, ἀλλὰ καὶ τὸν Ἡρακλείδην στε-
7 φανῶσαι διὰ τὴν ἔφοδον, ταῦτα δ' εἰρηκότες ἃ προφανῶς ἐστιν ἴδια τῶν ἡττημένων, ὅμως καὶ διὰ τῶν
κατὰ μέρος καὶ διὰ τῆς καθολικῆς ἀποφάσεως νικῶν-
8 τας ἀποφαίνουσι τοὺς Ῥοδίους, καὶ ταῦτα τῆς ἐπιστολῆς ἔτι μενούσης ἐν τῷ πρυτανείῳ τῆς ὑπ' αὐτοὺς
τοὺς καιροὺς ὑπὸ τοῦ ναυάρχου πεμφθείσης περὶ τούτων τῇ τε βουλῇ καὶ τοῖς πρυτάνεσιν, οὐ ταῖς Ἀντι-
σθένους καὶ Ζήνωνος ἀποφάσεσι ⟨συμφωνούσης⟩
ἀλλὰ ταῖς ἡμετέραις.
16. Ἑξῆς δὲ τοῖς προειρημένοις γράφουσι περὶ τοῦ
2 κατὰ Μεσσηνίους παρασπονδήματος. ἐν ᾧ φησιν ὁ
Ζήνων ὁρμήσαντα τὸν Νάβιν ἐκ τῆς Λακεδαίμονος
καὶ διαβάντα τὸν Εὐρώταν ποταμὸν παρὰ τὸν Ὁπλί-
την προσαγορευόμενον πορεύεσθαι διὰ τῆς ὁδοῦ τῆς
στενῆς παρὰ τὸ Πολιάσιον, ἕως ἐπὶ τοὺς κατὰ Σελλα-
3 σίαν ἀφίκετο τόπους· ἐντεῦθεν δ' ἐπὶ Θαλάμας ἐπι-
βαλόντα κατὰ Φαρὰς παραγενέσθαι πρὸς τὸν Πάμι-
4 σον ποταμόν. ὑπὲρ ὧν οὐκ οἶδα πῶς χρὴ λέγειν·

---

41 Doric island west of the Halicarnassian peninsula. Independent at the time, but leaning toward Rhodes. See S. Sherwin-
White, *Ancient Cos* (Göttingen 1978); C. Habicht, *Chiron* 37
(2007), 123–152.

driven by an unfavorable wind, anchored there, and next day put to sea again and crossed to Cos.[41] Meanwhile the enemy took the quinqueremes in tow and anchoring off Lade, spent the night near their own camp. They say also that the Milesians, in great alarm at what had happened, not only voted a crown to Philip for his brilliant attack, but another to Heraclides.[42] After telling us all these things, which obviously are symptoms of defeat, they nevertheless declare that the Rhodians were victorious both in the particular engagements and generally, and this in spite of the fact that the dispatch sent home by the admiral at the very time to the Rhodian senate and prytaneis, which is still preserved in the prytaneum[43] at Rhodes, does not confirm the pronouncements of Antisthenes and Zeno, but my own.

16. In the next place they speak of the treacherous attempt on Messene.[44] Here Zeno tells us that Nabis, setting out from Lacedaemon and crossing the Eurotas near the so-called Hoplites,[45] marched by the narrow road skirting Poliasion until he arrived at the district of Sellasia and thence passing Thalamae[46] reached the river Pamisus at Pharae.[47] I really am at a loss what to say about all this: for

[42] See n. on 13.4.1.

[43] The office of the *prytaneis*, for whom see n. on 13.5.1.

[44] See 13.1–3.

[45] Meaning and location are uncertain, as is the location of Poliasion.

[46] On the Messenian Gulf in Laconia. *RE* Thalamai 1187–1193 (F. Bölte).

[47] Modern Kalamata in south Messenia. *RE* Pharai 1801–1805 (F. Bölte).

τοιαύτην γὰρ φύσιν ἔχει τὰ προειρημένα πάντα συλλήβδην ὥστε μηδὲν διαφέρειν τοῦ λέγειν ὅτι ποιησά-
μενός τις ἐκ Κορίνθου τὴν ὁρμὴν καὶ διαπορευθεὶς
τὸν Ἰσθμὸν καὶ συνάψας ταῖς Σκειρωνίσιν εὐθέως ἐπὶ
τὴν Κοντοπορίαν ἐπέβαλε καὶ παρὰ τὰς Μυκήνας
ἐποιεῖτο τὴν πορείαν εἰς Ἄργος. ταῦτα γὰρ οὐχ οἷον
5 παρὰ μικρόν ἐστιν, ἀλλὰ τὴν ἐναντίαν διάθεσιν ἔχει
πρὸς ἄλληλα, καὶ τὰ μὲν κατὰ τὸν Ἰσθμόν ἐστι καὶ
τὰς Σκιράδας πρὸς ἀνατολὰς τοῦ Κορίνθου, τὰ δὲ
κατὰ τὴν Κοντοπορίαν καὶ Μυκήνας ἔγγιστα πρὸς
6 δύσεις χειμερινάς, ὥστ᾽ εἶναι τελέως ἀδύνατον ἀπὸ
τῶν προηγουμένων ἐπιβαλεῖν τοῖς προειρημένοις τό-
7 ποις. τὸ δ᾽ αὐτὸ καὶ περὶ τοὺς κατὰ τὴν Λακεδαίμονα
8 συμβέβηκεν· ὁ μὲν γὰρ Εὐρώτας καὶ τὰ περὶ τὴν
Σελλασίαν κεῖται τῆς Σπάρτης ὡς πρὸς τὰς θερινὰς
ἀνατολάς, τὰ δὲ κατὰ Θαλάμας καὶ Φαρὰς καὶ Πάμι-
9 σον ὡς πρὸς τὰς χειμερινὰς δύσεις, ὅθεν οὐχ οἷον ἐπὶ
τὴν Σελλασίαν, ἀλλ᾽ οὐδὲ τὸν Εὐρώταν δέον ἐστὶ διαβαίνειν τὸν προτιθέμενον παρὰ Θαλάμας ποιεῖσθαι
τὴν πορείαν εἰς τὴν Μεσσηνίαν.

17. Πρὸς δὲ τούτοις φησὶ τὴν ἐπάνοδον ἐκ τῆς
Μεσσήνης πεποιῆσθαι τὸν Νάβιν κατὰ τὴν πύλην
2 τὴν φέρουσαν ἐπὶ Τεγέαν. τοῦτο δ᾽ ἔστιν ἄλογον. πρόκειται γὰρ τῆς Τεγέας ἡ Μεγάλη πόλις ὡς πρὸς τὴν
Μεσσήνην, ὥστ᾽ ἀδύνατον εἶναι καλεῖσθαί τινα πύ-
3 λην παρὰ τοῖς Μεσσηνίοις ἐπὶ Τεγέαν. ἀλλ᾽ ἔστι παρ᾽
αὐτοῖς πύλη Τεγεᾶτις προσαγορευομένη, καθ᾽ ἣν
ἐποίησατο τὴν ἐπάνοδον Νάβις· ᾧ πλανηθεὶς ἔγγιον

the character of the description taken as a whole is exactly as if one were to say that a man setting out from Corinth and crossing the Isthmus and reaching the Scironic rocks at once entered the Contoporia and passing Mycenae proceeded toward Argos. For this is no slight error, but the places in question are in quite opposite quarters, the Isthmus and Scirades being to the east of Corinth while the Contoporia and Mycenae are very nearly southwest, so that it is absolutely impossible to reach the latter locality by the former. The same is the case with regard to the topography of Laconia. The Eurotas and Sellasia are northeast of Sparta, while Thalamae, Pharae, and the Pamisus are southwest. So that one who intends to march past Thalamae to Messenia not only need not go to Sellasia, but need not cross the Eurotas at all.

17. In addition to this he says that Nabis on returning from Messene quitted it by the gate leading to Tegea.[48] This is absurd, for between Messene and Tegea lies Megalopolis, so that none of the gates can possibly be called the gate leading to Tegea by the Messenians. There is, however, a gate they call the Tegean gate, by which Nabis did actually retire, and Zeno, deceived by this name, sup-

[48] This criticism is unfounded, as is the statement that Zeno was deceived.

4 ὑπέλαβε τὴν Τεγέαν εἶναι Μεσσηνίων. τὸ δ' ἔστιν οὐ
   τοιοῦτον, ἀλλ' ἡ Λακωνικὴ καὶ [ἡ] Μεγαλοπολῖτις
   χώρα μεταξὺ κεῖται τῆς Μεσσηνίας καὶ Τεγεάτιδος.
5 τὸ δὲ τελευταῖον· φησὶ γὰρ τὸν Ἀλφειὸν ἐκ τῆς πηγῆς
   εὐθέως κρυφθέντα καὶ πολὺν ἐνεχθέντα τόπον ὑπὸ
6 γῆς ἐκβάλλειν περὶ Λυκόαν τῆς Ἀρκαδίας. ὁ δὲ ποτα-
   μὸς οὐ πολὺν τόπον ἀποσχὼν τῆς πηγῆς, καὶ κρυφθεὶς
7 ἐπὶ δέκα στάδια, πάλιν ἐκπίπτει, καὶ τὸ λοιπὸν φερό-
   μενος διὰ τῆς Μεγαλοπολίτιδος τὰς μὲν ἀρχὰς ἐλα-
   φρός, εἶτα λαμβάνων αὔξησιν καὶ διανύσας ἐπιφανῶς
   πᾶσαν τὴν προειρημένην χώραν ἐπὶ διακοσίους σταδίους γίνεται πρὸς Λυκόαν, ἤδη προσειληφὼς καὶ τὸ
   τοῦ Λουσίου ῥεῦμα καὶ παντελῶς ἄβατος ὢν καὶ βα-
   ρύς. . . .
8 Οὐ μὴν ἀλλὰ καὶ πάντα μοι δοκεῖ τὰ προειρημένα
   διαπτώματα μὲν εἶναι, πρόφασιν δ' ἐπιδέχεσθαι καὶ
   παραίτησιν· τὰ μὲν γὰρ δι' ἄγνοιαν γέγονε, τὸ δὲ περὶ
   τὴν ναυμαχίαν διὰ τὴν πρὸς τὴν πατρίδα φιλοστορ-
9 γίαν. τί τις οὖν εἰκότως ἂν Ζήνωνι μέμψαιτο; διότι τὸ
   πλεῖον οὐ περὶ τὴν τῶν πραγμάτων ζήτησιν οὐδὲ περὶ
   τὸν χειρισμὸν τῆς ὑποθέσεως, ἀλλὰ περὶ τὴν τῆς λέξεως κατασκευὴν ἐσπούδακε, καὶ δῆλός ἐστι πολλάκις
   ἐπὶ τούτῳ σεμνυνόμενος, καθάπερ καὶ πλείους ἕτεροι
10 τῶν ἐπιφανῶν συγγραφέων. ἐγὼ δὲ φημὶ μὲν δεῖν
   πρόνοιαν ποιεῖσθαι καὶ σπουδάζειν ὑπὲρ τοῦ δέοντος
   ἐξαγγέλλειν τὰς πράξεις—δῆλον γὰρ ὡς οὐ μικρά,
   μεγάλα δὲ συμβάλλεται τοῦτο πρὸς τὴν ἱστορίαν—οὐ
   μὴν ἡγεμονικώτατόν γε καὶ πρῶτον αὐτὸ παρὰ τοῖς

posed that Tegea was in the neighborhood of Messene. This is not the case, but between Messenia and the territory of Tegea lie Laconia and the territory of Megalopolis. And last of all we are told that the Alpheius immediately below its source disappears and runs for a considerable distance underground, coming to the surface again near Lycoa[49] in Arcadia. The fact is that the river at no great distance from its source passes underground for about ten stades and afterward on emerging runs through the territory of Megalopolis, being at first of small volume but gradually increasing, and after traversing all that territory in full view for two hundred stades reaches Lycoa, having now been joined by the Lusius and become quite impassable, and rapid . . .

I think, however, that all the instances I have mentioned are errors indeed but admit of some explanation and excuse. Some of them are due to ignorance, and those concerning the sea battle are due to patriotic sentiment. Have we then any more valid reason for finding fault with Zeno? Yes: because he is not for the most part so much concerned with inquiry into facts and proper treatment of his material, as with elegance of style, a quality on which he, like several other famous authors, often shows that he prides himself. My own opinion is that we should indeed bestow care and concern on the proper manner of reporting events—for it is evident that this is no small thing but greatly contributes to the value of history—but we should not regard this as the first and leading object to be aimed

[49] North of Andritsaena in Arcadia. *RE* Lykaia 2229–2231 (E. Meyer).

THE HISTORIES OF POLYBIUS

11 μετρίοις ἀνδράσι τίθεσθαι· πολλοῦ γε δεῖν· ἄλλα γὰρ
ἂν εἴη καλλίω μέρη τῆς ἱστορίας, ἐφ᾽ οἷς ἂν μᾶλλον
σεμνυνθείη πολιτικὸς ἀνήρ.

18. Ὃ δὲ λέγειν βούλομαι, γένοιτ᾽ ἂν οὕτω μάλιστα
2 καταφανές. ἐξηγούμενος γὰρ ὁ προειρημένος συγ-
γραφεὺς τήν τε Γάζης πολιορκίαν καὶ τὴν γενομένην
παράταξιν Ἀντιόχου πρὸς Σκόπαν ἐν Κοίλῃ Συρίᾳ
περὶ τὸ Πάνιον, περὶ μὲν τὴν τῆς λέξεως κατασκευὴν
δῆλός ἐστιν ἐπὶ τοσοῦτον ἐσπουδακὼς ὡς ὑπερβολὴν
τερατείας μὴ καταλιπεῖν τοῖς τὰς ἐπιδεικτικὰς καὶ
πρὸς ἔκπληξιν τῶν πολλῶν συντάξεις ποιουμένοις,
3 τῶν γε μὴν πραγμάτων ἐπὶ τοσοῦτον ὠλιγώρηκεν
ὥστε πάλιν ἀνυπέρβλητον εἶναι τὴν εὐχέρειαν καὶ
4 τὴν ἀπειρίαν τοῦ συγγραφέως. προθέμενος γὰρ πρώτην διασαφεῖν τὴν τῶν περὶ τὸν Σκόπαν ἔκταξιν, τῷ
μὲν δεξιῷ κέρατί φησι τῆς ὑπωρείας ἔχεσθαι τὴν φάλαγγα μετ᾽ ὀλίγων ἱππέων, τὸ δ᾽ εὐώνυμον αὐτῆς καὶ
τοὺς ἱππεῖς πάντας τοὺς ἐπὶ τούτου τεταγμένους ἐν
5 τοῖς ἐπιπέδοις κεῖσθαι. τὸν δ᾽ Ἀντίοχον ἐπὶ μὲν τὴν
ἑωθινὴν ἐκπέμψαι φησὶ τὸν πρεσβύτερον υἱὸν Ἀντίοχον ἔχοντα μέρος τι τῆς δυνάμεως, ἵνα προκαταλά-
βηται τῆς ὀρεινῆς τοὺς ὑπερκειμένους τῶν πολεμίων
6 τόπους, τὴν δὲ λοιπὴν δύναμιν ἅμα τῷ φωτὶ διαβιβά-
σαντα τὸν ποταμὸν <τὸν> μεταξὺ τῶν στρατοπέδων ἐν

50 Sent by Agathocles in 204/3 to recruit mercenaries in
Greece (15.15.16), Scopas is now in command of the army in the
Fifth Syrian War. Antiochus besieged Gaza in 201.

42

at by sober-minded men. Not at all: there are, I think,
other excellences on which an historian who has been a
practical statesman should rather pride himself.

18. I will attempt to make my meaning clear by the
following instance. The above-mentioned author in narrating the siege of Gaza and the engagement between
Antiochus and Scopas[50] at the Panium[51] in Coele-Syria has
evidently taken so much pains about his style that the
extravagance of his language is not excelled by any of those
declamatory works written to produce a sensation among
the vulgar. He has, however, paid so little attention to facts
that his recklessness and lack of experience are again unsurpassed. Undertaking in the first place to describe Scopas' order of battle he tells us that the phalanx with a few
horsemen rested its right wing on the hills, while the left
wing and all the cavalry set apart for this purpose stood on
the level ground. Antiochus, he says, had at early dawn
sent off his elder son Antiochus[52] with a portion of his
forces to occupy the parts of the hill which commanded
the enemy, and when it was daylight he took the rest of
his army across the river which separated the two camps

---

[51] Near the source of the river Jordan, way north of Gaza.
Scopas must have driven back the Seleucid army. The battle of
Panium took place in 200. M. Holleaux, *Ét.* 3.317–331. W. Huss,
Ägypten in hellenistischer Zeit (Munich 2001), 489–492. To these
years date several documents of the dossier found at Scythopolis,
concerning Antiochus and Ptolemy, son of Thraseas (see n. on
5.65.3): *SEG* 29.1613 and 1808.

[52] Born in 220 and coregent with his father from 209 until his
death in 193.

τοῖς ἐπιπέδοις ἐκτάττειν, τιθέντα τοὺς μὲν φαλαγγίτας
ἐπὶ μίαν εὐθεῖαν κατὰ μέσην τὴν τῶν πολεμίων τάξιν,
τῶν δ᾿ ἱππέων τοὺς μὲν ἐπὶ τὸ λαιὸν κέρας τῆς φάλαγγος, τοὺς δ᾿ ἐπὶ τὸ δεξιόν, ἐν οἷς εἶναι καὶ τὴν
κατάφρακτον ἵππον, ἧς ἡγεῖτο πάσης ὁ νεώτερος Ἀν-
7 τίοχος τῶν υἱῶν. μετὰ δὲ ταῦτά φησι τὰ θηρία προ-
τάξαι τῆς φάλαγγος ἐν διαστήματι καὶ τοὺς μετ᾿
Ἀντιπάτρου Ταραντίνους, τὰ δὲ μεταξὺ τῶν θηρίων
πληρῶσαι τοῖς τοξόταις καὶ σφενδονήταις, αὐτὸν δὲ
μετὰ τῆς ἑταιρικῆς ἵππου καὶ τῶν ὑπασπιστῶν κατό-
8 πιν ἐπιστῆναι τοῖς θηρίοις. ταῦτα δ᾿ ὑποθέμενος, τὸν
μὲν νεώτερον Ἀντίοχόν φησιν, ὃν ἐν τοῖς ἐπιπέδοις
ἔθηκε κατὰ τὸ λαιὸν τῶν πολεμίων ἔχοντα τὴν κατάφρακτον ἵππον, τοῦτον ἐκ τῆς ὀρεινῆς ἐπενεχθέντα
τρέψασθαι τοὺς ἱππέας τοὺς περὶ τὸν Πτολεμαῖον τὸν
Ἀερόπου καὶ καταδιώκειν, ὃς ἐτύγχανε τοῖς Αἰτωλοῖς
ἐπιτεταγμένος ἐν τοῖς ἐπιπέδοις ἐπὶ τῶν εὐωνύμων,
9 τὰς δὲ φάλαγγας, ἐπεὶ συνέβαλλον ἀλλήλαις, μάχην
10 ποιεῖν ἰσχυράν. ὅτι δὲ συμβαλεῖν ἀδύνατον ἦν τῶν
θηρίων καὶ τῶν ἱππέων καὶ τῶν εὐζώνων προτεταγμέ-
νων, τοῦτ᾿ οὐκέτι συνορᾷ.

19. Μετὰ δὲ ταῦτά φησι καταπροτερουμένην τὴν
φάλαγγα ταῖς εὐχειρίαις καὶ πιεζομένην ὑπὸ τῶν Αἰτωλῶν ἀναχωρεῖν ἐπὶ πόδα, τὰ <δὲ> θηρία τοὺς ἐγ-
κλίνοντας ἐκδεχόμενα καὶ συμπίπτοντα τοῖς πολεμί-
2 οις μεγάλην παρέχεσθαι χρείαν. πῶς δὲ ταῦτα γέγονεν
3 ὀπίσω τῆς φάλαγγος οὐ ῥᾴδιον καταμαθεῖν, ἢ πῶς
γενόμενα παρείχετο χρείαν μεγάλην· ὅτε γὰρ ἅπαξ αἱ

and drew it up on the plain, placing the phalanx in one line opposite the enemy's centre and stationing some of his cavalry to the left of the phalanx and some to the right, among the latter being the troop of mailed horsemen which was all under the command of his younger son, Antiochus. Next he tells us that the king posted the elephants at some distance in advance of the phalanx together with Antipater's[53] Tarantines,[54] the spaces between the elephants being filled with bowmen and slingers, while he himself with his horse and foot guards took up a position behind the elephants. Such being their positions as laid down by him, he tells us that the younger Antiochus, whom he stationed in command of the mailed cavalry on the plain opposite the enemy's left, charged from the hill, routed and pursued the cavalry under Ptolemy, son of Aeropus,[55] who commanded the Aetolians in the plain and on the left, and that the two phalanxes met and fought stubbornly, forgetting that it was impossible for them to meet as the elephants, cavalry, and light-armed troops were stationed in front of them.

19. Next he states that the phalanx, proving inferior in fighting power and pressed hard by the Aetolians, retreated slowly, but that the elephants were of great service in receiving them in their retreat and engaging the enemy. It is not easy to see how this could happen in the rear of the phalanx, or how if it did happen great service was

[53] A member of the royal family: 5.79.12.

[54] See n. on 4.77.7.

[55] *PP* 5239.15237. A. B. Tataki, *Macedonians Abroad* (Athens 1998), 420, no. 147. He had been eponymous priest of Alexander and the *Theoi Adelphoi* in 217/6.

THE HISTORIES OF POLYBIUS

φάλαγγες συνέπεσον ἀλλήλαις, οὐκέτι δυνατὸν ἦν
κρῖναι τὰ θηρία τίς ⟨τῶν⟩ ὑποπιπτόντων φίλιος ἢ πο-
4 λεμιός ἐστι. πρὸς δὲ τούτοις φησὶ τοὺς Αἰτωλῶν ἱππέας δυσχρηστεῖσθαι κατὰ τὸν κίνδυνον διὰ τὴν
5 ἀσυνήθειαν τῆς τῶν θηρίων φαντασίας. ἀλλ' οἱ μὲν
ἐπὶ τοῦ δεξιοῦ ταχθέντες ἐξ ἀρχῆς ἀκέραιοι διέμενον,
ὡς αὐτός φησι· τὸ δὲ λοιπὸν πλῆθος τῶν ἱππέων τὸ
μερισθὲν ἐπὶ τὸ λαιὸν ἐπεφεύγει πᾶν ὑπὸ τῶν περὶ
6 τὸν Ἀντίοχον ἡττημένον. ποῖον οὖν μέρος τῶν ἱππέων
ἦν κατὰ μέσην τὴν φάλαγγα τὸ τοὺς ἐλέφαντας ἐκ-
7 πληττόμενον; ποῦ δ' ὁ βασιλεὺς γέγονεν, ἢ τίνα παρέσχηται χρείαν ἐν τῇ μάχῃ, τὸ κάλλιστον σύστημα
περὶ αὐτὸν ἐσχηκὼς καὶ τῶν πεζῶν καὶ τῶν ἱππέων;
8 ἁπλῶς γὰρ οὐδὲν εἴρηται περὶ τούτων. ποῦ δ' ὁ πρεσβύτερος τῶν υἱῶν Ἀντίοχος ὁ μετὰ μέρους τινὸς τῆς
δυνάμεως προκαταλαβόμενος τοὺς ὑπερδεξίους τό-
9 πους; οὗτος μὲν γὰρ οὐδ' εἰς τὴν στρατοπεδείαν ἀνα-
κεχώρηκεν αὐτῷ μετὰ τὴν μάχην. εἰκότως· δύο γὰρ
Ἀντιόχους ὑπέθετο τοῦ βασιλέως υἱούς, ὄντος ἑνὸς
10 τοῦ τότε συνεστρατευμένου. πῶς δ' ὁ Σκόπας ἅμα μὲν
αὐτῷ πρῶτος, ἅμα δ' ἔσχατος ἀναλέλυκεν ἐκ τοῦ κινδύνου; φησὶ γὰρ αὐτὸν ἰδόντα τοὺς περὶ τὸν νεώτερον
Ἀντίοχον ἐχ τοῦ διώγματος ἐπιφαινομένους κατὰ νώτου τοῖς φαλαγγίταις, καὶ διὰ τοῦτο τὰς τοῦ νικᾶν
11 ἐλπίδας ἀπογνόντα, ποιεῖσθαι τὴν ἀποχώρησιν· μετὰ
δὲ ταῦτα συστῆναι τὸν μέγιστον κίνδυνον, κυκλωθεί-
σης τῆς φάλαγγος ὑπό τε τῶν θηρίων καὶ τῶν ἱππέων,
καὶ τελευταῖον ἀποχωρῆσαι τὸν Σκόπαν ἀπὸ τοῦ κινδύνου.

rendered. For once the two phalanxes had met it was not possible for the elephants to distinguish friend from foe among those they encountered. In addition to this he says the Aetolian cavalry were put out of action in the battle because they were unaccustomed to the sight of the elephants. But the cavalry posted on the right remained unbroken from the beginning as he says himself, while the rest of the cavalry, which had been assigned to the left wing, had been vanquished and put to flight by Antiochus. What part of the cavalry, then, was it that was terrified by the elephants in the centre of the phalanx, and where was the king all this time and what service did he render in the action with the horse and foot he had about him, the finest in the army? We are not told a single word about this. Where again was the king's elder son Antiochus, who had occupied positions overlooking the enemy with a part of the army? Why! according to Zeno this young man did not even take part in the return to the camp after the battle; naturally not, for he supposes there were two Antiochi there, sons of the king, whereas there was only one with him in this campaign. And can he explain how Scopas was both the first and the last to leave the field? For he tells us that when he saw the younger Antiochus returning from the pursuit and threatening the phalanx from the rear he despaired of victory and retreated; but after this the hottest part of the battle began, upon the phalanx being surrounded by the elephants and cavalry, and now Scopas was the last to leave the field.

20. Ταῦτα δέ μοι δοκεῖ, καὶ καθόλου τὰ τοιαῦτα τῶν ἀλογημάτων, πολλὴν ἐπιφέρειν αἰσχύνην τοῖς συγ-
2 γραφεῦσι. διὸ δεῖ μάλιστα μὲν πειρᾶσθαι πάντων κρατεῖν τῶν τῆς ἱστορίας μερῶν· καλὸν γάρ· εἰ δὲ μὴ τοῦτο δυνατόν, τῶν ἀναγκαιοτάτων καὶ τῶν μεγίστων ἐν αὐτῇ πλείστην ποιεῖσθαι πρόνοιαν.

3 Ταῦτα μὲν οὖν προήχθην εἰπεῖν, θεωρῶν νῦν, καθά-
περ καὶ ἐπὶ τῶν ἄλλων τεχνῶν καὶ ἐπιτηδευμάτων, τὸ μὲν ἀληθινὸν καὶ πρὸς τὴν χρείαν ἀνῆκον ἐν ἑκάστοις
4 ἐπισεσυρμένον, τὸ δὲ πρὸς ἀλαζονείαν καὶ φαντασίαν ἐπαινούμενον καὶ ζηλούμενον, ὡς μέγα τι καὶ θαυμάσιον, ὃ καὶ τὴν κατασκευὴν ἔχει ῥᾳδιεστέραν καὶ τὴν εὐδόκησιν ὀλιγοδεεστέραν, καθάπερ αἱ λοιπαὶ τῶν
5 γραφῶν. περὶ δὲ τῆς τῶν τόπων ἀγνοίας τῶν κατὰ τὴν Λακωνικὴν διὰ τὸ μεγάλην εἶναι τὴν παράπτωσιν οὐκ
6 ὤκνησα γράψαι καὶ πρὸς αὐτὸν Ζήνωνα, κρίνων καλὸν εἶναι τὸ μὴ τὰς τῶν πέλας ἁμαρτίας ἴδια προτερή-
ματα νομίζειν, καθάπερ ἔνιοι ποιεῖν εἰώθασιν, ἀλλὰ μὴ μόνον τῶν ἰδίων ὑπομνημάτων, ἀλλὰ καὶ τῶν ἀλλοτρίων, καθ᾽ ὅσον οἷοί τ᾽ ἐσμέν, ποιεῖσθαι πρό-
7 νοιαν καὶ διόρθωσιν χάριν τῆς κοινῆς ὠφελείας. ὁ δὲ λαβὼν τὴν ἐπιστολήν, καὶ γνοὺς ἀδύνατον οὖσαν τὴν μετάθεσιν διὰ τὸ προεκδεδωκέναι τὰς συντάξεις, ἐλυ-
πήθη μὲν ὡς ἔνι μάλιστα, ποιεῖν δ᾽ οὐδὲν εἶχε, τήν γε
8 μὴν ἡμετέραν αἵρεσιν ἀπεδέξατο φιλοφρόνως. ὃ δὴ κἂν ἐγὼ παρακαλέσαιμι περὶ αὐτοῦ <τοὺς> καθ᾽ ἡμᾶς καὶ τοὺς ἐπιγινομένους, ἐὰν μὲν κατὰ πρόθεσιν εὑ-
ρισκώμεθά που κατὰ τὴν πραγματείαν διαψευδόμενοι

48

20. Writers it seems to me should be thoroughly ashamed of nonsensical errors like the above. They should therefore strive above all to become masters of the whole craft of history, for to do so is good; but if this be out of their power, they should give the closest attention to what is most necessary and important.

I was led to make these observations, because I observe that at the present day, as in the case of other arts and professions, what is true and really useful is always treated with neglect, while what is pretentious and showy is praised and coveted as if it were something great and wonderful, whereas it is both easier to produce and wins applause more cheaply, as is the case with all other written matter. As for Zeno's errors about the topography of Laconia, the faults were so glaring that I had no hesitation in writing to him personally[56] also, as I do not think it right to look upon the faults of others as virtues of one's own, as is the practice of some, but it appears to me we should as far as we can look after and correct not only our own works but those of others for the sake of the general advantage. Zeno received my letter, and knowing that it was impossible to make the change, as he had already published his work, was very much troubled, but could do nothing, while most courteously accepting my own criticism. And I too will beg both my contemporaries and future generations in pronouncing on my work, if they ever find me making misstatements or neglecting the truth intention-

[56] Zeno answered courteously. This exchange between two contemporary historians is most remarkable.

καὶ παρορῶντες τὴν ἀλήθειαν, ἀπαραιτήτως ἐπιτιμᾶν,
9 ἐὰν δὲ κατ᾽ ἄγνοιαν, συγγνώμην ἔχειν, καὶ μάλιστα
πάντων ἡμῖν διὰ τὸ μέγεθος τῆς συντάξεως καὶ διὰ
τὴν καθόλου περιβολὴν τῶν πραγμάτων.

III. RES AEGYPTI

21. Ὅτι ὁ Τληπόλεμος ὁ τὰ τῆς βασιλείας τῶν
Αἰγυπτίων πράγματα μεταχειριζόμενος ἦν μὲν κατὰ
τὴν ἡλικίαν νέος καὶ κατὰ τὸ συνεχὲς ἐν στρατιωτικῷ
2 βίῳ διεγεγόνει μετὰ φαντασίας, ἦν δὲ καὶ τῇ φύσει
μετέωρος καὶ φιλόδοξος, καὶ καθόλου πολλὰ μὲν εἰς
πραγμάτων λόγον ἀγαθὰ προσεφέρετο, πολλὰ δὲ καὶ
3 κακά. στρατηγεῖν μὲν γὰρ ἐν τοῖς ὑπαίθροις καὶ χειρίζειν πολεμικὰς πράξεις δυνατὸς ἦν, καὶ ...ἀνδρώδης
ὑπῆρχε τῇ φύσει, καὶ πρὸς τὰς στρατιωτικὰς ὁμιλίας
4 εὐφυῶς διέκειτο· πρὸς δὲ ποικίλων πραγμάτων χειρι-
σμόν, δεόμενον ἐπιστάσεως καὶ νήψεως, καὶ πρὸς
φυλακὴν χρημάτων καὶ καθόλου τὴν περὶ τὸ λυσιτελὲς
5 οἰκονομίαν, ἀφυέστατος ὑπῆρχε πάντων. ᾗ καὶ ταχέως
οὐ μόνον ἔσφηλεν, ἀλλὰ καὶ τὴν βασιλείαν ἠλάττωσε.
6 παραλαβὼν γὰρ τὴν τῶν χρημάτων ἐξουσίαν, τὸ μὲν
πλεῖστον μέρος τῆς ἡμέρας κατέτριβε σφαιρομαχῶν
καὶ πρὸς τὰ μειράκια διαμιλλώμενος ἐν τοῖς ὅπλοις,
7 ἀπὸ δὲ τούτων γινόμενος εὐθέως πότους συνῆγε καὶ
τὸ πλεῖον μέρος τοῦ βίου περὶ ταῦτα καὶ σὺν τούτοις
8 εἶχε τὴν διατριβήν. ὃν δέ ποτε χρόνον τῆς ἡμέρας
ἀπεμέριζε πρὸς ἐντεύξεις, ἐν τούτῳ διεδίδου, μᾶλλον

ally to censure me relentlessly, but if I merely err owing
to ignorance to pardon me, especially in view of the magnitude of the work and its comprehensive treatment of
events.

III. AFFAIRS OF EGYPT

Character of Tlepolemus

21. Tlepolemus,[57] who was at the head of the government of Egypt, was still young and had constantly lived the
life of a soldier addicted to ostentation. He was also by
nature too buoyant and fond of fame, and generally speaking many of the qualities he brought to bear on the management of affairs were good but many also were bad. As
regards campaigning and the conduct of war he was capable, and he was also naturally courageous and happy in
his intercourse with soldiers; but as for dealing with complicated questions of policy—a thing which requires ap-
plication and sobriety—and as for the charge of money
and in general all that concerned financial profit no one
was more poorly endowed; so that speedily he not only
came to grief but diminished the power of the kingdom.
For when he assumed the financial control, he spent the
most part of the day in sparring and fencing bouts with the
young men, and when he had finished this exercise, at
once invited them to drink with him, spending the greater
part of his life in this manner and with these associates.
During that portion of the day that he set apart for audiences he used to distribute, or rather, if one must speak

[57] See n. on 15.15.25.

δ', εἰ δεῖ τὸ φαινόμενον εἰπεῖν, διερρίπτει τὰ βασιλικὰ
χρήματα τοῖς ἀπὸ τῆς Ἑλλάδος παραγεγονόσι
πρεσβευταῖς καὶ τοῖς περὶ τὸν Διόνυσον τεχνίταις,
μάλιστα δὲ τοῖς περὶ τὴν αὐλὴν ἡγεμόσι καὶ στρατι-
9 ώταις. καθόλου γὰρ ἀνανεύειν οὐκ ᾔδει, τῷ δὲ πρὸς
10 χάριν ὁμιλήσαντι πᾶν ἐξ ἑτοίμου τὸ φανὲν ἐδίδου. τὸ
λοιπὸν ηὐξάνετο ⟨τὸ⟩ κακόν, ἐξ αὐτοῦ λαμβάνον τὴν
11 ἐπίδοσιν. πᾶς γὰρ ὁ παθὼν εὖ παρὰ τὴν προσδοκίαν
καὶ τοῦ γεγονότος χάριν καὶ τοῦ μέλλοντος ὑπερε-
12 βάλλετο ταῖς τῶν λόγων εὐχαριστίαις· ὁ δὲ πυνθανόμενος τὸν γινόμενον ἐκ πάντων ἔπαινον ὑπὲρ αὑτοῦ
καὶ τὰς ἐν τοῖς πότοις ἐπιχύσεις, ἔτι δὲ τὰς ἐπιγραφὰς
καὶ τὰ διὰ τῶν ἀκροαμάτων εἰς αὐτὸν ᾀδόμενα παί-
γνια καθ' ὅλην τὴν πόλιν, εἰς τέλος ἐχαυνοῦτο καὶ
μᾶλλον ἀεὶ καὶ μᾶλλον ἐξετυφοῦτο, καὶ προχειρότε-
ρος ἐγίνετο πρὸς τὰς ξενικὰς καὶ στρατιωτικὰς χάριτας.

22. ἐφ' οἷς οἱ περὶ τὴν αὐλὴν ἀσχάλλοντες πάντα
παρεσημαίνοντο καὶ βαρέως αὐτοῦ τὴν αὐθάδειαν ὑπ-
έφερον, τὸν δὲ Σωσίβιον ἐκ παραθέσεως ἐθαύμαζον.
2 ἐδόκει γὰρ οὗτος τοῦ τε βασιλέως προεστάναι φρονι-
μώτερον ἢ κατὰ τὴν ἡλικίαν, τήν τε πρὸς τοὺς ἐκτὸς
ἀπάντησιν ἀξίαν ποιεῖσθαι τῆς ἐγκεχειρισμένης αὐτῷ
πίστεως· αὕτη δ' ἦν ἡ σφραγὶς καὶ τὸ τοῦ βασιλέως
3 σῶμα. κατὰ δὲ τὸν καιρὸν τοῦτον ἀνακομιζόμενος
4 ἥκει παρὰ τοῦ Φιλίππου Πτολεμαῖος ὁ Σωσιβίου. καὶ
πρὶν μὲν οὖν ἐκ τῆς Ἀλεξανδρείας ἐκπλεῦσαι πλήρης

the plain truth, scatter the royal funds among the envoys who had come from Greece and the actors of the guild of Dionysus[58] and chiefly among the generals and soldiers present at court. For he was quite incapable of refusing and gave at once to anyone who made himself pleasant to him any sum he thought fit. So the evil went on growing and propagating itself. For every one who had received an unexpected favor was for the sake both of the past and of the future profuse in his expressions of thanks. Tlepolemus, when he heard these universal eulogies of himself and the toasts drunk to him at table, when he read the inscriptions in his honor and heard of the playful verses sung about him by musicians all through the town, became at length very vainglorious, and every day his self-conceit increased and he grew more lavish of gifts to foreigners and soldiers.

22. All this gave the courtiers much cause for complaint. They noted all his acts with disapproval, and found his arrogance hard to put up with, while Sosibius[59] when compared with him aroused their admiration. The latter, they thought, had shown a wisdom beyond his years in his guardianship of the king, and in his communications with foreign representatives had conducted himself in a manner worthy of the charge committed to him, the seal that is to say and the person of the king. At this time Ptolemaeus,[60] the son of Sosibius, arrived on his way back from the court of Philip. Even before leaving Alexandria he had

---

[58] See S. Aneziri, *Die Vereine der dionysischen Techniten im Kontext der hellenistischen Gesellschaft* . . . (Stuttgart 2003); B. le Guen, *L'association des Technites d'Athènes* . . . (Tours 2005).

[59] The younger S.; see 15.32.6.   [60] Mentioned 15.25.13.

ἦν τύφου διά τε τὴν ἰδίαν φύσιν καὶ διὰ τὴν προσγε-
5 γενημένην ἐκ τοῦ πατρὸς εὐκαιρίαν· ὡς δὲ καταπλεύσας εἰς τὴν Μακεδονίαν συνέμιξε τοῖς περὶ τὴν αὐλὴν
νεανίσκοις, ὑπολαβὼν εἶναι τὴν Μακεδόνων ἀνδρείαν
ἐν τῇ τῆς ὑποδέσεως καὶ τῇ τῆς ἐσθῆτος διαφορᾷ,
παρῆν ταῦτα πάντ᾽ ἐζηλωκὼς καὶ πεπεισμένος αὐτὸν
μὲν ἄνδρα γεγονέναι διὰ τὴν ἐκδημίαν καὶ διὰ τὸ Μακεδόσιν ὡμιληκέναι, τοὺς δὲ κατὰ τὴν Ἀλεξάνδρειαν
6 ἀνδράποδα καὶ βλᾶκας διαμένειν. διόπερ εὐθέως ἐζη-
7 λοτύπει καὶ παρετρίβετο πρὸς τὸν Τληπόλεμον. πάντων δ᾽ αὐτῷ συγκατατιθεμένων τῶν περὶ τὴν αὐλὴν
διὰ τὸ τὸν Τληπόλεμον καὶ τὰ πράγματα καὶ τὰ χρήματα μὴ ὡς ἐπίτροπον, ἀλλ᾽ ὡς κληρονόμον χειρίζειν,
8 ταχέως ηὐξήθη τὰ τῆς διαφορᾶς. καθ᾽ ὃν καιρὸν ὁ
Τληπόλεμος, προσπιπτόντων αὐτῷ λόγων δυσμενικῶν
ἐκ τῆς τῶν αὐλικῶν παρατηρήσεως καὶ κακοπραγμοσύνης, τὰς μὲν ἀρχὰς παρήκουε καὶ κατεφρόνει τῶν
9 λεγομένων. ὡς δέ ποτε καὶ κοινῇ συνεδρεύσαντες
ἐτόλμησαν ἐν τῷ μέσῳ καταμέμφεσθαι τὸν Τληπόλε-
10 μον, ὡς κακῶς χειρίζοντα τὰ κατὰ τὴν βασιλείαν, οὐ
παρόντος αὐτοῦ, τότε δὴ παροξυνθεὶς συνῆγε τὸ συνέδριον καὶ παρελθὼν ἐκείνους μὲν ἔφη λάθρᾳ καὶ κατ᾽
ἰδίαν ποιεῖσθαι κατ᾽ αὐτοῦ τὰς διαβολάς, αὐτὸς δ᾽
ἔκρινε κοινῇ καὶ κατὰ πρόσωπον αὐτῶν ποιήσασθαι
τὴν κατηγορίαν.

11   Ὅτι μετὰ τὴν δημηγορίαν ἔλαβε καὶ τὴν σφραγῖδα
παρὰ Σωσιβίου, καὶ ταύτην παρειληφὼς ὁ Τληπόλεμος λοιπὸν ἤδη πάντα τὰ πράγματα κατὰ τὴν αὐτοῦ
προαίρεσιν ἔπραττεν.

been full of conceit owing to his own nature and owing to the affluence he owed to his father. But when on arriving in Macedonia he met the young men at that court, conceiving that Macedonian manhood consisted in the superior elegance of their dress and footgear, he returned to Egypt full of admiration for all such things, and convinced that he alone was a man owing to his having travelled and come in contact with the Macedonians, while all the Alexandrians were still slaves and blockheads. In consequence he at once grew jealous of Tlepolemus and acted so as to cause friction between them; and as all the courtiers took his part, because Tlepolemus administered public affairs and finances more like an heir than like a trustee, the difference soon became more acute. And now Tlepolemus, when hostile utterances due to the captiousness and malignancy of the courtiers reached his ears, at first refused to listen to these and treated them with contempt; but when on some occasions they even held public meetings and ventured to blame him for his maladministration of the affairs of the kingdom and this in his absence, he became really incensed, and calling a meeting of the Council,[61] appeared in person and said that they brought false accusations against him secretly and in private, but that he thought proper to accuse them in public and to their faces.

After his speech he took the seal from Sosibius, and having taken possession of it continued henceforth to act in all matters exactly as he chose.

[61] Tlepolemus' quarrel was with Ptolemaeus, but Ptolemaeus' brother Sosibius was influential and popular; Tlepolemus wanted the backing of the Council.

THE HISTORIES OF POLYBIUS

IV. RES SYRIAE

(40)   22a. Ὅτι Ἀντιόχου τοῦ βασιλέως τὴν τῶν Γαζαίων
2   πόλιν πορθήσαντος φησὶν ὁ Πολύβιος· ἐμοὶ δὲ καὶ
    δίκαιον ἅμα καὶ πρέπον εἶναι δοκεῖ τὸ τοῖς Γαζαίοις
3   ἀποδοῦναι τὴν καθήκουσαν μαρτυρίαν. οὐδὲν γὰρ δια-
    φέροντες ἀνδρείᾳ τῶν κατὰ Κοίλην Συρίαν πρὸς τὰς
    πολεμικὰς πράξεις, ἐν κοινωνίᾳ πραγμάτων καὶ τῷ
    τηρεῖν τὴν πίστιν πολὺ διαφέρουσι καὶ συλλήβδην
4   ἀνυπόστατον ἔχουσι τὴν τόλμαν. κατὰ γὰρ τὴν Περ-
    σῶν ἔφοδον ἐκπλαγέντων τῶν ἄλλων διὰ τὸ μέγεθος
    τῆς δυναστείας, καὶ πάντων ἐγχειρισάντων σφᾶς αὐ-
    τοὺς καὶ τὰς πατρίδας Μήδοις, μόνοι τὸ δεινὸν ὑπ-
5   έμειναν πάντες, τὴν πολιορκίαν ἀναδεξάμενοι. κατὰ
    δὲ τὴν Ἀλεξάνδρου παρουσίαν οὐ μόνον τῶν ἄλλων
    παραδεδωκότων αὐτούς, ἀλλὰ καὶ Τυρίων ἐξηνδραπο-
    δισμένων μετὰ βίας, καὶ σχεδὸν ἀνελπίστου τῆς σω-
    τηρίας ὑπαρχούσης τοῖς ἐναντιουμένοις πρὸς τὴν
    ὁρμὴν καὶ βίαν τὴν Ἀλεξάνδρου, μόνοι τῶν κατὰ Συ-
    ρίαν ὑπέστησαν καὶ πάσας ἐξήλεγξαν τὰς ἐλπίδας.
6   τὸ δὲ παραπλήσιον ἐποίησαν καὶ κατὰ τοὺς ἐνεστῶτας
    καιρούς· οὐδὲν γὰρ ἀπέλειπον τῶν ἐνδεχομένων, σπου-
    δάζοντες διαφυλάξαι τὴν πρὸς τὸν Πτολεμαῖον πί-
7   στιν. διὸ καθάπερ καὶ κατ' ἰδίαν ἐπισημαινόμεθα τοὺς
    ἀγαθοὺς ἄνδρας ἐν τοῖς ὑπομνήμασι, τὸν αὐτὸν τρό-
    πον χρὴ καὶ κοινῇ τῶν πόλεων τὴν ἐπ' ἀγαθῷ ποιή-
    σασθαι μνήμην, ὅσαι τῶν καλῶν ἐκ παραδόσεώς τι
    καὶ προθέσεως πράττειν εἰώθασιν.

IV. AFFAIRS OF SYRIA

After King Antiochus Had Taken and Sacked the
City of Gaza Polybius Writes as Follows

22a. It seems to me both just and proper here to testify, as they merit, to the character of the people of Gaza. Although in war they display no more valor than the people of Coele-Syria in general, they are far superior as regards acting in unison and keeping their faith; and to put it shortly show a courage which is irresistible. For instance in the Persian invasion,[62] when all other towns were terrified by the vast power of the invaders and surrendered themselves and their homes to the Medes, they alone faced the danger as one man and submitted to a siege. Again on the arrival of Alexander,[63] when not only had other cities surrendered, but when Tyre had been stormed and her population enslaved;[64] when there seemed to be scarcely any hope of safety for those who opposed the impetuous force of Alexander's attack, they were the only people in Syria who dared to withstand him and exhausted every resource in doing so. At the present time they acted similarly; for they left no possible means of resistance untried in their effort to keep their faith to Ptolemy. Therefore, just as it is our duty to make separate mention of brave men in writing history, so we should give due credit to such whole cities as are wont to act nobly by tradition and principle.

[62] By King Cambyses in 525 (Hdt. 3.19.3).

[63] Gaza withstood Alexander's siege for two months (Arr., *An.* 2.26–27). *RE* Gaza 880–886 (I. Benzinger).

[64] See Arr., *An.* 2.24.2–6, after a siege of seven months.

V. RES ITALIAE

23. Πόπλιος δὲ Σκιπίων ἧκεν ἐκ Λιβύης οὐ πολὺ
2 κατόπιν τῶν προειρημένων καιρῶν. οὔσης δὲ τῆς
προσδοκίας τῶν πολλῶν ἀκολούθου τῷ μεγέθει τῶν
πράξεων, μεγάλην εἶναι συνέβαινε καὶ τὴν φαντασίαν περὶ τὸν ἄνδρα καὶ τὴν τοῦ πλήθους εὔνοιαν
3 πρὸς αὐτόν. καὶ τοῦτ᾽ εἰκότως ἐκ τῶν κατὰ λόγον ἐγί-
4 νετο καὶ καθηκόντως· οὐδέποτε γὰρ ἂν ἐλπίσαντες
Ἀννίβαν ἐκβαλεῖν ἐξ Ἰταλίας οὐδ᾽ ἀποτρίψασθαι τὸν
ὑπὲρ αὐτῶν καὶ τῶν ἀναγκαίων κίνδυνον, τότε δοκοῦντες ἤδη βεβαίως οὐ μόνον ἐκτὸς γεγονέναι παντὸς φόβου καὶ πάσης περιστάσεως, ἀλλὰ καὶ κρατεῖν
5 τῶν ἐχθρῶν, ὑπερβολὴν οὐ κατέλιπον χαρᾶς. ὡς δὲ
καὶ τὸν θρίαμβον εἰσῆγε, τότε καὶ μᾶλλον ἔτι διὰ τῆς
τῶν εἰσαγομένων ἐνεργείας μιμνησκόμενοι τῶν προγεγονότων κινδύνων ἐκπαθεῖς ἐγίνοντο κατά τε τὴν
πρὸς θεοὺς εὐχαριστίαν καὶ κατὰ τὴν πρὸς τὸν αἴτιον
6 τῆς τηλικαύτης μεταβολῆς εὔνοιαν. καὶ γὰρ ὁ Σύφαξ
ὁ τῶν Μασαισυλίων βασιλεὺς ἤχθη τότε διὰ τῆς πόλεως ἐν τῷ θριάμβῳ μετὰ τῶν αἰχμαλώτων· ὃς καὶ
μετά τινα χρόνον ἐν τῇ φυλακῇ τὸν βίον μετήλλαξε.
7 τούτων δὲ συντελεσθέντων οἱ μὲν ἐν τῇ Ῥώμῃ κατὰ
τὸ συνεχὲς ἐπὶ πολλὰς ἡμέρας ἀγῶνας ἦγον καὶ παν-
ηγύρεις ἐπιφανῶν, χορηγὸν ἔχοντες εἰς ταῦτα τὴν
Σκιπίωνος μεγαλοψυχίαν.

V. AFFAIRS OF ITALY

Scipio Returns to Rome. His Triumph

23. Publius Scipio arrived from Africa not long after the above date.[65] As the eagerness with which he was awaited by the people corresponded to the greatness of his achievements, the splendor of his reception and his popularity with the commons were both very great. And this was quite natural, reasonable, and proper. For while they had never hoped to expel Hannibal from Italy and be quit of the danger which menaced themselves and those dearest to them, the thought that now they were assuredly not only freed from all fear and peril but that they had overcome their foes caused a joy that knew no bounds. And when he entered Rome in triumph, they were reminded more vividly of their former peril by the actual spectacle of the prisoners who marched in the procession, and expressed with passionate fervor their thanks to the gods and their love for him who had brought about so great a change. For among the prisoners led through the town in the triumph was Syphax,[66] king of the Masaesylii, who shortly afterward died in prison. After the termination of the triumph the Roman populace continued for many days to celebrate games and hold festival, the funds for the purpose being provided by the bounty of Scipio.

201–200 B.C.

[65] Scipio returned to Rome late in 201 and celebrated his triumph; *MRR* 1.320–321.

[66] Last mentioned 15.5.13.

VI. RES MACEDONIAE ET GRAECIAE

24. Ὅτι Φίλιππος ὁ βασιλεὺς τοῦ χειμῶνος ἤδη
καταρχομένου, καθ᾿ ὃν Πόπλιος Σολπίκιος ὕπατος
κατεστάθη ἐν Ῥώμῃ, ποιούμενος τὴν διατριβὴν ἐν
τοῖς Βαργυλίοις, θεωρῶν καὶ τοὺς Ῥοδίους καὶ τὸν
Ἄτταλον οὐχ οἷον διαλύοντας τὸ ναυτικόν, ἀλλὰ καὶ
προσπληροῦντας ναῦς καὶ φιλοτιμότερον προσκειμένους ταῖς φυλακαῖς, δυσχρήστως διέκειτο καὶ πολλὰς
2 καὶ ποικίλας εἶχε περὶ τοῦ μέλλοντος ἐπινοίας. ἅμα
μὲν γὰρ ἠγωνία τὸν ἐκ τῶν Βαργυλίων ἔκπλουν καὶ
προεωρᾶτο τὸν κατὰ θάλατταν κίνδυνον, ἅμα δὲ τοῖς
κατὰ τὴν Μακεδονίαν πράγμασι διαπιστῶν οὐδαμῶς
ἐβούλετο παραχειμάζειν κατὰ τὴν Ἀσίαν, φοβούμενος
3 [μὲν οὖν] καὶ τοὺς Αἰτωλοὺς καὶ τοὺς Ῥωμαίους· καὶ
γὰρ οὐδ᾿ ἠγνόει τὰς ἐξαποστελλομένας κατ᾿ αὐτοῦ
πρεσβείας εἰς Ῥώμην, . . . διότι πέρας ἔχει τὰ κατὰ
4 τὴν Λιβύην. ἐξ ὧν ἐδυσχρηστεῖτο μὲν ὑπερβαλλόντως,
ἠναγκάζετο δὲ κατὰ τὸ παρὸν ἐπιμένων αὐτοῦ, τὸ δὴ
5 λεγόμενον, λύκου βίον ζῆν. παρ᾿ ὧν μὲν γὰρ ἁρπάζων
καὶ κλέπτων, τοὺς δ᾿ ἀποβιαζόμενος, ἐνίους δὲ παρὰ
φύσιν αἰκάλλων διὰ τὸ λιμώττειν αὐτῷ τὸ στράτευμα,
ποτὲ μὲν ἐσιτεῖτο κρέα, ποτὲ δὲ σῦκα, ποτὲ δὲ σιτάρια
6 βραχέα παντελῶς· ὧν τινὰ μὲν αὐτῷ Ζεῦξις ἐχορήγει,

---

67 The consul of 211, elected a second time for 200; *MRR*
1.323.

68 Philip was blockaded there by his enemies; the date is the
fall of 201.

VI. AFFAIRS OF MACEDONIA
AND GREECE

Philip in Caria

24. At the beginning of the winter in which Publius   201 B.C.
Sulpicius[67] was appointed consul in Rome, King Philip,
who remained at Bargylia,[68] when he saw that the Rhodians and Attalus were not only not dissolving their fleet but
were manning other ships and paying more earnest attention to the maintenance of their garrisons, was much em-
barrassed and felt for many reasons serious disquietude as
to the future. For one thing he dreaded setting sail from
Bargylia as he foresaw a naval battle, and in the next place
as he was not confident about the position of affairs in
Macedonia he did not at all wish to pass the winter in Asia,
being afraid both of the Aetolians and of the Romans. For
he was not ignorant of the embassies[69] which had been
sent to Rome to act against him ... because the war in
Africa had ended. All these things caused him exceeding
great disquietude, and for the present he was compelled
to remain where he was, leading the life of a wolf as the
saying is. By preying on some and robbing them, by putting pressure on others and by cringing to others contrary
to his nature, as his army was starving, he sometimes managed to get a supply of meat, sometimes of figs and sometimes a quite insignificant quantity of corn. Zeuxis[70] provided him with some of these things and others he got

[69] From Attalus and Rhodes (Livy 31.2.1), as well as from
Athens (Livy 31.1.10).
[70] He had done so before: 16.1.8–9.

τὰ δὲ Μυλασεῖς καὶ Ἀλαβανδεῖς καὶ Μάγνητες, οὕς,
ὁπότε μέν τι δοῖεν, ἔσαινεν, ὅτε δὲ μὴ δοῖεν, ὑλάκτει
7 καὶ ἐπεβούλευεν αὐτοῖς. τέλος ἐπὶ τὴν Μυλασέων πόλιν πράξεις συνεστήσατο διὰ Φιλοκλέους, ἐσφάλη δὲ
8 διὰ τὴν ἀλογίαν τῆς ἐπιβολῆς. τὴν δ᾽ Ἀλαβανδέων
χώραν ὡς πολεμίαν κατέφθειρε, φήσας ἀναγκαῖον
εἶναι πορίζειν τῷ στρατεύματι τὰ πρὸς τὴν τροφήν.

9   Πολύβιος δ᾽ ὁ Μεγαλοπολίτης ἐν τῇ ιϛ´ τῶν ἱστο-
ριῶν "Φίλιππος" φησὶν "ὁ Περσέως πατήρ, ὅτε τὴν
Ἀσίαν κατέτρεχεν, ἀπορῶν τροφῶν τοῖς στρατιώταις
παρὰ Μαγνήτων, ἐπεὶ σῖτον οὐκ εἶχον, σῦκα ἔλαβε.
διὸ καὶ Μυοῦντος κυριεύσας τοῖς Μάγνησιν ἐχαρίσατο
τὸ χωρίον ἀντὶ τῶν σύκων."

25. Ὅτι ὁ τῶν Ἀθηναίων δῆμος ἐξέπεμπε πρεσβευτὰς
πρὸς Ἄτταλον τὸν βασιλέα τοὺς ἅμα μὲν εὐχαριστή-

---

71 Modern Milas in Caria. Once a center of Maussolus' realm,
now in Philip's hand. The city had a little earlier, in 215/4, concluded a treaty of *isopoliteia* (W. Gawantka, *Isopolitie* [Munich
1975]) with Miletus (*Milet* I 3.146 and P. Herrmann, *Milet* VI 1,
p. 178–180).   72 P. uses the traditional name, although the
city had officially been renamed *Antiochia* in 270 (L. Robert,
BCH-Suppl. 1 [1973], 435–466; G. Cohen, *Hellenistic Settle-
ments in Europe, the Islands, and Asia Minor* [Berkeley 1995],
248–250) and resumed its old name again only after Antiochus'
defeat in 190. It had it when P. wrote. A. Meadows, *Alabanda in
Caria. A Hellenistic City and its Coinage* (forthcoming).
73 A little north of the Maeander River, east of Ephesus. Only
recently, in 207, the city had received some sixty-five letters from
kings and decrees of cities, declaring support for the reformed
festival in honor of Artemis, many also granting the city inviola-

from the people of Mylasa,[71] Alabanda,[72] and Magnesia,[73] whom he used to caress whenever they gave him anything, but if they did not he used to growl at them and make plots against them. Finally he arranged for Mylasa to be betrayed to him by Philocles,[74] but failed owing to the stupid way in which the design was managed. As for the territory of Alabanda he devastated it as if it were enemy soil, alleging that it was necessary for him to procure food for his army.

(From Athenaeus 3.78e–f)

King Philip, the father of Perseus, as Polybius tells us in his sixteenth book, when he overran Asia, being in want of food for his soldiers, obtained figs from the Magnesians as they had no corn, and on taking Myus[75] presented it to the Magnesians in return for the figs.

Attalus at Athens

25. The people of Athens sent an embassy to King Attalus[76] to thank him for what had happened and to invite

bility; K. Rigsby, *Asylia. Inviolability in the Hellenistic World* (Berkeley 1996), 179–279, no. 67–131.

[74] Commander and diplomat in Philip's service, one of the "First Friends," active for another twenty years, and finally executed by the king. *RE* Philokles 2491–2492 (P. Schoch); Tataki (19.8), 452, no. 53.   [75] One of the twelve Ionian cities (before the Aeolian Smyrna was admitted as the thirteenth member). In the 220s dependent of, later absorbed by, Miletus (P. Herrmann, *MDAI(I)* 15 [1965], 90–103).

[76] He happpened to be nearby, at Aegina (Livy 31.14.11), which he had acquired ten years earlier from the Aetolians.

σοντας ἐπὶ τοῖς γεγονόσιν, ἅμα δὲ παρακαλέσοντας
αὐτὸν ἐλθεῖν Ἀθήναζε χάριν τοῦ συνδιαλαβεῖν περὶ
2 τῶν ἐνεστώτων. ὁ δὲ βασιλεὺς μετά τινας ἡμέρας πυθόμενος καταπεπλευκέναι Ῥωμαίων πρεσβευτὰς εἰς
τὸν Πειραιᾶ, καὶ νομίζων ἀναγκαῖον εἶναι τὸ συμμῖξαι
3 τούτοις, ἀνήχθη κατὰ σπουδήν. ὁ δὲ τῶν Ἀθηναίων
δῆμος γνοὺς τὴν παρουσίαν αὐτοῦ μεγαλομερῶς ἐψηφίσατο περὶ τῆς ἀπαντήσεως καὶ τῆς ὅλης ἀποδοχῆς
4 τοῦ βασιλέως. Ἄτταλος δὲ καταπλεύσας εἰς τὸν Πειραιᾶ τὴν μὲν πρώτην ἡμέραν ἐχρημάτισε τοῖς ἐκ τῆς
Ῥώμης πρεσβευταῖς, θεωρῶν δ' αὐτοὺς καὶ τῆς προγεγενημένης κοινοπραγίας μνημονεύοντας καὶ πρὸς
τὸν κατὰ τοῦ Φιλίππου πόλεμον ἑτοίμους ὄντας περι-
5 χαρὴς ἦν. τῇ δ' ἐπαύριον ἅμα τοῖς Ῥωμαίοις καὶ τοῖς
τῶν Ἀθηναίων ἄρχουσιν ἀνέβαινεν εἰς ἄστυ μετὰ μεγάλης προστασίας· οὐ γὰρ μόνον οἱ τὰς ἀρχὰς ἔχοντες μετὰ τῶν ἱππέων, ἀλλὰ καὶ πάντες οἱ πολῖται μετὰ
6 τῶν τέκνων καὶ γυναικῶν ἀπήντων αὐτοῖς. ὡς δὲ συνέμιξαν, τοιαύτη παρὰ τῶν πολλῶν ἐγένετο κατὰ τὴν
ἀπάντησιν φιλανθρωπία πρός τε Ῥωμαίους καὶ ἔτι
μᾶλλον πρὸς τὸν Ἄτταλον ὥσθ' ὑπερβολὴν μὴ κατα-
7 λιπεῖν. ἐπεὶ δ' εἰσῄει κατὰ τὸ Δίπυλον, ἐξ ἑκατέρου
τοῦ μέρους παρέστησαν τὰς ἱερείας καὶ τοὺς ἱερεῖς.
μετὰ δὲ ταῦτα πάντας μὲν τοὺς ναοὺς ἀνέῳξαν, ἐπὶ δὲ
πᾶσι θύματα τοῖς βωμοῖς παραστήσαντες ἠξίωσαν
8 αὐτὸν θῦσαι. τὸ δὲ τελευταῖον ἐψηφίσαντο τιμὰς τη-

him to come to Athens to discuss the situation. The king, learning a few days afterward that a legation from Rome[77] had arrived at Piraeus, and thinking it necessary to meet them, sailed off in haste. The Athenians, hearing of his approaching arrival, made a most generous grant for the reception and the entertainment in general of the king. Attalus, on the first day after his arrival at Piraeus, had an interview with the Roman legates, and was highly gratified to find that they were both mindful of his joint action with Rome in the past, and ready to engage in war with Philip. Next day he went up to Athens[78] in great state accompanied by the Romans and the Athenian archons. For not only all the magistrates and the knights, but all the citizens with their wives and children went out to meet them, and when they joined them there was such a demonstration on the part of the people of their affection for the Romans and still more for Attalus that nothing could have exceeded it in heartiness. As he entered the Dipylon,[79] they drew up the priests and priestesses on either side of the road; after this they threw all the temples open and bringing victims up to all the altars begged him to perform sacrifice. Lastly they voted him such honors as they had

[77] This embassy had been appointed in 201; *MRR* 1.321 and 325.

[78] For his reception see E. Perrin-Saminadayar, *BCH* 128–129 (2004–2005), 351–375.

[79] One of the main gates where the road from Piraeus reached the city; *OCD* Dipylon 485 (R. Osborne).

λικαύτας ἡλίκας οὐδενὶ ταχέως τῶν πρότερον εἰς αὐ-
9 τοὺς εὐεργετῶν γεγονότων· πρὸς γὰρ τοῖς ἄλλοις καὶ
φυλὴν ἐπώνυμον ἐποίησαν Ἀττάλῳ, καὶ κατένειμαν
αὐτὸν εἰς τοὺς ἐπωνύμους τῶν ἀρχηγετῶν.

26. Μετὰ δὲ ταῦτα συναγαγόντες ἐκκλησίαν ἐκά-
2 λουν τὸν προειρημένον. παραιτουμένου δὲ καὶ φάσκοντος εἶναι φορτικὸν τὸ κατὰ πρόσωπον εἰσελθόντα
διαπορεύεσθαι τὰς εὐεργεσίας τὰς αὑτοῦ τοῖς εὖ πε-
3 πονθόσι, τῆς εἰσόδου παρῆκαν, γράψαντα δ' αὐτὸν
ἠξίουν ἐκδοῦναι περὶ ὧν ὑπολαμβάνει συμφέρειν
4 πρὸς τοὺς ἐνεστῶτας καιρούς. τοῦ δὲ πεισθέντος καὶ
γράψαντος εἰσήνεγκαν τὴν ἐπιστολὴν οἱ προεστῶτες.
5 ἦν δὲ ⟨τὰ⟩ κεφάλαια τῶν γεγραμμένων ἀνάμνησις
τῶν πρότερον ἐξ αὐτοῦ γεγονότων εὐεργετημάτων εἰς
τὸν δῆμον, ἐξαρίθμησις τῶν πεπραγμένων αὐτῷ πρὸς
6 Φίλιππον κατὰ τοὺς ἐνεστῶτας καιρούς, τελευταία δὲ
παράκλησις εἰς τὸν κατὰ Φιλίππου πόλεμον, καὶ δι-
ορκισμός, ὡς ἐὰν μὴ νῦν ἕλωνται συνεμβαίνειν εὐγε-
νῶς εἰς τὴν ἀπέχθειαν ἅμα Ῥοδίοις καὶ Ῥωμαίοις καὶ

---

80 Untrue: they had granted such honors to kings Antigonus
and Demetrius in 307 (C. Habicht, *Gottmenschentum und
griechische Städte*, 2nd. ed. [Munich 1970], 44–48) and to
Ptolemy III in 224/3 (the same, *Studien zur Geschichte Athens in
hellenistischer Zeit* [Göttingen 1982], 105–112). For each of these
kings a new tribe was created, and *Attalis* was now added to their
number, while *Antigonis* and *Demetrias* were abolished.

81 C. Habicht, "Athens and the Attalids in the second century
B.C.," *Hesp.* 59, 1990, 561–577. Among the gifts was the so-called
"small Attalid dedication," a group of bronze statues displayed at

never[80] readily paid to any former benefactors. For in addition to other distinctions they named one of the tribes Attalis after him and they added his name to the list of the heroes who gave their names to these tribes.

26. In the next place they summoned an assembly and invited the king to attend. But when he begged to be excused, saying that it would be bad taste on his part to appear in person and recite to the recipients all the benefits[81] he had conferred, they did not insist on his presence, but begged him to write a public statement of what he thought advisable under present circumstances. He agreed to this, and when he had written the letter the presidents[82] laid it before the assembly. The chief points in the letter were as follows. He first reminded them of the benefits he had formerly conferred on the people of Athens, in the next place he gave an account of his action against Philip at the present crisis, and finally he adjured them to take part in the war against Philip, giving them his sworn assurance that if they did not decide now upon nobly declaring that they shared the hostile sentiments of the Romans,[83]

the south wall of the Acropolis—if this was in fact his gift, as is usually assumed, and not that of his son, as other scholars think. See F. Queyrel, *Rev. Arch.* (1989), 278–283; A. Stewart, *Attalos, Athens, and the Acropolis. The Pergamene 'Little Barbarians' and their Roman and Renaissance Legacy* (Cambridge 2004).

[82] These are the *prohedroi,* one for each tribe, except the one in charge of daily affairs at the time. *RE* πρόεδρος 2296–2308 (H. Schaefer). A. S. Henry, *The Prescripts of Athenian Decrees* (Leiden 1977), 27 n. 32; 39.   [83] Attalus may have had assurances from the Roman envoys. It is, however, disputed whether or not the decision to go to war against Philip had already been made by the people (a first attempt of the consul Sulpicius was rejected).

αὐτῷ, μετὰ δὲ ταῦτα παρέντες τοὺς καιροὺς κοινωνεῖν
βούλωνται τῆς εἰρήνης, ἄλλων αὐτὴν κατεργασαμέ-
νων, ἀστοχήσειν αὐτοὺς τοῦ τῇ πατρίδι συμφέροντος.

7 τῆς δ᾽ ἐπιστολῆς ταύτης ἀναγνωσθείσης ἕτοιμον ἦν
τὸ πλῆθος ψηφίζεσθαι τὸν πόλεμον καὶ διὰ τὰ λεγό-

8 μενα καὶ διὰ τὴν εὔνοιαν τὴν πρὸς τὸν Ἄτταλον. οὐ
μὴν ἀλλὰ καὶ τῶν Ῥοδίων ἐπεισελθόντων καὶ πολλοὺς
πρὸς τὴν αὐτὴν ὑπόθεσιν διαθεμένων λόγους, ἔδοξε
τοῖς Ἀθηναίοις ἐκφέρειν τῷ Φιλίππῳ τὸν πόλεμον.

9 ἀπεδέξαντο δὲ καὶ τοὺς Ῥοδίους μεγαλομερῶς καὶ τόν
τε δῆμον ἐστεφάνωσαν ἀριστείῳ στεφάνῳ καὶ πᾶσι
Ῥοδίοις ἰσοπολιτείαν ἐψηφίσαντο διὰ τὸ κἀκείνους
αὐτοῖς χωρὶς τῶν ἄλλων τάς τε ναῦς ἀποκαταστῆσαι

10 τὰς αἰχμαλώτους γενομένας καὶ τοὺς ἄνδρας. οἱ μὲν
οὖν πρέσβεις οἱ παρὰ τῶν Ῥοδίων ταῦτα διαπράξαντες ἀνήχθησαν εἰς τὴν Κέων ἐπὶ τὰς νήσους μετὰ
τοῦ στόλου.

27. Ὅτι καθ᾽ ὃν χρόνον οἱ τῶν Ῥωμαίων πρέσβεις
ἐν ταῖς Ἀθήναις ἐποιοῦντο τὴν διατριβήν, Νικάνορος
τοῦ παρὰ Φιλίππου κατατρέχοντος τὴν Ἀττικὴν ἕως
τῆς Ἀκαδημείας, προδιαπεμψάμενοι πρὸς αὐτὸν οἱ

---

84 For *isopoliteia* granted by one state to the citizens of another, see Gawantka (24.6).   85 Four Athenian vessels, in-
tercepted by the Macedonians, but retrieved by the Rhodians
(Livy 31.15.5. Holleaux, *Ét.* 4.189 n. 1).

86 Island southeast of Attica. See also below, 40.6. The Rhodians were at this time engaged in extending their influence over
the Aegaean Islands, and their efforts resulted in their playing a

the Rhodians and himself, but later, after neglecting this chance, wished to share in a peace due to the efforts of others, they would fail to obtain what lay in the interest of their country. After this letter had been read the people were ready to vote for war, both owing to the tenor of what the king said and owing to their affection for him. And, in fact, when the Rhodians came forward and spoke at length in the same sense, the Athenians decided to make war on Philip. They gave the Rhodians also a magnificent reception, bestowing on the people of Rhodes a crown for conspicuous valor and on all citizens of Rhodes equal political rights[84] at Athens with her own citizens, in reward for their having in addition to other services returned to them the Athenian ships[85] that had been captured and the prisoners of war. The Rhodian ambassadors having accomplished this sailed back to Ceos[86] with their fleet to look after the islands.

Rome and Philip

27. At the time that the Roman legates were staying in Athens Nicanor,[87] Philip's general, overran Attica up to the Academy,[88] upon which the Romans, after sending

leading role in a new League of Islanders; R. Etienne, *Ténos et les Cyclades*, 2 (Paris 1990), 85–124; H.-U. Wiemer, *Krieg, Handel und Piraterie . . .* (Berlin 2002), 271–276.   [87] Possibly the same as in 18.24.2. Tataki (19.8), 382 no. 38–39.

[88] Some 1,200 meters northwest of the Dipylon gate. Sanctuary of Athena and other gods, also the site of Plato's Academy. R. E. Wycherley, *The Stones of Athens* (Princeton 1978), 219–226, and map p. 223. L. Threatte, *Inscribed Schist fragments from the Athenian Academy Excavations* (Athens 2007).

Ῥωμαῖοι κήρυκα συνέμιξαν αὐτῷ καὶ παρεκάλεσαν
2 ἀναγγεῖλαι τῷ Φιλίππῳ διότι Ῥωμαῖοι παρακαλοῦσι
τὸν βασιλέα τῶν μὲν Ἑλλήνων μηδενὶ πολεμεῖν, τῶν
δὲ γεγονότων εἰς Ἄτταλον ἀδικημάτων δίκας ὑπέχειν
3 ἐν ἴσῳ κριτηρίῳ, καὶ διότι πράξαντι μὲν ταῦτα τὴν
εἰρήνην ἄγειν ἔξεστι πρὸς Ῥωμαίους, μὴ βουλομένῳ
δὲ πείθεσθαι τἀναντία συνεξακολουθήσειν ἔφασαν. ὁ
4 μὲν οὖν Νικάνωρ ταῦτ᾽ ἀκούσας ἀπηλλάγη· τὸν αὐτὸν
δὲ λόγον τοῦτον οἱ Ῥωμαῖοι καὶ πρὸς Ἠπειρώτας
εἶπαν περὶ Φιλίππου παραπλέοντες ἐν Φοινίκῃ καὶ
πρὸς Ἀμύνανδρον ἀναβάντες εἰς Ἀθαμανίαν· παραπλησίως καὶ πρὸς Αἰτωλοὺς ἐν Ναυπάκτῳ καὶ πρὸς
5 τοὺς Ἀχαιοὺς ἐν Αἰγίῳ. τότε δὲ διὰ τοῦ Νικάνορος τῷ
Φιλίππῳ ταῦτα δηλώσαντες αὐτοὶ μὲν ἀπέπλευσαν
ὡς Ἀντίοχον καὶ Πτολεμαῖον ἐπὶ τὰς διαλύσεις.

28. Ἀλλ᾽ ἐμοὶ δοκεῖ τὸ μὲν ἄρξασθαι καλῶς καὶ
συνακμάσαι ταῖς ὁρμαῖς πρὸς τὴν τῶν πραγμάτων
2 αὔξησιν ἐπὶ πολλῶν ἤδη γεγονέναι, τὸ δ᾽ ἐπὶ τέλος
ἀγαγεῖν τὸ προτεθὲν καί που καὶ τῆς τύχης ἀντι-
πιπτούσης συνεκπληρῶσαι τῷ λογισμῷ τὸ τῆς προ-
3 θυμίας ἐλλιπὲς ἐπ᾽ ὀλίγων γίνεσθαι. διὸ καὶ τότε δικαίως ἄν τις τὴν μὲν Ἀττάλου καὶ Ῥοδίων ὀλιγοπονίαν
καταμέμψαιτο, τὸ δὲ Φιλίππου βασιλικὸν καὶ μεγαλό-
ψυχον καὶ τὸ τῆς προθέσεως ἐπίμονον ἀποδέξαιτο,
οὐχ ὡς καθόλου τὸν τρόπον ἐπαινῶν, ἀλλ᾽ ὡς τὴν

---

89 See n. on 2.5.3.
90 King of the Athamanes; see n. on 4.16.9.

a herald to him in the first place, met him and asked him to inform Philip that the Romans requested that king to make war on no Grecian state and also to give such compensation to Attalus for the injuries he had inflicted on him as a fair tribunal should pronounce to be just. If he acted so, they added, he might consider himself at peace with Rome, but if he refused to accede the consequences would be the reverse. Nicanor on hearing this departed. The Romans conveyed the contents of this communication to the Epirots at Phoenice[89] in sailing along that coast and to Amynander,[90] going up to Athamania for that purpose. They also apprised the Aetolians at Naupactus[91] and the Achaeans[92] at Aegium. After having made this statement to Philip through Nicanor they sailed away to meet Antiochus and Ptolemy for the purpose of coming to terms.[93]

28. But it seems to me that while there are many cases in which men have begun well and in which their spirit of enterprise has kept pace with the growth of the matter in hand, those who have succeeded in bringing their designs to a conclusion, and even when fortune has been adverse to them, have compensated for deficiency in ardor by the exercise of reason, are few. Therefore we should be right on this occasion in finding fault with the remissness of Attalus and the Rhodians and in approving Philip's truly kingly conduct, his magnanimity and fixity of purpose, not indeed praising his character as a whole, but noting with

[91] Aetolian city in western Locris, where in 217 was concluded the peace ending the Social War. *OCD* Naupactus 1029 (W. M. Murray). [92] Allies of the king of Macedon since 224: *StV* 506 and 507. [93] To end the Fifth Syrian War.

4 πρὸς τὸ παρὸν ὁρμὴν ἐπισημαινόμενος. ποιοῦμαι δὲ
τὴν τοιαύτην διαστολήν, ἵνα μή τις ἡμᾶς ὑπολάβῃ
μαχόμενα λέγειν ἑαυτοῖς, ἄρτι μὲν ἐπαινοῦντας Ἄτταλον καὶ Ῥοδίους, Φίλιππον δὲ καταμεμφομένους,
5 νῦν δὲ τοὐναντίον. τούτου γὰρ χάριν ἐν ἀρχαῖς τῆς
πραγματείας διεστειλάμην, φήσας ἀναγκαῖον εἶναι
6 ποτὲ μὲν εὐλογεῖν, ποτὲ δὲ ψέγειν τοὺς αὐτούς, ἐπειδὴ
πολλάκις μὲν αἱ πρὸς τὸ χεῖρον τῶν πραγμάτων
ῥοπαὶ καὶ περιστάσεις ἀλλοιοῦσι τὰς προαιρέσεις
7 τῶν ἀνθρώπων, πολλάκις δ᾽ αἱ πρὸς τὸ βέλτιον, ἔστι
δ᾽ ὅτε κατὰ τὴν ἰδίαν φύσιν ἄνθρωποι ποτὲ μὲν ἐπὶ
τὸ δέον ὁρμῶσι, ποτὲ δ᾽ ἐπὶ τοὐναντίον. ὧν ἕν τί μοι
8 δοκεῖ καὶ τότε γεγονέναι περὶ τὸν Φίλιππον· ἀσχάλλων
γὰρ ἐπὶ τοῖς γεγονόσιν ἐλαττώμασι, καὶ τὸ πλεῖον
ὀργῇ καὶ θυμῷ χρώμενος, παραστατικῶς καὶ δαιμονίως ἐνήρμοσεν εἰς τοὺς ἐνεστῶτας καιρούς, καὶ τούτῳ
τῷ τρόπῳ κατανέστη τῶν Ῥοδίων καὶ τοῦ βασιλέως
9 Ἀττάλου, καὶ καθίκετο τῶν ἑξῆς πράξεων. ταῦτα μὲν
οὖν προήχθην εἰπεῖν διὰ τὸ τινὰς μὲν πρὸς τῷ τέρ-
ματι, καθάπερ οἱ κακοὶ τῶν σταδιέων, ἐγκαταλιπεῖν
τὰς ἑαυτῶν προθέσεις, τινὰς δ᾽ ἐν τούτῳ μάλιστα νικᾶν τοὺς ἀντιπάλους.

29. Ὁ δὲ Φίλιππος ἐβούλετο παρελέσθαι Ῥωμαίων
τὰς ἐν τούτοις τοῖς τόποις ἀφορμὰς καὶ τὰς ἐπι-
βάθρας.

2 Ἵνα, ἐὰν πρόθηται διαβαίνειν αὖθις εἰς τὴν Ἀσίαν,
ἐπιβάθραν ἔχοι τὴν Ἄβυδον.

admiration his readiness to meet present circumstances. I make this express statement lest anyone should think I contradict myself, as but lately I praised Attalus and the Rhodians and blamed Philip, and now I do the reverse. For it was for this very reason that at the outset of this work I stated as a principle that it was necessary at times to praise and at times to blame the same person, since often the shifts and turns of circumstances for the worse or for the better change the resolves of men, and at times by their very nature men are impelled to act either as they should or as they should not. One or other of these things happened then to Philip. For in his vexation at his recent losses and prompted chiefly by anger and indignation, he adapted himself to the situation with frenzied and almost inspired vigor, and by this means was able to resume the struggle against the Rhodians and King Attalus and achieve the success which ensued. I was induced, then, to say this because some people, like bad racers, give up their determination near the end of the course while it is just then that others overcome their adversaries.

29. Philip wished to cut off the resources and stepping-stones of the Romans in those parts.

So that if he meant to cross again to Asia, he might have Abydus[94] as a stepping-stone.

[94] City on the Asiatic shore of the Hellespont, bridgehead to Europe for Xerxes in 480. *OCD* Abydos 1–2 (S. Mitchell).

3   Τὴν δὲ τῆς Ἀβύδου καὶ Σηστοῦ θέσιν καὶ τὴν εὐκαιρίαν τῶν πόλεων τὸ μὲν διὰ πλειόνων ἐξαριθμεῖσθαι
μάταιον εἶναί μοι δοκεῖ διὰ τὸ πάντας, ὧν καὶ μικρὸν

4   ὄφελος, ἱστορηκέναι διὰ τὴν ἰδιότητα τῶν τόπων· κεφαλαιωδῶς γε μὴν ὑπομνῆσαι τοὺς ἀναγινώσκοντας
ἐπιστάσεως χάριν οὐκ ἄχρηστον εἶναι νομίζω πρὸς

5   τὸ παρόν. γνοίη δ' ἄν τις τὰ περὶ τὰς προειρημένας
πόλεις οὐχ οὕτως ἐξ αὐτῶν τῶν ὑποκειμένων τόπων
ὡς ἐκ τῆς παραθέσεως καὶ συγκρίσεως τῶν λέγεσθαι

6   μελλόντων. καθάπερ γὰρ οὐδ' ἐκ τοῦ παρὰ μέν τισιν
Ὠκεανοῦ προσαγορευομένου, παρὰ δέ τισιν Ἀτλαντικοῦ
πελάγους, δυνατὸν εἰς τὴν καθ' ἡμᾶς θάλατταν εἰσ-
πλεῦσαι μὴ οὐχὶ διὰ τοῦ καθ' Ἡρακλέους στήλας

7   περαιωθέντα στόματος, οὕτως οὐδ' ἐκ τῆς καθ' ἡμᾶς
εἰς τὴν Προποντίδα καὶ τὸν Πόντον ἀφικέσθαι μὴ
οὐχὶ διὰ τοῦ μεταξὺ Σηστοῦ καὶ Ἀβύδου διαστήμα-

8   τος ποιησάμενον τὸν εἴσπλουν. ὥσπερ δὲ πρός τινα
λόγον τῆς τύχης ποιουμένης τὴν κατασκευὴν ἀμφοτέρων τῶν πορθμῶν, πολλαπλάσιον εἶναι συμβαίνει
τὸν καθ' Ἡρακλέους στήλας πόρον τοῦ κατὰ τὸν Ἑλ-

9   λήσποντον· ὁ μὲν γάρ ἐστιν ἑξήκοντα σταδίων, ὁ δὲ
κατὰ τὴν Ἄβυδον δυεῖν, ὡς ἂν εἴ τινος τεκμαιρομένου
διὰ τὸ πολλαπλασίαν εἶναι τὴν ἔξω θάλατταν τῆς

10 καθ' ἡμᾶς. εὐκαιρότερον μέντοι γε τοῦ καθ' Ἡρακλείους

11 στήλας στόματός ἐστι τὸ κατὰ τὴν Ἄβυδον. τὸ μὲν
γὰρ ἐξ ἀμφοῖν ὑπ' ἀνθρώπων οἰκούμενον πύλης ἔχει
διάθεσιν διὰ τὴν πρὸς ἀλλήλους ἐπιμιξίαν, ποτὲ μὲν

Siege of Abydus

To describe at length the position of Abydus and Sestus[95] and the peculiar advantages of those cities seems to me useless, as every one who has the least claim to intelligence has acquired some knowledge of them owing to the singularity of their position, but I think it of some use for my present purpose to recall it summarily to the minds of my readers so as to fix their attention on it. One can form an idea of the facts about these cities not so much from a study of their actual topography as from dwelling on the comparison I am about to adduce. For just as it is impossible to sail from the sea called by some the Ocean and by others the Atlantic Sea into our own sea except by passing through the mouth of it at the Pillars of Heracles, so no one can reach the Euxine and Propontis from our sea except by sailing through the passage between Sestus and Abydus. Now, just as if chance in forming these two straits had exercised a certain proportion, the passage at the Pillars of Heracles is far wider than the Hellespont, being sixty stades in width while the width of the latter at Abydus is two stades,[96] just as if this distance had been designed owing to the Ocean being many times the size of this sea of ours. The natural advantages, however, of the entrance at Abydus far excel those of that at the Pillars of Heracles. For the former, lying as it does between two inhabited districts, somewhat resembles a gate owing to the free intercourse it affords, being sometimes bridged

95 Opposite Abydus on the Thracian Chersonese. Map for both cities in *RE* Hellespontos 183–184 (L. Bürchner).

96 In fact, ten (1,950 meters).

γεφυρούμενον ὑπὸ τῶν πεζεύειν ἐπ᾽ ἀμφοτέρας τὰς
ἠπείρους προαιρουμένων, ποτὲ δὲ πλωτευόμενον συν-
12 εχῶς· τὸ δὲ καθ᾽ Ἡρακλείους στήλας σπάνιον ἔχει
τὴν χρῆσιν καὶ σπανίοις διὰ τὴν ἀνεπιμιξίαν τῶν
ἐθνῶν τῶν πρὸς τοῖς πέρασι κατοικούντων τῆς Λιβύης καὶ τῆς Εὐρώπης καὶ διὰ τὴν ἀγνωσίαν τῆς
13 ἐκτὸς θαλάττης. αὕτη δ᾽ ἡ τῶν Ἀβυδηνῶν πόλις περι-
έχεται μὲν ἐξ ἀμφοῖν τοῖν μεροῖν ὑπὸ τῶν τῆς Εὐρώπης ἀκρωτηρίων, ἔχει δὲ λιμένα δυνάμενον σκέπειν
14 ἀπὸ παντὸς ἀνέμου τοὺς ἐνορμοῦντας. ἐκτὸς δὲ τῆς
εἰς τὸν λιμένα καταγωγῆς οὐδαμῶς οὐδαμῇ δυνατόν
ἐστιν ὁρμῆσαι πρὸς τὴν πόλιν διὰ τὴν ὀξύτητα καὶ
βίαν τοῦ ῥοῦ τοῦ κατὰ τὸν πόρον.

30.Οὐ μὴν ἀλλ᾽ ὅ γε Φίλιππος τὰ μὲν ἀποσταυρώσας,
τὰ δὲ περιχαρακώσας τοὺς Ἀβυδηνοὺς ἐπολιόρκει καὶ
2 κατὰ γῆν ἅμα καὶ κατὰ θάλατταν. ἡ δὲ πρᾶξις αὕτη
κατὰ μὲν τὸ μέγεθος τῆς παρασκευῆς καὶ τὴν ποικι-
λίαν τῶν ἐν τοῖς ἔργοις ἐπινοημάτων, δι᾽ ὧν οἵ τε
<πολιορκοῦντες καὶ> πολιορκούμενοι πρὸς ἀλλήλους
3 εἰώθασιν ἀντιμηχανᾶσθαι καὶ φιλοτεχνεῖν, οὐ γέγονε
θαυμάσιος, κατὰ δὲ τὴν γενναιότητα τῶν πολιορκουμένων καὶ τὴν ὑπερβολὴν τῆς εὐψυχίας, εἰ καί τις
4 ἄλλη, μνήμης ἀξία καὶ παραδόσεως. τὰς μὲν γὰρ
ἀρχὰς πιστεύοντες αὑτοῖς οἱ τὴν Ἄβυδον κατοικοῦντες
ὑπέμενον ἐρρωμένως τὰς τοῦ Φιλίππου παρασκευάς,
καὶ τῶν τε κατὰ θάλατταν προσαχθέντων μηχανημάτων τὰ μὲν τοῖς πετροβόλοις τύπτοντες διεσάλευσαν,
τὰ δὲ τῷ πυρὶ διέφθειραν, οὕτως ὥστε καὶ τὰς ναῦς

over by those who intend to pass on foot from one continent to the other and at other times constantly traversed by boats, while the latter is used by few and rarely for passage either from sea to sea or from land to land, owing to the lack of intercourse between the peoples inhabiting the extremities of Africa and Europe and owing to our ignorance of the outer sea. The city of Abydus itself lies between two capes on the European shore and has a harbor which affords protection from all winds. Without putting in to the harbor it is absolutely impossible to anchor off the city owing to the swiftness and strength of the current in the straits.

30. Philip, however, now began the siege of Abydus by sea and land, planting piles at the entrance to the harbor and making an entrenchment all round the town. The siege was not so remarkable for the greatness of the preparations and the variety of the devices employed in the works—those artifices and contrivances by which besieged and besiegers usually try to defeat each other's aims—as for the bravery and exceptional spirit displayed by the besieged, which rendered it especially worthy of being remembered and described to posterity. For at first the inhabitants of the town with the utmost self-confidence valiantly withstood all Philip's elaborate efforts, smashing by catapults some of the machines he brought to bear by sea and destroying others by fire, so that the enemy with

μόλις ἀνασπάσαι τοὺς πολεμίους ἐκ τοῦ κινδύνου.
5 τοῖς δὲ κατὰ γῆν ἔργοις ἕως μέν τινος προσαντεῖχον
εὐψύχως, οὐκ ἀπελπίζοντες κατακρατήσειν τῶν πολε-
6 μίων. ἐπειδὴ δὲ τὸ μὲν ἐκτὸς τοῦ τείχους ἔπεσε διὰ
τῶν ὀρυγμάτων, μετὰ δὲ ταῦτα διὰ τῶν μετάλλων
ἤγγιζον οἱ Μακεδόνες τῷ κατὰ ⟨τὸ⟩ πεπτωκὸς ὑπὸ
7 τῶν ἔνδοθεν ἀντῳκοδομημένῳ τείχει, τὸ τηνικάδε πέμψαντες πρεσβευτὰς Ἰφιάδην καὶ Παντάγνωτον ἐκέλευον παραλαμβάνειν τὸν Φίλιππον τὴν πόλιν, τοὺς
μὲν στρατιώτας ὑποσπόνδους ἀφέντα τοὺς παρὰ Ῥοδίων καὶ παρ᾽ Ἀττάλου, τὰ δ᾽ ἐλεύθερα τῶν σωμάτων
ἐάσαντα σῴζεσθαι κατὰ δύναμιν οὗ ποτ᾽ ἂν ἕκαστος
8 προαιρῆται μετὰ τῆς ἐσθῆτος τῆς περὶ τὸ σῶμα. τοῦ
δὲ Φιλίππου προστάττοντος περὶ πάντων ἐπιτρέπειν
ἢ μάχεσθαι γενναίως, οὗτοι μὲν ἐπανῆλθον.

31. οἱ δ᾽ Ἀβυδηνοὶ πυθόμενοι τὰ λεγόμενα, συνελ-
θόντες εἰς ἐκκλησίαν ἐβουλεύοντο περὶ τῶν ἐνεστώτων
2 ἀπονοηθέντες ταῖς γνώμαις. ἔδοξεν οὖν αὐτοῖς πρῶτον
μὲν τοὺς δούλους ἐλευθεροῦν, ἵνα συναγωνιστὰς
ἔχοιεν ἀπροφασίστους, ἔπειτα συναθροῖσαι τὰς μὲν
γυναῖκας εἰς τὸ τῆς Ἀρτέμιδος ἱερὸν ἁπάσας, τὰ δὲ
3 τέκνα σὺν ταῖς τροφοῖς εἰς τὸ γυμνάσιον, ἑξῆς δὲ τούτοις τὸν ἄργυρον καὶ τὸν χρυσὸν εἰς τὴν ἀγορὰν συναγαγεῖν, ὁμοίως δὲ καὶ τὸν ἱματισμὸν τὸν ἀξιόλογον
εἰς τὴν τετρήρη ⟨τὴν⟩ τῶν Ῥοδίων καὶ τὴν τριήρη τὴν

---

97 Scion of a highly distinguished family of men with this
name in the fifth and fourth centuries. Ad. Wilhelm, *Anz. Akad.*

difficulty withdrew their ships from the danger zone. As for the besiegers' works on land, up to a certain point the Abydenes offered a gallant resistance there, not without hope of getting the better of their adversaries; but when the outer wall was undermined and fell, and when the Macedonian mines approached the wall they had built from inside to replace the fallen one, they at last sent Iphiades[97] and Pantagnotus as commissioners, inviting Philip to take possession of the town, if he should allow the soldiers sent by Attalus and the Rhodians to depart under flag of truce, and all free inhabitants to escape with the clothes on their backs to whatever place they severally chose. But when Philip ordered them either to surrender at discretion or to fight bravely the commissioners returned,

31. and the people of Abydus, when they heard the answer, summoned a public assembly and discussed the situation in a despairing mood. They decided first of all to liberate the slaves, that they might have no pretext for refusing to assist them in the defense, in the next place to assemble all the women in the temple of Artemis and the children with their nurses in the gymnasium, and finally to collect all their gold and silver in the marketplace and place all valuable articles of dress in the Rhodian quadrireme and the trireme of the Cyzicenians.[98] Having re-

Wien (1911), 170–179. E. Schütrumpf, H.-J. Gehrke, *Aristoteles. Politik* 3 (Berlin 1996), 497–498.   [98] Cyzicus, a colony of Miletus, at the south shore of the Sea of Marmara. The city had common interests with Rhodes. A. Avram, "Kyzikos," in *An Inventory of Archaic and Classical Poleis,* M. H. Hansen and Th. N. Nielsen, ed. (Oxford ca. 2004), 983–986.

4 τῶν Κυζικηνῶν. ταῦτα δὲ προθέμενοι καὶ πράξαντες
ὁμοθυμαδὸν κατὰ τὸ δόγμα πάλιν συνηθροίσθησαν
εἰς τὴν ἐκκλησίαν, καὶ πεντήκοντα προεχειρίσαντο
τῶν πρεσβυτέρων ἀνδρῶν καὶ μάλιστα πιστευομένων,
ἔτι δὲ τὴν σωματικὴν δύναμιν ἐχόντων πρὸς τὸ δύ-
5 νασθαι τὸ κριθὲν ἐπιτελεῖν, καὶ τούτους ἐξώρκισαν
ἐναντίον ἁπάντων τῶν πολιτῶν ἦ μήν, ἐὰν ἴδωσι τὸ
διατείχισμα καταλαμβανόμενον ὑπὸ τῶν ἐχθρῶν,
κατασφάξειν μὲν τὰ τέκνα καὶ τὰς γυναῖκας, ἐμπρή-
σειν δὲ τὰς προειρημένας ναῦς, ῥίψειν δὲ κατὰ τὰς
ἀρὰς τὸν ἄργυρον καὶ τὸν χρυσὸν εἰς τὴν θάλατταν.
6 μετὰ δὲ ταῦτα παραστησάμενοι τοὺς ἱερέας ὤμνυον
πάντες ἢ κρατήσειν τῶν ἐχθρῶν ἢ τελευτήσειν μαχό-
7 μενοι περὶ τῆς πατρίδος. ἐπὶ δὲ πᾶσι σφαγιασάμενοι
κατάρας ἠνάγκασαν ἐπὶ τῶν ἐμπύρων ποιεῖσθαι τοὺς
8 ἱερέας καὶ τὰς ἱερείας περὶ τῶν προειρημένων. ταῦτα
δ' ἐπικυρώσαντες τοῦ μὲν ἀντιμεταλλεύειν τοῖς πολεμίοις ἀπέστησαν, ἐπὶ δὲ τοιαύτην γνώμην κατέστησαν ὥστ' ἐπειδὰν πέσῃ τὸ διατείχισμα, τότ' ἐπὶ τοῦ
πτώματος διαμάχεσθαι καὶ διαποθνήσκειν πρὸς τοὺς
βιαζομένους.

32. Ἐξ ὧν εἴποι τις ἂν καὶ τὴν λεγομένην Φωκικὴν
ἀπόνοιαν καὶ τὴν Ἀκαρνάνων εὐψυχίαν ὑπερηρκέναι
2 τὴν τῶν Ἀβυδηνῶν τόλμαν. Φωκεῖς τε γὰρ δοκοῦσι τὰ
παραπλήσια βουλεύσασθαι περὶ τῶν ἀναγκαίων, οὐκ
εἰς τέλος ἀπηλπισμένας ἔχοντες τὰς τοῦ νικᾶν ἐλπίδας
διὰ τὸ μέλλειν ποιεῖσθαι τὸν κίνδυνον πρὸς τοὺς Θετ-

solved on this they unanimously put their decree into execution, and then calling another assembly they nominated fifty of the older and most trusted citizens, men who possessed sufficient bodily strength to carry out their decision, and made them swear in the presence of all the citizens that whenever they saw the inner wall in the possession of the enemy they would kill all the women and children, set fire to the ships I mentioned, and throw the gold and silver into the sea with their curses.[99] After this, calling the priests before them they all swore either to conquer the foe or die fighting for their country. Last of all they slew some victims and obliged the priests and priestesses to pronounce over the burning entrails curses on those who neglected to perform what they had sworn. Having thus made sure of everything they stopped countermining against the enemy and came to the decision that as soon as the cross wall fell they would fight on its ruins and resist the assailants to the death.

32. All this would induce one to say that the daring courage of the Abydenes surpassed even the famous desperation of the Phocians and the courageous resolve of the Acarnanians.[100] For the Phocians are said to have decided on the same course regarding their families at a time when they had by no means entirely given up the hope of victory, as they were about to engage the Thessalians in a set bat-

[99] On themselves should they fail to carry out their oath.

[100] These events belong to the decade between 491 and 481, before the invasion of Greece by Xerxes. The enemy of the Phocians were the Thessalians; the full story is told in Pausanias 10.1.3–11, shorter versions in other authors. The enemies of the Acarnanians were the Aetolians; see 9.40.4–6.

3 ταλοὺς ἐν τοῖς ὑπαίθροις ἐκ παρατάξεως· ὁμοίως δὲ
καὶ τὸ τῶν Ἀκαρνάνων ἔθνος, ὅτε προιδόμενοι τὴν
Αἰτωλῶν ἔφοδον, ἐβουλεύσαντο παραπλήσια περὶ τῶν
ἐνεστώτων· ὑπὲρ ὧν τὰ κατὰ μέρος ἡμεῖς ἐν τοῖς πρὸ
4 τούτων ἱστορήκαμεν. Ἀβυδηνοὶ δέ, συγκεκλεισμένοι
καὶ σχεδὸν ἀπηλπικότες τὴν σωτηρίαν, πανδημεὶ
προείλοντο τῆς εἱμαρμένης τυχεῖν μετὰ τῶν τέκνων
καὶ τῶν γυναικῶν μᾶλλον ἢ ζῶντες ἔτι πρόληψιν
ἔχειν τοῦ πεσεῖσθαι τὰ σφέτερα τέκνα καὶ τὰς γυναῖ-
5 κας ὑπὸ τὴν τῶν ἐχθρῶν ἐξουσίαν. διὸ καὶ μάλιστ' ἄν
τις ἐπὶ τῆς Ἀβυδηνῶν περιπετείας μέμψαιτο τῇ τύχῃ,
διότι τὰς μὲν τῶν προειρημένων συμφορὰς οἷον ἐλε-
ήσασα παραυτίκα διωρθώσατο, περιθεῖσα τὴν νίκην
ἅμα καὶ τὴν σωτηρίαν τοῖς ἀπηλπισμένοις, περὶ δ'
6 Ἀβυδηνῶν τὴν ἐναντίαν εἶχε διάληψιν. οἱ μὲν γὰρ
ἄνδρες ἀπέθανον, ἡ δὲ πόλις ἑάλω, τὰ δὲ τέκνα σὺν
αὐταῖς μητράσιν ἐγένετο τοῖς ἐχθροῖς ὑποχείρια.

33. Πεσόντος γὰρ τοῦ διατειχίσματος, ἐπιβάντες
ἐπὶ τὸ πτῶμα κατὰ τοὺς ὅρκους διεμάχοντο τοῖς πολεμίοις οὕτω τετολμηκότως ὥστε τὸν Φίλιππον, καίπερ ἐκ διαδοχῆς προβαλόμενον τοὺς Μακεδόνας ἕως
νυκτός, τέλος ἀποστῆναι τῆς μάχης, δυσελπιστήσαντα
2 καὶ περὶ τῆς ὅλης ἐπιβολῆς. οὐ γὰρ μόνον ἐπὶ τοὺς
θνήσκοντας τῶν πολεμίων ἐπιβαίνοντες ἠγωνίζοντο
μετὰ παραστάσεως οἱ προκινδυνεύοντες τῶν Ἀβυδηνῶν, οὐδὲ τοῖς ξίφεσι καὶ τοῖς δόρασιν αὐτοῖς
3 ἐμάχοντο παραβόλως, ἀλλ' ὅτε τι τούτων ἀχρειωθὲν
ἀδυνατήσειεν ἢ μετὰ βίας προοῖντ' ἐκ τῶν χειρῶν,

tle in the open, and very similar measures were resolved on by the Acarnanian nation when they foresaw that they were to be attacked by the Aetolians. I have told[101] both the stories in a previous part of this work. But the people of Abydus, when thus completely surrounded and with no hope of safety left, resolved to meet their fate and perish to a man together with their wives and children rather than to live under the apprehension that their families would fall into the power of their enemies. Therefore one feels strongly inclined in the case of the Abydenes to find fault with Fortune for having, as if in pity, set right at once the misfortunes of those other peoples by granting them the victory and safety they despaired of, but for choosing to do the opposite to the Abydenes. For the men perished, the city was taken and the children and their mothers fell into the hands of the enemy.

33. For after the fall of the cross wall, its defenders, mounting the ruins as they sworn, continued to fight with such courage that Philip, though he had thrown his Macedonians on them corps after corps until nightfall, finally abandoned the struggle, having even almost given up hope of success in the siege as a whole. For the foremost of the Abydenes not only mounted the bodies of their dead enemies and kept up the struggle thence with the utmost desperation, not only did they fight most fiercely with sword and spear alone, but whenever any of these weapons became unserviceable and powerless to inflict injury, or when they were forced to drop it, they took hold of the

[101] The part concerning the Phocians is not preserved; for the Acarnanians see previous n.

THE HISTORIES OF POLYBIUS

συμπλεκόμενοι τοῖς Μακεδόσιν οὓς μὲν ἀνέτρεπον
ὁμοῦ τοῖς ὅπλοις, ὧν δὲ συντρίβοντες τὰς σαρίσας
αὐτοῖς τοῖς ἐκείνων κλάσμασιν ἐκ διαλήψεως ⟨πατάσ-
σοντες καὶ⟩ τύπτοντες αὐτῶν ταῖς ἐπιδορατίσι τὰ
πρόσωπα καὶ τοὺς γυμνοὺς τόπους εἰς ὁλοσχερῆ δια-
4 τροπὴν ἦγον. ἐπιγενομένης δὲ τῆς νυκτὸς καὶ διαλυ-
θείσης τῆς μάχης, τῶν μὲν πλείστων τεθνεώτων ἐπὶ
τοῦ πτώματος, τῶν δὲ λοιπῶν ὑπὸ τοῦ κόπου καὶ τῶν
τραυμάτων ἀδυνατούντων, συναγαγόντες ὀλίγους τινὰς τῶν πρεσβυτέρων Γλαυκίδης καὶ Θεόγνητος κατ-
έβαλον τὸ σεμνὸν καὶ θαυμάσιον τῆς τῶν πολιτῶν
5 προαιρέσεως διὰ τὰς ἰδίας ἐλπίδας· ἐβουλεύσαντο
γὰρ τὰ μὲν τέκνα καὶ τὰς γυναῖκας ζωγρεῖν, ἅμα δὲ
τῷ φωτὶ τοὺς ἱερεῖς καὶ τὰς ἱερείας ἐκπέμπειν μετὰ
στεμμάτων πρὸς τὸν Φίλιππον, δεησομένους καὶ
παραδιδόντας αὐτῷ τὴν πόλιν.

34. Κατὰ δὲ τοὺς καιροὺς τούτους Ἄτταλος ὁ βασιλεὺς ἀκούσας πολιορκεῖσθαι τοὺς Ἀβυδηνούς, δι᾽ Αἰγαίου ποιησάμενος τὸν πλοῦν εἰς Τένεδον, ὁμοίως δὲ
καὶ τῶν Ῥωμαίων Μάρκος Αἰμίλιος ὁ νεώτατος ἧκε
2 καταπλέων εἰς αὐτὴν τὴν Ἄβυδον. οἱ γὰρ Ῥωμαῖοι τὸ
σαφὲς ἀκούσαντες ἐν τῇ Ῥόδῳ περὶ τῆς τῶν Ἀβυδηνῶν
πολιορκίας καὶ βουλόμενοι πρὸς αὐτὸν τὸν Φίλιππον
ποιήσασθαι τοὺς λόγους κατὰ τὰς ἐντολάς, ἐπιστή-
σαντες τὴν πρὸς τοὺς βασιλέας ὁρμὴν ἐξέπεμψαν τὸν
3 προειρημένον, ὃς καὶ συμμίξας περὶ τὴν Ἄβυδον διεσάφει τῷ βασιλεῖ διότι δέδοκται τῇ συγκλήτῳ παρακαλεῖν αὐτὸν μήτε τῶν Ἑλλήνων μηδενὶ πολεμεῖν

Macedonians with their hands and threw them down in their armor, or breaking their pikes, stabbing and hitting them repeatedly with the fragments or else striking them on the face or the exposed parts of the body with the points threw them into utter confusion. When night came on and the battle was suspended, as most of the defenders were lying dead on the ruins and the remainder were exhausted by wounds and toil, Glaucides and Theognetus, calling a meeting of a few of the elder citizens, sacrificed in hope of personal advantage all that was splendid and admirable in the resolution of the citizens by deciding to save the women and children alive and to send out as soon as it was light the priests and priestesses with supplicatory boughs to Philip to beg for mercy and surrender the city to him.

34. At this time King Attalus, on hearing that Abydus was being besieged, sailed through the Aegean to Tenedos, and on the part of the Romans the youngest of the envoys, Marcus Aemilius,[102] came likewise by sea to Abydus itself. For the Romans had heard the truth in Rhodes about the siege of Abydus, and wishing to address Philip personally, as they had been instructed,[103] deferred their project of going to see the other kings and sent off the above Marcus Aemilius on this mission. Meeting the king near Abydus he informed him that the Senate had passed a decree, begging him neither to make war on any of the Greeks, nor to lay hands on any of Ptolemy's possessions.[104]

[102] *RE* Aemilius no. 68, 552–553 (P. v. Rohden).

[103] Livy 31.8.3–4.

[104] This is a new demand compared to 27.2, as is also the following one concerning Rhodes. Rome was not an ally of either Ptolemy or Rhodes.

μήτε τοῖς Πτολεμαίου πράγμασιν ἐπιβάλλειν τὰς
χεῖρας, περὶ δὲ τῶν εἰς Ἄτταλον καὶ Ῥοδίους ἀδικη-
4 μάτων δίκας ὑποσχεῖν, καὶ διότι ταῦτα μὲν οὕτω
πράττοντι τὴν εἰρήνην ἄγειν ἐξέσται, μὴ βουλομένῳ
δὲ πειθαρχεῖν ἑτοίμως ὑπάρξειν τὸν πρὸς Ῥωμαίους
5 πόλεμον. τοῦ δὲ Φιλίππου βουλομένου διδάσκειν ὅτι
Ῥόδιοι τὰς χεῖρας ἐπιβάλοιεν αὐτῷ, μεσολαβήσας ὁ
Μάρκος ἤρετο "Τί δαὶ Ἀθηναῖοι; τί δαὶ Κιανοί; τί δαὶ
νῦν Ἀβυδηνοί; καὶ τούτων τίς" ἔφη "σοὶ πρότερος
6 ἐπέβαλε τὰς χεῖρας;" ὁ δὲ βασιλεὺς ἐξαπορήσας κατὰ
τρεῖς τρόπους ἔφησεν αὐτῷ συγγνώμην ἔχειν ὑπερη-
φάνως ὁμιλοῦντι, πρῶτον μὲν ὅτι νέος ἐστὶ καὶ πραγμάτων ἄπειρος, δεύτερον ὅτι κάλλιστος ὑπάρχει τῶν
καθ᾽ αὑτὸν—καὶ γὰρ ἦν τοῦτο κατ᾽ ἀλήθειαν—<μάλι-
7 στα δ᾽ ὅτι Ῥωμαῖος. "ἐγὼ δὲ> μάλιστα μὲν ἀξιῶ Ῥωμαίους" ἔφη "μὴ παραβαίνειν τὰς συνθήκας μηδὲ
πολεμεῖν ἡμῖν· ἐὰν δὲ καὶ τοῦτο ποιῶσιν, ἀμυνούμεθα
γενναίως, παρακαλέσαντες τοὺς θεούς."

Οὗτοι μὲν οὖν ταῦτ᾽ εἰπόντες διεχωρίσθησαν ἀπ᾽
8 ἀλλήλων· ὁ δὲ Φίλιππος κυριεύσας τῆς πόλεως, τὴν
ὕπαρξιν ἅπασαν καταλαβὼν συνηθροισμένην ὑπὸ
9 τῶν Ἀβυδηνῶν ἐξ ἑτοίμου παρέλαβε. θεωρῶν δὲ τὸ
πλῆθος καὶ τὴν ὁρμὴν τῶν σφᾶς αὐτοὺς καὶ τὰ τέκνα
καὶ τὰς γυναῖκας ἀποσφαττόντων, κατακαόντων, ἀπ-
10 αγχόντων, εἰς τὰ φρέατα ῥιπτούντων, κατακρημνιζόν-
των ἀπὸ τῶν τεγῶν, ἐκπλαγὴς ἦν, καὶ διαλγῶν ἐπὶ
τοῖς γινομένοις παρήγγειλε διότι τρεῖς ἡμέρας ἀναστροφὴν δίδωσι τοῖς βουλομένοις ἀπάγχεσθαι καὶ

He was also to submit to a tribunal the question of compensation for the damage he had done to Attalus and the Rhodians. If he acted so he would be allowed to remain at peace, but if he did not at once accept these terms he would find himself at war with Rome. When Philip wished to prove that the Rhodians were the aggressors, Marcus interrupted him and asked, "And what about the Athenians? What about the Cianians, and what about the Abydenes now? Did any of these attack you first?" The king was much taken aback and said that he pardoned him for speaking so haughtily for three reasons, first because he was young and inexperienced in affairs, next because he was the handsomest man of his time—and this was a fact—and chiefly because he was a Roman. "My principal request," he said, "to the Romans is not to violate our treaty[105] or to make war on me; but if nevertheless they do so, we will defend ourselves bravely, supplicating the gods to help us."

After exchanging these words they separated, and Philip on gaining possession of the city found all their valuables collected in a heap by the Abydenes ready for him to seize. But when he saw the number and the fury of those who destroyed themselves and their women and children, either by cutting their throats, or by burning or by hanging or by throwing themselves into wells or off the roofs, he was amazed, and grieving much thereat announced that he granted a respite of three days to those who wished

[105] The peace of Phoenice in 205, StV 543.

11 σφάττειν αὐτούς. οἱ δ᾽ Ἀβυδηνοί, προδιειληφότες ὑπὲρ
αὑτῶν κατὰ τὴν ἐξ ἀρχῆς στάσιν, καὶ νομίζοντες οἷον
εἰ προδόται γίνεσθαι τῶν ὑπὲρ τῆς πατρίδος ἠγω-
νισμένων καὶ τεθνεώτων, οὐδαμῶς ὑπέμενον τὸ ζῆν,
ὅσοι μὴ δεσμοῖς ἢ τοιαύταις ἀνάγκαις προκατελή-
12 φθησαν· οἱ δὲ λοιποὶ πάντες ὥρμων ἀμελλήτως κατὰ
συγγενείας ἐπὶ τὸν θάνατον.

35. Ὅτι παρῆσαν μετὰ τὴν ἅλωσιν Ἀβύδου παρὰ
τοῦ τῶν Ἀχαιῶν ἔθνους εἰς τὴν Ῥόδον πρεσβευταί,
παρακαλοῦντες τὸν δῆμον εἰς τὰς πρὸς τὸν Φίλιππον
2 διαλύσεις. οἷς ἐπελθόντων ⟨τῶν⟩ ἐκ τῆς Ῥώμης πρεσβευτῶν καὶ διαλεγομένων ὑπὲρ τοῦ μὴ ποιεῖσθαι
διαλύσεις πρὸς Φίλιππον ἄνευ Ῥωμαίων, ἔδοξε προσέχειν τῷ δήμῳ τοῖς Ῥωμαίοις καὶ στοχάζεσθαι τῆς
τούτων φιλίας.

36. Ὁ δὲ Φιλοποίμην ἐξελογίσατο τὰ διαστήματα
τῶν Ἀχαϊκῶν πόλεων ἁπασῶν καὶ ποῖαι δύνανται
κατὰ τὰς αὐτὰς ὁδοὺς εἰς τὴν Τεγέαν παραγίνεσθαι.
2 λοιπὸν ἐπιστολὰς ἔγραψε πρὸς πάσας τὰς πόλεις, καὶ
ταύτας διέδωκε ταῖς πορρωτάτω πόλεσι, μερίσας οὕτως ὥστε καθ᾽ ἑκάστην ἔχειν μὴ μόνον τὰς ἑαυτῆς,
ἀλλὰ καὶ τὰς τῶν ἄλλων πόλεων, ὅσαι κατὰ τὴν
3 αὐτὴν ὁδὸν ἔπιπτον. ἐγέγραπτο δ᾽ ἐν ταῖς πρώταις
τοῖς ἀποτελείοις τοιαῦτα. "ὅταν κομίσησθε τὴν ἐπιστολήν, παραχρῆμα ποιήσασθε τοὺς ἐν ταῖς ἡλικίαις

---

106 They had sent Marcus Aemilius from Rhodes to Philip and

to hang themselves and cut their throats. The Abydenes, maintaining the resolve they had originally formed concerning themselves, and regarding themselves as almost traitors to those who had fought and died for their country, by no means consented to live except those of them whose hands had been stayed by fetters or such forcible means, all the rest of them rushing without hesitation in whole families to their death.

35. After the fall of Abydus an embassy from the Achaean League reached Rhodes begging that people to come to terms with Philip. But when the legates[106] from Rome presented themselves after the Achaeans and requested the Rhodians not to make peace with Philip apart from the Romans, it was resolved to stand by the Roman people and aim at maintaining friendship with them.

Expedition of Philopoemen against Nabis

36. Philopoemen, after calculating the distances of all the Achaean cities and from which of them troops could reach Tegea by the same road, proceeded to write letters to all of them and distributed these among the most distant cities, arranging so that each city received not only its own letter but those of the other cities on the same line of road. In the first letters he wrote to the commanding officers[107] as follows: "On receiving this you will make all of military age assemble at once in the marketplace armed,

were still there when the embassy of the Achaeans, still allies of Philip, arrived.

[107] There were two Apoteleioi in each city, commanding the cavalry and infantry respectively.

ἔχοντας τὰ ὅπλα καὶ πένθ᾽ ἡμερῶν ἐφόδια καὶ πέντ᾽
ἀργύριον, ἀθροίζεσθαι παραυτίκα πάντας εἰς τὴν
4 ἀγοράν. ἐπειδὰν δὲ συλλεχθῶσιν οἱ παρόντες, ἀνα-
λαβόντες αὐτοὺς ἄγετ᾽ εἰς τὴν ἑξῆς πόλιν· ὅταν δ᾽
ἐκεῖ παραγένησθε, τὴν ἐπιστολὴν ἀπόδοτε τὴν ἐπιγε-
γραμμένην τῷ παρ᾽ ἐκείνων ἀποτελείῳ καὶ πειθαρχεῖτε
5 τοῖς ἐγγεγραμμένοις." ἐγγέγραπτο δ᾽ ἐν ταύτῃ ταὐτὰ
τοῖς πρόσθεν, πλὴν διότι τὸ τῆς ἑξῆς κειμένης ὄνομα
6 πόλεως οὐ ταὐτὸν εἶχεν, εἰς ἣν ἔδει προάγειν. τοιούτου
δὲ τοῦ χειρισμοῦ γενομένου κατὰ τὸ συνεχές, πρῶτον
μὲν οὐδεὶς ἐγίνωσκε πρὸς τίνα πρᾶξιν ἢ πρὸς ποίαν
ἐπιβολήν ἐστιν ἡ παρασκευή, εἶτα ποῦ πορεύεται,
7 πλὴν τῆς ἑξῆς πόλεως, οὐδεὶς ἁπλῶς ᾔδει, πάντες δὲ
διαποροῦντες καὶ παραλαμβάνοντες ἀλλήλους προῆ-
8 γον εἰς τοὔμπροσθεν. τῷ δὲ μὴ τὸ ἴσον ἀπέχειν τῆς
Τεγέας τὰς πορρωτάτω κειμένας πόλεις οὐχ ἅμα πάσαις ἀπεδόθη τὰ γράμματα ταύταις, ἀλλὰ κατὰ λό-
9 γον ἑκάσταις. ἐξ ὧν συνέβη, μήτε τῶν Τεγεατῶν εἰ-
δότων τὸ μέλλον μήτε τῶν παραγινομένων, ἅμα
πάντας τοὺς Ἀχαιοὺς καὶ κατὰ πάσας τὰς πύλας εἰς
τὴν Τεγέαν εἰσπορεύεσθαι σὺν τοῖς ὅπλοις.

37. ταῦτα δὲ διεστρατήγει καὶ περιεβάλλετο τῇ
διανοίᾳ διὰ τὸ πλῆθος τῶν ⟨ὠτ⟩ακουστῶν καὶ κατα-
σκόπων τοῦ τυράννου.

2 Κατὰ δὲ τὴν ἡμέραν, ἐν ᾗ συναθροίζεσθαι τὸ πλῆθος ἔμελλε τῶν Ἀχαιῶν εἰς Τεγέαν, ἐξαπέστειλε τοὺς
ἐπιλέκτους, ὥστε νυκτερεύσαντας περὶ Σελλασίαν
ἅμα τῷ φωτὶ κατὰ τὴν ἐπιοῦσαν ἡμέραν ἐπιτρέχειν

with provisions and money sufficient for five days. As soon as all those present in the town are collected you will march them to the next city, and on arrival there you will hand the letter addressed to it to their commanding officer and obey the instructions contained in it." The contents in this letter were the same as those of the former one except that the name of the city to which they were to advance was different. This proceeding being repeated in city after city, it resulted in the first place that none knew for what action or what purpose the preparations were being made, and next that absolutely no one was aware where he was marching to but simply the name of the next city on the list, so that all advanced picking each other up and wondering what it was all about. As the distances of Tegea from the most remote cities differ, the letters were not delivered to them simultaneously but at a date in proportion to the distance. The consequence was that without either the people at Tegea or those who arrived there knowing what was contemplated, all the Achaean forces with their arms marched into Tegea by all the gates simultaneously.

37. He contrived matters so and made this comprehensive plan owing to the number of eavesdroppers and spies employed by the tyrant.[108]

On the day on which the main body of the Achaeans would arrive in Tegea he dispatched his picked troops[109] to pass the night at Sellasia and next day at daybreak to

108 Nabis, last mentioned 16.1.
109 See n. on 2.65.3.

3 τὴν Λακωνικήν. ἐὰν δ' οἱ μισθοφόροι βοηθήσαντες
παρενοχλῶσιν αὐτούς, συνέταξε ποιεῖσθαι τὴν ἀποχώρησιν ἐπὶ τὸν Σκοτίταν καὶ τὰ λοιπὰ πειθαρχεῖν
Διδασκαλώνδᾳ τῷ Κρητί· τούτῳ γὰρ ἐπεπιστεύκει καὶ
4 διετέτακτο περὶ τῆς ὅλης ἐπιβολῆς. οὗτοι μὲν οὖν
προῆγον εὐθαρσῶς ἐπὶ τὸ συντεταγμένον· ὁ δὲ Φιλοποίμην ἐν ὥρᾳ παραγγείλας δειπνοποιεῖσθαι τοῖς
Ἀχαιοῖς ἐξῆγε τὴν δύναμιν ἐκ τῆς Τεγέας, καὶ νυκτο-
πορήσας ἐνεργῶς περὶ τὴν ἑωθινὴν ἐνεκάθισε τὴν
στρατιὰν ἐν τοῖς περὶ τὸν Σκοτίταν προσαγορευομέ-
νοις τόποις, ὅς ἐστι μεταξὺ τῆς Τεγέας καὶ τῆς Λακε-
5 δαίμονος. οἱ δ' ἐν τῇ Πελλήνῃ μισθοφόροι κατὰ τὴν
ἐπιοῦσαν ἡμέραν ἅμα τῷ σημῆναι τοὺς σκοποὺς τὴν
καταδρομὴν τῶν πολεμίων ἐκ χειρὸς ἐβοήθουν, καθάπερ ἔθος ἦν αὐτοῖς, καὶ προσέκειντο τοῖς ὑπεναντίοις.
6 τῶν δ' Ἀχαιῶν κατὰ τὸ συνταχθὲν ὑποχωρούντων εἵ-
ποντο κατόπιν ἐπικείμενοι θρασέως καὶ τετολμη-
7 κότως. ἅμα δὲ τῷ παραβάλλειν εἰς τοὺς κατὰ τὴν
ἐνέδραν τόπους, διαναστάντων τῶν Ἀχαιῶν οἱ μὲν
κατεκόπησαν, οἱ δ' ἑάλωσαν αὐτῶν.

38. Ὁ δὲ Φίλιππος ὁρῶν τοὺς Ἀχαιοὺς εὐλαβῶς
διακειμένους πρὸς τὸν κατὰ Ῥωμαίων πόλεμον, ἐσπούδαζε κατὰ πάντα τρόπον ἐμβιβάσαι αὐτοὺς εἰς ἀπέχθειαν.

---

110 An oak forest at the border between Laconia and the Ar-
golid, with a sanctuary of Zeus Skotitas. RE Skotitas, nos. 1–2,
612–613 (F. Geyer; Th. Kock).

commence a raid on Laconia. If the mercenaries came to protect the country and gave them trouble, he ordered them to retire on Scotitas[110] and afterward to place themselves under the orders of Didascalondas the Cretan, who had been taken into his confidence and had received full instructions about the whole enterprise. These picked troops, then, advanced confidently to carry out their orders. Philopoemen, ordering the Achaeans to take an early supper, led the army out of Tegea, and making a rapid night march, halted his forces at early dawn in the district called the country round Scotitas, a place which lies between Tegea and Sparta. The mercenaries at Pellene,[111] when their scouts reported the invasion of the enemy, at once, as is their custom, advanced and fell upon the latter. When the Achaeans, as they had been ordered, retreated, they followed them up, attacking them with great daring and confidence. But when they reached the place where the ambuscade had been placed and the Achaeans rose from it, some of them were cut to pieces and others made prisoners.

38.[112] Philip, when he saw that the Achaeans were chary of going to war with Rome, tried by every means to create animosity between the two peoples.

---

[111] Mentioned in 4.81.7. City in Laconia, whose site has not been determined. *RE* Pellana 350–352 (F. Bölte). Different from Pellene in Achaea (*RE* Pellene 354–356) and from Pellene in Arcadia (*RE* Pellene 366–367), these two articles by E. Meyer.

[112] This excerpt could belong to 199/8 or 198 instead of 200. The reason for assigning it to the earlier year (and to Book 16, not 17) is given by WC 2.25.

VII. RES ASIAE

39. Μαρτυρεῖ τούτοις ἡμῶν τοῖς λόγοις Πολύβιος
ὁ Μεγαλοπολίτης· ἐν γὰρ τῇ ἑξκαιδεκάτῃ τῶν ἱστο-
ριῶν αὐτοῦ φησιν οὕτως· "ὁ δὲ τοῦ Πτολεμαίου στρατηγὸς Σκόπας ὁρμήσας εἰς τοὺς ἄνω τόπους κατε-
στρέψατο ἐν τῷ χειμῶνι τὸ Ἰουδαίων ἔθνος."

2 Τῆς δὲ πολιορκίας ῥεμβώδους γενομένης ὁ μὲν
Σκόπας ἠδόξει καὶ διεβέβλητο νεανικῶς.

3 Λέγει δὲ ἐν τῇ αὐτῇ βίβλῳ ὡς "τοῦ Σκόπα νικηθέν-
τος ὑπ' Ἀντιόχου τὴν μὲν Βατανέαν καὶ Σαμάρειαν
4 καὶ Ἄβιλα καὶ Γάδαρα παρέλαβεν Ἀντίοχος· μετ'
ὀλίγον δὲ προσεχώρησαν αὐτῷ καὶ τῶν Ἰουδαίων οἱ
περὶ τὸ ἱερὸν τὸ προσαγορευόμενον Ἱεροσόλυμα κατ-
5 οικοῦντες. ὑπὲρ οὗ καὶ πλείω λέγειν ἔχοντες, καὶ μάλιστα περὶ τῆς γενομένης περὶ τὸ ἱερὸν ἐπιφανείας,
εἰς ἕτερον καιρὸν ὑπερθησόμεθα τὴν διήγησιν."

40.1 Βαβράντιον, τόπος περὶ Χῖον. Πολύβιος ἑκκαιδεκάτῳ.

40.2 Γίττα, πόλις Παλαιστίνης. Πολύβιος ἑκκαιδεκάτῳ.

---

113 For his counterattack against King Antiochus, see n. on
18.2 and 22a. More in J., *AJ* 12.131, and Hieron., *FGrH* 260 F 45
(winter 201/0).

114 It is not known which town was besieged.

115 His victory over Scopas at Paneium, near the source of the
Jordan River. *RE* Panias 594–600 (G. Hölscher).

VII. AFFAIRS OF ASIA

(From Josephus, *Ant. Jud.* 12.3.3)

39. Polybius of Megalopolis testifies to this. For he says in the sixteenth book of his *Histories*, "Scopas,[113] Ptolemy's general, set out into the upper country and destroyed the Jewish nation in this winter."

"The siege[114] having been negligently conducted, Scopas fell into disrepute and was violently assailed."

He says in the same book, "When Scopas was conquered by Antiochus,[115] that king occupied Batanea,[116] Samaria,[117] Abila, and Gadara,[118] and after a short time those Jews who inhabited the holy place called Jerusalem,[119] surrendered to him. Of this place and the splendor of the temple I have more to tell,[120] but defer my narrative for the present."

40.1 Babrantium, a place close to Chius. Polybius Book 16.

40.2 Gitta, city of Palestine. Polybius Book 16.

[116] Modern Hauran, east of the Sea of Genezareth. *RE* Batanaia 115–118 (I. Benzinger).

[117] The region north of Judaea, south of Galilaea.

[118] Cities of the Syrian Decapolis; see 5.71.2–3 and nn.

[119] King Antiochus, having become master of the city, granted the Jews freedom of religion and support for the maintenance of the temple. His ordinance, directed to Ptolemy, son of Thraseas (n. on 5.65.3), his first governor of the region, is preserved in J., *AJ* 12.138–144, discussed by E. Bikerman, *Rev. Ét. Juiv.* (1935), 4–35.

[120] Perhaps in connection with the history of Antiochus IV Epiphanes. L. Troiani, *Studi Ellenistici* 23 (2010), 113–117.

40.3 Ἕλλα, χωρίον Ἀσίας, Ἀττάλου βασιλέως ἐμπόριον. Πολύβιος ιϛ΄.

40.4 Ἴνσοβροι, ἔθνος Ἰταλικόν. Πολύβιος ιϛ΄.

40.5 Κάνδασα . . . φρούριον Καρίας. Πολύβιος ἑκκαιδεκάτῳ.

40.6 Κάρθαια, μία τῆς ἐν Κέῳ τετραπόλεως . . . οἱ οἰκοῦντες Καρθαεῖς. Πολύβιος ιϛ΄.

40.7 Μάντυα, πόλις Ῥωμαίων. τὸ ἐθνικὸν Μαντυανός. Πολύβιος ἑκκαιδεκάτῳ.

40.3 Hella, a place of Asia, trading station of King Attalus. Polybius Book 16.

40.4 Insubres,[121] an Italic nation. Polybius Book 16.

40.5 Candasa, a place in Caria. Polybius Book 16.

40.6 Carthaea,[122] one of the four towns of Ceos. Polybius Book 16.

40.7 Mantua,[123] a city of the Romans. The ethnic is Mantuanus. Polybius Book 16.

---

[121] A Celtic people in the area of Mediolanum. See map 7 in *CAH,* 2nd ed., 8 (1989), 108.

[122] City on Ceos (see 26.10). The other three cities of the island are Iulis, Poeessa, and Coresia. *IG* XII 5 and XII Supplement. For two important new decrees of Carthaea from mid-third century, see D. Knoepfler, *Chiron* 35 (2005), 285–308.

[123] City of the Celtic Cenomani, for which see the map quoted on 40.4. In P.'s time Mantua was not yet a Roman community, and the words "a city of the Romans" may not be his.

FRAGMENTA LIBRI XVIII

I. RES MACEDONIAE ET GRAECIAE

(17) 1. Ἐπελθόντος δὲ τοῦ τεταγμένου καιροῦ παρῆν ὁ μὲν Φίλιππος ἐκ Δημητριάδος ἀναχθεὶς εἰς τὸν Μηλιέα κόλπον, πέντε λέμβους ἔχων καὶ μίαν πρίστιν,
2 ἐφ' ἧς αὐτὸς ἐπέπλει. συνῆσαν δ' αὐτῷ Μακεδόνες μὲν Ἀπολλόδωρος καὶ Δημοσθένης οἱ γραμματεῖς, ἐκ Βοιωτίας Βραχύλλης, Ἀχαιὸς δὲ Κυκλιάδας, ἐκπεπτωκὼς ἐκ Πελοποννήσου διὰ τὰς πρότερον ὑφ' ἡμῶν εἰρη-
3 μένας αἰτίας. μετὰ δὲ τοῦ Τίτου παρῆν ὅ τε βασιλεὺς

---

[1] After several setbacks, culminating in the recent defection of the Achaeans to the Roman side, King Philip decided to negotiate. In November of 198 the parties met at Nicaea on the shore of the Malian Gulf. *RE* Nikaia 222–226 (Wm. M. Oldfather). P's report is followed by Livy 32.32.5–36.10, with the commentary of J. Briscoe, *A Commentary on Livy, books XXXI–XXXII* (Oxford 1973).

[2] See n. on 10.42.6.

[3] Son of Neon, citizen of Thebes, and member of one of the most distinguished Boeotian families, which for several decades was attached to the kings of Macedonia. S. N. Koumanoudes, Θηβαϊκὴ προσωπογραφία (Athens 1979), no. 372.

[4] Son of Damaretus, of Pharae. Strategus of the Achaeans and

FRAGMENTS OF BOOK XVIII[1]

I. AFFAIRS OF MACEDONIA
AND GREECE

Flamininus and Philip

1. When the time fixed for the conference came, Philip   198–197
arrived, having sailed from Demetrias[2] to the Malian Gulf   B.C.
with five galleys and a beaked ship in which he traveled
himself. He was accompanied by the Macedonians Apollodorus and Demosthenes, his secretaries, by Brachylles[3]
from Boeotia, and by Cycliadas[4] the Achaean, who had
had to leave the Peloponnese for the reasons stated
above. Flamininus[5] had with him King Amynander[6] and

author of a dedication in 210/9 after a campaign in Elis (*SEG*
36.397). Again elected strategus in 200, but soon exiled when
Achaea defected from Philip. P. must have narrated this in Book
17 ("stated above"). For Achaean history in this period, see A.
Bastini, *Der Achäische Bund als hellenische Mittelmacht. Geschichte des achäischen Koinon in der Symmachie mit Rom*
(Frankfurt am Main 1987).

[5] Titus Quinctius Flamininus, consul 198. *RE* Quinctius no.
45, 1047–1100 (H. Gundel). E. Badian, *Titus Quinctius Flamininus. Philhellenism and Realpolitik* (Cincinnati 1970). R. Pfeil-
schifter, *Titus Quinctius Flamininus* (Göttingen 2005).

[6] See n. on 4.16.9.

THE HISTORIES OF POLYBIUS

4 Ἀμύνανδρος καὶ παρ' Ἀττάλου Διονυσόδωρος, ἀπὸ δὲ
τῶν ἐθνῶν καὶ πόλεων τῶν μὲν Ἀχαιῶν Ἀρίσταινος
καὶ Ξενοφῶν, παρὰ δὲ Ῥοδίων Ἀκεσίμβροτος ὁ ναύαρχος, παρὰ δὲ τῶν Αἰτωλῶν Φαινέας ὁ στρατηγός,

5 καὶ πλείους δ' ἕτεροι τῶν πολιτευομένων. συνεγγίσαν-
τες δὲ κατὰ Νίκαιαν πρὸς τὴν θάλατταν, οἱ μὲν περὶ
τὸν Τίτον ἐπέστησαν παρ' αὐτὸν ⟨τὸν⟩ αἰγιαλόν, ὁ δὲ

6 Φίλιππος ἐγγίσας τῇ γῇ μετέωρος ἔμενε. τοῦ δὲ Τίτου
κελεύοντος αὐτὸν ἀποβαίνειν, διαναστὰς ἐκ τῆς νεὼς

7 οὐκ ἔφησεν ἀποβήσεσθαι. τοῦ δὲ πάλιν ἐρομένου τίνα
φοβεῖται, φοβεῖσθαι μὲν ἔπησεν ὁ Φίλιππος οὐδένα
πλὴν τοὺς θεούς, ἀπιστεῖν δὲ τοῖς πλείστοις τῶν παρ-

8 όντων, μάλιστα δ' Αἰτωλοῖς. τοῦ δὲ τῶν Ῥωμαίων
στρατηγοῦ θαυμάσαντος καὶ φήσαντος ἴσον εἶναι
πᾶσι τὸν κίνδυνον καὶ κοινὸν τὸν καιρόν, μεταλαβὼν

9 ὁ Φίλιππος οὐκ ἔφησεν αὐτὸν ὀρθῶς λέγειν· Φαινέου
μὲν γὰρ παθόντος τι πολλοὺς εἶναι τοὺς στρατηγή-
σοντας Αἰτωλῶν, Φιλίππου δ' ἀπολομένου κατὰ τὸ

10 παρὸν οὐκ εἶναι τὸν βασιλεύσοντα Μακεδόνων. ἐδόκει
μὲν οὖν πᾶσι φορτικῶς κατάρχεσθαι τῆς ὁμιλίας.
ὅμως δὲ λέγειν αὐτὸν ἐκέλευεν ὁ Τίτος ὑπὲρ ὧν πάρ-

11 εστιν. ὁ δὲ Φίλιππος οὐκ ἔφη τὸν λόγον αὐτῷ καθήκειν, ἀλλ' ἐκείνῳ· διαπερ ἠξίου διασαφεῖν τὸν Τίτον

12 τί δεῖ ποιήσαντα τὴν εἰρήνην ἄγειν. ὁ δὲ τῶν Ῥωμαίων

7 See n. on 16.3.6.　　8 Of Dyme, strategus in 199/8 as
successor to Cycliadas, instrumental in bringing the Achaeans to
the Roman side. See also n. on 11.11.7.

100

the representative of Attalus Dionysodorus,[7] and on the part of cities and nations Aristaenus[8] and Xenophon[9] from Achaea, Acesimbrotus,[10] the admiral, from Rhodes, and from Aetolia the strategus Phaeneas[11] and several other politicians. Flamininus and those with him reached the sea at Nicaea and waited standing on the beach, but Philip on approaching land remained afloat. When Flamininus asked him to come ashore he rose from his place on the ship and said he would not disembark. Upon Flamininus again asking him of whom he was afraid Philip said he was afraid of no one but the gods, but he was suspicious of most of those present and especially of the Aetolians. When the Roman general expressed his surprise and said that the danger was the same for all and the chances equal, Philip said he was not right; for if anything happened to Phaeneas, there were many who could be strategi of the Aetolians, but if Philip perished there was no one at present to occupy the throne of Macedon. He seemed to them all to have opened the conference with little dignity, but Flamininus, however, begged him to state his reasons for attending it. Philip said it was not his own business to speak first, but that of Flamininus, and he therefore asked him to explain what he should do to have peace. The Ro-

[9] Of Aegium. He, his father Euryleon, and his son Alcithus were distinguished politicians among the Achaeans between 211 and 168. *RE* Xenophon 1568 (H. H. Schmitt). He was *proxenos* at Delphi in 195/4 (*SIG* 585.29).

[10] On record as the Rhodian admiral in *SIG* 673.

[11] The Aetolian strategus of 198. *RE* Phaineas 1563–1565 (W. Hoffmann).

στρατηγὸς αὐτῷ μὲν ἁπλοῦν τινα λόγον ἔφη καθή-
13 κειν καὶ φαινόμενον. κελεύειν γὰρ αὐτὸν ἐκ μὲν τῆς
Ἑλλάδος ἁπάσης ἐκχωρεῖν, ἀποδόντα τοὺς αἰχμαλώ-
14 τους καὶ τοὺς αὐτομόλους ἑκάστοις οὓς ἔχει, τοὺς δὲ
κατὰ τὴν Ἰλλυρίδα τόπους παραδοῦναι Ῥωμαίοις, ὧν
γέγονε κύριος μετὰ τὰς ἐν Ἠπείρῳ διαλύσεις· ὁμοίως
δὲ καὶ Πτολεμαίῳ τὰς πόλεις ἀποκαταστῆσαι πάσας,
ἃς παρῄρηται μετὰ τὸν Πτολεμαίου τοῦ Φιλοπάτορος
θάνατον.

2. Ταῦτα δ᾽ εἰπὼν ὁ Τίτος αὐτὸς μὲν ἐπέσχε, πρὸς
(17 2) δὲ τοὺς ἄλλους ἐπιστραφεὶς ἐκέλευε λέγειν ἅπερ ἑκά-
2 στοις αὐτῶν οἱ πέμψαντες εἴησαν ἐντεταλμένοι. πρῶτος δὲ Διονυσόδωρος ὁ παρ᾽ Ἀττάλου μεταλαβὼν τὸν
λόγον τάς τε ναῦς ἔφη δεῖν αὐτὸν ἀποδοῦναι τὰς τοῦ
βασιλέως τὰς γενομένας αἰχμαλώτους ἐν τῇ περὶ
Χίον ναυμαχίᾳ καὶ τοὺς ἅμα ταύταις ἄνδρας, ἀποκαταστῆσαι δὲ καὶ τὸ τῆς Ἀφροδίτης ἱερὸν ἀκέραιον καὶ
3 τὸ Νικηφόριον, ἃ κατέφθειρε. μετὰ δὲ τοῦτον ὁ τῶν
Ῥοδίων ναύαρχος Ἀκεσίμβροτος τῆς μὲν Περαίας
ἐκέλευεν ἐκχωρεῖν τὸν Φίλιππον, ἧς αὐτῶν παρῄρηται,
τὰς δὲ φρουρὰς ἐξάγειν ἐξ Ἰασοῦ καὶ Βαργυλίων καὶ

---

12 This goes beyond the earlier Roman demands in 16.27.2
and 34.3–4 but is in line with what Flamininus had earlier demanded, according to Livy 32.10.3.

13 Most likely acquisitions that Philip had made after the
peace of Phoenice in 205. Illyria had been on his mind when he
concluded the alliance with Hannibal in 215: see 7.9.13.

14 Among those were Aenus in Thracia (Livy 31.16.40) and

man general said that what it was his duty to say was simple and obvious. He demanded that Philip should withdraw[12] from the whole of Greece after giving up to each power the prisoners and deserters in his hands; that he should surrender to the Romans the district of Illyria[13] that had fallen into his power after the treaty made in Epirus, and likewise restore to Ptolemy all the towns[14] that he had taken from him after the death of Ptolemy Philopator.

2. Flamininus after speaking thus stopped, and turning to the others bade them each speak as they had been instructed by those who had commissioned them. Dionysodorus, the representative of Attalus, was the first to speak. He said that Philip must give up those of the king's ships he had taken in the battle of Chios, together with the men captured in them, and that he must restore to their original condition the temple of Aphrodite[15] and the Nicephorium[16] which he had destroyed. Next Acesimbrotus, the Rhodian admiral, demanded that Philip should evacuate the Peraea[17] which he had taken from the Rhodians, withdraw his garrisons from Iasus,[18] Bargylia,[19] and Euro-

perhaps Samos, if not yet re-conquered by Ptolemaic forces (see n. on 16.2.4).   [15] E. Ohlemutz, *Die Kulte und Heiligtümer der Götter in Pergamon* (Würzburg 1940), 225–228.

[16] See n. on 16.1.6.

[17] Territories of Rhodes on the mainland, partly integrated into the Rhodian state, partly subject areas. P. M. Fraser and G. E. Bean, *The Rhodian Peraea and Islands* (Oxford 1954). V. Gabrielsen, *C&M* 51 (2000), 129–183. See also 16.11.2. C. Carusi, *Isole e Peree in Asia Minore* (Pisa 2003), deals mainly with the Peraeae of Lesbos, Chios, and Samos.

[18] See n. on 16.12.1.   [19] 16.24.1.

4 τῆς Εὐρωμέων πόλεως, ἀποκαταστῆσαι δὲ καὶ Περιν-
θίους εἰς τὴν Βυζαντίων συμπολιτείαν, παραχωρεῖν δὲ
καὶ Σηστοῦ καὶ Ἀβύδου καὶ τῶν ἐμπορίων καὶ λιμέ-
5 νων τῶν κατὰ τὴν Ἀσίαν ἁπάντων. ἐπὶ δὲ τοῖς Ῥοδίοις
Ἀχαιοὶ Κόρινθον ἀπῄτουν καὶ τὴν τῶν Ἀργείων πόλιν
6 ἀβλαβῆ. μετὰ δὲ τούτους Αἰτωλοὶ πρῶτον μὲν τῆς
Ἑλλάδος ἁπάσης ἐκέλευον ἐξίστασθαι, καθάπερ καὶ
Ῥωμαῖοι, δεύτερον αὐτοῖς ἀποκαθιστάναι τὰς πόλεις
ἀβλαβεῖς τὰς πρότερον μετασχούσας τῆς τῶν Αἰτωλῶν συμπολιτείας.

3. Ταῦτα δ᾽ εἰπόντος τοῦ Φαινέου τοῦ τῶν Αἰτωλῶν
(17 3) στρατηγοῦ, μεταλαβὼν Ἀλέξανδρος ὁ προσαγορευό-
μενος Ἴσιος, ἀνὴρ δοκῶν πραγματικὸς εἶναι καὶ λέ-
2 γειν ἱκανός, οὔτε διαλύεσθαι νῦν ἔφησε τὸν Φίλιππον
ἀληθινῶς οὔτε πολεμεῖν γενναίως, ὅταν δέῃ τοῦτο
πράττειν, ἀλλ᾽ ἐν μὲν τοῖς συλλόγοις καὶ ταῖς ὁμιλίαις
ἐνεδρεύειν καὶ παρατηρεῖν καὶ ποιεῖν τὰ τοῦ πολεμοῦντος ἔργα, κατ᾽ αὐτὸν δὲ τὸν πόλεμον ἀδίκως
3 ἵστασθαι καὶ λίαν ἀγεννῶς· ἀφέντα γὰρ τοῦ κατὰ
πρόσωπον ἀπαντᾶν τοῖς πολεμίοις, φεύγοντα τὰς πόλεις ἐμπιπράναι καὶ διαρπάζειν καὶ διὰ ταύτης τῆς
προαιρέσεως ἡττώμενον τὰ τῶν νικώντων ἆθλα λυ-
4 μαίνεσθαι. καίτοι γε τοὺς πρότερον Μακεδόνων βεβα-

---

20 Conquered by Philip in 201 and renamed "Philippoi": *SEG*
36.973; see also *SEG* 43.70. Cohen (16.24.6), 251.
21 *RE* Perinthos 802–817 (E. Oberhummer). M. H. Sayar,
Perinthus, Herakleia und Umgebung . . Geschichte, Testimonia,

mus,[20] permit the Perinthians[21] to resume their confederacy with Byzantium, and retire from Sestus[22] and Abydus[23] and all commercial depots and harbors in Asia. After the Rhodians the Achaeans demanded Corinth[24] and Argos[25] undamaged, and next the Aetolians first of all, as the Romans had done, bade him withdraw from the whole of Greece, and next asked him to restore to them undamaged the cities which were formerly members of the Aetolian League.

3. After Phaeneas, the strategus of the Aetolians, had spoken thus, Alexander called the Isian,[26] a man considered to be a practical statesman and an able speaker, took part in the debate and said that Philip neither sincerely desired peace at present nor did he make war bravely when he had to do so, but that in assemblies and conferences he laid traps and watched for opportunities and behaved as if he were at war, but in war itself adopted an unfair and very ungenerous course. For instead of meeting his enemies face to face he used to flee before them, burning and sacking cities, and by this course of conduct though beaten he spoilt the prizes of the victors. Not this but quite the reverse had been the object of the former

griechische und lateinische Inschriften (Vienna 1998). Philip had annexed the city in 202.

[22] 16.29.3.   [23] 16.29.2–35.2.

[24] The city received a garrison from King Antigonus Doson in 224, when his assistance was requested by the Achaeans against Cleomenes.

[25] Philip's general Philocles was called in soon after the controversial decision of the Achaeans to leave Philip for the Romans; Livy 32.25.1–12.

[26] First mentioned in 13.1a.1.

σιλευκότας οὐ ταύτην ἐσχηκέναι τὴν πρόθεσιν, ἀλλὰ
τὴν ἐναντίαν· μάχεσθαι μὲν γὰρ πρὸς ἀλλήλους συνεχῶς ἐν τοῖς ὑπαίθροις, τὰς δὲ πόλεις σπανίως
5 ἀναιρεῖν καὶ καταφθείρειν. τοῦτο δ᾽ εἶναι πᾶσι φανερὸν
ἔκ τε τοῦ πολέμου τοῦ περὶ τὴν Ἀσίαν, ὃν Ἀλέξανδρος
ἐπολέμησε πρὸς Δαρεῖον, ἔκ τε τῆς τῶν διαδεξαμένων
ἀμφισβητήσεως, καθ᾽ ἣν ἐπολέμησαν πάντες πρὸς
6 Ἀντίγονον ὑπὲρ τῆς Ἀσίας. παραπλησίως δὲ καὶ τοὺς
τούτους διαδεξαμένους μέχρι Πύρρου κεχρῆσθαι τῇ
7 προαιρέσει ταύτῃ· διακινδυνεύειν μὲν γὰρ πρὸς αὑτοὺς
ἐν τοῖς ὑπαίθροις προχείρως καὶ πάντα ποιεῖν εἰς τὸ
καταγωνίσασθαι διὰ τῶν ὅπλων ἀλλήλους, τῶν δὲ
πόλεων φείδεσθαι χάριν τοῦ τοὺς νικήσαντας ἡγεῖ-
σθαι τούτων καὶ τιμᾶσθαι παρὰ τοῖς ὑποταττομένοις.
8 τὸ δ᾽ ἀναιροῦντα περὶ ὧν ὁ πόλεμός ἐστι τὸν πόλεμον
αὐτὸν καταλιπεῖν μανίας ἔργον εἶναι, καὶ ταύτης ἐρ-
9 ρωμένης, ὃ νῦν ποιεῖν τὸν Φίλιππον· τοσαύτας γὰρ
διεφθαρκέναι πόλεις ἐν Θετταλίᾳ, φίλον ὄντα καὶ
σύμμαχον, καθ᾽ ὃν καιρὸν ἐκ τῶν ἐν Ἠπείρῳ στενῶν
ἐποιεῖτο τὴν σπουδήν, ὅσας οὐδείς ποτε τῶν Θετταλοῖς
10 πεπολεμηκότων διέφθειρε. πολλὰ δὲ καὶ ἕτερα πρὸς
ταύτην τὴν ὑπόθεσιν διαλεχθεὶς τελευταίοις ἐχρήσατο
11 τούτοις. ἤρετο γὰρ τὸν Φίλιππον διὰ τί Λυσιμάχειαν
μετ᾽ Λἰτωλῶν ταττομένην καὶ στρατηγὸν ἔχουσαν
παρ᾽ αὐτῶν ἐκβαλὼν τοῦτον κατάσχοι φρουρᾷ τὴν
12 πόλιν· διὰ τί δὲ Κιανούς, παραπλησίως μετ᾽ Αἰτωλῶν

---

27 Antigonus I the One-eyed. The reference is to the war of

kings of Macedon; for they used to fight constantly with each other in the field but very seldom destroyed or ruined cities. This was evident to everybody from the war that Alexander waged against Darius in Asia, and from that long dispute of his successors in which they all took up arms against Antigonus[27] for the mastery of Asia; and their successors again down to Pyrrhus had acted on the same principle; they had always been ready to give battle to each other in the open field and had done all in their power to overcome each other by force of arms, but they had spared cities, so that whoever conquered might be supreme in them and be honored by his subjects. But while destroying the objects of war, to leave war itself untouched was madness and very strong madness. And this was just what Philip was now doing. For when he was hurrying back from the pass in Epirus[28] he destroyed more cities in Thessaly, though he was the friend and ally of the Thessalians, than any of their enemies had ever destroyed. After adding much more to the same effect, he finally argued as follows. He asked Philip why, when Lysimachia[29] was a member of the Aetolian League and was in charge of a military governor sent by them, he had expelled the latter and placed a garrison of his own in the city; and why had he sold into slavery the people of Cius,[30] also a member of the Aetolian

---

27 to 311 when Lysimachus, Cassander, Ptolemy, and Seleucus were allied against him, and to their later war (except for Ptolemy), that ended with Antigonus' defeat and death at Ipsus in 301.

28 At the Aous (Viossa), where Philip was bypassed by the Roman army of Flamininus. For the cities in Thessaly, see F. W. Walbank, *Philip V* (Cambridge 1940), 153.

29 See n. on 15.23.8.   30 15.21.1–23.10.

συμπολιτευομένους ἐξανδραποδίσαιτο, φίλος ὑπάρχων
Αἰτωλοῖς· τί δὲ λέγων κατέχει νῦν Ἐχῖνον καὶ Θήβας
τὰς Φθίας καὶ Φάρσαλον καὶ Λάρισαν.

4. Ὁ μὲν οὖν Ἀλέξανδρος ταῦτ᾽ εἰπὼν ἀπεσιώπησεν.
(17 1) ὁ δὲ Φίλιππος ἐγγίσας τῇ γῇ μᾶλλον ἢ πρόσθεν καὶ
διαναστὰς ἐπὶ τῆς νεὼς Αἰτωλικὸν ἔφη καὶ θεατρικὸν
2 διατεθεῖσθαι τὸν Ἀλέξανδρον λόγον. σαφῶς γὰρ πάντας γινώσκειν ὅτι τοὺς ἰδίους συμμάχους ἑκὼν μὲν
οὐδεὶς διαφθείρει, κατὰ δὲ τὰς τῶν καιρῶν περιστάσεις πολλὰ ποιεῖν ἀναγκάζεσθαι τοὺς ἡγουμένους
3 παρὰ τὰς ἑαυτῶν προαιρέσεις. ἔτι δὲ ταῦτα λέγοντος
τοῦ βασιλέως ὁ Φαινέας, ἠλαττωμένος τοῖς ὄμμασιν
ἐπὶ πλεῖον, ὑπέκρουε τὸν Φίλιππον, φάσκων αὐτὸν
ληρεῖν· δεῖν γὰρ ἢ μαχόμενον νικᾶν ἢ ποιεῖν τοῖς
4 κρείττοσι τὸ προστατόμενον. ὁ δὲ Φίλιππος, καίπερ
ἐν κακοῖς ὤν, ὅμως οὐκ ἀπέσχετο τοῦ καθ᾽ αὑτὸν ἰδι-
ώματος, ἀλλ᾽ ἐπιστραφεὶς "τοῦτο μὲν" ἔφησεν "ὦ Φαινέα, καὶ τυφλῷ δῆλον." ἦν γὰρ εὔθικτος καὶ πρὸς
τοῦτο τὸ μέρος εὖ πεφυκὼς πρὸς τὸ διαχλευάζειν ἀν-
5 θρώπους. αὖθις δὲ πρὸς τὸν Ἀλέξανδρον ἐπιστρέψας
"ἐρωτᾷς με" φησίν "Ἀλέξανδρε, διὰ τί Λυσιμάχειαν
6 προσέλαβον; ἵνα μὴ διὰ τὴν ὑμετέραν ὀλιγωρίαν
ἀνάστατος ὑπὸ Θρᾳκῶν γένηται, καθάπερ νῦν γέγονεν ἡμῶν ἀπαγαγόντων τοὺς στρατιώτας διὰ τοῦτον
τὸν πόλεμον, οὐ τοὺς φρουροῦντας αὐτήν, ὡς σὺ φής,

---

31 For these cities, whose return Phaenaeas had already demanded (2.6), see *RE* Pharsalos (Suppl. 12), 1038–1084 (Y. Bé-

League, when he himself was on friendly terms with the
Aetolians? On what pretext did he now retain possession
of Echinus,[31] Phthiotic Thebes, Pharsalus, and Larisa?

4. When Alexander had ended this harangue, Philip
brought his ship nearer to the shore than it had been, and
standing up on the deck, said that Alexander's speech had
been truly Aetolian and theatrical. Everyone, he said, was
aware that no one ever of his own free will ruins his own
allies, but that by changes of circumstance commanders
are forced to do many things that they would have pre-
ferred not to do. The king had not finished speaking when
Phaeneas, whose sight was badly impaired, interrupted
him rudely, saying that he was talking nonsense, for he
must either fight and conquer or do the bidding of his
betters. Philip, though in an evil case, could not refrain
from his peculiar gift of raillery, but turning to him said,
"Even a blind man, Phaeneas, can see that";[32] for he was
ready and had a natural talent for scoffing at people. Then,
turning again to Alexander, "You ask me," he said, "Alexander, why I annexed Lysimachia. It was in order that it
should not, owing to your neglect, be depopulated by the
Thracians, as has actually happened since I withdrew to
serve in this war those of my troops who were acting not
as you say as its garrison, but as its guardians. As for the

quignon). Larisa is Larisa *cremaste* in Phthiotis. For the highly
complicated question of who had valid claims on these cities in
198, see J. Walsh, *CP.* 88 (1993), 35–46.

[32] Antigonus I (see 3.5), one of Philip's predecessors, who was
one-eyed, is said to have made fun of his handicap using that same
expression (Plu., *Moralia* 633 C).

7 ἀλλὰ τοὺς παραφυλάττοντας. Κιανοῖς δ' ἐγὼ μὲν οὐκ
ἐπολέμησα Προυσίου δὲ πολεμοῦντος βοηθῶν ἐκείνῳ

8 συνεξεῖλον αὐτούς, ὑμῶν αἰτίων γενομένων· πολλάκις
γὰρ κἀμοῦ καὶ τῶν ἄλλων Ἑλλήνων διαπρεσβευομέ-
νων πρὸς ὑμᾶς, ἵνα τὸν νόμον ἄρητε τὸν διδόντα τὴν
ἐξουσίαν ὑμῖν ἄγειν λάφυρον ἀπὸ λαφύρου, πρότερον
ἔφατε τὴν Αἰτωλίαν ἐκ τῆς Αἰτωλίας ἀρεῖν ἢ τοῦτον
τὸν νόμον."

5. Τοῦ δὲ Τίτου θαυμάσαντος τί τοῦτ' ἐστίν, ὁ
(175) βασιλεὺς ἐπειρᾶτο διασαφεῖν αὐτῷ, λέγων ὅτι τοῖς
Αἰτωλοῖς ἔθος ὑπάρχει μὴ μόνον πρὸς οὓς ἂν αὐτοὶ
πολεμῶσι, τούτους αὐτοὺς ἄγειν καὶ τὴν τούτων χώ-

2 ραν, ἀλλὰ κἂν ἕτεροί τινες πολεμῶσι πρὸς ἀλλήλους,
ὄντες Αἰτωλῶν φίλοι καὶ σύμμαχοι, μηδὲν ἧττον
ἐξεῖναι τοῖς Αἰτωλοῖς ἄνευ κοινοῦ δόγματος καὶ
παρ‹αβοηθεῖν› ἀμφοτέροις τοῖς πολεμοῦσι καὶ τὴν

3 χώραν ἄγειν τὴν ἀμφοτέρων, ὥστε παρὰ μὲν τοῖς
Αἰτωλοῖς μήτε φιλίας ὅρους ὑπάρχειν μήτ' ἔχθρας,
ἀλλὰ πᾶσι τοῖς ἀμφισβητοῦσι περί τινος ἑτοίμους

4 ἐχθροὺς εἶναι τούτους καὶ πολεμίους. "πόθεν οὖν ἔξεστι τούτοις ἐγκαλεῖν νῦν, εἰ φίλος ὑπάρχων Αἰτωλοῖς
ἐγώ, Προυσίου δὲ σύμμαχος, ἔπραξά τι κατὰ Κιανῶν,

5 βοηθῶν τοῖς αὑτοῦ συμμάχοις; τὸ δὲ δὴ πάντων δεινότατον, οἱ ποιοῦντες ἑαυτοὺς ἐφαμίλλους Ῥωμαίοις
καὶ κελεύοντες ἐκχωρεῖν Μακεδόνας ἁπάσης τῆς Ἑλ-

6 λάδος· τοῦτο γὰρ ἀναφθέγξασθαι καὶ καθόλου μέν
ἐστιν ὑπερήφανον, οὐ μὴν ἀλλὰ Ῥωμαίων μὲν λεγόν-

7 των ἀνεκτόν, Αἰτωλῶν δ' οὐκ ἀνεκτόν· ποίας δὲ κελεύ-

110

people of Cius, it was not I who made war on them, but when Prusias[33] did so I helped him to exterminate them, and all through your fault. For on many occasions when I and the other Greeks sent embassies to you begging you to remove from your statutes the law empowering you to get booty from booty, you replied that you would rather remove Aetolia from Aetolia than that law."[34]

5. When Flamininus said he wondered what that was, the king tried to explain to him, saying that the Aetolians have a custom not only to make booty of the persons and territory of those with whom they are themselves at war, but if any other peoples are at war with each other who are friends and allies of theirs, it is permissible nevertheless to the Aetolians without any public decree to help both belligerents and pillage the territory of both; so that with the Aetolians there is no precise definition of friendship and enmity, but they promptly treat as enemies and make war on all between whom there is a dispute about anything. "So what right have they," he continued, "to accuse me now, because, being a friend of the Aetolians and the ally of Prusias, I acted against the people of Cius in coming to the aid of my ally? But what is most insufferable of all is that they assume they are the equals of the Romans in demanding that the Macedonians should withdraw from the whole of Greece. To employ such language at all is indeed a sign of haughtiness, but while we may put up with it from the lips of Romans we cannot when the speakers are Aetolians. And what," he said, "is that Greece

33 15.22.1.

34 For what follows see J. Scholten, *The Politics of Plunder . . .* (Berkeley 2000), 4.21–22.

ετέ με" φησὶν "ἐκχωρεῖν Ἑλλάδος καὶ πῶς ἀφορίζετε
ταύτην; αὐτῶν γὰρ Αἰτωλῶν οὐκ εἰσὶν Ἕλληνες οἱ
8 πλείους· τὸ γὰρ τῶν Ἀγραῶν ἔθνος καὶ τὸ τῶν Ἀπο-
9 δωτῶν, ἔτι δὲ τῶν Ἀμφιλόχων, οὐκ ἔστιν Ἑλλάς. ἢ
τούτων μὲν παραχωρεῖτέ μοι;"

6. Τοῦ δὲ Τίτου γελάσαντος "ἀλλὰ δὴ πρὸς μὲν
(176) Αἰτωλοὺς ἀρκείτω μοι ταῦτ'" ἔφη· "πρὸς δὲ Ῥοδίους
καὶ πρὸς Ἄτταλον ἐν μὲν ἴσῳ κριτῇ δικαιότερον ἂν
νομισθείη τούτους ἡμῖν ἀποδιδόναι τὰς αἰχμαλώτους
2 ναῦς καὶ τοὺς ἄνδας ἤπερ ἡμᾶς τούτοις· οὐ γὰρ ἡμεῖς
Ἀττάλῳ πρότεροι καὶ Ῥοδίοις τὰς χεῖρας ἐπεβάλομεν,
3 οὗτοι δ' ἡμῖν ὁμολογουμένως. οὐ μὴν ἀλλὰ σοῦ κελεύοντος Ῥοδίοις μὲν ἀποδίδωμι τὴν Περαίαν, Ἀττάλῳ δὲ
4 τὰς ναῦς καὶ τοὺς ἄνδρας τοὺς διασῳζομένους. τὴν δὲ
τοῦ Νικηφορίου καταφθορὰν καὶ τοῦ τῆς Ἀφροδίτης
τεμένους ἄλλως μὲν οὐκ εἰμὶ δυνατὸς ἀποκαταστῆσαι,
φυτὰ δὲ καὶ κηπουροὺς πέμψω τοὺς φροντιοῦντας θεραπείας τοῦ τόπου καὶ τῆς αὐξήσεως τῶν ἐκκοπέντων
5 δένδρων." πάλιν δὲ τοῦ Τίτου γελάσαντος ἐπὶ τῷ
χλευασμῷ, μεταβὰς ὁ Φίλιππος ἐπὶ τοὺς Ἀχαιοὺς
πρῶτον μὲν τὰς εὐεργεσίας ἐξηριθμήσατο τὰς ἐξ Ἀν-
6 τιγόνου γεγενημένας εἰς αὐτούς, εἶτα τὰς ἰδίας· ἑξῆς
δὲ τούτοις προηνέγκατο τὸ μέγεθος τῶν τιμῶν τῶν
7 ἀπηντημένων αὐτοῖς παρὰ τῶν Ἀχαιῶν. τελευταῖον δ'

---

35 For the Amphilochians Th. 2.68.5: οἱ δ' ἄλλοι Ἀμφίλοχοι
βάρβαροί εἰσιν. The Aetolians as μιξοβάρβαροι: E., *Ph.* 134–
138. For the locations of the territories, see E. Oberhummer,

from which you order me to withdraw, and how do you define Greece? For most of the Aetolians themselves are not Greeks.[35] No! the countries of the Agraae, the Apodotae, and the Amphilochians are not Greece. Do you give me permission to remain in those countries?"

6. Upon Flamininus smiling, "That is all I have to say to the Aetolians," he said, "but my answer to the Romans and Attalus is that a fair judge would pronounce that it would be more just for them to give up the captured ships and men to me than for me to give them up to them. For it was not I[36] who first took up arms against Attalus and the Rhodians, but they cannot deny that they were the aggressors. However, at your bidding I cede the Peraea to the Rhodians and the ships and men who still survive to Attalus. As for the damage done to the Nicephorium and the sanctuary of Aphrodite, it is not in my power to repair it otherwise, but I will send plants and gardeners to cultivate the place and see to the growth of the trees that were cut down." Flamininus again smiled at the jest, and Philip now passed to the Achaeans.[37] He first enumerated all the favors they had received from Antigonus and those he himself had done them, next he recited the high honors[38] they had conferred on the Macedonian monarchs,

36 Philip was technically correct, as his hostile actions had not directly affected Attalus or Rhodes, but only their friends or interests, and were carried out by irregulars such as Heraclides of Tarentum (13.4.1–5.6).

37 Philip had reason to complain about them.

38 Especially to Antigonus Doson; see n. on 2.70.5.

ἀνέγνω τὸ περὶ τῆς ἀποστάσεως ψήφισμα καὶ τῆς
πρὸς Ῥωμαίους μεταθέσεως, ᾗ χρησάμενος ἀφορμῇ
πολλὰ κατὰ τῶν Ἀχαιῶν εἰς ἀθεσίαν εἶπε καὶ ἀχαρι-
8 στίαν. ὅμως δ᾽ ἔφη τὸ μὲν Ἄργος ἀποδώσειν, περὶ δὲ
τοῦ Κορίνθου βουλεύσεσθαι μετὰ τοῦ Τίτου.

7. Ταῦτα δὲ διαλεχθεὶς πρὸς τοὺς ἄλλους ἤρετο τὸν
(177) Τίτον, φήσας πρὸς ἐκεῖνον αὐτῷ τὸν λόγον εἶναι καὶ
πρὸς Ῥωμαίους, πότερον οἴεται δεῖν ἐκχωρεῖν ὧν ἐπ-
έκτηται πόλεων καὶ τόπων ἐν τοῖς Ἕλλησιν, ἢ καὶ
2 τούτων ὅσα παρὰ τῶν γονέων παρείληφε. τοῦ δ᾽ ἀπο-
σιωπήσαντος ἐκ χειρὸς ἀπαντᾶν οἷοί τ᾽ ἦσαν ὁ μὲν
Ἀρίσταινος ὑπὲρ τῶν Ἀχαιῶν, ὁ δὲ Φαινέας ὑπὲρ τῶν
3 Αἰτωλῶν. ἤδη δὲ τῆς ὥρας συγκλειούσης ὁ μὲν τούτων λόγος ἐκωλύθη διὰ τὸν καιρόν, ὁ δὲ Φίλιππος
ἠξίου γράψαντας αὐτῷ δοῦναι πάντας ἐφ᾽ οἷς δεήσει
γίνεσθαι τὴν εἰρήνην· μόνος γὰρ ὢν οὐκ ἔχειν μεθ᾽
4 ὧν βουλεύηται· διὸ θέλειν αὐτῷ λόγον δοῦναι περὶ
5 τῶν ἐπιταττομένων. ὁ δὲ Τίτος οὐκ ἀηδῶς μὲν ἤκουε
τοῦ Φιλίππου χλευάζοντος· μὴ βουλόμενος δὲ τοῖς
ἄλλοις [μὴ] δοκεῖν ἀντεπέσκωψε τὸν Φίλιππον εἰπὼν
6 οὕτως· "εἰκότως" ἔφη "Φίλιππε, μόνος εἶ νῦν· τοὺς γὰρ
φίλους τοὺς τὰ κράτιστά σοι συμβουλεύσοντας ἀπώ-
λεσας ἅπαντας." ὁ δὲ Μακεδὼν ὑπομειδιάσας σαρδά-
νιον ἀπεσιώπησε.

7 Καὶ τότε μὲν ἅπαντες, ἐγγράπτους δόντες τῷ Φι-

and finally he read the decree[39] in which they decided to abandon him and go over to the Romans, taking occasion thereby to dwell at length on their inconsistency and ingratitude. Still, he said, he would restore Argos to them, but would consult with Flamininus as to Corinth.

7. After speaking to the others in these terms he asked Flamininus, saying that he was now addressing himself and the Romans, whether he demanded his withdrawal from those towns and places in Greece which he had himself conquered or from those also which he had inherited from his forebears. Flamininus remained silent, but Aristaenus on the part of the Achaeans and Phaeneas on that of the Aetolians were at once ready with a reply. However, as the day was now drawing to a close, they were prevented from speaking owing to the hour, and Philip demanded that they should all furnish him with their terms for peace in writing; for he was alone and had no one to consult, so he wished to think over their demands. Flamininus was by no means displeased by Philip's jests, and not wishing the others to think he was so, rallied Philip in turn by saying, "Naturally you are alone now, Philip, for you have killed all those of your friends[40] who would give you the best advice." The Macedonian monarch smiled sardonically and made no reply.

They all now, after handing to Philip their decisions in

---

[39] Passed at Sicyon by a very slim majority, as Livy, following P., reports in 32.20.1–23.3.

[40] The "friends" (φίλοι) made up the Council of the Hellenistic king; see C. Habicht, *The Hellenistic Monarchies. Selected Papers* (Ann Arbor 2006), 26–40 (a paper of 1958 that starts from this very sentence of P.) and Addenda, p. 290.

λίππῳ τὰς ἑαυτῶν προαιρέσεις ἀκολούθως τοῖς προειρημένοις, ἐχωρίσθησαν, ταξάμενοι κατὰ τὴν ἐπιοῦ-
8 σαν εἰς Νίκαιαν πάλιν ἀπαντήσειν· τῇ δ᾽ αὔριον οἱ
μὲν περὶ τὸν Τίτον ἧκον ἐπὶ τὸν ταχθέντα τόπον ἐν
ὧ‹ρα› πάντες [ἦσαν], ὁ δὲ Φίλιππος οὐ παρεγίνετο.

8. Τῆς δ᾽ ἡμέρας ἤδη προαγούσης ἐπὶ πολὺ καὶ
(178) σχεδὸν ἀπεγνωκότων τῶν περὶ τὸν Τίτον, παρῆν ὁ
Φίλιππος δείλης ὀψίας ἐπιφαινόμενος μεθ᾽ ὧν καὶ
2 πρότερον, κατατετριφὼς τὴν ἡμέραν, ὡς μὲν αὐτὸς
ἔφη, διὰ τὴν ἀπορίαν καὶ δυσχρηστίαν τῶν ἐπιταττομένων, ὡς δὲ τοῖς ἄλλοις ἐδόκει, βουλόμενος ἐκκλεῖ-
σαι τῷ καιρῷ τήν τε τῶν Ἀχαιῶν καὶ τὴν τῶν Αἰτωλῶν
3 κατηγορίαν· ἑώρα γὰρ τῇ πρόσθεν ἀπαλλαττόμενος
ἀμφοτέρους τούτους ἑτοίμους ὄντας πρὸς τὸ συμπλέ-
4 κεσθαι καὶ μεμψιμοιρεῖν αὐτῷ. διὸ καὶ τότε συνεγγίσας ἠξίου τὸν τῶν Ῥωμαίων στρατηγὸν ἰδίᾳ πρὸς
αὐτὸν διαλεχθῆναι περὶ τῶν ἐνεστώτων, ἵνα μὴ λόγοι
γένωνται μόνον ἐξ ἀμφοτέρων ἀψιμαχούντων. ἀλλὰ
5 καὶ τέλος τι τοῖς ἀμφισβητουμένοις ἐπιτεθῇ, πλεονάκις δ᾽ αὐτοῦ παρακαλοῦντος καὶ προσαξιοῦντος, ἤρετο
6 τοὺς συμπαρόντας ὁ Τίτος τί δέον εἴη ποιεῖν. τῶν δὲ
κελευόντων συνελθεῖν καὶ διακοῦσαι τῶν λεγομένων,
παραλαβὼν ὁ Τίτος Ἄππιον Κλαύδιον χιλίαρχον
ὄντα τότε, τοῖς μὲν ἄλλοις μικρὸν ἀπὸ τῆς θαλάττης
ἀναχωρήσασιν εἶπεν αὐτόθι μένειν, αὐτὸς δὲ τὸν Φί-
7 λιππον ἐκέλευσεν ἐκβαίνειν. ὁ δὲ βασιλεὺς παραλαβὼν
Ἀπολλόδωρον καὶ Δημοσθένην ἀπέβη, συμμίξας δὲ
8 τῷ Τίτῳ διελέγετο καὶ πλείω χρόνον. τίνα μὲν οὖν ἦν

writing—decisions similar to those I have stated—separated, making an appointment to meet next day again at Nicaea. On the morrow Flamininus and all the others arrived punctually at the appointed place, but Philip did not put in an appearance.

8. When it was getting quite late in the day and Flamininus had nearly given up all hope, Philip appeared at dusk accompanied by the same people, having, as he himself asserted, spent the day in puzzling over the conditions and dealing with the difficult points, but in the opinion of others his object was to prevent, by cutting down the time, the accusations of the Achaeans and Aetolians. For on the previous day at the moment of his departure he saw they were both ready to join issue with him and load him with reproach. So that now, approaching nearer, he asked the Roman general to converse with him in private about the situation, so that there should not be a mere skirmishing with words on both sides but that an end of some kind should be put to the dispute. When he begged and demanded this repeatedly, Flamininus asked those present what he ought to do. Upon their bidding him meet Philip and hear what he had to say, Flamininus taking with him Appius Claudius,[41] then military tribune, told the rest, who had retired a short distance from the seashore, to remain where they were and asked Philip to come ashore. The king left the ship accompanied by Apollodorus and Demosthenes, and meeting Flamininus conversed with him for a considerable time. It is difficult to tell what each

[41] *MRR* 1.331 and nn. 4–5.

τὰ τότε ῥηθέντα παρ᾽ ἑκατέρου, δυσχερὲς εἰπεῖν· ἔφη
δ᾽ οὖν ὁ Τίτος μετὰ τὸ χωρισθῆναι τὸν Φίλιππον,
9 διασαφῶν τοῖς ἄλλοις τὰ παρὰ τοῦ βασιλέως, Αἰτωλοῖς μὲν ἀποδοῦναι Φάρσαλον καὶ Λάρισαν, Θήβας δ᾽ οὐκ ἀποδιδόναι, Ῥοδίοις δὲ τῆς μὲν Περαίας
παραχωρεῖν, Ἰασοῦ δὲ καὶ Βαργυλίων οὐκ ἐκχωρεῖν·
Ἀχαιοῖς δὲ παραδιδόναι τὸν Κόρινθον καὶ τὴν τῶν
10 Ἀργείων πόλιν. Ῥωμαίοις δὲ τὰ κατὰ τὴν Ἰλλυρίδα
φάναι παραδώσειν καὶ τοὺς αἰχμαλώτους πάντας,
Ἀττάλῳ δὲ τάς τε ναῦς ἀποκαταστήσειν καὶ τῶν
ἀνδρῶν τῶν ἐν ταῖς ναυμαχίαις ἁλόντων ὅσοι περί-
εισι.

9. Πάντων δὲ τῶν παρόντων δυσαρεστουμένων τῇ
(179) διαλύσει καὶ φασκόντων δεῖν τὸ κοινὸν ἐπίταγμα
πρῶτον ποιεῖν—τοῦτο δ᾽ ἦν ἁπάσης ἐκχωρεῖν τῆς
Ἑλλάδος—εἰ δὲ μή, διότι τὰ κατὰ μέρος μάταια γίνε-
2 ται καὶ πρὸς οὐδέν, θεωρῶν ὁ Φίλιππος τὴν ἐν αὐτοῖς
ἀμφισβήτησιν καὶ δεδιὼς ἅμα τὰς κατηγορίας, ἠξίου
τὸν Τίτον ὑπερθέσθαι τὴν σύνοδον εἰς τὴν αὔριον διὰ
τὸ καὶ τὴν ὥραν εἰς ὀψὲ συγκλείειν· ἢ γὰρ πείσειν ἢ
3 πεισθήσεσθαι τοῖς παρακαλουμένοις. τοῦ δὲ συγχωρήσαντος, ταξάμενοι συμπορεύεσθαι πρὸς τὸν κατὰ
Θρόνιον αἰγιαλόν, τότε μὲν ἐχωρίσθησαν, τῇ δ᾽ ὑστε-
4 ραίᾳ πάντες ἧκον ἐπὶ τὸν ταχθέντα τόπον ἐν ὥρα. καὶ
βραχέα διαλεχθεὶς ὁ Φίλιππος ἠξίου πάντας, μάλιστα δὲ τὸν Τίτον, μὴ διακόψαι τὴν διάλυσιν, τῶν γε

of them said on that occasion, but Flamininus, after Philip had left, in explaining to the rest the king's proposals, said that he would restore Pharsalus[42] and Larisa to the Aetolians, but not Thebes, he would give up the Peraea to the Rhodians, but would not withdraw from Iasus and Bargylia, but to the Achaeans he would surrender Corinth and Argos. To the Romans he would give up his possessions in Illyria and would hand over all prisoners of war, and restore also to Attalus his ships and all who survived of the men captured in the naval engagements.[43]

9. When all present expressed their dissatisfaction with these terms and maintained that Philip should in the first place execute their common demand—that is withdraw from the whole of Greece, apart from which the different concessions were absurd and worthless—Philip, noticing the discussion that was going on and fearing the complaints they would bring against him, proposed to Flamininus to adjourn the conference till next day because, apart from other things, it was getting late: then he said he would either convince them or be convinced of the justice of their demands. Flamininus yielded to this request and after agreeing to meet on the beach at Thronion[44] they separated, and all next day arrived in time at the appointed place. Philip now in a short speech begged them all and especially Flamininus not to break off negotiations now

---

[42] For the concessions offered (or denied) by Philip, see chapters 2–3. With Corinth Philip meant the town, not the citadel, as 11.13 will make clear.

[43] Attalus had in fact only taken part in one, that of Chius.

[44] City in eastern Locris, southeast of Nicaea. *RE* Thronion 609–613 (W. M. Oldfather).

5 δὴ πλείστων εἰς συμβατικὴν διάθεσιν ἠγμένων, ἀλλ᾽
εἰ μὲν ἐνδέχεται δι᾽ αὐτῶν συμφώνους γενέσθαι περὶ
τῶν ἀντιλεγομένων· εἰ δὲ μή, πρεσβεύσειν ἔφη πρὸς
τὴν σύγκλητον, κἀκείνην πείσειν περὶ τῶν ἀμφισβη-
6 τουμένων, ἢ ποιήσειν ὅτι ποτ᾽ ἂν ἐπιτάττῃ. ταῦτα δ᾽
αὐτοῦ προτείνοντος, οἱ μὲν ἄλλοι πάντες ἔφασαν δεῖν
πράττειν τὰ τοῦ πολέμου καὶ μὴ προσέχειν τοῖς ἀξι-
7 ουμένοις. ὁ δὲ τῶν Ῥωμαίων στρατηγὸς οὐκ ἀγνοεῖν
μὲν οὐδ᾽ αὐτὸς ἔφη διότι τὸν Φίλιππον οὐκ εἰκός ἐστι
8 ποιῆσαι τῶν παρακαλουμένων οὐδέν· τῷ δ᾽ ἁπλῶς μηδὲν ἐμποδίζειν τὰς σφετέρας πράξεις τὴν αἰτουμένην
χάριν ὑπὸ τοῦ βασιλέως ἐκποιεῖν ἔφη χαρίζεσθαι.
9 κυρωθῆναι μὲν γὰρ οὐδ᾽ ὡς εἶναι δυνατὸν οὐδὲν τῶν
νῦν λεγομένων ἄνευ τῆς συγκλήτου, πρὸς δὲ τὸ λαβεῖν
πεῖραν τῆς ἐκείνων γνώμης εὐφυῶς ἔχειν τὸν ἐπιφερό-
10 μενον καιρόν· τῶν γὰρ στρατοπέδων οὐδ᾽ ὡς δυναμένων οὐδὲν πράττειν διὰ τὸν χειμῶνα, τοῦτον ἀποθέσθαι
τὸν χρόνον εἰς τὸ προσανενεγκεῖν τῇ συγκλήτῳ περὶ
τῶν προσπιπτόντων, οὐκ ἄθετον, ἀλλ᾽ οἰκεῖον εἶναι
πᾶσι.

10. Ταχὺ δὲ συγκαταθεμένων ἁπάντων διὰ τὸ θεω-
(17 10) ρεῖν τὸν Τίτον οὐκ ἀλλότριον ὄντα τῆς ἐπὶ τὴν σύγ-
2 κλητον ἀναφορᾶς, ἔδοξε συγχωρεῖν τῷ Φιλίππῳ πρεσβεύειν εἰς τὴν Ῥώμην, ὁμοίως δὲ καὶ παρ᾽ αὐτῶν
πέμπειν ἑκάστους πρεσβευτὰς τοὺς διαλεχθησομέ-
νους τῇ συγκλήτῳ καὶ κατηγορήσοντας τοῦ Φιλίππου.

that most of the delegates[45] had arrived at a conciliatory mood, but if possible to come to an agreement among themselves about the disputed points. If not, however, he said he would send an embassy to the senate and either persuade that body about these points or do whatever it ordered him. On his making this proposal all the others said they ought to continue the war and not accede to the request; but the Roman general[46] said that while he too was quite aware that there was no probability of Philip's really doing anything they demanded, yet as the king's request in no way interfered with their own action, it perfectly suited them to grant it. For as things stood, nothing they now said could be made valid without consulting the senate,[47] and besides the general advantage of arriving at a knowledge of the will of the senate, the immediate future was a favorable time for taking this course. The armies, in fact, could do nothing owing to the winter, and therefore to devote this time to referring the matter to the senate was by no means useless, but in the interest of them all.

10. They all soon gave their consent as they saw that Flamininus was evidently not averse from referring things to the senate, and it was decided to allow Philip to send an embassy to Rome, and that they also should each send ambassadors to speak before the senate and accuse Philip.

[45] Not true, as 9.6 shows.

[46] For Flamininus' motives see Holleaux, *Ét.* 5.73–77.

[47] Wrongly pretended by Flamininus, who was playing for time in the interests of his career as elections in Rome approached, which could lead to his recall.

3   Τοῦ δὲ πράγματος τῷ Τίτῳ τοῦ κατὰ τὸν σύλλογον
κατὰ νοῦν καὶ κατὰ τοὺς ἐξ ἀρχῆς διαλογισμοὺς προ-
κεχωρηκότος, παραυτίκα τὸ συνεχὲς τῆς ἐπιβολῆς
ἐξύφαινε, τά τε καθ᾽ αὑτὸν ἀσφαλιζόμενος ἐπιμελῶς

4   καὶ πρόλημμα τῷ Φιλίππῳ ποιῶν οὐδέν. δοὺς γὰρ
ἀνοχὰς διμήνους αὐτῷ τὴν μὲν πρεσβείαν τὴν εἰς τὴν
Ῥώμην ἐν τούτῳ τῷ χρόνῳ συντελεῖν ἐπέταξε, τὰς δὲ
φρουρὰς ἐξάγειν παραχρῆμα τὰς ἐκ τῆς Φωκίδος καὶ

5   Λοκρίδος ἐκέλευσε. διετάξατο δὲ καὶ περὶ τῶν ἰδίων
συμμάχων φιλοτίμως, ἵνα κατὰ μηδένα τρόπον μηδὲν
εἰς αὐτοὺς ἀδίκημα γίνηται κατὰ τοῦτον τὸν χρόνον

6   ὑπὸ Μακεδόνων. ταῦτα δὲ ποιήσας πρὸς τὸν Φίλιππον
ἔγγραπτα, λοιπὸν αὐτὸς ἤδη δι᾽ αὑτοῦ τὸ προκείμενον

7   ἐπετέλει. καὶ τὸν μὲν Ἀμύνανδρον εἰς τὴν Ῥώμην ἐξέπεμπε παραχρῆμα, γινώσκων αὐτὸν εὐάγωγον μὲν
ὄντα καὶ ῥᾳδίως ἐξακολουθήσοντα τοῖς ἐκεῖ φίλοις,
ἐφ᾽ ὁπότερ᾽ ἂν ἄγωσιν αὐτόν, φαντασίαν δὲ ποιήσοντα

8   καὶ προσδοκίαν διὰ τὸ τῆς βασιλείας ὄνομα. μετὰ δὲ
τοῦτον ἐξέπεμπε τοὺς παρ᾽ αὑτοῦ πρέσβεις, Κόιντόν
τε τὸν Φάβιον, ὃς ἦν αὐτῷ τῆς γυναικὸς ἀδελφιδοῦς,
καὶ Κόιντον Φολούιον, σὺν δὲ τούτοις Ἄππιον Κλαύ-

9   διον ἐπικαλούμενον Νέρωνα. παρὰ δὲ τῶν Αἰτωλῶν
ἐπρέσβευον Ἀλέξανδρος Ἴσιος, Δαμόκριτος Καλυδώ-
νιος, Δικαίαρχος Τριχωνιεύς, Πολέμαρχος Ἀρσινοεύς,

10   Λάμιος Ἀμβρακιώτης, Νικόμαχος Ἀκαρνὰν τῶν ἐκ
Θουρίου πεφευγότων κατοικούντων δ᾽ ἐν Ἀμβρακίᾳ,

The conference having led to a result agreeable to Flamininus and in accordance with his original calculations, he at once set to work to complete the texture of his design, securing his own position and giving Philip no advantage. For granting him an armistice of two months he ordered him to finish with his embassy to Rome within that time and to withdraw at once his garrisons from Phocis and Locris.[48] He also took energetic steps on behalf of his own allies to guard against their suffering any wrong from the Macedonians during this period. Having communicated with Philip to this effect by writing, he henceforth went on carrying out his purpose without consulting anyone. He at once dispatched Amynander[49] to Rome, as he knew that he was of a pliable disposition and would be ready to follow the lead of his own friends there in whichever direction they chose to move, and that his regal title would add splendor to the proceedings and make people eager to see him. After him he sent his own legates,[50] Quintus Fabius, the nephew of his wife, Quintus Fulvius and Appius Claudius Nero. The ambassadors from Aetolia[51] were Alexander the Isian, Damocritus of Calydon, Dicaearchus of Trichonium, Polemarchus of Arsinoë, Lamius of Ambracia, Nicomachus, one of the Acarnanians who had been exiled from Thurium and resided in Ambra-

---

48 *RE* Phokis 474–496 (F. Schober). *RE* Lokris 1135–1288 (W. M. Oldfather).

49 See n. on 4.16.9; last mentions 16.1.3 and 27.4.

50 For their names see *MRR* 1.331.

51 For these men see J. D. Grainger, *Aitolian Prosopographical Studies* (Leiden 2000).

11 Θεόδοτος Φεραῖος, φυγὰς ἐκ Θετταλίας, κατοικῶν δ᾽
ἐν Στράτῳ, παρὰ δὲ τῶν Ἀχαιῶν Ξενοφῶν Αἰγιεύς,
παρὰ δὲ τοῦ βασιλέως Ἀττάλου μόνος Ἀλέξανδρος,
παρὰ δὲ τοῦ δήμου τῶν Ἀθηναίων οἱ περὶ Κηφισόδω-
ρον.

11. Οὗτοι δὲ παρεγενήθησαν εἰς τὴν Ῥώμην πρὸ
(17 11) τοῦ τὴν σύγκλητον διαλαβεῖν ὑπὲρ τῶν εἰς τοῦτον τὸν
ἐνιαυτὸν καθεσταμένων ὑπάτων, πότερον ἀμφοτέρους
εἰς τὴν Γαλατίαν ἢ τὸν ἕτερον αὐτῶν δεήσει πέμπειν
2 ἐπὶ Φίλιππον. πεπεισμένων δὲ τῶν τοῦ Τίτου φίλων
μένειν τοὺς ὑπάτους ἀμφοτέρους κατὰ τὴν Ἰταλίαν
διὰ τὸν ἀπὸ τῶν Κελτῶν φόβον, εἰσελθόντες εἰς τὴν
σύγκλητον πάντες κατηγόρουν ἀποτόμως τοῦ Φιλίπ-
3 που. τὰ μὲν οὖν ἄλλα παραπλήσια τοῖς καὶ πρὸς
4 αὐτὸν τὸν βασιλέα πρότερον εἰρημένοις ἦν· τοῦτο δ᾽
ἐπιμελῶς ἐντίκτειν ἐπειρῶντο τῇ συγκλήτῳ πάντες,
διότι τῆς Χαλκίδος καὶ τοῦ Κορίνθου καὶ τῆς Δημητριάδος ὑπὸ τῷ Μακεδόνι ταττομένων οὐχ οἷόν τε
5 τοὺς Ἕλληνας ἔννοιαν λαβεῖν ἐλευθερίας. ὃ γὰρ αὐτὸς Φίλιππος εἶπε, τοῦτο καὶ λίαν ἀληθὲς ἔφασαν
ὑπάρχειν· ὃς ἔφη τοὺς προειρημένους τόπους εἶναι
6 πέδας Ἑλληνικάς, ὀρθῶς ἀποφαινόμενος. οὔτε γὰρ
Πελοποννησίους ἀναπνεῦσαι δυνατὸν ἐν Κορίνθῳ βασιλικῆς φρουρᾶς ἐγκαθημένης, οὔτε Λοκροὺς καὶ Βοιωτοὺς καὶ Φωκέας θαρρῆσαι Φιλίππου Χαλκίδα κατ-
7 έχοντος καὶ τὴν ἄλλην Εὔβοιαν, οὐδὲ μὴν Θετταλοὺς

---

52 These two men from states allied with Philip but exiled,

cia, and Theodotus of Pherae,[52] who was exiled from Thessaly and lived in Stratus; the envoy of the Achaeans was Xenophon[53] of Aegium; Attalus sent Alexander alone, and the Athenian people Cephisodorus.[54]

11. The envoys arrived in Rome before the senate had decided whether the consuls of the year should be both sent to Gaul or one of them against Philip. But when the friends of Flamininus were assured that both consuls were to remain in Italy owing to the fear of the Celts,[55] all the envoys entered the senate house and roundly denounced Philip. Their accusations were in general similar to those they had brought against the king in person, but the point which they all took pains to impress upon the senate was that as long as Chalcis, Corinth, and Demetrias remained in Macedonian hands it was impossible for the Greeks to have any thought of liberty. For Philip's own expression when he pronounced these places to be the fetters of Greece,[56] was, they said, only too true, since neither could the Peloponnesians breathe freely with a royal garrison established in Corinth, nor could the Locrians, Boeotians, and Phocians have any confidence while Philip occupied Chalcis and the rest of Euboea, nor again could the Thes-

Theodotus living in Aetolia, Nicomachus in Thyrreion, Acarnania: *LGPN* III A, Nicomachus 12–14.   [53] 1.4.

[54] The leading Athenian statesman at the time. Paus. 1.36.5–6 records his achievements, his report confirmed by a decree in Cephisodorus' honor, *ISE* 33, now dated 184/3. C. Habicht, *Pausanias' Guide to Ancient Greece* (Berkeley 1985), 92–94, with pp. XV–XVI of the reimpression (1998).   [55] At this time mainly the Insubres; see n. on 2.17.3.   [56] It is not known when Philip used that phrase, recorded also by other authors.

οὐδὲ Μάγνητας δυνατὸν ἐπαύρασθαι τῆς ἐλευθερίας
οὐδέποτε, Δημητριάδα Φιλίππου κατέχοντος καὶ Μα-
8 κεδόνων. διὸ καὶ τὸ παραχωρεῖν τῶν ἄλλων τόπων τὸν
Φίλιππον φαντασίαν εἶναι χάριν τοῦ τὸν παρόντα
καιρὸν ἐκφυγεῖν· ᾗ δ' ἂν ἡμέρᾳ βουληθῇ, ῥᾳδίως πάλιν ὑφ' αὑτὸν ποιήσεσθαι τοὺς Ἕλληνας, ἐὰν κρατῇ
9 τῶν προειρημένων τόπων. διόπερ ἠξίουν τὴν σύγκλητον ἢ τούτων τῶν πόλεων ἀναγκάσαι τὸν Φίλιππον
ἐκχωρεῖν ἢ μένειν ἐπὶ τῶν ὑποκειμένων καὶ πολεμεῖν
10 ἐρρωμένως πρὸς αὐτόν. καὶ γὰρ ἠνύσθαι τὰ μέγιστα
τοῦ πολέμου, τῶν τε Μακεδόνων προηττημένων δὶς
ἤδη καὶ κατὰ γῆν πλείστων αὐτοῖς χορηγιῶν ἐκ-
11 δεδαπανημένων. ταῦτα δ' εἰπόντες παρεκάλουν μήτε
τοὺς Ἕλληνας ψεῦσαι τῶν περὶ τῆς ἐλευθερίας ἐλπίδων μήθ' ἑαυτοὺς ἀποστερῆσαι τῆς καλλίστης ἐπι-
12 γραφῆς. οἱ μὲν οὖν παρὰ τῶν Ἑλλήνων πρέσβεις
ταῦτα καὶ τούτοις παραπλήσια διελέχθησαν, οἱ δὲ
παρὰ τοῦ Φιλίππου παρεσκευάσαντο μὲν ὡς ἐπὶ
πλεῖον ποιησόμενοι τοὺς λόγους, ἐν ἀρχαῖς δ' εὐθέως
13 ἐκωλύθησαν· ἐρωτηθέντες γὰρ εἰ παραχωροῦσι Χαλκίδος καὶ Κορίνθου καὶ Δημητριάδος, ἀπεῖπαν μηδε-
14 μίαν ἔχειν περὶ τούτων ἐντολήν. Οὗτοι μὲν οὖν ἐπιτιμη-
θέντες οὕτως κατέπαυσαν τὸν λόγον.

12. ἡ δὲ σύγκλητος τοὺς μὲν ὑπάτους ἀμφοτέρους
(17 12) εἰς Γαλατίαν ἐξαπέστειλε, καθάπερ ἐπάνω προεῖπα,
τὸν δὲ πρὸς τὸν Φίλιππον πόλεμον ἐψηφίσατο κατά-
μονον εἶναι, δοῦσα τῷ Τίτῳ τὴν ἐπιτροπὴν ὑπὲρ τῶν
2 Ἑλληνικῶν. ταχὺ δὲ τούτων εἰς τὴν Ἑλλάδα διασα-

salians or Magnesians ever enjoy liberty while the Macedonians held Demetrias. Therefore his withdrawal from the other places was a mere show of concession on the part of Philip in order to get out of his present difficulty, and if he commanded the above places he could easily bring the Greeks under subjection any day he wished. They therefore demanded that the senate should either compel Philip to withdraw from these towns or abide by the agreement and fight against him with all their strength. For the hardest task of the war had been accomplished, as the Macedonians had now been twice beaten[57] and had expended most of their resources on land. After speaking thus they entreated the senate neither to cheat the Greeks out of their hope of liberty nor to deprive themselves of the noblest title to fame. Such or very nearly such were the words of the ambassadors. Philip's envoys had prepared a lengthy argument in reply, but were at once silenced; for when asked if they would give up Chalcis, Corinth, and Demetrias they replied that they had no instructions on the subject.[58]

12. Thus cut short they stopped speaking, and the senate now, as I above stated, dispatched both consuls to Gaul and voted to continue the war against Philip, appointing Flamininus their commissioner in the affairs of Greece. This information was rapidly conveyed to Greece, and

[57] In 199 at the pass leading to Eordaea in Macedonia (Livy 31.39.6–9), and in 198 at the Aous Pass (n. on 3.9).

[58] A possible explanation is that Flamininus had misled Philip to believe he might be allowed to keep them (WC 2.563).

φηθέντων ἐγεγόνει τῷ Τίτῳ πάντα κατὰ νοῦν, ἐπὶ
βραχὺ μὲν καὶ ταὐτομάτου συνεργήσαντος, τὸ δὲ
πολὺ διὰ τῆς αὑτοῦ προνοίας ἁπάντων κεχειρισμέ-
3 νων. πάνυ γὰρ ἀγχίνους, εἰ καί τις ἕτερος Ῥωμαίων,
4 [καὶ] ὁ προειρημένος ἀνὴρ γέγονεν· οὕτως γὰρ εὐστόχως ἐχείριζε καὶ νουνεχῶς οὐ μόνον τὰς κοινὰς
ἐπιβολάς, ἀλλὰ καὶ τὰς κατ᾽ ἰδίαν ἐντεύξεις, ὥσθ᾽
5 ὑπερβολὴν μὴ καταλιπεῖν. καίτοι γε [καὶ] νέος ἦν
κομιδῇ· πλείω γὰρ τῶν τριάκοντ᾽ ἐτῶν οὐκ εἶχε· καὶ
πρῶτος εἰς τὴν Ἑλλάδα διαβεβήκει μετὰ στρατοπέδων.

13. Ἔμοιγε πολλάκις μὲν καὶ ἐπὶ πολλοῖς θαυμά-
(17 13) ζειν ἐπέρχεται τῶν ἀνθρωπείων ἁμαρτημάτων, μάλι-
2 στα δ᾽ ἐπὶ τῷ κατὰ τοὺς προδότας. διὸ καὶ βούλομαι
τὰ πρέποντα τοῖς καιροῖς διαλεχθῆναι περὶ αὐτῶν.
3 καίτοι γ᾽ οὐκ ἀγνοῶ διότι δυσθεώρητον ὁ τόπος ἔχει
τι καὶ δυσπαράγραφον· τίνα γὰρ ὡς ἀληθῶς προδό-
4 την δεῖ νομίζειν, οὐ ῥᾴδιον ἀποφήνασθαι. δῆλον γὰρ
ὡς οὔτε τοὺς ἐξ ἀκεραίου συντιθεμένους τῶν ἀνδρῶν
πρός τινας βασιλεῖς ἢ δυνάστας κοινωνίαν πραγμά-
5 των εὐθέως προδότας νομιστέον, οὔτε τοὺς κατὰ ‹τὰς›
περιστάσεις μετατιθέντας τὰς αὐτῶν πατρίδας ἀπό
τινων ὑποκειμένων πρὸς ἑτέρας φιλίας καὶ συμμα-
6 χίας, οὐδὲ τούτους. πολλοῦ γε δεῖν· ἐπείτοι γε πολλάκις οἱ τοιοῦτοι τῶν μεγίστων ἀγαθῶν γεγόνασιν αἴ-

---

59 Flamininus had been quaestor, but neither *aedilis* nor prae-

now all had fallen out as Flamininus wished, chance having contributed little to help him, but nearly all being due to his own prudent management. For this general had shown a sagacity equal to that of any Roman, having managed both public enterprises and his own private dealings with consummate skill and good sense, and this although he was yet quite young, not being over thirty.[59] He was the first Roman who had crossed to Greece in command of an army.

Definition of Treachery

13. I have often had occasion to wonder where the truth lies about many mistakes men make and especially about the question of traitors. I therefore wish to say a few words on the subject appropriate to the times I am dealing with, although I am quite aware that it is one which is difficult to survey and define; it being by no means easy to decide whom we should really style a traitor. It is evident that we cannot pronounce offhand to be traitors men who take the initiative in engaging in common action with certain kings and princes, nor again those who at the bidding of circumstances induce their countries to exchange their established relations for other friendships and alliances. Far from it; in view of the fact that such men have often conferred the greatest benefit on their country. Not to

tor. Such cases were rare exceptions, but possible before the *Lex Villia Annalis* of 180. Mommsen, *Staatsr.* 1.538, n. 21. A. E. Astin, *The Lex annalis before Sulla* (Bruxelles 1958), 26–28. T. Corey Brennan, *The Praetorship of the Roman Republic* 1 (Oxford 2000), 170–171.

7 τιοι ταῖς ἰδίαις πατρίσιν. ἵνα δὲ μὴ πόρρωθεν τὰ
παραδείγματα φέρωμεν, ἐξ αὐτῶν τῶν ἐνεστώτων ῥᾳ-
8 δίως ἔσται τὸ λεγόμενον κατανοεῖν. εἰ γὰρ μὴ σὺν
καιρῷ τότε μετέρριψε τοὺς Ἀχαιοὺς Ἀρίσταινος ἀπὸ
τῆς Φιλίππου συμμαχίας πρὸς τὴν Ῥωμαίων, φανερῶς
9 ἄρδην ἀπολώλει τὸ ἔθνος. νῦν δὲ χωρὶς τῆς παρ'
αὐτὸν τὸν καιρὸν ἀσφαλείας ἑκάστοις περιγενομένης,
αὐξήσεως τῶν Ἀχαιῶν ὁμολογουμένως ὁ προειρημένος ἀνὴρ κἀκεῖνο τὸ διαβούλιον αἴτιος ἐδόκει γεγονέ-
10 ναι· διὸ καὶ πάντες αὐτὸν οὐχ ὡς προδότην, ἀλλ' ὡς
11 εὐεργέτην καὶ σωτῆρα τῆς χώρας ἐτίμων. ὁ δ' αὐτὸς
ἂν εἴη λόγος καὶ περὶ τῶν ἄλλων, ὅσοι κατὰ τὰς τῶν
καιρῶν περιστάσεις τὰ παραπλήσια τούτοις πολιτεύ-
ονται καὶ πράττουσιν.

14. Ἧι καὶ Δημοσθένην κατὰ πολλά τις ἂν ἐπαι-
(17 14) νέσας ἐν τούτῳ μέμψαιτο, διότι πικρότατον ὄνειδος
τοῖς ἐπιφανεστάτοις τῶν Ἑλλήνων εἰκῇ καὶ ἀκρίτως
2 προσέρριψε, φήσας ἐν μὲν Ἀρκαδίᾳ τοὺς περὶ Κερκι-
δᾶν καὶ Ἱερώνυμον καὶ Εὐκαμπίδαν προδότας γενέ-
3 σθαι τῆς Ἑλλάδος, ὅτι Φιλίππῳ συνεμάχουν, ἐν δὲ
Μεσσήνῃ τοὺς Φιλιάδου παῖδας Νέωνα καὶ Θρασύ-

---

60 See n. on 1.4. His role in the defection of the Achaeans
to Rome seems to have motivated this digression, although the
event had occurred somewhat earlier. A. Aymard, followed by
WC 2.564–565, prefers to connect the chapter with the betrayal
of Argos to Philip by some of its leaders. This may, in fact, have
prompted P. to insert this discussion here, but his primary aim
still seems to have been to exculpate the Achaeans for failing

draw examples from far-off times, what I say can easily be observed from the time we are dealing with. For if Aristaenus[60] had not then in good time made the Achaeans throw off their alliance with Philip and change it for that with Rome, the whole nation would evidently have suffered utter destruction. But now, apart from the temporary safety gained for all the members of the League, this man and that counsel were regarded as having beyond doubt contributed to the increase of the Achaean power; so that all agreed in honoring him not as a traitor, but as the benefactor and preserver of the land. And the same is the case with others who according to change of circumstances adopt a similar policy of action.

14. It is for this reason that while we must praise Demosthenes[61] for so many things, we must blame him for one, for having recklessly and injudiciously cast bitter reproach on the most distinguished men in Greece by saying that Cercidas,[62] Hieronymus, and Eucampidas in Arcadia were betrayers of Greece because they joined Philip, and for saying the same of Neon and Thrasylochus, the sons of

Philip who had not failed them. See also A. M. Eckstein, *CQ* 81 (1987), 140–162.   [61] P. discusses Greeks of the fourth century condemned as traitors by Demosthenes (esp. 18.295), because they had dealings with, or supported, Philip II. Of some, nothing or very little is known. Outstanding is Daochus II of Pharsalus, member of a family of tetrarchs and Olympic victors, whose monument at Delphi, a work of Lysippus, is very famous. See *FD* III 4.460 for the inscribed bases and for archaeological bibliography.   [62] Different from and much older than the other Arcadian of that name, who was a citizen of Megalopolis (see n. on 2.48.4). For the man attacked by Demosthenes, see *RE* Kerkidas 293–294 (G. A. Gerhard).

λοχον, ἐν Ἄργει δὲ τοὺς περὶ Μύρτιν καὶ Τελέδαμον
4 καὶ Μνασέαν, παραπλησίως ἐν Θετταλίᾳ μὲν τοὺς
περὶ Δάοχον καὶ Κινέαν, παρὰ δὲ Βοιωτοῖς τοὺς περὶ
5 Θεογείτονα καὶ Τιμόλαν· σὺν δὲ τούτοις καὶ πλείους
ἑτέρους ἐξηρίθμηται, κατὰ πόλιν ὀνομάζων, καίτοι γε
πάντων μὲν τῶν προειρημένων ἀνδρῶν πολὺν ἐχόντων
λόγον καὶ φαινόμενον ὑπὲρ τῶν καθ᾽ αὑτοὺς δικαίων,
6 πλεῖστον δὲ τῶν ἐξ Ἀρκαδίας καὶ Μεσσήνης. οὗτοι
γὰρ ἐπισπασάμενοι Φίλιππον εἰς Πελοπόννησον καὶ
ταπεινώσαντες Λακεδαιμονίους πρῶτον μὲν ἐποίησαν
ἀναπνεῦσαι καὶ λαβεῖν ἐλευθερίας ἔννοιαν πάντας
7 τοὺς τὴν Πελοπόννησον κατοικοῦντας, ἔπειτα δὲ τὴν
χώραν ἀνακομισάμενοι καὶ τὰς πόλεις, ἃς παρῄρηντο
Λακεδαιμόνιοι κατὰ τὴν εὐκαιρίαν Μεσσηνίων, Μεγα-
λοπολιτῶν, Τεγεατῶν, Ἀργείων, ηὔξησαν τὰς ἑαυτῶν
8 πατρίδας ὁμολογουμένως· ἀνθ᾽ ὧν οὐ πολεμεῖν ὤφει-
λον Φιλίππῳ καὶ Μακεδόσιν, ἀλλὰ πάντα κατὰ δύνα-
9 μιν ἐνεργεῖν ὅσα πρὸς δόξαν καὶ τιμὴν ἀνῆκεν. εἰ μὲν
οὖν ταῦτ᾽ ἔπραττον ἢ φρουρὰν παρὰ Φιλίππου δεχό-
μενοι ταῖς πατρίσιν ἢ καταλύοντες τοὺς νόμους ἀφῃ-
ροῦντο τὴν ἐλευθερίαν καὶ παρρησίαν τῶν πολιτῶν
χάριν τῆς ἰδίας πλεονεξίας ἢ δυναστείας, ἄξιοι τῆς
10 προσηγορίας ἦσαν ταύτης· εἰ δὲ τηροῦντες τὰ πρὸς
τὰς πατρίδας δίκαια κρίσει πραγμάτων διεφέροντο,
νομίζοντες οὐ ταὐτὸ συμφέρον Ἀθηναίοις εἶναι καὶ
ταῖς ἑαυτῶν πόλεσιν, οὐ δήπου διὰ τοῦτο καλεῖσθαι
11 προδότας ἐχρῆν αὐτοὺς ὑπὸ Δημοσθένους. ὁ δὲ πάντα
μετρῶν πρὸς τὸ τῆς ἰδίας πατρίδος συμφέρον, καὶ

Philiadas in Messene, Myrtis, Teledamus and Mnaseas in Argos, Daochus and Cineas[63] in Thessaly, Theogeiton and Timolas in Boeotia, and several others in different cities. But in fact all the above men were perfectly and clearly justified in thus defending their own rights, and more especially those from Arcadia and Messene. For the latter, by inducing Philip to enter the Peloponnese and humbling the Lacedaemonians, in the first place allowed all the inhabitants of the Peloponnese to breathe freely and to entertain the thought of liberty, and next recovering the territory and cities of which the Lacedaemonians in their prosperity had deprived the Messenians, Megalopolitans, Tegeans, and Argives, unquestionably increased the power of their native towns. In return for this it was their duty not to fight against Philip, but to take every step for their own honor and glory. Had they in acting thus either submitted to have their towns garrisoned by Philip, or abolished their laws and deprived the citizens of freedom of action and speech to serve their own ambition and place themselves in power, they would have deserved the name of traitor. But if preserving the rights of their respective countries, they simply differed in their judgment of facts, thinking that the interests of Athens[64] were not identical with those of their countries, they should, I maintain, not have been dubbed traitors for this reason by Demosthenes. Measuring everything by the interests of his own

[63] Several prominent Thessalians of that name are listed in *LGPN* III B, p. 230, among them the famous minister of King Pyrrhus. For Daochus see above on 14.1.

[64] P. herewith states that Demosthenes' policy was just Athenocentric.

πάντας ἡγούμενος δεῖν τοὺς Ἕλληνας ἀποβλέπειν
πρὸς Ἀθηναίους, εἰ δὲ μή, προδότας ἀποκαλῶν, ἀγνοεῖν
12 μοι δοκεῖ καὶ πολὺ παραπαίειν τῆς ἀληθείας [ὁ πεποίηκε Δημοσθένης], ἄλλως τε δὴ καὶ τῶν συμβάν-
των τότε τοῖς Ἕλλησιν οὐ Δημοσθένει μεμαρτυρη-
κότων ὅτι καλῶς προυνοήθη τοῦ μέλλοντος, ἀλλ᾽
Εὐκαμπίδᾳ καὶ Ἱερωνύμῳ καὶ Κερκιδᾷ καὶ τοῖς Φιλι-
13 άδου παισίν. Ἀθηναίοις μὲν γὰρ τῆς πρὸς Φίλιππον
ἀντιπαραγωγῆς τὸ τέλος ἀπέβη τὸ πεῖραν λαβεῖν τῶν
μεγίστων συμπτωμάτων πταίσασι τῇ μάχῃ τῇ περὶ
14 Χαιρώνειαν· εἰ δὲ μὴ διὰ τὴν τοῦ βασιλέως μεγαλοψυχίαν καὶ φιλοδοξίαν, καὶ πορρωτέρω τὰ τῆς ἀτυχίας
ἂν αὐτοῖς προύβη διὰ τὴν Δημοσθένους πολιτείαν.
15 διὰ δὲ τοὺς προειρημένους ἄνδρας κοινῇ μὲν Ἀρκάσι
καὶ Μεσσηνίοις ἀπὸ Λακεδαιμονίων ἀσφάλεια καὶ
ῥᾳστώνη παρεσκευάσθη, κατ᾽ ἰδίαν δὲ ταῖς αὐτῶν πατρίσι πολλὰ καὶ λυσιτελῆ συνεξηκολούθησε.

15. Τίσιν οὖν εἰκότως ἂν ἐπιφέροι τις τὴν ὀνομασίαν
(17 15) ταύτην, ἔστι μὲν δυσπαράγραφον· μάλιστα δ᾽ ἂν
2 προστρέχοι πρὸς τὴν ἀλήθειαν ἐπὶ τοὺς τοιούτους φέρων, ὅσοι τῶν ἀνδρῶν κατὰ τὰς ὁλοσχερεῖς περιστάσεις ἢ τῆς ἰδίας ἀσφαλείας καὶ λυσιτελείας χάριν ἢ
τῆς πρὸς τοὺς ἀντιπολιτευομένους διαφορᾶς ἐγχει-
3 ρίζουσι τοῖς ἐχθροῖς τὰς πόλεις, ἢ καὶ νὴ Δία πάλιν
ὅσοι φρουρὰν εἰσδεχόμενοι καὶ συγχρώμενοι ταῖς
ἔξωθεν ἐπικουρίαις πρὸς τὰς ἰδίας ὁρμὰς καὶ προθέσεις ὑποβάλλουσι τὰς πατρίδας ὑπὸ τὴν τῶν πλείον
4 δυναμένων ἐξουσίαν. τοὺς τοιούτους ὑπὸ τὸ τῆς προ-

city, thinking that the whole of Greece should have its eyes turned on Athens, and if people did not do so, calling them traitors, Demosthenes seems to me to have been very much mistaken and very far wide of the truth, especially as what actually befell the Greeks then does not testify to his own admirable foresight but rather to that of Eucampidas, Hieronymus, Cercidas, and the sons of Philiadas. For the opposition offered to Philip by the Athenians resulted in their being overtaken by the gravest disasters,[65] defeated as they were at the battle of Chaeronea. And had it not been for the king's magnanimity and love of glory, their misfortune would have been even more terrible and all due to the policy of Demosthenes. But it was owing to the men whose names I mentioned that the two states of Arcadia and Messene obtained common security and rest from Lacedaemonian aggression, and that so many individual advantages to their citizens resulted.

15. It is, then, difficult to define who are the men to whom we may legitimately give this name, but one would most nearly approach the truth by applying it to those who in a season of imminent danger, either for their own safety or advantage or owing to their differences with the opposite party, put their cities into the hands of the enemy, or still more justifiably to those who, admitting a garrison and employing external assistance to further their own inclinations and aims, submit their countries to the domination of a superior power. It would be quite fair to class

[65] P. here makes success the measure of good policy. WC 2.568 remarks: "A comparison between the views expressed here and P.'s criticism of Thebes for placing her safety first in IV 31.5 is instructive." The same is true for his criticism of the policy of Athens after 229 in 5.106.6–7.

5 δοσίας ὄνομα μετρίως ἄν τις ὑποτάττοι πάντας. οἷς
λυσιτελὲς μὲν ἀληθῶς ἢ καλὸν οὐδὲν οὐδέποτε συν-
6 εξηκολούθησε, τὰ δ᾽ ἐναντία πᾶσιν ὁμολογουμένως. ᾗ
καὶ θαυμάζειν ἔστι πρὸς τὸν ἐξ ἀρχῆς λόγον, πρὸς τί
ποτε βλέποντες ἢ τίσι χρώμενοι διαλογισμοῖς ὁρμῶσι
7 πρὸς τὴν τοιαύτην ἀτυχίαν. οὔτε γὰρ ἔλαθε πώποτε
προδοὺς οὐδεὶς πόλιν ἢ στρατόπεδον ἢ φρούριον,
ἀλλὰ κἂν παρ᾽ αὐτὸν τὸν τῆς πράξεως καιρὸν ἀγνοηθῇ
τις, ὅ γ᾽ ἐπιγονόμενος χρόνος ἐποίησε φανεροὺς ἅπαν-
8 τας· οὐδὲ μὴν γνωσθεὶς οὐδεὶς σὐδέποτε μακάριον
ἔσχε βίον, ἀλλ᾽ ὡς μὲν ἐπίπαν ὑπ᾽ αὐτῶν τούτων οἷς
χαρίζονται τυγχάνουσι τῆς ἁρμοζούσης τιμωρίας.
9 χρῶνται μὲν γὰρ τοῖς προδόταις οἱ στρατηγοὶ καὶ
δυνάσται πολλάκις διὰ τὸ συμφέρον· ὅταν γε μὴν
ἀποχρήσωνται, χρῶνται λοιπὸν ὡς προδόταις, κατὰ
10 τὸν Δημοσθένην, μάλ᾽ εἰκότως ἡγούμενοι τὸν ἐγχει-
ρίσαντα τοῖς ἐχθροῖς τὴν πατρίδα καὶ τοὺς ἐξ ἀρχῆς
φίλους μηδέποτ᾽ ἂν εὔνουν σφίσι γενέσθαι μηδὲ δια-
11 φυλάξαι τὴν πρὸς αὐτοὺς πίστιν. οὐ μὴν ἀλλ᾽ ἐὰν καὶ
τὰς τούτων διαφύγωσι χεῖρας, τάς γε δὴ τῶν παρα-
12 σπονδηθέντων οὐ ῥᾳδίως ἐκφυγγάνουσιν. ἐὰν δέ ποτε
καὶ τὰς ἀμφοτέρων τούτων ἐπιβουλὰς διολίσθωσιν, ἥ
γε παρὰ τοῖς ἄλλοις ἀνθρώποις φήμη τιμωρὸς αὐτοῖς
ἕπεται παρ᾽ ὅλον τὸν βίον, πολλοὺς μὲν φόβους
ψευδεῖς, πολλοὺς δ᾽ ἀληθεῖς παριστάνουσα καὶ νύκτωρ καὶ μεθ᾽ ἡμέραν, πᾶσι δὲ συνεργοῦσα καὶ συν-
υποδεικνύουσα τοῖς κακόν τι κατ᾽ ἐκείνων βουλευομέ-
13 νοις, τὸ δὲ τελευταῖον οὐδὲ κατὰ τοὺς ὕπνους ἐῶσα

all the above as traitors. The treachery of these men never
resulted in any real advantage or good to themselves, but
in every case, as no one can deny, just the reverse. And this
makes us wonder what their original motives are; with
what aim and reckoning on what they rush headlong into
such misfortune. For not a single man ever betrays a town
or an army or a fort without being found out, but even if
any be not detected at the actual moment, the progress of
time discovers them all at the end. Nor did any one of
them who had once been recognized ever lead a happy
life, but in most instances they meet with the punishment
they deserve at the hands of the very men with whom they
tried to ingratiate themselves. For generals and princes
often employ traitors to further their interest, but when
they have no further use for them they afterward, as Demosthenes says, treat them as traitors, very naturally
thinking that a man who has betrayed his country and his
original friends to the enemy could never become really
well disposed to themselves or keep faith with them. And
if they should happen to escape punishment at the hands
of their employers, it is by no means easy for them to escape it at the hands of those they betrayed. Should they,
however, give the slip to the retribution of both, their evil
name among other men clings to them for their whole life,
producing many false apprehensions and many real ones
by night and by day, aiding and abetting all who have evil
designs against them, and finally not allowing them even
in sleep to forget their offense, but compelling them to

λήθην αὐτοὺς ἔχειν τῶν ἡμαρτημένων, ἀλλ᾽ ὀνειρώττειν
ἀναγκάζουσα πᾶν γένος ἐπιβουλῆς καὶ περιπετείας,
ἅτε συνειδότας ἑαυτοῖς τὴν ὑπάρχουσαν ἐκ πάντων
14 ἀλλοτριότητα πρὸς σφᾶς καὶ τὸ κοινὸν μῖσος. ἀλλ᾽
ὅμως τούτων οὕτως ἐχόντων οὐδεὶς οὐδέποτε δεηθεὶς
15 ἠπόρησε προδότου πλὴν τελέως ὀλίγων τινῶν. ἐξ ὧν
εἰκότως εἴποι τις ἂν ὅτι τὸ τῶν ἀνθρώπων γένος,
δοκοῦν πανουργότατον εἶναι τῶν ζῴων, πολὺν ἔχει λό-
16 γον τοῦ φαυλότατον ὑπάρχειν. τὰ μὲν γὰρ ἄλλα ζῷα,
ταῖς τοῦ σώματος ἐπιθυμίαις αὐταῖς δουλεύοντα, διὰ
μόνας ταύτας σφάλλεται· τὸ δὲ τῶν ἀνθρώπων γένος,
καίπερ δεδοξοποιημένον, οὐχ ἧττον διὰ τὴν ἀλογιστίαν
17 ἢ διὰ τὴν φύσιν ἁμαρτάνει. καὶ ταῦτα μὲν ἡμῖν ἐπὶ
τοσοῦτον εἰρήσθω.

16. Ὅτι ὁ βασιλεὺς Ἄτταλος ἐτιμᾶτο μὲν καὶ πρό-
(17 16) τερον ὑπὸ τῆς τῶν Σικυωνίων πόλεως διαφερόντως, ἐξ
οὗ τὴν ἱερὰν χώραν τοῦ Ἀπόλλωνος ἐλυτρώσατο χρη-
2 μάτων αὐτοῖς οὐκ ὀλίγων, ἀνθ᾽ ὧν καὶ τὸν κολοσσὸν
αὐτοῦ τὸν δεκάπηχυν ἔστησαν παρὰ τὸν Ἀπόλλωνα
3 τὸν κατὰ τὴν ἀγοράν. τότε δὲ πάλιν αὐτοῦ δέκα τάλαντα δόντος καὶ μυρίους μεδίμνους πυρῶν, πολλαπλασίως ἐπιταθέντες ταῖς εὐνοίαις εἰκόνα τε χρυσῆν
ἐψηφίσαντο καὶ θυσίαν αὐτῷ συντελεῖν κατ᾽ ἔτος ἐνο-
4 μοθέτησαν. Ἄτταλος μὲν οὖν τυχὼν τῶν τιμῶν τούτων
ἀπῆρεν εἰς Κεγχρεάς.

---

66 When he attended the meeting of the Achaeans in October
198, which resulted in their joining Rome.

67 Pledging of sacred land to raise money in an emergency has

dream of every kind of plot and peril, conscious as they are of the estrangement of everybody and of men's universal hatred of them. But in spite of all this being so, no one ever, when he had need of one, failed to find a traitor, except in a very few cases. All this would justify us in saying that man, who is supposed to be the cleverest of the animals, may with good reason be called the least intelligent. For the other animals are the slaves of their bodily wants alone and only get into trouble owing to these, but man, for all the high opinion that has been formed of him, makes mistakes just as much owing to want of thought as owing to his physical impulses. I have now said enough on this subject.

Attalus at Sicyon

16. King Attalus had received exceptional honors on a former occasion[66] also from the Sicyonians after he had ransomed for them at considerable expense the land consecrated to Apollo,[67] in return for which they set up a colossal statue of him ten cubits high, next that of Apollo in their marketplace. And now again, upon his giving them ten talents and ten thousand medimni of wheat, his popularity increased fourfold, and they voted his portrait in gold and passed a law enjoining the performance of an annual sacrifice[68] to him. Attalus, then, having received these honors left for Cenchreae.

its parallels. Attalus repaid the debt. There were two temples of Apollo at Sicyon (Paus. 2.9.7; 11.2), one of which had been affected by the transaction.

[68] Attalus was to receive cult honors as he had at Athens in 200 (16.25.9).

17. Ὅτι Νάβις ὁ τύραννος ἀπολιπὼν ἐπὶ τῆς τῶν
(17 17) Ἀργείων πόλεως Τιμοκράτην τὸν Πελληνέα διὰ τὸ
μάλιστα τούτῳ πιστεύειν καὶ χρῆσθαι πρὸς τὰς ἐπι-
2 φανεστάτας πράξεις, ἐπανῆλθεν εἰς τὴν Σπάρτην, καὶ
μετά τινας ἡμέρας ἐξέπεμψε τὴν γυναῖκα, δοὺς ἐντολὰς
παραγενομένην εἰς Ἄργος περὶ πόρον γίνεσθαι χρη-
3 μάτων. ἡ δ᾽ ἀφικομένη πολὺ κατὰ τὴν ὠμότητα Νά-
4 βιν ὑπερέθετο· ἀνακαλεσαμένη γὰρ τῶν γυναικῶν
τινὰς μὲν κατ᾽ ἰδίαν, τινὰς δὲ κατὰ συγγένειαν, πᾶν
5 γένος αἰκίας καὶ βίας προσέφερε, μέχρι σχεδὸν ἁπασῶν οὐ μόνον τὸν χρυσοῦν ἀφείλετο κόσμον, ἀλλὰ
καὶ τὸν ἱματισμὸν τὸν πολυτελέστατον.

6   Ὁ δὲ Ἄτταλος περιβαλλόμενος πλείω λόγον, ὑπ-
εμίμνησκεν αὐτοὺς τῆς ἀνέκαθεν τῶν προγόνων ἀρε-
τῆς.

(1)   18. Ὁ δὲ Τίτος οὐ δυνάμενος ἐπιγνῶναι τοὺς πολεμίους ᾗ στρατοπεδεύουσι, τοῦτο δὲ σαφῶς εἰδὼς ὅτι
πάρεισιν εἰς Θετταλίαν, προσέταξε κόπτειν χάρακα
πᾶσιν ἕνεκα τοῦ παρακομίζειν μεθ᾽ αὐτῶν πρὸς τὰς
2 ἐκ τοῦ καιροῦ χρείας. τοῦτο δὲ κατὰ μὲν τὴν Ἑλληνικὴν
ἀγωγὴν δυνατὸν εἶναι δοκεῖ, κατὰ δὲ τὴν τῶν Ῥωμαίων
3 εὔκοπον. οἱ μὲν γὰρ Ἕλληνες μόλις αὐτῶν κρατοῦσι

---

69 He had just concluded a truce with the Achaeans, had betrayed Philip at Argos and joined the king's enemies.

70 See n. on 13.7.6.

71 The speech was given at Thebes (Livy 33.1.1 with 2.1) in
the spring of 197. The king had recently reminded the Athenians
of the benefits he conferred (16.26.5); at Thebes, he began with

Cruelty of the Wife of Nabis at Argos

17. Nabis[69] the tyrant, leaving Timocrates of Pellene in command of Argos, as he placed the greatest reliance on him and employed him in the most ambitious of his enterprises, returned to Sparta and after some days sent off his own wife,[70] ordering her upon reaching Argos to set about raising money. Upon her arrival she greatly surpassed Nabis in cruelty. For summoning the women, some of them singly and others with their families, she subjected them to every kind of outrage and violence until she had stripped them nearly all not only of their gold ornaments, but of their most precious clothing. . . .

Attalus,[71] discoursing at some length, reminded them of the valor his ancestors had always displayed.

Campaign of Flamininus in Thessaly and Battle of Cynoscephalae

18. Flamininus, not being able to discover where the enemy were encamped, but knowing for a certainty that they were in Thessaly, ordered all his soldiers to cut stakes for a palisade to carry with them for use when required. This appears to be impossible when the Greek usage is followed, but on the Roman system it is easy to cut them. For the Greeks have difficulty in holding only their pikes

those of his ancestors. Known are donations of Philetaerus, the founder of the dynasty, to Boeotian Thespiae: B. Virgilio, *Gli Attalidi di Pergamo* (Pisa 1993), 15–19. During his speech the king suffered a stroke and was partly paralyzed; he died the following autumn.

τῶν σαρισῶν ἐν ταῖς πορείαις καὶ μόλις ὑπομένουσι
4 τὸν ἀπὸ τούτων κόπον, Ῥωμαῖοι δὲ τοὺς μὲν θυρεοὺς
τοῖς ὀχεῦσι τοῖς σκυτίνοις ἐκ τῶν ὤμων ἐξηρτηκότες,
ταῖς δὲ χερσὶν αὐτοὺς τοὺς γαίσους φέροντες, ἐπι-
5 δέχονται τὴν παρακομιδὴν τοῦ χάρακος. ἅμα δὲ καὶ
6 μεγάλην εἶναι συμβαίνει τὴν διαφορὰν τούτων· οἱ μὲν
γὰρ Ἕλληνες τοῦτον ἡγοῦνται χάρακα βέλτιστον, ὃς
ἂν ἔχῃ πλείστας ἐκφύσεις καὶ μεγίστας πέριξ τοῦ
7 πρέμνου, παρὰ δὲ Ῥωμαίοις δύο κεραίας ἢ τρεῖς ἔχουσιν οἱ χάρακες, ὁ δὲ πλείστας τέτταρας· καὶ ταύτας
8 ...ἔχοντες λαμβάνονται ...οὐκ ἐναλλάξ. ἐκ δὲ τούτου
συμβαίνει τήν τε κομιδὴν εὐχερῆ γίνεσθαι τελέως—ὁ
γὰρ εἷς ἀνὴρ φέρει τρεῖς καὶ τέτταρας συνθεὶς ἐπ'
9 ἀλλήλους—τήν τε χρείαν ἀσφαλῆ διαφερόντως. ὁ μὲν
⟨γὰρ⟩ τῶν Ἑλλήνων ὅταν τεθῇ πρὸ τῆς παρεμβολῆς,
10 πρῶτον μέν ἐστιν εὐδιάσπαστος· ὅταν γὰρ τὸ μὲν
κρατοῦν καὶ πιεζούμενον ὑπὸ τῆς γῆς ἐν ὑπάρχῃ μόνον, αἱ δ' ἀποφύσεις ἐκ τούτου πολλαὶ καὶ μεγάλαι,
κἄπειτα δύο παραστάντες ἢ τρεῖς ἐκ τῶν ἀποφύσεων
ἐπισπάσωνται τὸν αὐτὸν χάρακα, ῥᾳδίως ἐκσπᾶται.
11 τούτου δὲ συμβάντος εὐθέως πύλη γίνεται διὰ τὸ μέγεθος καὶ τὰ παρακείμενα λέλυται, τῷ βραχείας τὰς
εἰς ἀλλήλους ἐμπλοκὰς καὶ τὰς ἐπαλλάξεις γίνεσθαι
12 τοῦ τοιούτου χάρακος. παρὰ δὲ Ῥωμαίοις συμβαίνει
τοὐναντίον. τιθέασι γὰρ εὐθέως ἐμπλέκοντες εἰς ἀλλήλους οὕτως ὥστε μήτε τὰς κεραίας εὐχερῶς ἐπιγνῶναι,
ποίας εἰσὶν ἐκφύσεως τῶν ἐν τῇ γῇ κατωρυγμένων,
13 μήτε τὰς ἐκφύσεις, ποίων κεραιῶν. λοιπὸν οὔτ' ἐπιλα-

142

when on the march and in supporting the fatigue caused by their weight, but the Romans, hanging their long shields from their shoulders by leather straps and only holding their javelins in their hands, can manage to carry the stakes besides. Also the stakes are quite different. For the Greeks consider that stake the best which has the most and the stoutest offshoots all round the main stem, while the stakes of the Romans have but two or three, or at the most four straight lateral prongs, and these all on one side and not alternating. The result of this is that they are quite easy to carry—for one man can carry three or four, making a bundle of them, and when put to use they are much more secure. For the Greek stakes, when planted round the camp, are in the first place easily pulled up; since when the portion of a stake that holds fast closely pressed by the earth is only one, and the offshoots from it are many and large, and when two or three men catch hold of the same stake by its lateral branches, it is easily pulled up. Upon this an entrance is at once created owing to its size, and the ones next to it are loosened, because in such a palisade the stakes are intertwined and crisscrossed in few places. With the Romans it is the reverse; for in planting them they so intertwine them that it is not easy to see to which of the branches, the lower ends of which are driven into the ground, the lateral prongs belong, nor to which prongs the branches belong. So, as these prongs are close together and adhere to each other, and as their points are

βέσθαι παρείραντα τὴν χεῖρα δυνατόν, ἅτε πυκνῶν
οὐσῶν καὶ προσπιπτουσῶν αὐταῖς, ἔτι δὲ φιλοπόνως
14 ἀπωξυμμένων τῶν κεραιῶν, οὔτ᾽ ἐπιλαβόμενον ἐκσπά-
σαι ῥᾴδιον διὰ τὸ πρῶτον μὲν πάσας τὰς προσβολὰς
σχεδὸν αὐτοκράτορα τὴν ἐκ τῆς γῆς δύναμιν ἔχειν,
15 δεύτερον δὲ τῷ τὸν μίαν ἐπισπώμενον κεραίαν πολλοὺς
ἀναγκάζεσθαι πειθομένους ἅμα βαστάζειν διὰ τὴν
εἰς ἀλλήλους ἐμπλοκήν· δύο δὲ καὶ τρεῖς ἐπιλαβέσθαι
16 ταὐτοῦ χάρακος οὐδ᾽ ὅλως εἰκός. ἐὰν δέ ποτε καὶ
κατακρατήσας ἐκσπάσῃ τις ἕνα καὶ δεύτερον, ἀνεπι-
17 γνώστως γίνεται τὸ διάστημα. διὸ καὶ μεγάλης <οὔ-
σης> διαφορᾶς τῷ καὶ τὴν εὕρεσιν ἑτοίμην εἶναι τοῦ
τοιούτου χάρακος καὶ τὴν κομιδὴν εὐχερῆ καὶ τὴν
18 χρείαν ἀσφαλῆ καὶ μόνιμον, φανερὸν ὡς εἰ καί τι τῶν
ἄλλων πολεμικῶν ἔργων ἄξιον ζήλου καὶ μιμήσεως
ὑπάρχει παρὰ Ῥωμαίοις, καὶ τοῦτο, κατά γε τὴν ἐμὴν
γνώμην.

(2) 19. Πλὴν ὅ γε Τίτος ἑτοιμασάμενος ταῦτα πρὸς τὰς
ἐκ τοῦ καιροῦ χρείας, προῆγε παντὶ τῷ στρατεύματι
βάδην, ἀποσχὼν δὲ περὶ πεντήκοντα στάδια τῆς τῶν
2 Φεραίων πόλεως αὐτοῦ παρενέβαλε. κατὰ δὲ τὴν ἐπιοῦσαν ὑπὸ τὴν ἑωθινὴν ἐξέπεμπε τοὺς κατοπτεύσον-
τας καὶ διερευνησομένους, εἴ τινα δυνηθεῖεν λαβεῖν
ἀφορμὴν εἰς τὸ γνῶναι ποῦ ποτ᾽ εἰσὶ καὶ τί πράττου-
3 σιν οἱ πολέμιοι. Φίλιππος δὲ [καὶ] κατὰ τὸν αὐτὸν
καιρὸν πυνθανόμενος τοὺς Ῥωμαίους στρατοπεδεύειν
περὶ τὰς Θήβας, ἐξάρας ἀπὸ τῆς Λαρίσης παντὶ τῷ
στρατεύματι προῆγε, ποιούμενος τὴν πορείαν ὡς ἐπὶ

carefully sharpened, it is not easy to pass one's hand through and grasp the stake, nor if one does get hold of it, is it easy to pull it up, as in the first place the power of resistance derived from the earth by all the portions open to attack is almost absolute, and next because a man who pulls at one prong is obliged to lift up numerous other stakes which give simultaneously under the strain owing to the way they are intertwined, and it is not at all probable that two or three men will get hold of the same stake. But if by main force a man succeeds in pulling up one or two, the gap is scarcely observable. Therefore, as the advantages of this kind of palisade are very great, the stakes being easy to find and easy to carry and the whole being more secure and more durable when constructed, it is evident that if any Roman military contrivance is worthy of our imitation and adoption this one certainly is, in my own opinion at least.

19. To resume—Flamininus, having prepared these stakes to be used when required, advanced slowly with his whole force and established his camp at a distance of about fifty stades from Pherae.[72] Next day at daybreak he sent out scouts to see if by observation and inquiry they could find any means of discovering where the enemy were and what they were about. Philip, at nearly the same time, on hearing that the Romans were encamped near Thebes, left Larisa with his entire army and advanced

---

[72] Modern Velestino in the Pelasgiotis. *RE* Pherai (Suppl. 7), 984–1026 (E. Kirsten).

4 τὰς Φεράς. ἀποσχὼν δὲ περὶ τριάκοντα στάδια, τότε
μὲν αὐτοῦ καταστρατοπεδεύσας ἐν ὥρᾳ παρήγγειλε
5 πᾶσι γίνεσθαι περὶ τὴν τοῦ σώματος θεραπείαν, ὑπὸ
δὲ τὴν ἑωθινὴν ἐξεγείρας τὴν δύναμιν τοὺς μὲν εἰθισμένους προπορεύεσθαι τῆς δυνάμεως προεξαπέστειλε,
συντάξας ὑπερβάλλειν τὰς ὑπὲρ τὰς Φερὰς ἀκρολο-
φίας, αὐτὸς δὲ τῆς ἡμέρας διαφαινούσης ἐκίνει τὴν
6 δύναμιν ἐκ τοῦ χάρακος. παρ᾽ ὀλίγον μὲν οὖν ἦλθον
ἀμφοτέρων οἱ προεξαπεσταλμένοι τοῦ συμπεσεῖν ἀλ-
7 λήλοις περὶ τὰς ὑπερβολάς· προϊδόμενοι γὰρ σφᾶς
αὐτοὺς ὑπὸ τὴν ὄρφνην ἐκ πάνυ βραχέος διαστήμα-
τος ἐπέστησαν, καὶ ταχέως ἔπεμπον, ἀποδηλοῦντες
ἀμφότεροι τοῖς ἡγεμόσι τὸ γεγονὸς καὶ πυνθανόμενοι
8 τί δέον εἴη ποιεῖν. . . . ἐπὶ τῶν ὑποκειμένων στρα-
9 τοπεδειῶν κἀκείνους ἀνακαλεῖσθαι. τῇ δ᾽ ἐπαύριον ἐξέπεμψαν ἀμφότεροι κατασκοπῆς ἕνεκα τῶν ἱππέων
καὶ τῶν εὐζώνων περὶ τριακοσίους ἑκατέρων, ἐν οἷς ὁ
Τίτος καὶ τῶν Αἰτωλῶν δύ᾽ οὐλαμοὺς ἐξαπέστειλε διὰ
10 τὴν ἐμπειρίαν τῶν τόπων· οἳ καὶ συμμίξαντες ἀλλήλοις ἐπὶ τάδε τῶν Φερῶν ὡς πρὸς Λάρισαν συνέβαλ-
11 λον ἐκθύμως. τῶν δὲ περὶ τὸν Εὐπόλεμον τὸν Αἰτωλὸν
εὐρώστως κινδυνευόντων καὶ συνεκκαλουμένων τοὺς
Ἰταλικοὺς πρὸς τὴν χρείαν, θλίβεσθαι συνέβαινε
12 τοὺς Μακεδόνας. καὶ τότε μὲν ἐπὶ πολὺν χρόνον ἀκρο-
βολισάμενοι διεχωρίσθησαν εἰς τὰς αὐτῶν παρεμβο-
λάς·

(3) 20. κατὰ δὲ τὴν ἐπιοῦσαν ἀμφότεροι δυσαρεστού-
μενοι τοῖς περὶ τὰς Φερὰς τόποις διὰ τὸ καταφύτους

marching in the direction of Pherae. When at a distance of thirty stades[73] from that town he encamped there while it was still early and ordered all his men to occupy themselves with the care of their persons. Next day at early dawn he aroused his men, and sending on in advance those accustomed to precede the main body with orders to cross the ridge above Pherae, he himself, when day began to break, moved the rest of his forces out of the camp. The advanced sections of both armies very nearly came into contact at the pass over the hills; for when in the darkness they caught sight of each other, they halted when already quite close and sent at once to inform their respective commanders of the fact and inquire what they should do. It was decided to remain for that day in their actual camp and to recall the advanced forces. Next day both commanders sent out some horse and light-armed infantry— about three hundred of either arm to reconnoiter. Among these Flamininus included two squadrons of Aetolians owing to their acquaintance with the country. The respective forces met on the near side of Pherae, in the direction of Larisa, and a desperate struggle ensued. As the force under Eupolemus[74] the Aetolian fought with great vigor and called up the Italians to take part in the action, the Macedonians found themselves hard pressed. For the present, after prolonged skirmishing, both forces separated and retired to their camps.

20. Next day both armies, dissatisfied with the ground near Pherae, as it was all under cultivation and covered

73 About six kilometers.
74 J. D. Grainger (10.9), 171. Later he was the leader of the anti-Roman faction in Aetolia and was deported to Rome.

2 εἶναι καὶ πλήρεις αἱμασιῶν καὶ κηπίων ἀνέζευξαν. ὁ
μὲν οὖν Φίλιππος ἐποιεῖτο τὴν πορείαν ὡς ἐπὶ τὴν
Σκοτοῦσσαν, σπεύδων ἐκ ταύτης τῆς πόλεως ἐφο-
διάσασθαι, μετὰ δὲ ταῦτα γενόμενος εὐτρεπὴς λαβεῖν

3 τόπους ἁρμόζοντας ταῖς αὑτοῦ δυνάμεσιν· ὁ δὲ Τίτος
ὑποπτεύσας τὸ μέλλον ἐκίνει τὴν δύναμιν ἅμα τῷ
Φιλίππῳ, σπεύδων προκαταφθεῖραι τὸν ἐν τῇ Σκο-

4 τουσσαίᾳ σῖτον. τῆς δ᾽ ἑκατέρων πορείας μεταξὺ κειμένων ὄχθων ὑψηλῶν, οὔθ᾽ οἱ Ῥωμαῖοι συνεώρων τοὺς
Μακεδόνας, ποῖ ποιοῦνται τὴν πορείαν, οὔθ᾽ οἱ Μακε-

5 δόνες τοὺς Ῥωμαίους. ταύτην μὲν ⟨οὖν⟩ τὴν ἡμέραν
ἑκάτεροι διανύσαντες, ὁ μὲν Τίτος ἐπὶ τὴν προσαγορευομένην Ἐρέτριαν τῆς ⟨Φθιώτιδος χώρας⟩, ὁ δὲ
Φίλιππος ἐπὶ τὸν Ὀγχηστὸν ποταμόν, αὐτοῦ κατέζευ-
ξαν, ἀγνοοῦντες ἀμφότεροι τὰς ἀλλήλων παρεμβο-

6 λάς· τῇ δ᾽ ὑστεραίᾳ προελθόντες ἐστρατοπέδευσαν,
Φίλιππος μὲν ἐπὶ τὸ Μελάμβιον προσαγορευόμενον
τῆς Σκοτουσσαίας, Τίτος δὲ περὶ τὸ Θετίδειον τῆς

7 Φαρσαλίας, ἀκμὴν ἀγνοοῦντες ἀλλήλους. ἐπιγενομένου
δ᾽ ὄμβρου καὶ βροντῶν ἐξαισίων, πάντα συνέβη τὸν
ἀέρα τὸν ἐκ τῶν νεφῶν κατὰ τὴν ἐπιοῦσαν ἡμέραν
ὑπὸ τὴν ἑωθινὴν πεσεῖν ἐπὶ τὴν γῆν, ὥστε διὰ τὸν
ἐφεστῶτα ζόφον μηδὲ τοὺς ἐν ποσὶ δύνασθαι βλέ-

8 πειν. οὐ μὴν ἀλλ᾽ ὅ γε Φίλιππος κατανύσαι σπεύδων
ἐπὶ τὸ προκείμενον, ἀναζεύξας προῆει μετὰ πάσης τῆς

9 στρατιᾶς. δυσχρηστούμενος δὲ κατὰ τὴν πορείαν διὰ
τὴν ὁμίχλην, βραχὺν τόπον διανύσας τὴν μὲν δύναμιν εἰς χάρακα παρενέβαλε, τὴν δ᾽ ἐφεδρείαν ἀπ-

with walls and small gardens, retired from it. Philip for his part began to march toward Scotussa,[75] hoping to procure supplies from that town and afterward when fully furnished to find ground suitable for his own army. But Flamininus, suspecting his purpose, put his army in motion at the same time as Philip with the object of destroying the corn in the territory of Scotussa before his adversary could get there. As there were high hills between the two armies in their march neither did the Romans perceive where the Macedonians were marching to nor the Macedonians the Romans. After marching all that day, Flamininus having reached the place called Eretria[76] in Phthiotis and Philip the river Onchestus, they both encamped at those spots, each ignorant of the position of the other's camp. Next day they again advanced and encamped, Philip at the place called Melambium in the territory of Scotussa and Flamininus at the sanctuary of Thetis in that of Pharsalus, being still in ignorance of each others' whereabouts. In the night there was a violent thunderstorm accompanied by rain, and next morning at early dawn all the mist from the clouds descended on the earth, so that owing to the darkness that prevailed one could not see even people who were close at hand. Philip, however, who was in a hurry to effect his purpose, broke up his camp and advanced with his whole army, but finding it difficult to march owing to the mist, after having made but little progress, he entrenched his army and sent off his

75 See n. on 10.42.3.
76 See map in WC 2.577, also for the area of the battle. The topographical details are often uncertain and controversial; a summary in WC 2.576–580.

ἔστειλε, συντάξας ἐπὶ τοὺς ἄκρους ἐπιβαλεῖν τῶν μεταξὺ κειμένων βουνῶν.

(4)   21. Ὁ δὲ Τίτος στρατοπεδεύων περὶ τὸ Θετίδειον, καὶ διαπορούμενος ὑπὲρ τῶν πολεμίων ποῦ ποτ᾽ εἰσί, δέκα προθέμενος οὐλαμοὺς καὶ τῶν εὐζώνων εἰς χιλίους ἐξαπέστειλε, παρακαλέσας εὐλαβῶς ἐξερευνωμέ-

2 νους ἐπιπορεύεσθαι τὴν χώραν· οἳ καὶ προάγοντες ὡς ἐπὶ τὰς ὑπερβολὰς ἔλαθον ἐμπεσόντες εἰς τὴν τῶν Μακεδόνων ἐφεδρείαν διὰ τὸ δύσοπτον τῆς ἡμέρας.

3 οὗτοι μὲν οὖν ἐν ταῖς ἀρχαῖς ἐπὶ βραχὺ διαταραχθέν-τες ἀμφότεροι μετ᾽ ὀλίγον ἤρξαντο καταπειράζειν ἀλλήλων, διεπέμψαντο δὲ καὶ πρὸς τοὺς ἑαυτῶν ἡγε-μόνας ἑκάτεροι τοὺς διασαφήσοντας τὸ γεγονός·

4 ἐπειδὴ δὲ κατὰ τὴν συμπλοκὴν οἱ Ῥωμαῖοι κατ-εβαροῦντο καὶ κακῶς ἔπασχον ὑπὸ τῆς τῶν Μακεδό-νων ἐφεδρείας, πέμποντες εἰς τὴν ἑαυτῶν παρεμβολὴν

5 ἐδέοντο σφίσι βοηθεῖν. ὁ δὲ Τίτος, παρακαλέσας τοὺς περὶ τὸν Ἀρχέδαμον καὶ τὸν Εὐπόλεμον Αἰτωλοὺς καὶ δύο τῶν παρ᾽ αὑτοῦ χιλιάρχων, ἐξέπεμψε μετὰ πεντα-

6 κοσίων ἱππέων καὶ δισχιλίων πεζῶν. ὧν προσγενομέ-νων τοῖς ἐξ ἀρχῆς ἀκροβολιζομένοις, παραυτίκα τὴν

7 ἐναντίαν ἔσχε διάθεσιν ὁ κίνδυνος· οἱ μὲν γὰρ Ῥω-μαῖοι, προσλαβόντες τὴν ἐκ τῆς βοηθείας ἐλπίδα δι-

8 πλασίως ἐπερρώσθησαν πρὸς τὴν χρείαν, οἱ δὲ Μα-κεδόνες ἠμύνοντο μὲν γενναίως, πιεζούμενοι δὲ πάλιν οὗτοι καὶ καταβαρούμενοι τοῖς ὅλοις προσέφυγον

covering force with orders to occupy the summits of the hills which lay between him and the enemy.

21. Flamininus lay still encamped near the sanctuary of Thetis[77] and, being in doubt as to where the enemy were, he pushed forward ten squadrons of horse and about a thousand light-armed infantry, sending them out with orders to go over the ground reconnoitering cautiously. In proceeding toward the pass over the hills they encountered the Macedonian covering force quite unexpectedly owing to the obscurity of the day. Both forces were thrown somewhat into disorder for a short time but soon began to take the offensive, sending to their respective commanders messengers to inform them of what had happened. When in the combat that ensued the Romans began to be overpowered and to suffer loss at the hands of the Macedonian covering force they sent to their camp begging for help, and Flamininus, calling upon Archedamus and Eupolemus[78] the Aetolians and two of his military tribunes, sent them off with five hundred horse and two thousand foot. When this force joined the original skirmishers the engagement at once took an entirely different turn. For the Romans, encouraged by the arrival of the reinforcements, fought with redoubled vigor, and the Macedonians, though defending themselves gallantly, were in their turn pressed hard, and upon being com-

---

[77] F. Stählin (3.12), 110 and 141; it belonged to Pharsalus.

[78] Grainger (10.9), 109 for Archedamus, 171 for Eupolemus, both influential politicians in Aetolia. As both men were deported to Rome just a little before P. was, one of them could have been P.'s source for the battle and responsible for his positive assessment of the Aetolian contribution to the victory.

πρὸς τοὺς ἄκρους καὶ διεπέμποντο πρὸς τὸν βασιλέα
περὶ βοηθείας.

(5)   22. Ὁ δὲ Φίλιππος οὐδέποτ᾽ ἂν ἐλπίσας κατ᾽ ἐκείνην
τὴν ἡμέραν ὁλοσχερῆ γενέσθαι κίνδυνον διὰ τὰς προειρημένας αἰτίας, ἀφεικὼς ἔτυχε καὶ πλείους ἐκ τῆς
2   παρεμβολῆς ἐπὶ χορτολογίαν. τότε δὲ πυνθανόμενος
τὰ συμβαίνοντα παρὰ τῶν διαποστελλομένων, καὶ
τῆς ὁμίχλης ἤδη διαφαινούσης, παρακαλέσας Ἡρακλείδην τε τὸν Γυρτώνιον, ὃς ἡγεῖτο τῆς Θετταλικῆς
ἵππου, καὶ Λέοντα τὸν τῶν Μακεδόνων ἱππάρχην ἐξέπεμπε, σὺν δὲ τούτοις Ἀθηναγόραν ἔχοντα πάντας
3   τοὺς μισθοφόρους πλὴν τῶν Θρακῶν. συναψάντων δὲ
τούτων τοῖς ἐν ταῖς ἐφεδρείαις, καὶ προσγενομένης
τοῖς Μακεδόσι βαρείας χειρός, ἐνέκειντο τοῖς πολεμί-
οις· καὶ πάλιν οὗτοι τοὺς Ῥωμαίους ἤλαυνον ἐκ μετα-
4   βολῆς ἀπὸ τῶν ἄκρων. μέγιστον δ᾽ αὐτοῖς ἐμπόδιον
ἦν τοῦ μὴ τρέψασθαι τοὺς πολεμίους ὁλοσχερῶς ἡ
τῶν Αἰτωλικῶν ἱππέων φιλοτιμία· πάνυ γὰρ ἐκθύμως
5   οὗτοι καὶ παραβόλως ἐκινδύνευον. Αἰτωλοὶ γάρ, καθ᾽
ὅσον ἐν τοῖς πεζικοῖς ἐλλιπεῖς εἰσι καὶ τῷ καθοπλισμῷ
καὶ τῇ συντάξει πρὸς τοὺς ὁλοσχερεῖς ἀγῶνας, κατὰ
τοσοῦτον τοῖς ἱππικοῖς διαφέρουσι πρὸς τὸ βέλτιον
τῶν ἄλλων Ἑλλήνων ἐν τοῖς κατὰ μέρος καὶ κατ᾽
6   ἰδίαν κινδύνοις. διὸ καὶ τότε τούτων παρακατασχόν-
των τὴν ἐπιφορὰν τῶν πολεμίων, οὐκέτι συνηλάσθη-
σαν ἕως εἰς τοὺς ἐπιπέδους τόπους, βραχὺ δ᾽ ἀποσχόντες
7   ἐκ μεταβολῆς ἔστησαν. ὁ δὲ Τίτος, θεωρῶν οὐ μόνον
τοὺς εὐζώνους καὶ τοὺς ἱππέας ἐγκεκλικότας, ἀλλὰ

pletely overmastered, fled to the summits and sent to the king for help.

22. Philip, who had never expected, for the reasons I have stated, that a general engagement would take place on that day, had even sent out a fair number of men from his camp to forage, and now when he heard of the turn affairs were taking from the messengers, and as the mist was beginning to clear, he called upon Heraclides of Gyrton, the commander of the Thessalian horse, and Leo, who was in command of the Macedonian horse, and dispatched them, together with all the mercenaries except those from Thrace, under the command of Athenagoras. Upon their joining the covering force the Macedonians, having received such a large reinforcement, pressed hard on the enemy and in their turn began to drive the Romans from the heights. But the chief obstacle to their putting the enemy entirely to rout was the high spirit of the Aetolian cavalry who fought with desperate gallantry. For by as much as the Aetolian infantry is inferior in the equipment and discipline required for a general engagement, by so much is their cavalry superior to that of other Greeks in detached and single combats. Thus on the present occasion they so far checked the spirit of the enemy's advance that the Romans were not as before driven down to the level ground, but when they were at a short distance from it turned and steadied themselves. Flamininus, upon seeing that not only had his light infantry and cavalry given

διὰ τούτους καὶ τὴν ὅλην δύναμιν ἐπτοημένην, ἐξῆγε
τὸ στράτευμα πᾶν καὶ παρενέβαλε πρὸς τοῖς βουνοῖς.
8 κατὰ δὲ τὸν αὐτὸν καιρὸν ἕτερος ἐφ᾽ ἑτέρῳ τῶν ἐκ τῆς
ἐφεδρείας Μακεδόνων ἔθει πρὸς τὸν Φίλιππον, ἀνα-
βοῶν "Βασιλεῦ, φεύγουσιν οἱ πολέμιοι· μὴ παρῇς τὸν
καιρόν· οὐ μένουσιν ἡμᾶς οἱ βάρβαροι· σὴ νῦν ἐστιν
9 ἡμέρα, σὸς ὁ καιρός." ὥστε τὸν Φίλιππον, καίπερ οὐκ
εὐδοκούμενον τοῖς τόποις, ὅμως ἐκκληθῆναι πρὸς τὸν
κίνδυνον. οἱ γὰρ προειρημένοι λόφοι καλοῦνται μὲν
Κυνὸς Κεφαλαί, τραχεῖς δ᾽ εἰσὶ καὶ περικεκλασμένοι
10 καὶ πρὸς ὕψος ἱκανὸν ἀνατείνοντες. διὸ καὶ προορώμενος ὁ Φίλιππος τὴν δυσχρηστίαν τῶν τόπων, ἐξ
ἀρχῆς μὲν οὐδαμῶς ἡρμόζετο πρὸς ἀγῶνα· τότε δὲ
παρορμηθεὶς διὰ τὴν ὑπερβολὴν τῆς εὐελπιστίας τῶν
ἀγγελλόντων ἕλκειν παρήγγελλε τὴν δύναμιν ἐκ τοῦ
χάρακος.
(6)   23. Ὁ δὲ Τίτος παρεμβαλὼν τὴν αὑτοῦ στρατιὰν
ἑξῆς ἅπασαν, ἅμα μὲν ἐφήδρευε τοῖς προκινδυνεύου-
2 σιν, ἅμα δὲ παρεκάλει τὰς τάξεις ἐπιπορευόμενος. ἡ
δὲ παράκλησις ἦν αὐτοῦ βραχεῖα μέν, ἐμφαντικὴ δὲ
καὶ γνώριμος τοῖς ἀκούουσιν. ἐναργῶς γὰρ ὑπὸ τὴν
ὄψιν ἐνδεικνύμενος ἔλεγε τοῖς αὑτοῦ στρατιώταις
3 "Οὐχ οὗτοι Μακεδόνες εἰσίν, ὦ ἄνδρες, οὓς ὑμεῖς προκατέχοντας ἐν Μακεδονίᾳ τὰς εἰς τὴν Ἐορδαίαν ὑπερβολὰς ἐκ τοῦ προφανοῦς μετὰ Σολπικίου βιασάμενοι
πρὸς τόπους ὑπερδεξίους ἐξεβάλετε, πολλοὺς αὐτῶν
4 ἀποκτείναντες; οὐχ οὗτοι Μακεδόνες εἰσίν, οὓς ὑμεῖς
προκατέχοντας τὰς ἀπηλπισμένας ἐν Ἠπείρῳ δυσ-

way, but that his whole army was flustered owing to this, led out all his forces and drew them up in order of battle close to the hills. At the same time one messenger after another from the covering force came running to Philip shouting, "Sire, the enemy are flying: do not lose the opportunity: the barbarians[79] cannot stand before us: the day is yours now: this is your time"; so that Philip, though he was not satisfied with the ground, still allowed himself to be provoked to do battle. The above-mentioned hills are, I should say, called "The Dog's Heads" (Cynoscephalae): they are very rough and broken and attain a considerable height. Philip, therefore, foreseeing what difficulties the ground would present, was at first by no means disposed to fight, but now urged on by these excessively sanguine reports he ordered his army to be led out of the entrenched camp.

23. Flamininus, having drawn up his whole army in line, both took steps to cover the retreat of his advanced force and walking along the ranks addressed his men. His address was brief, but vivid and easily understood by his hearers. For pointing to the enemy, who were now in full view, he said to his men, "Are these not the Macedonians whom, when they held the pass leading to Eordaea,[80] you under Sulpicius attacked in the open and forced to retreat to the higher ground after slaying many of them? Are these not the same Macedonians who when they held that desperately difficult position in Epirus[81] you compelled by

---

79 For the Romans called barbarians, see n. on 9.37.6.
80 See nn. on 3.9 and 11.10.
81 See nn. on 3.8 and 11.10.

χωρίας ἐκβιασάμενοι ταῖς ἑαυτῶν ἀρεταῖς φεύγειν
ἠναγκάσατε ῥίψαντας τὰ ὅπλα, τέως εἰς Μακεδονίαν
5 ἀνεκομίσθησαν; πῶς οὖν ὑμᾶς εὐλαβεῖσθαι καθήκει,
μέλλοντας ἐξ ἴσου ποιεῖσθαι τὸν κίνδυνον πρὸς τοὺς
αὐτούς; τί δὲ προορᾶσθαι τῶν προγεγονότων, ἀλλ' οὐ
6 τἀναντία δι' ἐκεῖνα καὶ νῦν θαρρεῖν; διόπερ, ὦ ἄνδρες,
παρακαλέσαντες σφᾶς αὐτοὺς ὁρμᾶσθε πρὸς τὸν κίνδυνον ἐρρωμένως· θεῶν γὰρ βουλομένων ταχέως πέ-
πεισμαι ταὐτὸ τέλος ἀποβήσεσθαι τῆς παρούσης
7 μάχης τοῖς προγεγονόσι κινδύνοις." οὗτος μὲν οὖν
ταῦτ' εἰπὼν τὸ μὲν δεξιὸν μέρος ἐκέλευε μένειν κατὰ
χώραν καὶ τὰ θηρία πρὸ τούτων, τῷ δ' εὐωνύμῳ μετὰ
8 τῶν εὐζώνων ἐπῄει σοβαρῶς τοῖς πολεμίοις· οἱ δὲ
προκινδυνεύοντες τῶν Ῥωμαίων, προσλαβόντες τὴν
τῶν πεζῶν στρατοπέδων ἐφεδρείαν, ἐκ μεταβολῆς
ἐνέκειντο τοῖς ὑπεναντίοις.

(7)   24. Φίλιππος δὲ κατὰ τὸν αὐτὸν καιρόν, ἐπειδὴ τὸ
πλέον μέρος ἤδη τῆς ἑαυτοῦ δυνάμεως ἑώρα παρεμ-
βεβληκὸς πρὸ τοῦ χάρακος, αὐτὸς μὲν ἀναλαβὼν
τοὺς πελταστὰς καὶ τὸ δεξιὸν τῆς φάλαγγος προῆγε,
σύντονον ποιούμενος τὴν πρὸς τοὺς λόφους ἀνάβασιν,
2 τοῖς δὲ περὶ τὸν Νικάνορα τὸν ἐπικαλούμενον ἐλέ-
φαντα συνέταξε φροντίζειν ἵνα τὸ λοιπὸν μέρος τῆς
3 δυνάμεως ἐκ ποδὸς ἕπηται. ἅμα δὲ τῷ τοὺς πρώτους
ἅψασθαι τῆς ὑπερβολῆς εὐθέως ἐξ ἀσπίδος παρενέβαλε καὶ προκατελάμβανε τοὺς ὑπερδεξίους· τῶν γὰρ
προκινδυνευόντων Μακεδόνων ἐπὶ πολὺ τεθλιφότων
τοὺς Ῥωμαίους ἐπὶ θάτερα μέρη τῶν λόφων, ἐρήμους

your valor to throw away their shields and take to flight, never stopping until they got home to Macedonia? What reason, then, have you to be timid now when you are about to do battle with the same men on equal terms? What need for you to dread a recurrence of former danger, when you should rather on the contrary derive confidence from memory of the past! And so, my men, encouraging each other dash on to the fray and put forth all your strength. For if it be the will of Heaven, I feel sure that this battle will end like the former ones." After speaking thus he ordered those on the right to remain where they were with the elephants in front of them, and taking with him the left half of his army, advanced to meet the enemy in imposing style. The advanced force of the Romans thus supported by the infantry of the legions now turned and fell upon their foes.

24. Philip at this same time, now that he saw the greater part of his army drawn up outside the entrenchment, advanced with the peltasts and the right wing of the phalanx, ascending energetically the slope that led to the hills and giving orders to Nicanor, who was nicknamed the elephant, to see that the rest of his army followed him at once. When the leading ranks reached the top of the pass, he wheeled to the left, and occupied the summits above it; for, as the Macedonian advanced force had pressed the Romans for a considerable distance down the oppo-

THE HISTORIES OF POLYBIUS

4 κατέλαβε τοὺς ἄκρους. ἔτι δὲ παρεμβάλλοντος αὐτοῦ
   τὰ δεξιὰ μέρη τῆς στρατιᾶς, παρῆσαν οἱ μισθοφόροι,
5 πιεζούμενοι κατὰ κράτος ὑπὸ τῶν πολεμίων· προσγε-
   νομένων γὰρ τοῖς τῶν Ῥωμαίων εὐζώνοις τῶν ἐν τοῖς
   βαρέσιν ὅπλοις ἀνδρῶν, καθάπερ ἀρτίως εἶπα, καὶ
   συνεργούντων κατὰ τὴν μάχην, προσλαβόντες οἷον εἰ
   σήκωμα τὴν τούτων χρείαν, βαρέως ἐπέκειντο τοῖς
6 πολεμίοις καὶ πολλοὺς αὐτῶν ἔκτεινον. ὁ δὲ βασιλεὺς
   ἐν μὲν ταῖς ἀρχαῖς, ὅτε παρεγίνετο, θεωρῶν οὐ μακρὰν
   τῆς τῶν πολεμίων παρεμβολῆς συνεστῶτα τὸν τῶν
7 εὐζώνων κίνδυνον περιχαρὴς ἦν· ὡς δὲ πάλιν ἐκ μεταβολῆς ἑώρα κλίνοντας τοὺς ἰδίους καὶ προσδεομένους
   ἐπικουρίας, ἠναγκάζετο βοηθεῖν καὶ κρίνειν ἐκ τοῦ
   καιροῦ τὰ ὅλα, καίπερ ἔτι τῶν πλείστων μερῶν τῆς
   φάλαγγος κατὰ πορείαν ὄντων καὶ προσβαινόντων
8 πρὸς τοὺς βουνούς. προσδεξάμενος δὲ τοὺς ἀγωνι-
   ζομένους, τούτους μὲν ἤθροιζε πάντας ἐπὶ τὸ δεξιὸν
   κέρας, καὶ τοὺς πεζοὺς καὶ τοὺς ἱππέας, τοῖς δὲ πελ-
   ταστοῖς καὶ τοῖς φαλαγγίταις παρήγγελλε διπλασι-
9 άζειν τὸ βάθος καὶ πυκνοῦν ἐπὶ τὸ δεξιόν. γενομένου
   δὲ τούτου, καὶ τῶν πολεμίων ἐν χερσὶν ὄντων, τοῖς μὲν
   φαλαγγίταις ἐδόθη παράγγελμα καταβαλοῦσι τὰς
10 σαρίσας ἐπάγειν, τοῖς δ' εὐζώνοις κερᾶν. κατὰ δὲ τὸν
   αὐτὸν καιρὸν καὶ Τίτος, δεξάμενος εἰς τὰ διαστήματα
   τῶν σημαιῶν τοὺς προκινδυνεύοντας, προσέβαλε τοῖς
   πολεμίοις.

(8) 25. Γενομένης δὲ τῆς ἐξ ἀμφοῖν συμπτώσεως μετὰ
     βίας καὶ κραυγῆς ὑπερβαλλούσης, ὡς ἂν ἀμφοτέρων

158

site side of the hills, he found these summits abandoned. While he was still deploying his force on the right his mercenaries appeared hotly pursued by the Romans. For when the heavy-armed Roman infantry had joined the light infantry, as I said, and gave them their support in the battle, they availed themselves of the additional weight thus thrown into the scale, and pressing heavily on the enemy killed many of them. When the king, just after his arrival, saw that the light infantry were engaged not far from the hostile camp he was overjoyed, but now on seeing his own men giving way in their turn and in urgent need of support, he was compelled to go to their assistance and thus decide the whole fate of the day on the spur of the moment, although the greater portion of the phalanx was still on the march and approaching the hills. Receiving those who were engaged with the enemy, he placed them all, both foot and horse, on his right wing and ordered the peltasts and that part of the phalanx he had with him to double their depth and close up toward the right. Upon this being done, the enemy being now close upon them, orders were sent to the men of the phalanx to lower their spears and charge, while the light infantry were ordered to place themselves on the flank. At the same moment Flamininus, having received his advanced force into the gaps between the maniples, fell upon the enemy.

25. As the encounter of the two armies was accompanied by deafening shouts and cries, both of them uttering

ὁμοῦ συναλαλαζόντων, ἅμα δὲ καὶ τῶν ἐκτὸς τῆς μάχης ἐπιβοώντων τοῖς ἀγωνιζομένοις, ἦν τὸ γινόμενον
2 ἐκπληκτικὸν καὶ παραστατικὸν ἀγωνίας. τὸ μὲν οὖν
δεξιὸν τοῦ Φιλίππου λαμπρῶς ἀπήλλατε κατὰ τὸν
κίνδυνον, ἅτε καὶ τὴν ἔφοδον ἐξ ὑπερδεξίου ποιούμενον καὶ τῷ βάρει τῆς συντάξεως ὑπερέχον καὶ τῇ
διαφορᾷ τοῦ καθοπλισμοῦ πρὸς τὴν ἐνεστῶσαν
3 χρείαν πολὺ παραλλάττον· τὰ δὲ λοιπὰ μέρη τῆς δυνάμεως αὐτῷ τὰ μὲν ἐχόμενα τῶν κινδυνευόντων ἐν
ἀποστάσει τῶν πολεμίων ἦν, τὰ δ᾽ ἐπὶ τῶν εὐωνύμων
ἄρτι διηνυκότα τὰς ὑπερβολὰς ἐπεφαίνετο τοῖς ἄκροις.
4 ὁ δὲ Τίτος, θεωρῶν οὐ δυναμένους τοὺς παρ᾽ αὑτοῦ
στέγειν τὴν τῆς φάλαγγος ἔφοδον, ἀλλ᾽ ἐκπιεζουμένους
τοὺς ἐπὶ τῶν εὐωνύμων, καὶ τοὺς μὲν ἀπολωλότας ἤδη,
τοὺς δ᾽ ἐπὶ πόδα ποιουμένους τὴν ἀναχώρησιν, ἐν δὲ
τοῖς δεξιοῖς μέρεσι καταλειπομένας τῆς σωτηρίας τὰς
5 ἐλπίδας, ταχέως ἀφορμήσας πρὸς τούτους, καὶ συνθεασάμενος [τῆς] τῶν πολεμίων τὰ μὲν συνεχῆ τοῖς
διαγωνιζομένοις ..., τὰ δ᾽ ἐκ τῶν ἄκρων ἀκμὴν ἐπι-
καταβαίνοντα, τὰ δ᾽ ἔτι τοῖς ἄκροις ἐφεστῶτα, προθέμενος τὰ θηρία προσῆγε τὰς σημαίας τοῖς πολεμί-
6 οις. οἱ δὲ Μακεδόνες, οὔτε τὸν παραγγελοῦντ᾽ ἔχοντες
οὔτε συστῆναι δυνάμενοι καὶ λαβεῖν τὸ τῆς φάλαγγος ἴδιον σχῆμα διά τε τὰς τῶν τόπων δυσχερείας
καὶ διὰ τὸ τοῖς ἀγωνιζομένοις ἑπόμενοι πορείας ἔχειν
7 διάθεσιν καὶ μὴ παρατάξεως, οὐδὲ προσεδέξαντο τοὺς
Ῥωμαίους εἰς τὰς χεῖρας ἔτι, δι᾽ αὐτῶν δὲ τῶν θηρίων
πτοηθέντες καὶ διασπασθέντες ἐνέκλιναν.

their war cry and those outside the battle also cheering the combatants, the spectacle was such as to inspire terror and acute anxiety. Philip's right wing acquitted themselves splendidly in the battle, as they were charging from higher ground and were superior in the weight of their formation, the nature of their arms also giving them a decided advantage on the present occasion. But as for the rest of his army, those next to the force actually engaged were still at a distance from the enemy and those on the left had only just surmounted the ridge and come into view of the summits. Flamininus, seeing that his men could not sustain the charge of the phalanx, but that since his left was being forced back, some of them having already perished and others retreating slowly, his only hope of safety lay in his right, hastened to place himself in command there, and observing that those of the enemy who were next to the actual combatants were idle, and that some of the rest were still descending to meet him from the summits and others had halted on the heights, placed his elephants in front and led on his maniples to the attack. The Macedonians now, having no one to give them orders and being unable to adopt the formation proper to the phalanx, in part owing to the difficulty of the ground and in part because they were trying to reach the combatants and were still in marching order and not in line, did not even wait until they were at close quarters with the Romans, but gave way thrown into confusion and broken up by the elephants alone.

(9)   26. Οἱ μὲν οὖν πλείους τῶν Ῥωμαίων ἑπόμενοι τού-

2   τους ἔκτεινον· εἷς δὲ τῶν χιλιάρχων τῶν ἅμα τούτοις,
σημαίας ἔχων οὐ πλείους εἴκοσι, καὶ παρ' αὐτὸν τὸν
τῆς χρείας καιρὸν συμφρονήσας ὃ δέον εἴη ποιεῖν,
μεγάλα συνεβάλετο πρὸς τὴν τῶν ὅλων κατόρθωσιν.

3   θεωρῶν γὰρ τοὺς περὶ τὸν Φίλιππον ἐπὶ πολὺ προπε-
πτωκότας τῶν ἄλλων καὶ πιεζοῦντας τῷ βάρει τὸ
σφέτερον εὐώνυμον, ἀπολιπὼν τοὺς ἐπὶ τοῦ δεξιοῦ
νικῶντας ἤδη καταφανῶς, ἐπιστρέψας ἐπὶ τοὺς ἀγω-
νιζομένους καὶ κατόπιν ἐπιγενόμενος προσέβαλλε

4   κατὰ νώτου τοῖς Μακεδόσι. τῆς δὲ τῶν φαλαγγιτῶν
χρείας ἀδυνάτου καθεστώσης ἐκ μεταβολῆς καὶ κατ'
ἄνδρα κινδυνεύειν, οὗτος μὲν ἐπέκειτο κτείνων τοὺς ἐν

5   ποσίν, οὐ δυναμένους αὑτοῖς βοηθεῖν, ἕως οὗ ῥίψαντες
τὰ ὅπλα φεύγειν ἠναγκάσθησαν οἱ Μακεδόνες, συν-
επιθεμένων αὐτοῖς ἐκ μεταβολῆς καὶ τῶν κατὰ πρόσ-

6   ωπον ἐγκεκλικότων. ὁ δὲ Φίλιππος ἐν μὲν ταῖς ἀρχαῖς,
καθάπερ εἶπα, τεκμαιρόμενος ἐκ τοῦ καθ' αὑτὸν μέ-

7   ρους ἐπέπειστο τελέως νικᾶν· τότε δὲ συνθεασάμενος
ἄφνω ῥιπτοῦντας τὰ ὅπλα τοὺς Μακεδόνας καὶ τοὺς
πολεμίους κατὰ νώτου προσβεβληκότας, βραχὺ γενόμενος ἐκ τοῦ κινδύνου μετ' ὀλίγων ἱππέων καὶ πεζῶν

8   συνεθεώρει τὰ ὅλα. κατανοήσας δὲ τοὺς Ῥωμαίους
κατὰ τὸ δίωγμα τοῦ λαιοῦ κέρως τοῖς ἄκροις ἤδη
προσπελάζοντας, ἐγίνετο ⟨πρὸς τὸ φεύγειν, ὅσους
ἐδύνατο⟩ πλείστους ἐκ τοῦ καιροῦ συναθροίσας τῶν

9   Θρακῶν καὶ Μακεδόνων. Τίτος δὲ τοῖς φεύγουσιν ἑπό-
μενος, καὶ καταλαβὼν ἐν ταῖς ὑπερβολαῖς ἄρτι τοῖς

26. Most of the Romans followed up these fugitives and continued to put them to the sword: but one of the tribunes with them, taking not more than twenty maniples and judging on the spur of the moment what ought to be done, contributed much to the total victory. For noticing that the Macedonians under Philip had advanced a long way in front of the rest, and were by their weight forcing back the Roman left, he quitted those on the right, who were now clearly victorious, and wheeling his force in the direction of the scene of combat and thus getting behind the Macedonians, he fell upon them in the rear. As it is impossible for the phalanx to turn right about face or to fight man to man, he now pressed his attack home, killing those he found in his way, who were incapable of protecting themselves, until the whole Macedonian force were compelled to throw away their arms and take to flight, attacked now also by the troops who had yielded before their frontal charge and who now turned and faced them. Philip at first, as I said, judging from the success of those under his own leadership, was convinced that his victory was complete, but now on suddenly seeing that the Macedonians were throwing away their arms and that the enemy had attacked them in the rear, retired with a small number of horse and foot to a short distance from the scene of action and remained to observe the whole scene. When he noticed that the Romans in pursuit of his left wing had already reached the summits, he decided to flee, collecting hastily as many Thracians and Macedonians as he could. Flamininus, pursuing the fugitives and finding when he reached the crest of the ridge that the ranks of

ἄκροις ἐπιβαλούσας τὰς εὐωνύμους τάξεις τῶν Μακεδόνων τὰς μὲν ⟨ἀρχὰς⟩ . . . ἐπέστη, τῶν πολεμίων
ὀρθὰς ἀνασχόντων τὰς σαρίσας, ὅπερ ἔθος ἐστὶ ποι-
10 εῖν τοῖς Μακεδόσιν, ὅταν ἢ παραδιδῶσιν αὑτοὺς ἢ
11 μεταβάλλωνται πρὸς τοὺς ὑπεναντίους· μετὰ δὲ ταῦτα
πυθόμενος τὴν αἰτίαν τοῦ συμβαίνοντος παρακατεῖχε
τοὺς μεθ᾽ αὑτοῦ φείσασθαι κρίνων τῶν ἀποδεδειλι-
12 ακότων. ἀκμὴν δὲ τοῦ Τίτου ταῦτα διανοουμένου τῶν
προηγουμένων τινὲς ἐπιπεσόντες αὐτοῖς ἐξ ὑπερδεξίου
προσέφερον τὰς χεῖρας, καὶ τοὺς μὲν πλείους διέφθει-
ρον, ὀλίγοι δέ τινες διέφυγον ῥίψαντες τὰ ὅπλα.

27. Πανταχόθεν δὲ τοῦ κινδύνου συντέλειαν εἰλη-
(10) φότος καὶ κρατούντων τῶν Ῥωμαίων, ὁ μὲν Φίλιππος
2 ἐποιεῖτο τὴν ἀποχώρησιν ὡς ἐπὶ τὰ Τέμπη. καὶ τῇ μὲν
πρώτῃ περὶ τὸν Ἀλεξάνδρου καλούμενον πύργον ηὐ-
λίσθη, τῇ δ᾽ ὑστεραίᾳ προελθὼν εἰς Γόννους ἐπὶ τὴν
εἰσβολὴν τῶν Τεμπῶν ἐπέμεινε, βουλόμενος ἀναδέξα-
3 σθαι τοὺς ἐκ τῆς φυγῆς ἀνασῳζομένους. οἱ δὲ Ῥωμαῖοι, μέχρι μέν τινος ἐπακολουθήσαντες τοῖς φεύγουσιν, οἱ μὲν ἐσκύλευον τοὺς τεθνεῶτας, οἱ δὲ τοὺς
αἰχμαλώτους ἤθροιζον, οἱ δὲ πλείους ὥρμησαν ἐπὶ
4 τὴν διαρπαγὴν τοῦ τῶν πολεμίων χάρακος· ἔνθα δὴ
καταλαβόντες τοὺς Αἰτωλοὺς προεμπεπτωκότας καὶ
δόξαντες στέρεσθαι τῆς σφίσι καθηκούσης ὠφελείας,
ἤρξαντο καταμέμφεσθαι τοὺς Αἰτωλοὺς καὶ λέγειν
πρὸς τὸν στρατηγὸν ὅτι τοὺς μὲν κινδύνους αὐτοῖς
5 ἐπιτάττει, τῆς δ᾽ ὠφελείας ἄλλοις παρακεχώρηκε. καὶ
τότε μὲν ἐπανελθόντες εἰς τὴν ἑαυτῶν στρατοπεδείαν

the Macedonian left were just attaining the summits, at first halted. The enemy were now holding up their spears, as is the Macedonian custom when they either surrender or go over to the enemy, and on learning the significance of this he kept back his men, thinking to spare the beaten force. But while he was still making up his mind some of the Romans who had advanced further fell on them from above and began to cut them down. Most of them perished, a very few escaping after throwing away their arms.

27. The battle being now over and the Romans everywhere victorious, Philip retreated toward Tempe. He spent the following night under canvas at a place called "Alexander's Tower" and next day went on to Gonni[82] at the entrance of Tempe, and remained there wishing to pick up the survivors of the rout. The Romans, after following up the fugitives for a certain distance, began, some of them, to strip the dead and others to collect prisoners, but most of them ran to plunder the enemy's camp. Finding, however, that the Aetolians had anticipated them there and considering themselves defrauded of the booty that was rightfully theirs, they began to find fault with the Aetolians and told their general that he imposed the risk on them and gave up the booty to others. For the present they returned to their own camp and retired to rest, and

[82] B. Helly, *Gonnoi*, 2 vols. (Amsterdam 1973). This Perrhaebian city controlled the route through Tempe. It has furnished a large number of important inscriptions, collected in Helly's volume 2.

ηὐλίσθησαν, εἰς δὲ τὴν ἐπαύριον ἅμα μὲν ἤθροιζον
τοὺς αἰχμαλώτους καὶ τὰ λειπόμενα τῶν σκύλων, ἅμα
δὲ προῆγον ποιούμενοι τὴν πορείαν ὡς ἐπὶ Λαρίσης.

6 ἔπεσον δὲ τῶν Ῥωμαίων πρὸς τοὺς ἑπτακοσίους· τῶν
δὲ Μακεδόνων ἀπέθανον μὲν οἱ πάντες εἰς ὀκτακισχι-
λίους, ζωγρίᾳ δ' ἑάλωσαν οὐκ ἐλάττους πεντακισχιλίων.

7 Καὶ τῆς μὲν ἐν Θετταλίᾳ γενομένης περὶ Κυνὸς
ἀπέβη τὸ τέλος·

28. ἐγὼ δὲ κατὰ μὲν τὴν ἕκτην βύβλον ἐν ἐπαγγελίᾳ
(11) καταλιπὼν ὅτι λαβὼν τὸν ἁρμόζοντα καιρὸν σύγκρισιν ποιήσομαι τοῦ καθοπλισμοῦ Ῥωμαίων καὶ Μακεδόνων, ὁμοίως δὲ καὶ τῆς συντάξεως τῆς ἑκατέρων, τί
διαφέρουσιν ἀλλήλων πρὸς τὸ χεῖρον καὶ τί πρὸς τὸ
βέλτιον, νῦν ἐπ' αὐτῶν τῶν πράξεων πειράσομαι τὴν
2 ἐπαγγελίαν ἐπὶ τέλος ἀγαγεῖν. ἐπεὶ γὰρ ἡ μὲν Μακεδόνων σύνταξις ἐν τοῖς πρὸ τοῦ χρόνοις, δι' αὐτῶν
τῶν ἔργων διδοῦσα τὴν πεῖραν, ἐκράτει τῶν τε κατὰ
τὴν Ἀσίαν καὶ τῶν Ἑλληνικῶν συντάξεων, ἡ δὲ Ῥωμαίων τῶν τε κατὰ τὴν Λιβύην καὶ τῶν κατὰ τὴν
3 Εὐρώπην προσεσπερίων ἐθνῶν ἁπάντων, ἐν δὲ τοῖς
καθ' ἡμᾶς καιροῖς οὐχ ἅπαξ, ἀλλὰ πλεονάκις γέγονε
τούτων τῶν τάξεων καὶ τῶν ἀνδρῶν πρὸς ἀλλήλους
4 διάκρισις, χρήσιμον καὶ καλὸν ἂν εἴη τὸ τὴν διαφορὰν
ἐρευνῆσαι, καὶ παρὰ τί συμβαίνει Ῥωμαίους ἐπικρα-

spent the next day in collecting prisoners and what was left of the spoil and also in advancing in the direction of Larisa. Of the Romans about seven hundred fell and the total Macedonian loss amounted to about eight thousand killed and not fewer than five thousand captured.[83]

Such was the result of the battle at Cynoscephalae between the Romans and Philip.

Advantages and Disadvantages of the Phalanx

28. In my sixth book I promised[84] that when a suitable occasion presented itself I would institute a comparison between the Roman and Macedonian equipment and formation, showing how they differ for better or worse, and I will, now that we see them both in actual practice, endeavor to fulfill this promise. For since the Macedonian formation in former times was proved by the experience of facts to be superior to other formations in use in Asia and Greece and that of the Romans likewise showed itself superior to those in use in Africa and among all the peoples of western Europe, and since now in our own times not once but frequently,[85] these two formations and the soldiers of both nations have been matched against each other, it will prove useful and beneficial to inquire into the difference, and into the reason why on the battlefield the

[83] It is impossible to say how close these figures are to the truth.   [84] The passage is lost.

[85] The major engagements happened in 197 (Cynoscephalae), 190 (Magnesia ad Sipylum), and 168 (Pydna). Corinth in 146, counted by WC 2.585, does not qualify, as the enemy of the Romans was not a Macedonian army.

τεῖν καὶ τὸ πρωτεῖον ἐκφέρεσθαι τῶν κατὰ πόλεμον
5 ἀγώνων, ἵνα μὴ τύχην λέγοντες μόνον μακαρίζωμεν
τοὺς κρατοῦντας ἀλόγως, καθάπερ οἱ μάταιοι τῶν
ἀνθρώπων, ἀλλ᾽ εἰδότες τὰς ἀληθεῖς αἰτίας ἐπαινῶμεν
καὶ θαυμάζωμεν κατὰ λόγον τοὺς ἡγουμένους.

6   Περὶ μὲν οὖν τῶν πρὸς Ἀννίβαν ἀγώνων γεγονότων
Ῥωμαίοις καὶ τῶν ἐν τούτοις ἐλαττωμάτων οὐδὲν ἂν
δέοι πλείω λέγειν· οὐ γὰρ παρὰ τὸν καθοπλισμὸν
οὐδὲ παρὰ τὴν σύνταξιν, ἀλλὰ παρὰ τὴν ἐπιδεξιότητα
τὴν Ἀννίβου καὶ τὴν ἀγχίνοιαν περιέπιπτον τοῖς
7 ἐλαττώμασι. δῆλον δὲ τοῦτο πεποιήκαμεν ἡμεῖς ἐπ᾽
8 αὐτῶν ὑποδεικνύοντες τῶν ἀγώνων. μαρτυρεῖ δὲ τοῖς
ἡμετέροις λόγοις πρῶτον μὲν τὸ τέλος τοῦ πολέμου·
προσγενομένου γὰρ στρατηγοῦ τοῖς Ῥωμαίοις παραπλησίαν δύναμιν ἔχοντος Ἀννίβᾳ, ταχέως καὶ τὸ
9 νικᾶν συνεξηκολούθησε τοῖς προειρημένοις· εἶτα καὶ
αὐτὸς Ἀννίβας ἀποδοκιμάσας τὸν ἐξ ἀρχῆς αὐτοῖς
ὑπάρχοντα καθοπλισμόν, ἅμα τῷ νικῆσαι τῇ πρώτῃ
μάχῃ παραχρῆμα τοῖς Ῥωμαίων ὅπλοις καθοπλίσας
τὰς οἰκείας δυνάμεις, τούτοις διετέλεσε χρώμενος τὸν
10 ἑξῆς χρόνον. Πύρρος γε μὴν οὐ μόνον ὅπλοις, ἀλλὰ
καὶ δυνάμεσιν Ἰταλικαῖς συγκέχρηται, τιθεὶς ἐναλλὰξ
σημαίαν καὶ σπεῖραν φαλαγγιτικὴν ἐν τοῖς πρὸς Ῥω-
11 μαίους ἀγῶσιν. ἀλλ᾽ ὅμως οὐδ᾽ οὕτως ἐδύνατο νικᾶν,
ἀλλ᾽ ἀεί πως ἀμφίδοξα τὰ τέλη τῶν κινδύνων αὐτοῖς
ἀπέβαινε.

12   Περὶ μὲν οὖν τούτων ἀναγκαῖον ἦν προειπεῖν χάριν

Romans have always had the upper hand and carried off the palm, so that we may not, like foolish men, talk simply of chance and felicitate the victors without giving any reason for it, but may, knowing the true causes of their success, give them a reasoned tribute of praise and admiration.

It will not be necessary to dilate upon the battles of the Romans with Hannibal and their defeats therein; for there they met with defeat not owing to their equipment and formation but owing to Hannibal's skill and cleverness. This I made sufficiently clear in dealing with the battles in question, and the best testimony to the justice of what I said was, first of all, the actual end of the war. For very soon when the Romans had the advantage of the services of a general of like capacity with Hannibal then victory was an immediate consequence of this. And secondly, Hannibal himself, discarding his original armament at once on winning the first battle, armed his own forces with the Roman weapons and continued to employ these up to the end. As for Pyrrhus he employed not only Italian arms but Italian forces, placing maniples of these and maniples composed of men from the phalanx in alternate order in his battles with the Romans. But still even by this means he could not gain a victory, but the result of all their battles was always more or less doubtful.[86]

It was necessary for me to preface my comparison by

[86] Only at Beneventum in 275, whereas Pyrrhus had been the winner in the two previous battles, at Heraclea and Asculum.

τοῦ μηδὲν ἀντεμφαίνειν ταῖς ἡμετέραις ἀποφάσεσιν·
ἐπάνειμι δ᾽ ἐπὶ τὴν προκειμένην σύγκρισιν.

29. Ὅτι μὲν ἐχούσης τῆς φάλαγγος τὴν αὑτῆς
(12) ἰδιότητα καὶ δύναμιν οὐδὲν ἂν ὑποσταίη κατὰ πρόσω
πον οὐδὲ μεῖναι τὴν ἔφοδον αὐτῆς, εὐχερὲς καταμαθεῖν
2 ἐκ πολλῶν. ἐπεὶ γὰρ ὁ μὲν ἀνὴρ ἵσταται σὺν τοῖς
ὅπλοις ἐν τρισὶ ποσὶ κατὰ τὰς ἐναγωνίους πυκνώσεις,
τὸ δὲ τῶν σαρισῶν μέγεθός ἐστι κατὰ μὲν τὴν ἐξ
ἀρχῆς ὑπόθεσιν ἑκκαίδεκα πηχῶν, κατὰ δὲ τὴν ἁρ
3 μογὴν τὴν πρὸς τὴν ἀλήθειαν δεκατεττάρων, τούτων
δὲ τοὺς τέτταρας ἀφαιρεῖ τὸ μεταξὺ τοῖν χεροῖν διά
4 στημα καὶ τὸ κατόπιν σήκωμα τῆς προβολῆς, φανερὸν
ὅτι τοὺς δέκα πήχεις προπίπτειν ἀνάγκη τὴν σάρισαν
πρὸ τῶν σωμάτων ἑκάστου τῶν ὁπλιτῶν, ὅταν ἴῃ δι᾽
ἀμφοῖν τοῖν χεροῖν προβαλόμενος ἐπὶ τοὺς πολεμί
5 ους. ἐκ δὲ τούτου συμβαίνει τὰς μὲν τοῦ δευτέρου καὶ
τρίτου καὶ τετάρτου πλεῖον, τὰς δὲ τοῦ πέμπτου ζυγοῦ
σαρίσας δύο προπίπτειν πήχεις πρὸ τῶν πρωτοστα
τῶν, ἐχούσης τῆς φάλαγγος τὴν αὑτῆς ἰδιότητα καὶ
6 πύκνωσιν κατ᾽ ἐπιστάτην καὶ κατὰ παραστάτην, ὡς
Ὅμηρος ὑποδείκνυσιν ἐν τούτοις·

ἀσπὶς ἄρ᾽ ἀσπίδ᾽ ἔρειδε, κόρυς κόρυν, ἀνέρα δ᾽
ἀνήρ·
ψαῦον δ᾽ ἱππόκομοι κόρυθες λαμπροῖσι φάλοισι
νευόντων· ὣς πυκνοὶ ἐφέστασαν ἀλλήλοισι.

these few words in order that my statements may meet with no contradiction. I will now proceed to the comparison itself.

29. That when the phalanx has its characteristic virtue and strength nothing can sustain its frontal attack or withstand the charge can be easily understood for many reasons. For since, when it has closed up for action, each man, with his arms, occupies a space of three feet in breadth, and the length of the pikes[87] is according to the original design sixteen cubits, but as adapted to actual needs fourteen cubits, from which we must subtract the distance between the bearer's two hands and the length of the weighted portion of the pike behind which serves to keep it couched—four cubits in all—it is evident that it must extend ten cubits beyond the body of each hoplite when he charges the enemy grasping it with both hands. The consequence is that while the pikes of the second, third, and fourth ranks extend farther than those of the fifth rank, those of that rank extend two cubits beyond the bodies of the men in the first rank, when the phalanx has its characteristic close order as regards both depth and breadth, as Homer expresses it in these verses:

> Spear crowded spear,
> Shield, helmet, man press'd helmet, man, and shield;
> The hairy crests of their resplendent casques
> Kiss'd close at every nod, so wedged they stood.[88]

---

[87] See M. Markle, "The Macedonian Sarissa, Spear, and Related Armor," *AJA* 81 (1977), 323–339.

[88] *Il.* 13.131–133. These lines have no relevance to the hoplite phalanx, still unknown to Homer.

7 τούτων δ' ἀληθινῶς καὶ καλῶς λεγομένων, δῆλον ὡς
ἀνάγκη καθ' ἕκαστον τῶν πρωτοστατῶν σαρίσας
προπίπτειν πέντε, δυσὶ πήχεσι διαφερούσας ἀλλήλων
κατὰ μῆκος.

30. Ἐκ δὲ τούτου ῥᾴδιον ὑπὸ τὴν ὄψιν λαβεῖν τὴν
(13) τῆς ὅλης φάλαγγος ἔφοδον καὶ προβολήν, ποίαν τιν'
εἰκὸς εἶναι καὶ τίνα δύναμιν ἔχειν, ἐφ' ἑκκαίδεκα τὸ
2 βάθος οὖσαν. ὧν ὅσοι <τὸ>πέμπτον ζυγὸν ὑπεραίρουσι,
ταῖς μὲν σαρίσαις οὐδὲν οἷοί τ' εἰσὶ συμβαλέσθαι
πρὸς τὸν κίνδυνον· διόπερ οὐδὲ ποιοῦνται κατ' ἄνδρα
3 τὴν προβολήν, παρὰ δὲ τοὺς ὤμους τῶν προηγουμένων ἀνανενευκυίας φέρουσι χάριν τοῦ τὸν κατὰ κορυ-
φὴν τόπον ἀσφαλίζειν τῆς ἐκτάξεως, εἰργουσῶν τῇ
πυκνώσει τῶν σαρισῶν ὅσα τῶν βελῶν ὑπερπετῆ τῶν
πρωτοστατῶν φερόμενα δύναται προσπίπτειν πρὸς
4 τοὺς ἐφεστῶτας. αὐτῷ γε μὴν τῷ τοῦ σώματος βάρει
κατὰ τὴν ἐπαγωγὴν πιεζοῦντες οὗτοι τοὺς προηγου-
μένους βιαίαν μὲν ποιοῦσι τὴν ἔφοδον, ἀδύνατον δὲ
τοῖς πρωτοστάταις τὴν εἰς τοὔπισθεν μεταβολήν.

5 Τοιαύτης περὶ τὴν φάλαγγα διαθέσεως καὶ καθόλου καὶ κατὰ μέρος <οὔσης>, ῥητέον ἂν εἴη καὶ τοῦ
Ῥωμαίων καθοπλισμοῦ καὶ τῆς ὅλης συντάξεως τὰς
6 ἰδιότητας καὶ διαφορὰς ἐκ παραθέσεως. ἵστανται μὲν
7 οὖν ἐν τρισὶ ποσὶ μετὰ τῶν ὅπλων καὶ Ῥωμαῖοι· τῆς
μάχης δ' αὐτοῖς κατ' ἄνδρα τὴν κίνησιν λαμβανούσης διὰ τὸ τῷ μὲν θυρεῷ σκέπειν τὸ σῶμα, συμμετα-
τιθεμένους αἰεὶ πρὸς τὸν τῆς πληγῆς καιρόν, τῇ
μαχαίρᾳ δ' ἐκ καταφορᾶς καὶ διαιρέσεως ποιεῖσθαι

My description is true and exact, and it is evident that each man of the first rank must have the points of five pikes extending beyond him, each at a distance of two cubits from the next.

30. From this we can easily conceive what is the nature and force of a charge by the whole phalanx when it is sixteen deep.[89] In this case those further back than the fifth rank cannot use their pikes so as to take any active part in the battle. They therefore do not level their pikes man against man, but hold them slanting up in the air over the shoulders of those in front of them, so as to protect the whole formation from above, keeping off by this serried mass of pikes all missiles which, passing over the heads of the first ranks, might fall on those immediately in front of and behind them. But these men by the sheer pressure of their bodily weight in the charge add to its force, and it is quite impossible for the first ranks to face about.

Such being in general and in detail the disposition of the phalanx, I have now, for purposes of comparison, to speak of the peculiarities of the Roman equipment and system of formation and the points of difference in both. Now in the case of the Romans also each soldier with his arms occupies a space of three feet in breadth, but as in their mode of fighting each man must move separately, as he has to cover his person with his long shield, turning to meet each expected blow, and as he uses his sword both for cutting and thrusting it is obvious that a looser order

[89] Sixteen ranks was the normal depth of the Macedonian phalanx.

8 τὴν μάχην προφανὲς ὅτι χάλασμα καὶ διάστασιν
ἀλλήλων ἔχειν δεήσει τοὺς ἄνδρας ἐλάχιστον τρεῖς
πόδας κατ᾽ ἐπιστάτην καὶ κατὰ παραστάτην, εἰ μέλ-
9 λουσιν εὐχρηστεῖν πρὸς τὸ δέον. ἐκ δὲ τούτου συμβήσεται τὸν ἕνα Ῥωμαῖον ἵστασθαι κατὰ δύο πρωτο-
στάτας τῶν φαλαγγιτῶν, ὥστε πρὸς δέκα σαρίσας
10 αὐτῷ γίνεσθαι τὴν ἀπάντησιν καὶ τὴν μάχην, ἃς οὔτε
κόπτοντα τὸν ἕνα καταταχῆσαι δυνατόν, ὅταν ἅπαξ
συνάψωσιν εἰς τὰς χεῖρας, οὔτε βιάσασθαι ῥᾴδιον,
μηδέν γε τῶν ἐφεστώτων δυναμένων συμβάλλεσθαι
τοῖς πρωτοστάταις μήτε πρὸς τὴν βίαν μήτε πρὸς τὴν
11 τῶν μαχαιρῶν ἐνέργειαν. ἐξ ὧν εὐκατανόητον ὡς οὐχ
οἷόν τε μεῖναι κατὰ πρόσωπον τὴν τῆς φάλαγγος
ἔφοδον οὐδέν, διατηρούσης τὴν αὑτῆς ἰδιότητα καὶ
δύναμιν, ὡς ἐν ἀρχαῖς εἶπα.

31. Τίς οὖν αἰτία τοῦ νικᾶν Ῥωμαίους καὶ τί τὸ
(14) σφάλλον ἐστὶ τοὺς ταῖς φάλαγξι χρωμένους; ὅτι
2 συμβαίνει τὸν μὲν πόλεμον ἀορίστους ἔχειν καὶ τοὺς
καιροὺς καὶ τοὺς τόπους τοὺς πρὸς τὴν χρείαν, τῆς δὲ
φάλαγγος ἕνα καιρὸν εἶναι καὶ τόπων ἓν γένος, ἐν οἷς
3 δύναται τὴν αὑτῆς χρείαν ἐπιτελεῖν. εἰ μὲν οὖν τις ἦν
ἀνάγκη τοῖς ἀντιπάλοις εἰς τοὺς τῆς φάλαγγος καιροὺς καὶ τόπους συγκαταβαίνειν, ὅτε μέλλοιεν κρίνε-
σθαι περὶ τῶν ὅλων, εἰκὸς ἦν κατὰ τὸν ἄρτι λόγον ἀεὶ
φέρεσθαι τὸ πρωτεῖον τοὺς ταῖς φάλαγξι χρωμένους·
4 εἰ δὲ δυνατὸν ἐκκλίνειν καὶ τοῦτο ποιεῖν ῥᾳδίως, πῶς
5 ἂν ἔτι φοβερὸν εἴη τὸ προειρημένον σύνταγμα; καὶ
μὴν ὅτι χρείαν ἔχει τόπων ἐπιπέδων καὶ ψιλῶν ἡ φά-

is required, and each man must be at a distance of at least three feet from the man next him in the same rank and those in front of and behind him, if they are to be of proper use. The consequence will be that one Roman must stand opposite two men in the first rank of the phalanx, so that he has to face and encounter ten pikes, and it is both impossible for a single man to cut through them all in time once they are at close quarters and by no means easy to force their points away, as the rear ranks can be of no help to the front rank either in thus forcing the pikes away or in the use of the sword. So it is easy to see that, as I said at the beginning, nothing can withstand the charge of the phalanx as long as it preserves its characteristic formation and force.

31. What then is the reason of the Roman success, and what is it that defeats[90] the purpose of those who use the phalanx? It is because in war the time and place of action is uncertain and the phalanx has only one time and one place in which it can perform its peculiar service. Now, if the enemy were obliged to adapt themselves to the times and places required by the phalanx when a decisive battle was impending, those who use the phalanx would in all probability, for the reasons I stated above, always get the better of their enemies; but if it is not only possible but easy to avoid its onset why should one any longer dread an attack of a body so constituted? Again, it is acknowledged that the phalanx requires level and clear ground with no

[90] The Achilles heel of the Macedonian phalanx was its inflexibility and inefficiency once its compact order was dissolved.

175

λαγξ, πρὸς δὲ τούτοις μηδὲν ἐμπόδιον ἐχόντων, λέγω
δ᾽ οἷον τάφρους, ἐκρήγματα, συναγκείας, ὀφρῦς, ῥεῖθρα
6 ποταμῶν, ὁμολογούμενόν ἐστι. πάντα γὰρ τὰ προειρημένα παραποδίζειν καὶ λύειν τὴν τοιαύτην τάξιν
7 ἱκανὰ γίνεται. διότι δ᾽ εὑρεῖν τόπους ποτὲ μὲν ἐπὶ σταδίους εἴκοσι, ποτὲ δὲ καὶ πλείους, ἐν οἷς μηδέν τι
τοιοῦτον ὑπάρχει, σχεδόν, ὡς εἰπεῖν, ἀδύνατόν ἐστιν,
εἰ δὲ μή γε, τελέως σπάνιον, καὶ τοῦτο πᾶς ἄν τις
8 ὁμολογήσειεν. οὐ μὴν ἀλλ᾽ ἔστω τόπους εὑρῆσθαι
τοιούτους. ἐὰν οὖν οἱ [μὲν] πολεμοῦντες εἰς μὲν τούτους μὴ συγκαταβαίνωσι, περιπορευόμενοι δὲ πορθῶσι
τὰς πόλεις καὶ τὴν χώραν τὴν τῶν συμμάχων, τί τῆς
9 τοιαύτης ὄφελος ἔσται συντάξεως; μένουσα μὲν γὰρ
ἐν τοῖς ἐπιτηδείοις αὐτῇ τόποις οὐχ οἷον ὠφελεῖν δύ-
10 ναιτ᾽ ἂν τοὺς φίλους, ἀλλ᾽ οὐδ᾽ ἑαυτὴν σῴζειν. αἱ γὰρ
τῶν ἐπιτηδείων παρακομιδαὶ κωλυθήσονται ῥᾳδίως
ὑπὸ τῶν πολεμίων, ὅταν ἀκονιτὶ κρατῶσι τῶν ὑπ-
11 αίθρων· ἐὰν δ᾽ ἀπολιποῦσα τοὺς οἰκείους τόπους βού-
ληταί τι πράττειν, εὐχείρωτος ἔσται τοῖς πολεμίοις.
12 οὐ μὴν ἀλλὰ κἂν εἰς τοὺς ἐπιπέδους συγκαταβάς τις
τόπους μὴ πᾶν ἅμα τὸ σφέτερον στρατόπεδον ὑπὸ
τὴν ἐπαγωγὴν τῆς φάλαγγος καὶ τὸν ἕνα καιρὸν ὑπο-
βάλῃ, βραχέα δὲ φυγομαχήσῃ κατ᾽ αὐτὸν τὸν τοῦ
κινδύνου καιρόν εὐθεώρητον γίνεται τὸ συμβησόμενον ἐξ ὧν ποιοῦσι Ῥωμαῖοι νῦν.

32. οὐκέτι γὰρ ἐκ τοῦ λόγου δεῖ τεκμαίρεσθαι τὸ
(15) νυνὶ λεγόμενον ὑφ᾽ ἡμῶν, ἀλλ᾽ ἐκ τῶν ἤδη γεγονότων.
2 οὐ γὰρ ἐξισώσαντες τὴν παράταξιν πᾶσιν ἅμα συμ-

obstacles such as ditches, clefts, depressions, ridges and water courses, all of which are sufficient to impede and break up such a formation. Every one would also acknowledge that it is almost impossible except in very rare cases to find spaces of say twenty stades or even more in length with no such obstacles. But even if we assume it to be possible, supposing those who are fighting against us refuse to meet us on such ground, but go round sacking the cities and devastating the territory of our allies, what is the use of such a formation? For by remaining on the ground that suits it, not only is it incapable of helping its friends but cannot even ensure its own safety. For the arrival of supplies will easily be prevented by the enemy, when they have undisturbed command of the open country. But if the phalanx leaves the ground proper to it and attempts any action, it will be easily overcome by the enemy. And again, if it is decided to engage the enemy on level ground, but instead of availing ourselves of our total force when the phalanx has its one opportunity for charging, we keep out of action even a small portion of it at the moment of the shock, it is easy to tell what will happen from what the Romans always do at present,

32. the likelihood of the result I now indicate requiring no argument but only the evidence of actual facts. For the Romans do not make their line equal in force to the enemy

βάλλουσι τοῖς στρατοπέδοις μετωπηδὸν πρὸς τὰς
φάλαγγας, ἀλλὰ τὰ μὲν ἐφεδρεύει τῶν μερῶν αὐτοῖς,
3 τὰ δὲ συμμίσγει τοῖς πολεμίοις. λοιπόν, ἄν τ᾽ ἐκ-
πιέσωσιν οἱ φαλαγγῖται τοὺς καθ᾽ αὑτοὺς προσβάλ-
4 λοντες ἄν τ᾽ ἐκπιεσθῶσιν ὑπὸ τούτων, λέλυται τὸ τῆς
φάλαγγος ἴδιον· ἢ γὰρ ἑπόμενοι τοῖς ὑποχωροῦσιν ἢ
φεύγοντες τοὺς προσκειμένους ἀπολείπουσι τὰ λοιπὰ
5 μέρη τῆς οἰκείας δυνάμεως, οὗ γενομένου δέδοται τοῖς
ἐφεδρεύουσι τῶν πολεμίων διάστημα καὶ τόπος, ὃν
οὗτοι κατεῖχον, πρὸς τὸ μηκέτι κατὰ πρόσωπον ὁρμᾶν,
ἀλλὰ παρεισπεσόντας πλαγίους παρίστασθαι καὶ
6 κατὰ νώτου τοῖς φαλαγγίταις. ὅταν δὲ τοὺς μὲν τῆς
φάλαγγος καιροὺς καὶ τὰ προτερήματα ῥάδιον ᾖ φυ-
λάξασθαι, τοὺς δὲ κατὰ τῆς φάλαγγος ἀδύνατον, πῶς
οὐ μεγάλην εἰκὸς εἶναι τὴν διαφορὰν ἐπὶ τῆς ἀληθείας
7 τῶν προειρημένων; καὶ μὴν πορευθῆναι διὰ τόπων
παντοδαπῶν ἀναγκαῖον τοὺς χρωμένους φάλαγγι καὶ
καταστρατοπεδεῦσαι, ἔτι δὲ τόπους εὐκαίρους προ-
καταλαβέσθαι καὶ πολιορκῆσαί τινας καὶ πολιορκηθῆ-
8 ναι καὶ παραδόξοις ἐπιφανείαις περιπεσεῖν· ἅπαντα
γὰρ ταῦτ᾽ ἐστὶ πολέμου μέρη καὶ ῥοπὰς ποιεῖ πρὸς
9 τὸ νικᾶν, ποτὲ μὲν ὁλοσχερεῖς, ποτὲ δὲ μεγάλας. ἐν οἷς
πᾶσιν ἡ μὲν Μακεδόνων ἐστὶ σύνταξις δύσχρηστος,
ποτὲ δ᾽ ἄχρηστος, διὰ τὸ μὴ δύνασθαι τὸν φαλαγγί-
την μήτε κατὰ τάγμα μήτε κατ᾽ ἄνδρα παρέχεσθαι
10 χρείαν, ἡ δὲ Ῥωμαίων εὔχρηστος· πᾶς γὰρ Ῥωμαῖος,
ὅταν ἅπαξ καθοπλισθεὶς ὁρμήσῃ πρὸς τὴν χρείαν,
ὁμοίως ἥρμοσται πρὸς πάντα τόπον καὶ καιρὸν καὶ

and expose all the legions to a frontal attack by the phalanx, but part of their forces remain in reserve and the rest
engage the enemy. Afterward whether the phalanx drives
back by its charge the force opposed to it or is repulsed by
this force, its own peculiar formation is broken up. For
either in following up a retreating foe or in flying before
an attacking foe, they leave behind the other parts of their
own army, upon which the enemy's reserve have room
enough in the space formerly held by the phalanx to attack
no longer in front but appearing by a lateral movement on
the flank and rear of the phalanx. When it is thus easy to
guard against the opportunities and advantages of the phalanx, but impossible to prevent the enemy from taking
advantage of the proper moment to act against it, the one
kind of formation naturally proves in reality superior to
the other. Again, those who employ the phalanx have to
march through and encamp in every variety of country;
they are compelled to occupy favorable positions in advance, to besiege certain positions and to be besieged in
others, and to meet attacks from quarters the least expected. For all such contingencies are parts of war, and
victory sometimes wholly and sometimes very largely de-
pends on them. Now in all these matters the Macedonian
formation is at times of little use and at times of no use at
all, because the phalanx soldier can be of service neither
in detachments nor singly, while the Roman formation is
efficient. For every Roman soldier, once he is armed and
sets about his business, can adapt himself equally well to
every place and time and can meet attack from every quar-

11 πρὸς πᾶσαν ἐπιφάνειαν. καὶ μὴν ἕτοιμός ἐστι καὶ τὴν
αὐτὴν ἔχει διάθεσιν, ἄν τε μετὰ πάντων δέῃ κινδυνεύειν ἄν τε μετὰ μέρους ἄν τε κατὰ σημαίαν ἄν τε καὶ
12 κατ' ἄνδρα. διὸ καὶ παρὰ πολὺ τῆς κατὰ μέρος εὐ-
χρηστίας διαφερούσης, παρὰ πολὺ καὶ τὰ τέλη συν-
εξακολουθεῖ ταῖς Ῥωμαίων προθέσεσι μᾶλλον ἢ ταῖς
13 τῶν ἄλλων. περὶ μὲν ⟨οὖν⟩ τούτων ἀναγκαῖον ἡγη-
σάμην εἶναι τὸ διὰ πλειόνων ποιήσασθαι μνήμην διὰ
τὸ καὶ παρ' αὐτὸν τὸν καιρὸν πολλοὺς τῶν Ἑλλήνων
διαλαμβάνειν, ὅτε Μακεδόνες ἡττήθησαν, ἀπίστῳ τὸ
γεγονὸς ἐοικέναι, καὶ μετὰ ταῦτα πολλοὺς διαπορή-
σειν διὰ τί καὶ πῶς λείπεται τὸ σύνταγμα τῆς φάλαγγος ὑπὸ τοῦ Ῥωμαίων καθοπλισμοῦ.

33. Φίλιππος δέ, τὰ δυνατὰ πεποιηκὼς πρὸς τὸν
(16) ἀγῶνα, τοῖς δ' ὅλοις πράγμασιν ἐσφαλμένος, ἀναδεξάμενος ὅσους ἐδύνατο πλείστους τῶν ἐκ τῆς μάχης ἀνασῳζομένων, αὐτὸς μὲν ὥρμησε διὰ τῶν Τεμ-
2 πῶν εἰς Μακεδονίαν. εἰς δὲ τὴν Λάρισαν ἔτι τῇ
προτεραίᾳ νυκτὶ διεπέμψατό τινα τῶν ὑπασπιστῶν,
ἐντειλάμενος ἀφανίσαι καὶ κατακαῦσαι τὰ βασιλικὰ
γράμματα, ποιῶν πρᾶγμα βασιλικὸν τὸ μηδ' ἐν τοῖς
3 δεινοῖς λήθην ποιεῖσθαι τοῦ καθήκοντος· σαφῶς γὰρ
ᾔδει διότι πολλὰς ἀφορμὰς δώσει τοῖς ἐχθροῖς καὶ
καθ' ἑαυτοῦ καὶ κατὰ τῶν φίλων, ἐὰν κρατήσωσι
4 Ῥωμαῖοι τῶν ὑπομνημάτων. ἴσως μὲν οὖν καὶ ἑτέροις
ἤδη τοῦτο συμβέβηκε, τὸ τὰς μὲν ἐν ταῖς ἐπιτυχίαις
ἐξουσίας μὴ δύνασθαι φέρειν ἀνθρωπίνως, ἐν δὲ
ταῖς περιπετείαις εὐλαβῶς ἵστασθαι καὶ νουνεχῶς·

ter. He is likewise equally prepared and equally in condition whether he has to fight together with the whole army or with a part of it or in maniples or singly. So since in all particulars the Romans are much more serviceable, Roman plans are much more apt to result in success than those of others. I thought it necessary to speak on this subject at some length because many Greeks on the actual occasions when the Macedonians suffered defeat considered the event as almost incredible, and many will still continue to wonder why and how the phalanx comes to be conquered by troops armed in the Roman fashion.

33. Philip had done his best in the battle, but on being thus thoroughly defeated, after first picking up as many as he could of the survivors from the battle himself hastily retired through Tempe to Macedonia. He had sent one of his aides-de-camp on the previous night to Larisa, with orders to destroy and burn the royal correspondence,[91] acting like a true king in not forgetting his duty even in the hour of disaster: for he well knew that if the documents[92] fell into the hands of the Romans he would be giving them much material to use against himself and his friends. Perhaps in the case of others also it has happened that in seasons of prosperity they have not been able to wear their authority with the moderation that befits a man, yet in the hour of danger have exercised due caution and kept

[91] Full of compromising material.
[92] The royal diaries, usually called *ephemerides*. *RE* Ephemerides 1749–1753 (J. Kaerst). Berve, *Alexanderreich*, 1.42–55.

5 ἐν τοῖς δὲ μάλιστα καὶ περὶ Φίλιππον τοῦτο γέγονε.
δῆλον δ᾽ ἔσται τοῦτο διὰ τῶν μετὰ ταῦτα ῥηθησομένων·
6 καθάπερ γὰρ καὶ τὰς ἐξ ἀρχῆς ὁρμὰς ἐπὶ τὸ δέον
αὐτοῦ σαφῶς ἐδηλώσαμεν, καὶ πάλιν τὴν ἐπὶ τὸ χεῖρον μεταβολήν, καὶ πότε καὶ διὰ τί καὶ πῶς ἐγένετο,
καὶ τὰς ἐν ταύτῃ πράξεις μετ᾽ ἀποδείξεως ἐξηγησάμεθα,
7 τὸν αὐτὸν τρόπον χρὴ καὶ τὴν μετάνοιαν αὐτοῦ
δηλῶσαι καὶ τὴν εὐστοχίαν, καθ᾽ ἣν μεταθέμενος τοῖς
ἐκ τῆς τύχης ἐλαττώμασιν εὐλογιστότατα δοκεῖ κεχρῆσθαι τοῖς καθ᾽ αὑτὸν καιροῖς.

8   Τίτος δὲ μετὰ τὴν μάχην ποιησάμενος τὴν καθήκουσαν πρόνοιαν περί τε τῶν αἰχμαλώτων καὶ τῶν
ἄλλων λαφύρων, ᾔει πρὸς Λάρισαν.

34. . . . καθόλου τῇ περὶ τὰ λάφυρα πλεονεξίᾳ τῶν
(17) Αἰτωλῶν . . . εἶτ᾽ οὐκ ἐβούλετο Φίλιππον ἐκβαλὼν ἐκ
τῆς ἀρχῆς Αἰτωλοὺς καταλιπεῖν δεσπότας τῶν Ἑλ-
2 λήνων. δυσχερῶς δ᾽ ἔφερε καὶ τὴν ἀλαζονείαν αὐτῶν,
θεωρῶν ἀντεπιγραφομένους ἐπὶ τὸ νίκημα καὶ πλη-
3 ροῦντας τὴν Ἑλλάδα τῆς αὐτῶν ἀνδραγαθίας. διὸ καὶ
κατά τε τὰς ἐντεύξεις ἀγερωχότερον αὐτοῖς ἀπήντα
καὶ περὶ τῶν κοινῶν ἀπεσιώπα, τὰ δὲ προκείμενα συν-
4 ετέλει καὶ δι᾽ αὑτοῦ καὶ διὰ τῶν ἰδίων φίλων. τοιαύτης
δ᾽ οὔσης δυσχρηστίας ἐν ἀμφοτέροις, ἧκον πρεσβευταὶ
μετά τινας ἡμέρας παρὰ τοῦ Φιλίππου Δημοσθένης

___

93 A famous epigram on the battle (*AP* 7.247), written by Alcaeus of Messene and hostile to Philip, named the Aetolians

their heads, but this was particularly so with Philip, as will be evident from what I am about to say. For just as I have clearly pointed out his early impulse to do what was right, and again the time, reasons, and circumstances of the change for the worse in him, narrating with documentary proofs his actions after this change, so must I in the same manner point out his new change of mind and the ability with which, adapting himself to the reverses of fortune, he faced the situation in which he found himself with exceptional prudence.

After the battle Flamininus took the requisite steps regarding the prisoners and other booty and then advanced toward Larisa. . . .

34. He was generally displeased with the overreaching conduct of the Aetolians about the booty, and did not wish to expel Philip from his kingdom and so leave them masters of Greece. Also he could ill brook their bragging,[93] when he saw them claiming equal credit with the Romans for the victory and filling the whole of Greece with the story of their prowess. In consequence he was somewhat brusque in his replies when he had interviews with them and kept silent about public affairs, carrying out his projects himself or with the aid of his friends. While these stiff relations on both sides still continued there came a few days after the battle a legation from Philip composed of

ahead of the Romans which also annoyed Flamininus, whom the poet thereupon extolled as the liberator of Greece, comparing him favorably to Xerxes who had come to enslave the Greeks (*AP* 16.5). See A. S. F. Gow and D. L. Page, *The Greek Anthology. Hellenistic Epigrams* (Cambridge 1965), 1.4, nos. 4–5 and 2.11–12.

5 καὶ Κυκλιάδας καὶ Λιμναῖος. πρὸς οὓς κοινολογηθεὶς
ὁ Τίτος ἐπὶ πλεῖον μετὰ τῶν χιλιάρχων πεντεκαιδεχη-
μέρους ἀνοχὰς ἐποιήσατο παραχρῆμα, συνετάξατο δὲ
καὶ συμπορεύεσθαι τῷ Φιλίππῳ κοινολογησόμενος
6 ὑπὲρ τῶν καθεστώτων ἐν ταύταις. γενομένης δὲ ταύτης τῆς ἐντεύξεως φιλανθρώπου, διπλασίως ἐξεκάετο
7 τὰ τῆς ὑποψίας κατὰ τοῦ Τίτου· ἤδη γὰρ κατὰ τὴν
Ἑλλάδα τῆς δωροδοκίας ἐπιπολαζούσης καὶ τοῦ μηδένα μηδὲν δωρεὰν πράττειν, καὶ τοῦ χαρακτῆρος τούτου νομιστευομένου παρὰ τοῖς Αἰτωλοῖς, οὐκ ἐδύναντο
πιστεύειν διότι χωρὶς δώρων ἡ τηλικαύτη μεταβολὴ
8 γέγονε τοῦ Τίτου πρὸς τὸν Φίλιππον, οὐκ εἰδότες τὰ
Ῥωμαίων ἔθη καὶ νόμιμα περὶ τοῦτο τὸ μέρος, ἀλλ'
ἐξ αὐτῶν τεκμαιρόμενοι καὶ συλλογιζόμενοι διότι τὸν
μὲν Φίλιππον εἰκὸς ἦν προτείνειν πλῆθος χρημάτων
διὰ τὸν καιρόν, τὸν δὲ Τίτον μὴ δύνασθαι τούτοις
ἀντοφθαλμεῖν.

35. Ἐγὼ δὲ κατὰ μὲν τοὺς ἀνωτέρω χρόνους καὶ
(18) κοινὴν ἂν ποιούμενος ἀπόφασιν ἐθάρρησα περὶ πάντων Ῥωμαίων εἰπεῖν ὡς οὐδὲν ἂν πράξειεν τοιοῦτον,
λέγω δὲ πρότερον ἢ τοῖς διαποντίοις αὐτοὺς ἐγχει-
ρῆσαι πολέμοις, ἕως ἐπὶ τῶν ἰδίων ἐθῶν καὶ νομίμων
2 ἔμενον. ἐν δὲ τοῖς νῦν καιροῖς περὶ πάντων μὲν οὐκ ἂν
τολμήσαιμι τοῦτ' εἰπεῖν· κατ' ἰδίαν μέντοι γε περὶ
πλειόνων ἀνδρῶν ἐν Ῥώμῃ θαρρήσαιμ' ἂν ἀποφήνασθαι διότι δύνανται τὴν πίστιν ἐν τούτῳ τῷ μέρει
3 διαφυλάττειν. μαρτυρίας δὲ χάριν ὁμολογούμενα δύ'
4 ὀνόματα . . . τοῦ μὴ δοκεῖν ἀδύνατα λέγειν. Λεύκιος

Demosthenes, Cycliades,[94] and Limnaeus. Flamininus, after conferring with them at some length in the presence
of his military tribunes, granted Philip an armistice of fifteen days at once, and arranged to have a meeting with
Philip to confer about the situation during the armistice.
As the interview had been conducted with perfect courtesy, the suspicions of Flamininus entertained by the Aetolians became twice as vehement. For since by this time
bribery and the notion that no one should do anything
gratis were very prevalent in Greece, and so to speak
quite current coin among the Aetolians, they could not
believe that Flamininus' complete change of attitude toward Philip could have been brought about without a
bribe, since they were ignorant of the Roman principles
and practice in this matter, but judged from their own, and
calculated that it was probable that Philip would offer a
very large sum owing to his actual situation and Flamininus would not be able to resist the temptation.

35. If I were dealing with earlier times, I would have
confidently asserted about all the Romans in general, that
no one of them would do such a thing; I speak of the years
before they undertook wars across the sea and during
which they preserved their own principles and practices.
At the present time, however, I would not venture to assert
this of all, but I could with perfect confidence say of many
particular men in Rome that in this matter they can maintain their faith. That I may not appear to be stating what
is impossible, I will cite as evidence the names of two men
regarding whom none will dispute my assertion. The first

[94] See 1.2.

THE HISTORIES OF POLYBIUS

μὲν γὰρ Αἰμίλιος ὁ Περσέα νικήσας, κύριος γενόμενος τῆς Μακεδόνων βασιλείας, ἐν ᾗ τῆς ἄλλης χωρὶς
κατασκευῆς καὶ χορηγίας ἐν αὐτοῖς εὑρέθη τοῖς θη-
σαυροῖς ἀργυρίου καὶ χρυσίου πλείω τῶν ἑξακισχιλίων
5 ταλάντων, οὐχ οἷον ἐπεθύμησε τούτων τινός, ἀλλ᾽ οὐδ᾽
αὐτόπτης ἠβουλήθη γενέσθαι, δι᾽ ἑτέρων δὲ τὸν χειρισμὸν ἐποιήσατο τῶν προειρημένων, καίτοι κατὰ τὸν
ἴδιον βίον οὐ περιττεύων τῇ χορηγίᾳ, τὸ δ᾽ ἐναντίον
6 ἐλλείπων μᾶλλον. μεταλλάξαντος γοῦν αὐτοῦ τὸν
βίον οὐ πολὺ κατόπιν τοῦ πολέμου, βουληθέντες οἱ
κατὰ φύσιν υἱοὶ Πόπλιος Σκιπίων καὶ Κόιντος Μάξι-
μος ἀποδοῦναι τῇ γυναικὶ τὴν φερνήν, εἴκοσι τάλαντα
καὶ πέντε, ἐπὶ τοσοῦτον ἐδυσχρηστήθησαν ὡς οὐδ᾽ εἰς
τέλος ἐδυνήθησαν, εἰ μὴ τὴν ἐνδουχίαν ἀπέδοντο καὶ
7 τὰ σώματα καὶ σὺν τούτοις ἔτι τινὰς τῶν κτήσεων. εἰ
δέ τισιν ἀπίστῳ τὸ λεγόμενον ἐοικέναι δόξει, ῥᾴδιον
8 ὑπὲρ τούτου λαβεῖν πίστιν· πολλῶν γὰρ ἀμφισβητουμένων παρὰ Ῥωμαίοις καὶ μάλιστα περὶ τοῦτο τὸ
μέρος διὰ τὰς πρὸς ἀλλήλους ἀντιπαραγωγάς, ὅμως
τὸ νῦν εἰρημένον ὑφ᾽ ἡμῶν ὁμολογούμενον εὑρήσει
9 παρὰ πᾶσιν ὁ ζητῶν. καὶ μὴν Πόπλιος Σκιπίων ὁ τούτου μὲν κατὰ φύσιν υἱός, Ποπλίου δὲ τοῦ μεγάλου
κληθέντος κατὰ θέσιν υἱωνός, κύριος γενόμενος τῆς

95 *OCD* Aemilius 21–22 (J. Briscoe).
96 In 160.
97 P. puts the younger son, with whom he developed a close
friendship, first.
98 If a marriage ended by the death of the man, the widow

is Lucius Aemilius Paullus,[95] the conqueror of Perseus.
For when he became master of the kingdom of the Macedonians, in which, apart from the splendid booty and other
riches, more than six thousand talents of gold and silver
were found in the treasury alone, not only did he not covet
any of his treasure, but did not even wish to look upon it,
and disposed of it all by the hands of others, and this although his private fortune was by no means ample, but on
the contrary rather meager. At least when he died[96] not
long after the war, and his sons by birth, Publius Scipio
and Quintus Fabius Maximus,[97] wished to give back to his
wife her dowry[98] of twenty-five talents they found such
difficulty in raising the sum that they could not possibly
have done it had they not sold the household goods, the
slaves, and some real property in addition. If what I say
seems incredible to anyone he can easily assure himself of
its truth. For though many facts and especially those concerning this matter are subjects of dispute at Rome owing
to their political dissensions, still on inquiry you will find
that the statement I have just made is acknowledged to be
true by all. Again, take the case of Publius Scipio, Aemilius' son by birth, but grandson by adoption of Publius
Scipio, known as the Great.[99] When he became master of

could request from his heirs that her *dos* be returned: M. Kaser,
Das römische Privatrecht, 2nd ed. (Munich 1971), 1.339, with
reference to this case.

[99] The elder Scipio Africanus. No Roman writer calls him so.
The exact meaning of the epithet is difficult to establish, as it is
for King Demetrius Poliorcetes (306–283), whom a decree of
Athenian volunteer soldiers calls "the Great," ὁ Μέγας (*ISE* 7.2),
or for Marc Antony in *OGI* 195 (private dedication).

Καρχηδόνος, ἥτις ἐδόκει πολυχρημονεστάτη τῶν
κατὰ τὴν οἰκουμένην εἶναι πόλεων, ἁπλῶς τῶν ἐξ ἐκείνης οὐδὲν εἰς τὸν ἴδιον βίον μετήγαγεν, οὔτ᾽ ὠνησά-
10 μενος οὔτ᾽ ἄλλῳ τρόπῳ κτησάμενος οὐδέν, καίπερ οὐχ
ὅλως εὐπορούμενος κατὰ τὸν βίον, ἀλλὰ μέτριος ὢν
11 κατὰ τὴν ὕπαρξιν, ὡς Ῥωμαῖος. οὐχ οἷον δὲ τῶν ἐξ
αὐτῆς τῆς Καρχηδόνος ἀπέσχετο μόνον, ἀλλὰ καὶ
καθόλου τῶν ἐκ τῆς Λιβύης οὐδὲν ἐπιμιχθῆναι πρὸς
12 τὸν ἴδιον εἴασε βίον. περὶ δὲ τούτου πάλιν τἀνδρὸς ὁ
ζητῶν ἀληθινῶς ἀναμφισβήτητον εὑρήσει παρὰ
Ῥωμαίοις τὴν περὶ τοῦτο τὸ μέρος δόξαν.

36. Ἀλλὰ γὰρ ὑπὲρ μὲν τούτων οἰκειότερον λαβόν-
(19) τες καιρὸν ποιησόμεθα ⟨τὴν⟩ ἐπὶ πλεῖον διαστολήν. ὁ
δὲ Τίτος ταξάμενος ἡμέραν πρὸς τὸν Φίλιππον τοῖς
μὲν συμμάχοις ἔγραψε παραχρῆμα, διασαφῶν πότε
δεήσει παρεῖναι πρὸς τὸν σύλλογον, αὐτὸς δὲ μετά
τινας ἡμέρας ἧκε πρὸς τὴν εἰσβολὴν τῶν Τεμπῶν εἰς
2 τὸν ταχθέντα χρόνον. ἀθροισθέντων δὲ τῶν συμμάχων καὶ τοῦ συνεδρίου συναχθέντος ἐξ αὐτῶν τούτων,
ἀναστὰς ὁ τῶν Ῥωμαίων στρατηγὸς ἐκέλευε λέγειν
ἕκαστον ἐφ᾽ οἷς δεῖ ποιεῖσθαι τὰς πρὸς τὸν Φίλιππον
3 διαλύσεις. Ἀμύνανδρος μὲν οὖν ὁ βασιλεὺς βραχέα
4 διαλεχθεὶς καὶ μέτρια κατέπαυσε τὸν λόγον· ἠξίου
γὰρ πρόνοιαν αὐτοῦ ποιήσασθαι πάντας, ἵνα μὴ χωρισθέντων Ῥωμαίων ἐκ τῆς Ἑλλάδος εἰς ἐκεῖνον ἀπ-
ερείδηται τὴν ὀργὴν ὁ Φίλιππος· εἶναι γὰρ εὐχειρώτους
Ἀθαμᾶνας αἰεὶ Μακεδόσι διά τε τὴν ἀσθένειαν καὶ
5 γειτνίασιν τῆς χώρας. μετὰ δὲ τοῦτον Ἀλέξανδρος ὁ

Carthage, which was considered the wealthiest city in the world, he took absolutely nothing from it to add to his own fortune, either by purchase or by any other means of acquisition, and this although he was not particularly well off, but only moderately so for a Roman. And not only did he keep his hands off the treasure in Carthage itself, but in general did not allow any of that from Africa to be mixed up with his private fortune. In the case of this man again anyone who really inquires will find that no one disputes his reputation at Rome in this respect.

36. But regarding these men, when I find a more suitable opportunity[100] I will speak more at large. Flamininus in the meanwhile, after fixing on a day to meet Philip, at once wrote to the allies instructing them at what date they should be present for the conference, and then a few days afterward came to the entrance of Tempe at the time determined on. When the allies had assembled, and while the council was exclusively composed of them, the Roman proconsul got up and asked them to state severally on what terms peace should be made with Philip. King Amynander[101] resumed his seat after speaking briefly and with moderation. For he begged them all to take steps for his protection, in case, when the Romans had left Greece, Philip might vent his anger on him. For, he said, the Athamanians were always easy victims of the Macedonians owing to their weakness and the closeness of the two countries. After him Alexander[102] the Aetolian got up. He

[100] 31.22.1–2.
[101] 1.3.
[102] 3.1.

Αἰτωλὸς ἀναστάς, καθότι μὲν ἤθροικε τοὺς συμμάχους ἐπὶ τὸ περὶ τῶν διαλύσεων διαβούλιον καὶ καθ-
6 όλου νῦν ἑκάστους ἀξιοῖ λέγειν τὸ φαινόμενον, ἐπήνεσε τὸν Τίτον, τοῖς δ᾽ ὅλοις πράγμασιν ἀγνοεῖν ἔφη
καὶ παραπίπτειν αὐτόν, εἰ πέπεισται διαλύσεις ποιησάμενος πρὸς Φίλιππον ἢ Ῥωμαίοις τὴν εἰρήνην ἢ
τοῖς Ἕλλησι τὴν ἐλευθερίαν βέβαιον ἀπολείψειν
7 οὐδέτερον γὰρ εἶναι τούτων δυνατόν, ἀλλ᾽ εἰ βούλεται
καὶ τὴν τῆς πατρίδος πρόθεσιν ἐπιτελῆ ποιεῖν καὶ τὰς
ἰδίας ὑποσχέσεις, ἃς ὑπέσχηται πᾶσι τοῖς Ἕλλησι,
μίαν ὑπάρχειν ἔφη διάλυσιν πρὸς Μακεδόνας τὸ Φί-
8 λιππον ἐκβάλλειν ἐκ τῆς ἀρχῆς. τοῦτο δ᾽ εἶναι καὶ
9 λίαν εὐχερές, ἐὰν μὴ παρῇ τὸν ἐνεστῶτα καιρόν. πλείω
δὲ πρὸς ταύτην τὴν ὑπόθεσιν διαλεχθεὶς κατέπαυσε
τὸν λόγον.

37. Ὁ δὲ Τίτος ἀναδεξάμενος ἀστοχεῖν αὐτὸν ἔφη-
(20) σεν οὐ μόνον τῆς Ῥωμαίων προαιρέσεως, ἀλλὰ καὶ
τῆς αὑτοῦ προθέσεως καὶ μάλιστα τοῦ τῶν Ἑλλήνων
2 συμφέροντος. οὔτε γὰρ Ῥωμαίους οὐδενὶ τὸ πρῶτον
πολεμήσαντας εὐθέως ἀναστάτους ποιεῖν τούτους·
3 πίστιν δ᾽ ἔχειν τὸ λεγόμενον ἔκ [τε] τῶν κατ᾽ Ἀννίβαν
καὶ Καρχηδονίους, ὑφ᾽ ὧν τὰ δεινότατα παθόντας
Ῥωμαίους, καὶ μετὰ ταῦτα γενομένους κυρίους ὃ βουληθεῖεν πρᾶξαι κατ᾽ αὐτῶν ἁπλῶς, οὐδὲν ἀνήκεστον
4 βουλεύσασθαι περὶ Καρχηδονίων· καὶ μὴν οὐδ᾽ αὐτὸς
οὐδέποτε ταύτην ἐσχηκέναι τὴν αἵρεσιν, ὅτι δεῖ πολεμεῖν πρὸς τὸν Φίλιππον ἀδιαλύτως· ἀλλ᾽ εἴπερ
ἐβουλήθη ποιεῖν τὰ παρακαλούμενα πρὸ τῆς μάχης,

praised Flamininus for having called the allies to take part in the Peace Conference and for inviting them now to give their several opinions, but he said he was much mistaken and wide of the mark if he believed that by coming to terms with Philip he would ensure either peace for the Romans or liberty for the Greeks. For neither of these results was possible; but if he wished to carry out completely the policy of his country and fulfill the promises he had given to all the Greeks, there was but one way of making peace with Macedonia and that was to depose Philip. To do so, he said, was really quite easy, if he did not let the present opportunity slip. After speaking at some length in the same sense he resumed his seat.

37. Flamininus spoke next. He said that Alexander was mistaken not only as to the policy of Rome, but as to his own particular design, and especially as to the interests of Greece. For neither did the Romans ever after a single war at once exterminate their adversaries, as was proved by their conduct toward Hannibal and the Carthaginians, at whose hands they had suffered injuries so grievous, but yet afterward, when it was in their power to treat them exactly as they chose, they had not resolved on any extreme measures. Nor, he said, had he himself ever entertained the idea that they should wage war on Philip without any hope of reconciliation; but if the king had consented to the conditions imposed on him before the

5 ἑτοίμως ἂν διαλελύσθαι πρὸς αὐτόν. διὸ καὶ θαυμάζειν ἔφη πῶς μετέχοντες τότε τῶν περὶ τῆς διαλύσεως

6 συλλόγων ἅπαντες νῦν ἀκαταλλάκτως ἔχουσιν. "ἢ
δῆλον ὅτι νενικήκαμεν; ἀλλὰ τοῦτό γ᾽ ἐστὶ πάντων

7 ἀγνωμονέστατον· πολεμοῦντας γὰρ δεῖ τοὺς ἀγαθοὺς
ἄνδρας βαρεῖς εἶναι καὶ θυμικούς, ἡττωμένους δὲ γεν-
ναίους καὶ μεγαλόφρονας, νικῶντάς γε μὴν μετρίους
καὶ πραεῖς καὶ φιλανθρώπους. ὑμεῖς δὲ τἀναντία

8 παρακαλεῖτε νῦν. ἀλλὰ μὴν καὶ τοῖς Ἕλλησι ταπει-
νωθῆναι μὲν ἐπὶ πολὺ συμφέρει τὴν Μακεδόνων ἀρ-

9 χήν, ἀρθῆναί γε μὴν οὐδαμῶς." τάχα γὰρ αὐτοὺς
πεῖραν λήψεσθαι τῆς Θρᾳκῶν καὶ Γαλατῶν παρανο-

10 μίας· τοῦτο γὰρ ἤδη καὶ πλεονάκις γεγονέναι. καθόλου δ᾽ αὐτὸς μὲν ἔφη καὶ τοὺς παρόντας Ῥωμαίων
κρίνειν, ἐὰν Φίλιππος ὑπομένῃ πάντα ποιεῖν τὰ πρότερον ὑπὸ τῶν συμμάχων ἐπιταττόμενα, διδόναι τὴν
εἰρήνην αὐτῷ, προσλαβόντας καὶ τὴν τῆς συγκλήτου
γνώμην· Αἰτωλοὺς δὲ κυρίους εἶναι βουλευομένους

11 ὑπὲρ σφῶν αὐτῶν. τοῦ δὲ Φαινέου μετὰ ταῦτα βουλομένου λέγειν ὅτι μάταια πάντα τὰ πρὸ τοῦ γέγονε·
τὸν γὰρ Φίλιππον, ἐὰν διολίσθῃ τὸν παρόντα καιρόν,

12 ἤδη πάλιν ἀρχὴν ἄλλην ποιήσεσθαι πραγμάτων· ὁ
Τίτος αὐτόθεν ἐξ ἕδρας καὶ θυμικῶς "παῦσαι" φησί
"Φαινέα, ληρῶν· ἐγὼ γὰρ οὕτως χειριῶ τὰς διαλύσεις
ὥστε μηδὲ βουληθέντα τὸν Φίλιππον ἀδικεῖν δύνασθαι τοὺς Ἕλληνας."

battle, he would gladly have made peace with him. "Therefore it indeed surprises me," he said, "that after taking part in the conferences for peace you are now all irreconcilable. Is it, as seems evident, because we won the battle? But nothing can be more unfeeling. Brave men should be hard on their foes and wroth with them in battle, when conquered they should be courageous and high-minded, but when they conquer, moderate, gentle and humane. What you exhort me to do now is exactly the reverse. Again it is in the interest of the Greeks[103] that the Macedonian dominion should be humbled for long, but by no means that it should be destroyed." For in that case, he said, they would very soon experience the lawless violence of the Thracians and Gauls, as they had on more than one occasion. On the whole, he continued, he and the other Romans present judged it proper, if Philip agreed to do everything that the allies had previously demanded, to grant him peace after first consulting the Senate. As for the Aetolians, they were at liberty to take their own counsel. When Phaeneas[104] after this attempted to say that all that had happened was of no use, for Philip, if he could wriggle out of the present crisis, would at once begin to reestablish his power, Flamininus interrupted him angrily and without rising[105] from his seat, exclaiming, "Stop talking nonsense, Phaeneas; for I will so manage the peace that Philip will not, even if he wishes it, be able to wrong the Greeks."

[103] Macedonia was considered a buffer against the threat to Greece from less civilized nations of the north, such as the Thracians and Celts (37.9).   [104] See n. on 1.4.   [105] A deliberate insult; this detail may come from an eyewitness.

38. Καὶ τότε μὲν ἐπὶ τούτοις ἐχωρίσθησαν. τῇ δ᾽

(21) ὑστεραίᾳ παραγενομένου τοῦ βασιλέως, καὶ τῇ τρίτῃ
πάντων εἰς τὸν σύλλογον ἀθροισθέντων, εἰσελθὼν ὁ
Φίλιππος εὐστόχως καὶ συνετῶς ὑπετέμετο τὰς πάν-

2 των ὁρμάς· ἔφη γὰρ τὰ μὲν πρότερον ὑπὸ Ῥωμαίων
καὶ τῶν συμμάχων ἐπιταττόμενα πάντα συγχωρεῖν
καὶ ποιήσειν, περὶ δὲ τῶν λοιπῶν διδόναι τῇ συγκλήτῳ

3 τὴν ἐπιτροπήν. τούτων δὲ ῥηθέντων οἱ μὲν ἄλλοι πάντες ἀπεσιώπησαν, ὁ δὲ τῶν Αἰτωλῶν Φαινέας "τί οὖν
ἡμῖν οὐκ ἀποδίδως, Φίλιππε" ἔφη "Λάρισαν τὴν Κρε-

4 μαστήν, Φάρσαλον, Θήβας τὰς Φθίας, Ἐχῖνον;" ὁ μὲν
οὖν Φίλιππος ἐκέλευε παραλαμβάνειν αὐτούς, ὁ δὲ
Τίτος τῶν μὲν ἄλλων οὐκ ἔφη δεῖν οὐδεμίαν, Θήβας

5 δὲ μόνον τὰς Φθίας· Θηβαίους γὰρ ἐγγίσαντος αὐτοῦ
μετὰ τῆς δυνάμεως καὶ παρακαλοῦντος σφᾶς εἰς τὴν
Ῥωμαίων πίστιν οὐ βουληθῆναι· διὸ νῦν, κατὰ πόλεμον ὑποχειρίων ὄντων, ἔχειν ἐξουσίαν ἔφη βουλεύε-

6 σθαι περὶ αὐτῶν ὡς ἂν προαιρῆται. τῶν δὲ περὶ τὸν
Φαινέαν ἀγανακτούντων, καὶ λεγόντων ὅτι δέον αὐτοὺς
εἴη, πρῶτον μέν, καθότι συνεπολέμησαν νῦν, κομίζεσθαι τὰς πόλεις τὰς πρότερον μεθ᾽ αὑτῶν συμπολι-

7 τευομένας, ἔπειτα κατὰ τὴν ἐξ ἀρχῆς συμμαχίαν, καθ᾽
ἣν ἔδει τῶν κατὰ πόλεμον ἁλόντων τὰ μὲν ἔπιπλα
Ῥωμαίων εἶναι, τὰς δὲ πόλεις Αἰτωλῶν, ὁ Τίτος

8 ἀγνοεῖν αὐτοὺς ἔφη κατ᾽ ἀμφότερα. τήν τε γὰρ συμμαχίαν λελύσθαι, καθ᾽ ὃν καιρὸν τὰς διαλύσεις ἐποιήσαντο πρὸς Φίλιππον ἐγκαταλείποντες Ῥωμαίους, εἴ

9 τε καὶ μένειν ἔτι τὴν συμμαχίαν, δεῖν αὐτοὺς κομίζε-

38. On that day they broke up on these terms. Next day the king arrived, and on the following day, when all had assembled at the conference, Philip entered and with great skill and sound sense cut away the ground on which they all based their violent demands by saying that he yielded to and would execute all the former demands of the Romans and the allies, and that he submitted all other questions to the decision of the Senate. After he had said this, all the others remained silent, but Phaeneas the Aetolian representative said, "Why then, Philip, do you not give up to us Larisa Cremaste, Pharsalus, Phthiotic Thebes, and Echinus?"[106] Philip told him to take them, but Flamininus said that they ought not to take any of the other towns, but only Phthiotic Thebes. For the Thebans, when on approaching the town with his army he demanded that they should submit to Rome, had refused. So that, now that they had been reduced by force of arms, he had a right to decide as he chose about them. When, upon this, Phaeneas grew indignant and said that in the first place the Aetolians should, as they had fought side by side with the Romans, receive back the towns which had formerly been members of their League, and next that the same resulted from the terms of their original alliance,[107] by which the mobile booty of cities captured in war were to go to the Romans and the towns to the Aetolians, Flamininus said they were mistaken on both points. For the alliance had been dissolved, when, deserting the Romans, they made terms[108] with Philip, and even if it still

106 See n. on 3.12.   107 Of 212 or 211, *StV* 536.
108 In 206, Livy 29.12.1.

σθαι καὶ παραλαμβάνειν, οὐκ εἴ τινες ἐθελοντὴν σφᾶς
εἰς τὴν Ῥωμαίων πίστιν ἐνεχείρισαν, ὅπερ αἱ κατὰ
Θετταλίαν πόλεις ἅπασαι πεποιήκασι νῦν, ἀλλ᾽ εἴ τινες κατὰ κράτος ἑάλωσαν.

39. Τοῖς μὲν οὖν ἄλλοις ὁ Τίτος ἤρεσκε ταῦτα λέ-
(22)   γων, οἱ δ᾽ Αἰτωλοὶ βαρέως ἤκουον καί τις οἷον ἀρχὴ
2   κακῶν ἐγεννᾶτο μεγάλων· ἐκ γὰρ ταύτης τῆς διαφορᾶς
καὶ τούτου τοῦ σπινθῆρος μετ᾽ ὀλίγον ὅ τε πρὸς Αἰ-
3   τωλοὺς ὅ τε πρὸς Ἀντίοχον ἐξεκαύθη πόλεμος. τὸ δὲ
συνέχον ἦν τῆς ὁρμῆς τῆς τοῦ Τίτου πρὸς τὰς διαλύσεις, ἐπυνθάνετο τὸν Ἀντίοχον ἀπὸ Συρίας ‹ἀν›ῆχθαι
μετὰ δυνάμεως, ποιούμενον τὴν ὁρμὴν ἐπὶ τὴν Εὐ-
4   ρώπην. διόπερ ἠγωνία μὴ ταύτης ὁ Φίλιππος τῆς
ἐλπίδος ἀντιλαμβανόμενος ἐπὶ τὸ πολιοφυλακεῖν ὁρμήσῃ καὶ τρίβειν τὸν πόλεμον, εἶθ᾽ ἑτέρου παραγενηθέντος ὑπάτου τὸ κεφάλαιον τῶν πράξεων εἰς ἐκεῖνον
5   ἀνακλασθῇ. διὸ συνεχωρήθη τῷ βασιλεῖ, καθάπερ
ἠξίου, λαβόντα τετραμήνους ἀνοχὰς παραχρῆμα μὲν
δοῦναι τῷ Τίτῳ τὰ διακόσια τάλαντα καὶ Δημήτριον
τὸν υἱὸν εἰς ὁμηρείαν καί τινας ἑτέρους τῶν φίλων,
περὶ δὲ τῶν ὅλων πέμπειν εἰς τὴν Ῥώμην καὶ διδόναι
6   τῇ συγκλήτῳ τὴν ἐπιτροπήν. καὶ τότε μὲν ἐχωρίσθησαν
πιστωσάμενοι περὶ τῶν ὅλων πρὸς ἀλλήλους, ἐφ᾽ ᾧ
Τίτον, ἐὰν μὴ συντελῆται τὰ κατὰ τὰς διαλύσεις,
ἀποδοῦναι Φιλίππῳ τὰ διακόσια τάλαντα καὶ τοὺς
ὁμήρους· μετὰ δὲ ταῦτα πάντες ἔπεμπον εἰς τὴν
7   Ῥώμην, οἱ μὲν συνεργοῦντες, οἱ δ᾽ ἀντειπράττοντες τῇ
διαλύσει. . . .

subsisted, they should receive back and occupy not the towns[109] which had surrendered to the Romans of their own free will, as all the Thessalian cities had now done, but any that had fallen by force of arms.

39. Flamininus, in speaking thus, pleased the others, but the Aetolians listened to him sullenly, and we may say that the prelude of great evils began to come into being. For it was the spark of this quarrel that set alight the war with the Aetolians and that with Antiochus. What chiefly urged Flamininus to hasten to make peace, was the news that had reached him of Antiochus' having put to sea in Syria with an army directed against Europe.[110] This made him fearful lest Philip, catching at this hope of support, might shut himself up in his towns and drag on the war, and that on the arrival of another consul, the principal glory of his achievement would be lost to him and reflected on his successor. He therefore yielded to the king's request and allowed him an armistice of four months. He was at once to pay Flamininus the two hundred talents and give as hostages his son Demetrius[111] with some other of his friends, sending to Rome to submit the whole question to the Senate. They now separated after exchanging mutual pledges about the whole question, Flamininus engaging, if the peace were not finally made, to return the two hundred talents and the hostages. After this all the parties sent to Rome, some working for the peace and others against it. . . .

---

[109] Flamininus' point is difficult to reconcile with lines 15–21 of that treaty, *StV* 536. See G. Klaffenbach, *SitzBerlin* 1954, no. 1, 13–19; J. Deininger, *Gnomon* 42 (1970), 66–67; P. Derow, *JRS* 69 (1979), 11–12.   [110] See 41.a.

[111] The younger of the king's sons, born ca. 208/7.

40. Τί δήποτ' ἐστὶν ὅτι τοῖς αὐτοῖς καὶ διὰ τῶν
(23) αὐτῶν ἀπατώμενοι πάντες οὐ δυνάμεθα λῆξαι ⟨τῆς⟩
2 ἀνοίας; τοῦτο γὰρ τὸ γένος τῆς ῥᾳδιουργίας πολλάκις
3 ὑπὸ πολλῶν ἤδη γέγονε· καὶ τὸ μὲν παρὰ τοῖς ἄλλοις
διαχωρεῖν ἴσως οὐ θαυμαστόν, τὸ δέ, παρ' οἷς ἡ πηγὴ
4 τῆς τοιαύτης ὑπάρχει κακοπραγμοσύνης. ἀλλ' ἔστιν
αἴτιον τὸ μὴ πρόχειρον ὑπάρχειν τὸ παρ' Ἐπιχάρμῳ
καλῶς εἰρημένον

νᾶφε καὶ μέμνασ' ἀπιστεῖν· ἄρθρα ταῦτα τᾶν
φρενῶν.

40.5 Μεδίων, πόλις πρὸς τῇ Αἰτολίᾳ. Πολύβιος
ὀκτωκαιδεκάτῳ.

II. RES ASIAE

40a.1 ** κωλύειν τὸν Ἀντίοχον παραλιπεῖν, οὐκ ἀπ-
εχθείσας χάριν, ἀλλ' ὑφορώμενοι μὴ Φιλίππῳ συν-
επισχύσας ἐμπόδιον γένηται τῇ τῶν Ἑλλήνων ἐλευ-
θερίᾳ.

40a.2 Ὅτι Ἀντίοχος ὁ βασιλεὺς πάνυ ὠρέγετο τῆς
Ἐφέσου διὰ τὴν εὐκαιρίαν, τῷ δοκεῖν μὲν κατὰ τῆς

---

112 WC 2.27 and 601 make a good case for transposing this
fragment after 43.13. But since it is just a reflection of the author
and of little weight, it seemed preferable not to disturb the traditional sequence of excerpts and fragments.   113 See n. on
2.3.1. At this time the city was once again a member of the Acarnanian Confederacy: IG IX 1².583, 21 (216). 582.4 and 46 (207).
114 Having victoriously ended the Fifth Syrian War, the king,

40. What can the reason be that we all, though deceived by the same means and through the same persons, cannot yet give over our folly? For this sort of fraud has been practiced often and by many. It is perhaps not surprising that it succeeds with others, but it is indeed astonishing that it does so with those who are the very fount of such trickery. The reason however is that we do not bear in mind Epicharmus' excellent advice,

> "Be sober and mindful to mistrust; these are the thews of the mind."[112]

40.5 Medion,[113] a city close to Aetolia. Polybius, Book 18.

II. AFFAIRS OF ASIA

Advantageous Site of Ephesus

40a.1 ** "to prevent Antiochus[114] from sailing along the shore, not because of enmity, but suspecting that he might, by assisting Philip, become an obstacle to the freedom of the Greeks."

40a.2 King Antiochus was very anxious to get possession of Ephesus[115] because of its favorable site, as it may   197 B.C.

with a large fleet, sailed along the southern coast of Asia Minor, but was confronted by the Rhodians with the demand not to sail beyond the Chelidonian Islands (Livy 33.20.2–3). On the news of Cynoscephalae they came to terms with him. Ma (16.1.8), 83. Wiemer (16.26.10), 44.

[115] The King soon gained it: H. H. Schmitt, *Untersuchungen zur Geschichte Antiochos' des Grossen und seiner Zeit* (Wiesbaden 1964), 282. 288.

Ἰωνίας καὶ τῶν ἐφ' Ἑλλησπόντου πόλεων καὶ κατὰ
γῆν καὶ κατὰ θάλατταν ἀκροπόλεως ἔχειν θέσιν, κατὰ
δὲ τῆς Εὐρώπης ἀμυντήριον ὑπάρχειν ἀεὶ τοῖς Ἀσίας
βασιλεῦσιν εὐκαιρότατον.

41. Ὅτι φησὶν ὁ Πολύβιος ἐν τῷ ιη' λόγῳ. ὅτι
(24) Ἄτταλος ἐτελεύτησε τὸν βίον· ὑπὲρ οὗ δίκαιόν ἐστι,
καθάπερ περὶ τῶν ἄλλων εἰθίσμεθα ποιεῖν, καὶ περὶ
τούτου νῦν ἐπιφθέγξασθαι τὸν ἁρμόζοντα λόγον.

2 ἐκείνῳ γὰρ ἐξ ἀρχῆς ἄλλο μὲν οὐδὲν ἐφόδιον ὑπῆρξε
3 πρὸς βασιλείαν τῶν ἐκτός, πλοῦτος δὲ μόνον, ὃς μετὰ
νοῦ μὲν καὶ τόλμης χειριζόμενος ὡς ἀληθῶς μεγάλην
παρέχεται χρείαν πρὸς πᾶσαν ἐπιβολήν, ἄνευ δὲ τῶν
προειρημένων τοῖς πλείστοις κακῶν παραίτιος πέφυκε
4 γίνεσθαι καὶ συλλήβδην ἀπωλείας. καὶ γὰρ φθόνους
γεννᾷ καὶ ἐπιβουλὰς καὶ πρὸς διαφθορὰν σώματος
καὶ ψυχῆς μεγίστας ἔχει ῥοπάς. ὀλίγαι δέ τινές εἰσι
ψυχαὶ παντάπασιν αἱ ταῦτα δυνάμεναι διωθεῖσθαι τῇ
5 τοῦ πλούτου δυνάμει. διὸ καὶ τοῦ προειρημένου ἄξιον
ἀγασθῆναι τὴν μεγαλοψυχίαν, ὅτι πρὸς οὐδὲν τῶν ἄλλων ἐπεβάλετο χρήσασθαι τοῖς χορηγίοις ἀλλὰ πρὸς
βασιλείας κατάκτησιν, οὗ μεῖζον ἢ κάλλιον οὐδὲν
6 οἷόν τ' ἐστὶν οὐδ' εἰπεῖν· ὃς τὴν ἀρχὴν ἐνεστήσατο
τῆς προειρημένης ἐπιβολῆς οὐ μόνον διὰ τῆς εἰς τοὺς
φίλους εὐεργεσίας καὶ χάριτος, ἀλλὰ καὶ διὰ τῶν
7 κατὰ πόλεμον ἔργων. νικήσας γὰρ μάχῃ Γαλάτας, ὃ
βαρύτατον καὶ μαχιμώτατον ἔθνος ἦν τότε κατὰ τὴν

be said to stand in the position of a citadel both by land and sea for anyone with designs on Ionia and the cities of the Hellespont, and is always a most favorable point of defense against Europe for the kings of Asia.

Character of Attalus

41. So died Attalus, and justice demands that, as is my practice in the case of others, I should pronounce a few befitting words over his grave. He possessed at the outset no other external resource that qualified him for a kingdom but wealth, a thing that when used with intelligence and daring is of real service in all enterprises but, when these virtues are absent, proves in most cases the cause of disaster and in fact of utter ruin. For it is the source of jealousy and plotting, and contributes more than anything else to the corruption of body and soul. Those souls indeed are few who can arrest these consequences by the mere power that riches give. We should therefore reverence this king's loftiness of mind, in that he did not attempt to use his great possessions for any other purpose than the attainment of sovereignty, a thing than which nothing greater or more splendid can be named. He laid the foundation of his design not only by the largesses and favors he conferred on his friends, but by his success in war. For having conquered the Gauls,[116] then the most formidable and

---

[116] See E. V. Hansen, *The Attalids of Pergamon*, 2nd ed. (Ithaca 1971), 26–33, and, from the vast bibliography on the victory monuments, e.g., H.-J. Schalles, *Untersuchungen zur Kulturpolitik der pergamenischen Herrscher im dritten Jahrhundert v. Chr.* (Tübingen 1985), 51–123.

Ἀσίαν, ταύτην ἀρχὴν ἐποιήσατο καὶ τότε πρῶτον

8 αὑτὸν ἔδειξε βασιλέα. τυχὼν δὲ τῆς τιμῆς ταύτης καὶ
βιώσας ἔτη δύο πρὸς τοῖς ἑβδομήκοντα, τούτων δὲ
βασιλεύσας τετταράκοντα καὶ τέτταρα, σωφρονέ-
στατα μὲν ἐβίωσε καὶ σεμνότατα πρὸς γυναῖκα καὶ

9 τέκνα, διεφύλαξε δὲ τὴν πρὸς πάντας τοὺς συμμάχους
καὶ φίλους πίστιν, ἐναπέθανε δ' ἐν αὐτοῖς τοῖς καλλί-
στοις ἔργοις, ἀγωνιζόμενος ὑπὲρ τῆς τῶν Ἑλλήνων

10 ἐλευθερίας. τὸ δὲ μέγιστον, τέτταρας υἱοὺς ἐν ἡλικίᾳ
καταλιπὼν οὕτως ἡρμόσατο τὰ κατὰ τὴν ἀρχὴν ὥστε
παισὶ παίδων ἀστασίαστον παραδοθῆναι τὴν βασιλείαν.

III. RES ITALIAE

42. Ὅτι ἐπὶ Μαρκέλλου Κλαυδίου ὑπάτου παρειλη-

(25) φότος τὴν ὕπατον ἀρχὴν ἧκον εἰς τὴν Ῥώμην οἵ τε
παρὰ τοῦ Φιλίππου πρέσβεις οἵ τε παρὰ τοῦ Τίτου
καὶ τῶν συμμάχων ὑπὲρ τῶν πρὸς Φίλιππον συν-

2 θηκῶν. λόγων δὲ πλειόνων γενομένων ἐν τῇ συγκλήτῳ,

3 ταύτῃ μὲν ἐδόκει βεβαιοῦν τὰς ὁμολογίας· εἰς δὲ τὸν
δῆμον εἰσενεχθέντος τοῦ διαβουλίου Μάρκος, αὐτὸς
ἐπιθυμῶν τῆς εἰς τὴν Ἑλλάδα διαβάσεως, ἀντέλεγε
καὶ πολλὴν ἐποιεῖτο σπουδὴν εἰς τὸ διακόψαι τὰς

4 συνθήκας. οὐ μὴν ἀλλ' ὅ γε δῆμος κατὰ τὴν τοῦ Τίτου

---

117 Of Apollonis, the daughter of a citizen of Cyzicus at the
south shore of the Sea of Marmara.

warlike nation in Asia Minor, he built upon this foundation, and then first showed he was really a king. And after
he had received this honorable title, he lived until the age
of seventy-two and reigned for forty-four years, ever most
virtuous and austere as husband[117] and father,[118] never
breaking his faith to his friends and allies, and finally dying
when engaged on his best work, fighting for the liberties[119]
of Greece. Add to this what is most remarkable of all, that
having four grown-up sons, he so disposed of his kingdom
that he handed on the crown in undisputed succession to
his children's children.

III. AFFAIRS OF ITALY

The Embassies to the Senate

42. After Claudius Marcellus,[120] the consul, had en-   196 B.C.
tered upon office there arrived in Rome the ambassadors
from Philip and also the legates sent by Flamininus and
the allies on the subject of the peace with Philip. After
considerable discussion in the Senate, that body resolved
to confirm the peace. But when the senatus consultum was
brought before the People, Marcus, who himself was desirous of crossing to Greece, spoke against it and did all in
his power to break off the negotiation. But in spite of this
the people yielded to the wishes of Flamininus and ratified

[118] Of four sons: Eumenes, Attalus, Philetaerus, and Athenaeus. The first two became kings themselves, Eumenes after
Attalus, Attalus after Eumenes' death.

[119] Certainly not the principal aim of his policy.

[120] Consul 196, *MRR* 1.335.

5 προαίρεσιν ἐπεκύρωσε τὰς διαλύσεις. ὧν ἐπιτελεσθει-
σῶν εὐθέως ἡ σύγκλητος ἄνδρας δέκα καταστήσασα
τῶν ἐπιφανῶν ἐξέπεμπε τοὺς χειριοῦντας τὰ κατὰ τὴν
Ἑλλάδα μετὰ τοῦ Τίτου καὶ βεβαιώσοντας τοῖς Ἕλ-
6 λησι τὴν ἐλευθερίαν. ἐποιήσαντο δὲ λόγους ἐν τῇ
συγκλήτῳ καὶ περὶ τῆς συμμαχίας οἱ παρὰ τῶν
7 Ἀχαιῶν πρέσβεις, οἱ περὶ Δαμόξενον τὸν Αἰγιέα· γενομένης δ᾽ ἀντιρρήσεως κατὰ τὸ παρὸν διὰ τὸ κατὰ
πρόσωπον Ἠλείους μὲν ἀμφισβητεῖν τοῖς Ἀχαιοῖς
ὑπὲρ τῆς Τριφυλίας, Μεσσηνίους δ᾽ ὑπὲρ Ἀσίνης καὶ
Πύλου, συμμάχους τότε Ῥωμαίων ὑπάρχοντας, Αἰτωλοὺς δὲ περὶ τῆς Ἡραιῶν πόλεως, ὑπέρθεσιν ἔλαβε τὸ
8 διαβούλιον ἐπὶ τοὺς δέκα. καὶ τὰ μὲν κατὰ τὴν σύγκλητον ἐπὶ τούτοις ἦν.

IV. RES GRAECIAE

43. Ὅτι κατὰ τὴν Ἑλλάδα μετὰ τὴν μάχην Τίτου
(26) παραχειμάζοντος ἐν Ἐλατείᾳ Βοιωτοί, σπουδάζοντες
ἀνακομίσασθαι τοὺς ἄνδρας τοὺς παρ᾽ αὐτῶν στρα-

---

[121] Eight of them are known, MRR 1.337–338.

[122] "not mentioned elsewhere" (WC 2.606). His name has,
however, been restored by Mezger in the peace treaty between
Miletus and Magnesia (Milet 148, 18), as one of those representing the Achaean League (as Damoxenus did in 196 at Rome):
Δα[μοξένου τοῦ – – – – –], a restoration accepted by Rehm and
others, but deemed "mere phantasy" by R. M. Errington, Chiron
19 (1989), 279, n. 5. Mezger's suggestion has been strengthened
by the dossier from Messene, dated to the years 182–180, as

the peace. Upon the conclusion of peace the Senate at once nominated ten[121] of its most distinguished members and sent them to manage Grecian affairs in conjunction with Flamininus, and to assure the liberties of the Greeks. The Achaean legate Damoxenus of Aegium[122] also spoke in the Senate on the subject of the alliance.[123] But since some opposition was raised for the time being, because the Eleans made a claim against the Achaeans for Triphylia, the Messenians (who were then the allies of Rome) for Asine and Pylus, and the Aetolians for the possession of Heraea, the decision was referred to the ten commissioners. Such was the result of the proceedings in the Senate.

IV. AFFAIRS OF GREECE

Conduct of the Boeotians

43. While Flamininus was wintering in Elatea[124] after the battle, the Boeotians, anxious to recover the men they

196 B.C.

printed by P. Themelis, *Proceedings of the International Symposium in honour of James Roy* (Stemnitza 2008), 212, lines 22–23: one of seventeen ἁγεμόνες of the League is Δαμόξενος Κλεοξένου Αἰγιεύς.

123 No formal treaty had been concluded, when the Achaeans changed sides in 198 and became allies of Rome. The Senate now denied them a treaty due to various protests from states claiming territory held by the Achaeans. Details in WC 2.606–608.

124 The principal city of Phocis. Its population had recently been expelled, by the Romans or the Aetolians, and had found shelter at Stymphalus in Arcadia, *ISE* 55 and additions, vol. 3 (2002), XVIII. See C. Habicht (10.11), 67–69.

τευσαμένους παρὰ τῷ Φιλίππῳ, διεπρεσβεύοντο περὶ

2 τῆς ἀσφαλείας αὐτῶν πρὸς Τίτον. ὁ δὲ βουλόμενος
ἐκκαλεῖσθαι τοὺς Βοιωτοὺς πρὸς τὴν σφετέραν εὔνοιαν διὰ τὸ προορᾶσθαι τὸν Ἀντίοχον, ἑτοίμως συν-

3 εχώρησεν. ταχὺ δὲ πάντων ἀνακομισθέντων ἐκ τῆς
Μακεδονίας, ἐν οἷς ἦν καὶ Βραχύλλης, τοῦτον μὲν
εὐθέως βοιωτάρχην κατέστησαν, παπαπλησίως δὲ
καὶ τοὺς ἄλλους τοὺς δοκοῦντας εἶναι φίλους τῆς Μακεδόνων οἰκίας ἐτίμων καὶ προῆγον οὐχ ἧττον ἢ πρό-

4 τερον. ἔπεμψαν δὲ καὶ πρεσβείαν πρὸς τὸν Φίλιππον
τὴν εὐχαριστήσουσαν ἐπὶ τῇ τῶν νεανίσκων ἐπανόδῳ,

5 λυμαινόμενοι τὴν τοῦ Τίτου χάριν. ἃ συνορῶντες οἱ
περὶ τὸν Ζεύξιππον καὶ Πεισίστρατον, καὶ πάντες οἱ
δοκοῦντες εἶναι Ῥωμαίοις φίλοι δυσχερῶς ἔφερον,
προορώμενοι τὸ μέλλον καὶ δεδιότες περὶ σφῶν αὐτῶν

6 καὶ τῶν ἀναγκαίων· σαφῶς γὰρ ᾔδεισαν ὡς, ἐὰν μὲν
οἱ Ῥωμαῖοι χωρισθῶσιν ἐκ τῆς Ἑλλάδος, ὁ δὲ Φίλιππος μένῃ παρὰ πλευράν, συνεπισχύων αἰεὶ τοῖς πρὸς
σφᾶς ἀντιπολιτευομένοις, οὐδαμῶς ἀσφαλῆ σφίσιν

7 ἐσομένην τὴν ἐν τῇ Βοιωτίᾳ πολιτείαν. διὸ καὶ συμ-
φρονήσαντες ἐπρέσβευον πρὸς Τίτον εἰς τὴν Ἐλά-

8 τειαν. συμμίξαντες δὲ τῷ προειρημένῳ πολλοὺς καὶ
ποικίλους εἰς τοῦτο τὸ μέρος διετίθεντο λόγους, ὑπο-
δεικνύντες τὴν ὁρμὴν τοῦ πλήθους τὴν οὖσαν ἤδη νῦν

9 καθ᾿ αὑτῶν καὶ τὴν ἀχαριστίαν τῶν ὄχλων. καὶ τέλος
ἐθάρρησαν εἰπεῖν ⟨ὡς⟩, ἐὰν μὴ τὸν Βραχύλλην ἐπ-
ανελόμενοι καταπλήξωνται τοὺς πολλούς, οὐκ ἔστιν

had sent to serve under Philip in the campaign, sent an embassy to Flamininus begging him to provide for their safety, and he gladly consented as, being apprehensive about Antiochus, he wished to conciliate the Boeotians. Upon all the men being very soon sent back from Macedonia, among them Brachylles,[125] they at once appointed the latter boeotarch,[126] and continued, no less than formerly, to advance and honor the others who were considered to be friends of the house of Macedon. They also sent an embassy to Philip thanking him for the return of the soldiers, thus depreciating the grace of Flamininus' act. When Zeuxippus,[127] Pisistratus and all who were considered the friends of Rome saw this, they were much displeased, as they foresaw what might happen and feared for themselves and their relatives. For they well knew that if the Romans quitted Greece and Philip remained on their flanks, his strength continuing to increase together with that of their political opponents, it would by no means be safe for them to take part in public life in Boeotia. They therefore clubbed together and sent envoys to Flamininus at Elatea. On meeting him they used a great variety of arguments, pointing out the violent feeling against them at present existing among the people and the noted ingratitude of a multitude, and finally they made bold to say that unless they struck terror into the populace by killing Brachylles there would be no security for the friends of

125 See n. on 1.2. He had been with King Philip at the conference in November 198.   126 Theirs was a board of seven, each representing one of the seven districts of Boeotia; D. Knoepfler, *Chiron* 32 (2002), 146–147.

127 *RE* Zeuxippos 380 (H. H. Schmitt).

ἀσφάλεια τοῖς Ῥωμαίων φίλοις χωρισθέντων τῶν
10 στρατοπέδων. ὁ δὲ Τίτος ταῦτα διακούσας αὐτὸς μὲν
    οὐκ ἔφη κοινωνεῖν τῆς πράξεως ταύτης, τοὺς δὲ βου-
11 λομένους πράττειν οὐ κωλύειν· καθόλου δὲ λαλεῖν αὐ-
    τοὺς ἐκέλευε περὶ τούτων Ἀλεξαμενῷ τῷ τῶν Αἰτωλῶν
12 στρατηγῷ. τῶν δὲ περὶ τὸν Ζεύξιππον πειθαρχησάν-
    των καὶ διαλεγομένων, ταχέως ὁ προειρημένος πει-
    σθεὶς καὶ συγκαταθέμενος τοῖς λεγομένοις τρεῖς μὲν
    τῶν Αἰτωλικῶν συνέστησε, τρεῖς δὲ τῶν Ἰταλικῶν
    νεανίσκων τοὺς προσοίσοντας τὰς χεῖρας τῷ Βρα-
    χύλλῃ. . . .
13 Οὐδεὶς γὰρ οὕτως οὔτε μάρτυς ἐστὶ φοβερὸς οὔτε
    κατήγορος δεινὸς ὡς ἡ σύνεσις ἡ κατοικοῦσ᾽ ἐν ταῖς
    ἑκάστων ψυχαῖς.

    44. Ὅτι κατὰ τὸν καιρὸν τοῦτον ἧκον ἐκ τῆς Ῥώμης
(27) οἱ δέκα, δι᾽ ὧν ἔμελλε χειρίζεσθαι τὰ κατὰ τοὺς Ἕλ-
    ληνας, κομίζοντες τὸ τῆς συγκλήτου <δόγμα> τὸ περὶ
2   τῆς πρὸς Φίλιππον εἰρήνης. ἦν δὲ τὰ συνέχοντα τοῦ
    δόγματος ταῦτα, τοὺς μὲν ἄλλους Ἕλληνας πάντας,
    τούς τε κατὰ τὴν Ἀσίαν καὶ κατὰ τὴν Εὐρώπην,
    ἐλευθέρους ὑπάρχειν καὶ νόμοις χρῆσθαι τοῖς ἰδίοις·
3   τοὺς δὲ ταττομένους ὑπὸ Φίλιππον καὶ τὰς πόλεις τὰς
    ἐμφρούρους παραδοῦναι Φίλιππον Ῥωμαίοις πρὸ τῆς
4   τῶν Ἰσθμίων πανηγύρεως, Εὔρωμον δὲ καὶ Πήδασα
    καὶ Βαργύλια καὶ τὴν Ἰασέων πόλιν, ὁμοίως Ἄβυδον,

---

128 Livy in telling the story of Brachylles' murder, is following
P. (33.27.5–29.12), but omits this detail that shows Flamininus'
involvement in the assassination plot (33.28.1).

the Romans once the legions had left. Flamininus,[128] after listening to this, said that he himself would take no part in this deed, but would put no obstacles in the way of anyone who wished to do so. He advised them on the whole to speak to Alexamenus, the Aetolian strategus. When Zeuxippus and the others acted on this advice and spoke about the matter, Alexamenus[129] was soon persuaded and agreeing to what they said, arranged for three Aetolians and three Italian soldiers to assassinate Brachylles. . . .

For no one is such a terrible witness or such a dread accuser as the conscience[130] that dwells in all our hearts.

Flamininus and the Roman Commissioners in Greece

44. At this time the ten commissioners who were to control the affairs of Greece arrived from Rome bringing the senatus consultum about the peace with Philip. Its principal contents were as follows: All the rest of the Greeks in Asia and Europe were to be free and subject to their own laws; Philip was to surrender to the Romans before the Isthmian games[131] those Greeks subject to his rule and the cities in which he had garrisons; he was to leave free, withdrawing his garrisons from them, the towns of Euromus, Pedasa, Bargylia, and Iasus,[132] as well as Aby-

---

[129] He was strategus for 197/6. In 192, he murdered Nabis of Sparta and was in turn killed by the Spartans (Livy 36.34–36).

[130] Livy 33.28.10 makes clear that Zeuxippus, a fugitive to Tanagra after the murder of Brachylles, was plagued by his conscience.   [131] Held at the Isthmus of Corinth every "even" year, such as 196.   [132] Carian cities; for Euromus see n. on 2.3; Iasus was perhaps already in Antiochus' hands.

Θάσον, Μύριναν, Πέρινθον, ἐλευθέρας ἀφεῖναι τὰς
5 φρουρὰς ἐξ αὐτῶν μεταστησάμενον· περὶ δὲ τῆς τῶν
Κιανῶν ἐλευθερώσεως Τίτον γράψαι πρὸς Προυσίαν
6 κατὰ τὸ δόγμα τῆς συγκλήτου· τὰ δ' αἰχμάλωτα καὶ
τοὺς αὐτομόλους ἅπαντας ἀποκαταστῆσαι Φίλιππον
Ῥωμαίοις ἐν τοῖς αὐτοῖς χρόνοις, ὁμοίως δὲ καὶ τὰς
καταφράκτους ναῦς πλὴν πέντε σκαφῶν καὶ τῆς ἑκ-
7 καιδεκήρους· δοῦναι δὲ καὶ χίλια τάλαντα, τούτων τὰ
μὲν ἡμίση παραυτίκα, τὰ δ' ἡμίση κατὰ φόρους ἐν
ἔτεσι δέκα.

45. Τούτου δὲ τοῦ δόγματος διαδοθέντος εἰς τοὺς
(28) Ἕλληνας οἱ μὲν ἄλλοι πάντες εὐθαρσεῖς ἦσαν καὶ
περιχαρεῖς, μόνοι δ' Αἰτωλοί, δυσχεραίνοντες ἐπὶ τῷ
μὴ τυγχάνειν ὧν ἤλπιζον, κατελάλουν τὸ δόγμα, φάσκοντες οὐ πραγμάτων, ἀλλὰ γραμμάτων μόνον ἔχειν
2 αὐτὸ διάθεσιν. καί τινας ἐλάμβανον πιθανότητας ἐξ
αὐτῶν τῶν ἐγγράπτων πρὸς τὸ διασείειν τοὺς ἀκού-
3 οντας τοιαύτας. ἔφασκον γὰρ εἶναι δύο γνώμας ἐν τῷ
δόγματι περὶ τῶν ὑπὸ Φιλίππου φρουρουμένων πόλεων, τὴν μὲν μίαν ἐπιτάττουσαν ἐξάγειν τὰς φρουρὰς
τὸν Φίλιππον, τὰς δὲ πόλεις παραδιδόναι Ῥωμαίοις,
τὴν δ' ἑτέραν ἐξάγοντα τὰς φρουρὰς ἐλευθεροῦν τὰς
4 πόλεις. τὰς μὲν οὖν ἐλευθερουμένας ἐπ' ὀνόματος δη-
λοῦσθαι, ταύτας δ' εἶναι τὰς κατὰ τὴν Ἀσίαν, τὰς δὲ

---

133 See 16.29.2–34.12; Myrina is one of the two towns on
Lemnus. It is not clear when Philip occupied it. The island was
mostly an Athenian possession. For Perinthus see n. on 2.4.

dus, Thasos, Myrina, and Perinthus;[133] Flamininus was to write to Prusias in the terms of the senatus consultum about restoring the freedom of Cius;[134] Philip was to restore to the Romans all prisoners of war and deserters before the same date, and to surrender to them all his warships with the exception of five light vessels and his great "sixteen";[135] he was to pay them a thousand talents, half at once and the other half by installments extending over ten years.

45. When the report of this senatus consultum was spread in Greece, all except the Aetolians were of good heart and overjoyed. The latter alone, disappointed at not obtaining what they had hoped for, spoke ill of the decree, saying that it contained an arrangement of words and not an arrangement of things. Even from the actual terms of the document they drew certain probable conclusions calculated to confuse the minds of those who listened to them. For they said there were two decisions in it about the cities garrisoned by Philip, one ordering him to withdraw his garrisons and surrender the cities to the Romans and the other to withdraw his garrisons and set the cities free. The towns to be set free were named and they were those in Asia, while evidently those to be surren-

---

134 See nn. on 15.21 and 22.2.

135 A very large ship, probably with oars grouped in pairs, eight men to an oar. This vessel was probably taken from Demetrius by Lysimachus in 288 (Plu. *Dem.* 43.4) and remained in Macedon until 168, when Aemilius Paullus after his victory over Perseus took it to Rome and paraded it up the Tiber (Livy 45.35.3).

παραδιδομένας Ῥωμαίοις φανερὸν ὅτι τὰς κατὰ τὴν
5 Εὐρώπην. εἶναι δὲ ταύτας Ὠρεόν, Ἐρέτριαν, Χαλκίδα,
6 Δημητριάδα, Κόρινθον. ἐκ δὲ τούτων εὐθεώρητον
ὑπάρχειν πᾶσιν ὅτι μεταλαμβάνουσι τὰς Ἑλληνικὰς
πέδας παρὰ Φιλίππου Ῥωμαῖοι, καὶ γίνεται μεθάρμο-
σις δεσποτῶν, οὐκ ἐλευθέρωσις τῶν Ἑλλήνων.

7   Ταῦτα μὲν οὖν ὑπ᾽ Αἰτωλῶν ἐλέγετο κατακόρως. ὁ
δὲ Τίτος ὁρμήσας ἐκ τῆς Ἐλατείας μετὰ τῶν δέκα καὶ
κατάρας εἰς τὴν Ἀντίκυραν, παραυτίκα διέπλευσεν εἰς
τὸν Κόρινθον, κἀκεῖ παραγενόμενος συνήδρευε μετὰ
8 τούτων καὶ διελάμβανε περὶ τῶν ὅλων. πλεοναζούσης
δὲ τῆς τῶν Αἰτωλῶν διαβολῆς καὶ πιστευομένης παρ᾽
ἐνίοις, πολλοὺς καὶ ποικίλους ἠναγκάζετο ποιεῖσθαι
9 λόγους ὁ Τίτος ἐν τῷ συνεδρίῳ, διδάσκων ὡς εἴπερ
βούλονται καὶ τὴν τῶν Ἑλλήνων εὔκλειαν ὁλόκληρον
περιποιήσασθαι, καὶ καθόλου πιστευθῆναι παρὰ πᾶσι
διότι καὶ τὴν ἐξ ἀρχῆς ἐποιήσαντο διάβασιν οὐ τοῦ
συμφέροντος ἕνεκεν, ἀλλὰ τῆς τῶν Ἑλλήνων ἐλευθερίας, ἐκχωρητέον εἴη πάντων τῶν τόπων καὶ πάσας
ἐλευθερωτέον τὰς πόλεις τὰς νῦν ὑπὸ Φιλίππου φρου-
10 ρουμένας. ταύτην δὲ συνέβαινε γίνεσθαι τὴν ἀπορίαν
ἐν τῷ συνεδρίῳ διὰ τὸ περὶ μὲν τῶν ἄλλων ἐν τῇ
Ῥώμῃ προδιειλῆφθαι καὶ ῥητὰς ἔχειν τοὺς δέκα παρὰ
τῆς συγκλήτου τὰς ἐντολάς, περὶ δὲ Χαλκίδος καὶ
Κορίνθου καὶ Δημητριάδος ἐπιτροπὴν αὐτοῖς δεδόσθαι διὰ τὸν Ἀντίοχον, ἵνα βλέποντες πρὸς τοὺς καιροὺς βουλεύωνται περὶ τῶν προειρημένων πόλεων
11 κατὰ τὰς αὐτῶν προαιρέσεις· ὁ γὰρ προειρημένος

dered to the Romans were those in Europe, that is to say Oreus, Eretria, Chalcis, Demetrias, and Corinth.[136] From this anyone could easily see that the Romans were taking over from Philip the fetters of Greece, and that what was happening was a readjustment of masters and not the delivery of Greece out of servitude.

Such things were being said by the Aetolians ad nauseam. But Flamininus, moving from Elatea with the ten commissioners, came down to Anticyra and at once sailed across to Corinth. On arriving there he sat in conference with the commissioners, deciding about the whole situation. As the slanderous reflections of the Aetolians were becoming more current and were credited by some, he was obliged to address his colleagues at length and in somewhat elaborate terms, pointing out to them that if they wished to gain universal renown in Greece and in general convince all that the Romans had originally crossed the sea not in their own interest but in that of the liberty of Greece, they must withdraw from every place and set free all the cities now garrisoned by Philip. The hesitation felt in the conference was due to the fact that, while a decision had been reached in Rome about all other questions, and the commissioners had definite instructions from the Senate on all other matters, the question of Chalcis, Corinth, and Demetrias had been left to their discretion owing to the fear of Antiochus, in order that with an eye to circumstances they should take any course on which they determined. For it was evident that Anti-

[136] The first three are cities of Euboea, the last three the "fetters of Greece" (see n. on 18.11.5). More below, 10–12.

βασιλεὺς δῆλος ἦν ἐπέχων πάλαι τοῖς κατὰ τὴν Εὐ-
12 ρώπην πράγμασιν. οὐ μὴν ἀλλὰ τὸν μὲν Κόρινθον ὁ
Τίτος ἔπεισε τὸ συνέδριον ἐλευθεροῦν παραχρῆμα καὶ
τοῖς Ἀχαιοῖς ἐγχειρίζειν διὰ τὰς ἐξ ἀρχῆς ὁμολογίας,
τὸν δ' Ἀκροκόρινθον καὶ Δημητριάδα καὶ Χαλκίδα
παρακατέσχεν.

46. Δοξάντων δὲ τούτων, καὶ τῆς Ἰσθμίων πανηγύ-
(29) ρεως ἐπελθούσης, καὶ σχεδὸν ἀπὸ πάσης τῆς οἰκουμένης τῶν ἐπιφανεστάτων ἀνδρῶν συνεληλυθότων
διὰ τὴν προσδοκίαν τῶν ἀποβησομένων, πολλοὶ καὶ
ποικίλοι καθ' ὅλην τὴν πανήγυριν ἐνέπιπτον λόγοι,
2 τῶν μὲν ἀδύνατον εἶναι φασκόντων Ῥωμαίους ἐνίων
ἀποστῆναι τόπων καὶ πόλεων, τῶν δὲ διοριζομένων
ὅτι τῶν μὲν ἐπιφανῶν εἶναι δοκούντων τόπων ἀποστή-
σονται, τοὺς δὲ φαντασίαν μὲν ἔχοντας ἐλάττω,
χρείαν δὲ τὴν αὐτὴν παρέχεσθαι δυναμένους καθ-
3 έξουσι. καὶ τούτους εὐθέως ἐπεδείκνυσαν αὐτοὶ καθ'
4 αὑτῶν διὰ τῆς πρὸς ἀλλήλους εὑρεσιλογίας. τοιαύτης
δ' οὔσης ἐν τοῖς ἀνθρώποις τῆς ἀπορίας, ἀθροισθέντος
τοῦ πλήθους εἰς τὸ στάδιον ἐπὶ τὸν ἀγῶνα, προελθὼν
ὁ κῆρυξ καὶ ⟨κατα⟩σιωπησάμενος τὰ πλήθη διὰ τοῦ
5 σαλπικτοῦ τόδε ⟨τὸ⟩ κήρυγμ' ἀνηγόρευσεν· "Ἡ σύγκλητος ἡ Ῥωμαίων καὶ Τίτος Κοΐντιος στρατηγὸς
ὕπατος, καταπολεμήσαντες βασιλέα Φίλιππον καὶ
Μακεδόνας, ἀφιᾶσιν ἐλευθέρους, ἀφρουρήτους, ἀφορολογήτους, νόμοις χρωμένους τοῖς πατρίοις, Κορινθί-
ους Φωκέας, Λοκρούς, Εὐβοεῖς, Ἀχαιοὺς τοὺς Φθιώ-
6 τας, Μάγνητας, Θετταλούς, Περραιβούς·" κρότου δ' ἐν

ochus had been for some time awaiting his opportunity to interfere in the affairs of Greece. However, Flamininus persuaded his colleagues to set Corinth[137] free at once, handing it over to the Achaeans, as had originally been agreed, while he remained in occupation of the Acrocorinth, Demetrias, and Chalcis.

46. This having been decided and the Isthmian games being now close at hand, the most distinguished men from almost the whole world having assembled there owing to their expectation of what would take place, many and various were the reports prevalent during the whole festival, some saying that it was impossible for the Romans to abandon certain places and cities, and others declaring that they would abandon the places which were considered famous, but would retain those which, while less illustrious, would serve their purpose equally well, even at once naming these latter out of their own heads, each more ingenious than the other. Such was the doubt in men's minds when, the crowd being now collected in the stadium to witness the games, the herald came forward and, having imposed universal silence by his bugler, read this proclamation:[138] "The senate of Rome and Titus Quinctius the proconsul having overcome King Philip and the Macedonians, leave the following peoples free, without garrisons and subject to no tribute and governed by their countries' laws—the Corinthians, Phocians, Locrians, Euboeans, Phthiotic Achaeans, Magnesians, Thes-

---

137 The town, not the citadel.

138 Some 260 years later imitated at the same spot by the emperor Nero declaring Greece free in a speech preserved on stone; Holleaux, *Ét.* 1.165–185.

ἀρχαῖς εὐθέως ἐξαισίου γενομένου τινὲς μὲν οὐδ᾽
ἤκουσαν τοῦ κηρύγματος, τινὲς δὲ πάλιν ἀκούειν
7 ἐβούλοντο. τὸ δὲ πολὺ μέρος τῶν ἀνθρώπων διαπι-
στούμενον καὶ δοκοῦν ὡς ἂν εἰ καθ᾽ ὕπνον ἀκούειν
τῶν λεγομένων διὰ τὸ παράδοξον τοῦ συμβαίνοντος,
8 πᾶς τις ἐξ ἄλλης ὁρμῆς ἐβόα προάγειν τὸν κήρυκα
καὶ τὸν σαλπικτὴν εἰς μέσον τὸ στάδιον καὶ λέγειν
πάλιν ὑπὲρ τῶν αὐτῶν, ὡς μὲν ἐμοὶ δοκεῖ, βουλομένων
τῶν ἀνθρώπων μὴ μόνον ἀκούειν, ἀλλὰ καὶ βλέπειν
τὸν λέγοντα διὰ τὴν ἀπιστίαν τῶν ἀναγορευομένων.
9 ὡς δὲ πάλιν ὁ κῆρυξ, προελθὼν εἰς τὸ μέσον καὶ κα-
τασιωπησάμενος διὰ τοῦ σαλπικτοῦ τὸν θόρυβον,
ἀνηγόρευσε ταὐτὰ καὶ ὡσαύτως τοῖς πρόσθεν, τηλικοῦτον συνέβη καταρραγῆναι τὸν κρότον ὥστε καὶ
μὴ ῥᾳδίως ἂν ὑπὸ τὴν ἔννοιαν ἀγαγεῖν τοῖς νῦν
10 ἀκούουσι τὸ γεγονός. ὡς δέ ποτε κατέληξεν ὁ κρότος,
τῶν μὲν ἀθλητῶν ἁπλῶς οὐδεὶς οὐδένα λόγον εἶχεν
ἔτι, πάντες δὲ διαλαλοῦντες, οἱ μὲν ἀλλήλοις, οἱ δὲ
πρὸς σφᾶς αὐτούς, οἷον εἰ παραστατικοὶ τὰς διανοίας
11 ἦσαν. ᾗ καὶ μετὰ τὸν ἀγῶνα διὰ τὴν ὑπερβολὴν τῆς
χαρᾶς μικροῦ διέφθειραν τὸν Τίτον εὐχαριστοῦντες·
12 οἱ μὲν γὰρ ἀντοφθαλμῆσαι κατὰ πρόσωπον καὶ σωτῆρα προσφωνῆσαι βουλόμενοι, τινὲς δὲ τῆς δεξιᾶς

---

139 The proclamation of 196 resulted in the re-foundation of
several Confederations of the Thessalians, the Perrhaebians, and
the Magnesians. See G. Kip, *Thessalische Studien* (Diss. Halle
1910). G. Busolt and H. Swoboda, *Griechische Staatskunde* 2,
(Munich 1926), 1478–1501.

140 The epithet puts the recipient in the sphere of heroes and

salians,[139] and Perrhaebians." At once at the very commencement a tremendous shout arose, and some did not even hear the proclamation, while others wanted to hear it again. But the greater part of the crowd, unable to believe their ears and thinking that they were listening to the words as if in a dream owing to the event being so unexpected, demanded loudly, each prompted by a different impulse, that the herald and bugler should advance into the middle of the stadium and repeat the announcement, wishing, as I suppose, not only to hear the speaker, but to see him owing to the incredible character of his proclamation. But when the herald, coming forward to the middle of the stadium and again silencing the noise by his bugler, made the same identical proclamation, such a mighty burst of cheering arose that those who listen to the tale today cannot easily conceive what it was. When at length the noise had subsided, not a soul took any further interest in the athletes, but all, talking either to their neighbors or to themselves, were almost like men beside themselves. So much so indeed that after the games were over they very nearly put an end to Flamininus by their expressions of thanks. For some of them, longing to look him in the face and call him their savior,[140] others in their anxiety to

gods. Dio of Syracuse was so hailed when he brought down the tyrant Dionysius II in 357 (Plu., *Dio* 46.1. D.S. 16.20.6). Antigonus Doson was "Savior" at Sparta and Mantinea: S. le Bohec, *Antigone Dôsôn, roi de Macédoine* (Nancy 1993), 458. Flamininus was also, within the years 196 to 191, the recipient of godlike honors in various Greek cities, such as Chalcis, Argos, and Gythium; see J.-L. Ferrary, *Actes du Xe Congrès International d'Épigraphie Grecque et Latine,* Nîmes, 4–9 Octobre 1992 (Paris 1997), 216.

ἄψασθαι σπουδάζοντες, οἱ δὲ πολλοὶ στεφάνους ἐπιρ-
ριπποῦντες καὶ λημνίσκους, παρ' ὀλίγον διέλυσαν τὸν
13 ἄνθρωπον. δοκούσης δὲ τῆς εὐχαριστίας ὑπερβολικῆς
γενέσθαι, θαρρῶν ἄν τις εἶπε διότι πολὺ καταδεεστέ-
14 ραν εἶναι συνέβαινε τοῦ τῆς πράξεως μεγέθους. θαυ-
μαστὸν γὰρ ἦν καὶ τὸ Ῥωμαίους ἐπὶ ταύτης γενέσθαι
τῆς προαιρέσεως καὶ τὸν ἡγούμενον αὐτῶν Τίτον,
ὥστε πᾶσαν ὑπομεῖναι δαπάνην καὶ πάντα κίνδυνον
χάριν τῆς τῶν Ἑλλήνων ἐλευθερίας· μέγα δὲ καὶ τὸ
δύναμιν ἀκόλουθον τῇ προαιρέσει προσενέγκασθαι·
15 τούτων δὲ μέγιστον ἔτι τὸ μηδὲν ἐκ τῆς τύχης ἀντι-
παῖσαι πρὸς τὴν ἐπιβολήν, ἀλλ' ἁπλῶς ἅπαντα πρὸς
ἕνα καιρὸν ἐκδραμεῖν, ὥστε διὰ κηρύγματος ἑνὸς
ἅπαντας καὶ τοὺς τὴν Ἀσίαν κατοικοῦντας Ἕλληνας
καὶ τοὺς τὴν Εὐρώπην ἐλευθέρους, ἀφρουρήτους, ἀφορολογήτους γενέσθαι, νόμοις χρωμένους τοῖς ἰδίοις.

47. Διελθούσης δὲ τῆς πανηγύρεως πρώτοις μὲν
(30) ἐχρημάτισαν τοῖς παρ' Ἀντιόχου πρεσβευταῖς, διακε-
λευόμενοι τῶν ἐπὶ τῆς Ἀσίας πόλεων τῶν μὲν αὐτονόμων ἀπέχεσθαι καὶ μηδεμιᾷ πολεμεῖν, ὅσας δὲ νῦν
παρείληφε τῶν ὑπὸ Πτολεμαῖον καὶ Φίλιππον ταττο-
2 μένων, ἐκχωρεῖν. σὺν δὲ τούτοις προηγόρευον μὴ δια-

---

141 They were Hegesianax and Lysias. Hegesianax, son of
Diogenes, a citizen of Alexandria Troas, was a poet and historian
(*FGrH* 45), a "friend" of King Antiochus, who often used him in
diplomatic missions. He was made a *proxenos* at Delphi in 193
(*SIG* 585, 43). *RE* Hegesianax 2602–2604 (F. Stähelin) and 2604–
2606 (F. Jacoby).

grasp his hand, and the greater number throwing crowns and fillets on him, they all but tore the man to pieces. But however excessive their gratitude may seem to have been, one may confidently say that it was far inferior to the greatness of the event. For it was a wonderful thing, to begin with, that the Romans and their general Flamininus should entertain this purpose incurring every expense and facing every danger for the freedom of Greece; it was a great thing that they brought into action a force adequate to the execution of their purpose; and greatest of all was the fact that no mischance of any kind counteracted their design, but everything without exception conduced to this one crowning moment, when by a single proclamation all the Greeks inhabiting Asia and Europe became free, ungarrisoned, subject to no tribute and governed by their own laws.

47. When the festival was over, the commissioners first gave audience to the ambassadors[141] of Antiochus. They ordered him, as regards the Asiatic cities, to keep his hands off those which were autonomous[142] and make war on none of them and to withdraw from those previously subject to Ptolemy[143] and Philip which he had recently taken. At the same time they enjoined him not to cross to

[142] In particular Smyrna and Lampsacus, both resisting Antiochus and both approaching Flamininus. For Lampsacus see *SIG* 591, where Flamininus and the ten Roman commissioners are mentioned in line 69.

[143] These were mainly cities along the south coast of Asia Minor.

βαίνειν εἰς τὴν Εὐρώπην μετὰ δυνάμεως· οὐδένα γὰρ
ἔτι τῶν Ἑλλήνων οὔτε πολεμεῖσθαι νῦν ὑπ᾽ οὐδενὸς
3 οὔτε δουλεύειν οὐδενί. καθόλου δὲ καὶ ἐξ αὐτῶν τινας
4 ἔφασαν ἥξειν πρὸς τὸν Ἀντίοχον. ταύτας μὲν οὖν οἱ
περὶ τὸν Ἡγησιάνακτα καὶ Λυσίαν λαβόντες τὰς
5 ἀποκρίσεις ἐπανῆλθον· μετὰ δὲ τούτους εἰσεκαλοῦντο
πάντας τοὺς ἀπὸ τῶν ἐθνῶν καὶ πόλεων παραγεγονό-
6 τας, καὶ τὰ δόξαντα τῷ συνεδρίῳ διεσάφουν. Μακεδόνων μὲν οὖν τοὺς Ὀρέστας καλουμένους διὰ τὸ
προσχωρῆσαι σφίσι κατὰ τὸν πόλεμον αὐτονόμους
ἀφεῖσαν, ἠλευθέρωσαν δὲ Περραιβοὺς καὶ Δόλοπας
7 καὶ Μάγνητας. Θετταλοῖς δὲ μετὰ τῆς ἐλευθερίας καὶ
τοὺς Ἀχαιοὺς τοὺς Φθιώτας προσένειμαν, ἀφελόμενοι
8 Θήβας τὰς Φθίας καὶ Φάρσαλον· οἱ γὰρ Αἰτωλοὶ
περί τε τῆς Φαρσάλου μεγάλην ἐποιοῦντο φιλοτιμίαν,
φάσκοντες αὑτῶν δεῖν ὑπάρχειν κατὰ τὰς ἐξ ἀρχῆς
9 συνθήκας, ὁμοίως δὲ καὶ περὶ Λευκάδος. οἱ δ᾽ ἐν τῷ
συνεδρίῳ περὶ μὲν τούτων τῶν πόλεων ὑπερέθεντο
τοῖς Αἰτωλοῖς τὸ διαβούλιον πάλιν ἐπὶ τὴν σύγκλητον, τοὺς δὲ Φωκέας καὶ τοὺς Λοκροὺς συνεχώρησαν
αὐτοῖς ἔχειν, καθάπερ εἶχον καὶ πρότερον, ἐν τῇ συμ-
10 πολιτείᾳ. Κόρινθον δὲ καὶ τὴν Τριφυλίαν καὶ <τὴν
Ἡραιῶν πόλιν Ἀχαιοῖς ἀπέδωκαν. Ὠρεὸν δ᾽>, ἔτι δὲ
τὴν Ἐρετριέων πόλιν ἐδόκει μὲν τοῖς πλείοσιν Εὐμένει
11 δοῦναι· Τίτου δὲ πρὸς τὸ συνέδριον διαστείλαντος

---

144 A tribe of disputed ethnicity, living in the Orestis, the valley of the Haliacmon (Vistritza), at the border between Macedo-

Europe with an army, for none of the Greeks were any longer being attacked by anyone or the subjects of anyone, and they announced in general terms that some of their own body would come to see Antiochus. Hegesianax and Lysias returned on receiving this answer, and after them the commissioners called before them all the representatives of different nations and cities, and explained to them the decisions of the board. As for Macedonia they gave autonomy to the tribe called Orestae[144] for having joined them during the war, and freed the Perrhaebians, Dolopes, and Magnesians.[145] Besides giving the Thessalians their freedom they assigned to Thessaly the Phthiotic Achaeans, taking away Phthiotic Thebes and Pharsalus; for the Aetolians were claiming Pharsalus with great vehemence, saying that it ought to be theirs according to the terms of the original treaty, and Leucas[146] as well. The members of the board deferred their decision until the Aetolians could lay the matter before the senate, but allowed them to include the Phocians and Locrians[147] in their League, as had formerly been the case. They gave Corinth, Triphylia, and Heraea[148] to the Achaeans, and most members were in favor of giving Oreus and Eretria[149] to Eumenes. But Flamininus having addressed the board

nia and Illyria. *RE* Orestis 960–965 (J. Schmidt). They had joined the Romans in 199 (Livy 31.40.3).

145 Thessalian *perioeci* or (the Dolopes) a Thessalian tribe. See Stählin, (3.12), 5–39 (Perrhaebia), 145–150 (Dolopia), 39–78 (Magnesia).   146 See n. on 5.5.12.

147 See n. on 10.4.

148 See 42.7.

149 See 47.5.

οὐκ ἐκυρώθη τὸ διαβούλιον· διὸ καὶ μετά τινα χρόνον
ἠλευθερώθησαν αἱ πόλεις αὗται διὰ τῆς συγκλήτου
12 καὶ σὺν ταύταις Κάρυστος. ἔδωκαν δὲ καὶ Πλευράτῳ
Λυχνίδα καὶ Πάρθον, οὔσας μὲν Ἰλλυρίδας, ὑπὸ Φί-
13 λιππον δὲ ταττομένας. Ἀμυνάνδρῳ δὲ συνεχώρησαν,
ὅσα παρεσπάσατο κατὰ πόλεμον ἐρύματα τοῦ Φιλίππου, κρατεῖν τούτων.

(31)   48. Ταῦτα δὲ διοικήσαντες ἐμέρισαν σφᾶς αὐτούς,
2 καὶ Πόπλιος μὲν Λέντλος εἰς Βαργύλια πλεύσας
ἠλευθέρωσε τούτους, Λεύκιος δὲ Στερτίνιος εἰς Ἡφαι-
στίαν καὶ Θάσον ἀφικόμενος καὶ τὰς ἐπὶ Θρᾴκης πό-
3 λεις ἐποίησε τὸ παραπλήσιον. πρὸς δὲ τὸν Ἀντίοχον
ὥρμησαν Πόπλιος Οὐίλλιος καὶ Λεύκιος Τερέντιος, οἱ
δὲ περὶ Γνάιον τὸν Κορνήλιον πρὸς τὸν βασιλέα Φί-
4 λιππον. ᾧ καὶ συμμίξαντες πρὸς τοῖς Τέμπεσι περί τε
τῶν ἄλλων διελέχθησαν ὑπὲρ ὧν εἶχον τὰς ἐντολάς,
καὶ συνεβούλευον αὐτῷ πρεσβευτὰς πέμπειν εἰς τὴν
Ῥώμην ὑπὲρ συμμαχίας, ἵνα μὴ δοκῇ τοῖς καιροῖς
ἐφεδρεύων ἀποκαραδοκεῖν τὴν Ἀντιόχου παρουσίαν.
5 τοῦ δὲ βασιλέως συγκαταθεμένου τοῖς ὑποδεικνυμένοις,
εὐθέως ἀπ᾽ ἐκείνου χωρισθέντες ἧκον ἐπὶ τὴν τῶν
6 Θερμικῶν σύνοδον, καὶ παρελθόντες εἰς τὰ πλήθη παρεκάλουν τοὺς Αἰτωλοὺς διὰ πλειόνων μένειν ἐπὶ τῆς

---

150 The southernmost city of Euboea.   151 10.41.4.

152 Lychnis is modern Ohrid at Lake Ohrid; Parthus is not
securely identified.   153 See n. on 4.16.1. Last mentioned
16.27.4 and 18.1.3. Among his recent acquisitions was the Thessalian city of Gomphi: Stählin (3.12), 125.

on that subject, the proposal was not ratified, so that after a short time these towns were set free by the senate as well as Carystus.[150] To Pleuratus[151] they gave Lychnis and Parthus,[152] which were Illyrian but subject to Philip, and they allowed Amynander[153] all the forts he had wrested from Philip in war.

48. After making these arrangements they separated. Publius Lentulus sailed to Bargylia and set it free, and Lucius Stertinius proceeded to Hephaestia,[154] Thasos and the Thracian cities[155] for the same purpose. Publius Villius[156] and Lucius Terentius[157] went to King Antiochus and Gnaeus Cornelius[158] to King Philip. Encountering him near Tempe he conveyed his other instructions to him and advised him to send an embassy to Rome to ask for an alliance, that they might not think he was watching for his opportunity and looking forward to the arrival of Antiochus. Upon the king's accepting this suggestion, Lentulus at once took leave of him and proceeded to Thermum,[159] where the general assembly of the Aetolians was in session. Appearing before the people he exhorted them, speaking at some length, to maintain their original atti-

---

[154] On Lemnus, the other town besides Myrina (44.4). A letter of Philip to Hephaestia: *Riv. Fil.*, n. s. 19 (1941), 179–193.

[155] Aenus and Maroneia, taken from Ptolemy in 200 (Livy 31.16.4).

[156] Publius Villius Tappulus, consul 199. *RE* Villius 2166–2177 (H. Gundel).

[157] Lucius Terentius Massaliota, a fairly young man who had a modest career. *RE* Terentius 665–666 (F. Münzer).

[158] Gnaeus Cornelius Lentulus, consul 201. *RE* Cornelius 1358–1361 (F. Münzer).

[159] See n. on 5.6.6.

ἐξ ἀρχῆς αἱρέσεως καὶ διαφυλάττειν τὴν πρὸς Ῥω-
7 μαίους εὔνοιαν. πολλῶν δὲ παρισταμένων, καὶ τῶν μὲν
πρᾴως καὶ πολιτικῶς μεμψιμοιρούντων αὐτοῖς ἐπὶ τῷ
μὴ κοινωνικῶς χρῆσθαι τοῖς εὐτυχήμασι μηδὲ τηρεῖν
8 τὰς ἐξ ἀρχῆς συνθήκας, τῶν δὲ λοιδορούντων καὶ φασκόντων οὔτ᾽ ἂν ἐπιβῆναι τῆς Ἑλλάδος οὐδέποτε
9 Ῥωμαίους οὔτ᾽ ἂν νικῆσαι Φίλιππον, εἰ μὴ δι᾽ ἑαυτούς,
τὸ μὲν ἀπολογεῖσθαι πρὸς ἕκαστα τούτων οἱ περὶ τὸν
Γνάιον ἀπεδοκίμασαν, παρεκάλουν δ᾽ αὐτοὺς πρεσβεύειν εἰς τὴν Ῥώμην, διότι πάντων παρὰ τῆς συγκλήτου
10 τεύξονται τῶν δικαίων· ὃ καὶ πεισθέντες ἐποίησαν. καὶ
τὸ μὲν τέλος τοῦ πρὸς Φίλιππον ⟨πολέμου⟩ τοιαύτην
ἔσχε διάθεσιν.

V. RES ASIAE

49. Ἐάν, τὸ δὴ λεγόμενον, τρέχωσι τὴν ἐσχάτην,
(35 6) ἐπὶ τοὺς Ῥωμαίους καταφεύξονται καὶ τούτοις ἐγχει-
ριοῦσι σφᾶς αὐτοὺς καὶ τὴν πόλιν.
(32 3) 2 Ὅτι προχωρούσης τῷ Ἀντιόχῳ κατὰ νοῦν τῆς ἐπιβολῆς παρόντι ἐν Θρᾴκῃ τῷ Ἀντιόχῳ κατέπλευσαν
3 (4) εἰς Σηλυβρίαν οἱ περὶ Λεύκιον Κορνήλιον. οὗτοι δ᾽
ἦσαν παρὰ τῆς συγκλήτου πρέσβεις ἐπὶ τὰς διαλύσεις ἐξαπεσταλμένοι

---

160 Of 212 or 211. See 38.7 and 47.8.

161 Perhaps the citizens of Lampsacus, pressed by Antiochus,
but this is uncertain.

tude and keep up their friendliness to Rome. Upon many speakers presenting themselves, some gently and diplomatically rebuking the Romans for not having used their success in a spirit of partnership or observed the terms of the original treaty,[160] while others spoke abusively saying that the Romans could never have landed in Greece or conquered Philip except through the Aetolians, he refrained from replying to these different accusations, but begged them to send an embassy, as they would obtain complete justice from the senate. This he persuaded them to do. Such was the situation at the end of the war against Philip.

V. AFFAIRS OF ASIA

49. If, as the phrase is, they are[161] at their last gasp, they will take refuge with the Romans and put themselves and the city in their hands.

196 B.C.

Antiochus and the Roman Envoys

Antiochus' project was going on as well as he could wish, and while he was in Thrace, Lucius Cornelius arrived by sea at Selymbria.[162] He was the ambassador sent by the Senate to establish peace between Antiochus and Ptolemy.

[162] City on the north shore of the Propontis, between Perinthus and Byzantium. *RE* Sely(m)bria 1324–1327 (E. Oberhummer).

(33)   50. τὰς Ἀντιόχου καὶ Πτολεμαίου. κατὰ δὲ τὸν αὐτὸν καιρὸν ἦκον καὶ τῶν δέκα Πόπλιος μὲν Λέντλος
2 ἐκ Βαργυλίων, Λεύκιος δὲ Τερέντιος καὶ Πόπλιος Οὐ-
3 ίλλιος ἐκ Θάσου. ταχὺ δὲ τῷ βασιλεῖ διασαφηθείσης
τῆς τούτων παρουσίας, πάντες ἐν ὀλίγαις ἡμέραις
ἠθροίσθησαν εἰς τὴν Λυσιμάχειαν. συνεκύρησαν δὲ
4 καὶ οἱ περὶ τὸν Ἡγησιάνακτα καὶ Λυσίαν οἱ πρὸς τὸν
Τίτον ἀποσταλέντες εἰς τὸν καιρὸν τοῦτον. αἱ μὲν οὖν
κατ' ἰδίαν ἐντεύξεις τοῦ τε βασιλέως καὶ τῶν Ῥωμαίων
5 τελέως ἦσαν ἀφελεῖς καὶ φιλάνθρωποι· μετὰ δὲ ταῦτα
γενομένης συνεδρείας κοινῆς ὑπὲρ τῶν ὅλων ἀλλοι-
οτέραν ἔλαβε τὰ πράγματα διάθεσιν. ὁ γὰρ Λεύκιος
ὁ Κορνήλιος ἠξίου μὲν καὶ τῶν ὑπὸ Πτολεμαῖον τατ-
6 τομένων πόλεων, ὅσας νῦν εἴληφε κατὰ τὴν Ἀσίαν,
παραχωρεῖν τὸν Ἀντίοχον, τῶν δ' ὑπὸ Φίλιππον διε-
μαρτύρετο φιλοτίμως ἐξίστασθαι· γελοῖον γὰρ εἶναι
τὰ Ῥωμαίων ἆθλα τοῦ γεγονότος αὐτοῖς πολέμου
πρὸς Φίλιππον Ἀντίοχον ἐπελθόντα παραλαμβάνειν.
7 παρῄνει δὲ καὶ τῶν αὐτονόμων ἀπέχεσθαι πόλεων.
8 καθόλου δ' ἔφη θαυμάζειν τίνι λόγῳ τοσαύταις μὲν
πεζικαῖς, τοσαύταις δὲ ναυτικαῖς δυνάμεσι πεποίηται
9 τὴν εἰς τὴν Εὐρώπην διάβασιν· πλὴν γὰρ τοῦ προτί-
θεσθαι Ῥωμαίοις ἐγχειεῖν αὐτόν, οὐδ' ἔννοιαν ἑτέραν
καταλείπεσθαι παρὰ τοῖς ὀρθῶς λογιζομένοις. οἱ μὲν
οὖν Ῥωμαῖοι ταῦτ' εἰπόντες ἀπεσιώπησαν·

(34)   51. ὁ δὲ βασιλεὺς πρῶτον μὲν διαπορεῖν ἔφη κατὰ
τίνα λόγον ἀμφισβητοῦσι πρὸς αὐτὸν ὑπὲρ τῶν ἐπὶ
τῆς Ἀσίας πόλεων· πᾶσι γὰρ μᾶλλον ἐπιβάλλειν

50. At the same time arrived three of the ten commissioners, Publius Lentulus[163] from Bargylia and Lucius Terentius and Publius Villius from Thasos. Their arrival was at once reported to the king and a few days afterward they all assembled at Lysimachia.[164] Hegesianax and Lysias, the envoys who had been sent to Flamininus, arrived there at the same time. In the unofficial interviews of the king and the Romans the conversation was simple and friendly, but afterward when an official conference about the situation in general was held, things assumed another aspect. For Lucius Cornelius asked Antiochus to retire from the cities previously subject to Ptolemy which he had taken possession of in Asia, while as to those previously subject to Philip he demanded with urgency that he should evacuate them. For it was a ridiculous thing, he said, that Antiochus should come in when all was over and take the prizes they had gained in their war with Philip. He also advised him to keep his hands off the autonomous cities. And generally speaking he said he wondered on what pretext the king had crossed to Europe with such large military and naval forces. For anyone who judged correctly could not suppose that the reason was any other than that he was proposing to attack the Romans. The Roman envoy having concluded his speech thus,

51. the king replied that in the first place he was at a loss to know by what right they disputed his possession of the Asiatic towns; they were the last people who had any

163 *RE* Cornelius 1379–1380 (F. Münzer).
164 See n. on 15.23.8.

THE HISTORIES OF POLYBIUS

2 τοῦτο ποιεῖν ἢ Ῥωμαίοις. δεύτερον δ᾽ ἠξίου μηδὲν
αὐτοὺς πολυπραγμονεῖν καθόλου τῶν κατὰ τὴν Ἀσίαν·
οὐδὲ γὰρ αὐτὸς περιεργάζεσθαι τῶν κατὰ τὴν Ἰταλίαν

3 ἁπλῶς οὐδέν. εἰς δὲ τὴν Εὐρώπην ἔφη διαβεβηκέναι
μετὰ τῶν δυνάμεων ἀνακτησόμενος τὰ κατὰ τὴν Χερρόνησον καὶ τὰς ἐπὶ Θρᾴκης πόλεις· τὴν γὰρ τῶν
τόπων τούτων ἀρχὴν μάλιστα πάντων αὐτῷ καθήκειν.

4 εἶναι μὲν γὰρ ἐξ ἀρχῆς τὴν δυναστείαν ταύτην Λυσιμάχου. Σελεύκου δὲ πολεμήσαντος πρὸς αὐτὸν καὶ
κρατήσαντος τῷ πολέμῳ πᾶσαν τὴν Λυσιμάχου βα-

5 σιλείαν δορίκτητον γενέσθαι Σελεύκου. κατὰ δὲ τοὺς
τῶν αὐτοῦ προγόνων περισπασμοὺς ἐν τοῖς ἑξῆς χρόνοις πρῶτον μὲν Πτολεμαῖον παρασπασάμενον σφε-
τερίσασθαι τοὺς τόπους τούτους, δεύτερον δὲ Φίλιπ-

6 πον. αὐτὸς δὲ νῦν οὐ κτᾶσθαι τοῖς Φιλίππου καιροῖς
συνεπιτιθέμενος, ἀλλ᾽ ἀνακτᾶσθαι τοῖς ἰδίοις δικαίοις

7 συγχρώμενος. Λυσιμαχεῖς δέ, παραλόγως ἀναστάτους
γεγονότας ὑπὸ Θρᾳκῶν, οὐκ ἀδικεῖν Ῥωμαίους κατά-

8 γων καὶ συνοικίζων· ποιεῖν γὰρ τοῦτ᾽ ἔφη βουλόμενος
οὐ Ῥωμαίοις τὰς χεῖρας ἐπιβαλεῖν, Σελεύκῳ δ᾽ οἰκη-

9 τήριον ἑτοιμάζειν. τὰς δ᾽ αὐτονόμους τῶν κατὰ τὴν
Ἀσίαν πόλεων οὐ διὰ τῆς Ῥωμαίων ἐπιταγῆς δέον
εἶναι τυγχάνειν τῆς ἐλευθερίας, ἀλλὰ διὰ τῆς αὐτοῦ

10 χάριτος. τὰ δὲ πρὸς Πτολεμαῖον αὐτὸς ἔφη διεξάξειν
εὐδοκουμένως ἐκείνῳ· κρίνειν γὰρ οὐ φιλίαν μόνον,

---

165 In 281, after the battle at Corupedium.

228

title to do so. Next he requested them not to trouble themselves at all about Asiatic affairs; for he himself did not in the least go out of his way to concern himself with the affairs of Italy. He said that he had crossed to Europe with his army for the purpose of recovering the Chersonese and the cities in Thrace, for he had a better title to the sovereignty of these places than anyone else. They originally formed part of Lysimachus' kingdom, but when Seleucus went to war with that prince and conquered him in the war, the whole of Lysimachus' kingdom came to Seleucus by right of conquest.[165] But during the years that followed, when his ancestors had their attention deflected elsewhere, first of all Ptolemy and then Philip had robbed them of those places and appropriated them. At present he was not possessing himself of them by taking advantage of Philip's difficulties, but he was repossessing himself of them by his right as well as by his might. As for the Lysimachians, who had been unexpectedly expelled from their homes by the Thracians, he was doing no injury to Rome in bringing them back and resettling them; for he did this not with the intention of doing violence to the Romans, but of providing a residence for Seleucus.[166] And regarding the autonomous cities of Asia it was not proper for them to receive their liberty by order of the Romans, but by his own act of grace. As for his relations with Ptolemy, he would himself settle everything in a manner agreeable to that king, for he had decided not only to establish

[166] The second of Antiochus' sons. After the death of the elder brother, Antiochus, in 193, he became the heir and followed his father on the throne in 187. He was installed by him as governor for the European possessions.

229

ἀλλὰ καὶ μετὰ τῆς φιλίας ἀναγκαιότητα συντίθεσθαι
πρὸς αὐτόν.

52. Τῶν δὲ περὶ τὸν Λεύκιον οἰομένων δεῖν καλεῖσθαι
(35) τοὺς Λαμψακηνοὺς καὶ τοὺς Σμυρναίους καὶ δοῦναι
2 λόγον αὐτοῖς, ἐγένετο τοῦτο. παρῆσαν δὲ παρὰ μὲν
Λαμψακηνῶν οἱ περὶ Παρμενίωνα καὶ Πυθόδωρον,
3 παρὰ δὲ Σμυρναίων οἱ περὶ Κοίρανον. ὧν μετὰ παρρησίας διαλεγομένων, δυσχεράνας ὁ βασιλεὺς ἐπὶ τῷ
δοκεῖν λόγον ὑπέχειν ἐπὶ Ῥωμαίων τοῖς πρὸς αὐτὸν
ἀμφισβητοῦσι, μεσολαβήσας τὸν Παρμενίωνα "παῦ-
4 σαι" φησὶ "τῶν πολλῶν· οὐ γὰρ ἐπὶ Ῥωμαίων, ἀλλ'
ἐπὶ Ῥοδίων ὑμῖν εὐδοκῶ διακριθῆναι περὶ τῶν ἀντι-
5 λεγομένων." καὶ τότε μὲν ἐπὶ τούτοις διέλυσαν τὸν
σύλλογον, οὐδαμῶς εὐδοκήσαντες ἀλλήλοις.

VI. RES AEGYPTI

(36) 53. Τῶν γὰρ παραβόλων καὶ καλῶν ἔργων ἐφίενται
2 μὲν πολλοί, τολμῶσι δ' ὀλίγοι ψαύειν. καίτοι πολὺ
καλλίους ἀφορμὰς εἶχε Σκόπας Κλεομένους πρὸς τὸ
3 παραβάλλεσθαι καὶ τολμᾶν. ἐκεῖνος μὲν γὰρ προκατα-
ληφθεὶς εἰς αὐτὰς συνεκλείσθη τὰς ἐν τοῖς ἰδίοις οἰ-
κέταις καὶ φίλοις ἐλπίδας· ἀλλ' ὅμως οὐδὲ ταύτας
ἐγκατέλιπεν, ἀλλ' ἐφ' ὅσον ἦν δυνατὸς ἐξήλεγξε, τὸ

---

167 He had just betrothed his daughter Cleopatra to King
Ptolemy V. The marriage followed in 194/3.
168 See n. on 47.1.
169 Probably none other than Pythodorus, son of Metrotimus,

friendship with him but to unite him to himself by a family alliance.[167]

52. Upon Lucius and his colleagues deciding to summon the representatives of Smyrna and Lampsacus[168] and give them a hearing, this was done. The Lampsacenes sent Parmenion and Pythodorus[169] and the Smyrnaeans Coeranus. When these envoys spoke with some freedom, the king, taking it amiss that he should seem to be submitting their dispute against him to a Roman tribunal, interrupted Parmenion, saying, "Enough of that long harangue: for it is my pleasure that our differences should be submitted to the Rhodians and not to the Romans." Hereupon they broke up the conference, by no means pleased with each other.

VI. AFFAIRS OF EGYPT

Scopas and Other Aetolians at Alexandria

53. There are many who crave after deeds of daring and renown, but few venture to set their hand to them. And yet Scopas[170] had better resources at his command for facing peril and acting boldly than Cleomenes.[171] For the latter, anticipated in his design, could hope for no support except from his own servants and friends, but yet instead of abandoning this slender hope, put it as far as it was in

196 B.C.

of Lampsacus, gymnasiarch ca. 200 at the festival for Athena Ilias, in a recently found decree (*SEG* 53.1373, line 60).

170 The Aetolian commander of the Ptolemaic army, defeated by Antiochus at Panium (16.18.2).

171 P. refers to his revolt and death, 5.33–39.

καλῶς ἀποθανεῖν τοῦ ζῆν αἰσχρῶς περὶ πλείονος ποι-
4 ησάμενος. Σκόπας δέ, καὶ χεῖρα βαρεῖαν ἔχων συνεργὸν καὶ καιρόν, ἅτε τοῦ βασιλέως ἔτι παιδὸς ὄντος,
5 μέλλων καὶ βουλευόμενος προκατελήφθη. γνόντες
γὰρ αὐτὸν οἱ περὶ τὸν Ἀριστομένην συναθροίζοντα
τοὺς φίλους εἰς τὴν ἰδίαν οἰκίαν καὶ συνεδρεύοντα
μετὰ τούτων, πέμψαντές τινας τῶν ὑπασπιστῶν ἐκά-
6 λουν εἰς τὸ συνέδριον. ὁ δ' οὕτω παρειστήκει τῶν
φρενῶν ὡς οὔτε πράττειν ἐτόλμα τῶν ἑξῆς οὐδὲν οὔτε
καλούμενος ὑπὸ τοῦ βασιλέως οἷός τ' ἦν πειθαρχεῖν,
7 ὃ πάντων ἐστὶν ἔσχατον, ἕως οἱ περὶ τὸν Ἀριστομένην
γνόντες αὐτοῦ τὴν ἀλογίαν τοὺς μὲν στρατιώτας καὶ
8 τὰ θηρία περιέστησαν περὶ τὴν οἰκίαν, Πτολεμαῖον δὲ
τὸν Εὐμένους πέμψαντες μετὰ νεανίσκων ἄγειν αὐτὸν
ἐκέλευον, ἐὰν μὲν ἑκὼν βούληται πειθαρχεῖν· εἰ δὲ μή,
9 μετὰ βίας. τοῦ δὲ Πτολεμαίου παρεισελθόντος εἰς τὴν
οἰκίαν καὶ δηλοῦντος ὅτι καλεῖ Σκόπαν ὁ βασιλεύς,
τὰς μὲν ἀρχὰς οὐ προσεῖχε τοῖς λεγομένοις, ἀλλὰ καὶ
βλέπων εἰς τὸν Πτολεμαῖον ἀτενὲς ἔμενε καὶ πλείω
χρόνον ὡς ἂν εἰ προσανατεινόμενος αὐτῷ καὶ θαυμά-
10 ζων τὴν τόλμαν. ὡς δ' ἐπελθὼν ὁ Πτολεμαῖος θρασέως ἐπελάβετο τῆς χλαμύδος αὐτοῦ, τότε βοηθεῖν
11 ἠξίου τοὺς παρόντας. ὄντων δὲ καὶ τῶν εἰσελθόντων
νεανίσκων πλειόνων καὶ τὴν ἔξω περίστασιν διασα-
φήσαντός τινος, συνείξας τοῖς παροῦσιν ἠκολούθει
μετὰ τῶν φίλων.

54. Ἅμα δὲ τῷ παρελθεῖν εἰς τὸ συνέδριον βραχέα
(37) μὲν ὁ βασιλεὺς κατηγόρησε, μετὰ δὲ τοῦτον Πολυ-

his power to the touch, valuing more highly a glorious death than a life of ignominy. Scopas, on the contrary, while he had a numerous band of supporters and a fine opportunity, as the king was still a child, was forestalled while still deferring and planning. For Aristomenes,[172] having discovered that he used to collect his friends in his own house and hold conferences there with them, sent some officers to summon him before the royal council. But he had so far lost his head that he neither dared to carry on his project, nor, worst of all, even felt himself capable of obeying when summoned by the king, until Aristomenes recognizing his confusion surrounded his house with soldiers and elephants. They then sent Ptolemy, the son of Eumenes, with some soldiers with orders to bring him, if he were willing to obey so much the better, but if not by force. When Ptolemy made his way into the house and announced that the king summoned Scopas, at first he paid no attention to what was said, but simply stared at Ptolemy for a considerable time, as if inclined to threaten him and astonished at his audacity. But when Ptolemy came up to him and boldly took hold of his cloak, he then called on those present to assist him. But as the number of soldiers who had entered the house was considerable, and as some one informed him that it was surrounded outside, he yielded to circumstances and followed Ptolemy accompanied by his friends.

54. When he entered the council chamber, the king first accused him in a few words and was followed by Poly-

172 The Acarnanian chancellor, successor to Tlepolemus. See n. on 15.31.6 and 7. He and Scopas had fought against each other in the Social War some twenty years earlier.

κράτης, ἄρτι παραγεγονὼς ἀπὸ Κύπρου, τελευταῖος δ'

2 Ἀριστομένης. ἦν δὲ τὰ μὲν ἄλλα παραπλήσιος ἡ κατηγορία πάντων τοῖς ἄρτι ῥηθεῖσι, προσετέθη δὲ τοῖς προειρημένοις ἡ μετὰ τῶν φίλων συνεδρεία καὶ τὸ μὴ

3 πειθαρχῆσαι καλούμενον ὑπὸ τοῦ βασιλέως. ἐφ' οἷς οὐ μόνον οἱ τοῦ συνεδρίου κατεγίγνωσκον αὐτοῦ πάντες, ἀλλὰ καὶ τῶν ἔξωθεν τῶν πρεσβευτῶν οἱ συμπαρ-

4 όντες. ὁ δ' Ἀριστομένης, ὅτε κατηγορεῖν ἔμελλε, πολλοὺς μὲν καὶ ἑτέρους παρέλαβε τῶν ἐπιφανῶν ἀνδρῶν ἀπὸ τῆς Ἑλλάδος, καὶ τοὺς παρὰ τῶν Αἰτωλῶν δὲ πρεσβεύοντας ἐπὶ τὰς διαλύσεις, ἐν οἷς ἦν καὶ Δωρί-

5 μαχος ὁ Νικοστράτου. ῥηθέντων δὲ τούτων μεταλαβὼν ὁ Σκόπας ἐπειρᾶτο μὲν φέρειν τινὰς ἀπολογισμούς, οὐδενὸς δὲ προσέχοντος αὐτῷ διὰ τὴν τῶν πραγμάτων ἀλογίαν, εὐθέως οὗτος μὲν εἰς φυλακὴν ἀπήγετο

6 μετὰ τῶν φίλων· ὁ δ' Ἀριστομένης ἐπιγενομένης τῆς νυκτὸς τὸν μὲν Σκόπαν καὶ τοὺς συγγενεῖς αὐτοῦ καὶ

7 φίλους πάντας διέφθειρε φαρμάκῳ, Δικαιάρχῳ δὲ καὶ στρέβλας καὶ μάστιγας προσαγαγὼν οὕτως αὐτὸν ἐπανείλετο, λαβὼν παρ' αὐτοῦ δίκην καθήκουσαν καὶ

8 κοινὴν ὑπὲρ πάντων τῶν Ἑλλήνων. ὁ γὰρ Δικαίαρχος οὗτος ἦν, ὃν Φίλιππος, ὅτε προέθετο παρασπονδεῖν τὰς Κυκλάδας νήσους καὶ τὰς ἐφ' Ἑλλησπόντου πόλεις, ἀπέδειξε τοῦ στόλου παντὸς ἡγεμόνα καὶ τῆς

9 ὅλης πράξεως προστάτην. ὃς ἐπὶ πρόδηλον ἀσέβειαν ἐκπεμπόμενος οὐχ οἷον ἄτοπόν τι πράττειν ἐνόμιζεν, ἀλλὰ τῇ τῆς ἀπονοίας ὑπερβολῇ καὶ τοὺς θεοὺς

crates[173] who had lately arrived from Cyprus, and last by Aristomenes. The accusations brought by all were similar to those I have just stated,[174] but in addition they mentioned his conferences with his friends and his refusal to obey the royal summons. He was condemned for these various reasons not only by the council but by those foreign ambassadors who were present. Aristomenes also, when about to impeach him, brought with him besides many other men of distinction from Greece, the Aetolian envoys also who had come to make peace,[175] one of whom was Dorimachus,[176] son of Nicostratus. The speeches of the accusers over, Scopas, speaking in his turn, attempted to offer some defense, but as no one paid any heed to him owing to the confusion of the circumstances he was at once led off to prison with his friends. Aristomenes after nightfall killed Scopas and all his friends by poison, but before killing Dicaearchus[177] he had him racked and scourged, thus punishing him as he deserved and on behalf of all the Greeks. For this Dicaearchus was the man whom Philip appointed to take command of all his fleet and direct the whole operation, when he decided on treacherously attacking the Cyclades and the cities on the Hellespont. Being thus sent forth on an evidently impious mission, he not only did not consider himself to be guilty of any exceptional wickedness, but by the excess of his

---

[173] Of Argos, one of the generals at the battle of Raphia in 217, later governor of Cyprus. See n. on 5.64.4.   [174] In a lost passage.   [175] Between Antiochus and Ptolemy.

[176] Once allied with Scopas in their Aetolian homeland; 13.1.1–3 and 1a.   [177] The Aetolian once used by Philip V against Rhodes (Holleaux, *Ét.* 4.124–145). See also n. on 13.4.1.

10 ὑπέλαβε καταπλήξεσθαι καὶ τοὺς ἀνθρώπους· οὗ γὰρ
   ὁρμίσειε τὰς ναῦς, δύο κατεσκεύαζε βωμούς, τὸν μὲν
   Ἀσεβείας, τὸν δὲ Παρανομίας, καὶ ἐπὶ τούτοις ἔθυε
11 καὶ τούτους προσεκύνει καθάπερ ἂν εἰ δαίμονας. διὸ
   καὶ δοκεῖ μοι τυχεῖν τῆς ἁρμοζούσης δίκης καὶ παρὰ
   θεῶν καὶ <παρ'> ἀνθρώπων· παρὰ φύσιν γὰρ ἐνστη-
   σάμενος τὸν αὑτοῦ βίον εἰκότως παρὰ φύσιν καὶ τῆς
12 εἱμαρμένης ἔτυχε. τῶν δὲ λοιπῶν Αἰτωλῶν τοὺς βου-
   λομένους εἰς τὴν οἰκείαν ἀπαλλάττεσθαι πάντας ἀπ-
   έλυσεν ὁ βασιλεὺς μετὰ τῶν ὑπαρχόντων.

   55. Σκόπα δὲ καὶ ζῶντος μὲν ἐπίσημος ἦν ἡ φιλαρ-
(38) γυρία—πολὺ γὰρ δή τι τοὺς ἄλλους ἀνθρώπους ὑπερέθετο κατὰ τὴν πλεονεξίαν—ἀποθανόντος δὲ καὶ μᾶλλον ἐγενήθη διὰ τοῦ πλήθους τοῦ χρυσίου καὶ τῆς
2 κατασκευῆς τῆς εὑρημένης παρ' αὐτῷ. λαβὼν γὰρ
   συνεργὸν τὴν ἀγριότητα τὴν Χαριμόρτου καὶ τὴν μέ-
   θην, ἄρδην ἐξετοιχωρύχησε τὴν βασιλείαν.
3 Ἐπειδὴ δὲ τὰ κατὰ τοὺς Αἰτωλοὺς ἔθεντο καλῶς οἱ
   περὶ τὴν αὐλήν, εὐθέως ἐγίνοντο περὶ τὸ ποιεῖν Ἀνα-
   κλητήρια τοῦ βασιλέως, οὐδέπω μὲν τῆς ἡλικίας κατ-
   επειγούσης, νομίζοντες δὲ λήψεσθαί τινα τὰ πράγματα κατάστασιν καὶ πάλιν ἀρχὴν τῆς ἐπὶ τὸ
   βέλτιον προκοπῆς, δόξαντος αὐτοκράτορος ἤδη γεγο-
4 νέναι τοῦ βασιλέως. χρησάμενοι δὲ ταῖς παρασκευαῖς
   μεγαλομερῶς, ἐπετέλουν τὴν πρᾶξιν ἀξίως τοῦ τῆς

---

178 PP 4428. He was strategus of Ptolemy IV for the hunting
of elephants (OGI 86) and is also mentioned by Str. 16.4.15. Usu-

insolence thought to terrify both gods and men: for wherever he anchored his ships he constructed two altars, one of Impiety and the other of Lawlessness, and on these he sacrificed and worshipped these powers as if they were divine. He therefore must be pronounced to have suffered the punishment he deserved at the hands of gods and men alike; for having regulated his life by unnatural principles he met likewise with no natural death. The other Aetolians who wished to leave for home, were all allowed by the king to depart with their property.

55. The avarice of Scopas had been notorious even when he was alive—for his rapacity much excelled that of any other man—but by his death it became more so owing to the quantity of money and precious objects found in his house. For, aided by the savagery and drunken violence of Charimortus[178] he had utterly stripped the palace like a burglar.

After the officials of the court had set to rights the matter of the Aetolians, they at once began to occupy themselves with the celebration of the king's Proclamation (Anacleteria).[179] Although his age was not such as to make it pressing, they thought that it would contribute to the settlement of affairs and be the beginning of a change for the better if the king were thought to be now invested with full authority. Having made preparations on a generous scale they carried out the ceremony in a manner worthy

ally taken to be Aetolian, but the name occurs so far only in Lato: *IC* 1.143, no. 34, line 6. See also L. Casson, "Ptolemy II and the Hunting of African Elephants," *TAPA* 123 (1993) 247–260.

[179] In the winter of 197/6. Huss (16.18.2), 504. The king was thirteen years old at the time.

βασιλείας προσχήματος, πλεῖστα Πολυκράτους δοκοῦντος εἰς τὴν ἐπιβολὴν ταύτην αὐτοῖς συνηργηκέ-
5 ναι. ὁ γὰρ προειρημένος ἀνὴρ καὶ κατὰ τὸν πατέρα
μὲν ἔτι νέος ὢν οὐδενὸς ἐδόκει τῶν περὶ τὴν αὐλὴν
δευτερεύειν οὔτε κατὰ τὴν πίστιν οὔτε κατὰ τὰς πρά-
6 ξεις, ὁμοίως δὲ κατὰ τὸν ἐνεστῶτα βασιλέα. πιστευθεὶς
γὰρ τῆς Κύπρου καὶ τῶν ἐν ταύτῃ προσόδων ἐν καιροῖς ἐπισφαλέσι καὶ ποικίλοις, οὐ μόνον διεφύλαξε
τῷ παιδὶ τὴν νῆσον, ἀλλὰ καὶ πλῆθος ἱκανὸν ἤθροισε
χρημάτων, ἃ τότε παραγεγόνει κομίζων τῷ βασιλεῖ,
παραδεδωκὼς τὴν ἀρχὴν τῆς Κύπρου Πτολεμαίῳ τῷ
7 Μεγαλοπολίτῃ. τυχὼν δὲ διὰ ταῦτα μεγάλης ἀποδοχῆς
καὶ περιουσίας ἐν τοῖς ἑξῆς χρόνοις, μετὰ ταῦτα προβαινούσης τῆς ἡλικίας ὁλοσχερῶς εἰς ἀσέλγειαν ἐξ-
8 ώκειλε καὶ βίον ἀσυρῆ. παραπλησίαν δέ τινα τούτῳ
φήμην ἐκληρονόμησεν ἐπὶ γήρως καὶ Πτολεμαῖος ὁ
9 Ἀγησάρχου. περὶ ὧν, ὅταν ἐπὶ τοὺς καιροὺς ἔλθωμεν,
οὐκ ὀκνήσομεν διασαφεῖν τὰ παρακολουθήσαντα ταῖς
ἐξουσίαις αὐτῶν ἀπρεπῆ.

of the dignity of the realm, Polycrates, as it appears, having taken the greatest share in furthering this scheme of theirs. This man had while still young, during the reign of the king's father, been considered second to none at court in loyalty and energy, and so he continued to be under the present king. For, being entrusted with the government of Cyprus and its revenue in hazardous and complicated circumstances, he had not only preserved the island for the boy but had collected a considerable sum of money, and had now come to Alexandria to bring this money to the king, having handed over the government of Cyprus to Ptolemaeus of Megalopolis.[180] Having, owing to this, been very well received and having amassed a large fortune in the years which followed, he afterward, as he grew older, entirely wrecked his good name by the licentiousness and depravity of his life. A very similar reputation was acquired in his old age by Ptolemy, son of Agesarchus. When I reach that period I will have no hesitation[181] in exposing the disgraceful circumstances attendant on their power.

[180] Ptolemy, son of Agesarchus. See n. on 15.25.14.
[181] The passage has been lost.

FRAGMENTA LIBRI XIX

1. Πολύβιος μέν γέ φησι τῶν ἐντὸς Βαίτιος ποταμοῦ πόλεων ἡμέρᾳ μιᾷ τὰ τείχη κελεύσαντος αὐτοῦ περιαιρεθῆναι· πάμπολλαι δ᾽ ἦσαν αὗται καὶ γέμουσαι μαχίμων ἀνδρῶν.

2. Ingens numerus erat bello Punico captorum, quos Hannibal, cum ab suis non redimerentur, venum dederat. multitudinis eorum argumentum est, quod Polybius scribit centum talentis eam rem Achaeis stetisse, cum quingenos denarios pretium in capita, quod redderetur dominis, statuissent.

FRAGMENTS OF BOOK XIX

(Plu. *Cat. Ma.* 10; cf. Livy 34.17.11)

1. Polybius says that at his (Cato's) command the walls of the cities this side of the river Baetis were razed to the ground on a single day. The number of these cities was very large, each full of able-bodied men.[1]

(Livy 34.50.5–6)

2. Enormous was the number of prisoners that Hannibal had captured in the war and whom he had sold, since their relatives did not pay ransom for them. The proof of how many they were is given by Polybius who wrote that their release cost the Achaeans one hundred talents, since they had fixed five hundred denarii per head as compensation for the previous owners.[2]

---

[1] Marcus Porcius Cato, as consul of 195, waged war in Spain: *MRR* 1.339. The reference to the river Baetis is in error.

[2] "The Roman slaves, taken prisoner in the Hannibalic War, were ransomed in response to an appeal made by Flamininus at a meeting of Greek delegations summoned to Corinth in spring 194 . . . Livy's 500 denarii stand for 500 drachmae" (WC 3.63).

FRAGMENTA LIBRI XX

I. RES GRAECIAE

1. Καὶ αὖθις Πολύβιος· τριάκοντα τῶν ἀποκλήτων προεχειρίσαντο τοὺς συνεδρεύσοντας μετὰ τοῦ βασιλέως. καὶ αὖθις· ὁ δὲ συνῆγε τοὺς ἀποκλήτους καὶ διαβούλιον ἀνεδίδου περὶ τῶν ἐνεστώτων.[1]—

2. Ὅτι Φιλίππου πρεσβεύσαντος πρὸς Βοιωτοὺς οἱ Βοιωτοὶ ἀπεκρίθησαν τοῖς πρεσβευταῖς διότι παραγενομένου τοῦ βασιλέως πρὸς αὐτούς, τότε βουλεύσονται περὶ τῶν παρακαλουμένων.[2]—

3. Ὅτι Ἀντιόχου διατρίβοντος ἐν τῇ Χαλκίδι καὶ τοῦ χειμῶνος καταρχομένου παρεγένοντο πρὸς αὐτὸν πρεσβευταὶ παρὰ μὲν τοῦ τῶν Ἠπειρωτῶν ἔθνους οἱ

[1] The Apocleti were a select council. See Livy 35.34. 2.
[2] The excerptor by mistake has substituted Philip for Antiochus.

---

[1] See n. on 4.5.9. The date is autumn 192, after Antiochus had landed at Demetrias.
[2] The Excerptor erroneously says "Philip"; the error was corrected by Reiske. The Boeotians soon joined the king.

FRAGMENTS OF BOOK XX

I. AFFAIRS OF GREECE

(Suda; cf. Livy 35.48.2)

1. "The Aetolians appointed thirty of the Apocleti[1] to sit with King Antiochus," and again, "He summoned the Apocleti to meet and submitted the situation to them." 192–191 B.C.

Antiochus and Boeotia

(Cf. Livy 35.50.5)

2. When Antiochus[2] sent an embassy to the Boeotians, they replied to the envoys that on the king presenting himself in person, they would take his demands into consideration.

Embassies to Antiochus from Epirus and Elis

(Cf. Livy 36.5.1–8)

3. While Antiochus was at Chalcis at the beginning of the winter, Charops[3] came to him as envoy on the part of the whole nation of Epirus, and Callistratus on that of the

---

[3] See P. Paschidis, *Between City and King* (Athens 2008), 349–353.

περὶ Χάροπα, παρὰ δὲ τῆς τῶν Ἠλείων πόλεως οἱ
2 περὶ Καλλίστρατον. οἱ μὲν οὖν Ἠπειρῶται παρεκάλουν αὐτὸν μὴ προεμβιβάζειν σφᾶς εἰς τὸν πρὸς
Ῥωμαίους πόλεμον, θεωροῦντα διότι πρόκεινται πά-
3 σης τῆς Ἑλλάδος πρὸς τὴν Ἰταλίαν· ἀλλ' εἰ μὲν
αὐτὸς δύναται προκαθίσας τῆς Ἠπείρου παρασκευά-
ζειν σφίσι τὴν ἀσφάλειαν, ἔφασαν αὐτὸν δέξασθαι
4 καὶ ταῖς πόλεσι καὶ τοῖς λιμέσιν· εἰ δὲ μὴ κρίνει
τοῦτο πράττειν κατὰ τὸ παρόν, συγγνώμην ἔχειν ἠξί-
5 ουν αὐτοῖς δεδιόσι τὸν ἀπὸ Ῥωμαίων πόλεμον. οἱ δ'
Ἠλεῖοι παρεκάλουν πέμπειν τῇ πόλει βοήθειαν· ἐψη-
φισμένων γὰρ τῶν Ἀχαιῶν τὸν πόλεμον εὐλαβεῖσθαι
6 τὴν τούτων ἔφοδον. ὁ δὲ βασιλεὺς τοῖς μὲν Ἠπειρώταις
ἀπεκρίθη διότι πέμψει πρεσβευτὰς τοὺς διαλεχθησο-
μένους αὐτοῖς ὑπὲρ τῶν κοινῇ συμφερόντων, τοῖς δ'
7 Ἠλείοις ἐξαπέστειλε χιλίους πεζούς, ἡγεμόνα συστήσας Εὐφάνη τὸν Κρῆτα.—

4. Ὅτι Βοιωτοὶ ἐκ πολλῶν ἤδη χρόνων καχεκτοῦντες
ἦσαν καὶ μεγάλην εἶχον διαφορὰν πρὸς τὴν γεγενη-
2 μένην εὐεξίαν καὶ δόξαν αὐτῶν τῆς πολιτείας. οὗτοι
γὰρ μεγάλην περιποιησάμενοι καὶ δόξαν καὶ δύναμιν

---

4 There were three large tribes in Epirus: Molossi, Chaones,
and Thesprotians. Charops was, contrary to the long held view,
not a Chaon, but a Thesprotian (*Bull. ép.* 1969, 347). He was the
son of Machatas, a friend of the Romans, and his help had allowed
Flamininus in 198 to outflank Philip at the Aous Pass (27.15.2).
Livy calls him *princeps Epirotarum* (32.11.10); as such, he repre-

city of Elis.[4] The Epirots begged him not to involve them in the first place in a war with Rome, exposed as they were to Italy in front of all Greece. If indeed he was capable of protecting Epirus and assuring their safety, they said they would be glad to receive him in their cities and harbors, but if he did not decide to do this at present they asked him to pardon them if they were afraid of war with Rome. The Eleans begged him to send succor to their city, for as the Achaeans[5] had voted for war, they were apprehensive of being attacked by them. The king replied to the Epirots that he would send envoys to speak to them on the subject of their joint interests, and to Elis he dispatched a force of a thousand infantry under the command of the Cretan Euphanes.

Decadence of Boeotia

(Cf. Livy 36.6)

4. For many years Boeotia had been in a morbid condition[6] very different from the former sound health and renown of that state. After the battle of Leuctra[7] the Boeo-

sented the country in an embassy to kings Antiochus and [Ptolemy], apparently in 192, just at the time that P. discusses here, *SEG* 37.709 with *Bull. ép.* 1988, 709.

[5] See R. M. Errington, *Philopoemen* (Oxford 1969), 115. They declared war on Antiochus four months before the Romans crossed to Greece (39.3.8).

[6] The following long digression with its severe criticism of the Boeotians has been criticized in turn as greatly exaggerated by D. Hennig, *Chiron* 7 (1977), 119–148.

[7] Their victory over the Spartans in 371.

ἐν τοῖς Λευκτρικοῖς καιροῖς, οὐκ οἶδ' ὅπως κατὰ τὸ
συνεχὲς ἐν τοῖς ἑξῆς χρόνοις ἀφῄρουν ἀμφοτέρων
αἰεὶ τῶν προειρημένων, ἔχοντες στρατηγὸν Ἀβαιόκρι-
3 τον. ἀπὸ δὲ τούτων τῶν καιρῶν οὐ μόνον ἀφῄρουν,
ἀλλ' ἁπλῶς εἰς τἀναντία τραπέντες καὶ τὴν πρὸ τοῦ
4 δόξαν ἐφ' ὅσον οἷοί τ' ἦσαν ἠμαύρωσαν. Ἀχαιῶν γὰρ
αὐτοὺς πρὸς Αἰτωλοὺς ἐκπολεμωσάντων, μετασχόντες
τούτοις τῆς αὐτῆς αἱρέσεως καὶ ποιησάμενοι συμμαχίαν, μετὰ ταῦτα κατὰ τὸ συνεχὲς ἐπολέμουν πρὸς
5 Αἰτωλούς. ἐμβαλόντων δὲ μετὰ δυνάμεως εἰς τὴν Βοιωτίαν τῶν Αἰτωλῶν ἐκστρατεύσαντες πανδημεί, καὶ
τῶν Ἀχαιῶν ἠθροισμένων καὶ μελλόντων παραβοηθεῖν
οὐκ ἐκδεξάμενοι τὴν τούτων παρουσίαν συνέβαλον
6 τοῖς Αἰτωλοῖς, ἡττηθέντες δὲ κατὰ τὸν κίνδυνον οὕτως
ἀνέπεσον ταῖς ψυχαῖς ὥστ' ἀπ' ἐκείνης τῆς χρείας
ἁπλῶς οὐδενὸς ἔτι τῶν καλῶν ἀμφισβητεῖν ἐτόλμησαν
οὐδ' ἐκοινώνησαν οὔτε πράξεως οὔτ' ἀγῶνος οὐδενὸς
7 ἔτι τοῖς Ἕλλησι μετὰ κοινοῦ δόγματος, ἀλλ' ὁρμή-
σαντες πρὸς εὐωχίαν καὶ μέθας οὐ μόνον τοῖς σώμα-
σιν ἐξελύθησαν, ἀλλὰ καὶ ταῖς ψυχαῖς.

5. Τὰ δὲ κεφάλαια τῆς κατὰ μέρος ἀγνοίας ἐχειρίσθη
2 παρ' αὐτοῖς τὸν τρόπον τοῦτον. μετὰ γὰρ τὴν προειρημένην ἧτταν εὐθέως ἐγκαταλιπόντες τοὺς Ἀχαιοὺς
3 προσένειμαν Αἰτωλοῖς τὸ ἔθνος. ἀνελομένων δὲ καὶ
τούτων πόλεμον μετά τινα χρόνον πρὸς Δημήτριον
τὸν Φιλίππου πατέρα, πάλιν ἐγκαταλιπόντες τούτους,

---

8 The son of Abaeodorus of Thebes. He was elected *proxenos*

tians had attained great celebrity and power, but by some means or other during the period which followed they proceeded to lose both gradually, ⟨particularly⟩ when Abaeocritus[8] was their general. From that time their reputation was completely reversed and they wiped out even the memory of their former glory. For when the Achaeans had succeeded in making them go to war with the Aetolians, they took the side of the former and made an alliance with them, after which they forthwith made war on the Aetolians. When the latter invaded Boeotia, they marched out in full force, and the Achaeans having collected their forces and being about to come to their help, without waiting for their arrival they engaged the Aetolians. When defeated in the battle they so much lost their spirit, that they never after that affair ventured to pretend to any honorable distinction, nor did they ever take part with the Greeks in any action or in any struggle by public decree, but abandoning themselves to good cheer and strong drink, sapped the energy not only of their bodies but of their minds.

5. The crowning act of all their individual follies came about as follows. After the defeat I mentioned they at once abandoned the Achaeans and attached their own League to that of the Aetolians. Shortly afterward, when the Aetolians undertook a war against Demetrius,[9] the father of Philip, the Boeotians again deserted them and on the ar-

at Delphi (*FD* III 3.194), where he was also a *naopoeus* for the Boeotians (*CID* II 122, II 8). As general in 245 he lost the battle (and his life) against the Aetolians at Chaeronea.

[9] King Demetrius II of Macedon (239–229). The war began in the king's first year.

καὶ παραγενομένου Δημητρίου μετὰ δυνάμεως εἰς τὴν
Βοιωτίαν οὐδενὸς πεῖραν λαβόντες τῶν δεινῶν, ὑπέ-
4 ταξαν σφᾶς αὐτοὺς ὁλοσχερῶς Μακεδόσι. βραχέος
⟨δ᾿⟩ αἰθύγματος ἐγκαταλειπομένου τῆς προγονικῆς
δόξης, ἦσάν τινες οἳ δυσηρεστοῦντο τῇ παρούσῃ κα-
5 ταστάσει καὶ τῷ πάντα πείθεσθαι Μακεδόσι. διὸ καὶ
μεγάλην ἀντιπολιτείαν εἶναι συνέβαινε τούτοις πρὸς
τοὺς περὶ τὸν Ἀσκώνδαν καὶ Νέωνα, τοὺς Βραχύλλου
προγόνους· οὗτοι γὰρ ἦσαν οἱ μάλιστα τότε μακεδο-
6 νίζοντες. οὐ μὴν ἀλλὰ τέλος κατίσχυσαν οἱ περὶ τὸν
7 Ἀσκώνδαν γενομένης τινὸς περιπετείας τοιαύτης. Ἀντίγονος μετὰ τὸν Δημητρίου θάνατον ἐπιτροπεύσας
Φιλίππου, πλέων ἐπί τινας πράξεις πρὸς τὰς ἐσχατιὰς
τῆς Βοιωτίας πρὸς Λάρυμναν, παραδόξου γενομένης
8 ἀμπώτεως ἐκάθισαν εἰς τὸ ξηρὸν αἱ νῆες αὐτοῦ. κατὰ
δὲ τὸν καιρὸν τοῦτον προσπεπτωκυίας φήμης ὅτι μέλλει κατατρέχειν τὴν χώραν Ἀντίγονος, Νέων, ἱππαρχῶν
τότε καὶ πάντας τοὺς Βοιωτῶν ἱππεῖς μεθ᾿ αὑτοῦ πε-
ριαγόμενος χάριν τοῦ παραφυλάττειν τὴν χώραν,
ἐπεγένετο τοῖς περὶ τὸν Ἀντίγονον ἀπορουμένοις καὶ
9 δυσχρηστουμένοις διὰ τὸ συμβεβηκός, καὶ δυνάμενος
μεγάλα βλάψαι τοὺς Μακεδόνας ἔδοξε φείσασθαι
10 παρὰ τὴν προσδοκίαν αὐτῶν. τοῖς μὲν οὖν ἄλλοις
Βοιωτοῖς ἤρεσκε τοῦτο πράξας, τοῖς δὲ Θηβαίοις οὐχ
11 ὅλως εὐδόκει τὸ γεγονός. ὁ δ᾿ Ἀντίγονος, ἐπελθούσης

10 Of Thebes; he, his son Neon, and his grandson Brachylles
were since the event at Larymna (5.7) closely associated with the

248

rival of Demetrius with his army in Boeotia would not face
any danger whatever but completely submitted to Macedonia. But as some slight sparks remained of their ances-
tral glory, some were by no means pleased with the present situation and this implicit obedience to the
Macedonians. There was in consequence a violent opposition on the part of these to Ascondas[10] and Neon, the
grandfather and father of Brachylles, who were then the
warmest partisans of Macedonia. However, in the
end, Ascondas and Neon got the upper hand owing to
the following accident. Antigonus, who after the death of
Demetrius had become Philip's guardian, was sailing on
some business to Larymna[11] at the extremity of Boeotia,
when owing to an extraordinarily low ebb tide his vessels
settled on the land. It had just been reported that Antigonus was about to raid the country, and Neon, who was then
hipparch and was on the move with the whole of the Boeotian cavalry with the object of protecting the country,
lighted upon Antigonus, who was in a state of dismay and
in a difficult position owing to the accident; and though it
was in his power to inflict much damage on the Macedonians, decided, contrary to their expectation, to spare
them. The other Boeotians approved of his conduct, but
the Thebans were not entirely pleased with it. Antigonus,

kings of Macedonia, as long as there were kings. For the family
see Paschidis 319–323. For Brachylles see 18.1.2. Neon was honored at Epidaurus: *SEG* 11 414 30.

11 The easternmost city of Locris. For the incident here reported, which happened in 227, see S. Le Bohec, *Antigone Dôsôn,
roi de Macédoine* (Nancy 1993), 189–194.

μετ᾽ ὀλίγον τῆς πλήμης καὶ κουφισθεισῶν τῶν νεῶν,
τῷ μὲν Νέωνι μεγάλην εἶχε χάριν ἐπὶ τῷ μὴ συνεπι-
τεθεῖσθαι σφίσι κατὰ τὴν περιπέτειαν, αὐτὸς δὲ τὸν
12 προκείμενον ἐτέλει πλοῦν εἰς τὴν Ἀσίαν. διὸ καὶ μετὰ
ταῦτα, νικήσας Κλεομένη τὸν Σπαρτιάτην καὶ κύριος
γενόμενος τῆς Λακεδαίμονος, ἐπιστάτην ἀπέλειπε τῆς
πόλεως Βραχύλλην, ταύτην αὐτῷ χάριν ἀποδιδοὺς
τῆς τοῦ πατρὸς Νέωνος εὐεργεσίας· ἐξ ὧν οὐδὲ κατὰ
μικρὸν συνέβη τὴν οἰκίαν ἐπανορθωθῆναι τὴν περὶ
13 τὸν Βραχύλλην. οὐ μόνον δὲ ταύτην αὐτῶν ἔσχε τὴν
πρόνοιαν, ἀλλὰ καὶ κατὰ τὸ συνεχές, ὁτὲ μὲν αὐτός,
ὁτὲ δὲ Φίλιππος, χορηγοῦντες καὶ συνεπισχύοντες
αἰεί, ταχέως κατηγωνίσαντο τοὺς ἐν ταῖς Θήβαις αὐτοῖς ἀντιπολιτευομένους καὶ πάντας ἠνάγκασαν μα-
κεδονίζειν πλὴν τελέως ὀλίγων τινῶν.
14   Τὰ μὲν οὖν κατὰ τὴν οἰκίαν τὴν Νέωνος τοιαύτην
ἔλαβε τὴν ἀρχὴν καὶ τῆς πρὸς Μακεδόνας συστάσεως καὶ τῆς κατὰ τὴν οὐσίαν ἐπιδόσεως·

    6. τὰ δὲ κοινὰ τῶν Βοιωτῶν εἰς τοσαύτην παραγε-
γόνει καχεξίαν ὥστε σχεδὸν εἴκοσι καὶ πέντ᾽ ἐτῶν τὸ
δίκαιον μὴ διεξῆχθαι παρ᾽ αὐτοῖς μήτε περὶ τῶν ἰδιω-
τικῶν συμβολαίων μήτε περὶ τῶν κοινῶν ἐγκλημάτων,
2 ἀλλ᾽ οἱ μὲν φρουρὰς παραγγέλλοντες τῶν ἀρχόντων,

---

12 The king was to begin his expedition to Caria, now beyond all doubt, due to inscriptions from Labraunda published by
J. Crampa, *Labraunda. The Greek Inscriptions*, 2 vols. (Lund
1969), 1972. For this expedition see Le Bohec (5.7), 327–361.

when the flood tide very shortly came in and his ships had been lightened, was very thankful to Neon for not having availed himself of the accident to attack him, and now continued the voyage to Asia[12] upon which he had set out. In consequence of this, when, at a later period, he had conquered Cleomenes of Sparta and become master[13] of Lacedaemon, he left Brachylles in that town as his commissioner,[14] bestowing this post on him out of gratitude for the kind service that Neon, the father of Brachylles had rendered him. This contributed no little to the fortunes of Brachylles and his house; and not only did Antigonus show him this mark of his regard, but ever afterward both he and Philip continued to furnish him with money and strengthen his position, and thus they soon crushed those opposed to them at Thebes and compelled all, with quite a few exceptions, to take the part of Macedon.

It was thus that the attachment of the house of Neon to Macedonia and the increase in its fortunes originated.

6. But public affairs in Boeotia had fallen into such a state of disorder[15] that for nearly twenty-five years justice, both civil and criminal, had ceased to be administered there, the magistrates by issuing orders, some of them for the dispatch of garrisons and others for general campaigns,

---

[13] After his victory at Sellasia in 222 (2.65–69).

[14] They are the *epistatai*. There has been a vivid discussion on their role and position with respect to the king. See most recently F. Papazoglou, *Ziva Antika* 50 (2000), 172–176. R. M. Errington, *Chiron* 32 (2002), 51–63. M. Hatzopoulos, *Tekmeria* 8 (2003 [2006]), 27–59.

[15] For criticism of P.'s bleak picture, see Hennig (4.1).

οἱ δὲ στρατείας κοινάς, ἐξέκοπτον ἀεὶ τὴν δικαιοδο-
σίαν· ἔνιοι δὲ τῶν στρατηγῶν καὶ μισθοδοσίας ἐποί-
3 ουν ἐκ τῶν κοινῶν τοῖς ἀπόροις τῶν ἀνθρώπων. ἐξ ὧν
ἐδιδάχθη τὰ πλήθη τούτοις προσέχειν καὶ τούτοις
περιποιεῖν τὰς ἀρχάς, δι᾽ ὧν ἔμελλε τῶν μὲν ἀδικημάτων καὶ τῶν ὀφειλημάτων οὐχ ὑφέξειν δίκας, προσλήψεσθαι ⟨δὲ⟩ τῶν κοινῶν αἰεί τι διὰ τὴν τῶν
4 ἀρχόντων χάριν. πλεῖστα δὲ συνεβάλετο πρὸς τὴν
τοιαύτην ... Ὀφέλτας, αἰεί τι προσεπινοῶν ὃ κατὰ τὸ
παρὸν ἐδόκει τοὺς πολλοὺς ὠφελεῖν, μετὰ δὲ ταῦτα
5 πάντας ἀπολεῖν ἔμελλεν ὁμολογουμένως. τούτοις δ᾽
ἠκολούθησε καὶ ἕτερος ζῆλος οὐκ εὐτυχής. οἱ μὲν γὰρ
ἄτεκνοι τὰς οὐσίας οὐ τοῖς κατὰ γένος ἐπιγενομένοις
τελευτῶντες ἀπέλειπον, ὅπερ ἦν ἔθος παρ᾽ αὐτοῖς πρότερον, ἀλλ᾽ εἰς εὐωχίας καὶ μέθας διετίθεντο καὶ κοι-
6 νὰς τοῖς φίλοις ἐποίουν· πολλοὶ δὲ καὶ τῶν ἐχόντων
γενεὰς ἀπεμέριζον τοῖς συσσιτίοις τὸ πλεῖον μέρος
τῆς οὐσίας, ὥστε πολλοὺς εἶναι Βοιωτῶν οἷς ὑπῆρχε
δεῖπνα τοῦ μηνὸς πλείω τῶν εἰς τὸν μῆνα διατε-
ταγμένων ἡμερῶν.

7   Διὸ καὶ Μεγαρεῖς, μισήσαντες μὲν τὴν τοιαύτην
κατάστασιν, μνησθέντες δὲ τῆς προγεγενημένης αὐτοῖς μετὰ τῶν Ἀχαιῶν συμπολιτείας, αὖτις ἀπένευσαν
8 πρὸς τοὺς Ἀχαιοὺς καὶ τὴν ἐκείνων αἵρεσιν. Μεγαρεῖς
γὰρ ἐξ ἀρχῆς μὲν ἐπολιτεύοντο μετὰ τῶν Ἀχαιῶν ἀπὸ
τῶν κατ᾽ Ἀντίγονον τὸν Γονατᾶν χρόνων· ὅτε δὲ Κλε-

---

16 The city was from ca. 243 a member of the Achaean Con-

always contriving to abolish legal proceedings. Certain strategi even provided payout of the public funds for the indigent, the populace thus learning to court and invest with power those men who would help them to escape the legal consequences of their crimes and debts and even in addition to get something out of the public funds as a favor from the magistrates. The chief abettor of these abuses was Opheltas, who was constantly contriving some scheme apparently calculated to benefit the populace for the moment, but perfectly sure to ruin everyone at the end. Incident upon all this was another most unfortunate mania. For childless men did not leave their property to their nearest heirs when they died, as had formerly been the custom there, but employed it for purposes of junketing and banqueting and made it the common property of their friends. Even many who had families distributed the greater part of their fortune among their clubs, so that there were many Boeotians who had each month more dinners than there were days in the calendar.

Defection of Megara[16] from the Boeotian League

One consequence of this was that the Megarians, detesting this state of affairs and mindful of their former confederacy with the Achaean League, once more inclined toward the Achaeans and their policy. For the Megarians had originally, from the days of Antigonus Gonatas, formed

federacy, then ca. 224, with the concurrence of the Achaeans, joined the Boeotian League, and returned ca. 206/5 (?) once again to that of the Achaeans. *RE* Megara 195–196 and Suppl. 12; 848–849 (E. Meyer); Errington (3. 5), 77.

ομένης εἰς τὸν Ἰσθμὸν προεκάθισεν, διακλεισθέντες
προσέθεντο τοῖς Βοιωτοῖς μετὰ τῆς τῶν Ἀχαιῶν γνώ-
9 μης. βραχὺ δὲ πρὸ τῶν νῦν λεγομένων καιρῶν δυσα-
ρεστήσαντες τῇ πολιτείᾳ τῶν Βοιωτῶν αὖτις ἀπένευ-
10 σαν πρὸς τοὺς Ἀχαιούς. οἱ δὲ Βοιωτοὶ διοργισθέντες
ἐπὶ τῷ καταφρονεῖσθαι δοκεῖν ἐξῆλθον ἐπὶ τοὺς Με-
11 γαρεῖς πανδημεὶ σὺν τοῖς ὅπλοις. οὐδένα δὲ ποιουμένων λόγον τῶν Μεγαρέων τῆς παρουσίας αὐτῶν, οὕτω
θυμωθέντες πολιορκεῖν ἐπεβάλοντο καὶ προσβολὰς
12 ποιεῖσθαι τῇ πόλει. πανικοῦ δ' ἐμπεσόντος αὐτοῖς καὶ
φήμης ὅτι πάρεστιν Φιλοποίμην τοὺς Ἀχαιοὺς ἔχων,
ἀπολιπόντες πρὸς τῷ τείχει τὰς κλίμακας ἔφυγον
προτροπάδην εἰς τὴν οἰκείαν.

7. Τοιαύτην δ' ἔχοντες οἱ Βοιωτοὶ τὴν διάθεσιν τῆς
πολιτείας, εὐτυχῶς πως διώλισθον καὶ τοὺς κατὰ Φί-
2 λιππον καὶ τοὺς κατ' Ἀντίοχον καιρούς. ἔν γε μὴν
τοῖς ἑξῆς οὐ διέφυγον, ἀλλ' ὥσπερ ἐπίτηδες ἀνταπόδοσιν ἡ τύχη ποιουμένη βαρέως ἔδοξεν αὐτοῖς
ἐπεμβαίνειν· ὑπὲρ ὧν ἡμεῖς ἐν τοῖς ἑξῆς ποιησόμεθα
μνήμην.

3 Ὅτι οἱ πολλοὶ πρόφασιν μὲν εἶχον τῆς πρὸς Ῥωμαίους ἀλλοτριότητος τὴν ἐπαναίρεσιν τὴν Βραχύλλου καὶ τὴν στρατείαν, ἣν ἐποιήσατο Τίτος ἐπὶ Κορώνειαν διὰ τοὺς ἐπιγινομένους φόνους ἐν ταῖς ὁδοῖς
4 τῶν Ῥωμαίων, τῇ δ' ἀληθείᾳ καχεκτοῦντες ⟨ἦσαν⟩
5 ταῖς ψυχαῖς διὰ τὰς προειρημένας αἰτίας. καὶ γὰρ τοῦ
βασιλέως συνεγγίζοντος ἐξῄεσαν ἐπὶ τὴν ἀπάντησιν

part of the Achaean League, but when Cleomenes inter-
cepted them by occupying the Isthmus, they were cut off,
and with the consent of the Achaeans, joined the Boeotian
League. But shortly before the time I am speaking of, they
became displeased with the conduct of affairs in Boeotia,
and again turned to the Achaeans. Hereupon the Boeotians, indignant at seeming to be flouted, marched out
with all their forces against Megara, and when the Megarians treated their arrival as of no importance, they began
in their anger to besiege Megara and make assaults on it.
But, being seized by panic owing to a report that Philopoemen with the Achaeans had arrived, they left their
ladders against the wall and fled in utter rout to their own
country.

7. Such being the condition of public affairs in Boeotia,
they were lucky enough to scrape through by some means
or other the critical period of Philip and Antiochus. Subsequently, however, they did not escape, but Fortune, it
seems as if purposely requiting them, fell heavily upon
them, as I shall tell in due course.[17]

(Cf. Livy 36.6)

Most of the Boeotian people assigned as a reason for
their hostility to Rome the assassination of Brachylles[18]
and the expedition made by Flamininus against Coronea
owing to the frequent murders of Romans on the roads;
but the real reason was that morbid condition of their
minds due to the causes I have mentioned. For when King
Antiochus was near at hand, the Boeotian magistrates

[17] 22.4.1–17.   [18] 18.43.1–13. Livy (36.6) has preserved
more of P.'s narrative.

οἱ τῶν Βοιωτῶν ἄρξαντες· συμμίξαντες δὲ καὶ φιλανθρώπως ὁμιλήσαντες ἦγον αὐτὸν εἰς τὰς Θήβας.

8. Ἀντίοχος δὲ ὁ μέγας ἐπικαλούμενος, ὃν Ῥωμαῖοι
καθεῖλον, ὡς ἱστορεῖ Πολύβιος ἐν τῇ εἰκοστῇ, παρελθὼν εἰς Χαλκίδα τῆς Εὐβοίας συνετέλει γάμους, πεντήκοντα μὲν ἔτη γεγονὼς καὶ δύο τὰ μέγιστα τῶν
ἔργων ἀνειληφώς, τήν τε τῶν Ἑλλήνων ἐλευθέρωσιν,
ὡς αὐτὸς ἐπηγγέλλετο, καὶ τὸν πρὸς Ῥωμαίους πόλε-
2 μον. ἐρασθεὶς οὖν παρθένου Χαλκιδικῆς κατὰ τὸν τοῦ
πολέμου καιρὸν ἐφιλοτιμήσατο γῆμαι αὐτήν, οἰνοπό-
3 της ὢν καὶ μέθαις χαίρων. ἦν δ' αὕτη Κλεοπτολέμου
μὲν θυγάτηρ, ἑνὸς τῶν ἐπιφανῶν, κάλλει δὲ πάσας
4 ὑπερβάλλουσα. καὶ τοὺς γάμους συντελῶν ἐν τῇ
Χαλκίδι αὐτόθι διέτριψε τὸν χειμῶνα, τῶν ἐνεστώτων
οὐδ' ἡντινοῦν ποιούμενος πρόνοιαν. ἔθετο δὲ καὶ τῇ
5 παιδὶ ὄνομα Εὔβοιαν. ἡττηθεὶς οὖν τῷ πολέμῳ ἔφυγεν
εἰς Ἔφεσον μετὰ τῆς νεογάμου.

6   Nec praeter quingentos, qui circa regem fuerunt, ex
toto exercitu quisquam effugit, etiam ex decem milibus

---

[19] See n. on 4.2.7. Attested in this way since 203.

[20] Antiochus had repudiated Laodice, who had borne him
three sons and four or five daughters. He had just very recently
established an official cult of her, with a high priest in every sa-
trapy of his realm. Three identical copies of his order to this effect, from various locations, have been preserved, dating from
spring 194; RC 36; L. Robert, Hellenica 7 (1949), 5–29, and the
same, CRAcad. Inscr. 1967, 281–297.

went out to meet him, and on joining him addressed him in courteous terms and brought him into Thebes.

Wedding of Antiochus

(From Athenaeus 10.439e, f)

8. Antiochus, surnamed the Great,[19] he whom the Romans overthrew, upon reaching Chalcis, as Polybius tells us in his twentieth book, celebrated his wedding.[20] He was then fifty years old,[21] and had undertaken two very serious tasks, one being the liberation of Greece, as he himself gave out, the other a war with Rome. He fell in love, then, with a maiden of Chalcis at the time of the war, and was most eager to make her his wife, being himself a wine-bibber and fond of getting drunk. She was the daughter of Cleoptolemus,[22] a noble Chalcidian, and of surpassing beauty. So celebrating his wedding at Chalcis, he spent the whole winter there not giving a moment's thought to the situation of affairs. He gave the girl the name Euboea, and when defeated in the war fled to Ephesus with his bride.

Battle of Thermopylae

(Cf. Livy 36.19.11)

Not a soul escaped[23] from the whole army except the five hundred who were round the king, and a very small

[21] Rather one or two years above that, as the authors who follow P. have it; something was probably omitted by Athenaeus.

[22] Paschidis 444–445.

[23] From the battle at Thermopylae in 191 (Livy 36.18–19), in which the consul Manius Acilius Glabrio defeated Antiochus.

militum, quos Polybio auctore traiecisse secum regem in
Graeciam scripsimus, exiguus numerus.

9. Ὅτι οἱ περὶ τὸν Φαινέαν τὸν τῶν Αἰτωλῶν στρατηγὸν μετὰ τὸ γενέσθαι τὴν Ἡράκλειαν ὑποχείριον
τοῖς Ῥωμαίοις, ὁρῶντες τὸν περιεστῶτα καιρὸν τὴν
Αἰτωλίαν καὶ λαμβάνοντες πρὸ ὀφθαλμῶν τὰ συμβη-
σόμενα ταῖς ἄλλαις πόλεσιν, ἔκριναν διαπέμπεσθαι
2 πρὸς τὸν Μάνιον ὑπὲρ ἀνοχῶν καὶ διαλύσεως. ταῦτα
δὲ διαλαβόντες ἐξαπέστειλαν Ἀρχέδαμον καὶ Παντα-
3 λέοντα καὶ Χάλεπον· οἳ συμμίξαντες τῷ στρατηγῷ
τῶν Ῥωμαίων προέθεντο μὲν καὶ πλείους ποιεῖσθαι
λόγους, μεσολαβηθέντες δὲ κατὰ τὴν ἔντευξιν ἐκωλύ-
4 θησαν. ὁ γὰρ Μάνιος κατὰ μὲν τὸ παρὸν οὐκ ἔφασκεν
εὐκαιρεῖν, περισπώμενος ὑπὸ τῆς τῶν ἐκ τῆς Ἡρα-
5 κλείας λαφύρων οἰκονομίας· δεχημέρους δὲ ποιησάμενος ἀνοχὰς ἐκπέμψειν ἔφη μετ᾽ αὐτῶν Λεύκιον, πρὸς
6 ὃν ἐκέλευε λέγειν ὑπὲρ ὧν ἂν δέοιντο. γενομένων δὲ
τῶν ἀνοχῶν, καὶ τοῦ Λευκίου συνελθόντος εἰς τὴν
Ὑπάταν, ἐγένοντο λόγοι καὶ πλείους ὑπὲρ τῶν ἐνεστώ-
7 των. οἱ μὲν οὖν Αἰτωλοὶ συνίσταντο τὴν δικαιολογίαν
ἀνέκαθεν προφερόμενοι τὰ προγεγονότα σφίσι φιλάν-

---

24 Heraclea Trachinia, founded by the Spartans in 426, was
forced to join the Aetolian Confederacy in 280 (Paus. 10.20.9).
Stählin (18.3.12), 206–209. For the siege by the consul, see Livy
36.22.5–24.12, and the inscription *M'. Acilius C. f. cos. Heraclea
cep(it)* in *AE* 1993, 643.

number of the ten thousand soldiers whom Polybius tells us he had brought over with him to Greece.

The Aetolians Make Peace

(Cf. Livy 36.27)

9. After Heraclea[24] had fallen into the hands of the Romans, Phaeneas, the strategus of the Aetolians, seeing Aetolia threatened with peril on all sides and realizing what was likely to happen to the other towns, decided to send an embassy to Manius Acilius Glabrio to beg for an armistice and peace. Having resolved on this he dispatched Archedamus,[25] Pantaleon, and Chalepus. They had intended on meeting the Roman general to address him at length, but at the interview they were cut short and prevented from doing so. For Glabrio told them that for the present he had no time as he was occupied by the disposal of the booty from Heraclea, but granting them a ten days' armistice, he said he would send back with them Lucius Valerius Flaccus,[26] to whom he bade them submit their request. The armistice having been made, and Flaccus having met them at Hypata,[27] there was considerable discussion of the situation. The Aetolians, in making out their case, went back to the very beginning, reciting all

[25] Aetolian strategus in 191/0 as successor to Phaeneas.

[26] Consul 195 with Cato, now serving, like Cato, in a minor military capacity. The Valerii were patrons of the Aetolians since the alliance concluded by Marcus Valerius Laevinus, the consul of 211, *StV* 536.

[27] The principal town of the Aenianes, northwest of Heraclea.

8 θρωπα πρὸς τοὺς Ῥωμαίους· ὁ δὲ Λεύκιος ἐπιτεμὼν
αὐτῶν τὴν ὁρμὴν οὐκ ἔφη τοῖς παροῦσι καιροῖς ἁρμό-
ζειν τοῦτο τὸ γένος τῆς δικαιολογίας· λελυμένων γὰρ
τῶν ἐξ ἀρχῆς φιλανθρώπων δι᾽ ἐκείνους, καὶ τῆς
ἐνεστώσης ἔχθρας δι᾽ Αἰτωλοὺς γεγενημένης, οὐδὲν
ἔτι συμβάλλεσθαι τὰ τότε φιλάνθρωπα πρὸς τοὺς νῦν
9 καιρούς. διόπερ ἀφεμένους τοῦ δικαιολογεῖσθαι συνε-
βούλευε τρέπεσθαι πρὸς τὸν ἀξιωματικὸν λόγον καὶ
δεῖσθαι τοῦ στρατηγοῦ συγγνώμης τυχεῖν ἐπὶ τοῖς
10 ἡμαρτημένοις. οἱ δ᾽ Αἰτωλοὶ καὶ πλείω λόγον ποιησάμενοι περὶ τῶν ὑποπιπτόντων ἔκριναν ἐπιτρέπειν τὰ
ὅλα Μανίῳ, δόντες αὑτοὺς εἰς τὴν Ῥωμαίων πίστιν,
11 οὐκ εἰδότες τίνα δύναμιν ἔχει τοῦτο, τῷ δὲ τῆς πίστεως ὀνόματι πλανηθέντες, ὡς ἂν διὰ τοῦτο τελειο-
12 τέρου σφίσιν ἐλέους ὑπάρξοντος. παρὰ ⟨δὲ⟩ Ῥωμαίοις
ἰσοδυναμεῖ τό τ᾽ εἰς τὴν πίστιν αὑτὸν ἐγχειρίσαι καὶ
τὸ τὴν ἐπιτροπὴν δοῦναι περὶ αὑτοῦ τῷ κρατοῦντι.

10. Πλὴν ταῦτα κρίναντες ἐξέπεμψαν ἅμα τῷ Λευ-
κίῳ τοὺς περὶ Φαινέαν διασαφήσοντας τὰ δεδογμένα
2 τῷ Μανίῳ κατὰ σπουδήν· οἳ καὶ συμμίξαντες τῷ
στρατηγῷ καὶ πάλιν ὁμοίως δικαιολογηθέντες ὑπὲρ
αὑτῶν, ἐπὶ καταστροφῆς εἶπαν διότι κέκριται τοῖς
Αἰτωλοῖς σφᾶς αὐτοὺς ἐγχειρίζειν εἰς τὴν Ῥωμαίων
3 πίστιν. ὁ δὲ Μάνιος μεταλαβὼν "οὐκοῦν οὕτως ἔχει
4 ταῦτα," φησίν, "ὦ ἄνδρες Αἰτωλοί;" τῶν δὲ κατανευσάν-
των, "τοιγαροῦν πρῶτον μὲν δεήσει μηδένα διαβαίνειν ὑμῶν εἰς τὴν Ἀσίαν, μήτε κατ᾽ ἰδίαν μήτε μετὰ
5 κοινοῦ δόγματος, δεύτερον Δικαίαρχον ἔκδοτον δοῦναι

their former deeds of kindness to the Romans, but Flaccus cut the flood of their eloquence short by saying that this sort of pleading did not suit present circumstances. For as it was they who had broken off their originally kind relations, and as their present enmity was entirely their own fault, former deeds of kindness no longer counted as an asset. Therefore he advised them to leave off trying to justify themselves and resort rather to deprecatory language, begging the consul to grant them pardon for their offenses. The Aetolians, after some further observations about the actual situation, decided to refer the whole matter to Glabrio, committing themselves "to the faith"[28] of the Romans, not knowing the exact meaning of the phrase, but deceived by the word "faith" as if they would thus obtain more complete pardon. But with the Romans to commit oneself to the faith of a victor is equivalent to surrendering at discretion.

10. However, having reached this decision they sent off Phaeneas and others to accompany Flaccus and convey it at once to Glabrio. On meeting the general, after again pleading in justification of their conduct, they wound up by saying that the Aetolians had decided to commit themselves to the faith of the Romans. Upon this Glabrio, taking them up, said, "So that is so, is it, ye men of Aetolia?" and when they assented, "Very well," he said, "then in the first place none of you must cross to Asia, either on his own account or by public decree; next you must surrender Di-

---

[28] Roman *fides*. The following episode has been widely discussed; see e.g., E. Gruen, *Athenaeum* 61–62 (1982), 50–68.

καὶ Μενέστρατον τὸν Ἠπειρώτην," ὃς ἐτύγχανε τότε
παραβεβοηθηκὼς εἰς Ναύπακτον, "σὺν δὲ τούτοις
Ἀμύνανδρον τὸν βασιλέα καὶ τῶν Ἀθαμάνων τοὺς

6 ἅμα τούτῳ συναποχωρήσαντας πρὸς αὑτούς." ὁ δὲ
Φαινέας μεσολαβήσας "ἀλλ' οὔτε δίκαιον," ἔφησεν,
"οὔθ᾽ Ἑλληνικόν ἐστιν, ὦ στρατηγέ, τὸ παρακαλούμε-

7 νον." ὁ δὲ Μάνιος οὐχ οὕτως ὀργισθεὶς ὡς βουλόμενος εἰς ἔννοιαν αὐτοὺς ἀγαγεῖν τῆς περιστάσεως καὶ
καταπλήξασθαι τοῖς ὅλοις, "ἔτι γὰρ ὑμεῖς ἑλληνοκο-
πεῖτε" φησί "καὶ περὶ τοῦ πρέποντος καὶ καθήκοντος
ποιεῖσθε λόγον, δεδωκότες ἑαυτοὺς εἰς τὴν πίστιν; οὓς
ἐγὼ δήσας εἰς τὴν ἅλυσιν ἀπάξω πάντας, ἂν τοῦτ᾽

8 ἐμοὶ δόξῃ." ταῦτα λέγων φέρειν ἅλυσιν ἐκέλευσε καὶ
σκύλακα σιδηροῦν ἑκάστῳ περιθεῖναι περὶ τὸν τρά-

9 χηλον. οἱ μὲν οὖν περὶ τὸν Φαινέαν ἔκθαμβοι γεγονότες ἔστασαν ἄφωνοι πάντες, οἱονεὶ παραλελυμένοι καὶ
τοῖς σώμασι καὶ ταῖς ψυχαῖς διὰ τὸ παράδοξον τῶν

10 ἀπαντωμένων· ὁ δὲ Λεύκιος καί τινες ἕτεροι τῶν συμ-
παρόντων χιλιάρχων ἐδέοντο τοῦ Μανίου μηδὲν βουλεύσασθαι δυσχερὲς ὑπὲρ τῶν παρόντων ἀνδρῶν, ἐπεὶ

11 τυγχάνουσιν ὄντες πρεσβευταί. τοῦ δὲ συγχωρήσαντος ἤρξατο λέγειν ὁ Φαινέας· ἔφη γὰρ αὑτὸν καὶ τοὺς
ἀποκλήτους ποιήσειν τὰ προστατττόμενα, προσδεῖσθαι
δὲ καὶ τῶν πολλῶν, εἰ μέλλει κυρωθῆναι τὰ παραγ-

12 γελλόμενα. τοῦ δὲ Μανίου φήσαντος αὐτὸν ὀρθῶς λέγειν, ἠξίου πάλιν ἀνοχὰς αὐτοῖς δοθῆναι δεχημέρους.
συγχωρηθέντος δὲ καὶ τούτου, τότε μὲν ἐπὶ τούτοις

13 ἐχωρίσθησαν· παραγενόμενοι δ' εἰς τὴν Ὑπάταν διε-

caearchus and Menestratus of Epirus" (the latter had recently come to their assistance at Naupactus) "and at the same time King Amynander[29] and all the Athamanians who went off to join you together with him." Phaeneas now interrupted him and said, "But what you demand, O General, is neither just nor Greek." Glabrio, not so much incensed, as wishing to make them conscious of the real situation they were in and thoroughly intimidate them, said: "So you still give yourselves Grecian airs and speak of what is meet and proper after surrendering unconditionally? I will have you all put in chains if I think fit." Saying this he ordered a chain to be brought and an iron collar to be put round the neck of each. Phaeneas and the rest were thunderstruck, and all stood there speechless as if paralyzed in body and mind by this extraordinary experience. But Flaccus and some of the other military tribunes who were present entreated Glabrio not to treat the men with excessive harshness, in view of the fact that they were ambassadors.[30] Upon his consenting, Phaeneas began to speak. He said that he and the Apocleti would do what Glabrio ordered, but that the consent of the people was required if the orders were to be enforced. Glabrio now said that he was right, upon which he called for a renewal of the armistice for ten days more. This request also was granted, and they parted on this understanding. On reaching Hypata the envoys informed the Apocleti of

[29] The king is now found on the side of Antiochus and the Aetolians; he was last mentioned in 18.47.13.

[30] Ambassadors, at the difference of heralds, were not protected by a guarantee of inviolability: see *RE* Presbeia (Suppl. 13), 544–546 (D. Kienast).

σάφουν τοῖς ἀποκλήτοις τὰ γεγονότα καὶ τοὺς ῥηθέντας λόγους. ὧν ἀκούσαντες τότε πρῶτον ἔννοιαν ἔλαβον Αἰτωλοὶ τῆς αὑτῶν ἀγνοίας καὶ τῆς ἐπιφερομένης
14 αὐτοῖς ἀνάγκης. διὸ γράφειν ἔδοξεν εἰς τὰς πόλεις καὶ
συγκαλεῖν τοὺς Αἰτωλοὺς χάριν τοῦ βουλεύσασθαι
15 περὶ τῶν προσταττομένων. διαδοθείσης δὲ τῆς φήμης
ὑπὲρ τῶν ἀπηντημένων τοῖς περὶ τὸν Φαινέαν, οὕτως
ἀπεθηριώθη τὸ πλῆθος ὥστ' οὐδ' ἀπαντᾶν οὐδεὶς ἐπ-
16 εβάλετο πρὸς τὸ διαβούλιον. τοῦ δ' ἀδυνάτου κωλύ-
σαντος βουλεύσασθαι περὶ τῶν ἐπιταττομένων, ἅμα
δὲ καὶ τοῦ Νικάνδρου κατὰ τὸν καιρὸν τοῦτον κατα-
πλεύσαντος ἐκ τῆς Ἀσίας εἰς τὰ Φάλαρα τοῦ κόλπου
τοῦ Μηλιέως, ὅθεν καὶ τὴν ὁρμὴν ἐποιήσατο, καὶ
διασαφοῦντος ⟨τὴν⟩ τοῦ βασιλέως εἰς αὑτὸν προθυμίαν καὶ τὰς εἰς τὸ μέλλον ἐπαγγελίας, ἔτι μᾶλλον
ὠλιγώρησαν, τοῦ μηδὲν γενέσθαι πέρας ὑπὲρ τῆς
17 εἰρήνης. ὅθεν ἅμα τῷ διελθεῖν τὰς ἐν ταῖς ἀνοχαῖς
ἡμέρας κατάμονος αὖθις ὁ πόλεμος ἐγεγόνει τοῖς Αἰτωλοῖς.

11. Περὶ δὲ τῆς συμβάσης τῷ Νικάνδρῳ περιπε-
2 τείας οὐκ ἄξιον παρασιωπῆσαι. παρεγενήθη μὲν γὰρ
ἐκ τῆς Ἐφέσου δωδεκαταῖος εἰς τὰ Φάλαρα πάλιν,
3 ἀφ' ἧς ὥρμηθ' ἡμέρας· καταλαβὼν δὲ τοὺς Ῥωμαίους
ἔτι περὶ τὴν Ἡράκλειαν, τοὺς ⟨δὲ⟩ Μακεδόνας
ἀφεστῶτας μὲν ἀπὸ τῆς Λαμίας, οὐ μακρὰν δὲ στρα-
4 τοπεδεύοντας τῆς πόλεως, τὰ μὲν χρήματ' εἰς τὴν Λα-

what had taken place and what had been said, and it was only now, on hearing all, that the Aetolians became conscious of their mistake and of the constraint now brought to bear on them. It was therefore decided to write to the towns and call an assembly of the nation to take the demands into consideration. When the report of what had befallen Phaeneas was spread abroad, the people became so savage that no one even would attend the meeting to discuss matters. As sheer impossibility thus prevented any discussion of the demands, and as at the same time Nicander[31] arrived from Asia Minor at Phalara[32] in the Malian Gulf, from which he had set forth, and informed them of King Antiochus' cordial reception of him and his promises of future assistance, they neglected the matter more and more; so that no steps tending to the conclusion of peace were taken. In consequence, after the termination of the armistice, the Aetolians remained as before *in statu belli*.

11. The dangerous experience that had befallen Nicander must not be passed over in silence. For starting from Ephesus he reached Phalara on the twelfth day after he had set sail from it. Finding that the Romans were still near Heraclea and that the Macedonians had retired from Lamia, but were encamped not far from the town, he man-

---

[31] Aetolian from Trichonium, who had a distinguished career and was three times strategus; Paschidis 339–341. In 193 he tried unsuccessfully to win Philip to the Aetolian side. The unexpected, very generous way the king treated him in 191 made him loyal to the royal house to its end; in 168 he was deported to Rome (11.10), where he may have been one of P.'s informants. *RE* Nikandros 247–249 (F. Stähelin).   [32] The harbor of Lamia, probably Stylis. *RE* Phalara 1647–1648 (E. Kirsten).

μίαν διεκόμισε παραδόξως, αὐτὸς δὲ τῆς νυκτὸς ἐπεβάλετο κατὰ τὸν μεταξὺ τόπον τῶν στρατοπέδων
5 διαπεσεῖν εἰς τὴν Ὑπάταν. ἐμπεσὼν δ' εἰς τοὺς προ-
κοίτους τῶν Μακεδόνων ἀνήγετο πρὸς τὸν Φίλιππον
ἔτι τῆς συνουσίας ἀκμαζούσης, προσδο<κῶν> πείσε-
σθαί τι δεινὸν πεσὼν ὑπὸ τοῦ Φιλίππου τὸν θυμὸν ἢ
6 παραδοθήσεσθαι τοῖς Ῥωμαίοις. τοῦ δὲ πράγματος
ἀγγελθέντος τῷ βασιλεῖ, ταχέως ἐκέλευσε τοὺς ἐπὶ
τούτων ὄντας θεραπεῦσαι τὸν Νίκανδρον καὶ τὴν λοι-
7 πὴν ἐπιμέλειαν αὐτοῦ ποιήσασθαι φιλάνθρωπον. μετὰ
δέ τινα χρόνον αὐτὸς ἐξαναστὰς συνέμιξε τῷ Νικάνδρῳ καὶ πολλὰ καταμεμψάμενος τὴν κοινὴν τῶν Αἰτωλῶν ἄγνοιαν, ἐξ ἀρχῆς μέν, ὅτι Ῥωμαίους ἐπαγά-
γοιεν τοῖς Ἕλλησι, μετὰ δὲ ταῦτα πάλιν Ἀντίοχον,
ὅμως ἔτι καὶ νῦν παρεκάλει λήθην ποιησαμένους τῶν
προγεγονότων ἀντέχεσθαι τῆς πρὸς αὐτὸν εὐνοίας
καὶ μὴ θελῆσαι συνεπεμβαίνειν τοῖς κατ' ἀλλήλων
8 καιροῖς. ταῦτα μὲν οὖν παρῄνει τοῖς προεστῶσι τῶν
Αἰτωλῶν ἀναγγέλλειν· αὐτὸν δὲ τὸν Νίκανδρον παρακαλέσας μνημονεύειν τῆς εἰς αὐτὸν γεγενημένης εὐεργεσίας ἐξέπεμπε μετὰ προπομπῆς ἱκανῆς, παραγγείλας τοῖς ἐπὶ τούτῳ τεταγμένοις ἀσφαλῶς εἰς τὴν
9 Ὑπάταν αὐτὸν ἀποκαταστῆσαι. ὁ δὲ Νίκανδρος, τελέως ἀνελπίστου καὶ παραδόξου φανείσης αὐτῷ τῆς
ἀπαντήσεως, τότε μὲν ἀνεκομίσθη πρὸς τοὺς οἰκείους,
κατὰ δὲ τὸν ἑξῆς χρόνον ἀπὸ ταύτης τῆς συστάσεως
10 εὔνους ὢν διετέλει τῇ Μακεδόνων οἰκίᾳ. διὸ καὶ μετὰ
ταῦτα κατὰ τοὺς Περσικοὺς καιροὺς ἐνδεδεμένος τῇ

aged by a wonder to convey the money to Lamia, and himself attempted at night to escape between the two armies to Hypata. Falling into the hands of the Macedonian sentries, he was being brought before Philip while the banquet was still at its height, quite expecting to suffer the worst at the hands of the enraged king, or to be given up to the Romans. But when the matter was reported to Philip,[33] he at once ordered those whose business this was, to attend to Nicander's personal wants and treat him kindly in every respect. After a little he himself rose from table and came to visit Nicander. He severely blamed the errors into which the Aetolian state had fallen, by calling in[34] first of all the Romans and subsequently Antiochus to attack the Greeks, but nevertheless he still implored them to forget the past, and to cultivate their friendship with himself, and not be ever disposed to take advantage of circumstances adverse to either. This message he begged him to convey to the leading Aetolian statesmen, and after exhorting Nicander himself to be ever mindful of the kindness he had shown him, sent him off with an adequate escort, ordering the officers whose duty it was to bring him back to Hypata in safety. Nicander, finding himself thus met by Philip in a spirit which he never dared to hope for or expect, was now restored to his relatives, and ever after this friendly approach remained well inclined to the house of Macedon. Thus even later in the time of Perseus still

[33] For his role in this war, see Walbank (18. 3.9), 186–222.
[34] When they concluded the treaty with them in 212/1.

προειρημένῃ χάριτι καὶ δυσχερῶς ἀντιπράττων ταῖς
τοῦ Περσέως ἐπιβολαῖς, εἰς ὑποψίας καὶ διαβολὰς
ἐμπεσὼν καὶ τέλος ἀνακληθεὶς εἰς Ῥώμην ἐκεῖ μετήλλαξε τὸν βίον.

11   Κόραξ, ὄρος μεταξὺ Καλλιπόλεως καὶ Ναυπάκτου.
Πολύβιος εἰκοστῷ.

12   Ἀπεράντεια, πόλις Θεσσαλίας. Πολύβιος εἰκοστῷ.

12. . . . ἐξ αὐτῶν τὸν ἐροῦντα περὶ τούτων πρὸς
(xxi.15) αὐτόν· ἀλλ' ὥσπερ ἐπὶ τῶν πλείστων ἐργολαβοῦντες
πολλοὶ προσφέρουσι τὰς τοιαύτας χάριτας καὶ ταύτην ἀρχὴν ποιοῦνται φιλίας καὶ συστάσεως, οὕτως
ἐπὶ Φιλοποίμενος ὁ προσοίσων ταύτην τὴν χάριν
2   ἑκὼν οὐχ εὑρίσκετο τὸ παράπαν, ἕως [ἂν] ἐξαπορή-
σαντες ψήφῳ προεχειρίσαντο Τιμόλαον, ὃς ὑπάρχων
καὶ ξένος πατρικὸς καὶ συνήθης ἐπὶ πολὺ τῷ Φιλο-
ποίμενι, δὶς εἰς τὴν Μεγάλην πόλιν ἐκδημήσας αὐτοῦ
τούτου χάριν οὐκ ἐτόλμησε φθέγξασθαι περὶ τούτων
οὐδέν, μέχρις ὅτε μυωπίσας ἑαυτὸν καὶ τρίτον ἐλθὼν
3   ἐθάρρησε μνησθῆναι τῆς δωρεᾶς. τοῦ δὲ Φιλοποίμε-

35 Modern Vardhousi. *RE* Korax 1378–1379 (Wm. Oldfather).
For the context see Livy 36.30.4.

36 Also called Callium, identified by W. Dittenberger from a
dedication to King Pyrrhus found there. Devastated in the invasion of the Celts in 279 (Paus. 10.22.3). See C. Habicht, *Pausanias*
(18.10.11), 32–35 and XIV. See also P. Pantos, Τὰ σφραγίσματα
τῆς Αἰτωλικῆς Καλλιπόλεως (Athens 1985).

37 Located close to the Achelous river, the exact site is not
known. Not Thessalian and certainly not called Thessalian by P.
Taken from Aetolia by Philip; Walbank (18.3.9), 207.

feeling the obligation he was under for this favor and ill disposed to oppose the projects of Perseus, he exposed himself to suspicion and obloquy, and finally was summoned to Rome and ended his days there.

Corax,[35] a mountain between Callipolis[36] and Naupactus. Polybius in Book 20.

Aperantia,[37] a city of Thessaly. Polybius in Book 20.

Philopoemen at Sparta

(Cf. Plutarch, *Philop.* 15)

12. The Spartans[38] wished to find one of their own citizens to speak to Philopoemen about this. But whereas on most occasions there are many ready to pursue their private advantages by offering such favors and thus take the first steps to recommend and establish friendship, in the case of Philopoemen they could not find a single man willing to offer him this favor, until at last being hard put to it they appointed by vote Timolaus, who though he was a family friend of Philopoemen and had been intimate with him for long, had visited Megalopolis twice for this very purpose without being able to summon up the courage to mention the matter to him, until spurring himself on and going there a third time he ventured to address him on the subject of the gift. When Philopoemen, as he never

[38] The following episode (12.1–7) is told in Paus. 8.51.1–2, and in Plu., *Phil.* 15. The events happened after Philopoemen had brought Sparta into the Achaean Confederacy, in 191 or already in 192. The fragment should, according to WC 3.2, stand between 8.5 and 8.6; other proposals are quoted by him.

νος παραδόξως αὐτὸν ἐπὶ τούτοις ἀποδεξαμένου καὶ
4 φιλανθρώπως, ὁ μὲν Τιμόλαος περιχαρὴς ἦν, ὑπολαβὼν καθῖχθαι τῆς ἐπιβολῆς, ὁ δὲ Φιλοποίμην ἥξειν
ἔφη μετ᾽ ὀλίγας ἡμέρας εἰς τὴν Λακεδαίμονα· θέλειν
γὰρ εὐχαριστῆσαι πᾶσι τοῖς ἄρχουσι περὶ τούτων.
5 ἐλθὼν δὲ μετὰ ταῦτα καὶ κληθεὶς εἰς τὸ συνέδριον
πάλαι μὲν ἔφη γινώσκειν τὴν τῶν Λακεδαιμονίων
πρὸς αὐτὸν εὔνοιαν, μάλιστα δ᾽ ἐκ τοῦ νῦν προτεινο-
6 μένου στεφάνου καὶ τῆς τοιαύτης τιμῆς. τὴν μὲν οὖν
προαίρεσιν αὐτῶν ἔφησεν ἀποδέχεσθαι, τῷ δὲ χει-
ρισμῷ δυσωπεῖσθαι. δεῖν γὰρ οὐ τοῖς φίλοις δίδοσθαι
τὰς τοιαύτας τιμὰς καὶ τοὺς στεφάνους, ἐξ ὧν ὁ περι-
7 θέμενος οὐδέποτε μὴ τὸν ἰὸν ἐκνίψηται, πολὺ δὲ μᾶλλον τοῖς ἐχθροῖς, ἵν᾽ οἱ μὲν φίλοι τηροῦντες τὴν
παρρησίαν πιστεύωνται παρὰ τοῖς Ἀχαιοῖς, ἐπὰν
προθῶνται τῇ πόλει βοηθεῖν, οἱ δ᾽ ἐχθροὶ καταπιόντες
τὸ δέλεαρ ἢ συνηγορεῖν αὐτοῖς ἀναγκάζωνται ἢ
σιωπῶντες μηδὲν δύνωνται βλάπτειν.

II. FRAGMENTUM INCERTAE SEDIS

8 Ὅτι οὐχ ὅμοιόν ἐστιν ἐξ ἀκοῆς περὶ πραγμάτων
διαλαμβάνειν καὶ γενόμενον αὐτόπτην, ἀλλὰ καὶ μεγάλα διαφέρει, πολὺ δέ τι συμβάλλεσθαι πέφυκεν
ἑκάστοις ἡ κατὰ τὴν ἐνάργειαν πίστις.

expected, received the proposal quite courteously, he was delighted, as he thought he had attained his object, and Philopoemen said he would come to Sparta in a few days, as he wished to thank all the magistrates for this favor. Upon his going there later and being invited to attend the Council, he said that he had long recognized the kind feelings the Spartans entertained for him and now did so more than ever from the crown and very high honor that they offered him. So, he said, he perfectly appreciated their intentions, but was a little abashed by the manner in which they proceeded. For such honors and such crowns, the rust of which he who once put them on would never wash off his head, should never be given to friends, but much rather to enemies, in order that their friends, retaining the right to speak their minds, might be trusted by the Achaeans when they proposed to help Sparta, while their enemies, who had swallowed the bait, might either be compelled to support the proposal or have to hold their tongues and be incapacitated from doing any harm.

II. A FRAGMENT, THE PLACE OF WHICH IS UNCERTAIN

It is not at all the same to judge of things from hearsay and from having actually witnessed them, but there is a great difference. In all matters a certainty founded on the evidence of one's eyes is of the greatest value.

FRAGMENTA LIBRI XXI

I. RES ITALIAE

1. Ὅτι κατὰ τὸν καιρὸν τοῦτον συνέβη καὶ τὴν ἐκ
(xx.21) τῆς Ῥώμης πρεσβείαν, ἣν ἀπέστειλαν οἱ Λακεδαιμό-
2 νιοι, παραγενέσθαι διεψευσμένην τῶν ἐλπίδων. ἐπρέ-
3 σβευον μὲν γὰρ περὶ τῶν ὁμήρων καὶ τῶν κωμῶν· ἡ
δὲ σύγκλητος περὶ μὲν τῶν κωμῶν ἔφησεν ἐντολὰς
δώσειν τοῖς παρ᾽ αὐτῶν ἀποστελλομένοις πρέσβεσιν,
4 περὶ δὲ τῶν ὁμήρων ἔτι βουλεύσασθαι θέλειν. περὶ δὲ
τῶν φυγάδων τῶν ἀρχαίων θαυμάζειν ἔφησαν, πῶς
οὐ κατάγουσιν αὐτοὺς εἰς τὴν οἰκείαν, ἠλευθερωμένης
τῆς Σπάρτης.

2. Ὅτι τοῖς Ῥωμαίοις τῆς κατὰ τὴν ναυμαχίαν
(3) (1) νίκης ἄρτι προσηγγελμένης, πρῶτον μὲν τῷ δήμῳ
2 παρήγγειλαν ἐλινύας ἄγειν ἡμέρας ἐννέα—τοῦτο δ᾽

---

¹ Summer or early autumn 191. It is disputed whether this fragment (1.1–4) in fact belongs to this book, or whether it should be placed after 20.12.1–7; see WC 3.88. ² Five Spartans turned over by Nabis at Flamininus' demand when he achieved peace in 195. ³ Some were handed over in trust to the Achaeans under the peace treaty of 195, but not returned when Sparta joined their Confederacy; see n. on 20.12.1.

FRAGMENTS OF BOOK XXI

I. AFFAIRS OF ITALY

Embassy of the Lacedaemonians to Rome

1. At this time[1] the embassy which the Lacedaemonians had sent to Rome arrived disappointed in their hopes. For they had been sent on the subject of the hostages[2] and villages,[3] but regarding the villages the senate replied that they would give orders to the legates sent by them, and as for the hostages they must consult further about the matter. As to the old exiles they said they wondered why the Spartans did not call them home, now that Sparta was free.[4]

Embassy of the Aetolians

2. Immediately upon the announcement of the naval victory,[5] the Romans ordered the people to observe nine days of rest,[6] i.e., to keep a general holiday and sacrifice

---

[4] After the assassination of Nabis. The "old exiles" were those banned by him.   [5] At Corycus, on the mainland opposite Chius, a Syrian fleet was defeated in autumn 191 by the Romans and King Eumenes II.

[6] A *supplicatio* of nine days.

ἔστιν σχολάζειν πανδημεὶ καὶ θύειν τοῖς θεοῖς χαρι-
3 στήρια τῶν εὐτυχημάτων—μετὰ δὲ ταῦτα τοὺς παρὰ
τῶν Αἰτωλῶν πρέσβεις καὶ τοὺς παρὰ τοῦ Μανίου
4 προσῆγον τῇ συγκλήτῳ. γενομένων δὲ πλειόνων παρ'
ἀμφοῖν λόγων, ἔδοξε τῷ συνεδρίῳ δύο προτείνειν γνώμας τοῖς Αἰτωλοῖς, ἢ διδόναι τὴν ἐπιτροπὴν περὶ πάντων τῶν καθ' αὑτοὺς ἢ χίλια τάλαντα παραχρῆμα
δοῦναι καὶ τὸν αὐτὸν ἐχθρὸν καὶ φίλον νομίζειν Ῥω-
5 μαίοις. τῶν δ' Αἰτωλῶν ἀξιούντων διασαφῆσαι ῥητῶς
ἐπὶ τίσι δεῖ διδόναι τὴν ἐπιτροπήν, οὐ προσδέχεται
6 τὴν διαστολὴν ἡ σύγκλητος. διὸ καὶ τούτοις γέγονε
κατάμονος ὁ πόλεμος.

(2) 3. Ὅτι κατὰ τοὺς αὐτοὺς καιροὺς ἡ σύγκλητος
(xx.13) ἐχρημάτισε τοῖς παρὰ Φιλίππου πρεσβευταῖς· ἧκον
2 γὰρ παρ' αὐτοῦ πρέσβεις ἀπολογιζόμενοι τὴν εὔνοιαν
καὶ προθυμίαν, ἣν παρέσχηται Ῥωμαίοις ὁ βασιλεὺς
3 ἐν τῷ πρὸς Ἀντίοχον πολέμῳ. ὧν διακούσασα τὸν μὲν
υἱὸν Δημήτριον ἀπέλυσε τῆς ὁμηρείας παραχρῆμα·
ὁμοίως δὲ καὶ τῶν φόρων ἐπηγγείλατο παραλύσειν,
διαφυλάξαντος αὐτοῦ τὴν πίστιν ἐν τοῖς ἐνεστῶσι
4 καιροῖς. παραπλησίως δὲ καὶ τοὺς τῶν Λακεδαιμονίων ὁμήρους ἀφῆκε πλὴν Ἀρμένα τοῦ Νάβιδος υἱοῦ·
τοῦτον δὲ μετὰ ταῦτα συνέβη νόσῳ μεταλλάξαι τὸν
βίον.

---

7 The Aetolian embassy of winter 191/0, during a truce
granted by Acilius, after he had besieged Naupactus for two
months.

to the gods in thanks for their success. After this they introduced into the Senate the Aetolian embassy[7] and the legates from Glabrio. After both had addressed them at some length, the senate decided to give the Aetolians the choice[8] of two courses, either to submit all matters to the decision of the senate or to pay at once a thousand talents and enter into an offensive and defensive alliance with Rome. When they demanded a definite statement of what matters were to be submitted to the senate's decision, that body refused to grant any explanation, and therefore the Aetolians remained *in statu belli*.

Embassy from Philip

3. At about the same time the senate gave a hearing to the envoys of Philip; for he had sent this embassy to call attention in his favor to the goodwill and readiness to help he had shown in the war with Antiochus. After listening to them the senate at once set free his son Demetrius,[9] who was their hostage, and also promised to relieve him of some of the payments due, if he kept his faith to them under present circumstances.[10] They also set free the Lacedaemonian hostages except Armenas, the son of Nabis, who soon after this sickened and died.

[8] The Aetolians were to choose between *deditio* and a *foedus*, in which they would be an unequal partner.

[9] The prince had been a hostage since the peace of 197. He was now about fifteen.

[10] The Roman army was about to march through Philip's territory on their way to fight Antiochus in Asia Minor.

II. RES GRAECIAE

3b. Ὅτι καὶ κατὰ τὴν Ἑλλάδα, πρεσβείας παραγε-
(9) (7) νομένης εἰς Ἀχαΐαν παρ' Εὐμένους τοῦ βασιλέως
2 ὑπὲρ συμμαχίας, ἀθροισθέντες εἰς ἐκκλησίαν οἱ πολλοὶ τῶν Ἀχαιῶν τήν τε συμμαχίαν ἐπεκύρωσαν καὶ
νεανίσκους ἐξαπέστειλαν, πεζοὺς μὲν χιλίους ἱππεῖς
δ' ἑκατόν, ὧν ἡγεῖτο Διοφάνης ὁ Μεγαλοπολίτης.

(2) 4. Ὅτι πολιορκουμένων τῶν Ἀμφισσέων ὑπὸ Μανίου τοῦ Ῥωμαίων στρατηγοῦ, κατὰ τὸν καιρὸν τοῦτον ὁ τῶν Ἀθηναίων δῆμος, πυνθανόμενος τήν τε τῶν
Ἀμφισσέων ταλαιπωρίαν καὶ τὴν τοῦ Ποπλίου παρουσίαν, ἐξαπέστειλε πρεσβευτὰς τοὺς περὶ τὸν
2 Ἐχέδημον, ἐντειλάμενος ἅμα μὲν ἀσπάσασθαι τοὺς
περὶ τὸν Λεύκιον καὶ Πόπλιον, ἅμα δὲ καταπειράζειν
3 τῆς πρὸς Αἰτωλοὺς διαλύσεως. ὧν παραγενομένων
ἀσμένως ἀποδεξάμενος ὁ Πόπλιος ἐφιλανθρώπει τοὺς
ἄνδρας, θεωρῶν ὅτι παρέξονται χρείαν αὐτῷ πρὸς τὰς
4 προκειμένας ἐπιβολάς. ὁ γὰρ προειρημένος ἀνὴρ
ἐβούλετο θέσθαι μὲν καλῶς τὰ κατὰ τοὺς Αἰτωλούς·
εἰ δὲ μὴ συνυπακούοιεν, πάντως διειλήφει παραλιπὼν
5 ταῦτα διαβαίνειν εἰς τὴν Ἀσίαν, σαφῶς γινώσκων δι-

---

11 He was engaged to defend his realm against Antiochus' son
Seleucus.

12 Son of Diaeus of Megalopolis, an able commander and influential politician, strategus 192/1, thereafter in charge of the
Achaeans sent to support Eumenes. More on him in 9.1–3.

II. AFFAIRS OF GREECE

Eumenes and Achaea

3b. In Greece, too, when an embassy reached Achaea from King Eumenes[11] about an alliance, the Achaean people meeting in a general assembly voted the alliance and sent off soldiers—a thousand foot and a hundred horse under the command of Diophanes[12] of Megalopolis.

The Aetolians and the Roman Governors

4. While Glabrio, the Roman general, was besieging Amphissa,[13] the Athenian people, hearing of the distress of the Amphissians and the arrival of Publius Scipio, sent an embassy at the head of which was Echedemus,[14] with instructions to salute Lucius and Publius Scipio and to attempt to procure terms of peace for the Aetolians. Publius was very glad of their arrival and paid much attention to them, as he saw they would be of service to him in the projects he entertained. For the general wished to settle the Aetolian matter, and even if the Aetolians did not submit, had in any case resolved to neglect them and cross to

[13] The largest city in Locris, some twelve kilometers northwest of Delphi. Acilius began its siege until he was succeeded by the consul of 190, Lucius Cornelius Scipio. With him was his brother Publius, the victor over Hannibal, as his *legatus*.

[14] A member of one of the leading families of Athens at the time. See C. Habicht (16.25.8), 189–193, and P. Pantos, *Hesp.* 58 (1989), 277–288.

ὅτι τὸ τέλος ἐστὶ τοῦ πολέμου καὶ τῆς ὅλης ἐπιβολῆς
οὐκ ἐν τῷ χειρώσασθαι τὸ τῶν Αἰτωλῶν ἔθνος, ἀλλ'
ἐν τῷ νικήσαντας τὸν Ἀντίοχον κρατῆσαι τῆς Ἀσίας.

6 διόπερ ἅμα τῷ μνησθῆναι τοὺς Ἀθηναίους ὑπὲρ τῆς
   διαλύσεως, ἑτοίμως προσδεξάμενος τοὺς λόγους ἐκέλευσε παραπλησίως πειράζειν αὐτοὺς καὶ τῶν Αἰτω-
7 λῶν. οἱ δὲ περὶ τὸν Ἐχέδημον, προδιαπεμψάμενοι καὶ
   μετὰ ταῦτα πορευθέντες εἰς τὴν Ὑπάταν αὐτοί, διελέγοντο περὶ τῆς διαλύσεως τοῖς ἄρχουσι τῶν Αἰτωλῶν.
8 ἑτοίμως δὲ κἀκείνων συννυπακουόντων κατεστάθησαν
9 οἱ συμμίξοντες τοῖς Ῥωμαίοις· οἳ καὶ παραγενόμενοι
   πρὸς τοὺς περὶ τὸν Πόπλιον, καταλαβόντες αὐτοὺς
   στρατοπεδεύοντας ἐν ἑξήκοντα σταδίοις ἀπὸ τῆς Ἀμ-
   φίσσης, πολλοὺς διετίθεντο λόγους, ἀναμιμνήσκοντες
   τῶν γεγονότων σφίσι φιλανθρώπων πρὸς Ῥωμαίους.
10 ἔτι δὲ πρᾳότερον καὶ φιλανθρωπότερον ὁμιλήσαντος
   τοῦ Ποπλίου καὶ προφερομένου τάς τε κατὰ τὴν
   Ἰβηρίαν καὶ τὴν Λιβύην πράξεις καὶ διασαφοῦντος
   τίνα τρόπον κέχρηται τοῖς κατ' ἐκείνους τοὺς τόπους
   αὐτῷ πιστεύσασιν καὶ τέλος οἰομένου δεῖν ἐγχειρίζειν
11 σφᾶς αὐτῷ καὶ πιστεύειν, τὰς μὲν ἀρχὰς ἅπαντες οἱ
   παρόντες εὐέλπιδες ἐγενήθησαν, ὡς αὐτίκα μάλα τε-
12 λεσιουργηθησομένης τῆς διαλύσεως· ἐπεὶ δέ, πυθομένων τῶν Αἰτωλῶν ἐπὶ τίσι δεῖ ποιεῖσθαι τὴν εἰρήνην,
   ὁ Λεύκιος διεσάφησεν διότι δυεῖν προκειμένων αὐτοῖς
13 αἵρεσις ὑπάρχει—δεῖν γὰρ ἢ τὴν ἐπιτροπὴν διδόναι
   περὶ πάντων τῶν καθ' αὑτοὺς ἢ χίλια τάλαντα παραχρῆμα καὶ τὸν αὐτὸν ἐχθρὸν αἱρεῖσθαι φίλον Ῥωμαί-

Asia, as he well knew that the object of the war and the whole expedition was not to subdue the Aetolian League but to conquer Antiochus and become masters of Asia.[15] Therefore as soon as the Athenians mentioned peace, he readily accepted the proposal, and told them to sound the Aetolians also. Echedemus, having sent a message in advance, proceeded himself to Hypata, and spoke about the question of peace to the Aetolian authorities. They also readily lent an ear, and delegates were appointed to meet the Romans. Upon reaching Publius, whom they found encamped at a distance of sixty stades from Amphissa, they made a long speech reminding him of all the kindness they had shown the Romans. When Scipio addressed them in a still milder and kinder tone, recounting his actions in Spain and Africa, and explaining how he had dealt with people in those countries who had relied on him, and when he finally expressed his opinion that they ought to place themselves in his hands and rely on him, all those present at first became most sanguine, thinking that peace would be at once concluded. But when, upon the Aetolians inquiring on what conditions they should make peace, Lucius Scipio informed them that there were two alternatives[16] open to them, either to submit entirely to Rome or to pay a thousand talents at once and make a de-

[15] This is P.'s interpretation of the Roman goal at the time.
[16] The same as in 2.4.

14 οις—ἐδυσχρήστησαν μὲν οἱ παρόντες τῶν Αἰτωλῶν
ὡς ἔνι μάλιστα διὰ τὸ μὴ γίνεσθαι τὴν ἀπόφασιν
ἀκόλουθον τῇ προγενομένῃ λαλιᾷ, πλὴν ἐπανοίσειν
ἔφασαν ὑπὲρ τῶν ἐπιταττομένων τοῖς Αἰτωλοῖς.

(3)   5. Οὗτοι μὲν οὖν ἐπανῄεσαν βουλευσόμενοι περὶ

2 τῶν προειρημένων· οἱ <δὲ> περὶ τὸν Ἐχέδημον συμμίξαντες τοῖς ἀποκλήτοις ἐβουλεύοντο περὶ τῶν προ-

3 ειρημένων. ἦν δὲ τῶν ἐπιταττομένων τὸ μὲν ἀδύνατον
διὰ τὸ πλῆθος τῶν χρημάτων, τὸ δὲ φοβερὸν διὰ τὸ
πρότερον αὐτοὺς ἀπατηθῆναι, καθ᾽ ὃν καιρὸν ἐπι-
νεύσαντες ὑπὲρ τῆς ἐπιτροπῆς παρὰ μικρὸν εἰς τὴν

4 ἄλυσιν ἐνέπεσον. διόπερ ἀπορούμενοι καὶ δυσχρη-
στούμενοι περὶ ταῦτα πάλιν ἐξέπεμπον τοὺς αὐτοὺς
δεησομένους ἢ τῶν χρημάτων ἀφελεῖν, ἵνα δύνωνται
τελεῖν, ἢ τῆς ἐπιτροπῆς ἐκτὸς ποιῆσαι τοὺς πολιτικοὺς

5 ἄνδρας καὶ τὰς γυναῖκας. οἳ καὶ συμμίξαντες τοῖς

6 περὶ τὸν Πόπλιον διεσάφουν τὰ δεδογμένα. τοῦ δὲ
Λευκίου φήσαντος ἐπὶ τούτοις ἔχειν παρὰ τῆς συγκλήτου τὴν ἐξουσίαν, ἐφ᾽ οἷς ἀρτίως εἶπεν, οὗτοι μὲν

7 αὖθις ἐπανῆλθον, οἱ δὲ περὶ τὸν Ἐχέδημον ἐπακολουθήσαντες εἰς τὴν Ὑπάταν συνεβούλευσαν τοῖς Αἰτωλοῖς, ἐπεὶ τὰ τῆς διαλύσεως ἐμποδίζοιτο κατὰ τὸ
παρόν, ἀνοχὰς αἰτησαμένους καὶ τῶν ἐνεστώτων κακῶν ὑπέρθεσιν ποιησαμένους πρεσβεύειν πρὸς τὴν
σύγκλητον, κἂν μὲν ἐπιτυγχάνωσι περὶ τῶν ἀξιου-

8 μένων· εἰ δὲ μή, τοῖς καιροῖς ἐφεδρεύειν. χείρω μὲν
9 γὰρ ἀδύνατον γενέσθαι τῶν ὑποκειμένων τὰ περὶ
σφᾶς, βελτίω γε μὴν οὐκ ἀδύνατον διὰ πολλὰς αἰτίας.

fensive and offensive alliance, the Aetolians present were exceedingly distressed to find that this decision was not at all conformable to their previous conversation. They, however, said they would submit the conditions to the people of Aetolia.

5. These delegates, then, returned home to discuss the matter, and Echedemus meeting the Apocleti also talked it over. One of the alternative conditions was impossible owing to the magnitude of the sum demanded, and the other frightened them owing to what had taken place on the occasion of their former mistake,[17] when after having assented to absolute submission they came very near to being placed in chains. Consequently, in their difficulty and distress, they sent off the same envoys again to beg either that the sum might be reduced so that they would be able to pay it, or that their citizens and their wives should be excluded from the total submission. Meeting Publius and his brother they communicated the decree of the Aetolians on the subject, but when Lucius said that he was only empowered by the senate to propose the conditions he had stated, they again returned to Aetolia, and Echedemus following them to Hypata, advised the Aetolians, since there was this obstacle at present to the conclusion of peace, to ask for an armistice and gaining thus a temporary relief from present ills, to send an embassy to the senate, when if they were successful in obtaining their request well and good, but if not they might watch for a change of circumstances. For it was impossible for their situation to be worse than it actually was, but there were

17 See 20.10.7.

10 φανέντων δὲ καλῶς λέγειν τῶν περὶ τὸν Ἐχέδημον,
ἔδοξε πρεσβεύειν τοῖς Αἰτωλοῖς ὑπὲρ τῶν ἀνοχῶν.
11 ἀφικόμενοι δὲ πρὸς τὸν Λεύκιον ἐδέοντο συγχωρηθῆναι
σφίσι κατὰ τὸ παρὸν ἑξαμήνους ἀνοχάς, ἵνα πρε-
12 σβεύσωσι πρὸς τὴν σύγκλητον. ὁ δὲ Πόπλιος, πάλαι
πρὸς τὰς κατὰ τὴν Ἀσίαν πράξεις παρωρμημένος,
ταχέως ἔπεισε τὸν ἀδελφὸν ὑπακοῦσαι τοῖς ἀξιουμέ-
13 νοις. γραφεισῶν δὲ τῶν ὁμολογιῶν, ὁ μὲν Μάνιος, λύ-
σας τὴν πολιορκίαν καὶ παραδοὺς ἅπαν τὸ στράτευμα
καὶ τὰς χορηγίας τοῖς περὶ τὸν Λεύκιον, εὐθέως ἀπηλ-
λάττετο μετὰ τῶν χιλιάρχων εἰς τὴν Ῥώμην.

III. RES ASIAE

(4) 6. Οἱ δὲ Φωκαιεῖς, τὰ μὲν ὑπὸ τῶν ἀπολειφθέντων
Ῥωμαίων ἐν ταῖς ναυσὶν ἐπισταθμευόμενοι, τὰ δὲ τὰς
ἐπιταγὰς δυσχερῶς φέροντες, ἐστασίαζον.

2 Ὅτι κατὰ τοὺς αὐτοὺς χρόνους οἱ τῶν Φωκαιέων
ἄρχοντες, δεδιότες τάς τε τῶν πολλῶν ὁρμὰς διὰ τὴν
σιτοδείαν καὶ τὴν τῶν Ἀντιοχιστῶν φιλοτιμίαν, ἐξέπεμψαν πρεσβευτὰς πρὸς Σέλευκον, ὄντα πρὸς τοῖς
3 ὅροις τῆς χώρας αὐτῶν, ἀξιοῦντες μὴ πελάζειν τῆς
πόλεως, ὅτι πρόκειται σφίσι τὴν ἡσυχίαν ἄγειν καὶ
καραδοκεῖν τὴν τῶν ὅλων κρίσιν, μετὰ δὲ ταῦτα πει-
4 θαρχεῖν τοῖς εἰρημένοις. ἦσαν δὲ τῶν πρεσβευτῶν

18 See 5.77.4. The city was in Roman hands after the sea
battle of Corycus (2.1).

many reasons why it might improve. Echedemus' advice seemed to them to be good, and it was decided to send envoys asking for a truce. So coming to Lucius they begged him to grant them for the present a truce for six months, in order to send an embassy to the Senate. Publius, who had for long been eager to play a part in Asiatic affairs, soon persuaded his brother to accede to the request. Upon the signature of the agreement, Glabrio, after raising the siege and handing over his whole army and his stores to Lucius, at once left for Rome with his military tribunes.

III. AFFAIRS OF ASIA

State of Phocaea

(Suda; cf. Livy 37.9.1)

6. The Phocaeans, partly because the Romans left in the ships were quartered upon them and partly because they objected to the enforced contributions, became disaffected.

At the same date the magistrates of Phocaea,[18] afraid both of the excited state the people were in owing to the dearth of corn and of the active propaganda of the partisans of Antiochus, sent envoys to Seleucus,[19] who was on the borders of their territory, begging him not to approach the town, as it was their intention to keep quiet and await the issue of events, after which they would yield obedience to orders given them. Of these envoys Aristarchus, Cas-

[19] See n. on 3b.1. He was his father's commander in Aeolis (Livy 37.8.5).

ἴδιοι μὲν τοῦ Σελεύκου καὶ ταύτης τῆς ὑποθέσεως
Ἀρίσταρχος καὶ Κάσσανδρος καὶ Ῥόδων, ἐναντίοι δὲ
καὶ πρὸς Ῥωμαίους ἀπονενευκότες Ἡγίας καὶ Γελίας.

5 ὧν συμμιξάντων ὁ Σέλευκος εὐθέως τοὺς μὲν περὶ τὸν
Ἀρίσταρχον ἀνὰ χεῖρας εἶχε, τοὺς δὲ περὶ τὸν Ἡγίαν

6 παρεώρα. πυθόμενος δὲ τὴν ὁρμὴν τῶν πολλῶν καὶ
τὴν σπάνιν τοῦ σίτου, παρεὶς τὸν χρηματισμὸν καὶ
τὴν ἔντευξιν τῶν παραγεγονότων προῆγε πρὸς τὴν
πόλιν.

7   Ἐξελθόντες μὲν Γάλλοι δύο μετὰ τύπων καὶ προσ-
τηθιδίων ἐδέοντο μηδὲν ἀνήκεστον βουλεύεσθαι περὶ
τῆς πόλεως.

(5)   7. Πυρφόρος, ᾧ ἐχρήσατο Παυσίστρατος ὁ τῶν

2 Ῥοδίων ναύαρχος. ἦν δὲ κημός· ἐξ ἑκατέρου δὲ τοῦ
μέρους τῆς πρώρρας ἀγκύλαι δύο παρέκειντο παρὰ
τὴν ἐντὸς ἐπιφάνειαν τῶν τοίχων, εἰς ἃς ἐνηρμόζοντο

3 κοντοὶ προτείνοντες τοῖς κέρασιν εἰς θάλατταν. ἐπὶ δὲ
τὸ τούτων ἄκρον ὁ κημὸς ἁλύσει σιδηρᾷ προσήρτητο

4 πλήρης πυρός, ὥστε κατὰ τὰς ἐμβολὰς καὶ παραβο-
λὰς εἰς μὲν τὴν πολεμίαν ναῦν ἐκτινάττεσθαι πῦρ,
ἀπὸ δὲ τῆς οἰκείας πολὺν ἀφεστάναι τόπον διὰ τὴν

5 ἔγκλισιν. Ὅτι Παμφιλίδας ὁ τῶν Ῥοδίων ναύαρχος
ἐδόκει πρὸς πάντας τοὺς καιροὺς εὐαρμοστότερος εἶ-

sander, and Rhodon were attached to Seleucus and his cause, while Hegias and Gelias were opposed to him and inclined to favor the Romans. Upon their meeting him, Seleucus at once admitted the three first into his intimacy, neglecting Hegias and Gelias. But when he heard of the excitement of the populace and the dearth of corn he advanced to the town without giving the envoys a formal audience.

(Suda.; cf. Livy 37.11.7)

Two Galli[20] or priests of Cybele with images and pectorals came out of the town, and besought them not to resort to extreme measures against the city.

Naval Matters

(Suda)

7. The engine for throwing fire used by Pausistratus,[21] the Rhodian admiral, was funnel-shaped. On each side of the ship's prow noosed ropes were run along the inner side of the hull, into which were fitted poles stretching out seaward with their extremities. From the extremity of each hung by an iron chain the funnel-shaped vessel full of fire, so that, in charging or passing, the fire was shot out of it into the enemy's ship, but was a long way from one's own ship owing to the inclination.

Pamphilidas,[22] the Rhodian admiral, was considered more adequate to any occasion than Pausistratus because

[20] Eunuch priests of Cybele. *RE* Gallos 674–682 (F. Cumont). A. S. F. Gow, *JHS* 80 (1960), 88–93 and pl. VIII.

[21] *RE* Pausistratos 2423–2425 (Th. Lenschau).

[22] This seems to be an error for Eudamus; cf. Livy 37.12.8–9.

ναι τοῦ Παυσιστράτου διὰ τὸ βαθύτερος τῇ φύσει καὶ
στασιμώτερος μᾶλλον ἢ τολμηρότερος ὑπάρχειν.
6 ἀγαθοὶ γὰρ οἱ πολλοὶ τῶν ἀνθρώπων οὐκ ἐκ τῶν κατὰ
λόγον, ἀλλ᾽ ἐκ τῶν συμβαινόντων ποιεῖσθαι τὰς δια-
7 λήψεις. ἄρτι γὰρ δι᾽ αὐτὸ τοῦτο προκεχειρισμένοι τὸν
Παυσίστρατον, διὰ τὸ πρᾶξιν ἔχειν τινὰ καὶ τόλμαν,
παραχρῆμα μετέπιπτον εἰς τἀναντία ταῖς γνώμαις
διὰ τὴν περιπέτειαν.

(6)   8. Ὅτι κατὰ τὸν καιρὸν τοῦτον εἰς τὴν Σάμον
προσέπεσε γράμματα τοῖς περὶ τὸν Λεύκιον καὶ τὸν
Εὐμένη παρά τε τοῦ Λευκίου τοῦ τὴν ὕπατον ἀρχὴν
2 ἔχοντος καὶ παρὰ Ποπλίου Σκιπίωνος, δηλοῦντα τὰς
πρὸς τοὺς Αἰτωλοὺς γεγενημένας συνθήκας ὑπὲρ τῶν
ἀνοχῶν καὶ τὴν ἐπὶ τὸν Ἑλλήσποντον πορείαν τῶν
πεζικῶν στρατοπέδων. ὁμοίως δὲ καὶ τοῖς περὶ τὸν
3 Ἀντίοχον καὶ Σέλευκον ταῦτα διεσαφεῖτο παρὰ τῶν
Αἰτωλῶν.

9. Ὅτι Διοφάνης ὁ Μεγαλοπολίτης μεγάλην ἕξιν
(7) (3) εἶχεν ἐν τοῖς πολεμικοῖς διὰ τὸ πολυχρονίου γεγονότος τοῦ πρὸς Νάβιν πολέμου τοῖς Μεγαλοπολίταις
ἀστυγείτονος πάντα συνεχῶς τὸν χρόνον ὑπὸ τὸν Φιλοποίμενα τεταγμένος τριβὴν ἐσχηκέναι τῶν κατὰ
2 (4) πόλεμον ἔργων ἀληθινήν. χωρίς τε τούτων κατὰ τὴν
ἐπιφάνειαν καὶ κατὰ τὴν σωματικὴν χρείαν ἦν ὁ προ-
3 (5) ειρημένος ἀνὴρ δυνατὸς καὶ καταπληκτικός. τὸ δὲ κυριώτατον, πρὸς πόλεμον ὑπῆρχεν ἀνὴρ ἀγαθὸς καὶ
τοῖς ὅπλοις ἐχρῆτο διαφερόντως.

he was by nature wise and steadfast rather than venturesome. For most men are good at judging a situation rather from what happens to occur than by reasoning things out. They had appointed Pausistratus for the very reason that he was energetic and daring, but all of a sudden they entirely changed their minds owing to his disaster.

8. At this time letters reached Samos addressed to Lucius Aemilius Regillus[23] and Eumenes from Lucius Scipio the consul and from Publius Scipio informing them of the truce made with the Aetolians and of the march of the Roman army toward the Hellespont. The Aetolians had also informed Antiochus and Seleucus of this.

Diophanes of Megalopolis

9. Diophanes of Megalopolis had had great practice in war, because during the long war against Nabis, which was waged in the immediate vicinity of Megalopolis, he had constantly served under Philopoemen and thus acquired actual experience in the methods of warfare. Add to this that the man I am speaking of was both in personal appearance and in personal combat very powerful and redoubtable. And, most important of all, he was a gallant man-at-arms and exceptionally skilled in their use.

---

[23] *MRR* 1.356. In 190 successor to Livius Salinator as commander of the Roman fleet.

(8)   10. Ὅτι Ἀντίοχος ὁ βασιλεὺς εἰς τὸν Πέργαμον
ἐμβαλών, πυθόμενος δὲ τὴν παρουσίαν Εὐμένους τοῦ
βασιλέως καὶ θεωρῶν οὐ μόνον τὰς ναυτικάς, ἀλλὰ
καὶ τὰς πεζικὰς δυνάμεις ἐπ᾿ αὐτὸν παραγινομένας,
ἐβουλεύετο λόγους ποιήσασθαι περὶ διαλύσεως ὁμοῦ
πρός τε Ῥωμαίους καὶ τὸν Εὐμένη καὶ τοὺς Ῥοδίους.

2   ἐξάρας οὖν ἅπαντι τῷ στρατεύματι παρῆν πρὸς τὴν
Ἐλαίαν καὶ λαβὼν λόφον τινὰ καταντικρὺ τῆς πόλεως τὸ μὲν πεζικὸν ἐπὶ τούτου κατέστησε, τοὺς δ᾿
ἱππεῖς παρ᾿ αὐτὴν τὴν πόλιν παρενέβαλε, πλείους

3   ὄντας ἑξακισχιλίων. αὐτὸς δὲ μεταξὺ τούτων γενόμενος διεπέμπετο πρὸς τοὺς περὶ τὸν Λεύκιον εἰς τὴν

4   πόλιν ὑπὲρ διαλύσεων. ὁ δὲ στρατηγὸς ὁ τῶν Ῥωμαίων
συναγαγὼν τούς τε Ῥοδίους καὶ τὸν Εὐμένην ἠξίου

5   λέγειν περὶ τῶν ἐνεστώτων τὸ φαινόμενον. οἱ μὲν οὖν
περὶ τὸν Εὔδαμον καὶ Παμφιλίδαν οὐκ ἀλλότριοι τῆς
διαλύσεως ἦσαν· ὁ δὲ βασιλεὺς οὔτ᾿ εὐσχήμονα τὴν
διάλυσιν οὔτε δυνατὴν ἔφησε κατὰ τὸ παρὸν εἶναι.

6   "εὐσχήμονα γάρ" ἔφη "πῶς οἷόν τε γίνεσθαι τὴν
ἔκβασιν, ἐὰν τειχήρεις ὄντες ποιώμεθα τὰς διαλύ-

7   σεις;" καὶ μὴν οὐδὲ δυνατὴν ἔφησε κατὰ τὸ παρόν·
"πῶς γὰρ ἐνδέχεται, μὴ προσδεξαμένους ὕπατον, ἄνευ
τῆς ἐκείνου γνώμης βεβαιῶσαι τὰς ὁμολογηθείσας

8   συνθήκας; χωρίς τε τούτων, ἐὰν ὅλως γένηταί τι σημεῖον ὁμολογίας πρὸς Ἀντίοχον, οὔτε τὰς ναυτικὰς
δυνάμεις δυνατὸν ἐπανελθεῖν δήπουθεν εἰς τὴν ἰδίαν

Antiochus Negotiates

(Cf. Livy 37.18.6)

10. King Antiochus had entered the territory of Pergamum, where hearing of the arrival of King Eumenes, and seeing that both the naval and military forces were coming up against him, was desirous of making proposals for peace simultaneously to the Romans, to Eumenes and to the Rhodians. Setting out, then, with his whole army he came to Elaea,[24] and seizing on an eminence opposite the town, established his infantry there, encamping his cavalry, more than six thousand in number, under the walls of the town. He accompanied the latter force, and sent a messenger to Lucius Aemilius, who was within the town, on the subject of peace. The Roman general, summoning Eumenes and the Rhodians to meet him, begged them to give him their view of the situation. Eudamus and Pamphilidas[25] were not opposed to peace, but the king said that, for the present, peace neither befitted their dignity nor was possible. "For how," he said, "can the result fail to be undignified if we make peace while we are shut up within the walls? And indeed how is it even possible for the present? For how can we, unless we await the arrival of a general of consular rank, confirm any agreement we arrive at without his consent? And, apart from this, if we manage at all to come to some semblance of an agreement with Antiochus, I scarcely suppose that your naval and military forces can return home, unless the Senate and

[24] The port of Pergamum and the kings' naval station.

[25] Cf. 7.5. The Rhodian admiral, successor to Eudamus. *RE* Pamphilidas 329–330 (Th. Lenschau).

οὔτε τὰς πεζικάς, ἐὰν μὴ πρότερον ὅ τε δῆμος ἥ τε

9 σύγκλητος ἐπικυρώσῃ τὰ δοχθέντα. λείπεται δὴ καρα-
δοκοῦντας τὴν ἐκείνων ἀπόφασιν παραχειμάζειν ἐν-
θάδε καὶ πράττειν μὲν μηδέν, ἐκδαπανᾶν δὲ τὰς τῶν

10 ἰδίων συμμάχων χορηγίας καὶ παρασκευάς· ἔπειτ', ἂν
μὴ σφίσι παρῇ τῇ συγκλήτῳ διαλύεσθαι, καινοποιεῖν
πάλιν ἀπ' ἀρχῆς τὸν πόλεμον, παρέντας τοὺς ἐνεστῶτας καιρούς, ἐν οἷς δυνάμεθα θεῶν βουλομένων

11 πέρας ἐπιθεῖναι τοῖς ὅλοις." ὁ μὲν οὖν Εὐμένης ταῦτ'
εἶπεν· ὁ δὲ Λεύκιος ἀποδεξάμενος τὴν συμβουλίαν,
ἀπεκρίθη τοῖς περὶ τὸν Ἀντίοχον ὅτι πρὸ τοῦ τὸν
ἀνθύπατον ἐλθεῖν οὐκ ἐνδέχεται γενέσθαι τὰς διαλύ-

12 σεις. ὧν ἀκούσαντες οἱ περὶ τὸν Ἀντίοχον παραυτίκα

13 μὲν ἐδῄουν τὴν τῶν Ἐλαϊτῶν χώραν· ἑξῆς δὲ τούτοις
Σέλευκος μὲν ἐπὶ τούτων ἔμεινε τῶν τόπων, Ἀντίοχος
δὲ κατὰ τὸ συνεχὲς ἐπιπορευόμενος ἐνέβαλεν εἰς τὸ

14 Θήβης καλούμενον πεδίον, καὶ παραβεβληκὼς εἰς
χώραν εὐδαίμονα καὶ γέμουσαν ἀγαθῶν ἐπλήρου τὴν
στρατιὰν παντοδαπῆς λείας.—

(9)   11. Ὅτι Ἀντίοχος ὁ βασιλεὺς παραγενόμενος εἰς
τὰς Σάρδεις ἀπὸ τῆς προρρηθείσης στρατείας διεπέμ-

2 πετο συνεχῶς πρὸς Προυσίαν, παρακαλῶν αὐτὸν εἰς
τὴν σφετέραν συμμαχίαν. ὁ δὲ Προυσίας κατὰ μὲν
τοὺς ἀνώτερον χρόνους οὐκ ἀλλότριος ἦν τοῦ κοινωνεῖν τοῖς περὶ τὸν Ἀντίοχον· πάνυ γὰρ ἐδεδίει τοὺς
Ῥωμαίους, μὴ ποιῶνται τὴν εἰς Ἀσίαν διάβασιν ἐπὶ

---

26 As Reiske saw, probably an error for "consul" (Lucius

People ratify your decision. All that will be left for you to do, then, is to spend the winter here awaiting their pronouncement, perfectly inactive, but exhausting the stores and material of your allies; and afterward, if the Senate does not approve of your making peace, you will have to begin the war afresh from the beginning, after having thrown away the present opportunity we have by the grace of God of putting an end to the whole business." Eumenes spoke so, and Aemilius, approving his advice, replied to Antiochus that it was impossible for peace to be made before the arrival of the proconsul.[26] Antiochus, on hearing this, at once began to lay waste the territory of Elaea. After this, while Seleucus remained in this neighborhood, Antiochus made constant incursions into the so-called plain of Thebe,[27] and lighting upon this most fertile district, abounding in produce, plentifully supplied his army with every variety of booty.

Antiochus Approaches Prusias

(Cf. Livy 37.25.4)

11. King Antiochus, on returning to Sardis from the expedition I have described, sent frequent messages to Prusias[28] inviting him to enter into alliance with him. Prusias previously had not been disinclined to join Antiochus, for he was very much afraid of the Romans crossing to Asia

Scipio); the Greek ought then to have ὕπατον instead of ἀνθύπατον.

[27] City in Mysia. *RE* Thebe 1595–1599 (E. Honigmann).

[28] King Prusias I of Bithynia. See nn. on 4.47.6 and 15.22.1. *RE* Prusias 1086–1107 (C. Habicht), esp. 1097–1099.

3 καταλύσει πάντων τῶν δυναστῶν. παραγενομένης δ'
ἐπιστολῆς αὐτῷ παρά τε Λευκίου καὶ Ποπλίου τῶν
ἀδελφῶν, κομισάμενος ταύτην καὶ διακναγνοὺς ἐπὶ
ποσὸν ἔστη τῇ διανοίᾳ καὶ προείδετο τὸ μέλλον ἐν-
4 δεχομένως, ἅτε τῶν περὶ τὸν Πόπλιον ἐναργέσι κε-
χρημένων καὶ πολλοῖς μαρτυρίοις πρὸς πίστιν διὰ
5 τῶν ἐγγράπτων. οὐ γὰρ μόνον ὑπὲρ τῆς ἰδίας προαιρέσεως ἔφερον ἀπολογισμούς, ἀλλὰ καὶ περὶ τῆς κοι-
6 νῆς ἁπάντων Ῥωμαίων, δι' ὧν παρεδείκνυον οὐχ οἷον
ἀφῃρημένοι τινὸς τῶν ἐξ ἀρχῆς βασιλέων τὰς δυναστείας, ἀλλὰ τινὰς μὲν καὶ προσκατεσκευακότες αὐτοὶ δυνάστας, ἐνίους δ' ηὐξηκότες καὶ πολλαπλασίους
7 αὐτῶν τὰς ἀρχὰς πεποιηκότες. ὧν κατὰ μὲν τὴν Ἰβηρίαν Ἀνδοβάλην καὶ Κολίχαντα προεφέροντο, κατὰ
δὲ τὴν Λιβύην Μασαννάσαν, ἐν δὲ τοῖς κατὰ τὴν
8 Ἰλλυρίδα τόποις Πλευρᾶτον· οὓς ἅπαντας ἔφασαν ἐξ
ἐλαφρῶν καὶ τῶν τυχόντων δυναστῶν πεποιηκέναι
9 βασιλεῖς ὁμολογουμένως. ὁμοίως κατὰ τὴν Ἑλλάδα
Φίλιππον καὶ Νάβιν, ὧν Φίλιππον μὲν καταπολεμήσαντες καὶ συγκλείσαντες εἰς ὅμηρα καὶ φόρους,
βραχεῖαν αὐτοῦ νῦν λαβόντες ἀπόδειξιν εὐνοίας ἀπο-
καθεστακέναι μὲν αὐτῷ τὸν υἱὸν καὶ τοὺς ἅμα τούτῳ
συννομηρεύοντας νεανίσκους, ἀπολελυκέναι δὲ τῶν φόρων, πολλὰς δὲ τῶν πόλεων ἀποδεδωκέναι τῶν ἁλου-
10 σῶν κατὰ πόλεμον· Νάβιν δὲ δυνηθέντες ἄρδην

29 The same argument was used by Flamininus in his answer
to the Aetolian Alexander in 18.37.1–10.

with the object of deposing all the princes there. But on a
letter reaching him from the brothers Publius and Lucius
Scipio, after having received and read it, he was consider-
ably relieved of his anxiety and foresaw tolerably well what
would happen, as the Scipios in their communication employed many clear arguments in confirmation of their assertions. For they not only pleaded their own policy but
the universal policy of Rome, pointing out[29] that not only
had the Romans deprived no former prince of his kingdom, but had even themselves created some new king-
doms, and had augmented the power of other princes,
making their dominion many times more extensive than
formerly. In Spain they cited the cases of Andobales[30] and
Colichas,[31] in Africa that of Massanissa,[32] and that of Pleuratus[33] in Illyria; all of whom they said they had made
real and acknowledged kings out of petty and insignificant[34] princelets. In Greece itself they adduced the cases
of Philip and Nabis.[35] As for Philip, after they had crushed
him in war and tied his hands by imposing hostages and
tribute on him, no sooner had they received from him a
slight proof of his goodwill than they had restored to him
his son and the other young men who were held as hostages together with Demetrius; they had remitted the tribute and given him back many of the cities taken in the
war. And while they could have utterly annihilated Nabis,

---

[30] Probably in 201. For him see nn. on 3.76.6 and 10.35.3.

[31] See 11.20.3–5.

[32] He was the main beneficiary of the peace of 202, *StV* 548.

[33] See 18.47.12.

[34] Exaggerated, at least for some.

[35] See nn. on 4.81.13 and 13.6.1.

ἐπανελέσθαι, τοῦτο μὲν οὐ ποιῆσαι, φείσασθαι δ᾽ αὐτοῦ, καίπερ ὄντος τυράννου, λαβόντες πίστεις τὰς εἰ-
11 θισμένας. εἰς ἃ βλέποντα παρεκάλουν τὸν Προυσίαν
διὰ τῆς ἐπιστολῆς μὴ δεδιέναι περὶ τῆς ἀρχῆς, θαρ-
ροῦντα δ᾽ αἱρεῖσθαι τὰ Ῥωμαίων· ἔσεσθαι γὰρ ἀμετα-
12 μέλητον αὐτῷ τὴν τοιαύτην προαίρεσιν. ὧν ὁ Προυσίας διακούσας ἐπ᾽ ἄλλης ἐγένετο γνώμης. ὡς δὲ
καὶ παρεγενήθησαν πρὸς αὐτὸν πρέσβεις οἱ περὶ τὸν
Γάιον Λίβιον, τελέως ἀπέστη τῶν κατὰ τὸν Ἀντίοχον
13 ἐλπίδων, συμμίξας τοῖς προειρημένοις ἀνδράσιν. Ἀντίοχος δὲ ταύτης ἀποπεσὼν τῆς ἐλπίδος παρῆν εἰς
Ἔφεσον καὶ συλλογιζόμενος ὅτι μόνως ἂν οὕτω δύ-
ναιτο κωλῦσαι τὴν τῶν πεζικῶν στρατοπέδων διάβασιν καὶ καθόλου τὸν πόλεμον ἀπὸ τῆς Ἀσίας ἀποτρίβεσθαι ...βεβαίως κρατοίη τῆς θαλάττης, προέθετο
ναυμαχεῖν καὶ κρίνειν τὰ πράγματα διὰ τῶν κατὰ θάλατταν κινδύνων.

12. Πολύβιος· οἱ δὲ πειραταὶ θεασάμενοι τὸν ἐπί-
πλουν τῶν Ῥωμαϊκῶν πλοίων, ἐκ μεταβολῆς ἐποιοῦντο
τὴν ἀναχώρησιν.—

(10)   13. Ὅτι ὁ Ἀντίοχος μετὰ τὴν κατὰ τὴν ναυμαχίαν
γενομένην ἧτταν ἐν ταῖς Σάρδεσιν παριεὶς τοὺς και-
2 ροὺς καὶ καταμέλλων ἐν τοῖς ὅλοις, ἅμα τῷ πυθέσθαι
τῶν πολεμίων τὴν διάβασιν συντριβεὶς τῇ διανοίᾳ

---

36 C. Livius Salinator, praetor 191 in charge of the fleet (*MRR*
1.353), ambassador to Prusias.

37 See Livy 37.27.4–5 for the context, the Roman victory at

they had not done so, but spared him, although he was a tyrant, on receipt of the usual pledges. They wrote begging Prusias, in view of this, not to be afraid about his kingdom, but confidently to take the side of the Romans, for he would never repent of his decision. Prusias, then, after reading the letter, changed his mind, and when Gaius Livius[36] also arrived on an embassy to him, after meeting that legate he entirely relinquished all hope in Antiochus. Antiochus thus disappointed, proceeded to Ephesus, and calculating that the only way to prevent the enemy's army from crossing and generally avert the war from Asia was to obtain definite command of the sea, determined to give battle by sea and thus decide matters.

Flight of the Pirates

(Suda)

12. The pirates,[37] when they saw the Roman fleet advancing on them, turned and fled.

Attempt of Antiochus to Make Peace

(Livy 37.34–36)

13. Antiochus, who, after his defeat in the naval engagement,[38] remained in Sardis neglecting his opportunities and generally deferring action of any kind, on learning that the enemy had crossed to Asia, was crushed in spirit

Myonnesus in Ionia over Antiochus' admiral Polyxenidas in 190. The pirates were fighting against the Romans. *RE* Μυόννησος 1080–1081 (J. Keil).

[38] In the bay of Teos. See Livy 37.30.

καὶ δυσελπιστήσας ἔκρινεν διαπέμπεσθαι πρὸς τοὺς
3 περὶ τὸν Λεύκιον καὶ Πόπλιον ὑπὲρ διαλύσεων. προ-
χειρισάμενος οὖν Ἡρακλείδην τὸν Βυζάντιον ἐξέπεμψε, δοὺς ἐντολὰς ὅτι παραχωρεῖ τῆς τε τῶν
Λαμψακηνῶν καὶ Σμυρναίων, ἔτι δὲ τῆς Ἀλεξανδρέων
4 πόλεως, ἐξ ὧν ὁ πόλεμος ἔλαβε τὰς ἀρχάς· ὁμοίως δὲ
κἄν τινας ἑτέρας ὑφαιρεῖσθαι βούλωνται τῶν κατὰ
τὴν Αἰολίδα καὶ τὴν Ἰωνίαν, ὅσαι τἀκείνων ᾕρηνται
5 κατὰ τὸν ἐνεστῶτα πόλεμον. πρὸς δὲ τούτοις ὅτι τὴν
ἡμίσειαν δώσει τῆς γεγενημένης σφίσι δαπάνης εἰς
6 τὴν πρὸς αὐτὸν διαφοράν. ταύτας μὲν οὖν ὁ πεμπόμε-
νος εἶχε τὰς ἐντολὰς πρὸς τὴν κατὰ κοινὸν ἔντευξιν,
ἰδίᾳ δὲ πρὸς τὸν Πόπλιον ἑτέρας, ὑπὲρ ὧν τὰ κατὰ
7 μέρος ἐν τοῖς ἑξῆς δηλώσομεν. ἀφικόμενος δ᾽ εἰς τὸν
Ἑλλήσποντον ὁ προειρημένος πρεσβευτὴς καὶ καταλαβὼν τοὺς Ῥωμαίους μένοντας ἐπὶ τῆς στρατοπεδείας, οὗ πρῶτον κατεσκήνωσαν ἀπὸ τῆς διαβάσεως,
8 τὰς μὲν ἀρχὰς ἥσθη, νομίζων αὐτῷ συνεργὸν εἶναι
πρὸς τὴν ἔντευξιν τὸ μένειν ἐπὶ τῶν ὑποκειμένων καὶ
πρὸς μηδὲν ὡρμηκέναι τῶν ἑξῆς τοὺς ὑπεναντίους,
9 πυθόμενος δὲ τὸν Πόπλιον ἔτι μένειν ἐν τῷ πέραν
ἐδυσχρήστησε διὰ τὸ τὴν πλείστην ῥοπὴν κεῖσθαι
10 τῶν πραγμάτων ἐν τῇ ᾽κείνου προαιρέσει. αἴτιον δ᾽ ἦν
καὶ τοῦ μένειν τὸ στρατόπεδον ἐπὶ τῆς πρώτης παρεμβολῆς καὶ τοῦ κεχωρίσθαι τὸν Πόπλιον ἀπὸ τῶν
δυνάμεων τὸ σάλιον εἶναι τὸν προειρημένον ἄνδρα.
11 τοῦτο δ᾽ ἔστιν, καθάπερ ἡμῖν ἐν τοῖς περὶ τῆς πολιτείας εἴρηται, τῶν τριῶν ἓν σύστημα, δι᾽ ὧν συμβαίνει

and, abandoning all hope, decided to send to the Scipios to beg for peace. He therefore appointed and dispatched Heracleides of Byzantium, instructing him to say that he gave up his claims to Lampsacus, Smyrna, and Alexandria Troas,[39] the towns which were the cause of the war, as well as such other places in Aeolis and Ionia as they chose to take among those which had sided with Rome in the present war. He also engaged to pay half the expenses which their war with him had caused them. These were the instructions that his envoy was to deliver in his public audience, and there were other private ones he was to convey to Publius Scipio[40] of which I will give a detailed account further on. Heracleides, on reaching the Hellespont and finding the Romans still encamped on the place where they had pitched their tents immediately after crossing, was at first glad of this, thinking that the fact that the enemy remained stationary and had as yet not attempted to make any progress would tell in his favor at the audience; but on learning that Publius Scipio still remained on the further side, he was distressed, as the result very largely depended on the intentions of that commander. The real reason why both the army remained in its first camp and Scipio was apart from it was that the latter was one of the Salii.[41] These are, as I said[42] in my book on the Roman constitution, one of the three colleges whose duty it is

[39] See n. on 18.47.1.

[40] See 15.1.

[41] A board of priests; *RE* Salii 1874–1894 (F. Geiger). K. Latte, *Römische Religionsgeschichte* (Munich 1960), 114–119.

[42] This passage is lost; cf. 6.1.9.

τὰς ἐπιφανεστάτας θυσίας ἐν τῇ Ῥώμῃ συντελεῖσθαι

12 τοῖς θεοῖς· ... τριακονθήμερον μὴ μεταβαίνειν κατὰ
τὸν καιρὸν τῆς θυσίας, ἐν ᾗ <ποτ'> ἂν χώρᾳ κατα-

13 ληφθῶσιν [οἱ σάλιοι οὗτοι]. ὃ καὶ τότε συνέβη γενέσθαι Ποπλίῳ· τῆς γὰρ δυνάμεως μελλούσης περαιοῦ-
σθαι κατέλαβεν αὐτὸν οὗτος ὁ χρόνος, ὥστε μὴ

14 δύνασθαι μεταβαλεῖν τὴν χώραν. διὸ συνέβη τόν τε
Σκιπίωνα χωρισθῆναι τῶν στρατοπέδων καὶ μεῖναι
κατὰ τὴν Εὐρώπην, τὰς δὲ δυνάμεις περαιωθείσας μένειν ἐπὶ τῶν ὑποκειμένων καὶ μὴ δύνασθαι πράττειν
τῶν ἑξῆς μηθέν, προσαναδεχομένας τὸν προειρημένον
ἄνδρα.

(11) 14. Ὁ δ' Ἡρακλείδης, μετά τινας ἡμέρας παραγενομένου τοῦ Ποπλίου, κληθεὶς πρὸς τὸ συνέδριον εἰς

2 ἔντευξιν διελέγετο περὶ ὧν εἶχε τὰς ἐντολάς, φάσκων
τῆς τε τῶν Λαμψακηνῶν καὶ Σμυρναίων, ἔτι δὲ τῆς
τῶν Ἀλεξανδρέων πόλεως ἐκχωρεῖν τὸν Ἀντίοχον,
ὁμοίως δὲ καὶ τῶν κατὰ τὴν Αἰολίδα καὶ τὴν Ἰωνίαν,

3 ὅσαι τυγχάνουσιν ᾑρημέναι τὰ Ῥωμαίων· πρὸς δὲ
τούτοις τὴν ἡμίσειαν ἀναδέχεσθαι τῆς γεγενημένης

4 αὐτοῖς δαπάνης εἰς τὸν ἐνεστῶτα πόλεμον. πολλὰ δὲ
καὶ ἕτερα πρὸς ταύτην τὴν ὑπόθεσιν διελέχθη, παρακαλῶν τοὺς Ῥωμαίους μήτε τὴν τύχην λίαν ἐξελέγχειν
ἀνθρώπους ὑπάρχοντας, μήτε τὸ μέγεθος τῆς αὑτῶν
ἐξουσίας ἀόριστον ποιεῖν, ἀλλὰ περιγράφειν, μάλιστα

5 μὲν τοῖς τῆς Εὐρώπης ὅροις· καὶ γὰρ ταύτην μεγάλην
ὑπάρχειν καὶ παράδοξον διὰ τὸ μηδένα καθῖχθαι τῶν

6 προγεγονότων αὐτῆς· εἰ δὲ πάντως καὶ τῆς Ἀσίας

to perform the principal sacrifices, and, no matter where they happen to be, it is forbidden for them to change their residence for thirty days during the celebration of the sacrifices. This was now the case with Scipio; for just as his army was crossing, he was caught by this period, so that he could not change his residence. The consequence was that he was separated from his army and stopped behind in Europe, while the legions after crossing remained inactive, and were unable to make any progress as they were awaiting his arrival.

14. When Scipio arrived a few days afterward, Heracleides was summoned for an audience to the Army Council and addressed them on the subject of his instructions, saying that Antiochus abandoned all claims to Lampsacus, Smyrna, and Alexandria, and such other cities of Aeolis and Ionia as had made common cause with Rome, and that he also offered to pay half the expenses they had incurred in the present war. He spoke at considerable length on the subject, exhorting the Romans first to remember that they were but men and not to test fortune too severely, and next to impose some limit on the extent of their empire, confining it if possible to Europe, for even so it was vast and unexampled, no people in the past having attained to this. But if they must at all hazards grasp for

βούλονταί τινα προσεπιδράττεσθαι, διορίσαι ταῦτα·
πρὸς πᾶν γὰρ τὸ δυνατὸν προσελεύσεσθαι τὸν βασι-
7 λέα. ῥηθέντων δὲ τούτων, ἔδοξε τῷ συνεδρίῳ τὸν
στρατηγὸν ἀποκριθῆναι διότι τῆς μὲν δαπάνης οὐ
τὴν ἡμίσειαν, ἀλλὰ πᾶσαν δίκαιόν ἐστιν Ἀντίοχον
ἀποδοῦναι· φῦναι γὰρ τὸν πόλεμον ἐξ ἀρχῆς οὐ δι'
8 αὑτούς, ἀλλὰ δι' ἐκεῖνον· τῶν δὲ πόλεων μὴ τὰς κατὰ
τὴν Αἰολίδα καὶ τὴν Ἰωνίαν μόνον ἐλευθεροῦν, ἀλλὰ
πάσης τῆς ἐπὶ τάδε τοῦ Ταύρου δυναστείας ἐκχωρεῖν.
9 ὁ μὲν οὖν πρεσβευτὴς ταῦτ' ἀκούσας παρὰ τοῦ συνεδρίου, διὰ τὸ πολὺ τῶν ἀξιουμένων τὰς ἐπιταγὰς
ὑπεραίρειν οὐδένα λόγον ποιησάμενος, τῆς μὲν κοινῆς
ἐντεύξεως ἀπέστη, τὸν δὲ Πόπλιον ἐθεράπευσε φιλοτίμως.

(12)   15. Λαβὼν δὲ καιρὸν ἁρμόζοντα διελέγετο περὶ ὧν
2 εἶχε τὰς ἐντολάς. αὗται δ' ἦσαν διότι πρῶτον μὲν
χωρὶς λύτρων ὁ βασιλεὺς αὐτῷ τὸν υἱὸν ἀποδώσει·
3 συνέβαινε γὰρ ἐν ἀρχαῖς τοῦ πολέμου τὸν υἱὸν τὸν
τοῦ Σκιπίωνος γεγονέναι τοῖς περὶ Ἀντίοχον ὑπο-
4 χείριον· δεύτερον δὲ διότι καὶ κατὰ τὸ παρὸν ἕτοιμός
ἐστιν ὁ βασιλεὺς ὅσον ἂν ἀποδείξῃ διδόναι πλῆθος
χρημάτων καὶ μετὰ ταῦτα κοινὴν ποιεῖν τὴν ἐκ τῆς
βασιλείας χορηγίαν, ἐὰν συνεργήσῃ ταῖς ὑπὸ τοῦ
5 βασιλέως προτεινομέναις διαλύσεσιν. ὁ δὲ Πόπλιος
τὴν μὲν κατὰ τὸν υἱὸν ἐπαγγελίαν ἔφη δέχεσθαι καὶ
μεγάλην χάριν ἕξειν ἐπὶ τούτοις, ἐὰν βεβαιώσῃ τὴν
6 ὑπόσχεσιν· περὶ δὲ τῶν ἄλλων ἀγνοεῖν αὐτὸν ἔφη καὶ
παραπαίειν ὁλοσχερῶς τοῦ σφετέρου συμφέροντος οὐ

themselves some portions of Asia in addition, let them definitely state which, for the king would accede to anything that was in his power. After this speech the council decided that the consul should answer that in justice Antiochus should pay not half the expense but the whole, for the war was originally due to him and not to them. He must also not only set free the cities of Aeolis and Ionia, but retire from all the country subject to him on this side[43] of the Taurus. Upon hearing this from the Council the envoy, as these demands far exceeded his offer, did not give them consideration, but withdrawing from the public audience devoted himself to cultivating relations with Publius Scipio.

15. As soon as he had a fitting opportunity, he spoke to Scipio according to his instructions. These were to tell him that in the first place the king would restore his son to him without ransom—for at the beginning of the war Scipio's son[44] had happened to fall into the hands of Antiochus; secondly that he was ready to give to Scipio at present any sum he named and afterward to share the revenue of his kingdom with him, if he helped him now to obtain the terms of peace he proposed. Scipio answered that he accepted the promise about his son, and would be most grateful to Antiochus if he fulfilled it; but as to the rest he made a great mistake and had entirely failed to recognize the king's own true interest not only in this private inter-

---

[43] This is all of Seleucid Asia Minor, except Cilicia.

[44] L. Cornelius Scipio, who never made it to the consulship and just barely became praetor in 174. *MRR* 1.404. *RE* Cornelius 1431–1433 (F. Münzer).

μόνον κατὰ τὴν πρὸς αὐτὸν ἔντευξιν, ἀλλὰ ⟨καὶ⟩ κατὰ

7 τὴν πρὸς τὸ συνέδριον. εἰ μὲν γὰρ ἔτι Λυσιμαχείας καὶ τῆς εἰς τὴν Χερρόνησον εἰσόδου κύριος ὑπάρχων

8 ταῦτα προύτεινε, ταχέως ἂν αὐτὸν ἐπιτυχεῖν. ὁμοίως, εἰ καὶ τούτων ἐκχωρήσας παραγεγόνει πρὸς τὸν Ἑλλήσποντον μετὰ τῆς δυνάμεως καὶ δῆλος ὢν ὅτι κωλύσει τὴν διάβασιν ἡμῶν ἐπρέσβευε περὶ τῶν αὐτῶν τούτων, ἣν ἂν οὕτως αὐτὸν ἐφικέσθαι τῶν ἀξιουμένων.

9 ὅτε δ᾽ ἐάσας ἐπιβῆναι τῆς Ἀσίας τὰς ἡμετέρας δυνάμεις καὶ προσδεξάμενος οὐ μόνον τὸν χαλινόν, ἀλλὰ καὶ τὸν ἀναβάτην παραγίνεται πρεσβεύων περὶ διαλύσεων ἴσων, εἰκότως αὐτὸν ἀποτυγχάνειν καὶ δι-

10 εψεῦσθαι τῶν ἐλπίδων. διόπερ αὐτῷ παρῄνει βέλτιον βουλεύεσθαι περὶ τῶν ἐνεστώτων καὶ βλέπειν τοὺς

11 καιροὺς ἀληθινῶς. ἀντὶ δὲ τῆς κατὰ τὸν υἱὸν ἐπαγγελίας ὑπισχνεῖτο δώσειν αὐτῷ συμβουλίαν ἀξίαν τῆς προτεινομένης χάριτος· παρεκάλει γὰρ αὐτὸν εἰς πᾶν συγκαταβαίνειν, μάχεσθαι δὲ κατὰ μηδένα τρό-

12 πον Ῥωμαίοις. ὁ μὲν ⟨οὖν⟩ Ἡρακλείδης ταῦτ᾽ ἀκούσας ἐπανῆλθε καὶ συμμίξας διεσάφει τῷ βασιλεῖ τὰ κατὰ

13 μέρος· Ἀντίοχος ⟨δὲ⟩ νομίσας οὐδὲν ἂν βαρύτερον αὐτῷ γενέσθαι πρόσταγμα τῶν νῦν ἐπιταττομένων, εἰ λειφθείη μαχόμενος, τῆς μὲν περὶ τὰς διαλύσεις ἀσχολίας ἀπέστη, τὰ δὲ πρὸς ἀγῶνα πάντα καὶ πανταχόθεν ἡτοίμαζεν.

(13) 16. Ὅτι μετὰ τὴν νίκην οἱ Ῥωμαῖοι τὴν αὐτῶν πρὸς Ἀντίοχον παρειληφότες καὶ τὰς Σάρδεις καὶ τὰς

---

45 At Magnesia near Sipylus, in December 190.

view with himself, but at his audience before the Council. For had he made these proposals while he was still master of Lysimachia and the approach to the Chersonese, he would soon have obtained his terms. Or again, even after retiring from those positions, had he proceeded to the Hellespont with his army, and showing that he would prevent our crossing, had sent to propose the same terms, it would still have been possible for him to obtain them. "But now," he said, "that he has allowed our army to land in Asia, when after letting himself not only be bitted but mounted he comes to us asking for peace on equal terms he naturally fails to get it and is foiled in his hopes." He advised him, therefore, to take better counsel in his present situation and look facts in the face. In return for his promise about his son, he would give him a piece of advice equal in value to the favor he offered, and that was to consent to everything and avoid at all cost a battle with the Romans. Heracleides, after listening to this, returned, and on joining the king, gave him a detailed report. But Antiochus, thinking that no more severe demands than the present could be imposed on him even if he were worsted in a battle, ceased to occupy himself with peace, and began to make every preparation and avail himself of every resource for the struggle.

Conditions Imposed by Scipio after the Battle of Magnesia

(Cf. Livy 37.45.3)

16. After the victory[45] gained by the Romans over Antiochus they occupied Sardis and its citadels, . . . and

ἀκροπόλεις ἄρτι . . . ἧκε Μουσαῖος ἐπικηρυκευόμενος
2 παρ' Ἀντιόχου. τῶν δὲ περὶ τὸν Πόπλιον φιλανθρώπως προσδεξαμένων αὐτόν, ἔφη βούλεσθαι τὸν Ἀντίοχον ἐξαποσταλῆναι πρεσβευτὰς τοὺς διαλεχθησο-
3 μένους ὑπὲρ τῶν ὅλων. διόπερ ἀσφάλειαν ἠξίου
4 δοθῆναι τοῖς παραγινομένοις. τῶν δὲ συγχωρησάντων
οὗτος μὲν ἐπανῆλθεν, μετὰ δέ τινας ἡμέρας ἧκον
πρέσβεις παρὰ τοῦ βασιλέως Ἀντιόχου Ζεῦξις ὁ πρότερον ὑπάρχων Λυδίας σατράπης καὶ Ἀντίπατρος
5 ἀδελφιδοῦς. οὗτοι δὲ πρῶτον μὲν ἔσπευδον ἐντυχεῖν
Εὐμένει τῷ βασιλεῖ, διευλαβούμενοι μὴ διὰ τὴν προ-
γεγενημένην παρατριβὴν φιλοτιμότερος ᾖ πρὸς τὸ
6 βλάπτειν αὐτούς. εὑρόντες δὲ παρὰ τὴν προσδοκίαν
μέτριον αὐτὸν καὶ πρᾷον, εὐθέως ἐγίνοντο περὶ τὴν
7 κοινὴν ἔντευξιν. κληθέντες δ' εἰς τὸ συνέδριον πολλὰ
μὲν καὶ ἕτερα διελέχθησαν, παρακαλοῦντες πράως
8 χρήσασθαι καὶ μεγαλοψύχως τοῖς εὐτυχήμασι, φάσκοντες οὐχ οὕτως Ἀντιόχῳ τοῦτο συμφέρειν ὡς αὐτοῖς Ῥωμαίοις, ἐπείπερ ἡ τύχη παρέδωκεν αὐτοῖς τὴν
9 τῆς οἰκουμένης ἀρχὴν καὶ δυναστείαν· τὸ δὲ συνέχον
ἠρώτων τί δεῖ ποιήσαντας τυχεῖν τῆς εἰρήνης καὶ τῆς
10 φιλίας τῆς πρὸς Ῥωμαίους. οἱ δ' ἐν τῷ συνεδρίῳ πρότερον ἤδη συνηδρευκότες καὶ βεβουλευμένοι περὶ
τούτων, τότ' ἐκέλευον διασαφεῖν τὰ δεδογμένα τὸν
Πόπλιον.

(14)   17. Ὁ δὲ προειρημένος ἀνὴρ οὔτε νικήσαντας ἔφη
Ῥωμαίους οὐδέποτε γενέσθαι βαρυτέρους ⟨οὔθ' ἡττη-

Musaeus came from Antiochus under a flag of truce. Upon Scipio receiving him courteously, he said that Antiochus wished to send envoys to discuss the whole situation. He therefore desired that a safe conduct should be given to this mission. Upon Scipio's consenting, he returned, and after a few days the king's envoys arrived. They were Zeuxis,[46] the former governor of Lydia, and Antipater[47] the king's nephew. They were anxious first of all to meet King Eumenes, as they were alarmed lest owing to previous friction[48] he might be somewhat disposed to do them injury. But on finding him, contrary to their expectation, quite reasonable and gentle, they at once took steps to obtain a public audience. Upon being summoned to the Army Council, they first of all made a general appeal of some length to the Romans, exhorting them to use their success mildly and magnanimously, and saying that this would not so much further the interest of Antiochus as that of the Romans themselves, now that Fortune had made them rulers and masters of the whole world.[49] But their main object was to ask what they must do in order to secure peace and alliance with Rome. The members of the Council had previously sat to consider this, and they now asked Publius Scipio to communicate their decision.

17. Scipio said that victory had never made the Romans more exacting <nor defeat less moderate>: therefore they

46 See nn. on 5.45.4 and 16.1.8 and Ma (16.1.8), 123–130.
47 5.79.12.
48 Eumenes had been attacked in his capital.
49 See 1.2.7, 15.15.1. See also 23.4.

2 θέντας μετριωτέρους.)¹ διὸ καὶ νῦν αὐτοῖς τὴν αὐτὴν
ἀπόκρισιν δοθήσεσθαι παρὰ Ῥωμαίων, ἣν καὶ πρότερον ἔλαβον, ὅτε πρὸ τῆς μάχης παρεγενήθησαν ἐπὶ
3 τὸν Ἑλλήσ<ποντον>. δεῖν γὰρ αὐτοὺς ἔκ τε τῆς Εὐρώπης ἐκχωρεῖν καὶ <τῆς Ἀσίας> τῆς ἐπὶ τάδε τοῦ
4 Ταύρου πάσης. πρὸς δὲ τούτοις Εὐβοϊκὰ τάλαντ' ἐπι-
δοῦναι μύρια καὶ πεντακισχίλια Ῥωμαίοις ἀντὶ τῆς
5 εἰς τὸν πόλεμον δαπάνης. τούτων δὲ πεντακόσια μὲν
παραχρῆμα, δισχίλια δὲ καὶ πεντακόσια πάλιν, ἐπει-
δὰς ὁ δῆμος κυρώσῃ τὰς διαλύσεις, τὰ δὲ λοιπὰ τελεῖν
ἐν ἔτεσι δώδεκα, διδόντα καθ' ἕκαστον ἔτος χίλια τά-
6 λαντα. ἀποδοῦναι δὲ καὶ Εὐμένει τετρακόσια τάλαντα
<τὰ> προσοφειλόμενα καὶ τὸν ἐλλείποντα σῖτον κατὰ
7 τὰς πρὸς τὸν πατέρα συνθήκας. σὺν δὲ τούτοις Ἀννίβαν ἐκδοῦναι τὸν Καρχηδόνιον καὶ Θόαντα τὸν Αἰτωλὸν καὶ Μνασίλοχον Ἀκαρνᾶνα καὶ Φίλωνα καὶ Εὐ-
8 βουλίδαν τοὺς Χαλκιδέας. πίστιν δὲ τούτων ὁμήρους
εἴκοσι δοῦναι παραχρῆμα τὸν Ἀντίοχον τοὺς παρα-
9 γραφέντας. ταῦτα μὲν οὖν ὁ Πόπλιος ἀπεφήναθ' ὑπὲρ
παντὸς τοῦ συνεδρίου. συγκαταθεμένων δὲ τῶν περὶ
τὸν Ἀντίπατρον καὶ Ζεῦξιν, ἔδοξε πᾶσιν ἐξαποστεῖλαι
πρεσβευτὰς εἰς τὴν Ῥώμην τοὺς παρακαλέσοντας
τὴν σύγκλητον καὶ τὸν δῆμον ἐπικυρῶσαι τὰς συνθή-
10 κας. καὶ τότε μὲν ἐπὶ τούτοις ἐχωρίσθησαν, ταῖς δ'

¹ Suppl. B-W.

would now give them the same answer as they had formerly received, when before the battle they came to the Hellespont. They must retire from Europe and from all Asia on this side of the Taurus: Antiochus must pay to the Romans for the expenses of the war 15,000 Euboean talents, 500 at once, 2,500 upon the peace being ratified by the People, and the remainder in twelve yearly installments of 1,000 talents each: he must also pay to Eumenes the 400 talents he still owed him and the corn he had not yet delivered according to the terms of his agreement[50] with his father Attalus. In addition he was to give up Hannibal[51] the Carthaginian, Thoas[52] the Aetolian, Mnasilochus[53] the Acarnanian, and Philo[54] and Eubulidas of Chalcis. As security Antiochus was to give at once the twenty hostages[55] whose names were appended. Such was the decision which Scipio pronounced in the name of the whole Council. Upon Antipater and Zeuxis accepting the terms, it was universally decided to send envoys to Rome to beg the Senate and People to ratify the peace, and on this understanding the envoys took leave. On the following

[50] Some take it as a reference to the understanding of 216 directed against Achaeus, others (including WC 3.110) to events of 198.

[51] He had left Carthage and gone to see Antiochus whom he met and joined in 195 at Ephesus. Holleaux, *Ét.* 5, 180–183.

[52] Aetolian with a career of over thirty-five years, four times strategus. Grainger (18.10.9), 321. Paschidis 334–338.

[53] He tried to bring the Acarnanian Confederacy to the side of Antiochus, Livy 36.11.8–12.11.

[54] He and Eubulides are not otherwise known.

[55] Among them was Antiochus' son Antiochus, later to become King Antiochus IV.

ἑξῆς ἡμέραις οἱ Ῥωμαῖοι διεῖλον τὰς δυνάμεις . . .
11 μετὰ δέ τινας ἡμέρας παραγενομένων ⟨τῶν⟩ ὁμήρων
εἰς τὴν Ἔφεσον, εὐθέως ἐγίνοντο περὶ τὸ πλεῖν εἰς
τὴν Ῥώμην ὅ τ' Εὐμένης οἵ τε παρ' Ἀντιόχου πρε-
12 σβευταί, παραπλησίως δὲ καὶ παρὰ Ῥοδίων καὶ παρὰ
Σμυρναίων καὶ σχεδὸν τῶν ἐπὶ τάδε τοῦ Ταύρου πάντων τῶν κατοικούντων ἐθνῶν καὶ πολιτευμάτων ἐπρέσβευον εἰς τὴν Ῥώμην.

IV. RES ITALIAE

18. Ὅτι ἤδη τῆς θερείας ἐνισταμένης μετὰ τὴν
(xxii.1) νίκην τῶν Ῥωμαίων τὴν πρὸς Ἀντίοχον παρῆν ὅ τε
βασιλεὺς Εὐμένης οἵ τε παρ' Ἀντιόχου πρέσβεις οἵ
τε παρὰ τῶν Ῥοδίων, ὁμοίως δὲ καὶ παρὰ τῶν ἄλλων·
2 σχεδὸν γὰρ ἅπαντες οἱ κατὰ τὴν Ἀσίαν εὐθέως μετὰ
τὸ γενέσθαι τὴν μάχην ἔπεμπον πρεσβευτὰς εἰς τὴν
Ῥώμην, διὰ τὸ πᾶσιν τότε καὶ πάσας τὰς ὑπὲρ τοῦ
3 μέλλοντος ἐλπίδας ἐν τῇ συγκλήτῳ κεῖσθαι. ἅπαντας
μὲν οὖν τοὺς παραγενομένους ἐπεδέχετο φιλανθρώπως ἡ σύγκλητος, μεγαλομερέστατα δὲ καὶ κατὰ τὴν
ἀπάντησιν καὶ τὰς τῶν ξενίων παροχὰς Εὐμένη τὸν
4 βασιλέα, μετὰ δὲ τοῦτον τοὺς Ῥοδίους. ἐπειδὴ δ' ὁ τῆς
ἐντεύξεως καιρὸς ἦλθεν, εἰσεκαλέσαντο πρῶτον τὸν
βασιλέα καὶ λέγειν ἠξίουν μετὰ παρρησίας ὧν βού-
5 λεται τυχεῖν παρὰ τῆς συγκλήτου. τοῦ δ' Εὐμένους
φήσαντος διότι εἰ καὶ παρ' ἑτέρων τυχεῖν τινος ἐβούλετο φιλανθρώπου, Ῥωμαίοις ἂν ἐχρήσατο συμβού-

days the Romans divided their forces . . . and a few days afterward, when the hostages arrived at Ephesus, Eumenes and the envoys of Antiochus prepared to sail for Rome, as well as embassies from Rhodes, Smyrna, and almost all peoples and states on this side of the Taurus.

IV. AFFAIRS OF ITALY

The Embassies at Rome

(Cf. Livy 37.52–56)

18. At the beginning of the summer following the victory of the Romans over Antiochus, King Eumenes, the envoys of Antiochus, and those from Rhodes and elsewhere arrived at Rome: for nearly all the communities of Asia Minor sent envoys to Rome immediately after the battle, as the whole future of all of them depended on the senate. The senate received all the arrivals courteously, but treated with especial splendor, both in the mode of their reception and the richness of the allowance provided, King Eumenes, and after him the Rhodians. When the date fixed for the audience arrived, they called in first the king and begged him to speak frankly stating what he wished the senate to do for him. Eumenes said that had he wished to ask a kindness of any other people, he would have taken the advice of the Romans so that he might

189 B.C.

λοις πρὸς τὸ μήτ᾽ ἐπιθυμεῖν μηδενὸς παρὰ τὸ δέον
6 μήτ᾽ ἀξιοῦν μηδ᾽ ἐν πέρα τοῦ καθήκοντος· ὁπότε δ᾽
αὐτῶν πάρεστι δεόμενος Ῥωμαίων, ἄριστον εἶναι νο-
μίζει τὸ διδόναι τὴν ἐπιτροπὴν ἐκείνοις καὶ περὶ αὑτοῦ
7 καὶ περὶ τῶν ἀδελφῶν· τῶν δὲ πρεσβυτέρων τινὸς
ἀναστάντος καὶ κελεύοντος μὴ κατορρωδεῖν, ἀλλὰ λέγειν τὸ φαινόμενον, διότι πρόκειται τῇ συγκλήτῳ πᾶν
αὐτῷ χαρίζεσθαι τὸ δυνατόν, ἔμεινεν ἐπὶ τῆς αὐτῆς
8 γνώμης. χρόνου δ᾽ ἐγγινομένου ὁ μὲν βασιλεὺς ἐξ-
9 εχώρησεν, ἡ δὲ ἐντὸς ἐβουλεύετο τί δεῖ ποιεῖν. ἔδοξεν
οὖν τὸν Εὐμένη παρακαλεῖν αὐτὸν ὑποδεικνύναι θαρ-
ροῦντα περὶ ὧν πάρεστιν· καὶ γὰρ εἰδέναι τὰ διαφέροντα τοῖς ἰδίοις πράγμασιν ἐκεῖνον ἀκριβέστερον τὰ
10 κατὰ τὴν Ἀσίαν. δοξάντων δὲ τούτων εἰσεκλήθη, καὶ
τῶν πρεσβυτέρων τινὸς ἀποδείξαντος τὰ δεδογμένα
λέγειν ἠναγκάσθη περὶ τῶν προκειμένων.

(xxii.2)   19. ἔφασκεν οὖν ἄλλο μὲν οὐδὲν ἂν εἰπεῖν περὶ τῶν
καθ᾽ αὑτόν, ἀλλὰ μεῖναι … τελέως διδοὺς ἐκείνοις τὴν
ἐξουσίαν· ἕνα δὲ τόπον ἀγωνιᾶν τὸν κατὰ τοὺς Ῥο-
2 δίους· διὸ καὶ προῆχθαι νῦν εἰς τὸ λέγειν ὑπὲρ τῶν
3 ἐνεστώτων. ἐκείνους γὰρ παρεῖναι μὲν οὐδὲν ἧττον
ὑπὲρ τῆς σφετέρας πατρίδος συμφερόντως σπουδάζον-
τας ἤπερ αὑτοὺς ὑπὲρ τῆς ἰδίας ἀρχῆς φιλοτιμεῖσθαι
4 κατὰ τὸ παρόν· τοὺς δὲ λόγους αὐτῶν τὴν ἐναντίαν
ἔμφασιν ἔχειν τῇ προθέσει τῇ κατὰ τὴν ἀλήθειαν.

56 For the speeches of Eumenes (19.1–21.11) and the Rhodians (22.5–23.12), opinions vary widely on the question of how

neither nourish any immoderate desire nor make any exorbitant demand, but now that he appeared as a suppliant before the Romans he thought it best to commit to them the decision about himself and his brothers. Here one of the senators interrupted him and bade him not to be afraid, but say what he thought, as the senate were resolved to grant him anything that was in their power, but Eumenes held to his opinion. After some time had elapsed, the king took his departure, and the senate considered what they should do. It was resolved to beg Eumenes to appear alone and indicate to them frankly the object of his visit. For he knew more accurately than anyone what was in his own interest so far as Asia was concerned. After this decision he was again called in; and, upon one of the senators showing him the decree, he was compelled to speak about the matter at issue.

19. He said,[56] then, that he had nothing further to say about what concerned him personally but adhered to his resolution, giving the senate complete authority to decide. But there was one point on which he was anxious, and that was the action of the Rhodians; and for this reason he had now been induced to speak about the situation. "For the Rhodians," he said, "have come to promote the interests of their country, with just as much warmth as we at the present crisis plead for our dominions. But at the present crisis, whatever they say is meant to give an impression quite contrary to their real purpose, and this you will eas-

reliable they are. See most recently Wiemer (16.5.1), 130–137. C. Habicht agrees with those who think that they are products of Polybius' imagination. He, nevertheless, may have had some reliable information.

5 τοῦτο δ᾿ εἶναι ῥᾴδιον καταμαθεῖν. ἐρεῖν μὲν γὰρ αὐτούς, ἐπειδὰν εἰσπορευθῶσιν, διότι πάρεισιν οὔτε παρ᾿
ὑμῶν αἰτούμενοι τὸ παράπαν οὐδὲν οὔθ᾿ ἡμᾶς βλάπτειν θέλοντες κατ᾿ οὐδένα τρόπον, πρεσβεύονται δὲ
περὶ τῆς ἐλευθερίας τῶν τὴν Ἀσίαν κατοικούντων

6 Ἑλλήνων. "τοῦτο δ᾿ οὐχ οὕτως αὐτοῖς εἶναι κεχαρι-
σμένον φήσουσιν ὡς ὑμῖν καθῆκον καὶ τοῖς γεγο-

7 νόσιν ἔργοις ἀκόλουθον. ἡ μὲν οὖν διὰ τῶν λόγων
φαντασία τοιαύτη τις αὐτῶν ἔσται· τὰ δὲ κατὰ τὴν
ἀλήθειαν τὴν ἐναντίαν ἔχοντα τούτοις εὑρεθήσεται

8 διάθεσιν. τῶν γὰρ πόλεων ἐλευθερωθεισῶν, ὡς αὐτοὶ
παρακαλοῦσιν, τὴν μὲν τούτων συμβήσεται δύναμιν
αὐξηθῆναι πολλαπλασίως, τὴν δ᾿ ἡμετέραν τρόπον

9 τινὰ καταλυθῆναι. τὸ γὰρ τῆς ἐλευθερίας ὄνομα καὶ
τῆς αὐτονομίας ἡμῖν μὲν ἄρδην ἀποσπάσει πάντας οὐ
μόνον τοὺς νῦν ἐλευθερωθησομένους, ἀλλὰ καὶ τοὺς
πρότερον ἡμῖν ὑποταττομένους, ἐπειδὰν ὑμεῖς ἐπὶ ταύτης ὄντες φανεροὶ γένησθε τῆς προαιρέσεως, τούτοις

10 δὲ προσθήσει πάντας. τὰ γὰρ πράγματα φύσιν ἔχει
τοιαύτην· δόξαντες γὰρ ἠλευθερῶσθαι διὰ τούτους
ὀνόματι μὲν ἔσονται σύμμαχοι τούτων, τῇ δ᾿ ἀληθείᾳ
πᾶν ποιήσουσι τὸ κελευόμενον ἑτοίμως, τῇ μεγίστῃ

11 χάριτι γεγονότες ὑπόχρεοι. διόπερ, ὦ ἄνδρες, ἀξιοῦμεν
ὑμᾶς τοῦτον τὸν τόπον ὑπιδέσθαι, μὴ λάθητε τοὺς μὲν
παρὰ τὸ δέον αὔξοντες, τοὺς δ᾿ ἐλαττοῦντες τῶν φίλων
ἀλόγως, ἅμα δὲ τούτοις τοὺς μὲν πολεμίους γεγονότας εὐεργετοῦντες, τοὺς δ᾿ ἀληθινοὺς φίλους παρορῶντες καὶ κατολιγωροῦντες τούτων.

ily discover. For when they enter this house they will say that they have come neither to beg for anything at all from you nor with the wish to harm me in any way, but that they send this embassy to plead for the freedom of the Greek inhabitants of Asia Minor. They will say that this is not so much a favor to themselves as your duty, and the natural consequence of what you have already achieved. Such will be the false impression their words will be meant to produce on you, but you will find that their actual intentions are of quite a different character. When the towns for which they plead are set at liberty their own power in Asia will be immensely increased, and mine will be more or less destroyed. For this fine name of freedom and autonomy will, the moment it becomes evident that you have decided to act so, entirely detach from me not only the cities now about to be liberated, but those previously subject to me, and add them all to the Rhodian dominion. For such is the nature of things: thinking that they owe their freedom to Rhodes, they will be nominally the allies of the Rhodians, but in reality ready to obey all their orders, feeling indebted to them for the greatest of services. Therefore, I beg you, sirs, to be suspicious on this point, in case unawares you strengthen some of your friends more than is meet and unwisely weaken others, at the same time conferring favors on your enemies and neglecting and making light of those who are truly your friends.

20. ἐγὼ δὲ περὶ μὲν τῶν ἄλλων, ὅτου δέοι, παντὸς ⟨ἂν⟩ παραχωρήσαιμι τοῖς πέλας ἀφιλονίκως, περὶ δὲ τῆς ὑμετέρας φιλίας καὶ τῆς εἰς ὑμᾶς εὐνοίας ἁπλῶς οὐδέποτ' ἂν οὐδενὶ τῶν ὄντων ἐκχωρήσαιμι κατὰ δύ-

2 ναμιν. δοκῶ δὲ καὶ τὸν πατέρα τὸν ἡμέτερον, εἴπερ

3 ἔζη, τὴν αὐτὴν ἂν προέσθαι φωνὴν ἐμοί. καὶ γὰρ ἐκεῖνος, πρῶτος μετασχὼν τῆς ὑμετέρας φιλίας καὶ συμμαχίας, σχεδὸν πάντων τῶν [κατὰ] τὴν Ἀσίαν καὶ τὴν Ἑλλάδα νεμομένων, εὐγενέστατα διεφύλαξε ταύτην ἕως τῆς τελευταίας ἡμέρας, οὐ μόνον κατὰ τὴν

4 προαίρεσιν, ἀλλὰ καὶ κατὰ τὰς πράξεις. πάντων γὰρ ὑμῖν ἐκοινώνησε τῶν κατὰ τὴν Ἑλλάδα πολέμων καὶ πλείστας μὲν εἰς τούτους καὶ πεζικὰς καὶ ναυτικὰς δυνάμεις παρέσχετο τῶν ἄλλων συμμάχων, πλείστην δὲ συνεβάλετο χορηγίαν καὶ μεγίστους ὑπέμεινε κιν-

5 δύνους· τέλος δ' εἰπεῖν, κατέστρεψε τὸν βίον ἐν αὐτοῖς τοῖς ἔργοις κατὰ τὸν Φιλιππικὸν πόλεμον, παρακαλῶν Βοιωτοὺς εἰς τὴν ὑμετέραν φιλίαν καὶ συμμαχίαν.

6 ἐγὼ δὲ διαδεξάμενος τὴν ἀρχὴν τὴν μὲν προαίρεσιν τὴν τοῦ πατρὸς διεφύλαξα—ταύτην γὰρ οὐχ οἷόν τ'

7 ἦν ὑπερθέσθαι—τοῖς δὲ πράγμασιν ὑπερεθέμην. οἱ γὰρ καιροὶ τὴν ἐκ πυρὸς βάσανον ἐμοὶ μᾶλλον ἢ

8 'κείνῳ προσῆγον. Ἀντιόχου γὰρ σπουδάζοντος ἡμῖν θυγατέρα δοῦναι καὶ συνοικειωθῆναι τοῖς ὅλοις, δι- δόντος ⟨δὲ⟩ παραχρῆμα μὲν τὰς πρότερον ἀπηλ- λοτριωμένας ἀφ' ἡμῶν πόλεις, μετὰ δὲ ταῦτα πᾶν ὑπισχνουμένου ποιήσειν, εἰ μετάσχοιμεν τοῦ πρὸς

9 ὑμᾶς πολέμου, τοσοῦτον ἀπέσχομεν τοῦ προσδέξα-

314

20. As for myself I would, as regards other matters, make any necessary concession to my neighbors without disputing it, but I would never, as long as I could help, yield to any man alive in my friendship with you and the goodwill I bear you. And I think my father, were he alive, would give utterance to the same words. For he, who was, I think, the first[57] of the inhabitants of Asia and Greece to gain your friendship and alliance, most nobly maintained these until the day of his death, and not only in principle, but by actual deeds, taking part in all your wars in Greece and furnishing for these wars larger military and naval forces than any other of your allies; contributing the greatest quantity of supplies and incurring the greatest danger; and finally ending his days in the field of action during the war with Philip, while he was actually exhorting the Boeotians[58] to become your friends and allies. On succeeding to the throne I adhered to my father's principles—those indeed it was impossible to surpass; but I surpassed him in putting them in practice; because the times were such as to try me as by fire in a way he never had been tried. For when Antiochus was anxious to give me his daughter in marriage,[59] and to cement our union in every respect, giving me back[60] at once the cities he had formerly alienated from me, and next promising to do everything for me if I would take part in the war against you, I was so far from

---

[57] During the First Macedonian War, not necessarily in a formal alliance (Livy 27.30.2).   [58] See n. on 18.17.6.

[59] The name of the girl and the date of the offer are not known.

[60] These places may have been taken from his (at that time: his father's) realm in 198.

σθαί τι τούτων, ὡς πλείσταις μὲν καὶ πεζικαῖς καὶ
ναυτικαῖς δυνάμεσιν τῶν ἄλλων συμμάχων ἠγω-
νίσμεθα μεθ᾽ ὑμῶν πρὸς Ἀντίοχον, πλείστας δὲ χορηγίας συμβεβλήμεθα πρὸς τὰς ὑμετέρας χρείας ἐν
τοῖς ἀναγκαιοτάτοις καιροῖς, εἰς πάντας δὲ τοὺς κινδύνους δεδώκαμεν αὑτοὺς ἀπροφασίστως μετά γε τῶν
10   ὑμετέρων ἡγεμόνων. τὸ δὲ τελευταῖον ὑπεμείναμεν
συγκλεισθέντες εἰς αὐτὸν τὸν Πέργαμον πολιορκεῖσθαι καὶ κινδυνεύειν ἅμα περὶ τοῦ βίου καὶ τῆς ἀρχῆς
διὰ τὴν πρὸς τὸν ὑμέτερον δῆμον εὔνοιαν.

21. ὥσθ᾽ ὑμᾶς, ἄνδρες Ῥωμαῖοι, πολλοὺς μὲν γεγο-
(xxii.4) νότας αὐτόπτας, πάντας δὲ γινώσκοντας διότι λέγο-
μεν ἀληθῆ, δίκαιόν ἐστι τὴν ἁρμόζουσαν πρόνοιαν
2   ποιήσασθαι περὶ ἡμῶν. καὶ γὰρ ἂν πάντων γένοιτο
δεινότατον, εἰ Μασαννάσαν μὲν τὸν οὐ μόνον ὑπάρ-
ξαντα πολέμιον ὑμῖν, ἀλλὰ καὶ τὸ τελευταῖον καταφυ-
γόντα πρὸς ὑμᾶς μετά τινων ἱππέων, τοῦτον, ὅτι καθ᾽
ἕνα πόλεμον τὸν πρὸς Καρχηδονίους ἐτήρησε τὴν πίστιν, βασιλέα τῶν πλείστων μερῶν τῆς Λιβύης πε-
3   ποιήκατε, Πλεύρατον δέ, πράξαντα μὲν ἁπλῶς οὐδέν,
διαφυλάξαντα δὲ μόνον τὴν πίστιν, μέγιστον τῶν
4   κατὰ τὴν Ἰλλυρίδα δυναστῶν ἀναδεδείχατε, ἡμᾶς δὲ
τοὺς διὰ προγόνων τὰ μέγιστα καὶ κάλλιστα τῶν ἔργων ὑμῖν συγκατειργασμένους παρ᾽ οὐδὲν ποιήσεσθε.
5   τί οὖν ἐστιν ὃ παρακαλῶ, καὶ τίνος φημὶ δεῖν ἡμᾶς
6   τυγχάνειν παρ᾽ ὑμῶν; ἐρῶ μετὰ παρρησίας, ἐπείπερ
ἡμᾶς ἐξεκαλέσασθε πρὸς τὸ λέγειν ὑμῖν τὸ φαινό-
7   μενον. εἰ μὲν αὐτοὶ κρίνετέ τινας τόπους διακατέχειν

316

accepting any of these offers that I fought at your side against Antiochus with larger naval and military forces than any other of your allies, and contributed the greatest quantity of supplies to meet your needs when they were most urgent: I shared unhesitatingly with your generals the danger of all the battles that were fought, and finally suffered myself to be besieged in Pergamum itself and risk my life as well as my kingdom, all for the sake of the good-will I bore to your people.

21. Therefore, ye men of Rome, many of whom saw with your own eyes and all of whom know that what I say is true, it is but just for you to take fitting thought for my welfare. For of all things it would be most shameful if after making Massanissa,[61] who was once your enemy and finally sought safety with you accompanied by only a few horsemen, king of the greater part of Africa, simply because he kept faith with you in one war against Carthage: if after making Pleuratus,[62] who did absolutely nothing except maintain his faith to you, the greatest prince in Illyria, you now ignore myself, who from my father's days onward have taken part in your greatest and most splendid achievements. What is it then that I beg of you and what do I think you ought to do for me? I will speak quite frankly, as you begged me to state my real opinion. If you decide to remain in occupation of certain parts of Asia on

[61] See n. on 11.7.
[62] See 11.7.

τῆς Ἀσίας τῶν ὄντων μὲν ἐπὶ τάδε τοῦ Ταύρου, ταττομένων δὲ πρότερον ὑπ᾽ Ἀντίοχον, τοῦτο καὶ μάλιστα
8 βουλοίμεθ᾽ ἂν ἰδεῖν γενόμενον· καὶ γὰρ ἀσφαλέστατα
βασιλεύσειν ὑμῖν γειτνιῶντες ὑπολαμβάνομεν καὶ
9 μάλιστα μετέχοντες τῆς ὑμετέρας ἐξουσίας. εἰ δὲ
τοῦτο μὴ κρίνετε ποιεῖν, ἀλλ᾽ ἐκχωρεῖν τῆς Ἀσίας
ὁλοσχερῶς, οὐδενί φαμεν δικαιότερον εἶναι παραχωρεῖν ὑμᾶς τῶν ἐκ τοῦ πολέμου γεγονότων ἄθλων ἤπερ
10 ἡμῖν. νὴ Δί᾽, ἀλλὰ κάλλιόν ἐστι τοὺς δουλεύοντας
ἐλευθεροῦν. εἴγε μὴ μετ᾽ Ἀντιόχου πολεμεῖν ὑμῖν ἐτόλ-
11 μησαν. ἐπεὶ δὲ τοῦθ᾽ ὑπέμειναν, πολλῷ κάλλιον τὸ
τοῖς ἀληθινοῖς φίλοις τὰς ἁρμοζούσας χάριτας ἀποδιδόναι μᾶλλον ἢ τοὺς πολεμίους γεγονότας εὐεργετεῖν.᾽᾽

(xxii.5) 22. Ὁ μὲν οὖν Εὐμένης ἱκανῶς εἰπὼν ἀπηλλάγη, τὸ
δὲ συνέδριον αὐτόν τε τὸν βασιλέα καὶ τὰ ῥηθέντα
2 φιλοφρόνως ἀπεδέχετο καὶ πᾶν τὸ δυνατὸν προθύμως
εἶχεν αὐτῷ χαρίζεσθαι. μετὰ δὲ τοῦτον ἐβούλοντο μὲν
εἰσάγειν Ῥοδίους. ἀφυστεροῦντος δέ τινος τῶν πρε-
3 σβευτῶν εἰσεκαλέσαντο τοὺς Σμυρναίους. οὗτοι δὲ
πολλοὺς μὲν ἀπολογισμοὺς εἰσήνεγκαν περὶ τῆς
αὑτῶν εὐνοίας καὶ προθυμίας, ἣν παρέσχηνται Ῥωμαί-
4 οις κατὰ τὸν ἐνεστῶτα πόλεμον· οὔσης δὲ τῆς περὶ
αὑτῶν δόξης ὁμολογουμένης, διότι γεγόνασι πάντων
ἐκτενέστατοι τῶν ἐπὶ τῆς Ἀσίας αὐτονομουμένων, οὐκ
ἀναγκαῖον ἡγούμεθ᾽ εἶναι τοὺς κατὰ μέρος ἐκτίθεσθαι
5 λόγους. ἐπὶ δὲ τούτοις εἰσῆλθον οἱ Ῥόδιοι καὶ βραχέα
προενεγκάμενοι περὶ τῶν κατ᾽ ἰδίαν σφίσι πεπραγμέ-

this side of the Taurus which were formerly subject to Antiochus, I should be exceedingly gratified to see that happen. For I think that my kingdom would be more secure with you on my frontiers, and a portion of your power falling to my share. But if you decide not to do this, but entirely to evacuate Asia, I think there is no one to whom you could cede the prizes of the war with more justice than to myself. But surely, you will be told, it is a finer thing to set free those in servitude. Well perhaps, if they had not ventured[63] to fight against you with Antiochus. But since they suffered themselves to do so it is far finer to give your true friends a fitting token of your gratitude than to confer favors on those who were your enemies."

22. Eumenes, after having spoken in this capable manner, withdrew. The senate gave a kind reception to the king himself and to his speech, and they were ready to grant him any favor in their power. After him they wished to call in the Rhodians; but as one of the envoys was late in appearing, they summoned those of Smyrna. The latter pleaded at length the goodwill and promptness they had shown in helping the Romans in the late war. But since it is universally agreed that of all the autonomous states of Asia they had been by far the most energetic supporters of Rome, I do not think it necessary to report their speech in detail. Next to them came the Rhodians, who after a brief reference to their particular services to Rome soon brought

[63] Most of these cities were unable to choose sides.

νων εἰς Ῥωμαίους, ταχέως εἰς τὸν περὶ τῆς πατρίδος

6 ἐπανῆλθον λόγον. ἐν ᾧ μέγιστον αὐτοῖς ἔφασαν γεγονέναι σύμπτωμα κατὰ τὴν πρεσβείαν, πρὸς ὃν
οἰκειότατα διάκεινται βασιλέα καὶ κοινῇ καὶ κατ᾽
ἰδίαν, πρὸς τοῦτον αὐτοῖς ἀντιπεπτωκέναι τὴν φύσιν

7 τῶν πραγμάτων. τῇ μὲν γὰρ αὐτῶν πατρίδι δοκεῖν
τοῦτο κάλλιστον εἶναι καὶ μάλιστα πρέπον Ῥωμαίοις,
τὸ τοὺς ἐπὶ τῆς Ἀσίας Ἕλληνας ἐλευθερωθῆναι ‹καὶ›
τυχεῖν τῆς αὐτονομίας τῆς ἅπασιν ἀνθρώποις προσ-
φιλεστάτης, Εὐμένει δὲ καὶ τοῖς ἀδελφοῖς ἥκιστα

8 τοῦτο συμφέρειν· φύσει γὰρ πᾶσαν μοναρχίαν τὸ μὲν
ἴσον ἐχθαίρειν, ζητεῖν δὲ πάντας, εἰ δὲ μή γ᾽ ὡς πλεί-

9 στους, ὑπηκόους εἶναι σφίσι καὶ πειθαρχεῖν. ἀλλὰ
καίπερ τοιούτων ὄντων τῶν πραγμάτων, ὅμως ἔφασαν
πεπεῖσθαι διότι καθίξονται τῆς προθέσεως, οὐ τῷ
πλεῖον Εὐμένους δύνασθαι παρὰ Ῥωμαίοις, ἀλλὰ τῷ
δικαιότερα φαίνεσθαι λέγοντες καὶ συμφορώτερα

10 πᾶσιν ὁμολογουμένως. εἰ μὲν γὰρ μὴ δυνατὸν ἦν
ἄλλως Εὐμένει χάριν ἀποδοῦναι Ῥωμαίους, εἰ μὴ
παραδοῖεν αὐτῷ τὰς αὐτονομουμένας πόλεις, ἀπορεῖν

11 εἰκὸς ἦν περὶ τῶν ἐνεστώτων· ἢ γὰρ φίλον ἀληθινὸν
ἔδει παριδεῖν, ἢ τοῦ καλοῦ καὶ καθήκοντος αὐτοῖς
ὀλιγωρῆσαι καὶ τὸ τέλος τῶν ἰδίων πράξεων ἀμαυ-

12 ρῶσαι καὶ καταβαλεῖν. "εἰ δ᾽ ἀμφοτέρων τούτων ἱκανῶς ἔξεστιν προνοηθῆναι, τίς ἂν ἔτι περὶ τούτου δια-

13 πορήσειεν; καὶ μὴν ὥσπερ ἐν δείπνῳ πολυτελεῖ, πάντ᾽

14 ἔνεστιν ἱκανὰ πᾶσιν καὶ πλείω τῶν ἱκανῶν. καὶ γὰρ
Λυκαονίαν καὶ Φρυγίαν τὴν ἐφ᾽ Ἑλλησπόντου καὶ

their speech round to the question of their country. Here, they said, their chief misfortune on the occasion of this embassy was that the very nature of things placed them in opposition to a prince with whom their relations both in public and in private were most close and cordial. To their country it seemed most noble and most worthy of Rome that the Greeks in Asia should be freed and obtain that autonomy which is nearest to the hearts of all men. But this was not at all in the interest of Eumenes and his brothers; for every monarchy by its nature hated equality and strove to make all men or at least as many as possible subject and obedient to it. But although the facts were so, still, they said, they were confident that they would attain their purpose, not because they had more influence with the Romans than Eumenes, but because their plea must appear indisputably the more just and more advantageous to every one concerned. For if the only way in which the Romans could show their gratitude to Eumenes was by giving up to him the autonomous cities, the question at issue admitted of some doubt; since they would have either to overlook a true friend, or else pay no heed to the call of honor and duty and tarnish and degrade the aim and purpose of their achievements. "But if," they said, "it is possible to provide satisfactorily for these two objects, why show any further hesitation? Nay, just as at a sumptuous banquet, there is surely enough and more than enough of everything for all. For Lycaonia,[64] Hellespontic Phry-

---

[64] This and the other areas here mentioned were outside of the principal interests of the Rhodians, which focused on regions not mentioned here, including Caria and Lycia.

τὴν Πισιδικήν, πρὸς δὲ ταύταις Χερρόνησον καὶ τὰ
προσοροῦντα ταύτῃ τῆς Εὐρώπης ἔξεστιν ὑμῖν οἷς ἂν
15 βούλησθε ... προστεθέντα πρὸς τὴν Εὐμένους βασιλείαν δεκαπλασίαν αὐτὴν δύναται ποιεῖν τῆς νῦν
ὑπαρχούσης· πάντων δὲ τούτων ἢ τῶν πλείστων αὐτῇ
προσμερισθέντων, οὐδεμιᾶς ἂν γένοιτο τῶν ἄλλων
δυναστειῶν καταδεεστέρα.

23. ἔξεστιν οὖν, ὦ ἄνδρες Ῥωμαῖοι, καὶ τοὺς φίλους
(xxii.6) μεγαλομερῶς σωματοποιῆσαι καὶ τὸ τῆς ἰδίας ὑπο-
2 θέσεως λαμπρὸν ⟨μὴ⟩ καταβαλεῖν. οὐ γὰρ ἐστιν ὑμῖν
καὶ τοῖς ἄλλοις ἀνθρώποις ταὐτὸν τέλος τῶν ἔργων,
3 ἀλλ᾽ ἕτερον. οἱ μὲν γὰρ ἄλλοι πάντες ὁρμῶσιν πρὸς
τὰς πράξεις ὀρεγόμενοι τοῦ καταστρέψασθαι καὶ
4 προσλαβεῖν πόλεις, χορηγίαν, ναῦς· ὑμᾶς δὲ πάντων
τούτων ἀπροσδεήτους ⟨οἱ θεοὶ⟩ πεποιήκασι, πάντα τὰ
κατὰ τὴν οἰκουμένην τεθεικότες [μὲν] ὑπὸ τὴν ὑμετέραν
5 ἐξουσίαν. τίνος οὖν ἔτι προσδεῖσθε, καὶ τίνος ἂν ἔτι
6 δέοι πρόνοιαν ὑμᾶς ποιεῖσθαι τὴν ἰσχυροτάτην; δῆλον
ὡς ἐπαίνου καὶ δόξης παρ᾽ ἀνθρώποις, ἃ καὶ κτήσα-
σθαι μέν ἐστι ⟨δυσχερές⟩, δυσχερέστερον δὲ κτησα-
μένους διαφυλάξαι. γνοίητε δ᾽ ἂν τὸ λεγόμενον οὕτως.
7 ἐπολεμήσατε πρὸς Φίλιππον καὶ πᾶν ὑπεμείνατε χάριν τῆς τῶν Ἑλλήνων ἐλευθερίας· τοῦτο γὰρ προέ-
θεσθε, καὶ τοῦθ᾽ ὑμῖν ἆθλον ἐξ ἐκείνου τοῦ πολέμου
8 περιγέγονεν, ἕτερον δ᾽ ἁπλῶς οὐδέν. ἀλλ᾽ ὅμως εὐδο-
κεῖτε τούτῳ μᾶλλον ἢ τοῖς παρὰ Καρχηδονίων φό-
9 ροις· καὶ μάλα δικαίως· τὸ μὲν γὰρ ἀργύριόν ἐστι
κοινόν τι πάντων ἀνθρώπων κτῆμα, τὸ δὲ καλὸν καὶ

gia, Pisidia, the Chersonese, and the parts of Europe adjacent thereto are at your disposal to give to whom you will. Any one of these, if added to the kingdom of Eumenes, would make it ten times as big as it is now, and if all or most of them were assigned to him, he would not be inferior to any other king.

23. So it is in your power, ye men of Rome, to give a magnificent accretion of strength to your friends, and yet not diminish the splendor of your own role. For the ends you propose to achieve are not the same as those of other people. Other men are impelled to armed action by the prospect of getting into their power and annexing cities, stores, or ships. But the gods have made all these things superfluous for you, by subjecting the whole world to your dominion. What is it, then, that you really are in want of, and what should you most intently study to obtain? Obviously praise and glory among men, things difficult indeed to acquire and still more difficult to keep when you have them. What we mean we will try to make plainer. You went to war with Philip and made every sacrifice for the sake of the liberty of Greece. For such was your purpose and this alone—absolutely nothing else—was the prize you won by that war. But yet you gained more glory by that than by the tribute you imposed on Carthage. For money is a possession common to all men, but what is good, glorious, and

πρὸς ἔπαινον καὶ τιμὴν ἀνῆκον θεῶν καὶ τῶν ἔγγιστα
10 τούτοις πεφυκότων ἀνδρῶν ἐστιν. τοιγαροῦν σεμνότα-
τον τῶν ὑμετέρων ἔργων ἡ τῶν Ἑλλήνων ἐλευθέρωσις.
τούτῳ νῦν ἐὰν μὲν προσθῆτε τἀκόλουθον, τελειωθήσε-
ται τὰ τῆς ὑμετέρας δόξης. ἐὰν δὲ παρίδητε, καὶ ⟨τὰ⟩
11 πρὶν ἐλαττωθήσεται φανερῶς. ἡμεῖς μὲν οὖν, ὦ ἄνδρες,
καὶ τῆς προαιρέσεως γεγονότες αἱρετισταὶ καὶ τῶν
μεγίστων ἀγώνων καὶ κινδύνων ἀληθινῶς ὑμῖν μετε-
σχηκότες, καὶ νῦν οὐκ ἐγκαταλείπομεν ⟨τὴν⟩ τῶν φί-
12 λων τάξιν, ἀλλ᾽ ἅ γε νομίζομεν ὑμῖν καὶ πρέπειν καὶ
συμφέρειν, οὐκ ὠκνήσαμεν ὑπομνῆσαι μετὰ παρρησίας, οὐδενὸς στοχασάμενοι τῶν ἄλλων οὐδὲ περὶ
πλείονος οὐδὲν ποιησάμενοι τοῦ καθήκοντος αὑτοῖς."
13   Οἱ μὲν οὖν Ῥόδιοι ταῦτ᾽ εἰπόντες πᾶσιν ἐδόκουν
μετρίως καὶ καλῶς διειλέχθαι περὶ τῶν προκειμένων.
(xxii.7) 24. ἐπὶ δὲ τούτοις εἰσήγαγον τοὺς παρ᾽ Ἀντιόχου
2 πρεσβευτὰς Ἀντίπατρον καὶ Ζεῦξιν. ὧν μετ᾽ ἀξιώσεως
καὶ παρακλήσεως ποιησαμένων τοὺς λόγους, εὐ-
δόκησαν ταῖς γεγενημέναις ὁμολογίαις πρὸς τοὺς
3 περὶ τὸν Σκιπίωνα κατὰ τὴν Ἀσίαν, καὶ μετά τινας
ἡμέρας τοῦ δήμου συνεπικυρώσαντος ἔτεμον ὅρκια
4 περὶ τούτων πρὸς τοὺς περὶ τὸν Ἀντίπατρον. μετὰ δὲ
ταῦτα καὶ τοὺς ἄλλους εἰσῆγον, ὅσοι παρῆσαν ἀπὸ
τῆς Ἀσίας πρεσβεύοντες· ὧν ἐπὶ βραχὺ μὲν διήκου-
5 σαν, ἅπασιν δὲ τὴν αὐτὴν ἔδωκαν ἀπόκρισιν. αὕτη δ᾽
ἦν ὅτι δέκα πρεσβεύοντας ἐξαποστελοῦσι τοὺς ὑπὲρ
ἁπάντων τῶν ἀμφισβητουμένων ταῖς πόλεσι διαγνω-
6 σομένους. δόντες δὲ ταύτας τὰς ἀποκρίσεις μετὰ

324

praiseworthy belongs only to the gods and those men who are by nature nearest to them. Therefore, as the noblest of the tasks you accomplished was the liberation of the Greeks, if you now thus supplement it, your glorious record will be complete; but if you neglect to do so, that glory you have already gained will obviously be diminished. We then, ye men of Rome, who have been the devoted supporters of your purpose, and who have taken a real part in your gravest struggles and dangers, do not now abandon our post in the ranks of your friends, but have not hesitated to remind you frankly of what we at least think to be your honor and advantage, aiming at nothing else and estimating nothing higher than our duty."

The Rhodians in this speech seemed to all the house to have expressed themselves modestly and well about the situation.

24. They next called in Antipater and Zeuxis,[65] the envoys of Antiochus. Upon their having spoken in a tone of supplication and entreaty, the senate voted its approval of the terms made with Scipio in Asia; and when, a few days afterward, the People also ratified the treaty, the oaths[66] of adherence to it were exchanged with Antipater and his colleague. After this the other envoys from Asia were introduced, and the Senate, having given them a short hearing, returned to all the same answer. This was that they would send ten legates to pronounce on all disputes between the towns. After giving this answer they appointed

---

[65] 16.4.

[66] See the long n. in WC 3.116–117 for the difficulties in determining when peace between these parties was finally concluded.

ταῦτα κατέστησαν δέκα πρεσβευτάς, οἷς περὶ μὲν τῶν

7 κατὰ μέρος ἔδωκαν τὴν ἐπιτροπήν, περὶ δὲ τῶν ὅλων
αὐτοὶ διέλαβον ὅτι δεῖ τῶν ἐπὶ τάδε τοῦ Ταύρου κατοικούντων, ὅσοι μὲν ὑπ' Ἀντίοχον ἐτάττοντο, τούτους
Εὐμένει δοθῆναι πλὴν Λυκίαν καὶ Καρίας τὰ μέχρι

8 τοῦ Μαιάνδρου ποταμοῦ, ταῦτα δὲ Ῥοδίων ὑπάρχειν,
τῶν <δὲ> πόλεων τῶν Ἑλληνίδων ὅσαι μὲν Ἀττάλῳ
φόρον ὑπετέλουν, ταύτας τὸν αὐτὸν Εὐμένει τελεῖν,
ὅσαι δ' Ἀντιόχῳ, μόνον ταύταις ἀφεῖσθαι τὸν φόρον.

9 δόντες δὲ τοὺς τύπους τούτους ὑπὲρ τῆς ὅλης διοική-
σεως, ἐξέπεμπον τοὺς δέκα πρὸς Γνάιον τὸν ὕπατον

10 εἰς τὴν Ἀσίαν. ἤδη δὲ τούτων διῳκημένων, προσῆλθον
αὖθις οἱ Ῥόδιοι πρὸς τὴν σύγκλητον, ἀξιοῦντες περὶ
Σόλων τῶν Κιλικίων· διὰ γὰρ τὴν συγγένειαν ἔφασαν

11 καθήκειν αὐτοῖς προνοεῖσθαι τῆς πόλεως ταύτης. εἶναι
γὰρ Ἀργείων ἀποίκους Σολεῖς, καθάπερ καὶ Ῥοδίους·
ἐξ ὧν ἀδελφικὴν οὖσαν ἀπεδείκνυον τὴν συγγένειαν

12 πρὸς ἀλλήλους. ὧν ἕνεκα δίκαιον ἔφασαν εἶναι τυχεῖν
αὐτοὺς τῆς ἐλευθερίας ὑπὸ Ῥωμαίων διὰ τῆς Ῥοδίων

13 χάριτος. ἡ δὲ σύγκλητος διακούσασα περὶ τούτων
εἰσεκαλέσατο τοὺς παρ' Ἀντιόχου πρεσβευτάς, καὶ τὸ
μὲν πρῶτον ἐπέταττε πάσης Κιλικίας ἐκχωρεῖν τὸν
Ἀντίοχον· οὐ προσδεχομένων δὲ τῶν περὶ τὸν Ἀντίπατρον διὰ τὸ παρὰ τὰς συνθήκας εἶναι, πάλιν ὑπὲρ

14 αὐτῶν Σόλων ἐποιοῦντο τὸν λόγον. φιλοτίμως δὲ πρὸς

---

67 *MRR* 1.363 with nn. 6–8. All ten are known, the only case
where there is such full information for a commission of ten.

the ten legates,[67] leaving matters of detail to their discretion, but themselves deciding on the following general scheme. Of the inhabitants of Asia on this side of the Taurus those provinces formerly subject to Antiochus were to be given to Eumenes, with the exception of Lycia and the part of Caria south of the Meander, which were to go to Rhodes: of the Greek cities those which formerly paid tribute to Attalus were to pay the same to Eumenes, and only in the case of those which were tributary to Antiochus was the tribute to be remitted. Having laid down these general principles for the government of Asia, they dispatched the ten legates there to join Gnaeus Manlius Vulso, the consul.[68] But after all had been thus arranged the Rhodians came before the Senate again on behalf of the people of Soli in Cilicia; for they said that owing to their tie of kinship with this city it was their duty to espouse its cause, the people of Soli[69] being colonists of Argos, like the Rhodians themselves; so that the two were in the position of sisters, which made it only just that the Solians should receive their freedom from Rome through the good graces of the Rhodians. The senate after listening to them summoned the envoys of Antiochus, and at first ordered him to withdraw from the whole of Cilicia; but when the envoys refused to assent to this, as it was contrary to the treaty,[70] they renewed the demand confining it to Soli alone. But upon the envoys stubbornly resisting

[68] *MRR* 1.360 and 366.

[69] City at the border between Cilicia Tracheia and Cilicia Pedias, west of today's Mersin. Originally a Phoenician settlement, then a colony of Rhodes. *RE* Soloi 935–938 (W. Ruge).

[70] Because being on the other side of the Taurus.

τοῦτο διερειδομένων τῶν πρεσβευτῶν, τούτους μὲν
ἀπέλυσαν, τοὺς δὲ Ῥοδίους εἰσκαλεσάμενοι διεσάφουν τὰ συναντώμενα παρὰ τῶν περὶ τὸν Ἀντίπατρον
καὶ προσεπέλεγον ὅτι πᾶν ὑπομενοῦσιν, εἰ πάντως
15 τοῦτο κέκριται Ῥοδίοις. τῶν δὲ πρεσβευτῶν εὐδοκου-
μένων τῇ φιλοτιμίᾳ τῆς συγκλήτου καὶ φασκόντων
οὐδὲν ἔτι πέρα ζητεῖν, ταῦτα μὲν ἐπὶ τῶν ὑποκειμένων
ἔμεινεν.

16   Ἤδη δὲ πρὸς ἀναζυγὴν τῶν δέκα καὶ τῶν ἄλλων
πρεσβευτῶν ὄντων, κατέπλευσαν τῆς Ἰταλίας εἰς
Βρεντέσιον οἵ τε περὶ τὸν Σκιπίωνα καὶ Λεύκιον οἱ τῇ
17 ναυμαχίᾳ νικήσαντες τὸν Ἀντίοχον· οἳ καὶ μετά τινας
ἡμέρας εἰσελθόντες εἰς τὴν Ῥώμην ἦγον θριάμβους.

V. RES GRAECIAE

25. Ὅτι Ἀμύνανδρος ὁ τῶν Ἀθαμάνων βασιλεύς,
(xxii.8) δοκῶν ἤδη τὴν ἀρχὴν ἀνειληφέναι βεβαίως, εἰς Ῥώμην ἐξέπεμπε πρεσβευτὰς καὶ πρὸς τοὺς Σκιπίωνας
εἰς τὴν Ἀσίαν—ἔτι γὰρ ἦσαν περὶ τοὺς κατὰ τὴν
2 Ἔφεσον τόπους—τὰ μὲν ἀπολογούμενος τῷ δοκεῖν δι'
Αἰτωλῶν πεποιῆσθαι τὴν κάθοδον, τὰ δὲ κατηγορῶν
τοῦ Φιλίππου, τὸ δὲ πολὺ παρακαλῶν προσδέξασθαι
3 πάλιν αὐτὸν εἰς τὴν συμμαχίαν. οἱ δ' Αἰτωλοὶ νομίσαντες ἔχειν εὐφυῆ καιρὸν πρὸς τὸ τὴν Ἀμφιλοχίαν

it, they dismissed them, and calling in the Rhodians informed them of the reply they had received from Antipater and his colleague, adding that they would go to any
extremity, if the Rhodians absolutely insisted on this. The
Rhodian envoys however were pleased with the cordial
attention of the senate and said that they would make no
further demand, so that this matter remained as it was.

The ten legates and the other envoys were preparing
to depart, when Lucius Scipio and Lucius Aemilius Regillus, who had defeated Antiochus in the sea battle, arrived
at Brundisium and after a few days entered Rome and
celebrated their triumphs.[71]

V. AFFAIRS OF GREECE

The Situation in Aetolia and Western Greece

(Cf. Livy 38.3)

25. Amynander,[72] the king of Athamania, thinking now
that he had for certainty recovered his kingdom, sent envoys both to Rome and to the Scipios in Asia—they were
still in the neighborhood of Ephesus—excusing himself
for having to all appearance returned to Athamania with
the help of the Aetolians, and also bringing accusations
against Philip, but chiefly begging them to receive him[73]
once more into their alliance. The Aetolians, thinking this
a favorable opportunity for recovering Amphilochia[74] and

---

[71] The exact dates, in autumn of 189, are known: *MRR*
1.362.   [72] See 20.10.5.

[73] This must have happened, as 29.2–3 shows.

[74] See n. on 18.5.8 and Walbank (18.3.9), 212–213.

καὶ τὴν Ἀπεραντίαν ἀνακτήσασθαι, προέθεντο στρα-
4 τεύειν εἰς τοὺς προειρημένους τόπους. ἀθροίσαντος
δὲ Νικάνδρου τοῦ στρατηγοῦ πάνδημον στρατιάν,
5 ἐνέβαλον εἰς τὴν Ἀμφιλοχίαν. τῶν δὲ πλείστων αὐτοῖς
ἐθελοντὴν προσχωρησάντων μετῆλθον εἰς τὴν Ἀπεραντίαν. καὶ τούτων δὲ προσθεμένων ἑκουσίως ἐστρά-
6 τευσαν εἰς τὴν Δολοπίαν. οὗτοι δὲ βραχὺν μέν τινα
χρόνον ὑπέδειξαν ὡς ἀντιποιησόμενοι, τηρήσαντες
τὴν πρὸς Φίλιππον πίστιν· λαβόντες δὲ πρὸ ὀφθαλμῶν
τὰ περὶ τοὺς Ἀθαμᾶνας καὶ τὴν τοῦ Φιλίππου . . .,
ταχέως μετενόησαν καὶ προσέθεντο πρὸς τοὺς Αἰτω-
7 λούς. γενομένης δὲ τῆς τῶν πραγμάτων εὐροίας τοιαύτης, ἀπήγαγε τὴν στρατιὰν ὁ Νίκανδρος εἰς τὴν
οἰκείαν, δοκῶν ἠσφαλίσθαι ⟨τὰ⟩ κατὰ τὴν Αἰτωλίαν
τοῖς προειρημένοις ἔθνεσι καὶ τόποις τοῦ μηδένα δύ-
8 νασθαι κακοποιεῖν τὴν χώραν αὐτῶν. ἄρτι δὲ τούτων
συμβεβηκότων καὶ τῶν Αἰτωλῶν ἐπὶ τοῖς γεγονόσι
φρονηματιζομένων, προσέπεσε φήμη περὶ τῆς κατὰ
τὴν Ἀσίαν μάχης, ἐν ᾗ γνόντες ἡττημένον ὁλοσχερῶς
9 τὸν Ἀντίοχον αὖθις ἀνετράπησαν ταῖς ψυχαῖς. ὡς δὲ
παραγενηθεὶς ἐκ τῆς Ῥώμης ὁ Δαμοτέλης τόν τε πόλεμον ἀνήγγειλε διότι μένει κατάμονος, καὶ τὴν τοῦ
Μάρκου καὶ τῶν δυνάμεων διάβασιν ἐπ' αὐτούς, τότε
δὴ παντελῶς εἰς ἀμηχανίαν ἐνέπιπτον καὶ διηπόρουν
πῶς δεῖ χρήσασθαι τοῖς ἐπιφερομένοις πράγμασιν
10 ἔδοξεν οὖν αὐτοῖς πρός τε Ῥοδίους πέμπειν καὶ πρὸς

Aperantia, decided on an expedition to the above districts and Nicander[75] their strategus having assembled their total forces, they invaded Amphilochia. Upon most of the inhabitants joining them of their own accord, they went on to Aperantia, and when the people there also voluntarily joined them, they invaded Dolopia.[76] The Dolopians made a show of resistance for a short time; but, with the fate of Athamania and the flight of Philip before their eyes, they soon changed their minds and also joined the Aetolians. After this unbroken series of successes Nicander took his army back to their own country, thinking that by the annexation of the above countries and peoples Aetolia was secured against damage from any quarter. But just after these occurrences, and while the Aetolians were still elated by their success, came the news of the battle in Asia, and when they learnt that Antiochus had been utterly defeated, their spirits were again dashed. And when now Damoteles[77] arrived from Rome and announced that the state of war still subsisted, and that Marcus Fulvius Nobilior[78] with his army was crossing to attack them, they fell into a state of utter helplessness, and were at their wits' end as to how they should meet the danger which threatened them. They decided, then, to send to Athens[79] and

---

[75] See n. on 20.10.16, also 20.11.1–10. On his campaign in 189, Walbank (25.3), 214.　　　[76] The Dolopians are a Thessalian tribe. Stählin (18.3.12), 145–150.　　　[77] Well-known Aetolian from Locris; see Grainger (18.10.9), 144–145.

[78] Consul 189. He was assigned the Aetolian War. *MRR* 1.360.　　　[79] The Athenians, on their own initiative, had the previous year intervened with the Scipios on behalf of the Aetolians: 4.1–5.13.

Ἀθηναίους, ἀξιοῦντας καὶ παρακαλοῦντας πρεσβεῦσαι
περὶ αὐτῶν εἰς τὴν Ῥώμην καὶ παραιτησαμένους τὴν
ὀργὴν τῶν Ῥωμαίων ποιήσασθαί τινα λύσιν τῶν
11   περιεστώτων κακῶν τὴν Αἰτωλίαν. ὁμοίως δὲ καὶ παρ'
αὐτῶν ἐξέπεμψαν πάλιν πρεσβευτὰς εἰς τὴν Ῥώμην,
Ἀλέξανδρον τὸν Ἴσιον ἐπικαλούμενον καὶ Φαινέαν,
σὺν δὲ τούτοις Χάλεπον, ἔτι δ' Ἄλυπον τὸν Ἀμβρα-
κιώτην καὶ Λύκωπον.

26. Ὅτι παραγενομένων πρὸς τὸν στρατηγὸν τῶν
(xxii.9)   Ῥωμαίων ἐξ ⟨Ἠπείρου⟩ πρεσβευτῶν, ἐκοινολογεῖτο
2   τούτοις περὶ τῆς ἐπὶ τοὺς Αἰτωλοὺς στρατείας. τῶν
δὲ πρεσβευτῶν στρατεύειν ἐπὶ τὴν Ἀμβρακίαν συμ-
βουλευόντων—συνέβαινε γὰρ τότε πολιτεύεσθαι τοὺς
3   Ἀμβρακιώτας μετὰ τῶν Αἰτωλῶν—καὶ φερόντων ἀπολογισμοὺς διότι καὶ πρὸς τὸ μάχεσθαι τοῖς στρατοπέδοις, ἐὰν εἰς τοῦτα βούλωνται συγκαταβαίνειν
Αἰτωλοί, καλλίστους εἶναι τόπους συμβαίνει περὶ τὴν
4   προειρημένην πόλιν, κἂν ἀποδειλιῶσιν, εὐφυῶς αὐτὴν
κεῖσθαι πρὸς πολιορκίαν· καὶ γὰρ ἀφθόνους ἔχειν τὴν
χώραν τὰς χορηγίας πρὸς τὰς τῶν ἔργων παρασκευάς, καὶ τὸν Ἄρατθον ποταμὸν ῥέοντα παρὰ τὴν
πόλιν συνεργήσειν πρός τε τὰς τοῦ στρατοπέδου
χρείας, ἅτε θέρους ὄντος, καὶ πρὸς τὴν τῶν ἔργων
5   ἀσφάλειαν· δοξάντων δὲ τῶν πρεσβευτῶν καλῶς
συμβουλεύειν, ἀναζεύξας ὁ στρατηγὸς ἦγε διὰ τῆς
6   Ἠπείρου τὸν στρατὸν ἐπὶ τὴν Ἀμβρακίαν. ἀφικόμενος
δέ, καὶ τῶν Αἰτωλῶν οὐ τολμώντων ἀπαντᾶν, περιῄει

Rhodes begging and imploring those states to send embassies to Rome to appease the anger of the Romans, and to avert by some means the evils that encompassed Aetolia. At the same time they dispatched to Rome envoys of their own, Alexander the Isian and Phaeneas[80] accompanied by Chalepus, Alypus of Ambracia[81] and Lycopus.

(Cf. Livy 38.3.9)

26. Upon envoys from Epirus reaching the Roman consul he took their advice about his expedition to Aetolia. These envoys recommended that he march on Ambracia—for at the time the Ambracians were members of the Aetolian League—alleging that if the Aetolians were disposed to meet his legions in the field, the country round that city was the best for the purpose; but that if they declined to give battle, the situation of the town itself made it easy to besiege it, since the country afforded abundant material for the construction of siege works and the river Aratthus, which ran under its walls, would be of help to him both as a source of water supply to his army, it being now summer, and a defense of their works. The advice they gave was considered good, and the consul set out and led his army through Epirus to Ambracia. On arriving there and on the Aetolians not venturing to meet him, he

80 For Alexander see 13.1a.1, 18.3.1, and 36.5, and below 26.9; for Phaeneas, 18.1.4 and 20.9.1.

81 Some time later ambassador for his city to the Thessalian League, C. Habicht in *Demetrias* 1 (Bonn 1976), 178, line 13. Ambracia (modern Arta), formerly the residence of King Pyrrhus, became Aetolian after the end of the monarchy around 230.

κατοπτεύων τὴν πόλιν καὶ ἐνήργει τὰ τῆς πολιορκίας
φιλοτίμως.

7   Καὶ οἱ ⟨μὲν ὑπὸ τῶν Αἰτωλῶν⟩ εἰς τὴν Ῥώμην
ἀποσταλέντες πρέσβεις, παρατηρηθέντες ὑπὸ Σιβύρ-
του τοῦ Πετραίου περὶ τὴν Κεφαλληνίαν, κατήχθη-
8   σαν εἰς Χάραδρον. τοῖς δ᾽ Ἠπειρώταις ἔδοξεν τὰς μὲν
ἀρχὰς εἰς Βούχετον ἀποθέσθαι καὶ φυλάττειν ἐπιμελῶς τοὺς ἄνδρας· μετὰ δέ τινας ἡμέρας ἀπήτουν
αὐτοὺς λύτρα διὰ τὸ πόλεμον ὑπάρχειν σφίσιν πρὸς
9   τοὺς Αἰτωλούς. συνέβαινε δὲ τὸν μὲν Ἀλέξανδρον
πλουσιώτατον εἶναι πάντων τῶν Ἑλλήνων, τοὺς δὲ
λοιποὺς ⟨οὐ⟩ καθυστερεῖν τοῖς βίοις, πολὺ δὲ λείπε-
10 σθαι τοῦ προειρημένου ταῖς οὐσίαις. καὶ τὸ μὲν πρῶτον ἐκέλευον ἕκαστον ἀποδοῦναι πέντε τάλαντα. τοῦτο
δὲ τοῖς μὲν ἄλλοις οὐδ᾽ ὅλως ἀπήρεσκεν, ἀλλ᾽ ἐβούλοντο, περὶ πλείστου ποιούμενοι τὴν σφῶν αὐτῶν σω-
11 τηρίαν· ὁ δ᾽ Ἀλέξανδρος οὐκ ἂν ἔφη συγχωρῆσαι,
πολὺ γὰρ εἶναι τἀργύριον [φαίνεται], καὶ τὰς νύκτας
διαγρυπνῶν διωλοφύρετο πρὸς αὐτόν, εἰ δεήσει πέντε
12 τάλαντα καταβάλλειν. οἱ δ᾽ Ἠπειρῶται προορώμενοι
τὸ μέλλον καὶ διαγωνιῶντες μὴ γνόντες οἱ Ῥωμαῖοι
διότι πρεσβεύοντας πρὸς αὐτοὺς κατεσχήκασι, κἄπειτα γράψαντες παρακαλῶσι καὶ κελεύωσιν ἀπολύ-
ειν τοὺς ἄνδρας, συγκαταβάντες τρία τάλαντα πάλιν
13 ἀπήτουν ἕκαστον. ἀσμένως δὲ τῶν ἄλλων προσδεξα-

---

82 "Charadrus must be a town" (WC 3.122), confirmed by the
recently published convention of ca. 165 between Ambracia and

went round the city to survey it and made energetic preparations for its siege.

Meanwhile the envoys sent by the Aetolians to Rome were observed and caught by Sibyrtes the son of Petraeus off Cephallenia and were brought in to Charadrus.[82] The Epirots at first decided to lodge them in Buchetus[83] and keep careful guard over them, but after some days they demanded ransom from them, as they were at war with the Aetolians. Alexander happened to be the richest man in Greece and the others were not badly off, but far poorer than he was. At first the Epirots demanded five talents from each, which the others were not entirely indisposed to pay, but rather wished to do so, as they valued their safety above all things. Alexander,[84] however, said he would not yield to the demand, as the sum was too large, and spent sleepless nights bewailing his mischance if he had to pay five talents. The Epirots, foreseeing what was, as a fact, about to happen, and fearing much lest the Romans, on learning that they had arrested envoys on their way to Rome, might write and demand their release, reduced their demand to three talents for each envoy. The others were only too glad to accept, and were allowed to

Charadrus (*SEG* 49.635) about their common border. Its location has been fixed at Palaia Philippias, northwest of Ambracia, by P. Cabanes and J. Andréou, *BCH* 109 (1985), 515, and map p. 528. The city has already been mentioned at 4.63.4–5.

[83] A colony of Elis, modern Rosous, west of Ambracia and south of Charadrus. From there comes a recently found dedication of three Epirots fighting under the Roman consul Marcus Perperna in 129 against Aristonicus of Pergamum (*ISE* 147).

[84] Alexander Isios; see n. on 13.1a.1; further 18.3.1 and 36.5.

μένων, οὗτοι μὲν διεγγυηθέντες ἐπανῆλθον, ὁ δ᾽ Ἀλέξανδρος οὐκ ἂν ἔφη δοῦναι πλεῖον ταλάντου· καὶ γὰρ
14 τοῦτ᾽ εἶναι πολύ. καὶ τέλος ἀπογνοὺς αὐτὸν ἔμεινεν ἐν
τῇ φυλακῇ, πρεσβύτερος ἄνθρωπος, πλειόνων ἢ δια-
κοσίων ταλάντων ἔχων οὐσίαν· καί μοι δοκεῖ κἂν
15 ἐκλιπεῖν τὸν βίον ἐφ᾽ ᾧ μὴ δοῦναι τὰ τρία τάλαντα. τοσ-
αύτη τις ἐνίοις πρὸς τὸ πλεῖον ὁρμὴ παρίσταται καὶ
16 προθυμία. τότε δ᾽ ἐκείνῳ καὶ ταὐτόματον συνήργησεν
πρὸς τὴν φιλαργυρίαν, ὥστε παρὰ πᾶσιν ἐπαίνου καὶ
συγκαταθέσεως τυχεῖν τὴν ἀλογιστίαν αὐτοῦ διὰ τὴν
17 περιπέτειαν· μετὰ γὰρ ὀλίγας ἡμέρας γραμμάτων
παραγενηθέντων ἐκ τῆς Ῥώμης περὶ τῆς ἀφέσεως,
18 αὐτὸς μόνος ἀπελύθη χωρὶς λύτρων. οἱ δ᾽ Αἰτωλοί,
γνόντες τὴν αὐτοῦ περιπέτειαν, Δαμοτέλη προεχειρί-
19 σαντο πάλιν εἰς τὴν Ῥώμην πρεσβευτήν. ὃς ἐκπλεύ-
σας μέχρι τῆς Λευκάδος καὶ γνοὺς προάγοντα διὰ
τῆς Ἠπείρου μετὰ τῶν δυνάμεων Μάρκον ἐπὶ τὴν Ἀμβρακίαν, ἀπογνοὺς τὴν πρεσβείαν αὖθις ἀνεχώρησεν
εἰς τὴν Αἰτωλίαν.

27. Αἰτωλοὶ ὑπὸ τοῦ τῶν Ῥωμαίων ὑπάτου Μάρκου
(xxii.10) πολιορκούμενοι τῇ προσβολῇ τῶν μηχανημάτων καὶ
2 τῶν κριῶν γενναίως ἀντιπαρετάξαντο. οὗτος γὰρ
ἀσφαλισάμενος τὰ κατὰ τὰς στρατοπεδείας συνίστατο
μεγαλομερῶς τὴν πολιορκίαν καὶ τρία μὲν ἔργα κατὰ
τὸ Πύρρειον προσῆγεν διὰ τῶν ἐπιπέδων [τόπων], δι-
εστῶτα μὲν ἀπ᾽ ἀλλήλων, παράλληλα δέ, τέταρτον δὲ
κατὰ τὸ Ἀσκληπιεῖον, πέμπτον δὲ κατὰ τὴν ἀκρόπολιν.
3 γινομένης δὲ τῆς προσαγωγῆς ἐνεργοῦ κατὰ πάντας

depart after giving surety, but Alexander said he would not
pay more than a talent, and even that was too much. Finally he gave up all hope, and remained in prison, being
then advanced in years and possessing a fortune of more
than two hundred talents. And, I think, he would have
perished rather than pay the three talents: so strong is the
impulse and so great the eagerness of some people to ac-
cumulate money. In this case, however, chance furthered
his cupidity, so that, owing to the unexpected outcome,
this foolish avarice met with universal praise and approval;
for a few days afterward a letter arrived from Rome ordering the envoys to be liberated, and he alone escaped without paying ransom. The Aetolians when they heard of the
misfortune that had befallen him appointed Damoteles
again ambassador to Rome; but having sailed as far as Leucas he heard that Marcus Fulvius was advancing through
Epirus with his army on Ambracia, and abandoning his
mission returned to Aetolia.

Siege of Ambracia

(From *Anon. de obsid. toll.* 169–174; *ep.* Livy 38.5)
27. The Aetolians, besieged in Ambracia by the Roman
consul Marcus Fulvius, gallantly resisted the assaults of
rams and other machines. For the consul, after securing
his camps, had begun siege operations on an extensive
scale. He brought up three machines through the level
country near the Pyrrheium at some distance from each
other but advancing on parallel lines, a fourth at the Aes-
culapium and a fifth at the acropolis. As the assault was
vigorously conducted at one and the same time in all these

ἅμα τοὺς τόπους, ἐκπληκτικὴν συνέβαινε γίνεσθαι
4 τοῖς ἔνδον τὴν τοῦ μέλλοντος προσδοκίαν. τῶν δὲ
κριῶν τυπτόντων ἐνεργῶς τὰ τείχη, καὶ τῶν δορυδρε-
πάνων ἀποσυρόντων τὰς ἐπάλξεις, ἐπειρῶντο μὲν οἱ
κατὰ τὴν πόλιν ἀντιμηχανᾶσθαι πρὸς ταῦτα, τοῖς μὲν
κριοῖς διὰ κεραιῶν ἐνιέντες σηκώματα μολιβδᾶ καὶ
5 λίθους καὶ στύπη δρύινα· τοῖς δὲ δρεπάνοις σιδηρᾶς
περιτιθέντες ἀγκύρας καὶ κατασπῶντες ταῦτ' ἔσω τοῦ
τείχους, ὥστ' ἐπὶ τὴν ἔπαλξιν συντριβέντος τοῦ δόρα-
6 τος ἐγκρατεῖς γίνεσθαι τῶν δρεπάνων. τὸ δὲ πλεῖον
ἐπεξιόντες ἐμάχοντο γενναίως, ποτὲ μὲν ἐπιτιθέμενοι
νύκτωρ τοῖς ἐπικοιτοῦσιν ἐπὶ τῶν ἔργων, ποτὲ δὲ τοῖς
ἐφημερεύουσι μεθ' ἡμέραν προφανῶς ἐγχειροῦντες,
καὶ τριβὴν ἐνεποίουν τῇ πολιορκίᾳ.

7   Τοῦ γὰρ Νικάνδρου ἐκτὸς ἀναστρεφομένου καὶ
πέμψαντος πεντακοσίους ἱππεῖς εἰς τὴν πόλιν, οἳ καὶ
παραβιασάμενοι τὸν μεταξὺ χάρακα τῶν πολεμίων
8 εἰσέφρησαν εἰς τὴν πόλιν, ... παραγγείλας, καθ' ἣν
ἐτάξαντο ἡμέραν, αὐτοὺς μὲν ἐξελθόντας ... ποιήσασθαι, συνεπιλαβέσθαι δὲ αὐτὸν τούτοις τοῦ κινδύνου.... αὐτῶν μὲν εὐψύχως τῆς πόλεως ἐξορμησάντων
καὶ γενναίως ἀγωνισαμένων, τοῦ δὲ Νικάνδρου καθυ-
στερήσαντος, εἴτε καταπλαγέντος τὸν κίνδυνον εἴτε
καὶ ἀναγκαῖα νομίσαντος τὰ ἐν οἷς διέτριβε πράγμασιν, ἡττήθησαν τῆς ἐπιβολῆς.

28. Οἱ δὲ Ῥωμαῖοι συνεχῶς ἐνεργοῦντες τοῖς κριοῖς
(xxii.11) ἀεί τι παρέλυον τῶν τειχῶν· οὐ μὴν εἴς γε τὴν πόλιν
2 ἐδύναντο βιάσασθαι διὰ τῶν πτωμάτων, τῷ καὶ τὴν

places, the besieged were terrified by the prospect of what awaited them. While the rams continued to batter the walls and the long sickle-shaped grapplers to drag down the battlements, the defenders of the city made efforts to counterengineer them, dropping by means of cranes leaden weights, stones, and stumps of trees on to the rams and after catching the sickles with iron anchors dragging them inside the wall, so that the pole of the apparatus was smashed against the battlement and the sickle itself remained in their hands. They also made frequent sallies, sometimes attacking by night those who slept on the machines, and sometimes openly attempting in daylight to dislodge the day shift, thus impeding the progress of the siege.

(From *Anon. de obsid. toll.* 97–99; *ep.* Livy 38.5–6)

Nicander,[85] who was hovering round outside the Roman lines, had sent five hundred horse to the town, who forced an entrance by breaking through the entrenchments of the enemy. He had ordered them on a day agreed upon to make a sortie and attack the Roman works, engaging to come to their assistance.... But although they made a gallant dash out of the city and fought bravely, the plan failed because Nicander failed to appear, either because he was afraid of the risk, or because he thought the task on which he was actually occupied more urgent.

(From *Anon. de obsid. toll.* 178–195; *ep.* Livy 38.7.4)

28. The Romans, working constantly with their rams, continued to break down portions of the wall, but they were not able to force their way in through the breach, as

[85] See 25.4, 28.18.

ἀντοικοδομίαν ὑπὸ τῶν ἔνδον ἐνεργὸν εἶναι καὶ μάχεσθαι γενναίως ἐπὶ τοῦ πίπτοντος μέρους τοὺς Αἰτω-
3 λούς. διόπερ ἀπορούμενοι κατήντησαν ἐπὶ τὸ μεταλ-
λεύειν καὶ χρῆσθαι τοῖς ὀρύγμασιν ὑπὸ γῆς.
4 ἀσφαλισάμενοι δὲ τὸ μέσον ἔργον τῶν τριῶν τῶν
προϋπαρχόντων καὶ σκεπάσαντες ἐπιμελῶς [τὴν σύ-
ριγγα] τοῖς γέρροις, προεβάλοντο στοὰν παράλληλον
5 τῷ τείχει σχεδὸν ἐπὶ δύο πλέθρα. καὶ λαβόντες ἀρχὴν
ἐκ ταύτης ὤρυττον ἀδιαπαύστως καὶ τὴν νύκτα καὶ
6 τὴν ἡμέραν ἐκ διαδοχῆς. ἐφ' ἱκανὰς μὲν οὖν ἡμέρας
ἐλάνθανον τοὺς ἔνδον φέροντες ἔξω τὸν χοῦν διὰ τῆς
7 σύριγγος. ὡς δὲ μέγας ὁ σωρὸς ἐγένετο τῆς ἐκ-
φερομένης γῆς καὶ σύνοπτος τοῖς ἐκ τῆς πόλεως, οἱ
προεστῶτες τῶν πολιορκουμένων ὤρυττον τάφρον
ἔσωθεν ἐνεργῶς παράλληλον τῷ τείχει καὶ τῇ στοᾷ
8 τῇ πρὸ τῶν πύργων. ἐπειδὴ δὲ βάθος ἔσχεν ἱκανόν,
ἑξῆς ἔθηκαν παρὰ τὸν ἕνα τοῖχον τῆς τάφρου τὸν
ἐγγὺς τῷ τείχει χαλκώματα συνεχῆ, λεπτότατα ταῖς
κατασκευαῖς, καὶ παρὰ ταῦτα διὰ τῆς τάφρου παριόν-
9 τες ἠκροῶντο τοῦ ψόφου τῶν ὀρυττόντων ἔξωθεν. ἐπεὶ
δ' ἐσημειώσαντο τὸν τόπον, καθ' ὃν ἐδήλου τινὰ τῶν
χαλκωμάτων διὰ τῆς συμπαθείας, ὤρυττον ἔσωθεν
ἐπικαρσίαν πρὸς τὴν ὑπάρχουσαν ἄλλην κατὰ γῆς
τάφρον ὑπὸ τὸ τεῖχος, στοχαζόμενοι τοῦ συμπεσεῖν
10 ἐναντίοι τοῖς πολεμίοις. ταχὺ δὲ τούτου γενομένου, διὰ
τὸ τοὺς Ῥωμαίους μὴ μόνον ἀφῖχθαι πρὸς τὸ τεῖχος
ὑπὸ γῆς, ἀλλὰ καὶ διεστυλωκέναι τόπον ἱκανὸν τοῦ
τείχους ἐφ' ἑκάτερον τὸ μέρος τοῦ μετάλλου, συνέπε-

the defenders worked hard at counterwalling, and fought gallantly on the ruins. So, as a last resource, they took to mining and digging underground. Having secured the middle one of the three machines they previously had on this site and covered it carefully with wattle screens, they constructed in front of it a covered gallery running parallel to the wall for about two hundred feet, from which they dug continuously by day and night, employing relays. For a good many days they carried out the earth by the underground passage without being noticed by the defenders, but when the heap of earth became considerable and visible to those in the city, the leaders of the besieged set vigorously to work to dig a trench inside the wall parallel to the wall itself and to the gallery in front of the towers. When it was sufficiently deep, they lined the side of the trench next the wall with exceedingly thin plates of bronze, and advancing along the trench with their ears close to these, listened for the noise made by the miners outside. When they had noted the spot indicated by the reverberation of some of the bronze plates, they began to dig from within another underground passage at right angles to the trench and passing under the wall, their object being to encounter the enemy. This they soon succeeded in doing, as the Roman miners had not only reached the wall but had underpinned a considerable part of it on both

THE HISTORIES OF POLYBIUS

11 σον ἀλλήλοις, καὶ τὸ μὲν πρῶτον ἐμάχοντο ταῖς σαρίσαις ὑπὸ γῆν· ἐπεὶ δ' οὐδὲν ἠδύναντο μέγα ποιεῖν
διὰ τὸ προβάλλεσθαι θυρεοὺς καὶ γέρρα πρὸ αὑτῶν

12 ἀμφότεροι, τὸ τηνικάδ' ὑπέθετό τις τοῖς πολιορκουμέ-
νοις πίθον προθεμένους ἁρμοστὸν κατὰ τὸ πλάτος τῷ
μετάλλῳ τρυπῆσαι τὸν πυθμένα καὶ διώσαντας αὐλίσκον σιδηροῦν ἴσον τῷ τεύχει πλῆσαι τὸν πίθον ὅλον
πτίλων λεπτῶν καὶ πυρὸς παντελῶς μικρὸν ἐμβαλεῖν

13 ὑπ' αὐτὸ τὸ τοῦ πίθου περιστόμιον· κἄπειτα σιδηροῦν
πῶμα τρημάτων πλῆρες τῷ στόματι περιθέντας
ἀσφαλῶς εἰσάγειν διὰ τοῦ μετάλλου, νεύοντι τῷ στό-

14 ματι πρὸς τοὺς ὑπεναντίους· ὁπότε δ' ἐγγίσαιεν τοῖς
πολεμίοις, περισάξαντας τὰ χείλη τοῦ πίθου πανταχόθεν τρήματα δύο καταλιπεῖν ἐξ ἑκατέρου τοῦ μέρους, δι' ὧν διωθοῦντες τὰς σαρίσας οὐκ ἐάσουσι

15 προσιέναι τῷ πίθῳ τοὺς ὑπεναντίους· μετὰ δὲ ταῦτα
λαβόντας ἀσκόν, ᾧπερ οἱ χαλκεῖς χρῶνται, καὶ προσ-
αρμόσαντας πρὸς τὸν αὐλὸν τὸν σιδηροῦν φυσᾶν
ἐνεργῶς τὸ πρὸς τῷ στόματι πῦρ ἐν τοῖς πτίλοις
ἐγκείμενον, κατὰ τοσοῦτον ἐπαγομένους ἀεὶ τὸν αὐλὸν

16 ἐκτός, καθ' ὅσον ἂν ἐκκάηται τὰ πτίλα. γενομένων δὲ
πάντων καθάπερ προείρηται, τό τε πλῆθος τοῦ καπνοῦ
συνέβαινε πολὺ γίνεσθαι καὶ τῇ δριμύτητι διαφέρον
διὰ τὴν φύσιν τῶν πτίλων, φέρεσθαί τε πᾶν εἰς τὸ τῶν

17 πολεμίων μέταλλον. ὥστε καὶ λίαν κακοπαθεῖν καὶ
δυσχρηστεῖσθαι τοὺς Ῥωμαίους, οὔτε κωλύειν οὔθ'
ὑπομένειν δυναμένους ἐν τοῖς ὀρύγμασι τὸν καπνόν.

18 τοιαύτην δὲ λαμβανούσης τριβὴν τῆς πολιορκίας ὁ

sides of their gallery of approach. On meeting, they first of all fought underground with their pikes, but when they found that they could not effect much by this, as on both sides they used bucklers and wattles to protect themselves, some one suggested to the besieged to put in front of them a large corn jar exactly broad enough to fit into the trench. They were to bore a hole in the bottom of it, and insert into this an iron tube as long as the jar: next they were to fill the whole jar with fine feathers and place a small amount of fire round its extreme edge: they were now to fit on to the mouth of the jar an iron lid full of holes and introduce the whole carefully into the mine with its mouth turned toward the enemy. When they reached the latter they were to stop up completely the space round the rim of the jar, leaving two holes, one on either side, through which they could push their pikes and prevent the enemy from approaching it. They were then to take a blacksmith's bellows and fitting it into the iron tube blow hard on the fire that was near the mouth of the vessel among the feathers, gradually, as the feathers caught fire, withdrawing the tube. Upon all those instructions being followed, a quantity of smoke, especially pungent owing to its being produced by feathers, was all carried up the enemy's mine, so that the Romans suffered much and were in an evil case, as they could neither prevent nor support the smoke in their diggings. While the siege thus continued to be pro-

στρατηγὸς τῶν Αἰτωλῶν πρεσβεύειν ἔγνω πρὸς τὸν στρατηγὸν τῶν Ῥωμαίων.

29. Ὅτι κατὰ τὸν καιρὸν τοῦτον οἱ παρὰ τῶν Ἀθη- (xxii.12) ναίων καὶ τῶν Ῥοδίων πρέσβεις ἧκον ἐπὶ τὸ στρατό- πεδον τῶν Ῥωμαίων, συνεπιληψόμενοι τῶν διαλύσεων.

2 ὅ τε βασιλεὺς τῶν Ἀθαμάνων Ἀμύνανδρος παρεγέ- νετο σπουδάζων ἐξελέσθαι τοὺς Ἀμβρακιώτας ἐκ τῶν περιεστώτων κακῶν, δοθείσης αὐτῷ τῆς ἀσφαλείας

3 ὑπὸ τοῦ Μάρκου διὰ τὸν καιρόν· πάνυ γὰρ οἰκείως εἶχε πρὸς τοὺς Ἀμβρακιώτας διὰ τὸ καὶ πλείω χρόνον

4 ἐν τῇ πόλει ταύτῃ διατετριφέναι κατὰ φυγήν. ἧκον δὲ καὶ παρὰ τῶν Ἀκαρνάνων μετ' ὀλίγας ἡμέρας ἄγοντές τινες τοὺς περὶ Δαμοτέλην· ὁ γὰρ Μάρκος πυθόμενος τὴν περιπέτειαν αὐτῶν ἔγραψε τοῖς Θυρρειεῦσιν ἀνα-

5 κομίζειν τοὺς ἄνδρας ὡς αὐτόν. πάντων δὲ τούτων ἠθροισμένων ἐνηργεῖτο φιλοτίμως τὰ πρὸς τὰς δια-

6 λύσεις. ὁ μὲν οὖν Ἀμύνανδρος κατὰ τὴν αὐτοῦ πρόθε- σιν εἴχετο τῶν Ἀμβρακιωτῶν, παρακαλῶν σῴζειν σφᾶς αὐτούς ... εἶναι δὲ τοῦτον οὐ μακράν, ἐὰν μὴ

7 βουλεύσωνται βέλτιον περὶ αὑτῶν. πλεονάκις δὲ προσπελάζοντος αὐτοῦ τῷ τείχει καὶ διαλεγομένου περὶ τούτων, ἔδοξε τοῖς Ἀμβρακιώταις εἰσκαλέσασθαι

8 τὸν Ἀμύνανδρον εἰς τὴν πόλιν. τοῦ δὲ στρατηγοῦ συγχωρήσαντος τῷ βασιλεῖ τὴν εἴσοδον, οὗτος μὲν εἰσελθὼν διελέγετο τοῖς Ἀμβρακιώταις περὶ τῶν ἐνε-

9 στώτων, οἱ δὲ παρὰ τῶν Ἀθηναίων καὶ τῶν Ῥοδίων πρέσβεις λαμβάνοντες εἰς τὰς χεῖρας τὸν στρατηγὸν τῶν Ῥωμαίων καὶ ποικίλως ὁμιλοῦντες, πραΰνειν ἐπει-

longed, the strategus of the Aetolians decided to send envoys to the Roman consul.

Peace Made with Aetolia

(Cf. Livy 38.9)

29. At this time the envoys from Athens and Rhodes arrived at the Roman camp to assist in making the peace. Amynander, the king of Athamania, also came to attempt to deliver the Ambraciots from their dangerous situation, having received a safe-conduct from Marcus Fulvius, who availed himself of the opportunity; for this king was on very good terms with the Ambraciots, having lived in the town for a considerable time during his exile. Some representatives of Acarnania also arrived a few days afterward bringing Damoteles and those with him; for Fulvius, on learning of their unfortunate situation, had written to the people of Thyrrheium[86] to send the men to him. All the above bodies having thus met, negotiations for peace proceeded energetically. Amynander, in pursuance of his purpose, approached the Ambraciots begging them to save themselves and not to run into the extremity of danger, which was not far off, unless they were better advised in their proceedings. After he had more than once ridden up to the wall and spoken to them, the Ambraciots decided to invite him to enter the city. Having received permission from the consul to do so, he went in and conversed with the Ambraciots about the situation. Meanwhile the envoys of Athens and Rhodes, approaching the Roman consul privately, attempted by various arguments to mitigate his

[86] City in Acarnania. *RE* Thyrreion 744–747 (K. Fiehn).

10 ρῶντο τὴν ὀργὴν αὐτοῦ. τοῖς δὲ περὶ τὸν Δαμοτέλη
καὶ Φαινέαν ὑπέθετό τις ἔχεσθαι καὶ θεραπεύειν τὸν
11 Γάιον Οὐαλέριον· οὗτος δ᾽ ἦν Μάρκου μὲν υἱὸς τοῦ
πρώτου συνθεμένου πρὸς Αἰτωλοὺς τὴν συμμαχίαν,
Μάρκου δὲ τοῦ τότε στρατηγοῦντος ἀδελφὸς ἐκ μη-
τρός· ἄλλως δὲ πρᾶξιν ἔχων νεανικὴν ἦν μάλιστα
12 παρὰ τῷ στρατηγῷ πιστευόμενος. ὃς παρακληθεὶς
ὑπὸ τῶν περὶ τὸν Δαμοτέλη καὶ νομίσας ἴδιον εἶναι
τὸ πρᾶγμα καὶ καθήκειν αὐτῷ τὸ προστατῆσαι τῶν
Αἰτωλῶν, πᾶσαν εἰσεφέρετο σπουδὴν καὶ φιλοτιμίαν,
ἐξελέσθαι σπουδάζων τὸ ἔθνος ἐκ τῶν περιεστώτων
13 κακῶν. ἐνεργῶς δὲ πανταχόθεν προσαγομένης τῆς φι-
14 λοτιμίας, ἔλαβε τὸ πρᾶγμα συντέλειαν. οἱ μὲν γὰρ
Ἀμβρακιῶται πεισθέντες ὑπὸ τοῦ βασιλέως ἐπέτρεψαν
τὰ καθ᾽ αὑτοὺς τῷ στρατηγῷ τῶν Ῥωμαίων καὶ παρ-
έδωκαν τὴν πόλιν ἐφ᾽ ᾧ τοὺς Αἰτωλοὺ ὑποσπόνδους
15 ἀπελθεῖν· τοῦτο γὰρ ὑφείλοντο πρῶτον, τηροῦντες τὴν
πρὸς τοὺς συμμάχους πίστιν.

30. ὁ δὲ Μάρκος συγκατέθετο τοῖς Αἰτωλοῖς ἐπὶ
(xxii.13) τούτῳ ποιήσασθαι τὰς διαλύσεις, ὥστε διακόσια μὲν
2 Εὐβοϊκὰ τάλαντα παραχρῆμα λαβεῖν, τριακόσια δ᾽ ἐν
3 ἔτεσιν ἕξ, πεντήκοντα καθ᾽ ἕκαστον ἔτος· ἀποκατασταθῆναι δὲ ⟨καὶ τοὺς αἰχμαλώτους⟩ καὶ τοὺς αὐτομόλους Ῥωμαίοις ἅπαντας τοὺς παρ᾽ αὐτοῖς ὄντας ἐν
4 ἓξ μησὶ χωρὶς λύτρων· πόλιν δὲ μηδεμίαν ἔχειν ἐν τῇ
συμπολιτείᾳ μηδὲ μετὰ ταῦτα προσλαβέσθαι τούτων,

346

anger. Some one also suggested to Damoteles and Phaeneas to address themselves to Gaius Valerius[87] and cultivate relations with him. He was the son of Marcus Valerius Laevinus, who had been the first to make an alliance with the Aetolians, and was brother by the mother's side of Marcus Fulvius the present consul, besides which, as he was young and active, he especially enjoyed the consul's confidence. Upon Damoteles and his colleague soliciting his good offices, thinking that it was his own business and his duty[88] to act as protector of the Aetolians, he exerted himself in every way, laboring to rescue that nation from the dangers that beset them. So that, as the matter was pushed forward energetically from all quarters, it was brought to a conclusion. For the Ambraciots, yielding to the advice of the king, placed themselves at the mercy of the Roman consul, and surrendered their city on condition that the Aetolians were allowed to depart under flag of truce. For this was the first condition they wrested from him, keeping faith to their allies.

30. Fulvius next agreed with the Aetolians to make peace on the following conditions.[89] They were to pay two hundred Euboic talents at once and three hundred more in six years in yearly installments of fifty; they were to restore to the Romans in six months without ransom the prisoners and deserters who were in their hands; they were neither to retain in their League nor to receive into it in future any of the cities which after the crossing of

[87] Gaius Valerius Laevinus. *RE* Valerius 44–45 (H. Volkmann).   [88] Because of his father's close relations to the Aetolians.   [89] They were milder than those offered by Lucius Scipio (4.12–14).

ὅσαι μετὰ τὴν Λευκίου Κορνηλίου διάβασιν ἑάλωσαν
ὑπὸ Ῥωμαίων ἢ φιλίαν ἐποιήσαντο πρὸς Ῥωμαίους·
5 Κεφαλληνίους δὲ πάντας ἐκσπόνδους εἶναι τούτων
τῶν συνθηκῶν.

6   Ταῦτα μὲν οὖν ὑπετυπώθη τότε κεφαλαιωδῶς περὶ
τῶν διαλύσεων· ἔδει δὲ τούτοις πρῶτον μὲν εὐδοκῆσαι
τοὺς Αἰτωλούς, μετὰ δὲ ταῦτα γίνεσθαι τὴν ἀναφορὰν
7 ἐπὶ Ῥωμαίους. οἱ μὲν οὖν Ἀθηναῖοι καὶ Ῥόδιοι παρέ-
μενον αὐτοῦ, καραδοκοῦντες τὴν τῶν Αἰτωλῶν ἀπό-
φασιν· οἱ δὲ περὶ τὸν Δαμοτέλην ἐπανελθόντες διεσά-
8 φουν τοῖς Αἰτωλοῖς περὶ τῶν συγκεχωρημένων. τοῖς
μὲν οὖν ὅλοις εὐδόκουν· καὶ γὰρ ἦν αὐτοῖς ἅπαντα
παρὰ τὴν προσδοκίαν· περὶ δὲ τῶν πόλεων τῶν πρότερον συμπολιτευομένων αὐτοῖς διαπορήσαντες ἐπὶ
9 ποσὸν τέλος συγκατέθεντο τοῖς προτεινομένοις. ὁ δὲ
Μάρκος παραλαβὼν τὴν Ἀμβρακίαν τοὺς μὲν Αἰτωλοὺς ἀφῆκεν ὑποσπόνδους, τὰ δ᾿ ἀγάλματα καὶ τοὺς
ἀνδριάντας καὶ τὰς γραφὰς ἀπήγαγεν ἐκ τῆς πόλεως,
ὄντα καὶ πλείω διὰ τὸ γεγονέναι βασίλειον Πύρρου
10 τὴν Ἀμβρακίαν. ἐδόθη δ᾿ αὐτῷ καὶ στέφανος ἀπὸ τα-
11 λάντων ἑκατὸν καὶ πεντήκοντα. ταῦτα δὲ διοικησάμε-
νος ἐποιεῖτο τὴν πορείαν εἰς τὴν μεσόγειον τῆς Αἰτωλίας, θαυμάζων ἐπὶ τῷ μηδὲν αὐτῷ παρὰ τῶν Αἰτωλῶν
12 ἀπαντᾶσθαι. παραγενόμενος δὲ πρὸς Ἄργος τὸ καλούμενον Ἀμφιλοχικὸν κατεστρατοπέδευσεν, ὅπερ ἀπέχει

Lucius Cornelius Scipio had been taken by the Romans or had entered into friendly relations with them; the whole of Cephallenia[90] was to be excluded from this treaty.

Such were the general conditions of peace then roughly sketched. They had first of all to be accepted by the Aetolians and then submitted to Rome. The Athenians and Rhodians remained on the spot awaiting the decision of the Aetolians, while Damoteles and Phaeneas returned home and explained the conditions. On the whole the people were satisfied with them, for they were all such as they had not hoped to obtain. For a certain time they hesitated about the cities belonging to their League; but finally agreed to the proposal. Fulvius, having entered Ambracia, allowed the Aetolians to depart under flag of truce; but carried away[91] all the decorative objects, statues, and pictures, of which there were a considerable number, as the town had once been the royal seat of Pyrrhus. A crown[92] of a hundred and fifty talents was also presented to him. Having settled everything there, he marched into the interior of Aetolia, being surprised at receiving no answer from the Aetolians. On arriving at Amphilochian Argos,[93] which is a hundred and eighty

90 See n. on 5.3.3. The island was also excluded from the final treaty (32.12).

91 The looting of Ambracia was, like that of Syracuse in 212, one of the most notorious cases of Roman art theft and criticized even in the Senate: Livy 38.43.5 and 39.5.15 (a list of artifacts paraded in Fulvius' triumph).

92 Actually a gift of precious metal, coined or not.

93 For Argos in Amphilochia, see N. G. L. Hammond, *Epirus* (Oxford 1967), 246 and map 10 on p. 238 (location).

13 τῆς Ἀμβρακίας ἑκατὸν ὀγδοήκοντα σταδίους. ἐκεῖ δὲ
συμμιξάντων αὐτῷ τῶν περὶ τὸν Δαμοτέλην καὶ διασαφούντων ὅτι δέδοκται τοῖς Αἰτωλοῖς βεβαιοῦν τὰς
δι᾿ ἑαυτῶν γεγενημένας ὁμολογίας, διεχωρίσθησαν,
Αἰτωλοὶ μὲν εἰς τὴν οἰκείαν, Μάρκος δ᾿ εἰς τὴν Ἀμ-
14 βρακίαν. κἀκεῖσε παραγενόμενος οὗτος μὲν ἐγίνετο
15 περὶ τὸ περαιοῦν τὴν δύναμιν εἰς τὴν Κεφαλληνίαν, οἱ
δ᾿ Αἰτωλοὶ προχειρισάμενοι Φαινέαν καὶ Νίκανδρον
πρεσβευτὰς ἐξέπεμψαν εἰς τὴν Ῥώμην περὶ τῆς εἰρή-
16 νης· ἁπλῶς γὰρ οὐδὲν ἦν κύριον τῶν προειρημένων,
εἰ μὴ καὶ τῷ δήμῳ δόξαι τῷ τῶν Ῥωμαίων.

31. Οὗτοι μὲν οὖν παραλαβόντες τούς τε Ῥοδίους
(xxii.14) καὶ τοὺς Ἀθηναίους ἔπλεον ἐπὶ τὸ προκείμενον· παρα-
2 πλησίως δὲ καὶ Μάρκος ἐξαπέστειλε Γάιον τὸν Οὐ-
αλέριον καί τινας ἑτέρους τῶν φίλων πράξοντας τὰ
3 περὶ τῆς εἰρήνης. ἀφικομένων δ᾿ εἰς τὴν Ῥώμην, πάλιν
ἐκαινοποιήθη τὰ τῆς ὀργῆς πρὸς Αἰτωλοὺς διὰ Φιλίπ-
4 που τοῦ βασιλέως· ἐκεῖνος γὰρ δοκῶν ἀδίκως ὑπὸ τῶν
Αἰτωλῶν ἀφῃρῆσθαι τὴν Ἀθαμανίαν καὶ τὴν Δολοπίαν διεπέμψατο πρὸς τοὺς φίλους, ἀξιῶν αὐτοὺς
συνοργισθῆναι καὶ μὴ προσδέξασθαι τὰς διαλύσεις.
5 διὸ καὶ τῶν μὲν Αἰτωλῶν εἰσπορευθέντων παρήκουεν
ἡ σύγκλητος, τῶν δὲ Ῥοδίων καὶ τῶν Ἀθηναίων ἀξι-
6 ούντων ἐνετράπη καὶ προσέσχε τὸν νοῦν. καὶ γὰρ
ἐδόκει ⟨μετὰ⟩ Δάμων᾿ ὁ Κιχησίου ⟨Λέ⟩ων ἄλλα τε
καλῶς εἰπεῖν καὶ παραδείγματι πρὸς τὸ παρὸν οἰκείῳ

---

94 Lost to Philip during Nicander's campaign (25.1–7).

stades distance from Ambracia, he encamped there. Here he was met by Damoteles, who informed him that the Aetolians had passed a decree ratifying the conditions he had agreed to; they then separated, the Aetolians returning home and Fulvius proceeding to Ambracia. He there occupied himself with preparations for taking his army across to Cephallenia; and the Aetolians appointed and dispatched Phaeneas and Nicander as envoys to Rome about the peace; for nothing at all in it was valid without the consent of the Roman People.

31. These envoys, then, taking with them those of Athens and Rhodes, sailed on their mission; and Fulvius also sent Gaius Valerius Laevinus and some others of his friends to further the peace. But when they reached Rome the anger of the People against Aetolia had been revived by King Philip, who, thinking that the Aetolians had unjustly deprived him of Athamania and Dolopia,[94] sent messages to his friends at Rome begging them to participate in his indignation and refuse to accept the peace. In consequence when the Aetolians were admitted, the senate paid little heed to them; but when the Rhodians and Athenians spoke on their behalf, they grew more respectful and listened to them with attention. And indeed Leon,[95] son of Kichesias, who followed Damon, was judged to have spoken well on the whole and to have employed in his

[95] There was perhaps only one speaker named, and he was Leon, son of Kichesias, of Aixone, who belonged to one of the five leading Athenian families at the time—C. Habicht (16.25.8), 194–197. The father's name, Kichesias, known from inscriptions, is badly corrupted in P., but only slightly in Livy 38.10.4: Leon Hicesiae; *leo cichensii.*

7 χρήσασθαι κατὰ τὸν λόγον. ἔφη γὰρ ὀργίζεσθαι μὲν
εἰκότως τοῖς Αἰτωλοῖς· πολλὰ γὰρ εὖ πεπονθότας
τοὺς Αἰτωλοὺς ὑπὸ Ῥωμαίων οὐ χάριν ἀποδεδωκέναι
τούτων, ἀλλ᾽ εἰς μέγαν ἐνηνοχέναι κίνδυνον τὴν Ῥωμαίων ἡγεμονίαν ἐκκαύσαντας τὸν πρὸς Ἀντίοχον
8 πόλεμον. ἐν τούτῳ δὲ διαμαρτάνειν τὴν σύγκλητον, ἐν
9 ᾧ τὴν ὀργὴν φέρειν ἐπὶ τοὺς πολλούς. εἶναι γὰρ τὸ
συμβαῖνον ἐν ταῖς πολιτείαις περὶ τὰ πλήθη παρα-
10 πλήσιον τῷ γινομένῳ περὶ τὴν θάλατταν. καὶ γὰρ
ἐκείνην κατὰ μὲν τὴν αὑτῆς φύσιν ἀεί ποτ᾽ εἶναι
γαληνὴν καὶ καθεστηκυῖαν καὶ συλλήβδην τοιαύτην
ὥστε μηδέποτ᾽ ἂν ἐνοχλῆσαι μηδένα τῶν προσπελα-
11 ζόντων αὐτῇ καὶ χρωμένων· ἐπειδὰν δ᾽ ἐμπεσόντες εἰς
αὐτὴν ἄνεμοι βίαιοι ταράξωσι καὶ παρὰ φύσιν ἀναγ-
κάσωσι κινεῖσθαι, τότε μηθὲν ἔτι δεινότερον εἶναι
μηδὲ φοβερώτερον θαλάττης· ὃ καὶ νῦν τοῖς κατὰ τὴν
12 Αἰτωλίαν συμπεσεῖν. "ἕως μὲν γὰρ ἦσαν ἀκέραιοι,
πάντων τῶν Ἑλλήνων ὑπῆρχον ὑμῖν εὐνούστατοι καὶ
13 βεβαιότατοι συνεργοὶ πρὸς τὰς πράξεις· ἐπεὶ δ᾽ ἀπὸ
μὲν τῆς Ἀσίας πνεύσαντες Θόας καὶ Δικαίαρχος, ἀπὸ
δὲ τῆς Εὐρώπης Μενεστᾶς καὶ Δαμόκριτος συνετάρα-
ξαν τοὺς ὄχλους καὶ παρὰ φύσιν ἠνάγκασαν πᾶν καὶ
14 λέγειν καὶ πράττειν, τότε δὴ κακῶς φρονοῦντες ἐβου-
λήθησαν μὲν ὑμῖν, ἐγένοντο δ᾽ αὑτοῖς αἴτιοι κακῶν.
15 ⟨ἀνθ᾽ ὧν ὑμᾶς⟩ δεῖ πρὸς ἐκείνους ἔχειν ἀπαραιτήτως,
ἐλεεῖν δὲ τοὺς πολλοὺς καὶ διαλύεσθαι πρὸς αὐτούς,
εἰδότας ὅτι γενόμενοι πάλιν ἀκέραιοι, καὶ πρὸς τοῖς
ἄλλοις ἔτι νῦν ὑφ᾽ ὑμῶν σωθέντες, εὐνούστατοι πάλιν

speech a similitude apt to the present case. He said that they were justified in being angry with the Aetolians; for that people after receiving many benefits from the Romans had not shown any gratitude for them but had much endangered the Roman supremacy by stirring up the war against Antiochus. In one respect, however, the senate was wrong and that was in being wroth with the populace. For what happened in states to the people was very much the same as what befalls the sea. The sea by its proper nature was always calm and at rest, and in general of such a character that it would never give trouble to any of those who approach it and make use of it; but when violent winds fall upon it and stir it up, compelling it to move contrary to its own nature, nothing was more terrible and appalling than the sea. "And this," he said, "is just what has happened to the Aetolians. As long as no one tampered with them, they were of all the Greeks your most warm and trustworthy supporters. But when Thoas[96] and Dicaearchus,[97] blowing from Asia, and Menestas[98] and Damocritus from Europe stirred up the people and compelled them, contrary to their nature, to become reckless in word and deed, then of a truth in their folly the Aetolians desired to do you evil but brought evil on their own heads. Therefore, while being implacable to the men who instigated them, you should take pity on the people, and make peace with them, well knowing, that when again they have none to tamper with them and now, in addition, owe their preservation to you, they will again be the best disposed to you of all the

---

[96] 17.7; Dicaearchus 20.10.5.   [97] Paschidis 334–338.

[98] 20.10.5 (Menestratus); (Damocritus) 18.10.9; he was the brother of Thoas.

16 ἔσονται πάντων Ἑλλήνων." ὁ μὲν οὖν Ἀθηναῖος ταῦτ'
εἰπὼν ἔπεισε τὴν σύγκλητον διαλύεσθαι πρὸς τοὺς
Αἰτωλούς.

32. Δόξαντος δὲ τῷ συνεδρίῳ, καὶ τοῦ δήμου συν-
(xxii.15) επιψηφίσαντος, ἐκυρώθη τὰ κατὰ τὰς διαλύσεις. τὰ δὲ
2 κατὰ μέρος ἦν τῶν συνθηκῶν ταῦτα. "ὁ δῆμος ὁ τῶν
Αἰτωλῶν τὴν ἀρχὴν καὶ τὴν δυναστείαν τοῦ δήμου
3 τῶν Ῥωμαίων.... ‹πολεμίους› μὴ διέτω διὰ τῆς χώρας καὶ τῶν πόλεων ἐπὶ Ῥωμαίους ἢ τοὺς συμμάχους
καὶ φίλους αὐτῶν, μηδὲ χορηγείτω μηδὲν δημοσίᾳ
4 βουλῇ.... καὶ ἐὰν πολεμῶσιν πρός τινας Ῥωμαῖοι,
πολεμείτω πρὸς αὐτοὺς ὁ δῆμος ὁ τῶν Αἰτωλῶν. τοὺς
5 δὲ ‹αὐτομόλους, τοὺς› δραπέτας, τοὺς αἰχμαλώτους
πάντας τοὺς Ῥωμαίων καὶ τῶν συμμάχων ἀποδότωσαν
6 Αἰτωλοί, χωρὶς τῶν ὅσοι κατὰ πόλεμον ἁλόντες εἰς
τὴν ἰδίαν ἀπῆλθον καὶ πάλιν ἑάλωσαν, καὶ χωρὶς τῶν
ὅσοι πολέμιοι Ῥωμαίων ἐγένοντο, καθ᾽ ὃν καιρὸν Αἰτωλοὶ μετὰ Ῥωμαίων συνεπολέμουν, ‹ἐν› ἡμέραις
ἑκατὸν ἀφ᾽ ἧς ἂν τὰ ὅρκια τελεσθῇ, τῷ ἄρχοντι τῷ ἐν
7 Κερκύρᾳ· ἐὰν δὲ μὴ εὑρεθῶσίν τινες ἐν τῷ χρόνῳ
τούτῳ, ὅταν ἐμφανεῖς γένωνται, τότε ἀποδότωσαν
χωρὶς δόλου· καὶ τούτοις μετὰ ‹τὰ› ὅρκια μὴ ἔστω
8 ἐπάνοδος εἰς τὴν Αἰτωλίαν. δότωσαν δὲ Αἰτωλοὶ ἀργυρίου μὴ χείρονος Ἀττικοῦ παραχρῆμα μὲν τάλαντα

---

99 The peace treaty, 32.1–14, for which see WC 3.131–136 and
Livy's adaptation of P's text (38.11.1–9). It is more or less standard, with the most notable exception of the opening clause.

100 This is the so-called "maiestas-clause," occurring here for

Greeks." By this speech the Athenian envoy persuaded the Senate to make peace with the Aetolians.

32. When the Senate had passed a consultum, and the people also had voted it, the peace was ratified. The particular conditions were as follows:[99] "The people of Aetolia shall preserve without fraud the empire and majesty of the Roman people:[100] they shall not permit any armed forces proceeding against the Romans, or their allies and friends, to pass through their territory or support such forces in any way by public consent: they shall have the same enemies as the Roman people, and on whomsoever the Romans make war the people of Aetolia shall make war likewise: the Aetolians shall surrender all deserters, fugitives, and prisoners belonging to the Romans and their allies, always excepting such as after being made prisoners of war returned to their own country and were afterward recaptured, and such as were enemies of the Romans during the time when the Aetolians were fighting in alliance with Rome; all the above to be surrendered, within a hundred days of the peace being sworn, to the chief magistrate of Corcyra;[101] but if some are not to be found up to that date, whenever they are discovered they shall be surrendered without fraud, and such shall not be permitted to return to Aetolia after peace has been sworn: the Aetolians shall pay in silver specie, not inferior to Attic money,

the first time. See E. Täubler, *Imperium Romanum* (Berlin 1913), 62, and most recently St. Mitchell, *The Treaty between Rome and Lycia of 46 BC (Papyrologica Florentina* 35 [Florence 2005]), 187–189, and P. Sánchez, *Chiron* 37 (2007), 363–381. It is not found in most of the other treaties Rome concluded; it meant for the Aetolians the loss of any independent foreign policy.

[101] See n. on 2.11.5.

Εὐβοϊκὰ διακόσια τῷ στρατηγῷ τῷ ἐν τῇ Ἑλλάδι,
ἀντὶ τρίτου μέρους τοῦ ἀργυρίου χρυσίον, ἐὰν βούλωνται, διδόντες, τῶν δέκα μνῶν ἀργυρίου χρυσίου μνᾶν

9 διδόντες, ἀφ' ἧς <δ'> ἂν ἡμέρας τὰ ὅρκια τμηθῇ ἐν
ἔτεσι τοῖς πρώτοις ἓξ κατὰ ἔτος ἕκαστον τάλαντα
πεντήκοντα· καὶ τὰ χρήματα καθιστάτωσαν ἐν Ῥώμῃ.

10 δότωσαν Αἰτωλοὶ ὁμήρους τῷ στρατηγῷ τετταράκοντα, μὴ νεωτέρους ἐτῶν δώδεκα μηδὲ πρεσβυτέρους
τετταράκοντα, εἰς ἔτη ἕξ, οὓς ἂν Ῥωμαῖοι προκρίνω-
σιν, χωρὶς στρατηγοῦ καὶ ἱππάρχου καὶ δημοσίου
γραμματέως καὶ τῶν ὡμηρευκότων ἐν Ῥώμῃ. καὶ τὰ

11 ὅμηρα καθιστάτωσαν εἰς Ῥώμην· ἐὰν δέ τις ἀποθάνῃ
12 τῶν ὁμήρων, ἄλλον ἀντικαθιστάτωσαν. περὶ δὲ Κε-
13 φαλληνίας μὴ ἔστω ἐν ταῖς συνθήκαις. ὅσαι χῶραι
καὶ πόλεις καὶ ἄνδρες, οἷς οὗτοι ἐχρῶντο, ἐπὶ Λευκίου
Κοϊντίου καὶ Γναΐου Δομετίου στρατηγῶν ἢ ὕστερον
ἑάλωσαν ἢ εἰς φιλίαν ἦλθον Ῥωμαίοις, τούτων τῶν
πόλεων καὶ τῶν ἐν ταύταις μηδένα προσλαβέτωσαν

14 Αἰτωλοί. ἡ δὲ πόλις καὶ ἡ χώρα ἡ τῶν Οἰνιαδῶν
15 Ἀκαρνάνων ἔστω." τμηθέντων δὲ τῶν ὁρκίων ἐπὶ τούτοις συνετετέλεστο τὰ τῆς εἰρήνης. καὶ τὰ μὲν κατὰ
τοὺς Αἰτωλοὺς καὶ καθόλου τοὺς Ἕλληνας τοιαύτην
ἔσχε τὴν ἐπιγραφήν.

32b. Ὁ δὲ Φολούιος πραξικοπήσας νυκτὸς κατέ-
(40) λαβε τὸ μέρος τῆς ἀκροπόλεως καὶ τοὺς Ῥωμαίους
(xxii.23) εἰσήγαγε.

---

102 See n. on 30.5.
103 Of 192.

two hundred Euboic talents at once to the consul then in Greece, paying a third part of the sum if they wish, in gold at the rate of one gold mina for ten silver minae; and for the first six years after the final conclusion of the treaty fifty talents per annum, this sum to be delivered in Rome: the Aetolians shall give the consul forty hostages each of more than twelve and less than forty years of age at the choice of the Romans and to serve as such for six years, none of them being either a strategus, a hipparch, or a public secretary or one who has previously served as hostage in Rome; these hostages also to be delivered in Rome, and any one of them who dies to be replaced: Cephallenia[102] is not to be included in the treaty: of the cities, villages, and men formerly belonging to Aetolia but captured by or entering into friendship with the Romans during or subsequent to the consulship[103] of Lucius Quintius Flamininus and Gnaeus Domitius Ahenobarbus none are to be annexed by the Aetolians: and the city and territory of Oeniadae[104] shall belong to Acarnania." After the oaths had been taken, peace was established on these conditions and such was the seal finally set on the affairs of Aetolia and Greece in general.

192 B.C.

Capture of Same in Cephallenia by Fulvius

(Suda; Livy 38.29.10)

32b. Fulvius by a secret understanding occupied part of the acropolis by night and introduced the Romans.[105]

189 B.C.

[104] See n. on 4.65.2.

[105] Livy 38.29.10 shows that this concerns the capture of Same at Cephallenia by the consul Fulvius in 189 or early 188. See *IG* IX 1², fasc. 4, p. 233.

32c. Ὅτι τὸ καλὸν καὶ τὸ συμφέρον σπανίως εἴωθε
(41) συντρέχειν, καὶ σπάνιοι τῶν ἀνδρῶν εἰσιν οἱ δυνάμε-
(xxi.16) νοι ταῦτα συνάγειν καὶ συναρμόζειν πρὸς ἄλληλα.
2 κατὰ μὲν γὰρ τὸ πολὺ πάντες ἴσμεν διότι τό τε καλὸν
φεύγει τὴν τοῦ παραυτίκα λυσιτελοῦς φύσιν καὶ τὸ
3 λυσιτελὲς τὴν τοῦ καλοῦ. πλὴν ὁ Φιλοποίμην προέθετο ταῦτα καὶ καθίκετο τῆς ἐπιβολῆς· καλὸν μὲν γὰρ
τὸ κατάγειν τοὺς αἰχμαλώτους φυγάδας εἰς τὴν Σπάρτην, συμφέρον δὲ τὸ ταπεινῶσαι τὴν τῶν Λακεδαιμονίων πόλιν, ⟨ἐξελάσαντ⟩α[2] τοὺς δεδορυφορηκότας τῇ
4 τῶν τυ⟨ράν⟩ν⟨ω⟩ν ⟨δυναστείᾳ⟩. θεωρῶν δ' ὅτι πάσης
βασιλείας ἐπανορθ⟨ώσεως αἴτια⟩ τὰ χρήματα ⟨γέγο-
νεν, ἅ⟩τε φύσει νουνεχὴν ὢν καὶ στρατηγικός, περι-
εβα .... |γένοιτο κομιδὴ τῶν ἔξω ⟨πορι⟩ζο-
μένων χρημάτων.

VI. RES ASIAE

33. Ὅτι καθ' ὃν καιρὸν ἐν τῇ Ῥώμῃ τὰ περὶ τὰς
(xxii.16) συνθήκας τὰς πρὸς Ἀντίοχον καὶ καθόλου περὶ τῆς
Ἀσίας αἱ πρεσβεῖαι διεπράττοντο, κατὰ δὲ τὴν Ἑλλάδα τὸ τῶν Αἰτωλῶν ἔθνος ἐπολεμεῖτο, κατὰ τοῦτον

2 Pédech

Wisdom of Philopoemen

(Livy 38.30)

32c. What is good very seldom coincides with what is advantageous, and few are those who can combine the two and adapt them to each other. Indeed we all know that for the most part the nature of immediate profit is repugnant to goodness and vice versa. But Philopoemen[106] made this his purpose and attained his object. For it was a good act to restore to their country the Spartan exiles who were prisoners, and it was an advantageous one to humble the city of Sparta by expelling the satellites of the tyrants. And being by nature a man of sound sense and a real leader, he saw that money is at the root of the reestablishment of all kingly power, and did his best to prevent the receipt of the sums advanced.[107]

VI. AFFAIRS OF ASIA

Manlius and the Gallic War

(Cf. Livy 38.12.1)

33. At the same time that the embassies were negotiating at Rome concerning the peace with Antiochus and the fate of Asia Minor in general, and while the war against the Aetolian League still continued in Greece, the war

---

[106] This is an excerpt concerning events at Sparta, as described by Livy (who is following P.'s account) 38.30.1–34.9. Errington (20.3.5), 137–147.

[107] Poorly preserved as the text is, it seems clear that Philopoemen's actions are seen through the eyes of an admirer.

THE HISTORIES OF POLYBIUS

συνέβη τὸν περὶ τὴν Ἀσίαν πρὸς τοὺς Γαλάτας πόλεμον ἐπιτελεσθῆναι, περὶ οὗ νῦν ἐνιστάμεθα τὴν διήγησιν.

2   Ὁ δὲ κατευδοκήσας τῷ νεανίσκῳ κατὰ τὴν ἀπάντησιν, τοῦτον ἀπέλυσε παραχρῆμ' εἰς τὸ Πέργαμον.

34. Ὅτι Μοαγέτης ἦν τύραννος Κιβύρας, ὠμὸς
(xxii.17) γεγονὼς καὶ δόλιος,καὶ οὐκ ἄξιός ἐστιν ἐκ παραδρομῆς,
2   ἀλλὰ μετ' ἐπιστάσεως τυχεῖν τῆς ἁρμοζούσης μνήμης.

3   Πλὴν συνεγγίζοντος Γναΐου ὑπάτου Ῥωμαίων τῇ
Κιβύρᾳ, καὶ τοῦ Ἑλουΐου πεμφθέντος εἰς ἀπόπειραν
ἐπὶ τίνος ἐστὶ γνώμης, πρεσβευτὰς ἐξέπεμψε, παρακαλῶν μὴ φθεῖραι τὴν χώραν, ὅτι φίλος ὑπάρχει
4   Ῥωμαίων καὶ πᾶν ποιήσει τὸ παραγγελλόμενον. καὶ
ταῦτα λέγων ἅμα προύτεινε στέφανον ἀπὸ πεντεκαί-
5   δεκα ταλάντων. ὧν ἀκούσας αὐτὸς μὲν ἀφέξεσθαι τῆς
χώρας ἔφη, πρὸς δὲ τὸν στρατηγὸν ἐκέλευσε πρεσβεύειν ὑπὲρ τῶν ὅλων· ἔπεσθαι γὰρ αὐτὸν μετὰ τῆς

---

108 The campaign of the consul Gnaeus Manlius Vulso (*MRR*
1.360) in 189. See J. Grainger, *Anat. St.* 45 (1996), 23–42, map in
WC 3.141. P.'s report, based on the account of an eyewitness, is
followed and supplemented by Livy 38.12–27. For the settle-
ments of the three Galatian tribes in Asia Minor, see K. Strobel,
Die Galater 1 (Berlin 1996), 252–257.

109 The second son of Attalus I, the later King Attalus II (158–
138). Eumenes was at the time in Rome.

110 It is not clear which of the various tyrants of Cibyra called
Moagetes is meant here. The Moagetes who figures in the decree
of Araxa (*JHS* 68 [1948], 46–56, no. 11) as dynast of Bubon, but

against the Gauls in Asia, which I am now about to describe, was begun and ended.[108]

(Suda; cf. Livy 38.12.7)

Manlius was favorably impressed by the young man, Attalus,[109] at this interview and at once sent him off to Pergamum.

(Cf. Livy 38.14.3)

34. Moagetes[110] was tyrant of Cibyra.[111] He was a cruel and treacherous man and worthy of more than a passing notice.

(Cf. Livy 38.14.4)

When Gnaeus Manlius Vulso, the Roman consul, approached Cibyra and sent Helvius[112] to find out what the mind of Moagetes was, the latter sent envoys begging Helvius not to lay the country waste as he was the friend of the Romans and ready to do anything they told him. He at the same time offered a gold crown[113] of fifteen talents. Helvius, after listening to those envoys, promised to spare the country himself, but referred them to the consul for a general settlement. Manlius, he said, was close behind

who is also connected to Cibyra, could be this man. The date of this decree, as established by R. M. Errington, *Chiron* 17 (1987), 114–118, is some time after 167; the events recorded may go back to the first two decades of the century. More on these questions in D. Rousset, *De Lycie en Cabalide* (Geneva 2010).

111 In southern Phrygia, the main city of a tetrapolis (not yet existing in 189), comprising also Bubon, Balbura, and Oenoanda.

112 Gaius Helvius, one of Vulso's lieutenants.

113 See n. on 30.10.

6   στρατείας κατὰ πόδας. γενομένου δὲ τούτου, καὶ πέμψαντος τοῦ Μοαγέτου μετὰ τῶν πρεσβευτῶν καὶ τὸν
ἀδελφόν, ἀπαντήσας κατὰ πορείαν ὁ Γνάιος ἀνατα-

7   τικῶς καὶ πικρῶς ὡμίλησε τοῖς πρεσβευταῖς, φάσκων
οὐ μόνον ἀλλοτριώτατον γεγονέναι Ῥωμαίων τὸν Μο-
αγέτην πάντων τῶν κατὰ τὴν Ἀσίαν δυναστῶν, ἀλλὰ
καὶ κατὰ τὴν ῥώμην ὅλην .. εἰς καθαίρεσιν τῆς ἀρχῆς

8   καὶ ἐπιστροφῆς εἶναι καὶ κολάσεως. οἱ δὲ πρεσβευταὶ
καταπλαγέντες τὴν ἐπίφασιν τῆς ὀργῆς τῶν μὲν ἄλλων ἐντολῶν ἀπέστησαν, ἠξίουν δ' αὐτὸν εἰς λόγους

9   ἐλθεῖν. συγχωρήσαντος δὲ τότε μὲν ἐπανῆλθον εἰς

10 τὴν Κιβύραν, εἰς δὲ τὴν ἐπαύριον ἐξῆλθεν μετὰ τῶν
φίλων ὁ τύραννος κατά τε τὴν ἐσθῆτα καὶ τὴν ἄλλην
προστασίαν λιτὸς καὶ ταπεινός, ἔν τε τοῖς ἀπολογισμοῖς
κατολοφυρόμενος τὴν ἀδυναμίαν τὴν αὑτοῦ καὶ τὴν
ἀσθένειαν ὧν ἐπῆρχε πόλεων, καὶ ἠξίου προσδέξα-

11 σθαι τὰ πεντεκαίδεκα τάλαντα τὸν Γνάιον· ἐκράτει δὲ

12 τῆς Κιβύρας καὶ Συλείου καὶ τῆς ἐν Λίμνῃ πόλεως. ὁ
δὲ Γνάιος καταπλαγεὶς τὴν ἀπόνοιαν ἄλλο μὲν οὐδὲν
εἶπε πρὸς αὐτόν, ἐὰν δὲ μὴ διδῷ πεντακόσια τάλαντα
μετὰ μεγάλης χάριτος, οὐ τὴν χώραν ἔφη φθερεῖν,
ἀλλὰ τὴν πόλιν αὐτὴν πολιορκήσειν καὶ διαρπάσειν.

13 ὅθεν ὁ Μοαγέτης κατορρωδήσας τὸ μέλλον ἐδεῖτο
μηδὲν ποιῆσαι τοιοῦτον, καὶ προσετίθει κατὰ βραχὺ
τῶν χρημάτων, καὶ τέλος ἔπεισε τὸν Γνάιον ἑκατὸν
τάλαντα καὶ μυρίους μεδίμνους λαβόντα πυρῶν προσδέξασθαι πρὸς τὴν φιλίαν αὐτόν.

him with his army. Upon this being done, Moagetes having sent his brother in addition to the other envoys, Manlius met them on his march and spoke to them in a threatening and severe manner, saying that not only had Moagetes proved more hostile to the Romans than any other Asiatic prince, but had done all in his power to subvert their rule, and therefore deserved animadversion and chastisement rather than friendship. The envoys, alarmed by the vehemence of his anger, neglected their other instructions and begged him to grant an interview to Moagetes himself. On his agreeing to this request they returned to Cibyra; and next day the tyrant and his friends came out to meet him dressed and escorted in the simplest and most unassuming manner, and in a submissive speech, bewailing his own powerlessness and the weakness of the towns subject to him, begged Manlius to accept the fifteen talents—the places he ruled over being, besides Cibyra, Syleium and that called the town in the Lake. Manlius, amazed at his impudence, said not another word, but merely that if he did not pay five hundred talents and thank his stars, he would not only lay waste his territory, but besiege and sack the city itself. So that Moagetes, in dread of the fate that threatened him, implored him to do nothing of the kind; and, raising his offer little by little, persuaded Manlius to accept a hundred talents and ten thousand medimni of wheat and to receive him into his alliance.

35. Ὅτι κατὰ τὸν καιρὸς ἡνίκα Γνάιος διῄει τὸν
(xxii.18) Κολοβάτον προσαγορευόμενον ποταμόν, ἦλθον πρὸς
αὐτὸν πρέσβεις ἐκ τῆς Ἰσίνδης προσαγορευομένης
2 πόλεως, δεόμενοι σφίσι βοηθῆσαι. τοὺς γὰρ Τερμησ-
σεῖς, ἐπισπασαμένους Φιλόμηλον, τήν τε χώραν ἔφασαν αὐτῶν ἀνάστατον πεποιηκέναι καὶ τὴν πόλιν
διηρπακέναι, νῦν τε πολιορκεῖν τὴν ἄκραν, συμπεφευ-
γότων εἰς αὐτὴν πάντων τῶν πολιτῶν ὁμοῦ γυναιξὶ
3 καὶ τέκνοις. ὧν διακούσας ὁ Γνάιος ἐκείνοις μὲν
ὑπέσχετο βοηθήσειν μετὰ μεγάλης χάριτος, αὐτὸς δὲ
νομίσας ἑρμαῖον εἶναι τὸ προσπεπτωκὸς ἐποιεῖτο τὴν
πορείαν ὡς ἐπὶ τῆς Παμφυλίας.
4 Ὁ δὲ Γνάιος συνεγγίσας τῇ Τερμησσῷ, πρὸς μὲν
τούτους συνέθετο φιλίαν, λαβὼν πεντήκοντα τάλαντα,
5 παραπλησίως δὲ καὶ πρὸς Ἀσπενδίους. ἀποδεξάμενος
δὲ καὶ τοὺς παρὰ τῶν ἄλλων πόλεων πρεσβευτὰς
κατὰ τὴν Παμφυλίαν καὶ τὴν προειρημένην δόξαν
ἐνεργασάμενος ἑκάστοις κατὰ τὰς ἐντεύξεις, ἅμα δὲ
καὶ τοὺς Ἰσινδεῖς ἐξελόμενος ἐκ τῆς πολιορκίας, αὖθις
ἐποιεῖτο τὴν πορείαν ὡς ἐπὶ τοὺς Γαλάτας.
36. Ὅτι Κύρμασα πόλιν λαβὼν ὁ Γνάιος καὶ λείαν
(xxii.19) ἄφθονον ἀνέζευξεν. προαγόντων δ' αὐτῶν παρὰ τὴν
2

---

114 Various suggestions have been made to identify the river;
see WC 3.144–145.   115 City in the Milyas. RE Isinda no. 3,
2083 (W. Ruge).   116 The citizens of Termessus *maior*, in
Pisidia. RE Termessos 732–775 (R. Heberdey). TAM III, fasc. 1.
    117 Dynast in Phrygia, perhaps founder of Philomelium, mod-
ern Aksehir. Cohen (16.24.6), 319–321. He recently became

(Cf. Livy 38.15.3)

35. While Manlius was crossing the river Colobatus,[114] envoys reached him from the city of Isinda[115] begging him to help them; for the Termessians,[116] summoning Philomelus[117] to their assistance, had devastated their territory and pillaged their city and were now besieging the citadel in which all the citizens with their wives and children had sought refuge. Manlius, after listening to their request, said he would be very pleased to come to their help; and, looking upon this chance as a godsend, began to march toward Pamphylia.

On approaching Termessus he received that people into his alliance on receipt of fifty talents, and likewise the people of Aspendus.[118] After receiving the envoys of the other Pamphylian cities, and producing on all of them on the occasion of their audiences an impression similar to that I have described, he first raised the siege of Isinda and then again began to march against the Gauls.[119]

(Cf. Livy 38.15.7)

36. Manlius, after capturing the city of Cyrmasa[120] and a quantity of booty, continued his march. While they were

known as a governor (of Phrygia) for Antiochus III in 209: *SEG* 54.1353. For him and other members of the dynasty, see J. Kobes, *"Kleine Könige." Untersuchungen zu den Lokaldynasten im hellenistischen Kleinasien (323–188 v.Chr.)* (St. Katherinen 1996), 156–163, 220, 256.   [118] City in Pamphylia (see n. on 5.73.3). The other principal cities are Perge, Side, and later Attaleia (modern Antalya).   [119] For this expedition see map in WC 3.141.   [120] For its location at Egnes, see G. E. Bean, *Anatolian Studies* 9 (1959), 91–97, and map p. 69. A bilingual inscription gives the name as Kormasa and Cormasa.

λίμνην, παρεγένοντο πρέσβεις ἐκ Λυσινόης διδόντες
3 αὐτοὺς εἰς τὴν πίστιν. οὓς προσδεξάμενος ἐνέβαλεν
εἰς τὴν τῶν Σαγαλασσέων γῆν καὶ πολὺ πλῆθος ἐξ-
ελασάμενος λείας ἀπεκαραδόκει τοὺς ἐκ τῆς πόλεως
4 ἐπὶ τίνος ἔσονται γνώμης. παραγενομένων δὲ πρεσβευτῶν ὡς αὐτόν, ἀποδεξάμενος τοὺς ἄνδρας καὶ λαβὼν
πεντήκοντα ταλάντων στέφανον καὶ δισμυρίους κρι-
θῶν μεδίμνους καὶ δισμυρίους πυρῶν, προσεδίξατο
τούτους εἰς τὴν φιλίαν.

37. Ὅτι Γνάιος ὁ στρατηγὸς τῶν Ῥωμαίων πρέ-
(xxii.20) σβεις ἐξαπέστειλε πρὸς τὸν Ἐποσόγνατον τὸν Γαλά-
την, ὅπως πρεσβεύσῃ πρὸς τοὺς τῶν Γαλατῶν βασι-
2 λεῖς. καὶ [ὁ] Ἐποσόγνατος ἔπεμψε πρὸς Γνάιον
πρέσβεις καὶ παρεκάλει [τὸν Γνάιον] τὸν τῶν Ῥωμαίων
στρατηγὸν μὴ προεξαναστῆναι μηδ' ἐπιβαλεῖν χεῖρας
3 τοῖς Τολιστοβογίοις Γαλάταις καὶ διότι πρεσβεύσει
πρὸς τοὺς βασιλεῖς αὐτῶν Ἐποσόγνατος καὶ ποιήσεται λόγους ὑπὲρ τῆς φιλίας, καὶ πεπεῖσθαι πρὸς πᾶν
αὐτοὺς παραστήσεσθαι τὸ καλῶς ἔχον.

4 Γνάιος ὁ ὕπατος Ῥωμαίων διερχόμενος ἐγεφύρωσε
τὸν Σαγγάριον ποταμόν, τελέως κοῖλον ὄντα καὶ
5 δύσβατον. καὶ παρ' αὐτὸν τὸν ποταμὸν στρατοπεδεύ-

---

121 RE Lysinia 40–41 (W. Ruge).   122 City in Pisidia,
modern Aghlasun. RE Sagalassos 1732–1733 (W. Ruge). For a
decree of the city honoring Manesas of Termessus, see TAM III
1, no. 7. M. Waelkens (ed.), Sagalassos. Reports 1986–1997 (Acta
archaeologica Lovanensia 5–7.9.11 [Leuven 1993–2000]). An important new document from Sagalassos in SEG 50.304.

advancing along the shore of the lake there came envoys
from Lysinoë[121] to announce its submission; and after receiving them he entered the territory of Sagalassus[122] and,
having carried off a large amount of booty, waited to see
what the mind of those in the city would be. Upon their
envoys reaching him he received them, and after accepting a crown[123] of fifty talents, twenty thousand medimni
of barley, and twenty thousand of wheat, admitted that city
into his alliance.

(Cf. Livy 38.18.1–3)

37. Manlius, the Roman consul, sent legates to the
Gaul Eposognatus asking him on his part to send envoys to the Galatian princes.[124] Eposognatus thereupon
sent envoys to Manlius begging him not to take the initiative in attacking the Galatian Tolistobogii,[125] as he would
communicate with their princes suggesting an alliance
with Rome, and was convinced that they would accept any
reasonable terms.

(Suda; cf. Livy 38.18.7)

Manlius, the Roman consul, on his passage through
Asia, bridged the river Sangarius[126] which here runs between deep banks and is very difficult to cross. As he was

---

[123] See n. on 30.10.

[124] The twelve tetrarchs, four from each tribe.

[125] One of the three Galatian tribes (the others are the Tectosagi and the Trocmi). Eposognatus belonged to them. They
dwelled in the valley of the upper Sangarius (37.4), with Pessinus
and Gordium their main cities. RE Tolistobogioi 1673–1677 (F.
Stähelin).

[126] Modern Sakarya. RE Sangarius 2269–2270 (W. Ruge).

σαμένου παραγίνονται Γάλλοι παρ' Ἄττιδος καὶ Βατ-
τάκου τῶν ἐκ Πεσσινοῦντος ἱερέων τῆς Μητρὸς τῶν
6 θεῶν, ἔχοντες προστηθίδια καὶ τύπους, φάσκοντες
7 προσαγγέλλειν τὴν θεὸν νίκην καὶ κράτος. οὓς ὁ Γνάιος φιλανθρώπως ὑπεδέξατο.

8 Ὄντος δὲ τοῦ Γναΐου πρὸς τὸ πολισμάτιον τὸ
καλούμενον Γορδίειον, ἧκον παρ' Ἐποσογνάτου πρέσβεις ἀποδηλοῦντες ὅτι πορευθεὶς διαλεχθείη τοῖς
9 τῶν Γαλατῶν βασιλεῦσιν, οἱ δ' ἁπλῶς εἰς οὐδὲν συγ-
καταβαίνοιεν φιλάνθρωπον, ἀλλ' ἠθροικότες ὁμοῦ τέκνα καὶ γυναῖκας καὶ τὴν ἄλλην κτῆσιν ἅπασαν εἰς
τὸ καλούμενον ὄρος Ὄλυμπον ἕτοιμοι πρὸς μάχην
εἰσίν.

38. Χιομάραν δὲ συνέβη τὴν Ὀρτιάγοντος αἰχμά-
(xxii.21) λωτον γενέσθαι μετὰ τῶν ἄλλων γυναικῶν, ὅτε Ῥωμαῖοι καὶ Γνάιος ἐνίκησαν μάχῃ τοὺς ἐν Ἀσίᾳ Γαλά-
2 τας. ὁ δὲ λαβὼν αὐτὴν ταξίαρχος ἐχρήσατο τῇ τύχῃ
3 στρατιωτικῶς καὶ κατῄσχυνεν. ἦν δ' ἄρα καὶ πρὸς
ἡδονὴν καὶ ἀργύριον ἀμαθὴς καὶ ἀκρατὴς ἄνθρωπος,

---

127 See n. on 6.7.

128 Modern Balhisar. Originally Phrygian like Gordium, a city
of the Tolistobogii. At P. was the main sanctuary of Cybele (*Magna
Mater*), whose sacred stone was transferred in 204 to Rome (P. J.
Burton, *Historia* 45 [1996], 21–35). *RE* Pessinus 1104–1113 (W.
Ruge). L. Boffo, *I re ellenistici e i centri religiosi dell' Asia Minore*
(Florence 1985), passim. B. Virgilio, *A&R* 26 (1981), 167–173. A
series of letters from Eumenes and Attalus II to the priest Attis
in *RC* 55–61. *I. Pessinous*, ed. J. Strubbe (Cologne 2005).

encamped close to the river, two Galli,[127] with pectorals and images, came on behalf of Attis and Battacus, the priests of the Mother of the Gods at Pessinus,[128] announcing that the goddess foretold his victory. Manlius gave them a courteous reception.

(Cf. Livy 38.18.10)

While Manlius was near the small town of Gordium[129] envoys from Eposognatus reached him informing him that he had gone in person to speak with the Galatian princes, but that they simply refused to make any advances: they had collected on Mount Olympus[130] their women and children and all their possessions, and were prepared to give battle.

(From Plutarch, *The Virtuous Deeds of Women* 22;
cf. Livy 38.24.2)

38. Chiomara, the wife of Ortiagon,[131] was captured with the other women when the Asiatic Gauls were defeated by the Romans under Manlius. The centurion into whose hands she fell took advantage of his capture with a soldier's brutality and did violence to her. The man was indeed an ill-bred lout, the slave both of gain and of lust,

[129] The old capital of Phrygia, at the upper Sangarius. R. S. Young, *Gordion. A Guide to the Excavations and Museum* (Ankara 1975).

[130] Somewhere between Gordium and Ancyra, its site not identified.

[131] Chieftain of the Tolistobogii. *RE* Ortiagon 1505–1506 (Th. Lenschau). After Vulso's campaign, he fought at the side of Prusias I and Hannibal against Eumenes. See *CAH* 8 (2nd ed.), 1989, 325–328 (C. Habicht).

ἡττήθη δ' ὅμως ὑπὸ τῆς φιλαργυρίας, καὶ χρυσίου
συχνοῦ διομολογηθέντος ὑπὲρ τῆς γυναικὸς ἦγεν
αὐτὴν ἀπολυτρώσων, ποταμοῦ τινος ἐν μέσῳ διείργον-
4 τος. ὡς δὲ διαβάντες οἱ Γαλάται τὸ χρυσίον ἔδωκαν
αὐτῷ καὶ παρελάμβανον τὴν Χιομάραν ἡ μὲν ἀπὸ
νεύματος προσέταξεν ἑνὶ παῖσαι τὸν Ῥωμαῖον ἀσπα-
5 ζόμενον αὐτὴν καὶ φιλοφρονούμενον, ἐκείνου δὲ πεισθέντος καὶ τὴν κεφαλὴν ἀποκόψαντος, ἀραμένη καὶ
6 περιστείλασα τοῖς κόλποις ἀπήλαυνεν. ὡς δ' ἦλθε
πρὸς τὸν ἄνδρα καὶ τὴν καφαλὴν αὐτῷ προύβαλεν,
ἐκείνου θαυμάσαντος καὶ εἰπόντος "ὦ γύναι, καλὸν ἡ
πίστις." "ναί," εἶπεν "ἀλλὰ κάλλιον ἕνα μόνον ζῆν
7 ἐμοὶ συγγεγενημένον." ταύτῃ μὲν ὁ Πολύβιός φησι
διὰ λόγων ἐν Σάρδεσι γενόμενος θαυμάσαι τό τε
φρόνημα καὶ τὴν σύνεσιν.

39. Ὅτι τῶν Ῥωμαίων μετὰ τὴν τῶν Γαλατῶν νίκην
(xxii.22) αὐτῶν πραχθεῖσαν στρατοπεδευόντων περὶ τὴν Ἄγ-
κυραν πόλιν, καὶ τοῦ Γναίου τοῦ στρατηγοῦ προάγειν
2 εἰς τοὔμπροσθεν μέλλοντος, παραγίνονται πρέσβεις
παρὰ τῶν Τεκτοσάγων, ἀξιοῦντες τὸν Γναῖον τὰς μὲν
δυνάμεις ἐᾶσαι κατὰ χώραν, αὐτὸν δὲ κατὰ τὴν ἐπιοῦσαν ἡμέραν προελθεῖν εἰς τὸν μεταξὺ τόπον τῶν
στρατοπέδων· ἥξειν δὲ καὶ τοὺς παρ' αὐτῶν βασιλεῖς
3 κοινολογησομένους ὑπὲρ τῶν διαλύσεων. τοῦ δὲ Γναίου συγκαταθεμένου καὶ παραγενηθέντος κατὰ τὸ

but his love of gain prevailed; and as a considerable sum had been promised him for the woman's ransom, he brought her to a certain place to deliver her up, a river running between him and the messengers. When the Gauls crossed and after handing him the money were taking possession of Chiomara, she signaled to one of them to strike the man as he was taking an affectionate leave of her. The man obeyed and cut off his head, which she took up and wrapped in the folds of her dress, and then drove off. When she came into the presence of her husband and threw the head at his feet, he was astonished and said, "Ah! my wife, it is good to keep faith." "Yes," she replied, "but it is better still that only one man who has lain with me should remain alive." Polybius tells us that he met and conversed with the lady at Sardis[132] and admired her high spirit and intelligence.

(Cf. Livy 38.25)

39. While the Romans after their victory over the Gauls were encamped near Ancyra[133] and Manlius the consul was about to advance, there came envoys from the Tectosages[134] begging him to leave his army where it was and to come out himself next day to the space between the camps, where their princes also would come and communicate with him about peace. Upon Manlius agreeing to this, and keeping the appointment accompanied by five

---

[132] It is not known when. For the whole story see Livy 38.24.2–11, a fuller version of P.'s report than Plutarch's given here as 38.1–7.   [133] The chief settlement of the Tectosagi, modern Ankara. C. Bosch, *Quellen zur Geschichte von Ankara im Altertum* (Ankara 1967). *OCD* Ancyra 87 (St. Mitchell).

[134] *RE* Tektosagen 171–173 (W. Ruge).

συνταχθὲν μετὰ πεντακοσίων ἱππέων, τότε μὲν οὐκ
4 ἦλθον οἱ βασιλεῖς· ἀνακεχωρηκότος δ' αὐτοῦ πρὸς
τὴν ἰδίαν παρεμβολήν, αὖθις ἧκον οἱ πρέσβεις ὑπὲρ
μὲν τῶν βασιλέων σκήψεις τινὰς λέγοντες, ἀξιοῦντες
δὲ πάλιν ἐλθεῖν αὐτόν, ἐπειδὴ τοὺς πρώτους ἄνδρας
5 ἐκπέμψουσιν κοινολογησομένους ὑπὲρ τῶν ὅλων. ὁ δὲ
Γνάιος κατανεύσας ἥξειν αὐτὸς μὲν ἔμεινεν ἐπὶ τῆς
ἰδίας στρατοπεδείας, Ἄτταλον δὲ καὶ τῶν χιλιάρχων
6 τινὰς ἐξαπέστειλεν μετὰ τριακοσίων ἱππέων. οἱ δὲ τῶν
Γαλατῶν ⟨πρέσβεις⟩ ἦλθον μὲν κατὰ τὸ συνταχθὲν
καὶ λόγους ἐποιήσαντο περὶ τῶν πραγμάτων, τέλος δ'
ἐπιθεῖναι τοῖς προειρημένοις ἢ κυρῶσαί τι τῶν δοξάν-
7 των οὐκ ἔφασαν εἶναι δυνατόν· τοὺς δὲ βασιλεῖς τῇ
κατὰ πόδας ἥξειν διωρίζοντο, συνθησομένους καὶ πέρας ἐπιθήσοντας, εἰ καὶ Γνάιος ὁ στρατηγὸς ἔλθοι
8 πρὸς αὐτούς. τῶν δὲ περὶ τὸν Ἄτταλον ἐπαγγειλαμένων
ἥξειν τὸν Γνάιον, τότε μὲν ἐπὶ τούτοις διελύθησαν.
9 ἐποιοῦντο δὲ ⟨τὰς⟩ ὑπερθέσεις ταύτας οἱ Γαλάται καὶ
διεστρατήγουν τοὺς Ῥωμαίους βουλόμενοι τῶν τε
σωμάτων τινὰ τῶν ἀναγκαίων καὶ τῶν χρημάτων
ὑπερθέσθαι πέραν Ἅλυος ποταμοῦ, μάλιστα δὲ τὸν
στρατηγὸν τῶν Ῥωμαίων, εἰ δυνηθεῖεν, λαβεῖν ὑπο-
10 χείριον· εἰ δὲ μή γε, πάντως ἀποκτεῖναι. ταῦτα δὲ προθέμενοι κατὰ τὴν ἐπιοῦσαν ἐκαραδόκουν τὴν παρουσίαν τῶν Ῥωμαίων, ἑτοίμους ἔχοντες ἱππεῖς εἰς
11 χιλίους. ὁ δὲ Γνάιος διακούσας τῶν περὶ τὸν Ἄτταλον
καὶ πεισθεὶς ἥξειν τοὺς βασιλεῖς, ἐξῆλθεν, καθάπερ
12 εἰώθει, μετὰ πεντακοσίων ἱππέων. συνέβη δὲ ταῖς πρό-

hundred horse, the princes did not come on that occasion, but after he had returned to his camp, the envoys came again offering some excuses on behalf of the princes, but begging him to come once more, as they would send out their leading men to exchange views about the whole situation. Manlius agreed to come, but himself remained in his own camp, sending out Attalus and some of the military tribunes with an escort of three hundred horse. The Gaulish envoys kept their appointment and spoke about the questions at issue, but said it was impossible then to come to a final agreement about matters or ratify anything that was decided. On the following day, however, they engaged that the princes should come to arrive at an agreement and complete the negotiations, if the consul Manlius met them in person. Attalus then promised that Manlius would come, and they separated on this understanding. The object of the Gauls in making these postponements and practicing these stratagems against the Romans was partly to gain time to transport certain of their relations and some of their property across the river Halys; but chiefly, if they could, to capture the Roman consul, or at any rate to kill him. With this intention they awaited next day the arrival of the Romans, keeping about a thousand horsemen in readiness. Manlius, after listening to Attalus and believing that the princes would come, went out as usual with an escort of five hundred horse. But it so

τερον ἡμέραις τοὺς ἐπὶ τὰς ξυλείας καὶ χορτολογίας
ἐκπορευομένους ἐκ τοῦ τῶν Ῥωμαίων χάρακος ἐπὶ
ταῦτα τὰ μέρη πεποιῆσθαι τὴν ἔξοδον, ἐφεδρείᾳ χρωμένους τοῖς ἐπὶ τὸν σύλλογον πορευομένοις ἱππεῦσιν.
13 οὗ καὶ τότε γενομένου καὶ πολλῶν ἐξεληλυθότων,
συνέταξαν οἱ χιλίαρχοι ⟨καὶ⟩ τοὺς εἰθισμένους ἐφεδρεύειν τοῖς προνομεύουσιν ἱππεῖς ἐπὶ ταῦτα τὰ μέρη
14 ποιήσασθαι τὴν ἔξοδον. ὧν ἐκπορευθέντων, αὐτομάτως
τὸ δέον ἐγενήθη πρὸς τὴν ἐπιφερομένην χρείαν.

40. Ἐν ... η ... τῆς | πράξεως τῆς περὶ τὸν Ἀριαράθην
εἰς τὴν παροιμίαν· ἔχοντες γὰρ π .. | διετε ..... οι τοῖς
πολεμίοις ἐγένοντο.

VII. RES ASIAE

(43)   41. Ὅτι κατὰ τοὺς καιροὺς τούτους κατὰ τὴν Ἀσίαν
(xxii.24) Γναίου τοῦ τῶν Ῥωμαίων στρατηγοῦ παραχειμάζοντος ἐν Ἐφέσῳ, κατὰ τὸν τελευταῖον ἐνιαυτὸν τῆς ὑπο-
κειμένης ὀλυμπιάδος, παρεγένοντο πρεσβεῖαι παρά τε
τῶν Ἑλληνίδων πόλεων τῶν ἐπὶ τῆς Ἀσίας καὶ παρ'
ἑτέρων πλειόνων, συμφοροῦσαι στεφάνους τῷ Γναίῳ
2 διὰ τὸ νενικηκέναι τοὺς Γαλάτας. ἅπαντες γὰρ οἱ τὴν
ἐπὶ τάδε τοῦ Ταύρου κατοικοῦντες οὐχ οὕτως ἐχάρησαν
Ἀντιόχου λειφθέντος ἐπὶ τῷ δοκεῖν ἀπολελύσθαι τινὲς
μὲν φόρων, οἱ δὲ φρουράς, καθόλου δὲ πάντες βασιλικῶν προσταγμάτων, ὡς ἐπὶ τῷ τὸν ἀπὸ τῶν βαρβάρων αὐτοῖς φόρον ἀφῃρῆσθαι καὶ δοκεῖν ἀπηλλάχθαι
3 τῆς τούτων ὕβρεως καὶ παρανομίας. ἦλθε δὲ καὶ παρ'

happened that on previous days the Romans who left their camp to collect wood and forage went out in this direction under cover of the cavalry who were going to the conference. On this day the same thing took place, the foragers being very numerous, and the tribunes ordered the cavalry which used to protect them to go out in this direction. This was done, and thus by chance the proper step was taken to meet the danger which menaced the consul.

VII. AFFAIRS OF ASIA

Further Negotiations with Manlius and the Peace with Antiochus

(Cf. Livy 38.37)

40.[135]

41. At this period,[136] while Gnaeus Manlius, the Roman consul, was wintering in Ephesus, in the last year of this Olympiad embassies arrived from the Greek cities in Asia and from several other quarters to confer crowns on him for his victories over the Gauls. For all the inhabitants of the country on this side of the Taurus were not so much pleased at the defeat of Antiochus and at the prospect of the liberation of some of them from tribute, of others from garrisons, and of all from royal injunctions, as at their release from the fear of the barbarians and at the thought that they were now delivered from the lawless violence of

189–188 B.C.

---

[135] A fragment of three very poorly preserved lines, mentioning King Ariarathes (41.4); "the text here is too faulty to allow confident restoration," WC 3.153.

[136] Winter 189/8.

Ἀντιόχου Μουσαῖος καὶ παρὰ τῶν Γαλατῶν πρεσβευταί, βουλόμενοι μαθεῖν ἐπὶ τίσιν αὐτοὺς δεῖ ποιεῖσθαι
4 τὴν φιλίαν. ὁμοίως δὲ καὶ παρ' Ἀριαράθου τοῦ τῶν
Καππαδοκῶν βασιλέως· καὶ γὰρ οὗτος, μετασχὼν
Ἀντιόχῳ τῶν αὐτῶν ἐλπίδων καὶ κοινωνήσας τῆς
πρὸς Ῥωμαίους μάχης, ἐδεδίει καὶ διηπορεῖτο περὶ
5 τῶν καθ' αὑτόν. διὸ καὶ πλεονάκις πέμπων πρεσβευτὰς
ἐβούλετο μαθεῖν τί δοὺς ἢ τί πράξας δύναιτ' ἂν παρ-
6 αιτήσασθαι τὴν σφετέραν ἄγνοιαν. ὁ δὲ στρατηγὸς
τὰς μὲν παρὰ τῶν πόλεων πρεσβείας πάσας ἐπαινέσας
καὶ φιλανθρώπως ἀποδεξάμενος ἐξαπέστειλε, τοῖς δὲ
Γαλάταις ἀπεκρίθη διότι προσδεξάμενος Εὐμένη τὸν
βασιλέα, τότε ποιήσεται τὰς πρὸς αὐτοὺς συνθήκας.
7 τοῖς δὲ περὶ Ἀριαράθην εἶπεν ἑξακόσια τάλαντα δόν-
8 τας τὴν εἰρήνην ἔχειν. πρὸς δὲ τὸν Ἀντιόχου πρεσβευτὴν συνετάξατο μετὰ τῆς δυνάμεως ἥξειν ἐπὶ τοὺς τῆς
Παμφυλίας ὅρους, τά τε δισχίλια τάλαντα καὶ πεντακόσια κομιούμενος καὶ τὸν σῖτον ὃν ἔδει δοῦναι τοῖς
στρατιώταις αὐτοῦ πρὸ τῶν συνθηκῶν κατὰ τὰς πρὸς
9 Λεύκιον ὁμολογίας. μετὰ δὲ ταῦτα καθαρμὸν ποιησάμενος τῆς δυνάμεως, καὶ τῆς ὥρας παραδιδούσης,
παραλαβὼν Ἄτταλον ἀνέζευξεν καὶ παραγενόμενος
εἰς Ἀπάμειαν ὀγδοαῖος ἐπέμεινε τρεῖς ἡμέρας, κατὰ δὲ
τὴν τετάρτην ἀναζεύξας προῆγε, χρώμενος ἐνεργοῖς
10 ταῖς πορείαις. ἀφικόμενος δὲ τριταῖος εἰς τὸν συν-
ταχθέντα τόπον τοῖς περὶ Ἀντίοχον, αὐτοῦ κατεστρα-

these tribes. Musaeus[137] also came on the part of Antiochus, and some envoys from the Gauls to discover on what terms they might be reconciled with Rome, and likewise an embassy from Ariarathes,[138] the king of Cappadocia; for he too had made common cause with Antiochus and had taken his part in the battle against the Romans, and he was now alarmed and doubtful as to what would befall him; so that he had sent several embassies to learn by what concessions or by what course of conduct he could atone for his error. The consul after thanking and courteously entertaining all the embassies from the towns, dismissed them and replied to the Gauls that he would wait for the arrival of King Eumenes before coming to terms with them. As for Ariarathes he told him to pay six hundred talents[139] and consider himself at peace. He arranged with the envoy of Antiochus to come with his army to the borders of Pamphylia to get the two thousand five hundred talents and the corn that Antiochus had to give to the Roman soldiers before peace was made, by the terms of his agreement with Lucius Scipio. After this he reviewed his army, and as the season admitted it, left Ephesus, taking Attalus with him, and reaching Apamea[140] in eight days, remained there for three days and on the fourth left that town and advanced by forced marches. Reaching the place he had agreed upon with Antiochus on the third day,

[137] 16.1.   [138] King Ariarathes IV, who had supported Antiochus and the Tectosagi.

[139] See 17.5.

[140] Modern Dinar. The old city of Celaenae, refounded by Antiochus I and named in honor of his mother, Apame. Cohen (16.24.6), 281–285.

11 τοπέδευσε. συμμιξάντων δὲ τῶν περὶ τὸν Μουσαῖον
καὶ παρακαλούντων αὐτὸν ἐπιμεῖναι, διότι καθυστεροῦ-
σιν αἵ θ' ἅμαξαι καὶ τὰ κτήνη τὰ παρακομίζοντα τὸν
σῖτον καὶ τὰ χρήματα, πεισθεὶς τούτοις ἐπέμεινε τρεῖς
12 ἡμέρας. τῆς δὲ χορηγίας ἐλθούσης τὸν μὲν σῖτον
ἐμέτρησε ταῖς δυνάμεσι, τὰ δὲ χρήματα παραδούς
τινι τῶν χιλιάρχων συνέταξεν παρακομίζειν εἰς Ἀπάμειαν.

(44)   42. Αὐτὸς δὲ πυνθανόμενος τὸν ἐπὶ τῆς Πέργης
(xxii.25) καθεσταμένον ὑπ' Ἀντιόχου φρούραρχον οὔτε τὴν
φρουρὰν ἐξάγειν οὔτ' αὐτὸν ἐκχωρεῖν ἐκ τῆς πόλεως,
2 ὥρμησε μετὰ τῆς δυνάμεως ἐπὶ τὴν Πέργην. ἐγγίζοντος
δ' αὐτοῦ τῇ πόλει, παρῆν ἀπαντῶν ὁ τεταγμένος ἐπὶ
τῆς φρουρᾶς, ἀξιῶν καὶ δεόμενος μὴ προκαταγινώ-
3 σκειν αὐτοῦ· ποιεῖν γὰρ ἕν τι τῶν καθηκόντων· παραλαβὼν γὰρ ἐν πίστει παρ' Ἀντιόχου τὴν πόλιν τηρεῖν
ἔφη ταύτην, ἕως ἂν διασαφηθῇ πάλιν παρὰ τοῦ πι-
στεύσαντος τί δεῖ ποιεῖν· μέχρι δὲ τοῦ νῦν ἁπλῶς
4 οὐδὲν αὐτῷ παρ' οὐδενὸς ἀποδεδηλῶσθαι. διόπερ
ἠξίου τριάκονθ' ἡμέρας χάριν τοῦ διαπεμψάμενος
5 ἐρέσθαι τὸν βασιλέα τί δεῖ πράττειν. ὁ δὲ Γνάιος,
θεωρῶν τὸν Ἀντίοχον ἐν πᾶσι τοῖς ἄλλοις εὐσυν-
θετοῦντα, συνεχώρησε πέμπειν καὶ πυνθάνεσθαι τοῦ
βασιλέως· καὶ μετά τινας ἡμέρας πυθόμενος παρέ-
δωκε τὴν πόλιν.

6   Κατὰ δὲ τὸν καιρὸν τοῦτον οἱ δέκα πρεσβευταὶ καὶ
[ὁ] βασιλεὺς Εὐμένης εἰς Ἔφεσον κατέπλευσαν, ἤδη
τῆς θερείας ἐναρχομένης· καὶ δύ' ἡμέρας ἐκ τοῦ πλοῦ

he encamped there. Upon Musaeus meeting him and begging him to have patience, as the carriages and animals which were bringing the corn and money were delayed on the road, he was persuaded to do so, and waited for three days. When the supplies came he divided the corn among his soldiers and handing over the money to one of his tribunes ordered him to convey it to Apamea.

42. Hearing now that the commander of the garrison at Perge[141] appointed by Antiochus was neither withdrawing the garrison nor leaving the town himself, he marched against that place with his army. When he was near it the commander came out to meet him, entreating him not to condemn him unheard; for he was doing what was part of his duty. He had been entrusted by Antiochus with the city and he was holding it until he was again informed by his master what he should do, but up to now he had received no instructions from anyone on the subject. He therefore asked for thirty days' grace in order that he might send and ask the king how to act. Manlius, as he saw that Antiochus was faithful to his obligations in all other respects, allowed him to send and inquire, and after a few days he received an answer and surrendered the town.

The ten legates[142] and King Eumenes arrived by sea at Ephesus in early summer, and after resting there for two days after their voyage, went up the country toward Apa-

---

[141] City of Pamphylia. *RE* Perge 694–704 (W. Ruge). It became part of Eumenes' realm. *I. Perge* 1 (1999), 2 (2004).

[142] See n. on 24.6.

προσαναλαβόντες αὐτοὺς ἀνέβαινον εἰς τὴν Ἀπάμειαν.

7 ὁ δὲ Γνάιος, προσπεσούσης αὐτῷ τῆς τούτων παρουσίας, Λεύκιον μὲν τὸν ἀδελφὸν μετὰ τετρακισχιλίων
ἐξαπέστειλε πρὸς τοὺς Ὀροανδεῖς, πειθανάγκης ἔχοντας διάθεσιν χάριν τοῦ κομίσασθαι τὰ προσοφειλό-
8 μενα τῶν ὁμολογηθέντων χρημάτων, αὐτὸς δὲ μετὰ
τῆς δυνάμεως ἀναζεύξας ἠπείγετο, σπεύδων συνάψαι
9 τοῖς περὶ τὸν Εὐμένη. παραγενόμενος δ᾽ εἰς τὴν
Ἀπάμειαν καὶ καταλαβὼν τόν τε βασιλέα καὶ τοὺς
δέκα, συνήδρευεν περὶ τῶν πραγμάτων. ἔδοξεν οὖν
10 αὐτοῖς κυρῶσαι πρῶτον τὰ πρὸς Ἀντίοχον ὅρκια καὶ
τὰς συνθήκας, ὑπὲρ ὧν οὐδὲν ἂν δέοι πλείω διατίθε-
σθαι λόγον, ἀλλ᾽ ἐξ αὐτῶν τῶν ἐγγράπτων ποιεῖσθαι
τὰς διαλήψεις.

(45) 43. Ἦν δὲ τοιαύτη τις ἡ τῶν κατὰ μέρος διάταξις·
(xxii.26) φιλίαν ὑπάρχειν Ἀντιόχῳ καὶ Ῥωμαίοις εἰς ἅπαντα
2 τὸν χρόνον ποιοῦντι τὰ κατὰ τὰς συνθήκας. μὴ διιέ-
ναι βασιλέα Ἀντίοχον καὶ τοὺς ὑποταττομένους διὰ
τῆς αὑτῶν χώρας ἐπὶ Ῥωμαίους καὶ τοὺς συμμάχους
3 πολεμίους μηδὲ χορηγεῖν αὐτοῖς μηδέν· ὁμοίως δὲ καὶ
Ῥωμαίους καὶ τοὺς συμμάχους ἐπ᾽ Ἀντίοχον καὶ τοὺς
4 ὑπ᾽ ἐκεῖνον ταττομένους. μὴ πολεμῆσαι δὲ Ἀντίοχον
5 τοῖς ἐπὶ ταῖς νήσοις μηδὲ τοῖς κατὰ τὴν Εὐρώπην.
6 ἐκχωρείτω δὲ πόλεων καὶ χώρας.... μὴ ἐξαγέτω μηδὲν

---

143 In Pisidia, perhaps not a city, but only the name of a tribe.
RE Oroandeis 1130–1132 (W. Ruge). WC 3.155–156.

mea. Manlius, on hearing of their arrival, dispatched his brother Lucius with four thousand men to Oroanda,[143] the iron hand in the velvet glove, to obtain payment[144] of the part still owing of the sum the people of that place had agreed to pay. He himself left in haste with his army, as he was anxious to meet Eumenes. Upon reaching Apamea and meeting Eumenes and the ten legates, he sat with them in council discussing the situation. It was decided in the first place to ratify the treaty with Antiochus, about the terms of which I need make no further remarks, but will quote the actual text.

43. The terms in detail were as follows:[145] "There shall be friendship between Antiochus and the Romans for all time if he fulfils the conditions of the treaty: King Antiochus and his subjects shall not permit the passage through their territory of any enemy marching against the Romans and their allies or furnish such enemy with any supplies: the Romans and their allies engage to act likewise toward Antiochus and his subjects: Antiochus shall not make war on the inhabitants of the islands or of Europe: he shall evacuate all cities, lands, ⟨villages, and forts on this side of the Taurus as far as the river Halys and all between the valley of the Taurus and the mountain ridges that descend to Lycaonia⟩:[146] from all such places he is to carry away

[144] The two hundred talents mentioned by Livy 38.18.2.

[145] Some passages that have been lost in the Greek have been supplied from Livy 38.38.2–18.

[146] There is a major lacuna in the text, supplemented from Livy 38.38.4 who, however, gives *Tanain amnem* instead of "river Halys." There is little certainty about P.'s original text. See WC 3.157–158.

πλὴν τῶν ὅπλων ὧν φέρουσιν οἱ στρατιῶται· εἰ δέ τι
τυγχάνουσιν ἀπενηνεγμένοι, καθιστάτωσαν πάλιν εἰς
7 τὰς αὐτὰς πόλεις. μηδ' ὑποδεχέσθωσαν τοὺς ἐκ τῆς
Εὐμένους τοῦ βασιλέως μήτε στρατιώτας μήτ' ἄλλον
8 μηδένα. εἰ δέ τινες ἐξ ὧν ἀπολαμβάνουσιν οἱ Ῥωμαῖοι
πόλεων μετὰ δυνάμεώς εἰσιν Ἀντιόχου, τούτους εἰς
9 Ἀπάμειαν ἀποκαταστησάτωσαν. τοῖς δὲ Ῥωμαίοις
καὶ τοῖς συμμάχοις εἴ τινες εἶεν ⟨ἐκ τῆς Ἀντιόχου
βασιλείας⟩, εἶναι τὴν ἐξουσίαν καὶ μένειν, εἰ βούλον-
10 ται, καὶ ἀποτρέχειν. τοὺς δὲ δούλους Ῥωμαίων καὶ
τῶν συμμάχων ἀποδότω Ἀντίοχος καὶ οἱ ὑπ' αὐτὸν
ταττόμενοι,καὶ τοὺς ἁλόντας καὶ τοὺς αὐτομολήσαντας,
11 καὶ εἴ τινα αἰχμαλώτον ποθεν εἰλήφασιν. ἀποδότω δὲ
Ἀντίοχος, ἐὰν ᾖ δυνατὸν αὐτῷ, καὶ Ἀννίβαν Ἀμίλκου
Καρχηδόνιον καὶ Μνασίλοχον Ἀκαρνᾶνα ⟨καὶ Θό-
αντα⟩ Αἰτωλόν, ⟨καὶ⟩ Εὐβουλίδαν καὶ Φίλωνα Χαλ-
κιδεῖς,καὶ τῶν Αἰτωλῶν ὅσοι κοινὰς εἰλήφασιν ἀρχάς,
12 καὶ τοὺς ἐλέφαντας τοὺς ἐν Ἀπαμείᾳ πάντας, καὶ μη-
13 κέτι ἄλλους ἐχέτω. ἀποδότω δὲ καὶ τὰς ναῦς τὰς
μακρὰς καὶ τὰ ἐκ τούτων ἄρμενα καὶ τὰ σκεύη, καὶ
μηκέτι ἐχέτω πλὴν δέκα ἀφράκτων ⟨ὧν⟩ μηδὲ⟨ν πλεί-
οσι⟩ τριάκοντα κωπῶν ἐχέτω ἐλαυνόμενον, μὴ δ' αὐτὰ
14 πολέμου ἕνεκεν, ⟨οὗ⟩ αὐτὸς κατάρχει. μηδὲ πλείτωσαν
ἐπὶ τάδε τοῦ Καλυκάδνου ⟨καὶ Σαρπηδονίου⟩ ἀκρω-

---

147 For all those named here see 17.7. None was a subject of
King Antiochus.   148 The text of this paragraph, containing
the naval clause, is faulty, both in P. and in Livy (38.38.8), result-

nothing except the arms borne by his soldiers, and if anything has been carried away, it is to be restored to the same
city: he shall not receive either soldiers or others from the
kingdom of Eumenes: if there be any men in the army of
Antiochus coming from the cities which the Romans take
over, he shall deliver them up at Apamea: if there be any
from the kingdom of Antiochus dwelling with the Romans
and their allies, they may remain or depart at their good
pleasure: Antiochus and his subjects shall give up the
slaves of the Romans and of their allies, both those taken
in war and those who deserted, and any prisoners of war
they have taken, if there be such: Antiochus shall give up,
if it be in his power, Hannibal[147] son of Hamilcar, the
Carthaginian, Mnasilochus the Acarnanian, Thoas the Aetolian, Eubulidas and Philo the Chalcidians, and all Aetolians who have held public office: he shall surrender[148] all
the elephants now in Apamea and not keep any in future:
he shall surrender his long ships with their gear and tackle
and in future he shall not possess more than ten undecked
ships of war, of which none is rowed by more than thirty
oars, and those not for a war in which he is the aggressor:
his ships shall not sail beyond the Calycadnus[149] and the
Sarpedonian promontory[150] unless conveying tribute, en-

ing in many uncertainties. See A. H. M. McDonald and F. W.
Walbank, *JRS* 59 (1969), 30–39, and, with additional remarks,
WC 3.159–160 for discussion and bibliography.

[149] The modern river Göksu. *RE* Kalykadnos 1767 (W. Ruge).
The emperor Frederick I Barbarossa drowned in that river in
1190.

[150] The cape south of the Calycadnus and of Silifke (Seleu-
cia).

τηρίου, εἰ μὴ φόρους ἢ πρέσβεις ἢ ὁμήρους ἄγοιεν.

15 μὴ ἐξέστω δὲ Ἀντιόχῳ μηδὲ ξενολογεῖν ἐκ τῆς ὑπὸ
Ῥωμαίους ταττομένης μηδ᾽ ὑποδέχεσθαι τοὺς φεύγον-

16 τας. ὅσαι δὲ οἰκίαι Ῥοδίων ἢ τῶν συμμάχων ἦσαν ἐν
τῇ ὑπὸ βασιλέα Ἀντίοχον ταττομένῃ ταύτας εἶναι

17 Ῥοδίων, ὡς καὶ πρὸ τοῦ ⟨τὸν πόλεμον⟩ ἐξενεγκεῖν. καὶ
εἴ τι χρῆμα ὀφείλετ᾽ αὐτοῖς, ὁμοίως ἔστω πράξιμον·
καὶ εἴ τι ἀπελήφθη ἀπ᾽ αὐτῶν, ἀναζητηθὲν ἀποδοθήτω.
ἀτελῆ δὲ ὁμοίως ⟨ὡς⟩ καὶ πρὸ τοῦ πολέμου τὰ πρὸς

18 τοὺς Ῥοδίους ὑπαρχέτω. εἰ δέ τινας τῶν πόλεων, ἃς
ἀποδοῦναι δεῖ Ἀντίοχον, ἑτέροις δέδωκεν Ἀντίοχος,
ἐξαγέτω καὶ ἐκ τούτων τὰς φρουρὰς καὶ τοὺς ἄνδρας.
ἐὰν δέ τινες ὕστερον ἀποτρέχειν βούλωνται, μὴ προσ-

19 δεχέσθω. ἀργυρίου δὲ δότω Ἀντίοχος Ἀττικοῦ Ῥωμαίοις ἀρίστου τάλαντα μύρια δισχίλια ἐν ἔτεσι δώδεκα, διδοὺς καθ᾽ ἕκαστον ἔτος χίλια· μὴ ἔλαττον δ᾽
ἑλκέτω τὸ τάλαντον λιτρῶν Ῥωμαϊκῶν ὀγδοήκοντα·
καὶ μοδίους σίτου πεντηκοντακισμυρίους καὶ τετρα-

20 κισμυρίους. ⟨δότω δὲ Εὐμένει τῷ βασιλεῖ τάλαντα⟩
τριακόσια πεντήκοντα ἐν ἔτεσι τοῖς πρώτοις πέντε,
⟨ἑβδομήκοντα⟩ κατὰ τὸ ἔτος, τῷ ἐπιβαλλομένῳ . .

21 καιρῷ, ⟨ᾧ⟩ καὶ τοῖς Ῥωμαίοις ἀποδίδωσι, καὶ τοῦ σίτου, καθὼς ἐτίμησεν ὁ βασιλεὺς Ἀντίοχος, τάλαντα
ἑκατὸν εἴκοσιν ἑπτὰ καὶ δραχμὰς χιλίας διακοσίας
ὀκτώ· ἃ συνεχώρησεν Εὐμένης λαβεῖν, γάζαν εὐαρε-

22 στουμένην ἑαυτῷ. ὁμήρους δὲ ⟨εἴκοσι⟩ διδότω Ἀντίοχος, δι᾽ ἐτῶν τριῶν ἄλλους ἀνταποστέλλων, μὴ
νεωτέρους ἐτῶν ὀκτωκαίδεκα μηδὲ πρεσβυτέρους τετ-

voys or hostages: Antiochus shall not have permission to hire mercenaries from the lands under the rule of the Romans, or to receive fugitives: all houses that belonged to the Rhodians and their allies in the dominions of Antiochus shall remain their property as they were before he made war on them; likewise if any money is owing to them they may exact payment, and if anything has been abstracted from them it shall be sought for and returned: merchandise meant for Rhodes shall be free from duties as before the war:[151] if any of the cities which Antiochus has to give up have been given by him to others, he shall withdraw from these also the garrisons and the men in possession of them: and if any cities afterward wish to desert to him, he shall not receive them: Antiochus shall pay to the Romans 12,000 talents of the best Attic money in twelve years, paying 1,000 talents a year, the talent not to weigh less than 80 Roman pounds, and 540,000 modii of corn: he shall pay to King Eumenes 350 talents in the next five years, paying 70 talents a year at the same time that he makes for his payments to the Romans and in lieu of the corn, as Antiochus estimated it—127 talents and 1,208 drachmas, the amount Eumenes agreed to accept as a sum of money acceptable to him: Antiochus shall give twenty hostages, replacing them every three years, not below eighteen years of age and not above forty-five: if any

[151] Seleucus II had exempted the Rhodians from custom dues for goods imported from his realm (5.89.8). Inversely, Antiochus IV exempted Milesian goods imported into his (*SEG* 36.1046, II, lines 1–3).

23 ταράκοντα πέντε. ἐὰν δέ τι διαφωνήσῃ τῶν ἀποδιδο-
24 μένων χρημάτων, τῷ ἐχομένῳ ἔτει ἀποδότωσαν. ἂν δέ
    τινες τῶν πόλεων ἢ τῶν ἐθνῶν, πρὸς ἃ γέγραπται μὴ
    πολεμεῖν Ἀντίοχον, πρότεροι ἐκφέρωσι πόλεμον, ἐξέ-
25 στω πολεμεῖν Ἀντιόχῳ. τῶν δὲ ἐθνῶν καὶ πόλεων τού-
    των μὴ ἐχέτω τὴν κυρίαν αὐτὸς μηδ' εἰς φιλίαν προσ-
26 αγέσθω. περὶ δὲ τῶν ἀδικημάτων τῶν πρὸς ἀλλήλους
27 γινομένων εἰς κρίσιν προκαλείσθωσαν. ἐὰν δέ τι θέ-
    λωσι πρὸς τὰς συνθήκας ἀμφότεροι κοινῷ δόγματι
    προστεθῆναι ἢ ἀφαιρεθῆναι ἀπ' αὐτῶν, ἐξέστω.

(46)   44. Τμηθέντων δὲ τῶν ὁρκίων ἐπὶ τούτοις, εὐθέως ὁ
(xxii.26, στρατηγὸς Κόιντον Μινύκιον Θέρμον καὶ Λεύκιον τὸν
28)   ἀδελφόν, ἄρτι κεκομικότα τὰ χρήματα παρὰ τῶν
2   Ὀροανδέων, εἰς Συρίαν ἐξαπέστειλε, συντάξας κομίζε-
          σθαι τοὺς ὅρκους παρὰ τοῦ βασιλέως καὶ διαβεβαι-
          ώσασθαι τὰ κατὰ μέρος ὑπὲρ τῶν συνθηκῶν. πρὸς δὲ
3   Κόιντον Φάβιον τὸν ἐπὶ τοῦ ναυτικοῦ στρατηγὸν ἐξ-
          έπεμψε γραμματοφόρους, κελεύων πάλιν πλεῖν αὐτὸν
          εἰς Πάταρα καὶ παραλαβόντα τὰς ὑπαρχούσας αὐτόθι
          ναῦς διαπρῆσαι.

(47)   45. Μάλιος ὁ ἀνθύπατος τριακόσια τάλαντα πρα-
          ξάμενος παρ' Ἀριαράθου φίλον αὐτὸν ἐποιήσατο Ῥω-
          μαίων.

---

152 He was one of the ten legates. RE Minucius 1967–1971 (F. Münzer).

153 MRR 1. 366. RE Fabius 1773–1775 (F. Münzer).

of the money he pays does not correspond to the above stipulations, he shall make it good in the following year if any of the cities or peoples against which Antiochus is forbidden by this treaty to make war begin first to make war on him, he may make war on such, provided he does not exercise sovereignty over any of them or receive them into his alliance: all grievances of both parties are to be submitted to a lawful tribunal: if both parties desire to add any clauses to this treaty or to remove any by common decree, they are at liberty to do so."

44. The general having sworn to this treaty he at once dispatched Quintus Minucius Thermus[152] and his own brother Lucius Manlius, who had just returned bringing the money from Oroanda, to Syria with orders to exact the oath from Antiochus and make sure that the treaty would be carried out in detail. He then sent dispatches to Quintus Fabius Labeo,[153] the commander of the fleet, ordering him to sail on to Patara,[154] and, taking possession of the ships there, to burn them.

(Suda; cf. Livy 38.39.6)

45. Manlius the proconsul exacting three hundred talents from Ariarathes[155] received him into the Roman alliance.

---

[154] City in Lycia at the mouth of the river Xanthus, with an important harbor. *RE* 18 (Nachträge), 2555–2561 (G. Radke). The importance of the harbor is emphasized by the already famous *Stadiasmos*, found in 1993 and published by Ş. Şahin and M. Adak, *Stadiasmus Patarensis* (Istanbul 2007).

[155] With Eumenes' assistance he had the sum imposed upon him (41.7) halved. His daughter Stratonice was now betrothed to Eumenes, whose ally he henceforth remained.

46. Ὅτι κατὰ τὴν Ἀπάμειαν οἵ τε δέκα καὶ Γνάιος
ὁ στρατηγὸς τῶν Ῥωμαίων, διακούσαντες πάντων
τῶν ἀπηντηκότων, τοῖς μὲν περὶ χώρας ἢ χρημάτων
ἤ τινος ἑτέρου διαφερομένοις πόλεις ἀπέδωκαν ὁμο-
λογουμένας ἀμφοτέροις, ἐν αἷς διακριθήσονται περὶ
τῶν ἀμφισβητουμένων· τὴν δὲ περὶ τῶν ὅλων ἐποι-
2 ήσαντο διάληψιν τοιαύτην. ὅσαι μὲν τῶν αὐτονόμων
πόλεων πρότερον ὑπετέλουν Ἀντιόχῳ φόρον, τότε δὲ
διεφύλαξαν τὴν πρὸς Ῥωμαίους πίστιν, ταύτας μὲν
ἀπέλυσαν τῶν φόρων· ὅσαι δ' Ἀττάλῳ σύνταξιν ἐτέ-
λουν, ταύταις ἐπέταξαν τὸν αὐτὸν Εὐμένει διδόναι
3 φόρον. εἰ δέ τινες ἀποστᾶσαι τῆς Ῥωμαίων φιλίας
Ἀντιόχῳ συνεπολέμουν, ταύτας ἐκέλευσαν Εὐμένει δι-
4 δόναι τοὺς Ἀντιόχῳ διατεταγμένους φόρους. ⟨Κολο-
φωνίους⟩ δὲ τοὺς τὸ Νότιον οἰκοῦντας καὶ Κυμαίους
5 καὶ Μυλασεῖς ἀφορολογήτους ἀφῆκαν, Κλαζομενίοις
δὲ καὶ δωρεὰν προσέθηκαν τὴν Δρυμοῦσσαν καλου-
μένην νῆσον, Μιλησίοις δὲ τὴν ἱερὰν χώραν ἀποκατέστησαν, ἧς διὰ τοὺς πολέμους πρότερον ἐξεχώρη-
6 σαν. Χίους δὲ καὶ Σμυρναίους, ἔτι δ' Ἐρυθραίους, ἔν
τε τοῖς ἄλλοις προῆγον καὶ χώραν προσένειμαν, ἧς
ἕκαστοι κατὰ τὸ παρὸν ἐπεθύμουν καὶ σφίσι καθήκειν ὑπελάμβανον, ἐντρεπόμενοι τὴν εὔνοιαν καὶ
σπουδήν, ἣν παρέσχηντο κατὰ τὸν πόλεμον αὐτοῖς.
7 ἀπέδωκαν δὲ καὶ Φωκαεῦσι τὸ πάτριον πολίτευμα
8 καὶ τὴν χώραν, ἣν καὶ πρότερον εἶχον. μετὰ δὲ ταῦτα
Ῥοδίοις ἐχρημάτισαν, διδόντες Λυκίαν καὶ Καρίας τὰ
9 μέχρι Μαιάνδρου ποταμοῦ πλὴν Τελμεσσοῦ. περὶ δὲ

Final Settlement of Asia Minor

(Cf. Livy 38.39.7–17)

46. In Apamea the ten legates and Manlius the proconsul, after listening to all the applicants, assigned, in cases
where the dispute was about land, money, or other property, cities agreed upon by both parties in which to settle their differences. The general dispositions they made
were as follows. All autonomous towns which formerly
paid tribute to Antiochus but had now remained faithful to Rome were freed from tribute: all which had paid
contributions to Attalus were to pay the same sum as tribute to Eumenes: any which had abandoned the Roman
alliance and joined Antiochus in the war were to pay to
Eumenes whatever tribute Antiochus had imposed on
them. They freed from tribute the Colophonians inhabiting Notium, the people of Cymae and Mylasa, and in addition to this immunity they gave to Clazomenae the island
called Drymussa and restored to the Milesians the holy
district, from which they had formerly retired owing to the
wars. They advanced in many ways Chios, Smyrna, and
Erythrae, and assigned to them the districts which they
desired to acquire at the time and considered to belong to
them by rights, out of regard for the goodwill and activity
they had displayed during the war, and they also restored
to Phocaea her ancient constitution and her former territory. In the next place they dealt with the claims of
Rhodes, giving her Lycia and Caria south of the Maeander,
except Telmessus. As for King Eumenes and his brothers

τοῦ βασιλέως Εὐμένους καὶ τῶν ἀδελφῶν ἔν τε ταῖς
πρὸς Ἀντίοχον συνθήκαις τὴν ἐνδεχομένην πρόνοιαν
ἐποιήσαντο καὶ τότε τῆς μὲν Εὐρώπης αὐτῷ προσέθηκαν Χερρόνησον καὶ Λυσιμάχειαν καὶ τὰ προσοροῦντα τούτοις ἐρύματα καὶ χώραν, ἧς Ἀντίοχος
10 ἐπῆρχεν· τῆς δ' Ἀσίας Φρυγίαν τὴν ἐφ' Ἑλλησπόντου,
Φρυγίαν τὴν μεγάλην, Μυσούς, οὓς ⟨Προυσίας⟩ πρότερον αὐτοῦ παρεσπάσατο, Λυκαονίαν, Μιλυάδα, Λυ-
11 δίαν, Τράλλεις, Ἔφεσον, Τελμεσσόν. ταύτας μὲν οὖν
ἔδωκαν Εὐμένει τὰς δωρεάς· περὶ δὲ τῆς Παμφυλίας,
Εὐμένους μὲν εἶναι φάσκοντος αὐτὴν ἐπὶ τάδε τοῦ
Ταύρου, τῶν ⟨δὲ⟩ παρ' Ἀντιόχου πρεσβευτῶν ἐπέκεινα,
διαπορήσαντες ἀνέθεντο περὶ τούτων εἰς τὴν σύγ-
12 κλητον. σχεδὸν δὲ τῶν ἀναγκαιοτάτων καὶ πλείστων
αὐτοῖς διῳκημένων, ἀναζεύξαντες προῆγον ἐφ' Ἑλλήσποντον, βουλόμενοι κατὰ τὴν πάροδον ἔτι τὰ πρὸς
τοὺς Γαλάτας ἀσφαλίσασθαι.

47. (Ὅ)τι τῶν Ῥωμαίων κατὰ τὴν ἐπάνοδον παρὰ
τῶν Θρᾳκῶν πολλὰ δεινά.................. | ναρ.. Ῥω-
μαίων στρατιω........................... | ....οὐκ ἂν
φήσειε κα........................... | εὐμαρὲς φῦλα...
δι........................... | ἂν περὶ τὰς ἰδίας
.... βαιν.................. | ..εστιν....ν.
...ησαμένους......ν.................. | εναιρομ..ν..ς
πράξεις.................. |

they had made all possible provision for them in their treaty with Antiochus, and they now added to their dominion the following: in Europe the Chersonese, Lysimachia and the adjacent forts and territory, and in Asia Hellespontic Phrygia, Greater Phrygia, that part of Mysia of which Prusias had formerly deprived Eumenes, Lycaonia, the Milyas, Lydia, Tralles, Ephesus, and Telmessus. Such were the gifts they gave to Eumenes. As for Pamphylia, since Eumenes maintained it was on this side of the Taurus, and the envoys of Antiochus said it was on the other, they were in doubt and referred the matter to the senate. Having thus settled nearly all the most important questions, they left Apamea and proceeded toward the Hellespont, intending on their way to put matters in Galatia on a safe footing.

47.[156]

[156] "This almost illegible extract. . . refers to the Roman return march through Thrace, described by Livy, 38.40.3–41.15" (WC 3.175). This was in autumn 188; the Romans were waylaid by various Thracian tribes and suffered heavy losses of men, including Quintus Marcius Thermus (44.1), and of booty.

FRAGMENTA LIBRI XXII

I. RES GRAECIAE

1   1. Ὅτι κατὰ τὴν ὀγδόην καὶ μ΄ ὀλυμπιάδα πρὸς
ταῖς ρ΄ πρεσβειῶν παρουσίαι ἐγένοντο πρὸς Ῥωμαίους
παρὰ Φιλίππου καὶ παρὰ τῶν προσορούντων τῇ
Μακεδονίᾳ. τὰ δόξαντα τῇ συγκλήτῳ περὶ τῶν
πρέσβεων.

2   Ὅτι κατὰ τὴν Ἑλλάδα Φιλίππου διαφορὰ πρὸς
Θετταλοὺς καὶ Περραιβοὺς περὶ τῶν πόλεων ὧν κατ-
εἶχε Φίλιππος ἐκ τῶν Ἀντιοχικῶν καιρῶν τῆς Θετ-
3   ταλίας καὶ Περραιβίας. ἡ γενομένη δικαιολογία περὶ
τούτων ἐπὶ Κοΐντου Καικιλίου περὶ τὰ Τέμπη. τὰ κρι-
θέντα διὰ (τῶν περὶ) τὸν Καικίλιον.

4   Κρίσις ἄλλη περὶ τῶν ἐπὶ Θράκης πόλεων Φιλίππῳ
πρὸς τοὺς παρ᾽ Εὐμένους πρεσβευτὰς καὶ τοὺς ἐκ
Μαρωνείας φυγάδας, καὶ τὰ ῥηθέντα περὶ τούτων ἐν
Θεσσαλονίκῃ καὶ τὰ δόξαντα τοῖς περὶ τὸν Καικίλιον.

5   Ἡ γενομένη σφαγὴ διὰ Φιλίππου τοῦ βασιλέως
ἐν Μαρωνείᾳ. παρουσία πρεσβευτῶν ἐκ Ῥώμης καὶ τὰ
προσταχθέντα διὰ τούτων. αἰτίαι δι᾽ ἃς ἐγένετο Ῥωμαίοις πρὸς Περσέα πόλεμος.

FRAGMENTS OF BOOK XXII[1]

I. AFFAIRS OF GREECE

1. In Olympiad 148 (188/7–185/4) embassies came to Rome from Philip and from the neighbors of Macedonia. The decrees of the Senate concerning these embassies.

Differences in Greece between Philip and the Thessalians and Perrhaebians concerning the cities of Thessaly and Perrhaebia that Philip possessed since the war against Antiochus. The pleading about these matters before Quintus Caecilius in the valley of Tempe. The verdict of Caecilius.

Another quarrel concerning the Thracian cities among Philip, the ambassadors of Eumenes and the exiled citizens of Maronea, the speeches about these matters delivered in Thessaloniki and the verdict of Caecilius.

The bloodbath engineered by King Philip at Maronea. The arrival of ambassadors from Rome and their orders. The causes for the war of the Romans against Perseus.

---

1 For this (and only this) book the excerpts are preceded by a list of topics, probably left in error with the manuscript. There are discrepancies between these lists and the contents of the book; see WC 3.7.

6   Κατὰ τὴν Πελοπόννησον πρεσβευτῶν παρουσία
παρά τε Πτολεμαίου τοῦ βασιλέως καὶ παρὰ Εὐμένους
7   καὶ παρὰ Σελεύκου. καὶ τὰ δόξαντα τοῖς Ἀχαιοῖς ὑπέρ
τε τῆς πρὸς Πτολεμαῖον συμμαχίας καὶ τῶν δωρεῶν
τῶν προτεινομένων αὐτοῖς ὑπὸ τῶν προειρημένων
8   βασιλέων. παρουσία Κοΐντου Καικιλίου καὶ μέμψις
ὑπὲρ τῶν (κατὰ) Λακεδαίμονα διῳκημένων.

9   Ὡς Ἀρεὺς καὶ Ἀλκιβιάδης ὄντες τῶν ἀρχαίων
φυγάδων ἐκ Λακεδαίμονος ἐπρέσβευσαν εἰς τὴν
Ῥώμην καὶ κατηγορίαν ἐποιήσαντο Φιλοποίμενος καὶ
τῶν Ἀχαιῶν.

2. Ὅτι κατὰ τὴν ὀγδόην καὶ μ΄ ὀλυμπιάδα πρὸς
ταῖς ρ΄ παρουσία ἐγένετο πρεσβευτῶν Ῥωμαίων εἰς
Κλείτορα καὶ σύνοδος τῶν Ἀχαιῶν. καὶ οἱ ῥηθέντες
ὑπὸ ἀμφοτέρων λόγοι περὶ τῶν κατὰ Λακεδαίμονα
πραγμάτων καὶ τὰ δόξαντα τοῖς Ἀχαιοῖς. ταῦτα κεφαλαιωδῶς.

3. Ὅτι μετὰ τὴν ἐν τῷ Κομπασίῳ τῶν ἀνθρώπων
(xxiii.1) ἐπαναίρεσιν δυσαρεστήσαντές τινες τῶν ἐν τῇ Λακεδαίμονι τοῖς γεγονόσι καὶ νομίσαντες ὑπὸ τοῦ Φιλοποίμενος ἅμα τὴν δύναμιν καὶ τὴν προστασίαν
καταλελύσθαι τὴν Ῥωμαίων, ἐλθόντες εἰς Ῥώμην
κατηγορίαν ἐποιήσαντο τῶν διῳκημένων καὶ τοῦ Φι-
2   λοποίμενος. καὶ τέλος ἐξεπορίσαντο γράμματα πρὸς
τοὺς Ἀχαιοὺς παρὰ Μάρκου Λεπέδου τοῦ μετὰ ταῦτα
γενηθέντος ἀρχιερέως, τότε δὲ τὴν ὕπατον ἀρχὴν
3   εἰληφότος· ὃς ἔγραφε τοῖς Ἀχαιοῖς, φάσκων οὐχ ὀρθῶς αὐτοὺς κεχειρικέναι τὰ κατὰ τοὺς Λακεδαιμονί-

At the Peloponnese ambassadors from King Ptolemy, from Eumenes and from Seleucus. The decrees of the Achaeans concerning their alliance with Ptolemy and about the offers made by the aforementioned kings. Presence of Quintus Caecilius and his reprimand concerning the events at Sparta.

Areus and Alcibiades, representing the "old exiles" of Sparta, came to Rome and accused Philopoemen and the Achaeans.

2. In Olympiad 148 Roman ambassadors came to Cleitor. Assembly of the Achaeans. The speeches delivered by both parties concerning the Spartan matters, also the decrees of the Achaeans. This a brief summary.

Philopoemen and Sparta

3. After the slaughter of the men at Compasium,[2] some   188 B.C.
of the Lacedaemonians, dissatisfied with what had taken place and thinking that the power and dignity of the Romans had been destroyed by Philopoemen, came to Rome and accused Philopoemen for the measures he had taken. They finally procured a letter from Marcus Lepidus,[3] the future pontifex maximus, who was then consul, in which he wrote to the Achaeans saying that they had not acted

---

[2] In Laconia where in the spring of 188 those Spartans responsible for the city's secession from the Achaeans were handed over to them and murdered, when Philopoemen was federal strategus. *RE* Philopoemen 88–89 (W. Hoffmann). Errington (20.3.5), 144–145.

[3] See n. on 16.34.1. He was consul in 187.

4   ους. ὧν πρεσβευόντων, εὐθέως ὁ Φιλοποίμην πρεσβευ-
    τὰς καταστήσας τοὺς περὶ Νικόδημον τὸν Ἠλεῖον
    ἐξέπεμψεν εἰς τὴν Ῥώμην.

5   Κατὰ δὲ τὸν καιρὸν τοῦτον ἧκε καὶ παρὰ Πτολε-
    μαίου πρεσβευτὴς Δημήτριος Ἀθηναῖος, ἀνανεωσόμε-
    νος τὴν προϋπάρχουσαν συμμαχίαν τῷ βασιλεῖ πρὸς
6   τὸ ἔθνος τῶν Ἀχαιῶν. <ὧν> προθύμως ἀναδεξαμένων
    τὴν ἀνανέωσιν, κατεστάθησαν πρεσβευταὶ πρὸς Πτο-
    λεμαῖον Λυκόρτας ὁ παρ' ἡμῶν πατὴρ καὶ Θεοδωρί-
    δας καὶ Ῥωσιτέλης Σικυώνιοι χάριν τοῦ δοῦναι τοὺς
    ὅρκους ὑπὲρ τῶν Ἀχαιῶν καὶ λαβεῖν παρὰ τοῦ βασι-
7   λέως. ἐγενήθη δέ τι κατὰ τὸν καιρὸν τοῦτον πάρεργον
    μὲν ἴσως, ἄξιον δὲ μνήμης. μετὰ γὰρ τὸ συντελεσθῆναι
    τὴν ἀνανέωσιν τῆς συμμαχίας, ὑπὲρ τῶν Ἀχαιῶν
8   ὑπεδέξατο τὸν πρεσβευτὴν ὁ Φιλοποίμην· γενομένης
    δὲ παρὰ τὴν συνουσίαν μνήμης τοῦ βασιλέως, ἐπι-
    βαλὼν ὁ πρεσβευτὴς πολλούς τινας διετίθετο λόγους
    ἐγκωμιάζων τὸν Πτολεμαῖον καί τινας ἀποδείξεις
    προεφέρετο τῆς τε περὶ τὰς κυνηγίας εὐχερείας καὶ
    τόλμης, ἑξῆς τε <τῆς> περὶ τοὺς ἵππους καὶ τὰ ὅπλα
9   δυνάμεως καὶ τῆς ἐν τούτοις ἀσκήσεως. τελευταίῳ δ'
    ἐχρήσατο μαρτυρίῳ πρὸς πίστιν τῶν εἰρημένων· ἔφη
    γὰρ αὐτὸν κυνηγετοῦντα ταῦρον βαλεῖν ἀφ' ἵππου
    μεσαγκύλῳ.

rightly in Sparta. While this embassy was still in Rome, Philopoemen, losing no time, sent Nicodemus of Elis[4] to represent him there.

Ptolemy Epiphanes and the Achaeans

At about the same time Demetrius of Athens, the representative of Ptolemy, also came to renew that king's existing alliance with the Achaean League. They readily consented to this, and Lycortas,[5] the writer's father, Theodoridas, and Rositeles[6] of Sicyon were appointed envoys to Ptolemy to take the oath on behalf of the Achaeans and receive that of the king. At this time there occurred something of minor importance perhaps, but worth mentioning. For after the renewal of the alliance[7] had been duly accomplished, Philopoemen entertained the king's envoy on behalf of the Achaeans. When mention was made of the king at the banquet the envoy, interjecting, was profuse in his praises of him, and cited some instances of his skill and daring in the chase, and afterward spoke of his expertness and training in horsemanship and the use of arms, the last proof he adduced of this being that he once in hunting hit a bull from horseback with a javelin.

---

[4] Elis had only become a member state of the Confederacy in 191. For the result of Nicodemus' mission see 7.5–7.

[5] P.'s father. *RE* Lykortas 2386–2390 (F. Stähelin).

[6] Reiske's suggestion that the name was, in fact, Sositeles seems to be correct.

[7] It is not certain when this alliance was concluded. The king is Ptolemy V Epiphanes (204–181).

4. Ὅτι κατὰ τὴν Βοιωτίαν μετὰ τὸ συντελεσθῆναι
(xxiii.2) τὰς πρὸς Ἀντίοχον Ῥωμαίοις συνθήκας ἀποκοπεισῶν
τῶν ἐλπίδων πᾶσι τοῖς καινοτομεῖν ἐπιβαλλομένοις,
ἄλλην ἀρχὴν καὶ διάθεσιν ἐλάμβανον αἱ πολιτεῖαι.

2 διὸ καὶ τῆς δικαιοδοσίας ἑλκομένης παρ᾽ αὐτοῖς
σχεδὸν ἐξ εἴκοσι καὶ πέντ᾽ ἐτῶν, τότε λόγοι διεδίδοντο
κατὰ τὰς πόλεις, φασκόντων τινῶν διότι δεῖ γίνεσθαι

3 διέξοδον καὶ συντέλειαν τῶν πρὸς ἀλλήλους. πολλῆς
δὲ περὶ τούτων ἀμφισβητήσεως ὑπαρχούσης διὰ τὸ
πλείους εἶναι τοὺς καχέκτας τῶν εὐπόρων, ἐγίνετό τι
συνέργημα τοῖς τὰ βέλτισθ᾽ αἱρουμένοις ἐκ ταὐτμάτου

4 τοιοῦτον. ὁ γὰρ Τίτος ἐν τῇ Ῥώμῃ πάλαι μὲν ἐσπούδαζε περὶ τοῦ καταπορευθῆναι τὸν Ζεύξιππον εἰς τὴν
Βοιωτίαν, ἅτε κεχρημένος αὐτῷ συνεργῷ πρὸς πολλὰ

5 κατὰ τοὺς Ἀντιοχικοὺς καὶ Φιλιππικοὺς καιρούς. κατὰ
δὲ τοὺς τότε χρόνους ἐξείργαστο γράψαι τὴν σύγκλητον τοῖς Βοιωτοῖς διότι δεῖ κατάγειν Ζεύξιππον καὶ

6 τοὺς ἅμ᾽ αὐτῷ φυγόντας εἰς τὴν οἰκείαν. ὧν προσπεσόντων, δείσαντες οἱ Βοιωτοὶ μὴ κατελθόντων τῶν
προειρημένων ἀποσπασθῶσιν ἀπὸ τῆς Μακεδόνων
εὐνοίας, βουλόμενοι κατακηρυχθῆναι τὰς κρίσεις τὰς
κατὰ τῶν περὶ τὸν Ζεύξιππον, ἃς ἦσαν πρότερον

7 αὐτοῖς ὑπογεγραμμένοι, . . . καὶ τούτῳ τῷ τρόπῳ τῶν
δικῶν μίαν μὲν αὐτῶν κατεδίκασαν ἱεροσυλίας, διότι
λεπίσαιεν τὴν τοῦ Διὸς τράπεζαν ἀργυρᾶν οὖσαν,

8 μίαν δὲ θανάτου διὰ τὸν Βραχύλλου φόνον. ταῦτα δὲ

---

8 See 20.6.1, also for the figure of twenty-five years.

*Troubles in Boeotia. Action of
Rome and of the Achaeans*

4. In Boeotia, after the peace between the Romans and
Antiochus had been signed, the hopes of all those who had
revolutionary aims were cut short, and there was a radical
change of character in the various states. The course of
justice had been at a standstill[8] there for nearly twenty-five
years, and now it was common matter of talk in the different cities that a final end must be put to all the disputes between the citizens. The matter, however, continued to be keenly disputed, as the politically disaffected
were much more numerous than those in affluent circumstances, when chance intervened as follows to support the
better disposed party. Flamininus had long been working
in Rome to secure the return of Zeuxippus[9] to Boeotia, as
he had been of much assistance to him at the time of the
wars with Philip and Antiochus, and at this juncture he
managed to get the senate to write to the Boeotians that
they must allow the return of Zeuxippus and the others
exiled together with him. When this message reached
them, the Boeotians, fearing lest the return of these exiles
might lead to the rupture of their good relations with
Macedonia, established a tribunal with the object of having judgment promulgated on the indictments against
Zeuxippus that they had already previously lodged, and
in this way he was condemned on one charge of sacrilege
for having stripped the holy table of Zeus of its silver plat-
ing and on another capital charge for the murder of
Brachylles.[10] Having managed matters so, they paid no

[9] See n. on 18.43.5.   [10] See nn. on 18.1.2 and 18.43.3.

διοικήσαντες οὐκέτι προσεῖχον τοῖς γραφομένοις,
ἀλλ' ἔπεμπον πρεσβευτὰς εἰς τὴν Ῥώμην τοὺς περὶ
Καλλίκριτον, φάσκοντες οὐ δύνασθαι τὰ κατὰ τοὺς
9   νόμους ᾠκονομημένα παρ' αὑτοῖς ἄκυρα ποιεῖν. ἐν δὲ
τοῖς καιροῖς τούτοις πρεσβεύσαντος αὐτοῦ τοῦ Ζευξ-
ίππου πρὸς τὴν σύγκλητον, οἱ Ῥωμαῖοι τὴν τῶν Βοιωτῶν προαίρεσιν ἔγραψαν πρός τε τοὺς Αἰτωλοὺς καὶ
πρὸς Ἀχαιούς, κελεύοντες κατάγειν Ζεύξιππον εἰς τὴν
10   οἰκείαν. οἱ δ' Ἀχαιοὶ τοῦ μὲν ⟨διὰ⟩ στρατοπέδων
ποιεῖσθαι τὴν ἔφοδον ἀπέσχον, πρεσβευτὰς δὲ προεχειρίσαντο πέμπειν τοὺς παρακαλέοντας τοὺς Βοιωτοὺς τοῖς λεγομένοις ὑπὸ τῶν Ῥωμαίων πειθαρχεῖν
καὶ τὴν δικαιοδοσίαν, καθάπερ καὶ τὴν ἐν αὑτοῖς,
11   οὕτω καὶ τὴν πρὸς αὑτοὺς ἐπὶ τέλος ἀγαγεῖν. συνέβαινε γὰρ καὶ τὰ πρὸς τούτους συναλλάγματα παρέλ-
12   κεσθαι πολὺν ἤδη χρόνον. ὧν διακούσαντες οἱ Βοιωτοί, στρατηγοῦντος Ἱππίου παρ' αὑτοῖς, παραχρῆμα
μὲν ὑπέσχοντο ποιήσειν τὰ παρακαλούμενα, μετ' ὀλί-
13   γον δὲ πάντων ὠλιγώρησαν. διόπερ ὁ Φιλοποίμην,
Ἱππίου μὲν ἀποτεθειμένου τὴν ἀρχήν, Ἀλκέτου δὲ
παρειληφότος, ἀπέδωκε τοῖς αἰτουμένοις τὰ ῥύσια
14   κατὰ τῶν Βοιωτῶν. ἐξ ὧν ἐγίνετο καταρχὴ διαφορᾶς
15   τοῖς ἔθνεσιν οὐκ εὐκαταφρόνητος. παραυτίκα γὰρ
ἔλαχε ... τῶν Μυρρίχου θρεμμάτων καὶ τοῦ Σίμωνος·
καὶ περὶ ταῦτα γενομένης συμπλοκῆς, οὐκέτι πολιτικῆς
διαφορᾶς, ἀλλὰ πολεμικῆς ἔχθρας ἐγένετο καταρχὴ
16   καὶ προοίμιον. εἰ μὲν οὖν ⟨ἡ⟩ σύγκλητος προσέθηκε
τἀκόλουθον περὶ τῆς καθόδου τῶν περὶ τὸν Ζεύξιπ-

further attention to the senate's letter, but sent Callicritus on an embassy to Rome to say that they could not set aside the legal decisions of their courts. At the same time Zeuxippus himself came to lay his case before the senate, and the Romans, informing the Aetolians and Achaeans by letter what was the policy of the Boeotians, bade them restore Zeuxippus to his home. The Achaeans refrained from proceeding to do so by armed force, but decided to send envoys to exhort the Boeotians to comply with the request of the Romans, and to beg them, as they had done in the case of their own legal proceedings, to bring to a conclusion also those to which Achaeans were parties; for a decision in suits between Boeotians and Achaeans had likewise been delayed for very long past. The Boeotians, on hearing these requests—Hippias was now their strategus—at once promised to accede to them, but in a very short time entirely neglected them; and owing to this Philopoemen, when Alcetas had succeeded Hippias in office, granted to all applicants right of seizure[11] of Boeotian property, which produced a by no means insignificant quarrel between the two nations. For . . . seized on the cattle of Myrrichus and Simon, and this leading to an armed conflict, proved to be the beginning and prelude of what was no longer a civil dispute but of a hatred characteristic of real war. Had the senate at this juncture followed up its order to restore Zeuxippus, war would soon have been set

[11] See B. Bravo, *ASNP* ser. 3, vol. 10 (1980) 675–987. A. Giovannini, *Les relations entre États dans la Grèce antique du temps d'Homère à l'intervention romaine (ca. 700–200 av. J.-C.)* (Wiesbaden 2007), 304–305.

17 πον, ταχέως ἂν ἐξεκαύθη πόλεμος· νῦν δ' ἐκείνη τε
παρεσιώπησεν, οἵ τε Μεγαρεῖς ἐπέσχον τὰ ῥύσια, δια-
πρεσβευσαμένων ... τοῖς συναλλάγμασιν.

5. Ὅτι ἐγένετο Λυκίοις διαφορὰ πρὸς Ῥοδίους διὰ
(xxiii.3) 2 τοιαύτας αἰτίας. καθ' οὓς καιροὺς οἱ δέκα διῴκουν τὰ
περὶ τὴν Ἀσίαν, τότε παρεγενήθησαν πρέσβεις, παρὰ
μὲν Ῥοδίων Θεαίδητος καὶ Φιλόφρων, ἀξιοῦντες αὐτοῖς δοθῆναι τὰ κατὰ Λυκίαν καὶ Καρίαν χάριν τῆς
εὐνοίας καὶ προθυμίας, ἣν παρέσχηνται σφίσι κατὰ
3 τὸν Ἀντιοχικὸν πόλεμον· παρὰ δὲ τῶν Ἰλιέων ἧκον
Ἵππαρχος καὶ Σάτυρος, ἀξιοῦντες διὰ τὴν πρὸς αὐτοὺς οἰκειότητα συγγνώμην δοθῆναι Λυκίοις τῶν
4 ἡμαρτημένων. ὧν οἱ δέκα διακούσαντες ἐπειράθησαν
ἑκατέρων στοχάσασθαι κατὰ τὸ δυνατόν. διὰ μὲν γὰρ
τοὺς Ἰλιεῖς οὐθὲν ἐβουλεύσαντο περὶ αὐτῶν ἀνήκεστον,
τοῖς δὲ Ῥοδίοις χαριζόμενοι προένειμαν ἐν δωρεᾷ
5 τοὺς Λυκίους. ἐκ ταύτης τῆς διαλήψεως ἐγενήθη στά-
σις καὶ διαφορὰ τοῖς Λυκίοις πρὸς αὐτοὺς τοὺς Ῥο-

---

12 This is of course an uncertain restoration.   13 For the
relations between Rhodes and Lycia after 188 see recently A.
Bresson, in: V. Gabrielsen (ed.) *Hellenistic Rhodes: Politics, Cul-
ture, and Society* (Aarhus 1999), 98–131. R. Behrwald, *Der lykis-
che Bund* (Bonn 2000), 89–105. Wiemer (16.26.10), 260–271.

14 Influential Rhodians, both with very long careers. *RE*
Theaidetos 1350–1351 (W. Schwahn). *RE* Philophron 76 (P.
Schoch).   15 For two contemporary citizens of Ilium with
that name, of which one could be the man named by P., see L.
Robert, *Monnaies antiques en Troade* (Geneva 1966), 29.

16 Clear testimonies for the notion that the Romans are de-
scendants of Aeneas occur first in the 190s (WC 3.182–183). A.

alight; but now the senate kept silence, and the Megarians put a stop to the seizures, the Boeotians (?) having applied to them through envoys, and having met the Achaean demand about the law suits.[12]

Dispute Between Rhodes and Lycia

5. A difference arose between the Lycians[13] and Rhodians owing to the following reasons. At the time when the ten commissioners were administering the affairs of Asia, two envoys, Theaedetus and Philophron,[14] arrived from Rhodes asking that Lycia and Caria should be given to the Rhodians in return for their goodwill and active assistance in the war with Antiochus; and at the same time two envoys from the people of Ilium, Hipparchus, and Satyrus,[15] came begging that, for the sake of the kinship[16] between Ilium and Rome, the offenses of the Lycians might be pardoned. The ten commissioners, after giving both embassies a hearing, attempted as far as possible to meet the requests of both. For to please the people of Ilium they took no very severe measures against the Lycians; but, as a favor to the Rhodians, they assigned Lycia to them as a gift.[17] Owing to this decision a quarrel of no trivial character arose between the Lycians and the Rhodians them-

Alföldi, *Die trojanischen Urahnen der Römer* (Basel 1957). G. K. Galinsky, *Aeneas, Sicily and Rome* (Princeton 1969). For this passage in P. see C. P. Jones, *Kinship Diplomacy in the Ancient World* (Cambridge, MA 1999), 70–71, with n. 14.

[17] So also 5.7: "as a present." The Senate, however, declared later that the report of the ten commissioners of 188 showed "that the Lycians had not been handed over to the Rhodians as a gift, but rather to be treated like friends and allies" (25.4.5).

6   δίους οὐκ εὐκαταφρόνητος. οἱ μὲν γὰρ Ἰλιεῖς ἐπιπορευόμενοι τὰς πόλεις αὐτῶν ἀπήγγελλον ὅτι παρήτηνται
τὴν ὀργὴν τῶν Ῥωμαίων καὶ παραίτιοι γεγόνασιν

7   αὐτοῖς τὴν ἐλευθερίας· οἱ δὲ περὶ τὸν Θεαίδητον ἐποιήσαντο τὴν ἀγγελίαν ἐν τῇ πατρίδι, φάσκοντες Λυκίαν καὶ Καρίας ⟨τὰ⟩ μέχρι τοῦ Μαιάνδρου δεδόσθαι

8   Ῥοδίοις ὑπὸ Ῥωμαίων ἐν δωρεᾷ. λοιπὸν οἱ μὲν Λύκιοι
πρεσβεύοντες ἧκον εἰς τὴν Ῥόδον ὑπὲρ συμμαχίας,
οἱ δὲ Ῥόδιοι προχειρισάμενοί τινας τῶν πολιτῶν
ἐξαπέστελλον τοὺς διατάξοντας ταῖς κατὰ Λυκίαν καὶ

9   Καρίαν πόλεσιν ὡς ἕκαστα δεῖ γενέσθαι. μεγάλης δ'
οὔσης τῆς παραλλαγῆς περὶ τὰς ἑκατέρων ὑπολήψεις,
ἕως μέν τινος οὐ πᾶσιν ἔκδηλος ἦν ἡ διαφορὰ τῶν

10   προειρημένων· ὡς δ' εἰσελθόντες εἰς τὴν ἐκκλησίαν οἱ
Λύκιοι διελέγοντο περὶ συμμαχίας, καὶ μετὰ τούτους
Ποθίων ὁ πρύτανις τῶν Ῥοδίων ἀναστὰς ἐφώτισε τὴν
ἑκατέρων αἵρεσιν καὶ προσεπετίμησε τοῖς Λυκίοις ...
πᾶν γὰρ ὑπομένειν ἔφασαν μᾶλλον ἢ ποιήσειν Ῥοδίοις τὸ προσταττόμενον.

II. RES ITALIAE

(9)   6. Ὅτι κατὰ τοὺς αὐτοὺς καιροὺς ἧκον εἰς τὴν
(xxiii.6)   Ῥώμην παρά τε τοῦ βασιλέως Εὐμένους πρεσβευταὶ
διασαφοῦντες τὸν ἐξιδιασμὸν τοῦ Φιλίππου τῶν ἐπὶ

2   Θρᾴκης πόλεων, καὶ παρὰ Μαρωνειτῶν οἱ φυγάδες

---

18 See n. on 13.5.1.   19 Greek city in Thrace, founded by
Chius. Philip took it and Aenus (6.7) from Ptolemy in 200, the

selves. For the representatives of Ilium, visiting the Lycian
cities, announced that they had softened the anger of the
Romans and had been instrumental in obtaining their
freedom. Theaedetus, however, and his colleague published in Rhodes the message that Lycia and Caria, south
of the Meander, had been given to Rhodes as a present by
the Romans. After this, envoys from Lycia came to Rhodes
to propose an alliance, but the Rhodians appointed some
of their citizens to proceed to the cities of Lycia and Caria
and give general orders as to what was to be done. Though
the conceptions formed on both sides were so widely di-
vergent, yet up to a certain point the difference between
them was not manifest to every one; but when the Lycians came into the Rhodian Assembly and began to talk
about alliance, and when afterward Pothion the Rhodian
prytanis[18] got up and after a clear statement of the two
views rebuked the Lycians, they . . . for they said they
would submit to anything rather than obey the orders of
the Rhodians.

II. AFFAIRS OF ITALY

Thracian Affairs before the Senate

(Cf. Livy 39.24.6)

6. At the same time envoys came from King Eumenes
to Rome conveying the news that Philip had appropriated
the Thracian cities. The exiles from Maronea[19] also arrived

186–185
B.C.

Romans declared it to be free in 196, but soon thereafter it was
garrisoned by Antiochus, then freed by the Romans in 189. All
testimonies about, and inscriptions of, Maronea in L. D. Louko-
poulou, Ἐπιγραφὲς τῆς Θρᾴκης τοῦ Αἰγαίου (Athens 2005).

κατηγοροῦντες καὶ τὴν αἰτίαν ἀναφέροντες τῆς αὑτῶν
ἐκπτώσεως ἐπὶ τὸν Φίλιππον, ἅμα δὲ τούτοις Ἀθα-
3 μᾶνες, Περραιβοί, Θετταλοί, φάσκοντες κομίζεσθαι
δεῖν αὑτοὺς τὰς πόλεις, ἃς παρείλετο Φίλιππος αὐτῶν
4 κατὰ τὸν Ἀντιοχικὸν πόλεμον. ἧκον δὲ καὶ παρὰ τοῦ
Φιλίππου πρέσβεις πρὸς ἅπαντας τοὺς κατηγορήσαν-
5 τας ἀπολογησόμενοι. γενομένων δὲ πλειόνων λόγων
πᾶσι τοῖς προειρημένοις πρὸς τοὺς παρὰ τοῦ Φιλίππου πρεσβευτάς, ἔδοξε τῇ συγκλήτῳ παραυτίκα κατα-
στῆσαι πρεσβείαν τὴν ἐπισκεψομένην τὰ κατὰ τὸν
Φίλιππον καὶ παρέξουσαν ἀσφάλειαν τοῖς βουλομένοις κατὰ πρόσωπον λέγειν τὸ φαινόμενον καὶ κατ-
6 ηγορεῖν τοῦ βασιλέως. καὶ κατεστάθησαν οἱ περὶ τὸν
Κόιντον Καικίλιον καὶ Μάρκον Βαίβιον καὶ Τεβέριον
Κλαύδιον.
7   Συνέβαινε τοὺς Αἰνίους πάλαι μὲν στασιάζειν, προσφάτως δ᾽ ἀπονεύειν τοὺς μὲν πρὸς Εὐμένη, τοὺς δὲ
πρὸς Μακεδονίαν.

III. RES GRAECIAE

(10)   7. Ὅτι κατὰ τὴν Πελοπόννησον ὡς μέν, ἔτι Φιλο-
(xxiii.7) ποίμενος στρατηγοῦντος, εἴς τε τὴν Ῥώμην ἐξαπέστειλε
πρεσβευτὰς τὸ τῶν Ἀχαιῶν ἔθνος ὑπὲρ τῆς Λακεδαιμονίων πόλεως πρός τε τὸν βασιλέα Πτολεμαῖον τοὺς
ἀνανεωσομένους τὴν προϋπάρχουσαν αὐτῷ συμμα-

accusing Philip of having been the cause of their banishment, and together with them representatives of the Athamanians, Perrhaebians, and Thessalians claiming that they should get back the towns of which Philip had despoiled them in the war with Antiochus. Philip also sent envoys to defend himself against all these accusations. After several discussions between all the above envoys and those of Philip, the senate decided to appoint at once a commission[20] to visit Philip's dominions and grant a safe-conduct to all who desired to state their case against Philip face to face. The commissioners appointed were Quintus Caecilius Metellus, Marcus Baebius Tamphilus, and Tiberius Claudius[21] Nero.

(Suda)

The people of Aenus[22] had long been at discord with each other, the one party inclining to Eumenes and the other to Macedonia.

III. AFFAIRS OF GREECE

The Achaean League and the Kings

7. I have already stated that while Philopoemen was still strategus, the Achaean League sent an embassy to Rome about Sparta, and other envoys to King Ptolemy to renew their existing alliance; and in the present year

187/6 B.C.

---

[20] *MRR* 1.373 and nn. 6–7.

[21] Livy gives instead (twice) "Tiberius Sempronius," which may be correct but then raises a question on his identity.

[22] In Thracia, modern Enez (in Turkey), at the mouth of the river Hebrus. *RE* Ainos 1028–1029 (G. Hirschfeld). J. M. F. May, *Ainos, its History and Coinage, 474–341 B. C.* (Oxford 1950).

THE HISTORIES OF POLYBIUS

2 χίαν, ἐδηλώσαμεν, φησὶν ὁ Πολύβιος. κατὰ δὲ τὸν
ἐνεστῶτα χρόνον, Ἀρισταίνου στρατηγοῦντος, οἵ τε
παρὰ Πτολεμαίου τοῦ βασιλέως ‹πρέσβεις ἧκον›, ἐν
Μεγάλῃ πόλει τῆς συνόδου τῶν Ἀχαιῶν ὑπαρχούσης·
3 ἐξαπεστάλκει δὲ ‹καὶ› ὁ βασιλεὺς Εὐμένης πρεσβευτάς, ἐπαγγελλόμενος ἑκατὸν καὶ εἴκοσι τάλαντα δώσειν τοῖς Ἀχαιοῖς, ἐφ᾽ ᾧ, δανειζομένων τούτων, ἐκ τῶν
τόκων μισθοδοτεῖσθαι τὴν βουλὴν τῶν Ἀχαιῶν ἐπὶ
4 ταῖς κοιναῖς συνόδοις. ἧκον δὲ καὶ παρὰ Σελεύκου τοῦ
βασιλέως πρεσβευταί, τήν τε φιλίαν ἀνανεωσόμενοι
καὶ δεκαναΐαν μακρῶν πλοίων ἐπαγγελλόμενοι δώ-
5 σειν τοῖς Ἀχαιοῖς. ἐχούσης δὲ τῆς συνόδου πραγμα-
τικῶς, πρῶτοι παρῆλθον οἱ περὶ Νικόδημον τὸν Ἠλεῖ-
ον καὶ τούς τε ῥηθέντας ἐν τῇ συγκλήτῳ λόγους ὑφ᾽
αὑτῶν ὑπὲρ τῆς τῶν Λακεδαιμονίων πόλεως διῆλθον
6 τοῖς Ἀχαιοῖς καὶ τὰς ἀποκρίσεις ἀνέγνωσαν, ἐξ ὧν ἦν
λαμβάνειν ἐκδοχὴν ὅτι δυσαρεστοῦνται μὲν καὶ τῇ
τῶν τειχῶν συντελέσει . . . καὶ τῇ καταλύσει . . . τῶν
ἐν τῷ Κομπασίῳ διαφθαρέντων, οὐ μὴν ἄκυρόν τι
7 ποιεῖν. οὐθενὸς δ᾽ οὔτ᾽ ἀντειπόντος οὔτε συνηγορήσαν-
τος, οὕτω πως παρεπέμφθη.
8   Μετὰ δὲ τούτους εἰσῆλθον οἱ παρ᾽ Εὐμένους πρέσβεις καὶ τήν τε συμμαχίαν τὴν πατρικὴν ἀνενεώσαντο
καὶ τὴν ὑπὲρ τῶν χρημάτων ἐπαγγελίαν διεσάφησαν
9 τοῖς πολλοῖς. καὶ πλείω δὲ πρὸς τούτας ‹τὰς› ὑπο-
θέσεις διαλεχθέντες καὶ μεγάλην εὔνοιαν καὶ φιλαν-
θρωπίαν τοῦ βασιλέως ἐμφήναντες πρὸς τὸ ἔθνος,
κατέπαυσαν τὸν λόγον.

408

when Aristaenus[23] was strategus the envoys came back
from Ptolemy during the session of the Achaean Assembly
at Megalopolis. King Eumenes had also sent envoys promising to give the Achaeans a hundred and twenty talents,
that they might lend it out and spend the interest in paying
the members of the Achaean Council during its session.
Envoys also came from King Seleucus[24] to renew friendship[25] with him, promising to give the Achaeans a flotilla
of ten long ships. The Assembly having set to work, Nicodemus[26] of Elis first came forward, and after reporting to
the Achaeans about the terms in which he had spoken
before the senate about Sparta, read the answer of the
senate, from which it was easy to infer that they were
displeased at the completion of the walls and at the . . . of
those executed at Compasium,[27] but that they did not re-
voke their previous decisions. As there was neither any
opposition or support the matter was shelved.

The envoys of Eumenes were the next to appear. They
renewed the alliance concluded with his father, informed
the Assembly of the promise of money and withdrew after
speaking at some length on both these subjects and expressing the great goodwill and friendly feelings of the
king toward the League.

[23] See 18.1.4 and 18.13.
[24] King Seleucus IV (187–175), who had just succeeded his
father Antiochus III. *CAH* (2nd ed.) 8 (1989), 338–341 (C.
Habicht). For recently found documents of his chancellery see
H. M. Cotton-M. Wörrle, *ZPE* 159 (2007), 191–207, and C. P.
Jones, *ZPE* 179 (2009), 100–104.
[25] This originated with the peace treaty of 188.
[26] 3.4.
[27] See n. on 3.1.

(11)
(xxiii.8)

8. μεθ᾽ οὓς Ἀπολλωνίδας ὁ Σικυώνιος ἀναστὰς κατὰ μὲν τὸ πλῆθος τῶν διδομένων χρημάτων ἀξίαν

2 ἔφη τὴν δωρεὰν τῶν Ἀχαιῶν, κατὰ δὲ τὴν προαίρεσιν τοῦ διδόντος καὶ τὴν χρείαν, εἰς ἣν δίδοται, πασῶν

3 αἰσχίστην καὶ παρανομωτάτην. τῶν γὰρ νόμων κωλυ- όντων μηθένα μήτε ⟨τῶν⟩ ἰδιωτῶν μήτε τῶν ἀρχόντων παρὰ βασιλέως δῶρα λαμβάνειν κατὰ μηδ᾽ ὁποίαν πρόφασιν, πάντας ἅμα δωροδοκεῖσθαι προφανῶς, προσδεξαμένους τὰ χρήματα, πάντων εἶναι παρανο- μώτατον, πρὸς δὲ τούτοις αἴσχιστον ὁμολογουμένως.

4 τὸ γὰρ ὀψωνιάζεσθαι τὴν βουλὴν ὑπ᾽ Εὐμένους καθ᾽ ἕκαστον ἔτος καὶ βουλεύεσθαι περὶ τῶν κοινῶν κατα- πεπωκότας οἰονεὶ δέλεαρ, πρόδηλον ἔχειν τὴν αἰσχύ-

5 νην καὶ τὴν βλάβην. νῦν μὲν γὰρ Εὐμένη διδόναι χρήματα, μετὰ δὲ ταῦτα Προυσίαν δώσειν, καὶ πάλιν

6 Σέλευκον. τῶν δὲ πραγμάτων ἐναντίαν φύσιν ἐχόντων τοῖς βασιλεῦσι καὶ ταῖς δημοκρατίαις, καὶ τῶν πλεί- στων καὶ μεγίστων διαβουλίων αἰεὶ γινομένων ⟨περὶ

7 τῶν⟩ πρὸς τοὺς βασιλεῖς ἡμῖν διαφερόντων, φανερῶς ἀνάγκη δυεῖν θάτερον ἢ τὸ τῶν βασιλέων λυσιτελὲς ἐπίπροσθεν γίνεσθαι τοῦ ⟨κατ᾽⟩ ἰδίαν συμφέροντος ἢ τούτου μὴ συμβαίνοντος ἀχαρίστους φαίνεσθαι

8 πᾶσιν, ἀντιπράττοντας τοῖς αὑτῶν μισθοδόταις. διὸ μὴ μόνον ἀπείπασθαι παρεκάλει τοὺς Ἀχαιούς, ἀλλὰ καὶ μισεῖν τὸν Εὐμένη διὰ τὴν ἐπίνοιαν τῆς δόσεως.

9 Μετὰ δὲ τοῦτον ἀναστὰς Κάσσανδρος Αἰγινήτης ἀνέμνησε τοὺς Ἀχαιοὺς τῆς Αἰγινητῶν ἀκληρίας, ᾗ

8. After their withdrawal Apollonidas[28] of Sicyon rose. He said that the sum offered by Eumenes was a gift not unworthy of the Achaeans' acceptance, but that the intention of the giver and the purpose to which it was to be applied were as disgraceful and illegal as could be. For, as it was forbidden by law for any private person or magistrate to receive gifts, on no matter what pretext, from a king, that all should be openly bribed by accepting this money was the most illegal thing conceivable, besides being confessedly the most disgraceful. For that the council should be in Eumenes' pay every year, and discuss public affairs after swallowing a bait, so to speak, would evidently involve disgrace and hurt. Now it was Eumenes who was giving them money; next time it would be Prusias, and after that Seleucus. "And," he said, "as the interests of democracies and kings are naturally opposed, and most debates and the most important deal with our differences with the kings, it is evident that perforce one or the other thing will happen: either the interests of the kings will take precedence of our own; or, if this is not so, we shall appear to every one to be ungrateful in acting against our paymasters." So he exhorted the Achaeans not only to refuse the gift, but to detest Eumenes for his purpose in offering it.

The next speaker was Cassander of Aegina, who reminded the Achaeans of the destitution which had over-

[28] Until recently only known from P., now on record in an unpublished inscription from Messene (*PAE* 2004 [2006], 42–46) as federal strategus ca. 180. He spoke about Eumenes' offer in the year of Aristaenus, either 186/5 (so WC 3.9–10) or 188/7 (so Errington (20. 3. 5), 150–162). The offer was a serious misstep on the part of Eumenes.

περιέπεσον διὰ τὸ μετὰ τῶν Ἀχαιῶν συμπολιτεύε-
σθαι, ὅτε Πόπλιος Σολπίκιος ἐπιπλεύσας τῷ στόλῳ
πάντας ἐξηνδραποδίσατο τοὺς ταλαιπώρους Αἰγινή-
10 τας· ὑπὲρ ὧν διεσαφήσαμεν, τίνα τρόπον Αἰτωλοί,
κύριοι γενόμενοι τῆς πόλεως κατὰ τὰς πρὸς Ῥωμαίους
συνθήκας, Ἀττάλῳ παραδοῖεν, τριάκοντα τάλαντα
11 παρ' αὐτοῦ λαβόντες. ταῦτ' οὖν τιθεὶς τοῖς Ἀχαιοῖς
πρὸ ὀφθαλμῶν ἠξίου τὸν Εὐμένη μὴ διάφορα προτεί-
νοντα θηρεύειν τὴν τῶν Ἀχαιῶν εὔνοιαν, ἀλλὰ τὴν
πόλιν ἀποδιδόντα τυγχάνειν πάντων τῶν φιλανθρώ-
12 πων ἀναντιρρήτως. τοὺς δ' Ἀχαιοὺς παρεκάλει μὴ
δέχεσθαι τοιαύτας δωρεάς, δι' ὧν φανήσονται καὶ τὰς
εἰς τὸ μέλλον ἐλπίδας ἀφαιρούμενοι τῆς Αἰγινητῶν
σωτηρίας.

13 Τοιούτων δὲ γενομένων λόγων, ἐπὶ τοσοῦτον παρέ-
στη τὸ πλῆθος ὥστε μὴ τολμῆσαι μηθένα συνειπεῖν
τῷ βασιλεῖ, πάντας δὲ μετὰ κραυγῆς ἐκβαλεῖν τὴν
προτεινομένην δωρεάν, καίτοι δοκούσης αὐτῆς ἔχειν
τι δυσαντοφθάλμητον διὰ τὸ πλῆθος τῶν προτεινομένων χρημάτων.

(12) 9. Ἐπὶ δὲ τοῖς προειρημένοις εἰσήχθη τὸ περὶ Πτο-
(xxiii.9) 2 λεμαίου διαβούλιον· ἐν ᾧ προκληθέντων τῶν ἀποστα-
λέντων πρεσβευτῶν ὑπὸ τῶν Ἀχαιῶν πρὸς Πτολεμαῖον,
προελθὼν Λυκόρτας μετὰ τῶν πρεσβευτῶν ἀπελογί-
σατο πρῶτον μὲν τίνα τρόπον καὶ δοῖεν καὶ λάβοιεν
3 τοὺς ὅρκους ὑπὲρ τῆς συμμαχίας, εἶτα <διότι κομί>-
ζοιεν δωρεὰν κοινῇ τοῖς Ἀχαιοῖς ἑξακισχίλια μὲν

taken the Aeginetans owing to their being members of the League at the time Publius Sulpicius Galba[29] had attacked Aegina with his fleet and sold into slavery all its unhappy inhabitants; and how, as I have narrated in a previous book,[30] the Aetolians gained possession of the town by their treaty with Rome, and handed it over to Attalus on receipt of thirty talents. Laying this before the eyes of the Achaeans, he begged Eumenes not to fish for the good offices of the Achaeans by making offers of money, but by giving up[31] the city of Aegina, to secure without a dissentient voice their complete devotion. He exhorted the Achaeans at the same time not to accept a gift which would clearly involve their depriving the Aeginetans of all hope of deliverance in the future.

In consequence of these speeches the people were so deeply moved that not a soul ventured to take the part of the king, but all with loud shouts rejected the proffered gift, although owing to the greatness of the sum the temptation seemed almost irresistible.

9. After the above debate the question of Ptolemy came on for discussion. The ambassadors sent by the Achaeans to Ptolemy having been summoned, Lycortas with his colleagues came forward, and reported in the first place how they had exchanged the oaths of alliance with Ptolemy, and next stated that they were the bearers of gifts to the Achaean nation consisting of six thousand bronze sets of

[29] See n. on 8.1.6. The speaker refers to events of 210.

[30] 9.42.5–8.

[31] It did not happen; Aegina remained with the monarchy until 133. There is a decree honoring King Attalus' II governor of the island, Cleon of Pergamum: *IG* IV.1².749.

ὅπλα χαλκᾶ πελταστικά, διακόσια δὲ τάλαντα νομί-
4 σματος ἐπισήμου χαλκοῦ· πρὸς δὲ τούτοις ἐπήνεσε
τὸν βασιλέα καὶ βραχέα περὶ τῆς εὐνοίας αὐτοῦ καὶ
προθυμίας τῆς εἰς τὸ ἔθνος εἰπὼν κατέστρεψε τὸν λό-
5 γον. ἐφ' οἷς ἀναστὰς ὁ τῶν Ἀχαιῶν στρατηγὸς Ἀρίσταινος ἤρετο τόν τε παρὰ τοῦ Πτολεμαίου πρεσβευτὴν
καὶ τοὺς ἐξαπεσταλμένους ὑπὸ τῶν Ἀχαιῶν ἐπὶ τὴν
ἀνανέωσιν, ποίαν ἧκε συμμαχίαν ἀνανεωσάμενος.
6 οὐδενὸς δ' ἀποκρινομένου, πάντων δὲ διαλαλούντων
πρὸς ἀλλήλους, πλῆρες ἦν τὸ βουλευτήριον ἀπορίας.
7 ἦν δὲ τὸ ποιοῦν τὴν ἀλογίαν τοιοῦτον. οὐσῶν καὶ
πλειόνων συμμαχιῶν τοῖς Ἀχαιοῖς πρὸς τὴν Πτολεμαίου βασιλείαν, καὶ τούτων ἐχουσῶν μεγάλας δια-
8 φορὰς κατὰ τὰς τῶν καιρῶν περιστάσεις, οὔθ' ὁ παρὰ
τοῦ Πτολεμαίου πρεσβευτὴς οὐδεμίαν ἐποιήσατο διαστολήν, ὅτ' ἀνενεοῦτο, καθολικῶς δὲ περὶ τοῦ πρά-
9 γματος ἐλάλησεν, οὔθ' οἱ πεμφθέντες πρέσβεις, ἀλλ'
ὡς μιᾶς ὑπαρχούσης αὐτοί τε τοὺς ὅρκους ἔδοσαν καὶ
10 παρὰ τοῦ βασιλέως ἔλαβον. ὅθεν προφερομένου τοῦ
στρατηγοῦ πάσας τὰς συμμαχίας καὶ κατὰ μέρος ἐν
ἑκάστῃ διαστελλομένου, μεγάλης οὔσης διαφορᾶς,
ἐζήτει τὸ πλῆθος εἰδέναι ποίαν ἀνανεοῖτο συμμαχίαν.
11 οὐ δυναμένου δὲ λόγον ὑποσχεῖν οὔτε τοῦ Φιλοποίμενος, ὃς ἐποιήσατο στρατηγῶν τὴν ἀνανέωσιν, οὔτε
τῶν περὶ τὸν Λυκόρταν τῶν πρεσβευσάντων εἰς τὴν
12 Ἀλεξάνδρειαν, οὗτοι μὲν ἐσχεδιακότες ἐφαίνοντο τοῖς
κοινοῖς πράγμασιν, ὁ δ' Ἀρίσταινος μεγάλην ἐφείλκετο
φαντασίαν ὡς μόνος εἰδὼς τί λέγει, καὶ τέλος οὐκ

arms for peltasts and two hundred talents weight of coined bronze. After expressing his thanks to the king and briefly touching on his friendly sentiments toward the League, he concluded his speech. The Achaean strategus Aristaenus now got up, and asked Ptolemy's ambassadors and those sent by the Achaeans to renew the alliance, which alliance had been renewed. When no one answered, but all the envoys began to talk between themselves, the house was at a loss to understand why. The cause of the confusion was as follows. There were several alliances between the Achaeans and the Ptolemaic kingdom, the terms of which varied widely with the variety of the circumstances under which they had been concluded; yet neither did Ptolemy's envoy make any distinction when the alliance was renewed but spoke in general terms on the subject, nor did the Achaean envoys do so, but exchanged oaths with the king as if there had only been one alliance. So that when the strategus produced all the alliances and explained in detail the points in which they differed, the divergences being very marked, the assembly demanded to know which alliance they were renewing. When neither Philopoemen, who had made the renewal during his year of office, nor Lycortas and his colleagues, who had been to Alexandria, could give any explanation, they were judged to have treated affairs of state in a perfunctory fashion,[32] but Aristaenus acquired a great reputation as being the only man who knew what he was speaking about. Finally he did not

[32] What was a major blunder committed by Philopoemen and Lycortas turned into a major achievement for Aristaenus. It is noteworthy that P. does not mitigate the fact damaging to his father's reputation.

εἴασε κυρωθῆναι τὸ διαβούλιον, ἀλλ᾽ εἰς ὑπέρθεσιν
13 ἤγαγε ⟨διὰ⟩ τὴν προειρημένην ἀλογίαν. τῶν δὲ παρὰ
τοῦ Σελεύκου πρέσβεων εἰσελθόντων, ἔδοξε τοῖς Ἀχαιοῖς τὴν μὲν φιλίαν ἀνανεώσασθαι ⟨πρὸς⟩ τὸν Σέλευκον, τὴν δὲ τῶν πλοίων δωρεὰν κατὰ τὸ παρὸν ἀπεί-
14 πασθαι. καὶ τότε μὲν περὶ τούτων βουλευσάμενοι
διέλυσαν εἰς τὰς ἰδίας ἕκαστοι πόλεις.

(13)   10. Μετὰ δὲ ταῦτα, τῆς πανηγύρεως ἀκμαζούσης,
(xxiii.10) ἦλθε Κόιντος Καικίλιος ἐκ Μακεδονίας, ἀνακάμπτων
ἀπὸ τῆς πρεσβείας ἧς ἐπρέσβευσε πρὸς Φίλιππον.
2 καὶ συναγαγόντος Ἀρισταίνου τοῦ στρατηγοῦ τὰς
ἀρχὰς εἰς τὴν τῶν Ἀργείων πόλιν, εἰσελθὼν ὁ Κόιντος
ἐμέμφετο, φάσκων αὐτοὺς βαρύτερον καὶ πικρότερον
τοῦ δέοντος κεχρῆσθαι τοῖς Λακεδαιμονίοις, καὶ παρεκάλει διὰ πλειόνων διορθώσασθαι τὴν προγεγενημέ-
3 νην ἄγνοιαν. ὁ μὲν οὖν Ἀρίσταινος εἶχε τὴν ἡσυχίαν,
δῆλος ὢν ἐξ αὐτοῦ τοῦ σιωπᾶν ὅτι δυσαρεστεῖται τοῖς
ᾠκονομημένοις καὶ συνευδοκεῖ τοῖς ὑπὸ Καικιλίου λε-
4 γομένοις· ὁ δὲ Διοφάνης ὁ Μεγαλοπολίτης, ἄνθρωπος
στρατιωτικώτερος ἢ πολιτικώτερος, ἀναστὰς οὐχ οἷον
ἀπελογήθη τι περὶ τῶν Ἀχαιῶν, ἀλλὰ καὶ προσυπέ-
δειξε τῷ Καικιλίῳ διὰ τὴν πρὸς τὸν Φιλοποίμενα
5 παρατριβὴν ἕτερον ἔγκλημα κατὰ τῶν Ἀχαιῶν. ἔφη
γὰρ οὐ μόνον τὰ κατὰ Λακεδαίμονα κεχειρίσθαι
6 κακῶς, ἀλλὰ καὶ τὰ κατὰ Μεσσήνην· ἦσαν δὲ περὶ
τῶν φυγαδικῶν τοῖς Μεσσηνίοις ἀντιρρήσεις τινὲς
πρὸς ἀλλήλους περὶ τὸ τοῦ Τίτου διάγραμμα καὶ τὴν
7 τοῦ Φιλοποίμενος διόρθωσιν. ὅθεν ὁ Καικίλιος, δοκῶν

allow the resolution to be ratified but adjourned the debate on it owing to the confusion I have explained. Upon the envoys from Seleucus entering the house the Achaeans voted to renew the friendship with that king, but to refuse the fleet of ships for the present. After these subjects had been discussed the assembly dissolved, the members returning to their cities.

10. After this, when the Nemean festival was at its height, Quintus Caecilius Metellus[33] came from Macedonia on his way back from his mission to Philip. Aristaenus, the strategus, having assembled the Achaean magistrates in Argos, Caecilius came in and found fault with them for having treated the Lacedaemonians with undue cruelty[34] and severity; and, addressing them at some length, exhorted them to correct their past errors. Aristaenus, for his part, remained silent, thus indicating his tacit disapproval of the management of matters there and his agreement with the remarks of Caecilius. Diophanes[35] of Megalopolis, who was more of a soldier than a man of politics, now got up, and not only did not offer any defense of the Achaeans, but, owing to his strained relations with Philopoemen, suggested to Caecilius another charge he might bring against the League. For he said that not only had matters been mismanaged at Sparta, but also at Messene, alluding to certain disputes about the exiles among the Messenians themselves on the subject of the edict[36] of Flamininus and Philopoemen's interference[37] with it. So

---

[33] See 6.5–6.   [34] At Compasium (3.1.).   [35] See n. on 21.36.2.   [36] See Livy 36.31.1–8, events of 191.

[37] For these events see *RE* Messenien (Suppl. 15), 274–275 (E. Meyer).

ἔχειν καὶ τῶν Ἀχαιῶν αὐτῶν τινας ὁμογνώμονας,
μᾶλλον ἠγανάκτει τῷ μὴ κατακολουθεῖν ἑτοίμως τοῖς
8 ὑπ᾽ αὐτοῦ παρακαλουμένοις τοὺς συνεληλυθότας. τοῦ
δὲ Φιλοποίμενος καὶ Λυκόρτα, σὺν ⟨δὲ⟩ τούτοις Ἄρχωνος, πολλοὺς καὶ ποικίλους διαθεμένων λόγους
ὑπὲρ τοῦ καλῶς μὲν διῳκῆσθαι τὰ κατὰ τὴν Σπάρτην
καὶ συμφερόντως αὐτοῖς μάλιστα τοῖς Λακεδαιμονίοις, ἀδύνατον δ᾽ εἶναι τὸ κινῆσαί τι τῶν ὑποκειμένων
ἄνευ τοῦ παραβῆναι καὶ τὰ πρὸς τοὺς ἀνθρώπους δί-
9 καια καὶ τὰ πρὸς τοὺς θεοὺς ὅσια, μένειν ἔδοξε τοῖς
παροῦσιν ἐπὶ τῶν ὑποκειμένων καὶ ταύτην δοῦναι τῷ
10 πρεσβευτῇ τὴν ἀπόκρισιν. ὁ δὲ Καικίλιος ὁρῶν τὴν
τούτων προαίρεσιν, ἠξίου τοὺς πολλοὺς αὐτῷ συν-
11 αγαγεῖν εἰς ἐκκλησίαν. οἱ δὲ τῶν Ἀχαιῶν ἄρχοντες
ἐκέλευον αὐτὸν δεῖξαι τὰς ἐντολάς, ἃς εἶχε παρὰ τῆς
συγκλήτου περὶ τούτων. τοῦ δὲ παρασιωπῶντος, οὐκ
12 ἔφασαν αὐτῷ συνάξειν τὴν ἐκκλησίαν· τοὺς γὰρ νόμους οὐκ ἐᾶν, ἐὰν μὴ φέρῃ τις ἔγγραπτα παρὰ τῆς
13 συγκλήτου, περὶ ὧν οἴεται δεῖν συνάγειν. ὁ δὲ Καικίλιος ἐπὶ τοσοῦτον ὠργίσθη διὰ τὸ μηθὲν αὐτῷ συγ-
χωρεῖσθαι τῶν ἀξιουμένων, ὥστ᾽ οὐδὲ τὴν ἀπόκρισιν
ἠβουλήθη δέξασθαι παρὰ τῶν ἀρχόντων, ἀλλ᾽ ἀναπό-
14 κριτος ἀπῆλθεν. οἱ δ᾽ Ἀχαιοὶ τὴν αἰτίαν ἀνέφερον καὶ
τῆς πρότερον παρουσίας ἅμα τῆς Μάρκου τοῦ Φολου-
ίου καὶ τῆς τότε τῶν περὶ τὸν Καικίλιον ἐπὶ τὸν Ἀρίσταινον καὶ τὸν Διοφάνην, ὡς τούτους ἀντισπασαμένους

that Caecilius, thinking that he had some of the Achaeans themselves in agreement with him, became still more vexed because the meeting of magistrates did not readily accede to his requests. After Philopoemen, Lycortas, and Archon[38] had spoken at length and employed various arguments to show that the management of affairs at Sparta had been good and particularly advantageous to the Spartans themselves, and that it was impossible to change anything in the established order of things there without violating the obligations of justice to men and piety to the gods, the meeting decided to make no change, and to convey this resolution to the legate. Caecilius, seeing how this meeting was disposed, demanded that the popular assembly should be summoned to meet him; but the magistrates asked him to show them the instructions he had from the senate on the subject; and, when he made no reply, refused to summon the assembly; for their laws did not allow it unless a written request was presented from the senate stating what matters it desired to submit to the assembly. Caecilius was so indignant[39] at none of his requests having been granted that he did not even consent to receive the answer of the magistrates, but went away without any. The Achaeans attributed both the former visit of Marcus Fulvius[40] and the present one of Caecilius to Aristaenus and Diophanes, alleging that these

[38] Of Aegira and, like his brother Xenarchus, influential and close to Philopoemen and Lycortas. J. Deininger, *Der politische Widerstand gegen Rom in Griechenland 217–86 v. Chr.* (Berlin 1971), 177–184.

[39] The Achaeans soon felt his anger: 12.5–10.

[40] See Livy 38.30.1. He is the consul of 189.

15 διὰ τὴν ἀντιπολιτείαν τὴν πρὸς τὸν Φιλοποίμενα· καί τις ἦν ὑποψία τῶν πολλῶν πρὸς τοὺς προειρημένους ἄνδρας. καὶ τὰ μὲν κατὰ Πελοπόννησον ἐν τούτοις ἦν.

IV. RES ITALIAE

(15) 11. Ὅτι τῶν περὶ τὸν Καικίλιον ἀνακεχωρηκότων
(xxiii.11) ἐκ τῆς Ἑλλάδος καὶ διασεσαφηκότων τῇ συγκλήτῳ περί τε τῶν κατὰ Μακεδονίαν καὶ τῶν κατὰ Πελοπόννησον, εἰσῆγον εἰς τὴν σύγκλητον τοὺς περὶ τούτων

2 ⟨παρα⟩γεγονότας πρεσβευτάς. εἰσελθόντων δὲ πρῶτον τῶν παρὰ τοῦ Φιλίππου καὶ παρ᾽ Εὐμένους, ἔτι δὲ τῶν ἐξ Αἴνου καὶ Μαρωνείας φυγάδων, καὶ ποιησαμένων τοὺς λόγους ἀκολούθως τοῖς ἐν Θεσσαλονίκῃ ῥηθεῖσιν

3 ἐπὶ τῶν περὶ τὸν Καικίλιον, ἔδοξε τῇ συγκλήτῳ πέμπειν πάλιν ἄλλους πρεσβευτὰς πρὸς τὸν Φίλιππον τοὺς ἐπισκεψομένους πρῶτον μὲν εἰ παρακεχώρηκε τῶν ἐν ⟨Θετταλίᾳ καὶ⟩ Περραιβίᾳ πόλεων κατὰ τὴν

4 τῶν περὶ τὸν Καικίλιον ἀπόκρισιν, εἶτα τοὺς ἐπιτάξοντας αὐτῷ τὰς φρουρὰς ἐξάγειν ἐξ Αἴνου καὶ Μαρωνείας, καὶ συλλήβδην ἀποβαίνειν ἀπὸ τῶν παραθαλαττίων τῆς Θρᾴκης ἐρυμάτων καὶ τόπων καὶ

5 πόλεων. μετὰ δὲ τούτους εἰσῆγον τοὺς ἀπὸ Πελοπον-
6 νήσου παραγεγονότας. οἵ τε γὰρ Ἀχαιοὶ πρεσβευτὰς ἀπεστάλκεισαν τοὺς περὶ Ἀπολλωνίδαν τὸν Σικυώνιον δικαιολογησομένους πρὸς τὸν Καικίλιον ὑπὲρ τοῦ μὴ λαβεῖν αὐτὸν ἀπόκρισιν καὶ καθόλου διδάξον-

two politicians had induced both to side with them owing to their political differences with Philopoemen, and they were viewed by the people with a certain suspicion. Such was the state of affairs in the Peloponnese.

IV. AFFAIRS OF ITALY

Treatment of Grecian Affairs by the Senate

(Cp. Livy 39.33)

11. After Caecilius and the other commissioners had left Greece and had reported to the senate about the affairs of Macedonia and the Peloponnese, the envoys who had come to Rome on these subjects were introduced.[41] The first to come in were the representatives of Philip and Eumenes and the exiles from Aenus and Maronea; and, upon their speaking in the same terms as they had done at Thessalonica before Caecilius, the senate decided to send fresh legates to Philip, to see in the first place if he had evacuated the cities in Thessaly and Perrhaebia, as Caecilius had stipulated in his reply to him, and next to order him to withdraw his garrisons from Aenus and Maronea and in general to quit all forts, places, and cities on the sea coast of Thrace. The envoys from the Peloponnese were the next to be introduced, the Achaeans having sent Apollonidas of Sicyon to justify themselves against Caecilius, because he had received no answer from them, and to

185–184
B.C.

---

[41] By the consuls of 184. *MRR* 1.374.

7 τας ὑπὲρ τῶν κατὰ Λακεδαίμονα πραγμάτων, ἔκ τε
τῆς Σπάρτης Ἀρεὺς καὶ Ἀλκιβιάδης ἐπρέσβευσαν·
οὗτοι δ' ἦσαν τῶν ἀρχαίων φυγάδων τῶν ὑπὸ τοῦ
Φιλοποίμενος καὶ τῶν Ἀχαιῶν νεωστὶ κατηγμένων εἰς

8 τὴν οἰκείαν. ὃ καὶ μάλιστα τοὺς Ἀχαιοὺς εἰς ὀργὴν
ἦγε τῷ δοκεῖν, μεγάλης οὔσης καὶ προσφάτου τῆς
εἰς τοὺς φυγάδας εὐεργεσίας, ἐξ αὐτῆς ἐπὶ τοσοῦτον
ἀχαριστεῖσθαι παρ' αὐτοῖς ὥστε καὶ καταπρεσβεύειν
καὶ κατηγορίαν ποιεῖσθαι πρὸς τοὺς κρατοῦντας τῶν
ἀνελπίστως αὐτοὺς σωσάντων καὶ καταγαγόντων εἰς
τὴν πατρίδα.

(16)   12. ποιησαμένων δὲ καὶ τούτων πρὸς ἀλλήλους ἐκ
(xxiii.12) συγκαταθέσεως τὴν δικαιολογίαν, καὶ διδασκόντων
τὴν σύγκλητον τῶν μὲν περὶ τὸν Ἀπολλωνίδαν τὸν
Σικυώνιον ὡς ἀδύνατον εἴη τὸ παράπαν ἄμεινον χειρισθῆναι τὰ κατὰ τὴν Σπάρτην ἢ νῦν κεχείρισται διὰ

2 τῶν Ἀχαιῶν καὶ διὰ Φιλοποίμενος, τῶν δὲ περὶ τὸν
Ἀρέα τἀναντία πειρωμένων λέγειν καὶ φασκόντων
πρῶτον μὲν καταλελύσθαι τὴν τῆς πόλεως δύναμιν
ἐξηγμένου τοῦ πλήθους μετὰ βίας, εἶτ' ἐν αὐτοῖς
ἐπισφαλῆ καὶ ἀπαρρησίαστον καταλείπεσθαι τὴν πο-

3 λιτείαν, ἐπισφαλῆ μὲν ὀλίγοις οὖσιν καὶ τούτοις τῶν
τειχῶν περιῃρημένων, ἀπαρρησίαστον δὲ διὰ τὸ μὴ
μόνον τοῖς κοινοῖς δόγμασιν τῶν Ἀχαιῶν πειθαρχεῖν,
ἀλλὰ καὶ κατ' ἰδίαν ὑπηρετεῖν τοῖς ἀεὶ καθισταμένοις

4 ἄρχουσιν, διακούσασα καὶ τούτων ἡ σύγκλητος ἔκρινε τοῖς αὐτοῖς πρεσβευταῖς δοῦναι καὶ περὶ τούτων
ἐντολάς, καὶ κατέστησεν πρεσβευτὰς ἐπὶ τὴν ‹Μακε-

speak in general on the affairs of Sparta, and Areus and Alcibiades[42] being the representatives of Sparta. These men both belonged to those old exiles who had recently been restored to their country by Philopoemen and the Achaeans; and it particularly excited the anger of the Achaeans that, after so great and recent a kindness as they had shown the exiles, they at once met with such flagrant ingratitude from them that they came on a mission against them to the ruling power and accused those who had so unexpectedly saved them and restored them to their homes.

12. Both parties, by common agreement, pleaded against each other. While Apollonidas of Sicyon argued in the Senate that it was quite impossible for the affairs of Sparta to have been managed better than they had been managed by the Achaeans and Philopoemen, Areus and his colleague attempted to prove the reverse, stating that in the first place the power of the city had been reduced by the forcible expulsion of the populace, and that then, in the state as left to those who remained, there was neither security nor liberty of speech, no security because they were few and their walls had been destroyed, and no liberty of speech because they not only had to obey the public decrees of the Achaeans but were as individuals obliged to be at the beck and call of the magistrates appointed from time to time. The senate, after hearing both sides, decided to give the same legates instructions on this subject, and appointed for Macedonia and Greece a com-

[42] Representatives of the "old exiles." See Errington (20.3.5), 175–179.

δονίαν καὶ τὴν〉 Ἑλλάδα τοὺς περὶ Ἄππιον Κλαύδιον.

5   Ἀπελογήθησαν δὲ καὶ πρὸς τὸν Καικίλιον ὑπὲρ
τῶν ἀρχόντων οἱ παρὰ τῶν Ἀχαιῶν πρέσβεις ἐν τῇ
συγκλήτῳ, φάσκοντες οὐθὲν ἀδικεῖν αὐτοὺς οὐδ᾽ ἀξίους ἐγκλήματος ὑπάρχειν ἐπὶ τῷ μὴ συνάγειν τὴν
6   ἐκκλησίαν· νόμον γὰρ εἶναι παρὰ τοῖς Ἀχαιοῖς μὴ
συγκαλεῖν τοὺς πολλούς, ἐὰν μὴ περὶ συμμαχίας ἢ
πολέμου δέῃ γίνεσθαι διαβούλιον ἢ παρὰ 〈τῆς〉 συγ-
7   κλήτου τις ἐνέγκῃ γράμματα. διὸ καὶ δικαίως τότε
βουλεύσασθαι μὲν τοὺς ἄρχοντας συγκαλεῖν τοὺς
Ἀχαιοὺς εἰς ἐκκλησίαν, κωλύεσθαι δ᾽ ὑπὸ τῶν νόμων
διὰ τὸ μήτε γράμματα φέρειν αὐτὸν παρὰ 〈τῆς〉 συγκλήτου μήτε τὰς ἐντολὰς ἐγγράπτους ἐθέλειν δοῦναι
8   τοῖς ἄρχουσιν. ὧν ῥηθέντων ἀναστὰς Καικίλιος τῶν
τε περὶ τὸν Φιλοποίμενα καὶ Λυκόρταν κατηγόρησεν
καὶ καθόλου τῶν Ἀχαιῶν καὶ τῆς οἰκονομίας, ᾗ περὶ
9   τῆς τῶν Λακεδαιμονίων ἐκέχρηντο πόλεως. ἡ δὲ σύγκλητος διακούσασα τῶν λεγομένων ἔδωκε τοῖς Ἀχαιοῖς ἀπόκρισιν ὅτι περὶ μὲν τῶν κατὰ Λακεδαίμονα
10   πέμψει τοὺς ἐπισκεψουένους· τοῖς δὲ πρεσβευταῖς τοῖς
αἰεὶ παρ᾽ ἑαυτῶν ἐκπεμπομένοις παρῄνει προσέχειν
τὸν νοῦν καὶ καταλογὴν ποιεῖσθαι τὴν ἁρμόζουσαν,
καθάπερ καὶ Ῥωμαῖοι ποιοῦνται τῶν παραγινομένων
πρὸς αὐτοὺς πρεσβευτῶν.

mission at the head of which was Appius Claudius Pulcher.[43]

The envoys from Achaea also spoke in the Senate defending their magistrates against Caecilius. They maintained that the magistrates had done nothing wrong and were deserving of no censure in not having summoned the assembly to meet, the Achaean law being that the popular assembly is not to be summoned unless a resolution has to be passed regarding alliance or war, or unless anyone brings a letter from the senate. Their magistrates had therefore been right on that occasion; for while they had considered summoning the Achaeans to a general assembly they were prevented from doing so by the laws, as Caecilius was neither the bearer of letters from the senate nor would he show to their magistrates his written instructions. After their speech Caecilius got up, and accusing Philopoemen and Lycortas and the Achaeans in general, condemned their management of the affairs of Sparta. The senate, after listening to the speeches, gave the following answer to the Achaeans. They would send a commission to inquire into Lacedaemonian affairs, and they advised the Achaeans to pay due attention and accord appropriate honors to all legates dispatched by them, just as the Romans do in the case of embassies arriving in Rome.

[43] Appius Claudius Pulcher, the consul of the previous year 185; *MRR* 1.376–377.

V. RES MACEDONIAE

(17)　　13. Ὅτι Φίλιππος ὁ βασιλεύς, διαπεμψαμένων πρὸς
(xxiii.13)　αὐτὸν ἐκ τῆς Ῥώμης τῶν ἰδίων πρεσβευτῶν καὶ δη-
2　λούντων ὅτι δεήσει κατ᾽ ἀνάγκην ἀποβαίνειν ἀπὸ τῶν
ἐπὶ Θρᾴκης πόλεων, πυθόμενος ταῦτα καὶ βαρέως φέρων ἐπὶ τῷ δοκεῖν πανταχόθεν αὐτοῦ περιτέμνεσθαι
τὴν ἀρχήν, ἐναπηρείσατο τὴν ὀργὴν εἰς τοὺς ταλαι-
3　πώρους Μαρωνείτας. μεταπεμψάμενος γὰρ Ὀνόμαστον
τὸν ἐπὶ Θρᾴκης τεταγμένον ἐκοινολογήθη τούτῳ περὶ
4　τῆς πράξεως. ὁ δ᾽ Ὀνόμαστος ἀναχωρήσας ἐξαπέστειλε
Κάσσανδρον εἰς Μαρώνειαν, συνήθη τοῖς πολλοῖς
5　ὑπάρχοντα διὰ τὸ ποιεῖσθαι τὸν πλείονα χρόνον ἐκεῖ
τὴν διατριβήν, ἅτε τοῦ Φιλίππου πάλαι τοὺς αὐλικοὺς
ἐγκαθεικότος εἰς τὰς πόλεις ταύτας καὶ συνήθεις πε-
6　ποιηκότος τοὺς ἐγχωρίους ταῖς τούτων παρεπιδημί-
αις. μετὰ δέ τινας ἡμέρας ἑτοιμασθέντων τῶν Θρᾳκῶν,
καὶ τούτων ἐπεισελθόντων διὰ τοῦ Κασσάνδρου νυ-
7　κτός, ἐγένετο μεγάλη σφαγὴ καὶ πολλοὶ τῶν Μαρωνειτῶν ἀπέθανον. κολασάμενος δὲ τῷ τοιούτῳ τρόπῳ
τοὺς ἀντιπράττοντας ὁ Φίλιππος καὶ πληρώσας τὸν
ἴδιον θυμόν, ἐκαραδόκει τὴν τῶν πρεσβευτῶν παρου-
8　σίαν [πεπεισμένος μηδένα τολμήσειν κατηγορήσειν
αὐτοῦ διὰ τὸν φόβον][1]. μετὰ δέ τινα χρόνον παραγενομένων τῶν περὶ τὸν Ἄππιον καὶ ταχέως πυθομένων
τὰ γεγονότα κατὰ τὴν Μαρώνειαν καὶ πικρῶς τῷ
9　Φιλίππῳ μεμψιμοιρούντων ἐπὶ τούτοις, ἐβούλετο μὲν

V. AFFAIRS OF MACEDONIA

Massacre at Maronea

(Cf. Livy 39.34–35)

13. King Philip, when his envoys sent a message to him   184 B.C.
from Rome that it would be necessary for him to evacuate[44] the Thracian cities; upon learning this he was much
embittered by the thought that he was being docked of his
dominions on every side, and vented his fury on the unhappy people of Maronea. Sending for Onomastus,[45] the
governor of Thrace, he communicated his intentions to
him. Onomastus upon leaving sent to Maronea Cassander,
who was familiar with the people, as he usually resided
there, Philip having for long been in the habit of settling
members of his court in these cities and accustoming the
inhabitants to their stay. After a few days, when the Thracians had been got ready and introduced into the town at
night by Cassander, a great massacre took place, and many
of the citizens perished. Philip, having thus chastised his
opponents and satisfied his vengeance, waited for the arrival of the legates [convinced that no one would dare to
accuse him owing to fear]; but shortly afterward when
Appius and his colleagues arrived, and, having soon heard
what had happened at Maronea, rebuked Philip severely
for his conduct, he tried to excuse himself by stating that

[44] 11.4.
[45] A close friend and advisor of the king. See also 14.1–5.

---

[1] Del. Naber, since the phrase recurs in 13.11, where it belongs, as Livy 39.34.5 shows.

ἀπολογεῖσθαι, φάσκων μὴ κεκοινωνηκέναι τῆς παρανομίας, ἀλλ' αὐτοὺς ἐν αὑτοῖς στασιάζοντας Μαρωνείτας, [καὶ] τοὺς μὲν ἀποκλίνοντας ⟨πρὸς⟩ Εὐμένη
κατὰ τὴν εὔνοιαν, τοὺς δὲ πρὸς ἑαυτόν, εἰς ταύτην
10 ἐμπεπτωκέναι τὴν ἀτυχίαν. καλεῖν δ' ἐκέλευε κατὰ
11 πρόσωπον, εἴ τις αὑτοῦ κατηγορεῖ. τοῦτο δ' ἐποίει πεπεισμένος μηδένα τολμήσειν διὰ τὸν φόβον, τῷ δοκεῖν
τὴν μὲν ἐκ Φιλίππου τιμωρίαν ἐκ χειρὸς ἔσεσθαι τοῖς
ἀντιπράξασιν, τὴν δὲ Ῥωμαίων ἐπικουρίαν μακρὰν
12 ἀφεστάναι. τῶν δὲ περὶ τὸν Ἄππιον οὐ φασκόντων
προσδεῖσθαι δικαιολογίας, σαφῶς γὰρ εἰδέναι τὰ γεγονότα καὶ τὸν αἴτιον τούτων, εἰς ἀπορίαν ἐνέπιπτεν
13 ὁ Φίλιππος. καὶ τὴν μὲν πρώτην ἔντευξιν ἄχρι τούτου
προβάντες ἔλυσαν·

(18)   14. κατὰ δὲ τὴν ἐπιοῦσαν ἡμέραν οἱ περὶ τὸν Ἄπ-
(xxiii.14) πιον πέμπειν ἐπέταττον τῷ Φιλίππῳ τὸν Ὀνόμαστον
καὶ τὸν Κάσσανδρον ἐξ αὐτῆς εἰς τὴν Ῥώμην [ἵνα
2 πύθηται περὶ τῶν γεγονότων]. ὁ δὲ βασιλεύς, δια-
τραπεὶς ὡς ἔνι μάλιστα καὶ ἀπορήσας ἐπὶ πολὺν χρόνον, τὸν μὲν Κάσσανδρον ἔφη πέμψειν, τὸν αὐθέντην
γεγονότα τῆς πράξεως, ὡς ἐκεῖνοί φασιν, ἵνα πύθηται
3 παρὰ τούτου τὰς ἀληθείας ἡ σύγκλητος. τὸν δ' Ὀνόμαστον ἐξῃρεῖτο καὶ παρ' αὐτὰ καὶ μετὰ ταῦτα τοῖς
πρεσβευταῖς ἐντυγχάνων, ἀφορμῇ μὲν χρώμενος τῷ
μὴ οἷον ἐν τῇ Μαρωνείᾳ παραγεγονέναι τὸν Ὀνό-
4 μαστον κατὰ τὸν τῆς σφαγῆς καιρόν, ἀλλὰ μηδ' ἐπὶ
τῶν σύνεγγυς τόπων γεγονέναι, τῇ δ' ἀληθείᾳ δεδιὼς
μὴ παραγενηθεὶς εἰς τὴν Ῥώμην, καὶ πολλῶν ἔργων

he had taken no part in the outrage, but that the people of Maronea themselves who were at discord, some of them being inclined to favor Eumenes and some himself, had brought this calamity on themselves; and he invited them to summon anyone who wished to accuse him to meet him. This he did owing to his conviction that no one would venture to do so, as all would think that Philip's vengeance on his opponents would be summary, while the help of Rome was remote. But when the commissioners said that any further defense on his part was superfluous, as they quite well knew what had happened and who was the cause of it, Philip was at a loss what to reply.

14. They broke up their first interview at this point, and on the next day the commissioners ordered Philip to send Onomastus and Cassander instantly to Rome [so that the matter be investigated]. Philip was exceedingly taken aback by this, and after hesitating for long, said he would send Cassander, the author of the deed, as they said, in order that the senate might learn the truth from him. Both now and at subsequent interviews with the legates he exculpated Onomastus on the pretext that not only had he not been present at Maronea on the occasion of the massacre, but had not even been in the neighborhood; fearing in fact that on arriving at Rome this officer, who had taken

αὐτῷ κεκοινωνηκὼς τοιούτων, οὐ μόνον τὰ κατὰ τοὺς
Μαρωνείτας, ἀλλὰ καὶ τἆλλα πάντα διασαφήσῃ τοῖς
5 Ῥωμαίοις. καὶ τέλος τὸν μὲν Ὀνόμαστον ἐξείλετο, τὸν
δὲ Κάσσανδρον μετὰ τὸ τοὺς πρεσβευτὰς ἀπελθεῖν
ἀποστείλας καὶ παραπέμψας ἕως Ἠπείρου φαρμάκῳ
6 διέφθειρεν. οἱ δὲ περὶ τὸν Ἄππιον, κατεγνωκότες τοῦ
Φιλίππου καὶ περὶ τῆς εἰς τοὺς Μαρωνείτας παρανομίας καὶ περὶ τῆς πρὸς Ῥωμαίους ἀλλοτριότητος, τοιαύτας ἔχοντες διαλήψεις ἐχωρίσθησαν.

7 Ὁ δὲ βασιλεὺς γενόμενος καθ᾽ ἑαυτὸν καὶ συμ-
μεταδοὺς τῶν φίλων Ἀπελλῇ καὶ Φιλοκλεῖ περὶ τῶν
ἐνεστώτων, ἔγνω σαφῶς ἐπὶ πολὺ προβεβηκυῖαν αὐτοῦ τὴν πρὸς Ῥωμαίους διαφοράν, καὶ ταύτην οὐκέτι
λανθάνουσαν, ἀλλὰ καταφανῆ τοῖς πλείστοις οὖσαν.
8 καθόλου μὲν οὖν πρόθυμος ἦν εἰς τὸ κατὰ πάντα τρόπον ἀμύνασθαι καὶ μετελθεῖν αὐτούς· πρὸς ἔνια δὲ
τῶν ἐπινοουμένων ἀπόχειρος ὢν ἐπεβάλετο πῶς ἂν ἔτι
γένοιτό τις ἀναστροφὴ καὶ λάβοι χρόνον πρὸς τὰς
9 εἰς τὸν πόλεμον παρασκευάς. ἔδοξεν οὖν αὐτῷ τὸν
νεώτατον υἱὸν Δημήτριον πέμπειν εἰς τὴν Ῥώμην, τὰ
μὲν ἀπολογησόμενον ὑπὲρ τῶν ἐγκαλουμένων, τὰ δὲ
καὶ παραιτησόμενον, εἰ καί τις ἄγνοιά ‹ποτ᾽› ἐγεγόνει
10 περὶ αὐτόν. πάνυ γὰρ ἐπέπειστο διὰ τούτου πᾶν τὸ
προτεθὲν ἀνύεσθαι παρὰ τῆς συγκλήτου διὰ τὴν

46 Both among the "First friends" of Philip, both later executed, Philocles by Philip, Apelles by Perseus. Walbank (18.3.9),
253, n.1.

430

part in many similar deeds, might inform the Romans not only about what had happened at Maronea, but about all the rest. Finally he got Onomastus excused; but sent off Cassander after the departure of the legates and giving him an escort as far as Epirus killed him there by poison. But Appius and the other legates, after condemning Philip for his outrage at Maronea and for his spirit of enmity to Rome, left him with this opinion of him.

The king, left by himself, confessed in his confidential intercourse with his friends Apelles and Philocles[46] that he saw clearly that his difference with the Romans had become very acute and that this did not escape the eyes of others but was patent to most people. He was therefore in general quite eager to resist and attack them by any and every means. But as he had not sufficient forces to execute some of his projects, he set himself to consider how he might put off matters for a little and gain time for warlike preparations.[47] He decided, then, to send his youngest son Demetrius[48] to Rome, in the first place to offer a defense against the charges brought against him, and next to ask for pardon if indeed he had inadvertently erred in any respect. For he felt quite convinced that through him he would get the senate to accede to anything he proposed

[47] Philip always, before and after his defeat at Cynoscephalae, wanted to have his army as a highly effective instrument. See M. Hatzopoulos, *L'organisation de l'armée macédonienne sous les Antigonides* (Athens 2001), esp. the Epigraphical Appendix, pp. 149–167.

[48] See 18.39.5 and 21.3.3, with notes. He had been held hostage in Rome from 197 to 191.

ὑπεροχὴν τὴν γεγενημένην τοῦ νεανίσκου κατὰ τὴν
11 ὁμηρείαν. ταῦτα δὲ διανοηθεὶς ἅμα μὲν ἐγίνετο περὶ
τὴν ἐκπομπὴν τούτου καὶ τῶν ἅμα τούτῳ συνεξαπο-
12 σταλησομένων φίλων, ἅμα δὲ τοῖς Βυζαντίοις ὑπέσχετο βοηθήσειν, οὐχ οὕτως ἐκείνων στοχαζόμενος
ὡς ἐπὶ τῇ 'κείνων προφάσει βουλόμενος καταπλήξασθαι τοὺς τῶν Θρᾳκῶν δυνάστας τῶν ὑπὲρ τὴν Προποντίδα κατοικούντων χάριν τῆς προκειμένης ἐπιβολῆς.

VI. RES GRAECIAE

(19)   15. Ὅτι κατὰ τὴν Κρήτην, κοσμοῦντος ἐν Γορτύνῃ
(xxiii.15) Κύδα τοῦ Ἀντάλκους, κατὰ πάντα τρόπον ἐλαττούμε-
νοι Γορτύνιοι τοὺς Κνωσίους, ἀποτεμόμενοι τῆς χώρας αὐτῶν τὸ μὲν καλούμενον Λυκάστιον προσένει-
2 μαν Ῥαυκίοις, τὸ ‹δὲ› Διατόνιον Λυττίοις. κατὰ δὲ τὸν
καιρὸν τοῦτον παραγενομένων πρεσβευτῶν ἐκ τῆς
Ῥώμης εἰς τὴν Κρήτην τῶν περὶ τὸν Ἄππιον χάριν
τοῦ διαλῦσαι τὰς ἐνεστώσας αὐτοῖς πρὸς ἀλλήλους
διαφοράς, καὶ ποιησαμένων λόγους ὑπὲρ τούτων ‹ἐν›
τῇ Κνωσίων καὶ Γορτυνίων, πεισθέντες οἱ Κρηταιεῖς

---

49 Their city had come under increased pressure from the
Thracians after Antiochus' withdrawal from the area.

50 The cosmoi were local boards of high officials in the cities
of Crete. Busolt-Swoboda (18.46.5), 747–749, and H. van Effen-
terre, *La Crète et le monde grec de Platon à Polybe* (Paris 1948),
100–103.

owing to the high esteem the young man had won while serving as a hostage. Having thought of this he occupied himself with the dispatch of Demetrius and the friends he was about to send in company with him, and also promised to help the Byzantines,[49] not so much with the view of gratifying them, as wishing upon this pretext to strike terror into the Thracian chiefs north of the Propontis and thus further the project he meant to execute.

VI. AFFAIRS OF GREECE

Quarrel of Gortyna and Cnosus

15. In Crete, when Cydas the son of Antalces held the office of Cosmos[50] at Gortyn,[51] the people of that city, exerting themselves to diminish in every way the power of the Cnosians,[52] parceled off from their territory the so-called Lycastium and assigned it to Rhaucus and the Diatonium to Lyttus. At this time[53] Appius Claudius and the other commissioners arrived in Crete from Rome, for the purpose of settling the disputes existing in the island. When they had spoken on the subject in Cnosus and Gortyn, the Cretans gave ear to them and put their affairs

184 B.C.

[51] For the city see the Preface of M. Guarducci to *IC* 4, pp. 1–39, and the inscriptions there collected, close to six hundred. For Crete in general during that time A. Chaniotis, *Die Verträge zwischen kretischen Poleis in der hellenistischen Zeit* (Stuttgart 1996).

[52] For Cnosus, Rhaucus, and Lyttus see *IC* 1, furthermore for Lyttus *RE* Lyttos (Suppl. 7), 427–436 (E. Kirsten).

[53] In 184; *MRR* 1.377.

3 ἐπέτρεψαν τὰ καθ᾽ αὑτοὺς τοῖς περὶ τὸν Ἄππιον. οἱ δὲ
[πεισθέντες] Κνωσίοις μὲν ἀποκατέστησαν τὴν χώραν, Κυδωνιάταις δὲ προσέταξαν τοὺς μὲν ὁμήρους
ἀπολαβεῖν, οὓς ἐγκατέλειπον δόντες τοῖς περὶ Χαρμί-
ωνα πρότερον, τὴν δὲ Φαλάσαρναν ἀφεῖναι μηδὲν ἐξ
4 αὐτῆς νοσφισαμένους. περὶ δὲ τῶν κατὰ κοινοδίκιον
συνεχώρησαν αὐτοῖς βουλομένοις μὲν [αὐτοῖς] ἐξεῖναι
5 μετέχειν, μὴ βουλομένοις δὲ καὶ τοῦτ᾽ ἐξεῖναι, πάσης
6 ἀπεχομένοις τῆς ἄλλης Κρήτης αὐτοῖς τε καὶ τοῖς ἐκ
Φαλασάρνης φυγάσιν. . . . ἀπέκτειναν τοὺς περὶ Με-
νοίτιον, ἐπιφανεστάτους ὄντας τῶν πολιτῶν.

VII. RES AEGYPTI

(6) 2   16. . . . ϛ θαυμάζουσι μὲν πάντες Φίλιππον διὰ τὴν
(xxi.16)   οπ . . . ϛ μεγαλοψυχίαν ὅτι κακῶς οὐ μόνον ἀκούων,
ἀλλὰ καὶ πάσχων ὑπ᾽ Ἀθηναίων, νικήσας αὐτοὺς τὴν
περὶ Χαιρώνειαν μάχην τοσοῦτον ἀπέσχε τοῦ χρήσασθαι τῷ καιρῷ πρὸς τὴν κατὰ τῶν ἐχθρῶν βλάβην
ὥστε τοὺς μὲν τεθνεῶτας τῶν Ἀθηναίων κηδεύσας
ἔθαψε, τοὺς δ᾽ αἰχμαλώτους χωρὶς λύτρων προσαμφι-
3 έσας ἐξαπέστειλε τοῖς ἀναγκαίοις· μιμοῦνται δ᾽ ἥκιστα τὴν τοιαύτην προαίρεσιν, ἁμιλλῶνται δὲ τοῖς

---

54 See for both cities *IC* 2. Phalasarna is the westernmost city
of Crete. *RE* Phalasarna 1653–1658 (E. Kirsten)

55 16.1 consists of some twelve lines, nearly all very fragmen-
tary. Not a single sentence can be made out. There is talk of

434

into their hands. They restored the territory to Cnosus: they ordered the Cydoniats to take back the hostages they had formerly left in Charmion's hands, and to leave Phalasarna[54] without taking anything away from it. As for the joint court, they allowed them, if they wished, to take part in it, and if they did not wish, to refuse on condition that they and the exiles from Phalasarna left the rest of Crete untouched. The . . . killed Menoetius and others, the most notable of their citizens.

VII. AFFAIRS OF EGYPT

16.[55] All admire King Philip the Second for his magnanimity, in that although the Athenians had injured him both by word and deed, when he overcame them at the battle of Chaeronea, he was so far from availing himself of his success to injure his enemies, that he buried with due rites the Athenian dead, and sent the prisoners back to their relations without ransom and clad in new raiment. But now far from imitating[56] such conduct men vie in

186–185
B.C.

guarantees violated and of unjust acts committed. Praise of the conduct of Philip II after his victory at Chaeronea follows in 16.2 and chapter 17 discusses the war of Ptolemy V against rebels in Egypt. All of this strongly suggests that this king is the culprit who is condemned by P. See Huss (16.18.2), 506–513. G. Hölbl, *Geschichte des Ptolemäerreiches* (Darmstadt 1994), 135–140 and A.-E. Veïsse, *Les révoltes égyptiennes* (*Studia Hellenistica* 41) (Leuven 2004), 160–161.

[56] The subjects seem to be Ptolemy V and unnamed contemporaries, but the rest of the sentence, probably not written by P., remains obscure.

θυμοῖς καὶ ταῖς τιμωρίαις πρὸς τούτους, οἷς πολεμοῦσι
τούτων αὐτῶν ἕνεκα. . . .

(7)   17. Ὅτι Πτολεμαῖος ὁ βασιλεὺς Αἰγύπτου ὅτε τὴν
(xxiii.16) Λύκων πόλιν ἐπολιόρκησε, καταπλαγέντες τὸ γεγονὸς
οἱ δυνάσται τῶν Αἰγυπτίων ἔδωκαν σφᾶς αὐτοὺς εἰς
2   τὴν τοῦ βασιλέως πίστιν. οἷς κακῶς ἐχρήσατο καὶ εἰς
3   κινδύνους πολλοὺς ἐνέπεσεν. παραπλήσιον δέ τι συνέβη καὶ κατὰ τοὺς καιρούς, ἡνίκα Πολυκράτης τοὺς
4   ἀποστάτας ἐχειρώσατο. οἱ γὰρ περὶ τὸν Ἀθίνιν καὶ
Παυσίραν καὶ Χέσουφον καὶ τὸν Ἰρόβαστον, οἵπερ
ἦσαν ἔτι διασωζόμενοι τῶν δυναστῶν, εἴξαντες τοῖς
πράγμασι παρῆσαν εἰς τὴν Σάιν, σφᾶς αὐτοὺς εἰς
5   τὴν τοῦ βασιλέως ἐγχειρίζοντες ⟨πίστιν⟩· ὁ δὲ Πτολεμαῖος ἀθετήσας τὰς πίστεις καὶ δήσας τοὺς ἀνθρώπους
γυμνοὺς ταῖς ἁμάξαις εἷλκε καὶ μετὰ ταῦτα τιμωρη-
6   σάμενος ἀπέκτεινεν. καὶ παραγενόμενος εἰς τὴν Ναύ-
κρατιν μετὰ τῆς στρατιᾶς, καὶ παραστήσαντος αὐτῷ
τοὺς ἐξενολογημένους ἄνδρας ἐκ τῆς Ἑλλάδος Ἀρι-
στονίκου, προσδεξάμενος τούτους ἀπέπλευσεν εἰς
7   Ἀλεξάνδρειαν, τῶν μὲν τοῦ πολέμου πράξεων οὐδεμιᾶς
κεκοινωνηκὼς διὰ τὴν Πολυκράτους ἀδικοδοξίαν, καίπερ ἔχων ἔτη πέντε καὶ εἴκοσιν.

anger and thirst for vengeance with those on whom they are making war to suppress these very sentiments. . . .

17. When Ptolemy the king of Egypt laid siege to the city of Lycopolis,[57] the Egyptian chiefs in terror surrendered at discretion. He used them ill and incurred great danger (sic). Much the same thing happened when Polycrates[58] got the rebels into his power. For Athinis, Pausiras, Chesufus and Irobastus, the surviving chieftains, forced by circumstances, came to Sais[59] to entrust themselves to the king's good faith. But Ptolemy, violating his faith, tied the men naked to carts, and, after dragging them through the streets and torturing them, put them to death. On reaching Naucratis[60] with his army, when Aristonicus[61] had presented to him the mercenaries he had raised in Greece, he took them and sailed off to Alexandria, having taken no part in any action in the war owing to the unfairness of Polycrates, although he was now twenty-five years old.

[57] Events of 197: *OGI* 90.22 and nn. 71–72.

[58] See n. on 5.64.4. He is mentioned also 15.29.10; 18.54.1; 18.55.9.

[59] City in Lower Egypt, perhaps once residence. *RE* Sais 1758–1759 (H. Kees).

[60] City on the Canopic branch of the Nile, southeast of Alexandria. Founded in the 7th century by numerous Greek states, it was an important trade station. *OCD* Naucratis 1028–1029 (W. E. H. Cockle), and various authors in *Topoi* 12–13 (2005), 133–257 (with bibliography).

[61] Eunuch and high-ranking officer in the service of Ptolemy V. L. Mooren, *The Aulic Titulature in Ptolemaic Egypt* (Brussels 1975), 146–149. *PP* 2152 and 2194. P. praises him in 22.1–5, below.

VIII. RES MACEDONIAE ET GRAECIAE

(8) 18. Ὅτι φησὶν ὁ Πολύβιος ἐν τῷ εἰκοστῷ δευτέρῳ·
(xxii.22a) περὶ δὲ τὴν τῶν ἐν Μακεδονίᾳ βασιλέων οἰκίαν ἤδη
2 τις ἀπὸ τούτων τῶν καιρῶν ἐφύετο κακῶν ἀνηκέστων
ἀρχή. καίτοι γ' οὐκ ἀγνοῶ διότι τινὲς τῶν συγγραφόν-
των περὶ τοῦ ⟨συστάντος⟩ Ῥωμαίοις πολέμου πρὸς
Περσέα, βουλόμενοι τὰς αἰτίας ἡμῖν ἐπιδεικνύναι τῆς
διαφορᾶς, πρῶτον μὲν ἀποφαίνουσι τὴν Ἀβρουπόλιος
ἔκπτωσιν ἐκ τῆς ἰδίας δυναστείας, ὡς καταδραμόντος
3 αὐτοῦ τὰ περὶ τὸ Πάγγαιον μέταλλα μετὰ τὸν τοῦ
Φιλίππου θάνατον· Περσεὺς δὲ παραβοηθήσας καὶ
τρεψάμενος ὁλοσχερῶς ἐξέβαλε τὸν προειρημένον ἐκ
4 τῆς ἰδίας ἀρχῆς· ἑξῆς δὲ ταύτῃ τὴν εἰς Δολοπίαν
εἰσβολὴν καὶ τὴν εἰς Δελφοὺς παρουσίαν Περσέως,
5 ἔτι δὲ τὴν κατ' Εὐμένους τοῦ βασιλέως ἐπιβουλὴν
γενομένην ἐν Δελφοῖς καὶ τὴν τῶν ἐκ Βοιωτίας πρεσβευτῶν ἐπαναίρεσιν, ἐξ ὧν ἔνιοί φασι φῦναι Περσεῖ
6 τὸν πρὸς Ῥωμαίους πόλεμον. ἐγὼ δέ φημι κυριώτατον
μὲν εἶναι καὶ τοῖς συγγράφουσι καὶ τοῖς φιλομαθοῦσι
τὸ γινώσκειν τὰς αἰτίας, ἐξ ὧν ἕκαστα γεννᾶται καὶ

---

62 186/5. 63 The execution of prince Demetrius and the
Third Macedonian War.

64 King of the Thracian Sapaei who dwelled on both sides of
the Nestus (Mesta). *RE* Sapaioi (Suppl. 6), 647–648 (G. Kazarov).
See also *RE* Thrake 437 (B. Lenk).

65 Mountain rich in silver and gold mines. For Abrupolis' attack and expulsion see *RE* Perseus 1000–1001 (F. Geyer).

VIII. AFFAIRS OF MACEDONIA
AND GREECE

(Cf. Livy 39.23.5)

18. From this time[62] forward dates the commencement
of the catastrophes[63] that were fatal to the royal house of
Macedon. I am not indeed unaware that some of the authors who have written about the war of the Romans with
Perseus, wishing to indicate the causes of the quarrel, at-
tribute it first to the expulsion of Abrupolis[64] from his
principality on the pretext that he had overrun the mines
on Mount Pangaeus[65] after the death of Philip, upon
which Perseus, coming to protect them and having utterly
routed him, expelled him, as I said, from his principality.
The next cause they give is the invasion of Dolopia[66] by
Perseus and his coming to Delphi, and further the plot[67]
formed at Delphi against King Eumenes, and the killing
of the envoys[68] from Boeotia, these latter events being
asserted by some to have been the causes of the war. Now
I maintain that it is most essential both for writers and for
students to know the causes from which all events spring

186–185
B.C.

179 B.C.

[66] *RE* Perseus 1001–1002.

[67] The assassination attempt on Eumenes at Delphi in March
172. Perseus probably had nothing to do with it.

[68] The alliance that the Boeotians concluded with Perseus (in
173?) was opposed by the city of Thebes, which sent two citizens
to Rome to report it. They died en route and Perseus was blamed
for their death. The five points of accusations against Perseus
given in 18.2–5 all recur on an inscription at Delphi, *RDGE* 40.
J. Bousquet, *BCH* 105 (1981) 407–416, recognized this as a letter
of (probably) Publius Licinius Crassus, the consul of 171, to the
city of Delphi, and found its beginning in *SIG* 613 B.

φύεται τῶν πραγμάτων· συγκέχυται δὲ ταῦτα παρὰ
τοῖς πλείστοις τῶν συγγραφέων διὰ τὸ μὴ κρατεῖσθαι
τίνι διαφέρει πρόφασις αἰτίας καὶ πάλιν προφάσεως

7 ἀρχὴ πολέμου. καὶ νῦν δὲ τῶν πραγμάτων αὐτῶν
προσυπομιμνησκόντων ἠνάγκασμαι πάλιν ἀνανεώσα-

8 σθαι τὸν αὐτὸν λόγον. τῶν γὰρ ἄρτι ῥηθέντων πραγμάτων τὰ μὲν πρῶτα προφάσεις εἰσί, τὰ δὲ τελευταῖα
<τὰ> περὶ τὴν <κατὰ> τοῦ βασιλέως Εὐμένους ἐπι-
βουλὴν καὶ τὰ περὶ <τὴν> τῶν πρεσβευτῶν ἀναίρεσιν
καὶ τούτοις ἕτερα παραπλήσια τῶν κατὰ τοὺς αὐτοὺς
καιροὺς γεγονότων ἀρχαὶ πρόδηλοι τοῦ συστάντος
Ῥωμαίοις καὶ Περσεῖ πολέμου καὶ τοῦ καταλυθῆναι
τὴν Μακεδόνων ἀρχήν· αἰτία δὲ τούτων ἁπλῶς ἐστιν

9 οὐδεμία. δῆλον δὲ τοῦτ' ἔσται διὰ τῶν ἑξῆς ῥηθη-
10 σομένων. καθάπερ γὰρ εἴπομεν Φίλιππον τὸν Ἀμύντου
διανοηθῆναι καὶ προθέσθαι συντελεῖν τὸν πρὸς τοὺς
Πέρσας πόλεμον, Ἀλέξανδρον δὲ τοῖς ὑπ' ἐκείνου κε-
κριμένοις <ἐπιγενέσθαι> χειριστὴν τῶν πράξεων, οὕτω
καὶ νῦν Φίλιππον μὲν τὸν Δημητρίου φαμὲν διανοηθῆναι πρότερον πολεμεῖν Ῥωμαίοις τὸν τελευταῖον
πόλεμον καὶ τὰς παρασκευὰς ἑτοίμας πάσας πρὸς
ταύτην ἔχειν τὴν ἐπιβολήν, ἐκείνου δ' ἐκχωρήσαντος

11 Περσέα γενέσθαι χειριστὴν τῶν πράξεων· εἰ δὲ τοῦτ'
ἀληθές, κἀκεῖνο σαφές· οὐ γὰρ οἷόν τε τὰς αἰτίας
ὕστερον γενέσθαι τῆς τελευτῆς τοῦ κρίναντος καὶ
προθεμένου πολεμεῖν· ὃ συμβαίνει τοῖς ὑπὸ τῶν ἄλλων συγγραφέων εἰρημένοις· πάντα γάρ ἐστι τὰ λεγόμενα παρ' αὐτοῖς ὕστερα τῆς Φιλίππου τελευτῆς.

and grow. But most writers are guilty of confusion in this matter, owing to their not observing the difference between a pretext and a cause, and between the beginning of a war and the pretext for it. I am therefore, as the circumstances themselves recall to my mind what I said on a previous occasion, compelled to repeat myself.[69] For of the events I just mentioned the first are pretexts, but the last—the plot against Eumenes and the murder of the envoys and other similar things that took place at the same time—constitute indeed evidently the actual beginning of the war between the Romans and Perseus and the consequent fall of the Macedonian power, but not a single one of them was its cause. This will be evident from what I am about to say. For just as I said[70] that Philip,[71] son of Amyntas, conceived and meant to carry out the war against Persia, but that it was Alexander who put his decision into execution, so now I maintain that Philip, son of Demetrius, first conceived the notion of entering on the last war against Rome, and had prepared everything for the purpose, but upon his death Perseus was the executor of the design. Now if one of these things is true, the other error also is evident. It is not surely possible that the causes of a war can be subsequent to the death of the man who decided on it and purposed to make it; and this is what other writers maintain; for all the things they mention are subsequent to the death of Philip.

[69] P. rehearses at length his discussion of 3.6.1 ff. on the causes, pretexts, and beginnings of war.   [70] 3.6.5.

[71] P. makes Philip responsible for the Third Macedonian War in the same way that he made Hamilcar Barcas responsible for the Second Punic War in 3.14.10. See also 23.9.6 and 23.10.4.

(14)
(xxiii.10a)

19. Ὅτι Φιλοποίμην πρὸς Ἄρχωνα τὸν στρατηγὸν λόγοις τισὶ διεφέρετο. ὁ μὲν οὖν Φιλοποίμην εὐδοκήσας ἐκ τοῦ καιροῦ τοῖς λεγομένοις καὶ μεταγνοὺς ἐπήνει τὸν Ἄρχωνα φιλοφρόνως, ὡς ἐντρεχῶς καὶ

2 πανούργως τῷ καιρῷ κεχρημένον. ἔμοιγε μήν, φησὶν ὁ Πολύβιος, οὔτε τότε παρόντι τὸ ῥηθὲν εὐηρέστησεν, ὥστ᾽ ἐπαινοῦντά τινα κακῶς ἅμα ποιεῖν, οὔτε μετὰ

3 ταῦτα τῆς ἡλικίας προβαινούσης· πολὺ γὰρ δή τι μοι δοκεῖ κεχωρίσθαι κατὰ τὴν αἵρεσιν ὁ πραγματικὸς ἀνὴρ τοῦ κακοπράγμονος καὶ παραπλησίαν ἔχειν διαφορὰν τῷ κακεντρεχεῖ πρὸς τὸν ἐντρεχῆ· ἃ μὲν γάρ ἐστι κ‹άλλ›ιστα τῶν ὄντων ὡς ἔπος εἰπεῖν, ἃ δὲ

4 τοὐναντίον· ἀλλὰ διὰ τὴν νῦν ἐπιπολάζουσαν ἀκρισίαν βραχείας ἔχοντα κοινότητας τὰ προειρημένα τῆς αὐτῆς ἐπισημασίας καὶ ζήλου τυγχάνει παρὰ τοῖς ἀνθρώποις.

IX. RES ASIAE

(xxiii.18)

20. Ὅτι Ἀπολλωνίς, ἡ Ἀττάλου τοῦ πατρὸς Εὐμένους τοῦ βασιλέως γαμετή, Κυζικηνὴ ἦν, γυνὴ διὰ πλείους

2 αἰτίας ἀξία μνήμης καὶ παρασημασίας. καὶ γὰρ ὅτι δημότις ὑπάρχουσα βασίλισσα ἐγεγόνει καὶ ταύτην

---

72 See n. on 10.8 and for his terms as general of the Achaeans, Errington (20.3.5), 300–301. As 19.2 shows, the praise was ironical. P. disapproved of that, a rare instance where he criticizes his model.

19. Philopoemen had a verbal dispute with Archon the strategus. Suddenly agreeing with what he said, he changed his attitude and praised Archon[72] warmly for having acted under the circumstances in an adroit and smart manner. But I myself, who happened to be present, neither approved at the time of what he said, lauding a man and at the same time doing him injury, nor do I think so now when I am of riper age. For in my opinion there is a wide difference in the character of a forceful man and an unscrupulous one, almost as great as that between an adroit and a mischievous one. The one quality may be said to be the best in the world and the other just the opposite. But owing to our prevalent lack of judgment, the two, having some points in common, meet with equal approbation and admiration.

IX. AFFAIRS OF ASIA

20. Apollonis,[73] the wife of Attalus, father of King Eumenes, was a native of Cyzicus, and for several reasons a very remarkable and praiseworthy woman. For the fact that being a simple citizen she became a queen and pre-

[73] The daughter of a citizen of Cyzicus, mother of the four sons of Attalus I. She was the recipient of cults at Hierapolis in Phrygia (*OGI* 308) and Teos in Ionia (*OGI* 309). A temple in her honor was erected at Cyzicus by her sons, decorated with reliefs depicting mythical scenes of children's love for their mother. The temple is celebrated by a series of epigrams (*AP* 3, nos. 1–19. F. Maltomini, *ASNP* 2002, 17–33 and 1.2a). An Athenian decree of 175/4 (*OGI* 248) praised her and Attalus for the exemplary education of their sons. She was given the epithet *Eusebes* (the Pious One) while she lived.

διεφύλαξε τὴν ὑπεροχὴν μέχρι τῆς τελευταίας, οὐχ
ἑταιρικὴν προσφερομένη πιθανότητα, σωφρονικὴν δὲ
καὶ πολιτικὴν σεμνότητα καὶ καλοκαγαθίαν, δικαία
3 τυγχάνειν τῆς ἐπ᾽ ἀγαθῷ μνήμης ἐστίν, καὶ καθότι
τέτταρας υἱοὺς γεννήσασα πρὸς πάντας τούτους
ἀνυπέρβλητον διεφύλαξε τὴν εὔνοιαν καὶ φιλοστορ-
γίαν μέχρι τῆς τοῦ βίου καταστροφῆς, καίτοι χρόνον
4 οὐκ ὀλίγον ὑπερβιώσασα τἀνδρός. πλὴν οἵγε περὶ τὸν
Ἄτταλον ἐν τῇ παρεπιδημίᾳ καλὴν περιεποιήσαντο
φήμην, ἀποδιδόντες τῇ μητρὶ τὴν καθήκουσαν χάριτα
5 καὶ τιμήν. ἄγοντες γὰρ ἐξ ἀμφοῖν τοῖν χεροῖν μέσην
αὐτῶν τὴν μητέρα περιῄεσαν τά θ᾽ ἱερὰ καὶ τὴν πόλιν
6 μετὰ τῆς θεραπείας. ἐφ᾽ οἷς οἱ θεώμενοι μεγάλως τοὺς
7 νεανίσκους ἀπεδέχοντο καὶ κατηξίουν καὶ μνημονεύ-
οντες τῶν περὶ τὸν Κλέοβιν καὶ Βίτωνα συνέκρινον
τὰς αἱρέσεις αὐτῶν, καὶ τὸ τῆς προθυμίας τῆς ἐκείνων
λαμπρὸν τῷ τῆς ὑπεροχῆς τῶν βασιλέων ἀξιώματι
8 συναναπληροῦντες. ταῦτα δ᾽ ἐτελέσθη ἐν Κυζίκῳ μετὰ
τὴν διάλυσιν τὴν πρὸς Προυσίαν τὸν βασιλέα.

21. Ὅτι Ὀρτιάγων ὁ Γαλάτης, τῶν ἐν τῇ Ἀσίᾳ
(xxii.21) βασιλεύων, ἐπεβάλετο τὴν ἁπάντων τῶν Γαλατῶν δυ-
2 ναστείαν εἰς αὑτὸν μεταστῆσαι, καὶ πολλὰ πρὸς
τοῦτο τὸ μέρος ἐφόδια προσεφέρετο καὶ φύσει καὶ
3 τριβῇ. καὶ γὰρ εὐεργετικὸς ἦν καὶ μεγαλόψυχος καὶ

---

74 Either Philetaerus or Athenaeus. Philetaerus was the first
of the brothers to die: *RE* Philetairos 2162 (W. Hoffmann).

75 Herodotus (1.31.1–5) has Solon tell King Croesus the story

served this dignity until the end without employing any seductive and meretricious art, but always exhibiting the gravity and excellence of a woman strict in her life and courteous in her demeanor, makes her worthy of honorable mention. Add to this that having given birth to four sons, she cherished for all of them up to her dying day an unsurpassed regard and affection, although she survived her husband for a considerable time. And Attalus and his brother[74] on their visit to the town showed due gratitude and respect to their mother. For, placing her between them and taking both her hands, they went round the temples and the city accompanied by their suites. All who witnessed it applauded and honored the young men for this, and, mindful of the story of Cleobis and Biton,[75] compared their conduct to this, and were thought to have made up for the splendor of the devotion of those with their exalted and royal status. This all happened in Cyzicus after the peace with King Prusias.[76]

(Suda)

21. Ortiagon,[77] one of the Galatian princes, formed the project of subjecting the whole of Galatia to his dominion; and for this purpose he possessed many advantages both natural and acquired. For he was munificent and mag-

of these brothers from Argos: what they did for her mother, how they were rewarded, and that a group representing them was dedicated by the citizens of Argos and dedicated to Delphi; this group has long been identified: A. Stewart, *Greek Sculpture* (New Haven 1990), 112. 342 and figs. 56–57.

[76] The peace was concluded in spring 183 (C. Habicht, *Hermes* 84 [1956] 96–100).

[77] See n. on 21.38.1.

4 κατὰ τὰς ἐντεύξεις εὔχαρις καὶ συνετός, τὸ δὲ συνέχον παρὰ Γαλάταις, ἀνδρώδης ἦν καὶ δυναμικὸς πρὸς
τὰς πολεμικὰς χρείας.

X. RES AEGYPTI

22. Ὅτι Ἀριστόνικος ὁ τοῦ Πτολεμαίου τοῦ βασι-
(xxiii.17) λέως Αἰγύπτου εὐνοῦχος μὲν ἦν, ἐκ παιδίου δ᾽ ἐγεγόνει
2 σύντροφος τῷ βασιλεῖ. τῆς δ᾽ ἡλικίας προβαινούσης
ἀνδρωδεστέραν εἶχεν ἢ κατ᾽ εὐνοῦχον τόλμαν καὶ
3 προαίρεσιν. καὶ γὰρ φύσει στρατιωτικὸς ἦν καὶ τὴν
πλείστην ἐποιεῖτο διατριβὴν ἐν τούτοις καὶ περὶ
4 ταῦτα. παραπλησίως δὲ καὶ κατὰ τὰς ἐντεύξεις ἱκανὸς
5 ὑπῆρχε καὶ τὸν κοινὸν νοῦν εἶχεν, ὃ σπάνιόν ἐστι. πρὸς
δὲ τούτοις πρὸς εὐεργεσίαν ἀνθρώπων πεφύκει καλῶς.

nanimous, his conversation was both charming and intelligent, and, what is most important among Gauls, he was brave and skilled in the art of war.

X. AFFAIRS OF EGYPT

(Suda)

22. Aristonicus[78] the servant of Ptolemy, king of Egypt, was a eunuch, but from childhood upward had been the king's intimate companion. As he grew older he showed himself more of a man in courage and general character than eunuchs generally are. For he was a born soldier, and spent most of his time with military men and in the study of military matters. He was also capable in conversation and he was liberal-minded, which is rare, and in addition to this he was naturally disposed to be beneficent.

[78] See n. on 17.6.

FRAGMENTA LIBRI XXIII

I. RES ITALIAE

1. Ὅτι κατὰ τὴν ἐνάτην καὶ τετταρακοστὴν ὀλυμ-
(xxiv.1) πιάδα πρὸς ταῖς ἑκατὸν εἰς τὴν Ῥώμην ἠθροίσθησαν
πρεσβειῶν πλῆθος ἀπὸ τῆς Ἑλλάδος, ὅσον οὐ ταχέως
2 πρότερον. τοῦ γὰρ Φιλίππου συγκλεισθέντος εἰς τὴν
κατὰ τὸ σύμβολον δικαιοδοσίαν πρὸς τοὺς ἀστυγεί-
τονας, καὶ τῶν Ῥωμαίων γνωσθέντων ὅτι προσδέ-
χονται τὰς κατὰ Φιλίππου κατηγορίας καὶ πρόνοιαν
ποιοῦνται τῆς ἀσφαλείας ⟨τῶν⟩ πρὸς αὐτὸν ἀμφισβη-
3 τούντων, ἅπαντες οἱ παρακείμενοι τῇ Μακεδονίᾳ παρῆσαν, οἱ μὲν κατ᾽ ἰδίαν, οἱ δὲ κατὰ πόλιν, οἱ δὲ κατὰ
4 τὰς ἐθνικὰς συστάσεις, ἐγκαλοῦντες τῷ Φιλίππῳ. σὺν
δὲ τούτοις οἱ παρ᾽ Εὐμένους ἧκον ἅμ᾽ Ἀθηναίῳ τῷ τοῦ
βασιλέως ἀδελφῷ, κατηγορήσοντες αὐτοῦ περί τε τῶν
ἐπὶ Θρᾴκης πόλεων καὶ περὶ τῆς ἀποσταλείσης
5 Προυσίᾳ βοηθείας. ἧκε δὲ καὶ Δημήτριος ὁ τοῦ Φιλίππου πρὸς πάντας τούτους ἀπολογησόμενος, ἔχων
Ἀπελλῆν καὶ Φιλοκλῆ μεθ᾽ αὑτοῦ, τοὺς τότε δοκοῦντας
6 εἶναι πρώτους φίλους τοῦ βασιλέως. παρῆσαν δὲ καὶ
παρὰ Λακεδαιμονίων πρέσβεις, ἀφ᾽ ἑκάστου γένους

FRAGMENTS OF BOOK XXIII

I. AFFAIRS OF ITALY

Embassies from Greece to Rome

(Cf. Livy 39.46.6)

1. In the 149th Olympiad so large a number of missions from Greece were assembled in Rome as had, perhaps, never been previously seen. For as Philip was strictly confined to the legal procedures prescribed in the conventions in dealing with his neighbors, and as it was known that the Romans were ready to listen to complaints against him, and looked after the safety of those who were at issue with him, all those on the frontiers of Macedonia had come, some individually and some representing cities or tribal groups, to accuse the king. Envoys also came from Eumenes, with Athenaeus, that king's brother, at their head, to bring charges against Philip on the subject of the Thracian cities and of the help he had sent to Prusias.[1] Demetrius, Philip's son, also appeared to defend his father against all the above, accompanied by Apelles and Philocles, who were then considered to be the chief friends of the king. There were also envoys from Lacedaemon rep-

---

[1] In the war between Eumenes and Prusias, for which see C. Habicht (18.7.6), 1–12 and 289.

7   τῶν ἐν τῇ πόλει. πρῶτον μὲν οὖν ἡ σύγκλητος εἰσεκαλέσατο τὸν Ἀθήναιον καὶ δεξαμένη τὸν στέφανον,
ὃν ἐκόμιζεν ἀπὸ μυρίων καὶ πεντακισχιλίων χρυσῶν,
ἐπῄνεσέ τε μεγαλομερῶς τὸν Εὐμένη καὶ τοὺς ἀδελφοὺς διὰ τῆς ἀποκρίσεως καὶ παρεκάλεσε μένειν ἐπὶ
8   τῆς αὐτῆς αἱρέσεως. ἐπὶ δὲ τούτῳ τὸν Δημήτριον εἰσ-
αγαγόντες οἱ στρατηγοὶ παρεκαλέσαντο τοὺς κατηγο-
ροῦντας τοῦ Φιλίππου πάντας καὶ παρῆγον κατὰ
9   μίαν πρεσβείαν. οὐσῶν δὲ τῶν πρεσβειῶν πολλῶν,
καὶ τῆς εἰσόδου τούτων γενομένης ἐπὶ τρεῖς ἡμέρας,
εἰς ἀπορίαν ἐνέπιπτεν ἡ σύγκλητος περὶ τοῦ πῶς δεῖ
10 χειρισθῆναι τὰ κατὰ μέρος. παρά τε γὰρ Θετταλῶν
καὶ κατὰ κοινὸν ἧκον καὶ κατ᾽ ἰδίαν ἀφ᾽ ἑκάστης πόλεως πρεσβευταί, παρά τε Περραιβῶν, ὁμοίως δὲ καὶ
παρ᾽ Ἀθαμάνων καὶ παρ᾽ Ἠπειρωτῶν καὶ παρ᾽ Ἰλ-
11 λυριῶν· ⟨ὧν⟩ οἱ μὲν περὶ χώρας, οἱ δὲ περὶ σωμάτων,
οἱ δὲ περὶ θρεμμάτων ἧκον ἀμφισβητοῦντες, ἔνιοι δὲ
περὶ συμβολαίων καὶ τῶν εἰς αὐτοὺς ἀδικημάτων,
12 τινὲς μὲν οὐ φάσκοντες δύνασθαι τυχεῖν τοῦ δικαίου
κατὰ τὸ σύμβολον διὰ τὸ τὸν Φίλιππον ἐκκόπτειν τὴν
δικαιοδοσίαν, τινὲς δ᾽ ἐγκαλοῦντες τοῖς κρίμασιν ὡς
παραβεβραβευμένοι, διαφθείραντος τοῦ Φιλίππου
13 τοὺς δικαστάς. καθόλου δὲ ποικίλη τις ἦν ἀκρισία καὶ
δυσχώρητος ἐκ τῶν κατηγορουμένων.

2. Ὅθεν ἡ σύγκλητος, οὔτ᾽ αὐτὴ δυναμένη διευ-
(xxiv.2)   κρινεῖν οὔτε τὸν Δημήτριον κρίνουσα δεῖν ἑκάστοις

450

resenting all the different factions[2] in that town. The senate summoned Athenaeus[3] in the first place, and, having received the crown he brought of the value of fifteen thousand gold staters, thanked Eumenes and his brothers profusely for their reply, and exhorted them to continue to maintain the same attitude. In the next place the consuls introduced Demetrius, and inviting all Philip's accusers to come forward, brought them in one by one. As these embassies were so numerous that it took three days to introduce them all, the senate was at a loss how to deal with all the details. For from Thessaly there was one embassy from the Confederacy[4] and particular ones from each town, and there were also embassies from Perrhaebia, Athamania, Epirus, and Illyria, some of them claiming territory, some slaves and some cattle, and others with complaints about the injustice they had suffered in their actions for the recovery of money, maintaining in some cases that they could not get justice in the authorized tribunals, as Philip quashed the proceedings, and in others finding fault with the decisions on the ground that the rulings were unfair, Philip having bribed the judges. So that on the whole the various accusations resulted in a confused and inextricable imbroglio.

2. Therefore the senate, unable itself to decide about all these matters, and thinking that Demetrius should not

2 There were four at the time; see 4.1–5.

3 The youngest brother of Eumenes.

4 Reorganized in 196, it received (some) laws by Flamininus: *SIG* 674, 63–64. H. Kramolisch, *Die Strategen des Thessalischen Bundes vom Jahr 196 v. Chr. bis zum Ausgang der römischen Republik* (Bonn 1978).

2 τούτων λόγον ὑπέχειν, ἅτε καὶ φιλανθρώπως πρὸς
αὐτὸν διακειμένη καὶ θεωροῦσα νέον ὄντα κομιδῇ καὶ
πολὺ τῆς τοιαύτης συστροφῆς καὶ ποικιλίας ἀπολει-
3 πόμενον, μάλιστα δὲ βουλομένη μὴ τῶν Δημητρίου
λόγων ἀκούειν, ἀλλὰ τῆς Φιλίππου γνώμης ἀληθινὴν
4 λαβεῖν πεῖραν, αὐτὸν Δημήτριον παρέλυσε τῆς δικαιολογίας, ἤρετο ⟨δὲ⟩ τὸν νεανίσκον καὶ τοὺς σὺν αὐτῷ
φίλους εἴ τινα περὶ τούτων ὑπομνηματισμὸν ἔχουσι
5 παρὰ τοῦ βασιλέως. τοῦ δὲ Δημητρίου φήσαντος
ἔχειν καὶ προτείναντός τι βυβλίδιον οὐ μέγα, λέγειν
αὐτὸν ἐκέλευσεν ἥνπερ τὰ ὑπομνήματα περιεῖχε πρὸς
ἕκαστον τῶν κατηγορουμένων ἀπόφασιν κεφαλαιώδη.
6 ὁ δὲ τὸ μὲν πεποιηκέναι τὸ προσταχθὲν ὑπὸ Ῥωμαίων
ἔφασκεν, ἢ τὴν αἰτίαν τοῦ μὴ πεπρᾶχθαι τοῖς ἐγκα-
7 λοῦσιν ἀνετίθει. προσέκειτο δὲ πρὸς ταῖς πλείσταις
ἀποφάσεσι "καίτοι οὐκ ἴσως χρησαμένων ἡμῖν τῶν
πρεσβευτῶν τῶν περὶ Καικίλιον ἐν τούτοις" καὶ πάλιν
8 "καίτοι γε οὐ δικαίως ἡμῶν ταῦτα πασχόντων." τοιαύτης δ᾽ οὔσης τῆς Φιλίππου γνώμης ἐν πάσαις ταῖς
ἀποφάσεσι, διακούσασα τῶν παραγεγονότων ἡ σύγ-
9 κλητος μίαν ἐποιήσατο περὶ πάντων διάληψιν. ἀποδε-
ξαμένη γὰρ τὸν Δημήτριον μεγαλομερῶς καὶ φιλανθρώπως διὰ τοῦ στρατηγοῦ, πολλοὺς καὶ παρακλητικοὺς
πρὸς αὐτὸν διαθεμένη λόγους, ἀπόκρισιν ἔδωκε διότι
περὶ πάντων καὶ τῶν εἰρημένων ὑπ᾽ αὐτοῦ καὶ τῶν
ἀνεγνωσμένων Δημητρίῳ πιστεύει διότι τὰ μὲν γέ-
10 γονε, τὰ δ᾽ ἔσται, καθάπερ δίκαιόν ἐστι γίνεσθαι. ἵνα
δὲ καὶ Φίλιππος εἰδῇ διότι τὴν χάριν ταύτην ἡ σύγ-

be forced to meet all these charges, as they were well
disposed toward him and saw that he was still quite young[5]
and very far from being competent to face such a whirl
of complications, and wishing particularly not to hear
speeches from Demetrius but to obtain some true test of
Philip's views, relieved the young man from pleading in
justification himself, but asked him and his friends who
were with him if they had any notes on all these matters
from the king. On Demetrius replying in the affirmative
and presenting a little notebook, they bade him give them
the general sense of the suggestions noted therein as a
reply to each of the charges. Philip in each case either
maintained that he had executed the orders of the Romans, or, if he had not done so, cast the blame on his accusers. He had added to most of his statements, "Although
Caecilius and the other legates did not deal fairly with us
in this case"; or again, "Although we were unjustly treated
in this case." Such being the tone of all Philip's statements, the senate, after listening to the envoys who had
arrived, came to one decision about all the questions. Having through the consul accorded a splendid and cordial
reception to Demetrius, and addressed him at length in
terms of encouragement, they gave as an answer that regarding all the matters on which he had spoken or read his
father's notes they accepted his word that strict justice
either had been done or would be done. And, that Philip
might see that this was a favor granted by the senate to

[5] He was in his early twenties.

κλητος Δημητρίῳ δίδωσιν, ἐξαποστελεῖν ἔφη πρεσβευτὰς ἐποψομένους εἰ γίνεται πάντα κατὰ τὴν τῆς συγκλήτου βούλησιν, ἅμα δὲ διασαφήσοντας τῷ βασιλεῖ
διότι τῆς συμπεριφορᾶς τυγχάνει ταύτης διὰ Δημή-
11 τριον. καὶ ταῦτα μὲν τοιαύτης ἔτυχε διεξαγωγῆς.

3. Μετὰ δὲ τούτους εἰσῆλθον οἱ παρ' Εὐμένους
(xxiv.3) πρέσβεις ⟨καὶ⟩περί τε τῆς βοηθείας τῆς ἀποσταλείσης
ὑπὸ τοῦ Φιλίππου τῷ Προυσίᾳ κατηγόρησαν καὶ περὶ
τῶν ἐπὶ Θρᾴκης τόπων, φάσκοντες οὐδ' ἔτι καὶ νῦν
2 αὐτὸν ἐξαγηοχέναι τὰς φρουρὰς ἐκ τῶν πόλεων. τοῦ
δὲ Φιλοκλέους ὑπὲρ τούτων βουληθέντος ἀπολογεῖσθαι
διὰ τὸ καὶ πρὸς τὸν Προυσίαν ⟨πε⟩πρεσβευκέναι καὶ
τότε περὶ τούτων ἐξαπεστάλθαι πρὸς τὴν σύγκλητον
3 ὑπὸ τοῦ Φιλίππου, βραχύν τινα χρόνον ἡ σύγκλητος
ἐπιδεξαμένη τοὺς λόγους ἔδωκεν ἀπόκρισιν διότι, τῶν
ἐπὶ Θρᾴκης τόπων ἐὰν μὴ καταλάβωσιν οἱ πρεσβευταὶ
πάντα διῳκημένα κατὰ τὴν τῆς συγκλήτου γνώμην
καὶ πάσας τὰς πόλεις εἰς τὴν Εὐμένους πίστιν ἐγκε-
χειρισμένας, οὐκέτι δυνήσεται φέρειν οὐδὲ καρτερεῖν
παρακουομένη περὶ τούτων.

4 Καὶ τῆς μὲν Φιλίππου καὶ Ῥωμαίων παρατριβῆς
ἐπὶ πολὺ προβαινούσης ἐπίστασις ἐγενήθη κατὰ τὸ
5 παρὸν διὰ τὴν τοῦ Δημητρίου παρουσίαν· πρὸς μέντοι γε τὴν καθόλου τῆς οἰκίας ἀτυχίαν οὐ μικρὰ συνέβη τὴν εἰς τὴν Ῥώμην τοῦ νεανίσκου πρεσβείαν
6 συμβαλέσθαι. ἥ τε γὰρ σύγκλητος ἀπερεισαμένη τὴν
χάριν ἐπὶ τὸν Δημήτριον ἐμετεώρισε μὲν τὸ μειράκιον, ἐλύπησε δὲ καὶ τὸν Περσέα καὶ τὸν Φίλιππον

Demetrius, they said that they would dispatch a commission to see if everything was being done as the senate desired and to inform the king at the same time that he met with this indulgence owing to Demetrius. Such was the issue of this matter.

3. The envoys of Eumenes were the next to enter. Their accusations related to the armed support sent by Philip to Prusias and to his treatment of the places in Thrace, where they said he had not even yet withdrawn his garrisons from the towns. Upon Philocles expressing his desire to offer a defense on these subjects, as he had both been on a mission to Prusias and had now been sent to the senate by Philip expressly for this purpose, the senate, after listening for a short time to what he said, gave him the following reply. If their commissioners did not find that all their wishes had been carried out, and all the cities put into the hands of Eumenes, they would no longer be able to submit to delay or tolerate disobedience in this matter.

The friction between Philip and the senate was becoming very acute when for the present it was thus arrested by the presence in Rome of Demetrius. The young man's embassy, however, contributed in no small measure to the ultimate misfortunes of the House of Macedon. For the senate, by granting this favor to Demetrius, turned that young man's head and gravely offended both Perseus and

ἰσχυρῶς τῷ δοκεῖν μὴ δι' αὐτούς, ἀλλὰ διὰ Δημήτριον

7 τυγχάνειν τῆς παρὰ Ῥωμαίων φιλανθρωπίας. ὅ τε Τίτος ἐκκαλεσάμενος τὸ μειράκιον καὶ προβιβάσας εἰς
λόγους ἀπορρήτους, οὐκ ὀλίγα συνεβάλετο πρὸς τὴν

8 αὐτὴν ὑπόθεσιν. τόν τε γὰρ νεανίσκον ἐψυχαγώγησεν,
ὡς αὐτίκα μάλα συγκατασκευασόντων αὐτῷ Ῥωμαίων
τὴν βασιλείαν, τούς τε περὶ τὸν Φίλιππον ἠρέθισε,
γράψας ἐξ αὐτῆς τὸν Δημήτριον ἀποστέλλειν πάλιν
εἰς τὴν Ῥώμην μετὰ τῶν φίλων ὡς πλείστων καὶ χρη-

9 σιμωτάτων. ταύταις γὰρ ταῖς ἀφορμαῖς χρησάμενος
ὁ Περσεὺς μετ' ὀλίγον ἔπεισε τὸν πατέρα συγκαταθέ-

10 σθαι τῷ Δημητρίου θανάτῳ. Περὶ μὲν οὖν τούτων ὡς
ἐχειρίσθη τὰ κατὰ μέρος ἐν τοῖς ἑξῆς δηλώσομεν.

(xxiv.4)   4. ἐπὶ δὲ τούτοις εἰσεκλήθησαν οἱ παρὰ τῶν Λακε-

2 δαιμονίων πρέσβεις. τούτων δ' ἦσαν διαφοραὶ τέτ-
ταρες. οἱ μὲν γὰρ περὶ Λῦσιν ἥκοντες ⟨ὑπὲρ⟩ τῶν
ἀρχαίων φυγάδων ἐπρέσβευον, φάσκοντες δεῖν ἔχειν
αὐτοὺς πάσας τὰς κτήσεις, ἀφ' ὧν ἐξ ἀρχῆς ἔφυγον·

3 οἱ δὲ περὶ τὸν Ἀρέα καὶ τὸν Ἀλκιβιάδην, ἐφ' ᾧ ταλαν-
τιαίαν λαβόντες κτῆσιν ἐκ τῶν ἰδίων τὰ λοιπὰ διαδοῦ-

4 ναι τοῖς ἀξίοις τῆς πολιτείας. Σήριππος δ' ἐπρέσβευε
περὶ τοῦ μένειν τὴν ὑποκειμένην κατάστασιν, ἣν ἔχοντές

5 ποτε συνεπολιτεύοντο μετὰ τῶν Ἀχαιῶν. ἀπὸ δὲ τῶν
τεθανατωμένων καὶ τῶν ἐκπεπτωκότων κατὰ τὰ τῶν
Ἀχαιῶν δόγματα παρῆσαν οἱ περὶ Χαίρωνα, κάθοδον
αὐτοῖς ἀξιοῦντες συγχωρηθῆναι καὶ τὴν πολιτείαν

6 ἀποκατασταθῆναι τοιαύτην, . . . ἐποιοῦντο πρὸς τοὺς

7 Ἀχαιοὺς οἰκείους ταῖς ἰδίαις ὑποθέσεσι λόγους. οὐ

Philip by the thought that the Romans had shown them kindness not for their own sakes but for that of Demetrius. Flamininus also, by inviting the young man's confidences and eliciting his secrets, contributed much to the same result, as he deluded him into cherishing the idea that the Romans were about to secure the throne for him at once, at the same time irritating Philip by writing to him to send Demetrius at once back to Rome with as many of his most serviceable friends as possible. For this was the pretext that Perseus soon after used to persuade his father to consent to the death of Demetrius.

4. How all this was brought about I will show in detail further on. The next envoys to be introduced were those from the Spartans. Of these there were four sets. Lysis and others came on behalf of the old exiles,[6] maintaining that they ought to recover all the property they had when first exiled: Areus and Alcibiades proposed that they should, upon receiving back their own property to the value of a talent, distribute the rest among those worthy of citizenship. Serippus[7] was in favor of the present conditions, which they had been enjoying during such time as they were members of the Achaean Confederacy, while Chaeron[8] and others appeared on behalf of those condemned to death or exiled by the decree of the Achaeans, demanding their recall and the restoration of the constitution . . . they addressed the Achaeans in terms which suited

[6] Represented by Lysis and (for a splinter group) by Areus and Alcibiades (4.3). See also 5.18.   [7] He spoke for the pro-Achaean Spartans; Errington (20.3.5), 180–181.

[8] He acted for those Spartans that were condemned or exiled by the Achaeans; Errington (previous n.) 181.

δυναμένη ⟨δὲ⟩ διευκρινεῖν ἡ σύγκλητος τὰς κατὰ μέρος διαφοράς, προεχειρίσατο τρεῖς ἄνδρας τοὺς καὶ
πρότερον ἤδη πεπρεσβευκότας περὶ τούτων εἰς τὴν
Πελοπόννησον· οὗτοι δ᾽ ἦσαν Τίτος, Κόιντος Καικί-
8 λιος, ⟨Ἄππιος Κλαύδιος⟩. ἐφ᾽ οἷς γενομένων λόγων
πλειόνων, ὑπὲρ μὲν τοῦ καταπορεύεσθαι τοὺς πεφευ-
γότας καὶ τεθανατωμένους καὶ περὶ τοῦ μένειν τὴν
9 πόλιν μετὰ τῶν Ἀχαιῶν ἐγένετο πᾶσι σύμφωνον, περὶ
δὲ τῶν κτήσεων, πότερον δεῖ τὸ τάλαντον εἰς ἑκάστους
τοὺς φυγάδας ἐκ τῶν ἰδίων ἐκλέξασθαι ..., περὶ τού-
10 των διημφισβήτουν πρὸς ἀλλήλους. ἵνα δὲ μὴ πάλιν
ἐξ ἀκεραίου περὶ πάντων ἀντιλέγοιεν, ἔγγραπτον ὑπὲρ
τῶν ὁμολογουμένων ..., ἐφ᾽ ὃ πάντες ἐπέβαλοντο τὰς
11 ἰδίας σφραγῖδας. οἱ δὲ περὶ τὸν Τίτον βουλόμενοι καὶ
τοὺς Ἀχαιοὺς εἰς τὴν ὁμολογίαν ἐμπλέξαι, προσεκα-
12 λέσαντο τοὺς περὶ Ξέναρχον. οὗτοι γὰρ ἐπρέσβευον
τότε παρὰ τῶν Ἀχαιῶν, ἅμα μὲν ἀνανεούμενοι τὴν
συμμαχίαν, ἅμα δὲ τῇ τῶν Λακεδαιμονίων διαφορᾷ
13 προσεδρεύοντες. καὶ παρὰ τὴν προσδοκίαν ἐρωτώμενοι
περὶ τῶν γραφομένων, εἰ συνευδοκοῦσιν, οὐκ οἶδ᾽ ὅπως
14 εἰς ἀπορίαν ἐνέπεσον. δυσηρεστοῦντο μὲν γὰρ τῇ
καθόδῳ τῶν φυγάδων καὶ τῶν τεθανατωμένων διὰ τὸ
γίνεσθαι παρὰ τὰ τῶν Ἀχαιῶν δόγματα καὶ παρὰ τὴν
στήλην, εὐδοκοῦντο δὲ τοῖς ὅλοις τῷ γράφεσθαι διότι
⟨δεῖ⟩ τὴν πόλιν τῶν Λακεδαιμονίων πολιτεύειν μετὰ
15 τῶν Ἀχαιῶν. καὶ πέρας τὰ μὲν ἀπορούμενοι, τὰ δὲ
καταπληττόμενοι τοὺς ἄνδρας, ἐπεβάλοντο τὴν σφρα-
16 γῖδα. ἡ δὲ σύγκλητος προχειρισαμένη Κόιντον Μάρ-

their own views. The senate, unable to come to a decision about these various differences, delegated that duty to three men who had formerly acted as commissioners[9] in the Peloponnese, Flamininus, Quintus Caecilius, and Appius Claudius. After listening to various arguments, they were all in agreement as to the restoration of the exiles and those condemned to death, and as to Sparta's remaining a member of the Achaean League: but on the question of the property—whether the talent's worth of his own property should be assigned to each exile or whether . . . they differed. But in order that the whole matter should not be rediscussed from the beginning, they drew up a written agreement about the points not in dispute to which all the parties affixed their seals. Flamininus and his colleagues, wishing to involve the Achaeans in this agreement, invited Xenarchus[10] to meet them along with the others who had been sent as envoys at the time by the Achaeans, partly to renew the alliance and partly to watch the result of the various demands made by the Spartans. Contrary to his expectation, when asked if they approved of the written agreement they for some reason or other hesitated. On the one hand they were not pleased with the recall of the exiles and of those put to death, because it was contrary to the Achaean decree as inscribed on the column; but they were on the whole pleased, because it was written in the agreement that Sparta was to remain a member of the Achaean League. At length, however, partly out of inability to decide, and partly from fear of Flamininus and his colleagues, they affixed their seal. The senate now ap-

9 *MRR* 1.380.   10 *RE* Xenarchos 1420–1421 (C. Habicht). He was the brother of Archon of Aegira (n. on 22.10.8).

κιον πρεσβευτὴν ἐξαπέστελλεν ἐπί τε τὰ κατὰ Μακεδονίαν καὶ τὰ κατὰ Πελοπόννησον.

5. Ὅτι Δεινοκράτης ὁ Μεσσήνιος παραγενόμενος
(xxiv.5) εἰς τὴν Ῥώμην πρεσβευτὴς καὶ καταλαβὼν τὸν Τίτον
πρεσβευτὴν καθεσταμένον ὑπὸ τῆς συγκλήτου πρός
2 τε Προυσίαν καὶ τὸν Σέλευκον, περιχαρὴς ἐγενήθη, νομίζων τὸν Τίτον διά τε τὴν πρὸς αὐτὸν φιλίαν—ἐγεγόνει γὰρ αὐτῷ συνήθης κατὰ τὸν Λακωνικὸν πόλεμον—καὶ διὰ τὴν πρὸς τὸν Φιλοποίμενα διαφοράν,
παραγενόμενον εἰς τὴν Ἑλλάδα, χειριεῖν τὰ κατὰ τὴν
3 Μεσσήνην πάντα κατὰ τὴν αὐτοῦ προαίρεσιν. διὸ καὶ
παρεὶς τἆλλα προσεκαρτέρει τῷ Τίτῳ καὶ πάσας εἰς
τοῦτον ἀπηρείσατο τὰς ἐλπίδας.

4 Ὅτι Δεινοκράτης ὁ Μεσσήνιος ἦν οὐ μόνον κατὰ
τὴν τριβήν, ἀλλὰ καὶ κατὰ τὴν φύσιν αὐλικὸς καὶ
5 στρατιωτικὸς ἄνθρωπος. τὸν δὲ πραγματικὸν τρόπον
ἐπέφαινε μὲν τέλειον, ἦν δὲ ψευδεπίγραφος καὶ ῥωπι-
6 κός. ἔν τε γὰρ τοῖς πολεμικοῖς κατὰ μὲν τὴν εὐχέρειαν
καὶ τὴν τόλμαν πολὺ διέφερε τῶν ἄλλων καὶ λαμπρὸς
7 ἦν ἐν τοῖς κατ᾽ ἰδίαν κινδύνοις. ὁμοίως δὲ καὶ κατὰ
τὴν ἄλλην διάθεσιν ἐν μὲν ταῖς ὁμιλίαις εὔχαρις καὶ
πρόχειρος ἦν, παρά τε τὰς συνουσίας εὐτράπελος καὶ
8 πολιτικός, ἅμα δὲ τούτοις φιλέραστος, περὶ δὲ κοινῶν
ἢ πολιτικῶν πραγμάτων ἀτενίσαι καὶ προϊδέσθαι τὸ
μέλλον ἀσφαλῶς, ἔτι δὲ παρασκευάσασθαι καὶ δια-

---

[11] Quintus Marcius Philippus, consul 186 and 169. *MRR*
1.379.

pointed Quintus Marcius Philippus[11] their legate, and dispatched him to Macedonia and the Peloponnese.

Deinocrates of Messene

(Cf. Livy 39.51)

5. Deinocrates[12] of Messene, on arriving at Rome on a mission from his country and learning that Flamininus had been appointed by the senate its legate to Prusias and Seleucus, was overjoyed, thinking that Flamininus, both owing to his personal friendship with himself—for they had become well acquainted during the war[13] in Laconia—and owing to his difference with Philopoemen, would upon arriving in Greece manage the affairs of Messene entirely as he himself desired. So neglecting to take any other steps he remained in close attendance on Flamininus and rested all his hopes on him.

Deinocrates of Messene was a soldier and a courtier not only by practice but by nature. He gave one perfectly the impression of being a capable man, but his capacity was but counterfeit and pinchbeck. For in war, to begin with, he was highly distinguished by his courageous daring, and was magnificent in particular engagements; and similarly, as regards his other qualities, his conversation was charming and unembarrassed, and in convivial society he was versatile and urbane and also fond of lovemaking. But as regards public or political affairs he was perfectly incapable of concentrated attention and clear insight into

[12] The leading Messenian since ca. 195; *RE* Messenien (Suppl. 15), 275–277 (E. Meyer).

[13] Against Nabis in 195 (Livy 39.24.5–40.4).

9 λεχθῆναι πρὸς πλῆθος, εἰς τέλος ἀδύνατος. καὶ τότε
κεκινηκὼς ἀρχὴν μεγάλων κακῶν τῇ πατρίδι, τελείως
οὐδὲν ᾤετο ποιεῖν, ἀλλὰ τὴν αὐτὴν ἀγωγὴν ἦγε τοῦ
βίου, προορώμενος οὐδὲν τῶν μελλόντων, ἐρῶν δὲ καὶ
κωθωνιζόμενος ἀφ᾽ ἡμέρας καὶ τοῖς ἀκροάμασι τὰς
10 ἀκοὰς ἀνατεθεικώς. βραχεῖαν δέ τινα τῆς περιστά-
11 σεως ἔμφασιν ὁ Τίτος αὐτὸν ἠνάγκασε λαβεῖν. ἰδὼν
γὰρ αὐτὸν παρὰ πότον ἐν μακροῖς ἱματίοις ὀρχούμενον,
παρ᾽ αὐτὰ μὲν ἐσιώπησε, τῇ δ᾽ αὔριον ἐντυγχάνοντος
αὐτοῦ καί τι περὶ τῆς πατρίδος ἀξιοῦντος "ἐγὼ μέν, ὦ
12 Δεινοκράτη, πᾶν" ἔφη "ποιήσω τὸ δυνατόν· ἐπὶ δὲ σοῦ
θαυμάζω πῶς δύνῃ παρὰ πότον ὀρχεῖσθαι, τηλικού-
των πραγμάτων ἀρχὴν κεκινηκὼς ἐν τοῖς Ἕλλησιν."
13 ἐδόκει δὲ τότε βραχύ τι συσταλῆναι καὶ μαθεῖν ὡς
ἀνοίκειον ὑπόθεσιν τῆς ἰδίας αἱρέσεως καὶ φύσεως
ἀποδέδωκε.

Πλὴν τότε παρῆν εἰς τὴν Ἑλλάδα μετὰ τοῦ Τίτου
14 πεπεισμένος ἐξ ἐφόδου τὰ κατὰ τὴν Μεσσήνην χει-
ρισθήσεσθαι κατὰ τὴν αὑτοῦ βούλησιν. οἱ δὲ περὶ
τὸν Φιλοποίμενα, σαφῶς ἐπεγνωκότες ὅτι περὶ τῶν
15 Ἑλληνικῶν ὁ Τίτος οὐδεμίαν ἐντολὴν ἔχει παρὰ τῆς
συγκλήτου, τὴν ἡσυχίαν εἶχον, καραδοκοῦντες αὐτοῦ
16 τὴν παρουσίαν. ἐπεὶ δὲ καταπλεύσας εἰς Ναύπακτον
ἔγραψε τῷ στρατηγῷ καὶ τοῖς δαμιουργοῖς τῶν
Ἀχαιῶν, καλέων συνάγειν τοὺς Ἀχαιοὺς εἰς ἐκκλη-
17 σίαν, ἀντέγραψαν αὐτῷ διότι ποιήσουσιν, ἂν γράψῃ

the future, as well as of preparing and delivering a speech to the people. At present, when he had just begun a series of terrible calamities for his country, he simply fancied that his action was of no importance, and went on living in his usual manner, foreseeing nothing of what would happen, but occupied with love affairs, drinking deep from an early hour, and listening to musicians. Flamininus, however, compelled him to realize in a measure the real situation; for once when he saw him at a party dancing in a long robe, he held his peace at the time, but next day, when Deinocrates came to see him and made some request about Messene, he said, "I, Deinocrates, will do what I can; but as for you I am surprised how you can dance at parties, after having set afoot matters of such import for Greece." He then for a time appeared to put a check on himself and realize that he had given an unsuitable impression of his own character and nature.

However, he appeared now in Greece with Flamininus, convinced that he had only to show his face for the affairs of Messene to be arranged as he wished. But Philopoemen, well knowing that Flamininus had no instructions from the senate regarding the affairs of Greece, kept quiet awaiting his arrival, and when, on disembarking at Naupactus, he wrote to the strategus and damiurges[14] of the Achaeans, ordering them to call the general assembly of the Achaeans, they replied that they would do so upon his informing them on what subjects he wished to

[14] Board of magistrates, ten at the time; J. A. O. Larsen, *Greek Federal States* (Oxford 1968), 221–223. Ch. Veligianni-Terzi, *Damiurgen. Zur Entwicklung einer Magistratur* (Diss. Heidelberg 1977), 106–107.

περὶ τίνων βούλεται διαλεχθῆναι τοῖς Ἀχαιοῖς· τοὺς
γὰρ νόμους ταῦτα τοῖς ἄρχουσιν ἐπιτάττειν. τοῦ δὲ μὴ
18 τολμῶντος γράφειν, αἱ μὲν τοῦ Δεινοκράτους ἐλπίδες
καὶ τῶν ἀρχαίων λεγομένων φυγάδων, τότε δὲ προσφάτως ἐκ τῆς Λακεδαίμονος ἐκπεπτωκότων, καὶ συλλήβδην ἡ τοῦ Τίτου παρουσία καὶ προσδοκία τοῦτον
τὸν τρόπον διέπεσεν.

II. RES GRAECIAE

6. Ὅτι κατὰ τοὺς αὐτοὺς καιροὺς ἐξαπεστάλησαν
(xxiv.11) ὑπὸ τῶν ἐκ Λακεδαίμονος φυγάδων πρέσβεις εἰς τὴν
Ῥώμην, ἐν οἷς ἦν Ἀρκεσίλαος καὶ Ἀγησίπολις, ὃς ἔτι
2 παῖς ὢν ἐγενήθη βασιλεὺς ἐν τῇ Σπάρτῃ. τούτους μὲν
οὖν λῃσταί τινες περιπεσόντες ἐν τῷ πελάγει διέφθει-
3 ραν, οἱ δὲ μετὰ τούτων κατασταθέντες διεκομίσθησαν
εἰς τὴν Ῥώμην.

III. RES MACEDONIAE

7. Ὅτι τοῦ Δημητρίου παραγενηθέντος ἐκ τῆς
(xxiii.7) Ῥώμης εἰς τὴν Μακεδονίαν καὶ κομίζοντος τὰς ἀποκρίσεις, ἐν αἷς οἱ Ῥωμαῖοι πᾶσαν τὴν ἐξ αὐτῶν χάριν
καὶ πίστιν εἰς τὸν Δημήτριον ἀπηρείδοντο καὶ διὰ
2 τοῦτον ἔφασαν πάντα πεποιηκέναι καὶ ποιήσειν, οἱ
μὲν Μακεδόνες ἀπεδέχοντο τὸν Δημήτριον, μεγάλων
3 ὑπολαμβάνοντες ἀπολελύσθαι φόβων καὶ κινδύνων—
προσεδόκων γὰρ ὅσον οὔπω τὸν ἀπὸ Ῥωμαίων πόλε-

address the Achaeans; for that was the course imposed on the magistrates by their laws. As Flamininus did not venture to reply, the hopes of Deinocrates and of the "old exiles," as they were called, who had then quite recently been exiled from Sparta, and in general the expectations created by Flamininus' arrival came to nothing.

II. AFFAIRS OF GREECE

The Spartan Envoys

6. At the same time envoys were sent by the Lacedaemonian exiles to Rome, among them being Arcesilaus and Agesipolis,[15] who as a boy had been king of Sparta. They were both caught and murdered at sea by some pirates, but their colleagues were conveyed to Rome.

184/3 B.C.

III. AFFAIRS OF MACEDONIA

(Cp. Livy 39.53)

7. When Demetrius reached Macedonia from Rome, bringing the reply in which the Romans attributed to this prince all the favor and confidence they had shown, saying that all that they had done or would do was for his sake, the Macedonians gave him a good reception, thinking that they had thus been freed from great apprehension and peril—for they had quite expected that owing to the fric-

184/3 B.C.

---

[15] The former is otherwise unknown, Agesipolis had briefly been king in 219: 4.35.10–14.

4 μον ἐπ᾽ αὐτοὺς ἥξειν διὰ τὰς τοῦ Φιλίππου παρα-
τριβάς—ὁ δὲ Φίλιππος καὶ Περσεὺς οὐχ ἡδέως ἑώρων
τὸ γινόμενον, οὐδ᾽ ἤρεσεν αὐτοῖς τὸ δοκεῖν τοὺς
Ῥωμαίους αὐτῶν μὲν μηθένα λόγον ποιεῖσθαι, τῷ δὲ
5 Δημητρίῳ πᾶσαν ἀνατιθέναι τὴν ἐξ αὐτῶν χάριν. οὐ
μὴν <ἀλλ᾽> ὁ μὲν Φίλιππος ἐπεκρύπτετο τὴν ἐπὶ τούτοις δυσαρέστησιν, ὁ δὲ Περσεύς, οὐ μόνον ἐν τῇ
πρὸς Ῥωμαίους εὐνοίᾳ παρὰ πολὺ τἀδελφοῦ λειπόμε-
νος, ἀλλὰ καὶ περὶ τἄλλα πάντα καθυστερῶν καὶ τῇ
6 φύσει καὶ τῇ κατασκευῇ, δυσχερῶς ἔφερε· τὸ δὲ συνέχον, ἐδεδίει περὶ τῆς ἀρχῆς, μὴ πρεσβύτερος ὢν
7 ἐξωσθῇ διὰ τὰς προειρημένας αἰτίας. διὸ τούς τε φίλους ἔφθειρε τοὺς τοῦ Δημητρίου . . .

8. Ὅτι τῶν περὶ τὸν Κόιντον τὸν Μάρκιον πρεσβευ-
(xxiv.6) σάντων εἰς Μακεδονίαν, ἀπέβη μὲν ἀπὸ τῶν ἐπὶ Θράκης Ἑλληνίδων πόλεων ὁλοσχερῶς ὁ Φίλιππος καὶ
τὰς φρουρὰς ἐξήγαγεν, ἀπέβη δὲ βαρυνόμενος καὶ
2 στένων. διωρθώσατο δὲ καὶ τἄλλα πάντα, περὶ ὧν
οἱ Ῥωμαῖοι ἐπέταττον, βουλόμενος ἐκείνοις μὲν μηδεμίαν ἔμφασιν ποιεῖν ἀλλοτριότητος, λαμβάνειν
δ᾽ ἀναστροφὴν πρὸς τὰς εἰς τὸν πόλεμον παρασκευάς.
3 τηρῶν δὲ τὴν προκειμένην ὑπόθεσιν, ἐξῆγε στρατιὰν
4 ἐπὶ τοὺς βαρβάρους. διελθὼν δὲ διὰ μέσης τῆς
Θράκης ἐνέβαλεν εἰς Ὀδρύσας <καὶ> Βέσσους καὶ
5 Δενθηλήτους. παραγενόμενος δ᾽ ἐπὶ τὴν προσαγορευ-

---

16 The passage is lost. Perseus was not a legitimate son of
Philip: Livy 39.53.3.

tion between Philip and the Romans a war with Rome was immediately imminent; but Philip and Perseus viewed it all with no favorable eyes, as it did not please them to think that the Romans treated them as if of no account, but credited Demetrius with all the favor they had shown. Philip, however, continued to conceal his displeasure; but Perseus, who was much less well disposed to the Romans than his brother, and much inferior to him in all other respects both by nature and by training, was deeply aggrieved. His principal fear was for the throne, lest, although the elder son, he might be excluded from it for the above reasons.[16] He therefore not only corrupted the friends of Demetrius . . .

(Cf. Livy, 39.53)

8. Upon the arrival in Macedonia of Quintus Marcius and the other Roman legates, Philip entirely evacuated the Greek towns in Thrace, withdrawing his garrisons, but he relinquished them in a sullen and grumbling spirit and with many sighs. He also set right all the other matters about which the Romans directed him, as he wished to give them no sign of hostility and thus gain time to make his preparations for war. Adhering to his resolve he now made an expedition against the barbarians. Passing through central Thrace he invaded the country of the Odrysians, the Bessi, and the Dentheleti.[17] On his arrival at Philippopolis,[18] the inhabitants fled to the hills, and he

---

[17] For the various Thracian tribes, see *RE* Thrake 405–406; for Philip's campaign of 183, ibid. 436–437 (B. Lenk). Z. H. Archibald, *The Odrysian Kingdom of Thrace* . . . (Oxford 1998).

[18] Today Plovdiv, founded by Philip II. *RE* Philippopolis 2244–2263 (Ch. M. Danoff). The inscriptions from the city and its territory, close to seven hundred, collected in *IGBulg.* III 1.

ομένην Φιλίππου πόλιν, φυγόντων τῶν ἐνοικούντων
6 εἰς τὰς ἀκρωρείας, ἐξ ἐφόδου κατέσχε τὴν πόλιν. μετὰ
δὲ ταῦτα πᾶν τὸ πεδίον ἐπιδραμὼν καὶ τοὺς μὲν
ἐκπορθήσας, παρ' ὧν δὲ πίστεις λαβών, ἐπανῆλθε,
7 φρουρὰν καταλιπὼν ἐν τῇ Φιλίππου πόλει. ταύτην δὲ
συνέβη μετά τινα χρόνον ἐκπεσεῖν ὑπὸ τῶν Ὀδρυσῶν,
ἀθετησάντων τὰς πρὸς τὸν βασιλέα πίστεις.

IV. RES ITALIAE

9. Ὅτι κατὰ τὸ δεύτερον ἔτος ἡ σύγκλητος, παρα-
(xxiv.10) γενομένων πρέσβεων παρ' Εὐμένους καὶ Φαρνάκου
<καὶ Φιλίππου> καὶ παρὰ τοῦ τῶν Ἀχαιῶν ἔθνους, ἔτι
δὲ παρὰ τῶν ἐκ τῆς Λακεδαίμονος ἐκπεπτωκότων καὶ
παρὰ τῶν κατεχόντων τὴν πόλιν, ἐχρημάτισε τούτοις.
2 ἧκον δὲ καὶ Ῥόδιοι πρεσβεύοντες ὑπὲρ τῆς Σινωπέων
3 ἀτυχίας. τούτοις μὲν οὖν καὶ τοῖς παρ' Εὐμένους καὶ
Φαρνάκου πρεσβεύουσιν ἡ σύγκλητος ἀπεκρίθη διότι
πέμψει πρεσβευτὰς τοὺς ἐπισκεψομένους περί τε Σινωπέων καὶ περὶ τῶν τοῖς βασιλεῦσιν ἀμφισβητου-
4 μένων. τοῦ δὲ Κοΐντου Μαρκίου προσφάτως ἐκ τῆς

---

[19] Pharnaces I, king of Pontus. He was king in the year of the
Athenian archon Tychandrus *I Délos* 1497 *bis*, who is now dated
to 196/5 (St. V. Tracy, *MDAI (A)* 107 [1992], 307–314). He died
in 170/69, as P. 27.17 indicates (the note on this in WC 3.318 is
no longer valid).   [20] See H. Heinen in A. Coşkun (ed.),
*Roms auswärtige Freunde in der späten Republik und im frühen
Prinzipat* (Göttingen 2005), 31–44.

took the city at once. After this he raided the whole plain, and, after devastating the lands of some and receiving the submission of others, he returned, leaving in Philippopolis a garrison which was shortly afterward expelled by the Odrysians, who broke their pledges to the king.

IV. AFFAIRS OF ITALY

Greek Embassies in Rome. Report of Marcius

(Cf. Livy 40.2.6)

9. In the second year of this Olympiad (149) upon the arrival in Rome of embassies from Eumenes, Pharnaces[19] and Philip, from the Achaean League, and from both the exiled Lacedaemonians and those in possession of the city, the senate gave them all audience.[20] Envoys also came from Rhodes on the subject of the calamity that had overtaken Sinope.[21] To these last and the envoys of Eumenes and Pharnaces the Senate replied that they would send legates to inquire about Sinope and about the disputes between the two kings. Quintus Marcius[22] had recently

183–182 B.C.

[21] The city had been attacked in 220 by King Mithridates II of Pontus, but successfully defended, with support from Rhodes (4.56.1–9 and nn.). Pharnaces, however, seized it in 183, which led to the war against Eumenes, Prusias II, and Ariarathes of Cappadocia, for which see *CAH* (2nd ed.) 8 (1989), 328–330 (C. Habicht), with the important correction in Habicht (18.7.6), p. 296, n. 14: The traditional date for the peace treaty *(IPE* 1^2 402) of 179 is, after all, correct. See, however, now Chr. Müller, *D'Olbia à Tanais* (Bordeaux 2010), 93–95 and nn. 104–130.

[22] 4.16.

Ἑλλάδος παραγεγονότος καὶ περί τε τῶν ἐν Μακεδονίᾳ
καὶ περὶ τῶν ἐν Πελοποννήσῳ διασεσαφηκότος, οὐκέτι
5 πολλῶν προσεδεήθη λόγων ἡ σύγκλητος, ἀλλ᾽ εἰσ-
καλεσαμένη καὶ τοὺς ἀπὸ Πελοποννήσου καὶ Μακεδονίας πρεσβεύοντας διήκουσε μὲν τῶν λόγων, τάς γε
μὴν ἀποκρίσεις ἔδωκε καὶ τὴν διάληψιν ἐποιήσατο
τῶν πραγμάτων οὐ πρὸς τοὺς τῶν πρεσβευτῶν λόγους, ἀλλὰ πρὸς τὴν ἀποπρεσβείαν ἁρμοσαμένη τοῦ
6 Μαρκίου. ὃς ὑπὲρ μὲν τοῦ Φιλίππου τοῦ βασιλέως
ἀπηγγέλκει διότι πεποίηκε μὲν τὰ προσταττόμενα,
πεποίηκε δὲ τὰ πάντα βαρυνόμενος, καὶ <καθ>ότι
7 λαβὼν καιρὸν πᾶν τι ποιήσει κατὰ Ῥωμαίων. διὸ καὶ
τοῖς μὲν παρὰ τοῦ Φιλίππου πρεσβευταῖς τοιαύτην
ἔδωκε τὴν ἀπόκρισιν, δι᾽ ἧς ἐπὶ μὲν τοῖς γεγονόσιν
ἐπῄνει τὸν Φίλιππον, εἰς δὲ τὸ λοιπὸν ᾤετο δεῖν προσέχειν αὐτὸν ἵνα μηδὲν ὑπεναντίον φαίνηται πράττων
8 Ῥωμαίοις. περὶ δὲ τῶν κατὰ Πελοπόννησον ὁ Μάρ-
κιος τοιαύτην ἐπεποίητο τὴν ἀπαγγελίαν διότι, τῶν
Ἀχαιῶν οὐ βουλομένων ἀναφέρειν οὐδὲν ἐπὶ τὴν σύγκλητον, ἀλλὰ φρονηματιζομένων καὶ πάντα δι᾽ ἑαυτῶν
9 πράττειν ἐπιβαλλομένων, ἐὰν παρακούσωσι μόνον
αὐτῶν κατὰ τὸ παρὸν καὶ βραχεῖαν ἔμφασιν ποιήσω-
σιν δυσαρεστήσεως, ταχέως ἡ Λακεδαίμων τῇ Μεσ-
10 σήνῃ συμφρονήσει. τούτου δὲ γενομένου μετὰ μεγάλης χάριτος ἥξειν τοὺς Ἀχαιοὺς ἔφη καταπεφευγότας
11 ἐπὶ Ῥωμαίους. διότι τοῖς μὲν ἐκ τῆς Λακεδαίμονος
ἀπεκρίθησαν τοῖς περὶ Σήριππον, βουλόμενοι μετέωρον ἐᾶσαι τὴν πόλιν, διότι πάντα πεποιήκασιν αὐτοῖς

returned from Greece, and upon his presenting his report on the subject of Macedonia and the Peloponnese, the Senate no longer required further debate, but summoning the envoys from the Peloponnese and Macedonia, listened, it is true, to their speeches, but drew up their reply and took their decision on the matter not with reference to the arguments of the envoys, but in accordance with the report of Marcius. He had reported regarding Philip that he had executed the Roman order, but he had done so grudgingly; and that as soon as he had the opportunity he would do all he could against Rome. The answer given by the senate to Philip's envoys was therefore as follows. They thanked him for what had been done, and in future they warned him to take care not to appear to be acting in any way in opposition to Rome. As regards the Peloponnese Marcius had reported that as the Achaeans[23] did not wish to refer anything to the senate, but had a great opinion of themselves and were attempting to act in all matters on their own initiative, if the senate paid no attention to their request for the present, and expressed their displeasure in moderate terms, Sparta would soon come to an understanding with Messene,[24] upon which the Achaeans would be only too glad to come asking for help from the Romans. So they replied to Serippus, the representative of Sparta, as they wished the city to remain in suspense, that they had done all in their power for the Spartans, but at pres-

[23] In 183 Messene seceded from the Confederacy.
[24] Implied is the expectation that Sparta too would secede.

τὰ δυνατά, κατὰ δὲ τὸ παρὸν οὐ νομίζουσιν εἶναι
12 τοῦτο τὸ πρᾶγμα πρὸς αὑτούς. τῶν δ' Ἀχαιῶν παρακαλούντων, εἰ μὲν δυνατόν ἐστιν, βοήθειαν αὐτοῖς
πέμψαι κατὰ τὴν συμμαχίαν ἐπὶ τοὺς Μεσσηνίους, εἰ
δὲ μή, προνοηθῆναι ‹γ'› ἵνα μηθεὶς τῶν ἐξ Ἰταλίας
μήθ' ὅπλα μήτε σῖτον εἰς τὴν Μεσσήνην εἰσαγάγῃ,
13 τούτων μὲν οὐδενὶ προσεῖχον, ἀπεκρίθησαν δὲ διότι
οὐδ' ἂν ὁ Λακεδαιμονίων ἢ Κορινθίων ἢ ‹τῶν› Ἀργείων ἀφίσταται δῆμος, οὐ δεήσει τοὺς Ἀχαιοὺς θαυ-
14 μάζειν ἐὰν μὴ πρὸς αὐτοὺς ἡγῶνται. ταύτην δὲ τὴν
ἀπόκρισιν ἐκθέμενοι, κηρύγματος ἔχουσαν διάθεσιν
τοῖς βουλομένοις ἕνεκεν Ῥωμαίων ἀφίστασθαι τῆς
τῶν Ἀχαιῶν πολιτείας, λοιπὸν τοὺς πρεσβευτὰς παρα-
κατεῖχον, καραδοκοῦντες τὰ κατὰ τὴν Μεσσήνην, πῶς
15 προχωρήσει τοῖς Ἀχαιοῖς. καὶ τὰ μὲν κατὰ τὴν Ἰταλίαν ἐν τούτοις ἦν.

V. RES MACEDONIAE

10. Ὅτι τῷ βασιλεῖ Φιλίππῳ καὶ τῇ συμπάσῃ
(xxiv.8) Μακεδονίᾳ κατὰ τοῦτον τὸν καιρὸν δεινή τις ἀρχὴ
κακῶν ἐνέπεσε καὶ πολλῆς ἐπιστάσεως καὶ μνήμης
2 ἀξία. καθάπερ γὰρ ἂν εἰ δίκην ἡ τύχη βουλομένη
λαβεῖν καιρῷ παρ' αὐτοῦ πάντων τῶν ἀσεβημάτων
καὶ παρανομημάτων ὧν εἰργάσατο κατὰ τὸν βίον,
τότε παρέστησέ τινας ἐρινῦς καὶ ποινὰς καὶ προστρο-
3 παίους τῶν δι' ἐκεῖνον ἠτυχηκότων· οἱ συνόντες αὐτῷ
καὶ νύκτωρ καὶ μεθ' ἡμέραν τοιαύτας ἔλαβον παρ'

ent they did not think that the matter concerned them.[25]
When the Achaeans begged them, if it were possible, to
send a force in virtue of their alliance to help them against
the Messenians, or if not to see to it that no one coming
from Italy should import arms or food to Messene, they
paid no attention to either request, and answered them
that not even if the people of Sparta, Corinth or Argos
deserted the League should the Achaeans be surprised if
the senate did not think it concerned them. Giving full
publicity to this reply, which was a sort of proclamation
that the Romans would not interfere with those who
wished to desert the Achaean League, they continued to
detain the envoys, waiting to see how the Achaeans would
get on at Messene.[26] Such was the situation in Italy.

V. AFFAIRS OF MACEDONIA

(Cf. Livy 40.3.3)

10. This year witnessed the first outbreak of terrible
misfortunes[27] for King Philip and the whole of Macedonia,
an event fully worthy of attention and careful record. For
it was now that Fortune, as if she meant to punish him at
one and the same time for all the wicked and criminal acts
he had committed in his life, sent to haunt him a host of
the furies, tormentors and avenging spirits of his victims,
phantoms that never leaving him by day and by night,

[25] An unnecessarily harsh and provocative reply.

[26] Secession was followed by war (see 12.1–9; 16.1–17.4).

[27] For the conflict between Philip's sons, see Livy's much
fuller account (40.5.2–16.3), derived from the once complete text
of P.

αὐτοῦ τιμωρίας, ἕως οὗ τὸ ζῆν ἐξέλιπεν, ὡς καὶ πάντας
ἀνθρώπους ὁμολογῆσαι διότι κατὰ τὴν παροιμίαν
ἔστι τις Δίκης ὀφθαλμός, ἧς μηδέποτε δεῖ καταφρονεῖν
4 ἀνθρώπους ὑπάρχοντας. πρῶτον μὲν γὰρ αὐτῷ ταύτην
παρεστήσαντο τὴν ἔννοιαν ὅτι δεῖ μέλλοντα πολεμεῖν
πρὸς Ῥωμαίους ἐκ τῶν ἐπιφανεστάτων καὶ παραθαλαττίων πόλεων τοὺς μὲν πολιτικοὺς ἄνδρας μετὰ
τέκνων καὶ γυναικῶν ἀναστάτους ποιήσαντα μετ-
αγαγεῖν εἰς τὴν νῦν μὲν Ἠμαθίαν, τὸ δὲ παλαιὸν Παι-
ονίαν προσαγορευομένην, πληρῶσαι ⟨δὲ⟩ καὶ Θρᾳκῶν
5 καὶ βαρβάρων τὰς πόλεις, ὡς βεβαιοτέρας αὐτῷ τῆς
ἐκ τούτων πίστεως ὑπαρξούσης κατὰ τὰς περιστά-
6 σεις. οὗ συντελουμένου, καὶ τῶν ἀνθρώπων ἀνασπά-
στων γινομένων, τηλικοῦτο συνέβη γενέσθαι πένθος
καὶ τηλικοῦτον θόρυβον ὥστε δοριάλωτον δοκεῖν
7 ἅπασαν γίνεσθαι. ἐξ ὧν κατάραι καὶ θεοκλυτήσεις
ἐγίνοντο κατὰ τοῦ βασιλέως, οὐκέτι λάθρᾳ μόνον,
8 ἀλλὰ καὶ φανερῶς. μετὰ δὲ ταῦτα βουληθεὶς μηδὲν
ἀλλότριον ὑποκαθέσθαι μηδὲ δυσμενὲς μηδὲν ἀπο-
λιπεῖν τὴν βασιλείαν, ἔγραψε τοῖς ἐπὶ τῶν πόλεων
διατεταγμένοις ἀναζητήσασι τοὺς υἱοὺς καὶ τὰς θυ-
9 γατέρας τῶν ὑπ’ αὐτοῦ Μακεδόνων ἀνῃρημένων, εἰς
φυλακὴν ἀποθέσθαι, μάλιστα μὲν φέρων ἐπὶ τοὺς
περὶ Ἄδμητον καὶ Πύρριχον καὶ Σάμον καὶ τοὺς μετὰ

---

28 *Paroemiogr.* 2.366, no. 8; parallels in Hesiod, tragedy, and
comedy.   29 The area of Macedonia that included Pella,
Beroea, and Edessa. *RE* Emathia 2480 (E. Oberhummer).

tortured him so terribly up to the day of his death that all men acknowledged that, as the proverb[28] says, "Justice has an eye" and we who are but men should never scorn her. For first of all the furies and tormenting spirits inspired him with the notion that now he was about to make war on Rome he ought to deport with their whole families from the principal cities and from those on the coast all men who took part in politics, and transfer them to the country now called Emathia[29] and formerly Paeonia,[30] filling the cities with Thracians and barbarians whose fidelity to him would be surer in the season of danger. While this project was being executed, and the men were being deported, there arose such mourning and such commotion that one would have said the whole country was being led into captivity. And in consequence were heard curses and imprecations against the king uttered no longer in secret but openly. In the next place, wishing to tolerate no disaffection and to leave no hostile element in his kingdom, he wrote to the officers[31] in whose charge the cities were, to search for the sons and daughters of the Macedonians he had killed and imprison them, referring chiefly to Admetus,[32] Pyrrhichus,[33] Samus[34] and the others put to death at

---

[30] The area west of the Strymon, including Stobi. *RE* Paiones 2403–2408 (B. Lenk).   [31] Probably *epistatai* (WC 3.231). See 5.26.5 and n. on 20.5.12.

[32] Macedonian rather than Larisaean; C. Habicht (18.7.6), 140–144. See, however, Tataki (16.19.8), 221–222, no. 27.

[33] Probably the elder brother of Samus; see following n. Tataki (previous n.), 104, no. 17.

[34] Son of the Chrysogonus honored by Larisa ca. 217 (5.9.4); Tataki 105, no. 20.

10 τούτων ἀπολομένους· ἅμα δὲ τούτοις συμπεριέλαβε
καὶ τοὺς ἄλλους ἅπαντας, ὅσοι κατὰ βασιλικὸν πρόσταγμα τοῦ ζῆν ἐστερήθησαν, ἐπιφθεγξάμενος, ὥς
φασι, τὸν στίχον τοῦτον·

11 νήπιος ὃς πατέρα κτείνας υἱοὺς καταλείπει. ὄντων
δὲ τῶν πλείστων ἐπιφανῶν διὰ τὰς τῶν πατέρων προ-
αγωγάς, ἐπιφανῆ καὶ τὴν τούτων ἀτυχίαν συνέβαινε

12 γίνεσθαι καὶ παρὰ πᾶσιν ἐλεεινήν. τρίτον δ᾽ ἡ τύχη
δρᾶμα κατὰ τὸν αὐτὸν καιρὸν ἐπεισήγαγεν τὸ κατὰ

13 τοὺς υἱούς, ἐν ᾧ τῶν μὲν νεανίσκων ἀλλήλοις ἐπι-
βουλευόντων, τῆς δ᾽ ἀναφορᾶς περὶ τούτων ἐπ᾽ αὐτὸν
γινομένης, καὶ δέον διαλαμβάνειν ποτέρου δεῖ γίνεσθαι τῶν υἱῶν φονέα καὶ πότερον αὐτῶν δεδιέναι
μᾶλλον κατὰ τὸν ἑξῆς βίον, μὴ γηράσκων αὐτὸς
πάθῃ τὸ παραπλήσιον, ἐστροβεῖτο νύκτωρ καὶ μεθ᾽

14 ἡμέραν περὶ τούτων διανοούμενος. ἐν τοιαύταις δ᾽
οὔσης ἀτυχίαις καὶ ταραχαῖς τῆς αὐτοῦ ψυχῆς, τίς
οὐκ ἂν εἰκότως ὑπολάβοι θεῶν τινων αὐτῷ μῆνιν εἰς
τὸ γῆρας κατασκῆψαι διὰ τὰς ἐν τῷ προγεγονότι βίῳ

15 παρανομίας; τοῦτο δ᾽ ἔτι μᾶλλον ἔσται δῆλον ἐκ τῶν
ἑξῆς ῥηθησομένων.

Ὅτι Φίλιππος ὁ Μακεδόνων βασιλεὺς πολλοὺς τῶν
Μακεδόνων ἀνελὼν καὶ τοὺς υἱοὺς αὐτῶν ἐπανεῖλεν,
ὥς φασι, τὸν στίχον τοῦτον εἰπών·

νήπιος ὃς πατέρα κτείνας υἱοὺς καταλείπει.

16 . . . καὶ διὰ ταῦτα τῆς ψυχῆς οἱονεὶ λυττώσης αὐτοῦ,
καὶ τὸ κατὰ τοὺς υἱοὺς νεῖκος ἅμα τοῖς προειρημένοις

the same time, but including all others who had suffered death by royal command, quoting, as they say, the line—A fool is he who slays the sire and leaves the sons alive.

As most of these young people were notable owing to the high stations their fathers had held, their misfortune too became notable, and excited the pity of all. And the third tragedy which Fortune produced at the same time was that concerning his sons. The young men were plotting against each other, and as the matter was referred to him, and it fell to him to decide of which of them he had to be the murderer and which of them he had to fear most for the rest of his life, lest he in his old age should suffer the same fate, he was disturbed night and day by this thought. Who can help thinking that, his mind being thus afflicted and troubled, it was the wrath of heaven which had descended on his old age, owing to the crimes of his past life? And this will be still more evident from what follows.

Philip of Macedon after putting many Macedonians to death, killed their sons also,[35] quoting as they say, the verse:

> A fool is he who slays the sire and leaves the sons alive.[36]

. . . And while his mind was almost maddened by this thought, the quarrel of his sons burst into flame at the

[35] For the sequel see Livy 40.5–24.

[36] A verse from the *Cypria*, quoted also by Aristotle, and ascribed to Stasinus by Clem. Alex. *Strom.* 6.2.19. See *RE* Kyklos 2394–2395 (A. Rzach), and M. L. West, *Greek Epic Fragments*, (Cambridge, MA 2003), 106–107, no. 31.

ἐξεκαύθη, τῆς τύχης ὥσπερ ἐπίτηδες ἀναβιβαζούσης
ἐπὶ σκηνὴν ἐν ἑνὶ καιρῷ τὰς τούτων συμφοράς.

17   Ἐναγίζουσιν οὖν τῷ Ξανθῷ Μακεδόνες καὶ καθαρμὸν ποιοῦσι σὺν ἵπποις ὡπλισμένοις.

11. Ὅτι "δεῖ μὴ μόνον ἀναγινώσκειν τὰς τραγῳδίας

(xxiv.8a)   καὶ τοὺς μύθους καὶ τὰς ἱστορίας, ἀλλὰ καὶ γινώσκειν

2   καὶ συνεφιστάνειν ἐπὶ τοῦτο τὸ μέρος. ἐν οἷς ἅπασιν
ἔστιν ὁρᾶν, ὅσοι μὲν τῶν ἀδελφῶν εἰς τὴν πρὸς
ἀλλήλους ὀργὴν καὶ φιλονικίαν ἐμπεσόντες ἐπὶ πολὺ
προύβησαν, ἅπαντας τοὺς τοιούτους οὐ μόνον σφᾶς
ἀπολωλεκότας, ἀλλὰ καὶ βίον καὶ τέκνα καὶ πόλεις

3   ἄρδην κατεστραφότας, ὅσοι δὲ μετρίως ἐζήλωσαν τὸ
στέργειν αὑτοὺς καὶ φέρειν τὰς ἀλλήλων ἀγνοίας,
τούτους ἅπαντας σωτῆρας γεγονότας ὧν ἀρτίως εἶπον
καὶ μετὰ τῆς καλλίστης φήμης καὶ δόξης βεβιωκό-

4   τας. καὶ μὴν ἐπὶ τοὺς ἐν τῇ Λακεδαίμονι βασιλεῖς
πολλάκις ὑμᾶς ἐπέστησα, λέγων ὅτι τοσοῦτον χρόνον
διετήρησαν σφῶν τῇ πατρίδι τὴν τῶν Ἑλλήνων
ἡμεμονίαν ὅσον πειθαρχοῦντες ὥσπερ γονεῦσι τοῖς

5   ἐφόροις ἠνείχοντο συμβασιλεύοντες ἀλλήλοις· ὅτε δὲ
<δια>φωνήσαντες εἰς μοναρχίαν τὰ πράγματα μετέ-

6   στησαν, τότε πάντων ἅμα τῶν κακῶν πεῖραν ἐποίησαν
λαβεῖν τὴν Σπάρτην· τὸ δὲ τελευταῖον ὡσανεὶ κατ'
ἔνδειξιν ὑμῖν λέγων καὶ τιθεὶς ἐναργῶς ὑπὸ τὴν ὄψιν

same time, Fortune as if of set purpose bringing their misfortunes on the stage at one and the same time.

(Suda)

The Macedonians offer sacrifices to Xanthus[37] and make a piacular offering to him with armed horses.

Fragment of a Speech of Philip to His Sons

(Cf. Livy 40.8)

11. You should not only read tragedies, myths, and stories but know well and ponder over such things. In all of them we see that those brothers[38] who, giving way to wrath and discord, carried their quarrel to excess, not only in every case brought destruction on themselves but utterly subverted their substance, their families and their cities; while those who studied even in moderation to love each other and tolerate each other's errors, were the preservers of all these things, and lived in the greatest glory and honor. Have I not often called your attention to the case of the kings of Sparta, pointing out how they preserved for their country her supremacy in Greece, as long as they obeyed the ephors as if they were their fathers, and were content to share the throne, but when once they fell out and changed the constitution to a monarchy,[39] then they caused Sparta to experience every evil? And finally, I constantly as a cogent proof of this kept before your eyes these

[37] Macedonian hero who received sacrifices during the rite of purification of the Macedonian army: M. Hatzopoulos, *Cultes et rites de passage en Macédoine* (Athens 1994), 89–92.

[38] Eteocles and Polynices, for instance.

[39] In 2.47.3 it is "into a tyranny."

διετέλουν τούτους τοὺς περὶ τὸν Εὐμένη καὶ τὸν
7 Ἄτταλον, ὅτι παραλαβόντες οὗτοι μικρὰν ἀρχὴν καὶ
τὴν τυχοῦσαν ηὐξήκασι ταύτην, ὥστε μηδεμιᾶς εἶναι
καταδεεστέραν, δι᾽ οὐθὲν ἕτερον ἢ διὰ τὴν πρὸς αὑτοὺς
ὁμόνοιαν καὶ συμφωνίαν καὶ τὸ δύνασθαι καταξίωσιν
8 ἀλλήλοις διαφυλάττειν· ὧν ὑμεῖς ἀκούοντες οὐχ οἷον
εἰς νοῦν ἐλαμβάνετε, τὸ δ᾽ ἐναντίον ἠκονᾶτ᾽, ἐμοὶ
δοκεῖ, τοὺς κατ᾽ ἀλλήλων θυμούς."

V. RES GRAECIAE

12. Πολύβιος. ὁ δ᾽ ἐξαναστὰς προῆγε, τὰ μὲν ὑπὸ
(xxiv.8b) τῆς ἀρρωστίας, τὰ δ᾽ ὑπὸ τῆς ἡλικίας βαρυνόμενος·
2 εἶχε γὰρ ἑβδομηκοστὸν ἔτος. Πολύβιος· διαβιασάμε-
νος δὲ τὴν ἀσθένειαν τῇ συνηθείᾳ τῇ πρὸ τοῦ παρῆν
ἐξ Ἄργους εἰς Μεγάλην πόλιν αὐθημερόν.

3 Ὅτι Φιλοποίμην ὁ τῶν Ἀχαιῶν στρατηγὸς συλ-
ληφθεὶς ὑπὸ Μεσσηνίων ἀνῃρέθη φαρμάκῳ, ἀνὴρ γενόμενος οὐδενὸς τῶν πρὸ τοῦ κατ᾽ ἀρετὴν δεύτερος,
τῆς τύχης μέντοι γ᾽ ἥττων, καίτοι δόξας ἐν παντὶ τῷ
4 πρὸ τοῦ βίῳ συνεργὸν ἐσχηκέναι ταύτην· ἀλλά μοι
δοκεῖ κατὰ τὴν κοινὴν παροιμίαν εὐτυχῆσαι μὲν
ἄνθρωπον ὄντα δυνατόν, διευτυχῆσαί γε μὴν ἀδύνατον·
5 διὸ καὶ μακαριστέον τῶν προγεγονότων οὐχ ὡς διευ-
τυχηκότας τινάς· τίς γὰρ ἀνάγκη ψευδεῖ λόγῳ χρω-

our contemporaries Eumenes and Attalus, telling you how, inheriting a small and insignificant kingdom, they increased it so much that it is now inferior to none, simply by their concord and agreement and their faculty of mutual respect. You listened to all this; but, far from its sinking into your minds, you, on the contrary, as it seems to me, whetted your passion against each other.

V. AFFAIRS OF GREECE

Philopoemen

(Suda)

12. Philopoemen arose and advanced although bowed down by sickness and the weight of years, being now in his seventieth year . . . but on getting over his ailment he recovered his former activity and reached Megalopolis from Argos in one day.

Philopoemen,[40] the strategus of the Achaeans, was captured by the Messenians and put to death by poison. He was a man second to none of his predecessors in virtue, but succumbed to Fortune, although he was thought to have always been favored by her in all his previous life. But my opinion is that, as the vulgar proverb says, it is possible for a human being to be fortunate, but impossible for him to be constantly so. Therefore we should regard some of our predecessors as blessed, not because they enjoyed constant good fortune—for what need is there by

---

[40] He attacked Messene after its secession. For a suggestion that he was not killed in captivity, but may have died of old age and internal injuries, see Errington (20.3.5), 191–193.

6 μένοις ματαίως προσκυνεῖν τὴν τύχην; ἀλλὰ τοὺς ὡς
πλεῖστον χρόνον ἐν τῷ ζῆν ἵλεων ἔχοντας ταύτην, κἄν
ποτε μετανοῇ, μετρίαις περιπεσόντας συμφοραῖς.

7   Μετ[ὰ δ᾽ εἵλοντο vel sim.] Λυκόρταν, ὃς ἦν οὐδὲν
ἥττων τούτου.

8   Ὅτι Φιλοποίμην τετταράκοντ᾽ ἔτη συνεχῶς φι-
(xxiv.9) λοδοξήσας ἐν δημοκρατικῷ καὶ πολυειδεῖ πολιτεύ-
9 ματι, πάντῃ πάντως διέφυγε τὸν τῶν πολλῶν φθόνον,
τὸ πλεῖον οὐ πρὸς χάριν, ἀλλὰ μετὰ παρρησίας πο-
λιτευόμενος· ὃ σπανίως ἂν εὕροι τις γεγονός.

13. Ὅτι θαυμαστόν ἐστι καὶ μέγιστον σημεῖον
(xxiv.9) γεγονέναι τῇ φύσει τὸν ἄνδρα τοῦτον ἡγεμονικὸν καὶ
πολύ τι διαφέροντα τῶν ἄλλων πρὸς τὸν πραγματικὸν
2 τρόπον· ἑπτακαίδεκα γὰρ ἔτη μείνας ἐν τοῖς ὑπαίθροις
πλεῖστά τ᾽ ἔθνη καὶ βάρβαρα διεξελθὼν καὶ πλείστοις ἀνδράσιν ἀλλοφύλοις καὶ ἑτερογλώττοις χρησάμενος συνεργοῖς πρὸς ἀπηλπισμένας καὶ παρα-
δόξους ἐπιβολάς, ὑπ᾽ οὐθενὸς οὔτ᾽ ἐπεβουλεύθη τὸ
παράπαν οὔτ᾽ ἐγκατελείφθη τῶν ἅπαξ αὐτῷ κοινωνη-
σάντων καὶ δόντων ἑαυτοὺς εἰς χεῖρας.

14. Ὅτι Πόπλιος φιλοδοξήσας ἐν ἀριστοκρατικῷ
(xxiv.9) πολιτεύματι τηλικαύτην περιεποιήσατο παρὰ μὲν τοῖς
2 ὄχλοις εὔνοιαν παρὰ δὲ τῷ συνεδρίῳ πίστιν ὥστ᾽, ἐν
μὲν τῷ δήμῳ κρίνειν τινὸς ἐπιβαλομένου κατὰ τὰ

41 The opposite of the democratic state of Philopoemen
(12.6).   42 See Th. Mommsen, "Die Scipionenprozesse,"
Röm. Forsch. 2 (Berlin 1879), 417–510. *RE* Cornelius 1475 (F.
Münzer). WC 3.243–245.

stating what is false to pay foolish worship to Fortune? But they are blessed to whom Fortune was kind for the greater part of their lives, and who, when she deserted them, only met with moderate misfortunes.

Thereafter [they elected] Lycortas, who was by no means inferior to him.

Philopoemen spent forty successive years in the pursuit of glory in a democratic state composed of various elements, and he avoided incurring the ill will of the people in any way or on any occasion, although in his conduct of affairs he usually did not court favor but spoke his mind: a thing we seldom find.

Hannibal

(Suda)

13. It is a remarkable and very cogent proof of Hannibal's having been by nature a real leader and far superior to anyone else in statesmanship, that though he spent seventeen years in the field, passed through so many barbarous countries, and employed to aid him in desperate and extraordinary enterprises numbers of men of different nations and languages, no one ever dreamt of conspiring against him, nor was he ever deserted by those who had once joined him or submitted to him.

Scipio

(Cf. Suda)

14. Publius Scipio, who pursued fame in an aristocratic state,[41] gained so completely the affection of the people and the confidence of the senate that when some one attempted to bring him to trial[42] before the people accord-

Ῥωμαίων ἔθη καὶ πολλὰ κατηγορήσαντος καὶ πικρῶς,
3   ἄλλο μὲν οὐθὲν εἶπε προελθών, οὐκ ἔφη δὲ πρέπον
εἶναι τῷ δήμῳ τῶν Ῥωμαίων οὐθενὸς ἀκούειν κατηγο-
ροῦντος Ποπλίου Κορνηλίου Σκιπίωνος, δι᾽ ὃν αὐτὴν
4   τὴν τοῦ λέγειν ἐξουσίαν ἔχουσιν οἱ κατηγοροῦντες. ὧν
ἀκούσαντες οἱ πολλοὶ παραχρῆμα διελύθησαν πάντες
ἐκ τῆς ἐκκλησίας, ἀπολιπόντες τὸν κατηγοροῦντα μόνον.

5   Ὅτι Πόπλιος ἐν τῷ συνεδρίῳ χρείας ποτὲ χρημά-
(xxiv.9a) των οὔσης εἴς τινα κατεπείγουσαν οἰκονομίαν, τοῦ δὲ
ταμίου διά τινα νόμον οὐ φάσκοντος ἀνοίξειν τὸ
ταμιεῖον κατ᾽ ἐκείνην τὴν ἡμέραν, αὐτὸς ἔφη λαβὼν
6   τὰς κλεῖς ἀνοίξειν· αὐτὸς γὰρ αἴτιος γεγονέναι καὶ
7   τοῦ κλείεσθαι τὸ ταμιεῖον. πάλιν δέ ποτε λόγον ἀπαι-
τοῦντός τινος ἐν τῷ συνεδρίῳ τῶν χρημάτων ὧν ἔλαβε
παρ᾽ Ἀντιόχου πρὸ τῶν συνθηκῶν <εἰς> τὴν τοῦ στρατοπέδου μισθοδοσίαν, ἔχειν μὲν ἔφη τὸν λογισμόν, οὐ
8   δεῖν δ᾽ αὐτὸν ὑποσχεῖν οὐδενὶ λόγον· τοῦ δ᾽ ἐπικειμένου
καὶ κελεύοντος φέρειν ἠξίωσε τὸν ἀδελφὸν ἐνεγκεῖν·
κομισθέντος δὲ τοῦ βυβλίου, προτείνας αὐτὸ καὶ
κατασπαράξας πάντων ὁρώντων τὸν μὲν ἀπαιτοῦντα
9   τὸν λόγον ἐκ τούτων ζητεῖν ἐκέλευσε, τοὺς δ᾽ ἄλλους
ἤρετο πῶς τῶν μὲν τρισχιλίων ταλάντων τὸν λόγον
ἐπιζητοῦσι πῶς ἐδαπανήθη καὶ διὰ τίνων, τῶν δὲ μυρίων καθόλου καὶ πεντακισχιλίων ὧν παρ᾽ Ἀντιόχου
λαμβάνουσιν, οὐκέτι ζητοῦσι πῶς εἰσπορεύεται καὶ
10 διὰ τίνων, οὐδὲ πῶς τῆς Ἀσίας καὶ τῆς Λιβύης, ἔτι δὲ

ing to the Roman practice, making many bitter accusations, he said nothing more when he came forward to defend himself, but that it was not proper for the Roman people to listen to anyone who accused Publius Cornelius Scipio, to whom his accusers owed the power of speech at all. All the people on hearing this at once dispersed, leaving the accuser alone.

Publius Scipio once in the senate when funds were required for an urgent outlay, and the quaestor owing to some law refused to open the treasury on that day, took the keys and said he would open it himself; saying it was owing to him that it was shut. On another occasion when someone in the senate asked him to render an account of the moneys he had received from Antiochus before the peace for the pay of his army, he said he had the account, but he was not obliged to render an account to anyone. When the senator in question pressed his demand and ordered him to bring it, he asked his brother to get it; and, when the book was brought to him, he held it out and tore it to bits in the sight of every one, telling the man who had asked for it to search among the pieces for the account. At the same time he asked the rest of the house why they demanded an account of how and by whom the three thousand talents had been spent, while they had not inquired how and by whose hands the fifteen thousand talents they were receiving from Antiochus were coming into the treasury, nor how they had become masters of Asia,

11   τῆς Ἰβηρίας κεκυριεύκασιν. ὥστε μὴ μόνον κατα-
πλαγῆναι πάντας, ἀλλὰ καὶ τὸν ζητήσαντα τὸν λόγον
ἀποσιωπῆσαι.

12   Ταῦτα μὲν οὖν ἡμῖν εἰρήσθω τῆς τε τῶν μετηλλα-
χότων ἀνδρῶν εὐκλείας ἕνεκεν καὶ τῆς τῶν ἐπιγινο-
μένων παρορμήσεως πρὸς τὰ καλὰ τῶν ἔργων.

15. Ὅτι οὐ καλὸν τὸ φθείρειν τοὺς καρποὺς τῶν
(xxv.3a) ὑπεναντίων· φησὶ γὰρ ὁ Πολύβιος οὐδέποτε δ᾽ ἐγὼ
συντίθεμαι τὴν γνώμην τοῖς ἐπὶ τοσοῦτον διατιθεμέ-
νοις τὴν ὀργὴν εἰς τοὺς ὁμοφύλους ὥστε μὴ μόνον
τοὺς ἐπετείους καρποὺς παραιρεῖσθαι τῶν πολεμίων,
ἀλλὰ καὶ τὰ δένδρα καὶ τὰ κατασκευάσματα διαφθεί-
2   ρειν, μηδὲ μεταμελείας καταλείποντας τόπον. ἀλλά
μοι δοκοῦσι μεγαλείως ἀγνοεῖν οἱ ταῦτα πράττοντες·
3   καθ᾽ ὅσον γὰρ ὑπολαμβάνουσι καταπλήττεσθαι τοὺς
πολεμίους λυμαινόμενοι τὴν χώραν καὶ παραιρούμε-
νοι πάσας, οὐ μόνον τὰς κατὰ τὸ παρόν, ἀλλὰ καὶ τὰς
εἰς τὸ μέλλον ἐλπίδας τῶν πρὸς τὸν βίον ἀναγκαίων,
κατὰ τοσοῦτον ἀποθηριοῦντες τοὺς ἀνθρώπους ἀμετά-
θετον ποιοῦσι τὴν πρὸς αὐτοὺς ὀργὴν τῶν ἅπαξ ἐξ-
αμαρτόντων.

16. Ὅτι ὁ Λυκόρτας ὁ τῶν Ἀχαιῶν στρατηγὸς τοὺς
(xxiv.12) Μεσσηνίους καταπληξάμενος τῷ πολέμῳ . . . πάλαι
2   μὲν οἱ Μεσσήνιοι καταπεπληγμένοι τὸν πρὸ τοῦ χρόνον τοὺς προεστῶτας, τότε μόλις ἐθάρρησάν τινες

---

43 P. assumes the role of an instructor of the Romans.

Africa, and Spain. So not only were all abashed, but he who had demanded the account kept silent.

I have related[43] these anecdotes for the sake of the good fame of the departed and to incite their successors to achieve noble deeds.

15. It is not right to destroy the harvest of one's enemies as Polybius says:[44] I never can share[45] the sentiment of those who indulge their anger on those of their own race to such an extent that they not only deprive the enemy of the year's harvest, but destroy trees and agricultural installations, leaving no room for redress. On the contrary in my opinion those who act thus make a very serious mistake. For the more they think to terrorize the enemy by spoiling their country and depriving them not only of all present but of all future hope of procuring the means of existence, the more they make the men savage, and in those who have committed but a single offense inspire an ineradicable hatred of themselves.

Messene Surrenders to the Achaeans

(Cf. Livy 39.50.9)

16. Lycortas, the strategus of the Achaeans, having cowed the Messenians by the war . . . The Messenians had long been overawed by their leaders, but now certain of them just ventured to open their mouths, relying on the

[44] Up to here, the excerptor speaks, not P.

[45] P. criticizes the devastation of Messene by the Achaeans under Philopoemen's successor Lycortas. See A. Chaniotis, *War in the Hellenistic World* (Oxford 2003), 121–129: "War and Agriculture." See also 24.2.3. P. has also criticized his father in 23.9.

αὐτῶν φωνὴν ἀφιέναι, πιστεύσαντες τῇ τῶν πολεμίων
ἐφεδρείᾳ, καὶ λέγειν ὅτι δεῖ πρεσβεύειν ὑπὲρ διαλύ-
3 σεως. οἱ μὲν οὖν περὶ τὸν Δεινοκράτην οὐκέτι δυνάμενοι πρὸς τὸ πλῆθος ἀντοφθαλμεῖν διὰ τὸ περιέχεσθαι
. . . τοῖς πράγμασιν εἴξαντες ἀνεχώρησαν εἰς τὰς
4 ἰδίας οἰκήσεις. οἱ δὲ πολλοὶ παρακληθέντες ὑπό τε
τῶν πρεσβυτέρων καὶ μάλιστα τῶν ἐκ Βοιωτίας
5 πρεσβευτῶν, οἳ πρότερον ἤδη παραγεγονότες ἐπὶ τὰς
διαλύσεις, Ἐπαίνετος καὶ Ἀπολλόδωρος, εὐκαίρως
τότε παρέτυχον ἐν τῇ Μεσσήνῃ, ταχέως ἐπακολουθήσαντες ἐπὶ τὰς διαλύσεις [οἱ Μεσσήνιοι] κατέστησαν πρεσβευτὰς καὶ τούτους ἐξέπεμψαν, δεόμενοι
6 τυχεῖν συγγνώμης ἐπὶ τοῖς ἡμαρτημένοις. ὁ δὲ στρατηγὸς τῶν Ἀχαιῶν παραλαβὼν τοὺς συνάρχοντας καὶ
διακούσας τῶν παραγεγονότων μίαν ἔφη Μεσσηνίοις
7 πρὸς τὸ ἔθνος εἶναι διάλυσιν, ἐὰν μὲν τοὺς αἰτίους τῆς
ἀποστάσεως καὶ τῆς Φιλοποίμενος ἀναιρέσεως ἤδη
παραδῶσιν αὐτῷ, περὶ δὲ τῶν ἄλλων ἁπάντων ἐπιτροπὴν δῶσιν τοῖς Ἀχαιοῖς, εἰς δὲ τὴν ἄκραν εἰσ-
8 δέξωνται παραχρῆμα φυλακήν. ἀναγγελθέντων δὲ
τούτων εἰς τοὺς ὄχλους, οἱ μὲν πάλαι πικρῶς διακείμενοι πρὸς τοὺς αἰτίους τοῦ πολέμου πρόθυμοι
τούτους ἦσαν ἐκδιδόναι καὶ συλλαμβάνειν, οἱ δὲ πε-
πεισμένοι μηδὲν πείσεσθαι δεινὸν ὑπὸ τῶν Ἀχαιῶν
ἑτοίμως συγκατέβαινον εἰς τὴν ὑπὲρ τῶν ὅλων ἐπι-
9 τροπήν. τὸ δὲ συνέχον, οὐκ ἔχοντες αἵρεσιν περὶ τῶν
10 παρόντων ὁμοθυμαδὸν ἐδέξαντο τὰ προτεινόμενα. τὴν
μὲν οὖν ἄκραν εὐθέως παραλαβὼν ὁ στρατηγὸς τοὺς

protection of the enemy, and to advise sending an embassy to ask for peace. Deinocrates and the others in power, no longer daring to face the people, as they were encompassed by perils, yielded to circumstances and retired to their own dwellings. The people now, entreated by the elders and chiefly by the Boeotian envoys Epaenetus and Apollodorus, who had arrived earlier to make peace, and by a happy chance were still in Messene, readily gave ear, and appointed and dispatched envoys craving pardon for the errors they had committed. The strategus of the Achaeans summoned his colleagues, and after listening to the envoys replied that the Messenians could make peace with the League on no other terms than by giving up to him now the authors of their defection and of the murder of Philopoemen, and by submitting all other matters to the discretion of the Achaeans and at once admitting a garrison into their citadel. When these terms were announced to the people, those who had been throughout hostile to the authors of the war were ready to arrest and surrender the latter, while all who were convinced that they would not be harshly treated by the Achaeans gladly agreed to the unconditional submission; and as, above all, they had no choice in the matter, they unanimously accepted the proposal. The strategus upon this at once took over the

11 πελταστὰς εἰς αὐτὴν παρήγαγεν, μετὰ δὲ ταῦτα προσ-
λαβὼν τοὺς ἐπιτηδείους ἐκ τοῦ στρατοπέδου παρῆλθεν
εἰς τὴν πόλιν καὶ συναγαγὼν τοὺς ὄχλους παρεκάλεσε τὰ πρέποντα τοῖς ἐνεστῶσι καιροῖς, ἐπαγγελ-
12 λόμενος ἀμεταμέλητον αὐτοῖς ἔσεσθαι τὴν πίστιν. τῆς
μὲν οὖν ὑπὲρ τῶν ὅλων διαλήψεως τὴν ἀναφορὰν ἐπὶ
τὸ ἔθνος ἐποιήσατο—καὶ γὰρ ὥσπερ ἐπίτηδες συνέβαινε τότε πάλιν συνάγεσθαι τοὺς Ἀχαιοὺς εἰς Με-
13 γάλην πόλιν ἐπὶ τὴν δευτέραν σύνοδον—τῶν δ' ἐν
ταῖς αἰτίαις ὅσοι μὲν μετέσχον τοῦ παρ' αὐτὸν τὸν
καιρὸν ἐπανελέσθαι τὸν Φιλοποίμενα, τούτοις ἐπέταξε
παραχρῆμα πάντας αὐτοὺς ἐξάγειν ἐκ τοῦ ζῆν.

17. Ὅτι οἱ Μεσσήνιοι διὰ τὴν αὐτῶν ἄγνοιαν εἰς
(xxv.1) τὴν ἐσχάτην παραγενόμενοι διάθεσιν ἀποκατέστησαν εἰς τὴν ἐξ ἀρχῆς κατάστασιν τῆς συμπολιτείας
2 διὰ τὴν Λυκόρτα καὶ τῶν Ἀχαιῶν μεγαλοψυχίαν. ἡ δ'
Ἀβία καὶ Θουρία καὶ Φαραὶ κατὰ τὸν καιρὸν τοῦτον
ἀπὸ μὲν τῆς Μεσσήνης ἐχωρίσθησαν, ἰδίᾳ <δὲ> θέμε-
ναι στήλην ἑκάστη μετεῖχεν τῆς κοινῆς συμπολιτείας.

3 Ῥωμαῖοι δὲ πυθόμενοι κατὰ λόγον κεχωρηκέναι
τοῖς Ἀχαιοῖς τὰ κατὰ τὴν Μεσσήνην, οὐδένα λόγον
ποιησάμενοι τῆς πρότερον ἀποφάσεως ἄλλην ἔδωκαν
τοῖς αὐτοῖς πρεσβευταῖς ἀπόκρισιν, διασαφοῦντες ὅτι
πρόνοιαν πεποίηνται τοῦ μηθένα τῶν ἐξ Ἰταλίας μήθ'
4 ὅπλα μήτε σῖτον εἰσάγειν εἰς τὴν Μεσσήνην. ἐξ οὗ
καταφανεῖς ἅπασιν ἐγενήθησαν ὅτι τοσοῦτον ἀπέχου-

citadel and introduced the peltasts into it, and after this, accompanied by competent members of his force, he entered the city, and summoning the populace addressed them in terms suitable to the occasion, promising that they would never repent of having entrusted their future to him. He referred the whole question to the League—it happened that at that very time the Achaeans, as if for this very purpose, were assembling again at Megalopolis for their second meeting—ordering those among the guilty Messenians who had actually participated in the death of Philopoemen at the time, to put an end to their own lives without delay.

17. The Messenians, having by their own error been reduced to the worst condition, were restored to their original position[46] in the League by the generosity of Lycortas and the Achaeans. Abia, Thuria, and Pharae[47] at this time separated from Messene and each setting up a separate inscribed pillar became members of the League.

The Romans, on hearing that the Messenian revolt had ended in a manner favorable to the Achaeans, entirely ignoring their former answer,[48] gave another reply to the same envoys, informing them that they had provided that no one should import from Italy arms and corn to Messene. This made it patent to every one that so far from

[46] That of *sympoliteia*. See Giovannini (22.4.13), 229–230. The fact is recorded with these same words at the very beginning of an unpublished dossier of documents found at Messene: P. Themelis, ΠΑΕ 2004 [2007] 42.   [47] This is the Messenian city, different from those of the same name in Achaea and Laconia: *RE* Pharai 1801–1805 (W. Brandenstein).

[48] 9.13–14.

σιν τοῦ τὰ μὴ λίαν ἀναγκαῖα τῶν ἐκτὸς πραγμάτων
ἀποτρίβεσθαι καὶ παρορᾶν, ὡς τοὐναντίον καὶ δυσχε-
ραίνουσιν ἐπὶ τῷ μὴ πάντων τὴν ἀναφορὰν ἐφ᾽ ἑαυτοὺς γίνεσθαι καὶ πάντα πράττεσθαι μετὰ τῆς αὑτῶν
γνώμης.

5   Εἰς δὲ τὴν λακεδαίμονα παραγενομένων τῶν πρεσβευτῶν ἐκ τῆς Ῥώμης καὶ κομιζόντων τὴν ἀπόκρισιν,
εὐθέως ὁ στρατηγὸς τῶν Ἀχαιῶν μετὰ τὸ συντελέσαι
τὰ κατὰ τὴν Μεσσήνην συνῆγε τοὺς πολλοὺς εἰς τὴν
6   τῶν Σικυωνίων πόλιν. ἀθροισθέντων δὲ τῶν Ἀχαιῶν
⟨ἀν⟩εδίδου διαβούλιον ὑπὲρ τοῦ προσλαβέσθαι ⟨τὴν
7   Σπάρτην⟩ εἰς τὴν συμπολιτείαν, φάσκων Ῥωμαίους
μὲν ἀποτρίβεσθαι τὴν πρότερον αὐτοῖς δοθεῖσαν ἐπιτροπὴν ὑπὲρ τῆς πόλεως ταύτης· ἀποκεκρίσθαι γὰρ
αὐτοὺς νῦν μηθὲν εἶναι τῶν κατὰ Λακεδαίμονα πρα-
8   γμάτων πρὸς αὐτούς· τοὺς δὲ κυριεύοντας τῆς Σπάρτης κατὰ τὸ παρὸν βούλεσθαι σφίσιν μετέχειν τῆς
9   συμπολιτείας. διὸ παρεκάλει προσδέχεσθαι τὴν πό-
λιν· εἶναι γὰρ τοῦτο κατὰ δύο τρόπους συμφέρον,
καθ᾽ ἕνα μέν, ὅτι τούτους ⟨μέλλουσι⟩ προσλήψεσθαι
10   τοὺς διατετηρηκότας τὴν πρὸς τὸ ἔθνος πίστιν, καθ᾽
ἕτερον δέ, διότι τῶν ἀρχαίων φυγάδων τοὺς ἀχαρίστως
καὶ ἀσεβῶς ἀνεστραμμένους εἰς αὐτοὺς οὐχ ἕξουσι
κοινωνοὺς τῆς πολιτείας, ἀλλ᾽ ἑτέρων αὐτοὺς ἐκκεκλει-
κότων τῆς πόλεως, βεβαιώσαντες τὰς ἐκείνων προαιρέσεις ἅμα τὴν ἁρμόζουσαν αὐτοῖς χάριν ἀποδώσουσι
11   μετὰ τῆς τῶν θεῶν προνοίας. ὁ μὲν οὖν Λυκόρτας
ταῦτα καὶ τὰ τοιαῦτα λέγων παρεκάλει τοὺς Ἀχαιοὺς

shirking and neglecting less important items of foreign affairs, they were on the contrary displeased if all matters were not submitted to them and if all was not done in accordance with their decision.

Readmission of Sparta to the Achaean League

When the envoys returned from Rome to Sparta with the reply, the strategus[49] of the Achaeans at once, after finally arranging the affairs of Messene, summoned the general assembly to meet at Sicyon. Upon its meeting, he initiated a debate about receiving Sparta into the League, saying that on the one hand the Romans had relieved themselves of the engagement formerly imposed on them to decide about this city, since they had answered[50] that Spartan affairs did not concern them, and on the other that the present rulers of Sparta wished to join the League. He therefore begged them to accept the adherence of that city. It was, he said, advantageous in two ways; because they would be including in the League those who had kept their faith to it, next because those of the old exiles who had behaved with such ingratitude and impiety to them would not be members of the League, but as they had been expelled from the city by others, they would both confirm the decision of these latter and pay them by the gods' providence the debt of thanks they deserved. Such were the words in which Lycortas recommended that the

49 Lycortas.
50 9.13.

προσδέξασθαι τὴν πόλιν· ὁ δὲ Διοφάνης καί τινες
12 ἕτεροι βοηθεῖν ἐπειρῶντο τοῖς φυγάσι καὶ παρεκάλουν τοὺς Ἀχαιοὺς μὴ συνεπιθέσθαι τοῖς ἐκπεπτωκό-
σιν μηδὲ δι’ ὀλίγους ἀνθρώπους συνεπισχῦσαι τοῖς
ἀσεβῶς καὶ παρανόμως αὐτοὺς ἐκ τῆς πατρίδος ἐκ-
βεβληκόσιν. τοιαῦτα μὲν ἦν τὰ ῥηθέντα παρ’ ἑκατέρων.

(xxv.2)   18. οἱ δ’ Ἀχαιοὶ διακούσαντες ἀμφοτέρων ἔκριναν
προσλαβέσθαι τὴν πόλιν, καὶ μετὰ ταῦτα στήλης
προγραφείσης συνεπολιτεύετο μετὰ τῶν Ἀχαιῶν ἡ
2 Σπάρτη, προσδεξαμένων τῶν ἐν τῇ πόλει τούτους τῶν
ἀρχαίων φυγάδων, ὅσοι μηδὲν ἐδόκουν ἄγνωμον πεποιηκέναι κατὰ τοῦ τῶν Ἀχαιῶν ἔθνους.
3   Οἱ δ’ Ἀχαιοὶ ταῦτα κυρώσαντες πρεσβευτὰς ἀπέστειλαν εἰς τὴν Ῥώμην τοὺς περὶ Βίππον τὸν Ἀργεῖον,
4 διασαφήσοντας τῇ συγκλήτῳ περὶ πάντων. ὁμοίως δὲ
καὶ Λακεδαιμόνιοι τοὺς περὶ Χαίρωνα κατέστησαν.
5 ἐξαπέστειλαν δ’ οἱ φυγάδες ⟨τοὺς περὶ⟩ Κλῆτιν καὶ
Διακτόριον τοὺς ⟨συγ⟩καταστησομένους ἐν τῇ συγκλήτῳ πρὸς τοὺς παρὰ τῶν Ἀχαιῶν πρεσβευτάς.

Achaeans admit Sparta. Diophanes,[51] however, and some others tried to take the part of the exiles, and begged the Achaeans not to join in their persecution, and for the sake of a few men to lend additional support to those who had wickedly and illegally driven them from their country.

18. Such were the arguments on each side. The Achaeans, after listening to both, decided to admit the town, and afterward, the inscription for a stone having been drawn up, Sparta became a member of the Achaean League, those in the town having agreed to receive such of the old exiles as had not been guilty of any ingratitude to the League.

The Achaeans having ratified this measure sent Bippus of Argos at the head of an embassy to Rome to inform the Senate about everything. The Lacedaemonians also appointed Chaeron as their envoy and the exiles Cletis and Diactorius to represent their interests in the senate against the Achaean envoys.

[51] See n. on 21.3b.2.

FRAGMENTA LIBRI XXIV

I. RES ITALIAE

(xxv.2.6)

1. Εἰς δὲ τὴν Ῥώμην παραγεγονότων τῶν πρεσβευτῶν παρά τε τῶν ⟨Λακεδαιμονίων καὶ τῶν⟩ ἐκ Λακεδαίμονος φυγάδων, ⟨ἔτι δὲ⟩ παρὰ τῶν Ἀχαιῶν, ἅμα δὲ καὶ τῶν παρ᾽ Εὐμένους καὶ παρ᾽ Ἀριαράθου τοῦ βασιλέως ἡκόντων καὶ τῶν παρὰ Φαρνάκου, τού-
2 τοις πρῶτον ἐχρημάτισεν ἡ σύγκλητος. βραχεῖ δὲ χρόνῳ πρότερον ἀνηγγελκότων τῶν περὶ τὸν Μάρκον πρεσβευτῶν, οὓς ἀπεστάλκεισαν ἐπὶ τὸν Εὐμένει καὶ
3 Φαρνάκῃ συνεστηκότα πόλεμον, καὶ διασεσαφηκότων περί τε τῆς Εὐμένους μετριότητος ἐν πᾶσιν καὶ περὶ τῆς Φαρνάκου πλεονεξίας καὶ καθόλου τῆς ὑπερηφανίας, οὐκέτι πολλῶν προσεδεήθη λόγων ἡ σύγκλητος διακούσασα τῶν παραγεγονότων, ἀπεκρίθη δὲ διότι πάλιν πέμψει πρεσβευτὰς τοὺς φιλοτιμότερον ἐπισκεψομένους ὑπὲρ τῶν διαφερόντων ⟨τοῖς⟩ προειρημένοις.
4 μετὰ δὲ ταῦτα τῶν ἐκ τῆς Λακεδαίμονος φυγάδων εἰσπορευθέντων καὶ τῶν ἐκ τῆς πόλεως ἅμα τούτοις, ἐπὶ πολὺ διακούσασα τοῖς μὲν ἐκ τῆς πόλεως οὐδὲν
5 ἐπετίμησε περὶ τῶν γεγονότων, τοῖς δὲ φυγάσιν ἐπηγ-

FRAGMENTS OF BOOK XXIV

I. AFFAIRS OF ITALY

Various Embassies at Rome

(Cf. Livy 40.20)

1. Upon the arrival in Rome of the envoys from the Lacedaemonians and from their exiles, from the Achaeans, from Eumenes, from King Ariarathes, and from Pharnaces, the senate first gave audience to the last named. A short time previously Marcus[1] and the other commissioners whom they had sent to inquire into the circumstances of the war between Eumenes and Pharnaces had presented their report, in which they pointed out the moderation of Eumenes in all matters, and the rapacious and generally overbearing conduct of Pharnaces. The senate, after listening to the envoys, had no need to debate the matter at length, but replied that they would send legates again to inquire with more diligence into the dispute of the two kings. The next to enter were the Spartan exiles together with those from the city; and after giving them a long hearing, the senate, without censuring the citizens at all for what had occurred, promised the exiles to write to

182–181 B.C.

---

[1] His identity is not known. The war is that mentioned in 23.9.2–3.

497

γείλατο γράψειν πρὸς τοὺς Ἀχαιοὺς περὶ τοῦ κατελθεῖν

6 αὐτοὺς εἰς τὴν οἰκείαν. μετὰ δέ τινας ἡμέρας εἰσπορευθέντων ⟨τῶν⟩ περὶ Βίππον τὸν Ἀργεῖον, οὓς
ἀπεστάλκει τὸ τῶν Ἀχαιῶν ἔθνος, καὶ διασαφούντων

7 περὶ τῆς Μεσσηνίων ἀποκαταστάσεως, οὐθενὶ δυσα-
ρεστήσασα περὶ τῶν οἰκονομουμένων ἡ σύγκλητος ἀπεδέξατο φιλανθρώπως τοὺς πρεσβευτάς.

II. RES GRAECIAE

2. Ὅτι κατὰ τὴν Πελοπόννησον παραγενομένων ἐκ
(xxv.3) Ῥώμης τῶν ἐκ τῆς Λακεδαίμονος φυγάδων καὶ κομιζόντων παρὰ τῆς συγκλήτου γράμματα τοῖς Ἀχαιοῖς
ὑπὲρ τοῦ προνοηθῆναι περὶ τῆς αὐτῶν καθόδου καὶ

2 σωτηρίας εἰς τὴν οἰκείαν, ἔδοξε τοῖς Ἀχαιοῖς ὑπερθέσθαι τὸ διαβούλιον, ἕως ἂν οἱ παρ' αὐτῶν ἔλθωσι

3 πρεσβευταί. ταῦτα δὲ τοῖς φυγάσιν ἀποκριθέντες
συνέθεντο τὴν πρὸς Μεσσηνίους στήλην, συγχωρή-
σαντες αὐτοῖς πρὸς τοῖς ἄλλοις φιλανθρώποις καὶ
τριῶν ἐτῶν ἀτέλειαν, ὥστε τὴν τῆς χώρας καταφθορὰν
μηδὲν ἧττον βλάψαι τοὺς Ἀχαιοὺς ἢ Μεσσηνίους.

4 τῶν δὲ περὶ τὸν Βίππον παραγενομένων ἐκ τῆς Ῥώμης
καὶ διασαφούντων γραφῆναι τὰ γράμματα περὶ τῶν
φυγάδων οὐ διὰ τὴν τῆς συγκλήτου σπουδήν, ἀλλὰ

5 διὰ τὴν τῶν φυγάδων φιλοτιμίαν, ἔδοξε τοῖς Ἀχαιοῖς
μένειν ἐπὶ τῶν ὑποκειμένων.

(4) 3. Κατὰ δὲ τὴν Κρήτην ἀρχὴ πραγμάτων ἐκινεῖτο
(xxv.3) μεγάλων, εἰ χρὴ λέγειν ἀρχὴν πραγμά⟨των⟩ ἐν

the Achaeans begging for their return to their country. A few days afterward when Bippus of Argos and the others sent by the Achaean League appeared before them and explained about the restoration of order at Messene,[2] the senate gave them a courteous reception, expressing no displeasure with anyone for the conduct of the matter.

II. AFFAIRS OF GREECE

2. In the Peloponnese when the Lacedaemonian exiles arrived bearing a letter from the senate to the Achaeans asking them to take measures for their safe return to their country, the Achaeans decided to adjourn the debate until the arrival of their own envoys. After giving the exiles this answer, they drew up an inscription to be engraved on the stone recording their agreement with the Messenians, and granting them among other favors a three-years exemption from taxes, so that the devastation[3] of the Messenian territory injured the Achaeans no less than the Messenians. Upon Bippus and the envoys returning from Rome and reporting that the letter on the subject of the exiles had been written not owing to the senate's interest in them, but owing to their importunity, the Achaeans decided to take no step.

3. This year witnessed the beginning of great troubles in Crete,[4] if indeed one can talk of a beginning of trouble

[2] The measures taken by Lycortas, 23.16–17.

[3] 23.15.1, also 24.9.1.

[4] This very sentence stands at the beginning of A. Chaniotis' book *Die Verträge der kretischen Poleis in der hellenistischen Zeit* (Stuttgart 1996); the events are discussed pp. 44–49.

Κρήτῃ· διὰ γὰρ τὴν συνέχειαν τῶν ἐμφυλίων πολέμων καὶ τὴν ὑπερβολὴν τῆς εἰς ἀλλήλους ὠμότητος
ταὐτὸν ἀρχὴ καὶ τέλος ἐστὶν ἐν Κρήτῃ, καὶ τὸ δοκοῦν
παραδόξως τισὶν εἰρῆσθαι τοῦτ᾽ ἐκεῖ θεωρεῖται συνεχῶς [τὸ] γινόμενον.

4. Πρὸς μὲν οὖν τῷ Πόντῳ τὸ Αἷμόν ἐστιν ὄρος,
μέγιστον τῶν ταύτῃ καὶ ὑψηλότατον, μέσην πως δια-
ροῦν τὴν Θρᾴκην· ἀφ᾽ οὗ φησι Πολύβιος ἀμφοτέρας
καθορᾶσθαι τὰς θαλάττας, οὐκ ἀληθῆ λέγων· καὶ γὰρ
τὸ διάστημα μέγα τὸ πρὸς τὸν Ἀδρίαν καὶ τὰ ἐπι-
σκοτοῦντα πολλά.

III. RES ITALIAE

5. Ὅτι γενομένων συνθηκῶν πρὸς ἀλλήλους Φαρνάκου καὶ Ἀττάλου καὶ τῶν λοιπῶν, ἅπαντες μετὰ τῶν
οἰκείων δυνάμεων ἀνεχώρησαν εἰς τὴν οἰκείαν. Εὐμένης δὲ κατὰ τὸν καιρὸν τοῦτον ἀπολελυμένος τῆς ἀρρωστίας καὶ διατρίβων ἐν Περγάμῳ, παραγενομένου
τἀδελφοῦ καὶ διασαφοῦντος περὶ τῶν ᾠκονομημένων,
εὐδοκήσας τοῖς γεγονόσιν προέθετο πέμπειν τοὺς
ἀδελφοὺς ἅπαντας εἰς τὴν Ῥώμην, ἅμα μὲν ἐλπίζων
πέρας ἐπιθήσειν τῷ πρὸς τὸν Φαρνάκην πολέμῳ διὰ
τῆς τούτων πρεσβείας, ἅμα δὲ συστῆσαι σπουδάζων
τοὺς ἀδελφοὺς τοῖς τ᾽ ἰδίᾳ φίλοις καὶ ξένοις ὑπάρχουσιν αὐτῶν ἐν τῇ Ῥώμῃ καὶ τῇ συγκλήτῳ κατὰ
κοινόν. προθύμων δὲ καὶ τῶν περὶ τὸν Ἄτταλον ὑπαρχόντων, ἐγένοντο περὶ τὴν ἐκδημίαν. καὶ τούτων πα-

(xxv.6)

2

3

4
5

in Crete. For owing to the constant succession of their civil wars and their excessive cruelty to each other, beginning and end mean the same thing in Crete, and what is regarded by some as a paradoxical utterance is there constantly a matter of fact.

4. At the Pontus the Haemus Mountain ends, the largest and highest in this area, which dissects Thrace somehow in the middle. Polybius says one could see from there both seas, which is not true. The distance to the Adriatic is too large and there is much that blocks the view.[5]

III. AFFAIRS OF ITALY

The Brothers of Eumenes in Rome

5. After the agreement between Pharnaces and Attalus and the others, they all returned home with their forces. Eumenes at this time had recovered from his sickness, and was living in Pergamum; and when his brother arrived and informed him how he had managed matters, he was pleased at what had happened, and resolved to send all his brothers[6] to Rome, hoping by this mission to put an end to the War between himself and Pharnaces, and at the same time wishing to recommend his brothers to the personal friends and former guests of himself and his house in Rome and to the senate in general. Attalus and the others gladly consented and prepared for the journey. Upon

181/180
B.C.

[5] This corresponds to Livy 40.21.2 and 22.4; the occasion is Philip's campaign of 181.

[6] Attalus, Philetaerus, and Athenaeus.

ραγενομένων εἰς τὴν Ῥώμην, καὶ κατ᾽ ἰδίαν μὲν πάντες ἀπεδέχοντο τοὺς νεανίσκους φιλανθρώπως, ἅτε
συνήθειαν ἐσχηκότες ἐν ταῖς περὶ τὴν Ἀσίαν στρα-
τείαις, ἔτι δὲ μεγαλομερέστερον ἡ σύγκλητος ἀπεδέ-
6 ξατο τὴν παρουσίαν αὐτῶν· καὶ γὰρ ξένια καὶ παροχὰς τὰς μεγίστας ἐξέθηκεν αὐτοῖς καὶ πρὸς τὴν
7 ἔντευξιν καλῶς ἀπήντησεν. οἱ δὲ περὶ τὸν Ἄτταλον
εἰσελθόντες εἰς τὴν σύγκλητον τά τε προϋπάρχοντα
φιλάνθρωπα διὰ πλειόνων λόγων ἀνενεώσαντο καὶ τοῦ
Φαρνάκου κατηγορήσαντες παρεκάλουν ἐπιστροφήν
τινα ποιήσασθαι, δι᾽ ἧς τεύξεται τῆς ἁρμοζούσης δί-
8 κης. ἡ δὲ σύγκλητος διακούσασα φιλανθρώπως ἀπεκρίθη διότι πέμψει πρεσβευτὰς τοὺς κατὰ πάντα τρόπον λύσοντας τὸν πόλεμον. καὶ τὰ μὲν κατὰ τὴν
Ἰταλίαν οὕτως εἶχεν.

IV. RES GRAECIAE

6. Ὅτι περὶ τοὺς αὐτοὺς καιροὺς Πτολεμαῖος ὁ
(xxv.7) βασιλεύς, βουλόμενος ἐμπλέκεσθαι τῷ τῶν Ἀχαιῶν
ἔθνει, διεπέμψατο πρεσβευτήν, ἐπαγγελλόμενος δεκα-
2 ναΐαν δώσειν ἐντελῆ πεντηκοντηρικῶν πλοίων. οἱ δ᾽
Ἀχαιοὶ καὶ διὰ τὸ δοκεῖν τὴν δωρεὰν ἀξίαν εἶναι χάριτος ἀσμένως ἀπεδέξαντο τὴν ἐπαγγελίαν. δοκεῖ γὰρ
3 ἡ δαπάνη οὐ πολὺ λείπειν τῶν δέκα ταλάντων. ταῦτα
δὲ βουλευσάμενοι προεχειρίσαντο πρεσβευτὰς Λυκόρταν καὶ Πολύβιον καὶ σὺν τούτοις Ἄρατον, υἱὸν
Ἀράτου τοῦ Σικυωνίου, τοὺς ἅμα μὲν εὐχαριστήσοντας

their arrival in Rome, all their friends gave the young men the kindest reception in their houses, as they had become intimate with them in their campaigns in Asia,[7] and the senate greeted them upon their arrival on a magnificent scale, with rich gifts and luxurious accommodations, and replying most satisfactorily to them at their official audience. Attalus and his brothers on entering the Curia spoke at some length in renewal of their former amicable relations and, accusing Pharnaces, begged the senate to take measures to inflict on him the punishment he merited. The senate, after giving them a courteous hearing, replied that they would send legates who would by some means or other put an end to the war. Such was the condition of affairs in Italy.

IV. AFFAIRS OF GREECE

Ptolemy and the Achaeans

6. At the same period[8] King Ptolemy, wishing to ingratiate himself with the Achaean League, sent an envoy promising to give them a full squadron of pentekonteres. The Achaeans, chiefly because they thought the gift one for which real thanks were due, gladly accepted it, for the cost was not much less than ten talents. Having decided on this, they appointed as envoys Lycortas, Polybius, and Aratus, son of Aratus of Sicyon, to thank the king[9] for

---

[7] Attested for Attalus 21.39.5–11, for Athenaeus by Livy 38.2.8, nowhere for Philetaerus.

[8] Spring 180.

[9] Somewhat belatedly, see 22.9.3.

τῷ βασιλεῖ περί τε τῶν ὅπλων ὧν πρότερον ἀπέστειλε
καὶ τοῦ νομίσματος, ἅμα δὲ παραληψομένους τὰ
πλοῖα καὶ πρόνοιαν ποιησομένους περὶ τῆς ἀποκομιδῆς

4 αὐτῶν. κατέστησαν δὲ τὸν μὲν Λυκόρταν διὰ τὸ κατὰ
τὸν καιρόν, καθ᾽ ὃν ἐποιεῖτο τὴν ἀνανέωσιν τῆς συμμαχίας ὁ Πτολεμαῖος, στρατηγοῦντα τότε συνεργῆσαι

5 φιλοτίμως αὐτῷ, τὸν δὲ Πολύβιον, νεώτερον ὄντα τῆς
κατὰ τοὺς νόμους ἡλικίας, διὰ τὸ τήν τε συμμαχίαν
αὐτοῦ τὸν πατέρα πρεσβεύσαντα πρὸς Πτολεμαῖον
ἀνανεώσασθαι καὶ τὴν δωρεὰν τῶν ὅπλων καὶ τοῦ

6 νομίσματος ἀγαγεῖν τοῖς Ἀχαιοῖς, παραπλησίως δὲ
καὶ τὸν Ἄρατον διὰ τὰς προγονικὰς συστάσεις πρὸς

7 τὴν βασιλείαν. οὐ μὴν συνέβη γε τὴν πρεσβείαν ταύτην ἐξελθεῖν διὰ τὸ μεταλλάξαι τὸν Πτολεμαῖον περὶ
τοὺς καιροὺς τούτους.

7. Ὅτι κατὰ τοὺς αὐτοὺς καιροὺς ἦν τις ἐν τῇ Λα-
(xxv.8) κεδαίμονι Χαίρων, ὃς ἐτύγχανε τῷ πρότερον ἔτει πε-
πρεσβευκὼς εἰς τὴν Ῥώμην, ἄνθρωπος ἀγχίνους μὲν
καὶ πρακτικός, νέος δὲ καὶ ταπεινὸς καὶ δημοτικῆς

2 ἀγωγῆς τετευχώς. οὗτος ὀχλαγωγῶν καὶ κινήσας ὁ
μηθεὶς ἕτερος ἐθάρρει, ταχέως περιεποιήσατο φαντα-

3 σίαν παρὰ τοῖς πολλοῖς. καὶ τὸ μὲν πρῶτον ἀφελόμενος
τὴν χώραν, ἣν οἱ τύραννοι συνεχώρησαν ταῖς ὑπο-
λειφθείσαις τῶν φυγάδων ἀδελφαῖς καὶ γυναιξὶ καὶ
μητράσι καὶ τέκνοις, ταύτην διέδωκε τοῖς λεπτοῖς εἰκῇ

4 καὶ ἀνίσως κατὰ τὴν ἰδίαν ἐξουσίαν· μετὰ δὲ ταῦτα

the arms and coined money he had previously sent, and
to receive the ships and look after their dispatch. They
appointed Lycortas because, at the time[10] when Ptolemy
renewed the alliance, he had been strategus, and had done
his best to consult the king's interests, and Polybius,[11] who
had not attained the legal age for such a post, because his
father had gone on an embassy to Ptolemy to renew the
alliance, and to bring back the gift of arms and money.
Aratus was chosen owing to his family's relations[12] with the
king. This embassy, however, never came off, owing to the
death of Ptolemy[13] which occurred about this time.

Chaeron of Sparta

(Cf. Suda)

7. Just about the same time there was in Sparta a certain Chaeron, who had been a member of the embassy to
Rome in the previous year.[14] He was a sharp and able
man, but he was young and of humble station, and had
received a vulgar education. This man, courting the mob
and making innovations upon which no one else ventured,
soon acquired some reputation with the populace. The
first thing he did was to take away from the sisters, wives,
mothers, and children that the exiles had left behind
the property granted them by the tyrants, and distribute
it among men of slender means at random, unfairly, and
just as he chose. After this he began to use public moneys

---

[10] The choice seems to be between 186/5 and 182/1.
[11] Then barely twenty years old.   [12] Going back at least
eighty-five years.   [13] September 180; Huss (16.18.2), 536.
[14] 23.18.4.

τοῖς κοινοῖς ὡς ἰδίοις χρώμενος ἐξεδαπάνα τὰς προσ-
όδους, οὐ νόμου στοχαζόμενος, οὐ κοινοῦ δόγματος,
5 οὐκ ἄρχοντος. ἐφ᾿ οἷς τινες ἀγανακτήσαντες ἐσπού-
δαζον κατασταθῆναι δοκιμαστῆρες τῶν κοινῶν κατὰ
6 τοὺς νόμους. ὁ δὲ Χαίρων θεωρῶν τὸ γινόμενον καὶ
συνειδὼς αὑτῷ κακῶς κεχειρικότι τὰ τῆς πόλεως, τὸν
ἐπιφανέστατον τῶν δοκιμαστήρων Ἀπολλωνίδαν καὶ
μάλιστα δυνάμενον ἐρευνῆσαι τὴν πλεονεξίαν αὐτοῦ,
τοῦτον ἀποπορευόμενον ἡμέρας ἐκ βαλανείου προσ-
7 πέμψας τινὰς ἐξεκέντησεν. ὧν προσπεσόντων τοῖς
Ἀχαιοῖς, καὶ τοῦ πλήθους ἀγανακτήσαντος ἐπὶ τοῖς
γεγονόσιν, ἐξ αὐτῆς ὁ στρατηγὸς ὁρμήσας καὶ παραγενόμενος εἰς τὴν Λακεδαίμονα τόν τε Χαίρωνα παρήγαγεν εἰς κρίσιν ὑπὲρ τοῦ φόνου τοῦ κατὰ τὸν
8 Ἀπολλωνίδαν καὶ κατακρίνας ἐποίησε δέσμιον, τούς
τε λοιποὺς δοκιματσήρας παρώξυνε πρὸς τὸ ποιεῖσθαι
τὴν ζήτησιν τῶν δημοσίων ἀληθινήν, φροντίσαι δὲ
καὶ περὶ τοῦ κομίσασθαι τὰς οὐσίας τοὺς τῶν φυγάδων ἀναγκαίους πάλιν, ἃς ὁ Χαίρων αὐτῶν ἀφείλετο
βραχεῖ χρόνῳ πρότερον.

(10)   8. Ὅτι κατὰ τὸν καιρὸν τοῦτον ἀναδόντος Ὑπερ-
(xxvi.1) βάτου τοῦ στρατηγοῦ διαβούλιον ὑπὲρ τῶν γραφομένων παρὰ Ῥωμαίων ὑπὲρ τῆς τῶν ἐκ Λακεδαίμονος
2 φυγάδων ⟨καθόδου⟩ τί δεῖ ποιεῖν, οἱ μὲν περὶ τὸν Λυκόρταν παρεκάλουν μένειν ἐπὶ τῶν ὑποκειμένων, διότι
Ῥωμαῖοι ποιοῦσι μὲν τὸ καθῆκον αὐτοῖς, συνυπακού-
οντες τοῖς ἀκληρεῖν δοκοῦσιν εἰς τὰ μέτρια τῶν ἀξι-

as if they were his own, and spent all the revenue without reference to laws, public decrees, or magistrates. Some citizens were indignant at this and took steps to get themselves appointed auditors[15] of the public accounts as the law enjoined. Chaeron, seeing this and conscious that he had misused the public funds, when Apollonidas, the most notable of the auditors and most capable of exposing his rapacity, was on his way from a bath one day in broad daylight, sent some men and killed him. Upon this becoming known to the Achaeans, the people were exceedingly indignant, and the strategus[16] started off at once for Sparta, where he put Chaeron on trial for the murder of Apollonidas, and upon his being found guilty, put him in prison, encouraging at the same time the other auditors to inquire seriously into the management of the public funds and to see that the relatives of the exiles recovered the property of which Chaeron had recently robbed them.

The Achaeans and Rome

8. At this time, when Hyperbatus the strategus submitted to the Achaeans' Assembly the question of how to act upon the Roman communication regarding the return of the Spartan exiles, Lycortas advised them to take no steps, because while it was true that the Romans were doing their duty in lending an ear to reasonable requests made by persons whom they regarded as bereft of their rights,

---

[15] Δοκιμαστήρ is a *hapax*, usually δοκιμαστής "scrutineer." See P. Fröhlich, *Les cités grecques et le contrôle des magistrats* (Geneva 2004), 234–235: "commissaires extraordinaires dans le koinon achéen."   [16] Probably Hyperbatus; see 8.1.

3 ουμένων· ὅταν μέντοι γε διδάξῃ τις αὐτοὺς ὅτι τῶν
παρακαλουμένων τὰ μέν ἐστιν ἀδύνατα, τὰ δὲ μεγάλην αἰσχύνην ἐπιφέροντα καὶ βλάβην τοῖς φίλοις,
οὔτε φιλονικεῖν εἰώθασιν οὔτε παραβιάζεσθαι περὶ
4 τῶν τοιούτων. διὸ καὶ νῦν, ἐάν τις αὐτοὺς διδάξῃ
⟨δι⟩ότι συμβήσεται τοῖς Ἀχαιοῖς, ἂν πειθαρχήσωσι
τοῖς γραφομένοις, παραβῆναι τοὺς ὅρκους, τοὺς νόμους, τὰς στήλας, ἃ συνέχει τὴν κοινὴν συμπολιτείαν
5 ἡμῶν, ἀναχωρήσουσιν καὶ συγκαταθήσονται διότι
καλῶς ἐπέχομεν καὶ παραιτούμεθα περὶ τῶν γραφο-
6 μένων. ταῦτα μὲν οὖν οἱ περὶ τὸν Λυκόρταν ἔλεγον· οἱ
δὲ περὶ τὸν Ὑπέρβατον καὶ Καλλικράτην πειθαρχεῖν
τοῖς γραφομένοις παρῄνουν καὶ μήτε νόμον μήτε
στήλην μήτ' ἄλλο μηθὲν τούτου νομίζειν ἀναγκαι-
7 ότερον. τοιαύτης δ' οὔσης τῆς ἀντιλογίας ἔδοξε τοῖς
Ἀχαιοῖς πρεσβευτὰς ἐξαποστεῖλαι πρὸς τὴν σύγκλη-
8 τον τοὺς διδάξοντας ἃ Λυκόρτας λέγει. καὶ παραυτίκα
κατέστησαν πρεσβευτὰς Καλλικράτην Λεοντήσιον,
Λυδιάδαν Μεγαλοπολίτην, Ἄρατον Σικυώνιον· καὶ
δόντες ἐντολὰς ἀκολούθους τοῖς προειρημένοις ἐξαπέ-
9 στειλαν. ὧν παραγενομένων εἰς τὴν Ῥώμην, εἰσελθὼν
ὁ Καλλικράτης εἰς τὴν σύγκλητον τοσοῦτον ἀπέσχε
τοῦ ταῖς ἐντολαῖς ἀκολούθως διδάσκειν τὸ συνέδριον

---

17 He is becoming the spokesman for those favoring obedience to Rome. He is also on record in the new dossier from
Messene dating to these years (see n. on 23.17.1). Deininger
(22.10.8), 135–145.

18 Grandson of the homonymous tyrant of Megalopolis. He

yet if it were pointed out to them that some of these requests were impossible to grant, and others would entail
great injury and disgrace on their friends, it was not their
habit in such matters to contend that they were right or
enforce compliance. "So," he said, "at present, if it is
pointed out to them that we Achaeans by acceding to their
written request will violate our oaths, our laws, and the
inscribed conventions that hold our League together, they
will withdraw their demand and agree that we are right in
hesitating and begging to be excused for noncompliance."
Lycortas spoke in this sense; but Hyperbatus and Callicrates[17] were in favor of compliance with the request, saying that neither laws nor inscribed agreements nor anything else should be considered more binding than the will
of Rome. Such being the different views advanced, the
Achaeans decided to send envoys to the senate to point
out what Lycortas urged, and they at once appointed Callicrates of Leontium, Lydiadas[18] of Megalopolis, and Aratus of Sicyon, and sent them off with instructions[19] con-
forming to what I have stated. Upon their arrival in
Rome, Callicrates on entering the senate house was so
far from addressing that body in the terms of his instruc-

abdicated, brought the city into the League, and was killed in
battle against king Cleomenes in 227. New documents on him
and his family were recently published: A. Stavrianopoulou, *Tekmeria* 7 (2002), 117–156, for Lydiadas II 152–154. For the chro-
nology WC 3.17–19.

[19] It is not clear what these instructions were, and whether (or
to what degree) Callicrates deviated from them. See on him P.
Derow, *Essays presented to C. M. Bowra* (The Alden Press for
Wadham College, Oxford 1970), 12–23.

ὥστε τοὐναντίον ἐκ καταβολῆς ἐπεχείρησεν οὐ μόνον
τῶν ἀντιπολιτευομένων κατηγορεῖν θρασέως, ἀλλὰ
καὶ τὴν σύγκλητον νουθετεῖν.

(11)   9. ἔφη γὰρ αὐτοὺς τοὺς Ῥωμαίους αἰτίους εἶναι τοῦ
(xxvi.2) μὴ πειθαρχεῖν αὐτοῖς τοὺς Ἕλληνας, ἀλλὰ παρακού-
ειν καὶ τῶν γραφομένων καὶ τῶν παραγγελλομένων.

2   δυεῖν γὰρ οὐσῶν αἱρέσεων κατὰ τὸ παρὸν ἐν πάσαις
ταῖς δημοκρατικαῖς πολιτείαις, καὶ τῶν μὲν φασκόντων δεῖν ἀκολουθεῖν τοῖς γραφομένοις ὑπὸ Ῥωμαίων
καὶ μήτε νόμον μήτε στήλην μήτ᾽ ἄλλο μηθὲν προυρ-

3   γιαίτερον νομίζειν τῆς Ῥωμαίων προαιρέσεως, τῶν δὲ
τοὺς νόμους προφερομένων καὶ τοὺς ὅρκους καὶ στήλας καὶ παρακαλούντων τὰ πλήθη μὴ ῥᾳδίως ταῦτα

4   παραβαίνειν, ἀχαϊκωτέραν εἶναι παρὰ πολὺ ταύτην
5   τὴν ὑπόθεσιν καὶ νικητικωτέραν ἐν τοῖς πολλοῖς. ἐξ
οὗ τοῖς μὲν αἱρουμένοις τὰ Ῥωμαίων ἀδοξίαν συν-
εξακολουθεῖν παρὰ τοῖς ὄχλοις καὶ διαβολήν, τοῖς δ᾽

6   ἀντιπράττουσιν τἀναντία. ἐὰν μὲν οὖν ὑπὸ τῆς συγκλήτου γίνηταί τις ἐπισημασία, ταχέως καὶ τοὺς πολιτευομένους μεταθέσθαι πρὸς τὴν Ῥωμαίων αἵρεσιν,
καὶ τοὺς πολλοὺς τούτοις ἐπακολουθήσειν διὰ τὸν φό-

7   βον. ἐὰν δὲ παρορᾶται τοῦτο τὸ μέρος, ἅπαντας ἀπο-
νεύσειν ἐπ᾽ ἐκείνην τὴν ὑπόθεσιν· ἐνδοξοτέραν γὰρ

8   εἶναι καὶ καλλίω παρὰ τοῖς ὄχλοις. διὸ καὶ νῦν ἤδη
τινὰς οὐθὲν ἕτερον προσφερομένους δίκαιον πρὸς φιλοδοξίαν, δι᾽ αὐτὸ τοῦτο τῶν μεγίστων τυγχάνειν
τιμῶν παρὰ τοῖς ἰδίοις πολιτεύμασιν διὰ τὸ δοκεῖν
ἀντιλέγειν τοῖς ὑφ᾽ ὑμῶν γραφομένοις, χάριν τοῦ δια-

tions, that on the contrary, from the very outset of his speech, he not only attempted to bring audacious accusations against his political opponents, but to lecture the senate.

9. For he said that it was the fault of the Romans themselves that the Greeks, instead of complying with their wishes, disobeyed their communications and orders. There were, he said, two parties at present in all democratic states, one of which maintained that the written requests of the Romans should be executed, and that neither laws, inscribed agreements, nor anything else should take precedence to the wishes of Rome, while the other appealed to laws, sworn treaties, and inscriptions, and implored the people not to violate these lightly; and this latter view, he said, was much more popular in Achaea and carried the day with the multitude, the consequence being that the partisans of Rome were constantly exposed to the contempt and slander of the mob, while it was the reverse with their opponents. If the senate now gave some token of their disapproval the political leaders would soon go over to the side of Rome, and the populace would follow them out of fear. But in the event of the senate neglecting to do so, every one would change and adopt the other attitude, which in the eyes of the mob was more dignified and honorable. "Even now," he said, "certain persons, who have no other just claim to distinction, have received the highest honors in their several states simply for the reason that they are thought to oppose your injunctions for the

μένειν τοὺς νόμους ἰσχυροὺς καὶ τὰ δόγματα τὰ γι-
9 νόμενα παρ᾽ αὐτοῖς. εἰ μὲν οὖν <ἀ>διαφόρως ἔχουσιν
ὑπὲρ τοῦ πειθαρχεῖν αὐτοῖς τοὺς Ἕλληνας καὶ συνυπακούειν τοῖς γραφομένοις, ἄγειν αὐτοὺς ἐκέλευε τὴν
10 ἀγωγήν, ἣν καὶ νῦν ἄγουσιν· εἰ δὲ βούλονται γίνεσθαι σφίσι τὰ παραγγελλόμενα καὶ μηθένα καταφρονεῖν τῶν γραφομένων, ἐπιστροφὴν ποιήσασθαι
11 παρεκάλει τοῦ μέρους τούτου τὴν ἐνδεχομένην. εἰ δὲ
μή, σαφῶς εἰδέναι δεῖν ὅτι τἀναντία συμβήσεται ταῖς
12 ἐπινοίαις αὐτῶν· ὃ καὶ νῦν ἤδη γεγονέναι. πρῴην μὲν
γὰρ ἐν τοῖς Μεσσηνιακοῖς πολλὰ ποιήσαντος Κοΐντου Μαρκίου πρὸς τὸ μηδὲν τοὺς Ἀχαιοὺς βουλεύσασθαι περὶ Μεσσηνίων ἄνευ τῆς Ῥωμαίων προαιρέ-
13 σεως, παρακούσαντας καὶ ψηφισαμένους αὐτοὺς τὸν
πόλεμον οὐ μόνον τὴν χώραν αὐτῶν καταφθεῖραι
πᾶσαν ἀδίκως, ἀλλὰ καὶ τοὺς ἐπιφανεστάτους τῶν
πολιτῶν οὓς μὲν φυγαδεῦσαι, τινὰς δ᾽ αὐτῶν ἐκδότους
λαβόντας αἰκισαμένους πᾶσαν αἰκίαν ἀποκτεῖναι, διότι προεκαλοῦντο περὶ τῶν ἀμφισβητουμένων ἐπὶ
14 Ῥωμαίους. νῦν δὲ πάλιν ἐκ πλείονος χρόνου γραφόντων αὐτῶν ὑπὲρ τῆς καθόδου τῶν ἐκ Λακεδαίμονος
φυγάδων, τοσοῦτον ἀπέχειν τοῦ πειθαρχεῖν ὡς καὶ
στήλην τεθεῖσθαι καὶ πεποιῆσθαι πρὸς τοὺς κατέχοντας τὴν πόλιν ὅρκους ὑπὲρ τοῦ μηδέποτε κατελεύσε-
15 σθαι τοὺς φυγάδας. εἰς ἃ βλέποντας αὐτοὺς ἠξίου
πρόνοιαν ποιεῖσθαι τοῦ μέλλοντος.

(12)   10. Ὁ μὲν οὖν Καλλικράτης ταῦτα καὶ τοιαῦτ᾽ εἰ-
(xxvi.3)

512

sake of maintaining the force of their laws and decrees. If, then, it is a matter of indifference to you whether or not the Greeks obey you and comply with your instructions, continue to act as you do now; but if you wish your orders to be executed and none to treat your communications with contempt, you should give all possible attention to this matter. For you may be quite sure that, if you do not, just the opposite will happen to what you contemplate, as has already been the case. For when quite lately in the Messenian difficulty Quintus Marcius[20] did his best to ensure that the Achaeans should take no steps regarding Messene without the initiative of Rome, they paid no attention to him; but, after voting for war on their own accord, not only most unjustly devastated the whole of Messenia,[21] but sent into exile some of its most distinguished citizens; and, when others were delivered up to them, put them to death after inflicting every variety of torture on them, just because they had appealed to Rome to judge the dispute. And now for some time while you have been writing to them about the return of the Spartan exiles, they are so far from complying that a solemn inscribed agreement has been made with the party that holds Sparta and oaths taken that the exiles shall never be allowed to return." So he begged them in view of all this to take precautions for the future.

10. Callicrates retired after speaking in these or similar

---

20 23.9.4; 9.8.

21 Callicrates' description sharply contrasts with P.'s own assessment (23.16.6–17.1) of how his father treated the Messenians.

πῶν ἀπῆλθεν. οἱ φυγάδες δ' ἐπεισελθόντες καὶ βρα-
2 χέα περὶ αὑτῶν διδάξαντες καί τινα τῶν πρὸς τὸν
3 κοινὸν ἔλεον εἰπόντες ἀνεχώρησαν. ἡ δὲ σύγκλητος
δόξασα τὸν Καλλικράτην λέγειν τι τῶν αὐτῇ συμφερόντων καὶ διδαχθεῖσα διότι δεῖ τοὺς μὲν τοῖς αὑτῆς
δόγμασιν συνηγοροῦντας αὔξειν, τοὺς δ' ἀντιλέγοντας
4 ταπεινοῦν, οὕτως καὶ τότε πρῶτον ἐπεβάλετο τοὺς μὲν
κατὰ τὸ βέλτιστον ἱσταμένους ἐν τοῖς ἰδίοις πολιτεύμασιν ἐλαττοῦν, τοὺς δὲ καὶ δικαίως ⟨καὶ ἀδίκως⟩
5 προστρέχοντας αὐτῇ σωματοποιεῖν. ἐξ ὧν αὐτῇ συνέβη κατὰ βραχύ, τοῦ χρόνου προβαίνοντος, κολάκων
6 μὲν εὐπορεῖν, φίλων δὲ σπανίζειν ἀληθινῶν. οὐ μὴν
ἀλλὰ τότε περὶ μὲν τῆς καθόδου τῶν φυγάδων οὐ
μόνον τοῖς Ἀχαιοῖς ἔγραψε, παρακαλοῦσα συνεπι-
σχύειν, ἀλλὰ καὶ τοῖς Αἰτωλοῖς καὶ τοῖς Ἠπειρώταις,
σὺν δὲ τούτοις Ἀθηναίοις, Βοιωτοῖς, Ἀκαρνᾶσιν, πάντας ὡσανεὶ προσδιαμαρτυρομένη χάριν τοῦ συντρῖψαι
7 τοὺς Ἀχαιούς. περὶ δὲ τοῦ Καλλικράτους αὐτοῦ κατ'
ἰδίαν παρασιωπήσασα τοὺς συμπρεσβευτὰς κατέτα-
ξεν εἰς τὴν ἀπόκρισιν διότι δεῖ τοιούτους ὑπάρχειν ἐν
8 τοῖς πολιτεύμασιν ἄνδρας οἷός ἐστι Καλλικράτης. ὁ
δὲ προειρημένος ἔχων τὰς ἀποκρίσεις ταύτας παρῆν
εἰς τὴν Ἑλλάδα περιχαρής, οὐκ εἰδὼς ὅτι μεγάλων
κακῶν ἀρχηγὸς γέγονε πᾶσι μὲν τοῖς Ἕλλησι, μάλι-
9 στα δὲ τοῖς Ἀχαιοῖς. ἔτι γὰρ τούτοις ἐξῆν καὶ κατ'
ἐκείνους τοὺς χρόνους κατὰ ποσὸν ἰσολογίαν ἔχειν

---

22 P. clearly composed the speech himself. So Callicrates' ad-

terms.[22] The exiles entered next, and, after stating their case in a few words and making a general appeal for compassion, withdrew. The senate, thinking that what Callicrates had said was in their interest, and learning from him that they should exalt those who supported their decrees and humble those who opposed them, now first began the policy[23] of weakening those members of the several states who worked for the best, and of strengthening those, who, no matter whether rightly or wrongly, appealed to its authority. The consequence of this was that gradually, as time went on, they had plenty of flatterers but very few true friends. They actually went so far on the present occasion as to write not only to the Achaeans on the subject of the return of the exiles, begging them to help these men, but to the Aetolians, Epirots, Athenians, Boeotians, and Acarnanians,[24] calling them all to witness as if for the express purpose of crushing the Achaeans. Speaking of Callicrates alone with no mention of the other envoys, they wrote in their official answer that there ought to be more men like Callicrates in the several states. He now returned in high spirits to Greece with this answer, quite unaware that he had been the initiator of great calamities for all Greece, and especially for the Achaeans. For it was still possible for the Achaeans even at this period to deal with Rome on more or less equal terms,

mission that he expressed a minority view (9.4) is rather what P. makes him say.   [23] P. finds in this debate the beginning of a deliberate policy of the Senate to weaken Greek attempts at preserving some independence.   [24] Four of the five states are Confederacies, with Athens the exception, although the city was hardly inferior to any of the other four.

πρὸς Ῥωμαίους διὰ τὸ τετηρηκέναι τὴν πίστιν ἐν τοῖς
ἐπιφανεστάτοις καιροῖς, ἐξ οὗ τὰ Ῥωμαίων εἵλοντο,
10 λέγω δὲ τοῖς κατὰ Φίλιππον καὶ Ἀντίοχον, οὕτω δὲ
τοῦ τῶν Ἀχαιῶν ἔθνους ηὐξημένου καὶ προκοπὴν εἰ-
ληφότος κατὰ τὸ βέλτιστον ἀφ' ὧν ἡμεῖς ἱστοροῦμεν
χρόνων, αὕτη πάλιν ἀρχὴ τῆς ἐπὶ τὸ χεῖρον ἐγένετο
11 μεταβολῆς, τὸ Καλλικράτους θράσος . . . Ῥωμαῖοι
ὄντες ἄνθρωποι καὶ ψυχῇ χρώμενοι λαμπρᾷ καὶ προαιρέσει καλῇ πάντας μὲν ἐλεοῦσι τοὺς ἐπταικότας καὶ
πᾶσι πειρῶνται χαρίζεσθαι τοῖς καταφεύγουσιν ὡς
12 αὑτούς· ὅταν μέντοι γέ τις ὑπέμνησε τῶν δικαίων,
τετηρηκὼς τὴν πίστιν, ἀνατρέχουσι καὶ διορθοῦνται
13 σφᾶς αὐτοὺς κατὰ δύναμιν ἐν τοῖς πλείστοις. ὁ δὲ
Καλλικράτης πρεσβεύσας κατὰ τοὺς ἐνεστῶτας καιροὺς εἰς τὴν Ῥώμην χάριν τοῦ λέγειν τὰ δίκαια περὶ
τῶν Ἀχαιῶν, χρησάμενος κατὰ τοὐναντίον τοῖς πράγμασιν καὶ συνεπισπασάμενος ⟨τὰ⟩ κατὰ Μεσσηνίους, ὑπὲρ ὧν οὐδ' ἐνεκάλουν Ῥωμαῖοι, παρῆν εἰς
Ἀχαΐαν προσανατεινόμενος τὸν ἀπὸ Ῥωμαίων φόβον·
14 καὶ διὰ τὴν ἀποπρεσβείαν καταπληξάμενος καὶ συν-
τρίψας τοὺς ὄχλους διὰ τὸ μηδὲν εἰδέναι τῶν ὑπ' αὐτοῦ κατ' ἀλήθειαν εἰρημένων ἐν τῇ συγκλήτῳ τοὺς
πολλούς, πρῶτον μὲν ᾑρέθη στρατηγός, πρὸς τοῖς
15 ἄλλοις κακοῖς καὶ δωροδοκηθείς, ἑξῆς δὲ τούτοις
παραλαβὼν τὴν ἀρχὴν κατῆγε τοὺς ἐκ τῆς Λακεδαίμονος καὶ τοὺς ἐκ τῆς Μεσσήνης φυγάδας.

as they had remained faithful to her ever since they had taken her part in the most important times—I mean the wars with Philip and Antiochus—but now after the Achaean League had become stronger and more prosperous than at any time during the period covered by my history, this effrontery of Callicrates was the beginning of a change for the worse. . . . The Romans are men, and with their noble disposition and high principles pity all who are in misfortune and appeal to them; but, when anyone who has remained true to them reminds them of the claims of justice, they usually draw back and correct themselves as far as they can. On the present occasion Callicrates, who had been sent to Rome to state the just claims of Achaea, did exactly the opposite, and having dragged in the Messenian question, about which the Romans did not even raise any complaint, returned to Achaea armed with threats of Roman displeasure. By his report he overawed and crushed the spirits of the people, who were perfectly ignorant of the words he had actually used in the Senate; first of all he was elected strategus,[25] taking bribes in addition to all his other misconduct, and next, on entering upon office, brought back the Spartan and Messenian exiles.

[25] The election marks Callicrates' ascendancy within Achaea. In office, he restored the Spartan and Messenian exiles. The former honored him with a statue at Olympia, *IvO* 300.

(13)　　11. Ὅτι Φιλοποίμενα καὶ Ἀρίσταινον τοὺς Ἀχαιοὺς
(xxv.9)　συνέβη οὔτε τὴν φύσιν ὁμοίαν σχεῖν οὔτε τὴν αἵρεσιν
2　τῆς πολιτείας. ἦν γὰρ ὁ μὲν Φιλοποίμην εὖ πεφυκὼς
πρὸς τὰς πολεμικὰς χρείας καὶ κατὰ τὸ σῶμα καὶ
κατὰ τὴν ψυχήν, ὁ δ' ἕτερος πρὸς τὰ πολιτικὰ τῶν
3　διαβουλίων. τῇ δ' αἱρέσει κατὰ τὴν πολιτείαν τοῦτο
διέφερον ἀλλήλων. τῆς γὰρ Ῥωμαίων ὑπεροχῆς ἤδη
τοῖς Ἑλληνικοῖς πράγμασιν ἐμπλεκομένης ὁλοσχερῶς
κατά τε τοὺς Φιλιππικοὺς καὶ τοὺς Ἀντιοχικοὺς και-
4　ρούς, ⟨ὁ μὲν⟩ Ἀρίσταινος ἦγε τὴν ἀγωγὴν τῆς πολιτείας οὕτως ὥστε πᾶν τὸ πρόσφορον Ῥωμαίοις ἐξ
ἑτοίμου ποιεῖν, ἔνια δὲ καὶ πρὶν ἢ προστάξαι 'κείνους.
5　ἐπειρᾶτο μέντοι γε τῶν νόμων ἔχεσθαι δοκεῖν καὶ τὴν
τοιαύτην ἐφείλκετο φαντασίαν, εἴκων, ὁπότε τούτων
ἀντιπίπτοι τις προδήλως τοῖς ὑπὸ Ῥωμαίων γραφο-
6　μένοις. ὁ δὲ Φιλοποίμην, ὅσα μὲν εἴη τῶν παρακαλουμένων ἀκόλουθα τοῖς νόμοις καὶ τῇ συμμαχίᾳ, πάντα
7　συγκατήνει καὶ συνέπραττεν ἀπροφασίστως, ὅσα δὲ
τούτων ἐκτὸς ἐπιτάττοιεν, οὐχ οἷός τ' ἦν ἐθελοντὴν
συνυπακούειν, ἀλλὰ τὰς μὲν ἀρχὰς ἔφη δεῖν δικαι-
8　ολογεῖσθαι, μετὰ δὲ ταῦτα πάλιν ἀξιοῦν· εἰ δὲ μηδ'
οὕτως πείθοιεν, τέλος οἷον ἐπιμαρτυρομένους εἴκειν
καὶ τότε ποιεῖν τὸ παραγγελλόμενον.

(14)　　12. Ὅτι τοιούτοις ἀπολογισμοῖς Ἀρίσταινος ἐχρῆτο
(xxxv.9a)　πρὸς τοὺς Ἀχαιοὺς περὶ τῆς ἰδίας αἱρέσεως· ἔφη γὰρ
οὐκ εἶναι δυνατὸν καὶ ⟨τὸ⟩ δόρυ καὶ τὸ κηρύκειον ἅμα

―――――――――

26 The comparison with Aristaenus (11–13) culminates in

Comparison between Philopoemen and Aristaenus

(Cf. Suda)

11. Philopoemen[26] and Aristaenus the Achaeans were alike neither in nature nor in their political convictions. Philopoemen indeed was exceptionally capable both physically and mentally in the field of war, Aristaenus in that of politics; and the difference in their political convictions was as follows. Now that, during the wars with Philip and Antiochus, Roman supremacy had definitely asserted itself in the affairs of Greece, Aristaenus in conducting affairs of state was ever ready to do what was agreeable to the Romans, sometimes even anticipating their orders, but yet he aimed at a seeming adherence to the law, and strove to acquire a reputation for doing so, though giving way whenever any law was in evident opposition to the Roman instructions. Philopoemen, on the other hand, cordially accepted and helped to execute, without raising any objection, all requests which were in accordance with the laws and the terms of the alliance; but when the requests were not so, could never induce himself to comply with them willingly, but said that the magistrates first ought to argue their point of view, and after that go on to put it as a request. If, however, they failed even by this means to convince the Romans, they should finally give way more or less under protest and execute the order.

12. Aristaenus offered to the Achaeans the following defense, more or less, of his policy. He said it was impossible to maintain their friendship with Rome, by holding

"two fictitious speeches condensing arguments which they employed on several occasions" (WC 3.265).

προτεινομένους συνέχειν τὴν πρὸς Ῥωμαίους φιλίαν·
"ἀλλ' εἰ μὲν οἷοί τ' ἐσμὲν ἀντοφθαλμεῖν καὶ δυνάμεθα
τοῦτο ποιεῖν..............⟨εἰ δὲ μηδ'⟩ ὁ Φιλοποίμην

2 εἰπεῖν τοῦτο τολμᾷ........καιροῖς ἕνα Ῥωμαίοις, διὰ
τί ἀδυνάτων ὀρεγόμενοι τὰ δυνατὰ παρίεμεν;" δύο γὰρ
ἔφη σκοποὺς εἶναι πάσης πολιτείας, τό τε καλὸν καὶ
τὸ συμφέρον. οἷς μὲν οὖν ἐφικτός ἐστιν ἡ τοῦ καλοῦ
κτῆσις, ταύτης ἀντέχεσθαι δεῖν τοὺς ὀρθῶς πολιτευο-
μένους· οἷς δ' ἀδύνατος, ἐπὶ τὴν τοῦ συμφέροντος

3 μερίδα καταφεύγειν· τὸ δ' ἑκατέρων ἀποτυγχάνειν μέγιστον εἶναι τεκμήριον ἀβουλίας. πάσχειν δὲ τοῦτο
προφανῶς τοὺς ἀπροφασίστως ὁμολογοῦντας μὲν
πᾶν τὸ παραγγελλόμενον, ἀκουσίως δὲ τοῦτο πράττον-

4 τας καὶ μετὰ προσκοπῆς· διόπερ ἢ τοῦτ' εἶναι δεικ-
τέον ὡς ἐσμὲν ἱκανοὶ πρὸς τὸ μὴ πειθαρχεῖν ἢ μηδὲ
λέγειν τοῦτο τολμῶντας ὑπακουστέον ἑτοίμως εἶναι
πᾶσι τοῖς παραγγελλομένοις.

(15) 13. Ὁ δὲ Φιλοποίμην οὐκ ἐπὶ τοσοῦτον ἔφη δεῖν
(xxv.9b) ἀμαθίαν αὑτοῦ ⟨καταγινώσκειν ὥστε τὸ μὴ δύνασθαι μετρεῖν μήτε τὴν διαφορὰν τοῦ πολιτεύματος
τῶν Ῥωμαίων καὶ τῶν Ἀχαιῶν μήτε τὴν ὑπερβολὴν

2 τῆς δυνάμεως "ἀλλὰ πάσης ὑπεροχῆς φύσιν ἐχούσης
ἀεὶ βαρύτερον χρῆσθαι τοῖς ὑποταττομένοις, πότερον" ἔφη "συμφέρει συνεργεῖν ταῖς ὁρμαῖς ταῖς τῶν
κρατούντων καὶ μηθὲν ἐμποδὼν ποιεῖν, ἵν' ὡς τάχιστα
πεῖραν λάβωμεν τῶν βαρυτάτων ἐπιταγμάτων, ἢ
τοὐναντίον, καθ' ὅσον οἷοί τ' ἐσμέν, συμπαλαίοντας
προσαντέχειν ἐπὶ τοσοῦτον, ἐφ' ὅσον μέλλομεν τελέ-

out the sword and the olive branch[27] at one and the same
time. "If," he said, "we are strong enough to face them and
can really do so, very well; but if even Philopoemen does
not venture to maintain this . . . why striving for the impossible do we neglect the possible?" There were, he said, two
aims in all policy, honor and interest. For those in whose
power it lies to gain honor, the right policy is to aim at this;
but those who are powerless to do so must take refuge in
the attainment of their interest. But to fail in both aims
was the highest proof of incompetence; and this was evidently the case with those who made no objection to any
demand, but complied with it against their wills and in a
manner calculated to give offense. "Therefore," he said,
"either it must be proved that we are capable of refusing
compliance, or, if no one dares to say this, we must readily
obey all orders."

13. The reply of Philopoemen was that they must not
think he was so stupid as to be incapable of measuring the
difference between the two states, Rome and Achaea, and
the superiority of the Roman power. "But," he continued,
"as a stronger power is naturally disposed to press ever
harder on those who submit to it, is it in our interest by
encouraging the whims of our masters, and not opposing
them in any way, to have to yield as soon as possible to the
most tyrannical behests? Should we not rather, as far as it
is in our power, wrestle with them, and hold out until we
are completely exhausted? And should they issue illegal

27 "The spear and the herald's staff."

521

3 ὡς.......κἂν ἐπιτάττωσιν . ...καὶ τούτων ὑπο-
μιμνήσκοντες αὐτοὺς ἐπιλαμβανόμεθα τῆς ὁρμῆς,
παρακαθέξομεν ἐπὶ ποσὸν τὸ πικρὸν αὐτῶν τῆς ἐξουσίας, ἄλλως τε δὴ καὶ περὶ πλείονος ποιουμένων Ῥωμαίων ἕως γε τοῦ νῦν, ὡς αὐτὸς φής, Ἀρίσταινε, τὸ
τηρεῖν τοὺς ὅρκους καὶ τὰς συνθήκας καὶ τὴν πρὸς
4 τοὺς συμμάχους πίστιν. ἐὰν δ᾽ αὐτοὶ καταγνόντες τῶν
ἰδίων δικαίων αὐτόθεν εὐθέως καθάπερ οἱ δοριάλωτοι
πρὸς πᾶν τὸ κελευόμενον ἑτοίμους ἡμᾶς αὐτοὺς παρα-
σκευάζωμεν, τί διοίσει τὸ τῶν Ἀχαιῶν ἔθνος Σικελι-
ωτῶν καὶ Καπυανῶν τῶν ὁμολογουμένως καὶ πάλαι
5 δουλευόντων;" διόπερ ἔφη δεῖν ἢ τοῦτο συγχωρεῖν ὡς
οὐδὲν ἰσχύει δίκαιον παρὰ Ῥωμαίοις ἢ μηδὲ τολμῶντας τοῦτο λέγειν χρῆσθαι τοῖς δικαίοις καὶ μὴ προΐεσθαι σφᾶς, ἔχοντάς γε δὴ μεγίστας καὶ καλλίστας
6 ἀφορμὰς πρὸς Ῥωμαίους. ὅτι μὲν γὰρ ἥξει ποτὲ τοῖς
Ἕλλησιν ὁ καιρὸς οὗτος, ἐν ᾧ δεήσει ποιεῖν κατ᾽
ἀνάγκην πᾶν τὸ παραγγελλόμενον, σαφῶς ἔφη γινώ-
σκειν· "ἀλλὰ πότερα τοῦτον ὡς τάχιστά τις ἂν ἰδεῖν
βουληθείη ⟨γενόμενον⟩ ἢ τοὐναντίον ὡς βραδύτατα;
7 δοκῶ μὲν γὰρ ὡς βραδύτατα." διὸ καὶ τούτῳ διαφέρειν ἔφη τὴν Ἀρισταίνου πολιτείαν τῆς ἑαυτοῦ· ἐκεῖνον
μὲν γὰρ σπουδάζειν ὡς τάχιστα τὸ χρεὼν ἰδεῖν γενόμενον καὶ συνεργεῖν τούτῳ κατὰ δύναμιν· αὐτὸς δὲ
πρὸς τοῦτ᾽ ἀντερείδειν καὶ διωθεῖσθαι, καθ᾽ ὅσον ἐστὶ
δυνατός.
8 Οὐ μὴν ἀλλ᾽ ἐκ τῶν προειρημένων δῆλον ὡς συνέβαινε γίνεσθαι τοῦ μὲν καλήν, τοῦ δ᾽ εὐσχήμονα τὴν

orders,[28] if, by pointing this out to them, we put some
check on their arbitrary conduct, we shall at least in a
measure curb the extreme severity of their dominion, especially since, as you yourself, Aristaenus, acknowledge,
the Romans, up to now at least, set a very high value on
fidelity to oaths, treaties, and contracts with allies. But if
we ourselves, ignoring our own rights, instantly without
protest make ourselves subservient, like prisoners of war,
to any and every order, what difference will there be between the Achaean League and the people of Sicily and
Capua, who have long been the acknowledged slaves of
Rome?" Therefore, he said, either they must confess that
with the Romans justice is impotent, or if they did not go
so far as to say this, they must stand by their rights, and
not give themselves away, especially as they had very great
and honorable claims on Rome. "I know too well," he said,
"that the time will come[29] when the Greeks will be forced
to yield complete obedience to Rome; but do we wish this
time to be as near as possible or as distant as possible?
Surely as distant as possible." So in this respect, he said,
the policy of Aristaenus differed from his own. Aristaenus
was anxious to see their fate overtake them as soon as possible, and worked for this end with all his might; but he
himself did all he could to strive against it and avert it.

I think it must be confessed from what I have said that
the policy of Philopoemen was honorable, and that of Aris-

---

[28] Heyse supplies ἐκτὸς νόμων τι.
[29] This sounds as if written after 146.

9 πολιτείαν, ἀμφοτέρας γε μὴν ἀσφαλεῖς· τοιγαροῦν
μεγίστων καιρῶν τότε περιστάντων καὶ Ῥωμαίους
καὶ τοὺς Ἕλληνας τῶν τε κατὰ Φίλιππον καὶ κατ'
Ἀντίοχον, ὅμως ἀμφότεροι διετήρησαν ἀκέραια τὰ δί-
10 καια τοῖς Ἀχαιοῖς πρὸς Ῥωμαίους· φήμη δέ τις ἐνέ-
τρεχεν ὡς Ἀρισταίνου Ῥωμαίοις εὐνουστέρου μᾶλλον
ἢ Φιλοποίμενος ὑπάρχοντος.

V. RES ASIAE

(8)   14. Ὅτι κατὰ τὴν Ἀσίαν Φαρνάκης ὁ βασιλεύς,
(xxv.4) πάλιν ὀλιγωρήσας τῆς γεγενημένης ἐπὶ Ῥωμαίους
ἀναφορᾶς, Λεώκριτον μὲν ἔτι κατὰ χειμῶνα μετὰ μυρίων στρατιωτῶν ἐξαπέστειλε πορθήσοντα τὴν Γαλα-
2 τίαν, αὐτὸς δὲ τῆς ἐαρινῆς ὥρας ὑποφαινούσης
ἤθροιζε τὰς δυνάμεις, ὡς ἐμβαλῶν εἰς τὴν Καππαδο-
3 κίαν. ἃ πυνθανόμενος Εὐμένης δυσχερῶς μὲν ἔφερε τὸ
συμβαῖνον διὰ τὸ πάντας τοὺς τῆς πίστεως ὅρους
ὑπερβαίνειν τὸν Φαρνάκην, ἠναγκάζετο δὲ τὸ παρα-
4 πλήσιον ποιεῖν. ἤδη δ' αὐτοῦ συνηθροικότος τὰς
δυνάμεις, κατέπλευσαν ἐκ τῆς Ῥώμης οἱ περὶ τὸν
5 Ἄτταλον. ὁμοῦ δὲ γενόμενοι καὶ κοινολογηθέντες
ἀλλήλοις ἀνέζευξαν παραχρῆμα μετὰ τῆς στρατιᾶς.
6 ἀφικόμενοι δ' εἰς τὴν Γαλατίαν τὸν μὲν Λεώκριτον
οὐκέτι κατέλαβον· τοῦ δὲ Κασσιγνάτου καὶ τοῦ Γαι-
ζατόριγος διαπεμπομένων πρὸς αὐτοὺς ὑπὲρ ἀσφαλείας, οἵτινες ἐτύγχανον ἔτει πρότερον ᾑρημένοι τὰ
Φαρνάκου, καὶ πᾶν ὑπισχνουμένων ποιήσειν τὸ προσ-

taenus plausible, but that both were safe. So that when, in the wars with Philip and Antiochus, great dangers at that time threatened both Rome and Greece, yet the one statesman and the other equally protected the rights of Achaea against Rome. But the report gained currency that Aristaenus was more favorably disposed to the Romans than Philopoemen.

V. AFFAIRS OF ASIA

War between Eumenes and Pharnaces

14. In Asia King Pharnaces, again treating the reference of the matter to Rome with contempt, sent Leocritus[30] in the winter with ten thousand troops to lay Galatia waste, and himself, when spring began to set in, collected his forces with the object of invading Cappadocia. Eumenes, on learning of this, was highly incensed, as Pharnaces was overstepping all the bounds of good faith, but he was forced to do the same thing himself. When he had already collected his troops, Attalus and his brothers returned from Rome. After meeting and conversing, the brothers at once left with their army. On arriving in Galatia they found that Leocritus was no longer there, but Cassignatus[31] and Gaezatorix,[32] who a year previously had taken the part of Pharnaces, sent to them asking for pro-

[30] For his role in this war, see D. S. 29.23, based on P.

[31] He reappears later as "dux Gallorum" in Eumenes' army during the war against Perseus and was killed in action (Livy 42.57.7 and 9).   [32] Another Celt, "king of the Gaesates," Stähelin (21.33.1), 49, n. 5.

7 ταττόμενον, ἀπειπάμενοι τούτους διὰ τὴν προγεγενη-
μένην ἀθεσίαν, ἐξάραντες παντὶ τῷ στρατεύματι
8 προῆγον ἐπὶ τὸν Φαρνάκην. παραγενόμενοι δ' ἐκ
Καλπίτου πεμπταῖοι πρὸς τὸν Ἅλυν ποταμὸν ἑκταῖοι
9 πάλιν ἀνέζευξαν εἰς Παρνασσόν. ἔνθα καὶ Ἀριαράθης
ὁ τῶν Καππαδοκῶν βασιλεὺς συνέμιξεν αὐτοῖς μετὰ
τῆς οἰκείας δυνάμεως, καὶ ἦλθον εἰς τὴν Μωκισσέων
10 χώραν. ἄρτι δὲ κατεστρατοπεδευκότων αὐτῶν προσέπεσε παραγενέσθαι τοὺς ἐκ τῆς Ῥώμης πρεσβευτὰς
11 ἐπὶ τὰς διαλύσεις. ὧν ἀκούσας ὁ βασιλεὺς Εὐμένης
Ἄτταλον μὲν ἐξαπέστειλε τούτους ἐκδεξόμενον, αὐτὸς
δὲ τὰς δυνάμεις ἐδιπλασίαζε καὶ διεκόσμει φιλοτίμως, ἅμα μὲν ἁρμοζόμενος πρὸς τὰς ἀληθινὰς χρείας,
ἅμα δὲ βουλόμενος ἐνδείκνυσθαι τοῖς Ῥωμαίοις ὅτι
δι' αὐτοῦ δυνατός ἐστι τὸν Φαρνάκην ἀμύνασθαι καὶ
καταπολεμεῖν.

(9)
(xxv.5) 15. παραγενομένων δὲ τῶν πρέσβεων καὶ παρακαλούντων λύειν τὸν πόλεμον, ἔφασαν μὲν οἱ περὶ τὸν
Εὐμένη καὶ τὸν Ἀριαράθην ἕτοιμοι πρὸς πᾶν εἶναι τὸ
2 παρακαλούμενον, ἠξίουν δὲ τοὺς Ῥωμαίους, εἰ μέν
ἐστι δυνατόν, ⟨εἰς⟩ σύλλογον αὐτοὺς συναγαγεῖν πρὸς
τὸν Φαρνάκην, ἵνα κατὰ πρόσωπον λεγομένων τῶν
λόγων ἴδωσι τὴν ἀθεσίαν αὐτοῦ καὶ τὴν ὠμότητα διὰ
3 πλειόνων· εἰ δὲ μὴ τοῦτ' εἴη δυνατόν, αὐτοὺς γενέσθαι
4 κριτὰς τῶν πραγμάτων ἴσους καὶ δικαίους. τῶν δὲ
πρεσβευτῶν ἀναδεχομένων πάντα τὰ δυνατὰ καὶ

---

33 See nn. on 21.41.4 and 21.45.1.

tection, and promising to submit to all their orders. Rejecting these overtures owing to the previous infidelity of these chiefs, they left with their whole army and advanced to meet Pharnaces. From Calpitus (?) they reached the Halys in four days, and next day left for Parnassus, where Ariarathes,[33] the king of Cappadocia, joined them with his own forces, upon which they advanced to the territory of Mocissus.[34] Just after they had encamped there the news reached them that the legates[35] from Rome had arrived to arrange a peace. On hearing this King Eumenes sent off Attalus to receive them, but himself doubled his forces and drilled them energetically; both for the purpose of meeting actual exigencies and to show the Romans that he was capable without any assistance of defending himself against Pharnaces and overcoming him.

15. When the legates arrived and begged the kings to put an end to the war, Eumenes and Ariarathes said they were quite ready to accede to this and any other request; but they asked the Romans if possible to contrive a meeting between them and Pharnaces, so that when he was brought face to face with them and they all spoke, his infidelity and cruelty might be fully revealed to them. If, however, this was beyond their power, they begged the legates themselves to act as fair and just judges in the matter. The legates consented to do all in their power that was

---

[34] *RE* Mokis(s)os 1514–1515 (W. Ruge), near the Halys and southwest of Mazaca (later Caesarea). The MS, however, gives κάμησην and κάμισιν respectively, which may stand for Καμισηνὴν or Καμισηνῶν (sc. γῆν) and indicate that P. spoke of Camisa, the area on the right bank of the upper Halys: *RE* Kamisa 1841 (W. Ruge).   [35] Their identity is not known.

καλῶς ἔχοντα ποιήσειν, ἀξιούντων δὲ τὴν στρατιὰν
5 ἀπάγειν ἐκ τῆς χώρας· ἄτοπον γὰρ εἶναι παρόντων
⟨πρέσβεων⟩ καὶ λόγους ποιουμένων ὑπὲρ διαλύσεων,
ἅμα παρεῖναι τὰ τοῦ πολέμου καὶ κακοποιεῖν ἀλλή-
6 λους· συνεχώρησαν οἱ περὶ τὸν Εὐμένη, καὶ τῇ κατὰ
πόδας εὐθέως ἀναζεύξαντες οὗτοι προῆγον ὡς ἐπὶ Γα-
7 λατίας. οἱ δὲ Ῥωμαῖοι πρὸς τὸν Φαρνάκην συμμίξαντες πρῶτον μὲν ἠξίουν αὐτὸν εἰς λόγους ἐλθεῖν τοῖς
περὶ τὸν Εὐμένη· μάλιστα γὰρ ἂν οὕτω τυχεῖν τὰ
8 πράγματα διεξαγωγῆς. τοῦ δὲ πρὸς τοῦτο τὸ μέρος
ἀντιβαίνοντος καὶ τέλος ἀπειπαμένου, δῆλον μὲν εὐθέως ἦν τοῦτο καὶ Ῥωμαίοις ὅτι καταγινώσκει
προφανῶς ἑαυτοῦ καὶ διαπιστεῖ τοῖς σφετέροις πράγ-
9 μασι· πάντῃ δὲ πάντως βουλόμενοι λῦσαι τὸν πόλεμον προσεκαρτέρουν, ἕως οὗ συνεχώρησε πέμψειν
αὐτοκράτορας ἐπὶ ⟨τὸν Πέργαμον κατὰ⟩ θάλατταν
τοὺς συνθησομένους τὴν εἰρήνην, ἐφ' οἷς ἂν οἱ
10 πρεσβευταὶ κελεύσωσιν. ἀφικομένων ⟨δὲ⟩ τῶν πρέσβεων, καὶ συνελθόντων ὁμοῦ τῶν τε Ῥωμαίων καὶ
τῶν περὶ Εὐμένη, καὶ τούτων μὲν εἰς ἅπαν ἑτοίμως
συγκαταβαινόντων χάριν τοῦ συντελεσθῆναι τὴν εἰ-
11 ρήνην, τῶν δὲ παρὰ τοῦ Φαρνάκου πρὸς πᾶν διαφε-
ρομένων καὶ τοῖς ὁμολογηθεῖσιν οὐκ ἐμμενόντων, ἀλλ'
αἰεί τι προσεπιζητούντων καὶ μεταμελομένων, ταχέως
τοῖς Ῥωμαίοις ἐγένετο δῆλον ὅτι ματαιοπονοῦσιν. οὐ
γὰρ οἷός τ' ἦν συγκαταβαίνειν ὁ Φαρνάκης εἰς τὰς
12 διαλύσεις. ὅθεν ἀπράκτου γενομένης τῆς κοινολογίας,
καὶ τῶν Ῥωμαίων ἀπαλλαγέντων ἐκ τοῦ Περγάμου,

proper, but demanded that the army be withdrawn from the country: for they said it was irregular that when a mission was acting for peace there should at the same time be present all the apparatus of war, the kings inflicting damage on each other. Eumenes consented, and the very next day he and Ariarathes broke up their camp and advanced toward Galatia. The Romans in the first place met Pharnaces, and begged him to have an interview with Eumenes, for this was the surest way of arranging matters. When he objected to this and finally refused, the Romans also at once saw that he clearly condemned himself and had no confidence in his case; but as they wished by any and every means to put an end to the war, they went on insisting until he consented to send by sea to Pergamum plenipotentiaries empowered to make peace on the terms dictated by the legates. On the arrival of the envoys, the Romans and Eumenes met them. They were ready to make any concessions for peace; but, as the envoys of Pharnaces differed with them on every point, did not adhere to their agreements, continued raising fresh demands and withdrawing from their concessions, the Romans soon saw that all their efforts were in vain, as Pharnaces was not in the least inclined to make peace. So that, as the conference had no result, as the Romans left

καὶ τῶν παρὰ τοῦ Φαρνάκου πρέσβεων ἀπολυθέντων εἰς τὴν οἰκείαν, ὁ μὲν πόλεμος ἐγεγένητο κατάμονος, οἱ δὲ περὶ τὸν Εὐμένη πάλιν ἐγίνοντο περὶ τὰς εἰς 13 τοῦτον παρασκευάς. ἐν ᾧ καιρῷ τῶν Ῥοδίων ἐπισπασμένων τὸν Εὐμένη [καὶ] φιλοτίμως, οὗτος μὲν ἐξώρμησε μετὰ πολλῆς σπουδῆς, πράξων τὰ κατὰ τοὺς Λυκίους. . . .

Pergamum, and as the envoys of Pharnaces returned to their own country, the war continued and Eumenes began to continue his preparations for it. At the same time the Rhodians[36] did their best to gain the assistance of Eumenes, and he hurriedly left to lend them a hand in Lycia. . . .

[36] In their new possession of Lycia (21.24.7–8; 46.8), they faced great difficulties in form of a revolt. See A. Bresson in Gabrielsen (22.5.1), 294–330.

FRAGMENTA LIBRI XXV

I. RES ASIAE

1. Πολυβίου δ᾽ εἰπόντος τριακοσίας αὐτῶν καταλῦσαι πόλεις Τεβέριον Γράκχον, κωμῳδῶν φησι
τοῦτο τῷ Γράκχῳ χαρίσασθαι τὸν ἄνδρα, τοὺς πύρ-
γους καλοῦντα πόλεις, ὥσπερ ἐν ταῖς θριαμβικαῖς
2 πομπαῖς. καὶ ἴσως οὐκ ἄπιστον τοῦτο λέγει· καὶ γὰρ
οἱ στρατηγοὶ καὶ οἱ συγγραφεῖς ῥᾳδίως ἐπὶ τοῦτο
φέρονται τὸ ψεῦσμα, καλλωπίζοντες τὰς πράξεις.

2. Ὅτι ὁ Φαρνάκης, ἐξαπιναίου καὶ βαρείας αὐτῷ
(xxvi.6) τῆς ἐφόδου γενομένης, ἕτοιμος ἦν πρὸς πᾶν τὸ προ-
τεινόμενον· πρέσβεις γὰρ ἐξαπέστειλε πρὸς Εὐμένη
2 καὶ Ἀριαράθην. τῶν δὲ περὶ Εὐμένη καὶ Ἀριαράθην
προσδεξαμένων τοὺς λόγους καὶ παραχρῆμα συν-
εξαποστειλάντων πρεσβευτὰς παρ᾽ αὐτῶν πρὸς τὸν
Φαρνάκην, καὶ τούτου γενομένου πλεονάκις παρ᾽ ἑκα-
3 τέρων, ἐκυρώθησαν αἱ διαλύσεις ἐπὶ τούτοις· εἰρήνην
ὑπάρχειν Εὐμένει καὶ Προυσίᾳ καὶ Ἀριαράθῃ πρὸς

---

1 For details see *RE* triumphus 502–503 (H. Strasburger).
M. Beard, The *Roman Triumph* (Cambridge, MA 2007). J.-L.
Bastien, *Le triomphe romain et son utilisation politique* (Rome
2007).

FRAGMENTS OF BOOK XXV

I. AFFAIRS OF ASIA

Conclusion of the Above War

1. ‹Posidonius› mocks Polybius' statement that Tiberius Gracchus demolished three hundred cities, saying that he had, in order to please Gracchus, called fortified villages "cities," as happens in triumphs.[1] And this is convincing, since generals and historians, embellishing the events, are easily carried to such lies.[2]

2. Pharnaces, when thus suddenly attacked in force, was ready to entertain any proposals, as he showed by sending envoys to Eumenes and Ariarathes.[3] These kings, after listening to his overtures, themselves sent envoys to Pharnaces, and after this had been done several times on both sides, peace was agreed to on the following terms.[4] "There shall be peace between Eumenes, Prusias,[5] and

180–179
B.C.

[2] This refers to the campaign of Tiberius Gracchus in Spain in 179 (*MRR* 1.393); see Livy 40.44.4–5 and 47.1–50.5.

[3] For the war in Asia Minor see 23.9.1–3, and from Book 24: 1.1–3, 14.1, 15.12. For Ariarathes see n. on 24.14.9. The peace was concluded in 179.   [4] P. quotes the treaty partly *verbatim,* partly in paraphrase (2.11–14).

[5] Prusias II, 182–149. *RE* Prusias 1107–1127 (C. Habicht).

533

4 Φαρνάκην καὶ Μιθριδάτην εἰς τὸν πάντα χρόνον. Γα-
λατίας μὴ ἐπιβαίνειν Φαρνάκην κατὰ μηδένα τρόπον.
ὅσαι γεγόνασιν πρότερον συνθῆκαι Φαρνάκῃ πρὸς
5 Γαλάτας, ἀκύρους ὑπάρχειν. ὁμοίως Παφλαγονίας ἐκχωρεῖν, ἀποκαταστήσαντα τοὺς οἰκήτορας, οὓς πρότερον ἐξαγηόχει, σὺν δὲ τούτοις ὅπλα καὶ βέλη καὶ τὰς
6 ἄλλας παρασκευάς. ἀποδοῦναι δὲ καὶ Ἀριαράθῃ τῶν
τε χωρίων ὅσα παρῄρητο μετὰ τῆς προϋπαρχούσης
7 κατασκευῆς καὶ τοὺς ὁμήρους. ἀποδοῦναι δὲ καὶ Τή-
ιον παρὰ τὸν Πόντον, ὃν μετά τινα χρόνον Εὐμένης
8 ἔδωκε Προυσίᾳ πεισθεὶς μετὰ μεγάλης χάριτος. ἐγράφη
δὲ καὶ τοὺς αἰχμαλώτους ἀποκαταστῆσαι Φαρνάκην
9 χωρὶς λύτρων καὶ τοὺς αὐτομόλους ἅπαντας· πρὸς δὲ
τούτοις τῶν χρημάτων καὶ τῆς γάζης, ἧς ἀπήνεγκε
παρὰ Μορζίου καὶ Ἀριαράθου, ἀποδοῦναι τοῖς προει-
10 ρημένοις βασιλεῦσιν ἐνακόσια τάλαντα, καὶ τοῖς περὶ
τὸν Εὐμένη τριακόσια προσθεῖναι τῆς εἰς τὸν πόλε-
11 μον δαπάνης. ἐπεγράφη δὲ καὶ Μιθριδάτῃ τῷ τῆς
Ἀρμενίας σατράπῃ τριακόσια τάλαντα, διότι παραβὰς
τὰς πρὸς Εὐμένη συνθήκας ἐπολέμησεν Ἀριαράθῃ.
12 περιελήφθησαν δὲ ταῖς συνθήκαις τῶν μὲν κατὰ τὴν
Ἀσίαν δυναστῶν Ἀρταξίας ὁ τῆς πλείστης Ἀρμενίας
13 ἄρχων καὶ Ἀκουσίλοχος, τῶν δὲ κατὰ τὴν Εὐρώπην
Γάταλος ὁ Σαρμάτης, τῶν δ' αὐτονομουμένων Ἡρα-

---

6 West of Pontus, east of Bithynia, north of Galatia. RE
Paphlagonia, vol. 18, 2486–2550 (W. Ruge, K. Bittel).

7 Dynast of Gangra in Paphlagonia.

8 Ruler of Lesser Armenia, perhaps nephew of Antiochus III
(8.23.3).

Ariarathes on the one hand and Pharnaces and Mithridates on the other for all time: Pharnaces shall not invade Galatia on any pretext: all treaties previously made between Pharnaces and the Galatians are revoked: he shall likewise retire from Paphlagonia,[6] restoring to their homes those of the inhabitants whom he had formerly deported, and restoring at the same time all weapons, missiles, and material of war: he shall give up to Ariarathes all the places of which he robbed him in the same condition as he found them, and he shall return the hostages: he shall also give up Teium on the Pontus"—this city was shortly afterward very gladly presented by Eumenes to Prusias who begged for it: "Pharnaces shall return all prisoners of war without ransom and all deserters. Likewise out of the money and treasure he carried off from Morzius[7] and Ariarathes, he shall repay to the above kings nine hundred talents, paying in addition to Eumenes three hundred talents toward the expenses of the war." A fine of three hundred talents was also imposed on Mithridates,[8] satrap of Armenia, because violating his treaty with Eumenes he had made war on Ariarathes. Of the Asiatic princelets Artaxias,[9] the ruler of the greater part of Armenia, and Acusilochus were included in the treaty; of those in Europe Gatalus the Sarmatian; also the following free cities,[10] Heraclia, Mesem-

[9] Ruler of eastern Armenia and founder of Artaxata. V. Tscherikower, *Die hellenistischen Städtegründungen von Alexander dem Grossen bis auf die Römerzeit* (Leipzig 1927), 82.

[10] The first three are cities in the Black Sea area; Cyzicus (22.20) is a peninsula at the shore of the Sea of Marmara. Pharnaces concluded an alliance with Chersonesus in the year of the peace, *IPE* 1² 402; for the date see n. on 23.9.2.

κλεῶται, Μεσημβριανοί, Χερρονησῖται, σὺν δὲ τούτοις
Κυζικηνοί. περὶ δὲ τῶν ὁμήρων τελευταῖον ἐγράφη
14 πόσους δεήσει καὶ τίνας δοῦναι τὸν Φαρνάκην· ὧν καὶ
15 παραγενηθέντων ἐξ αὐτῆς ἀνέζευξαν αἱ δυνάμεις. καὶ
τοῦ μὲν Εὐμένει καὶ Ἀριαράθῃ πρὸς Φαρνάκην συστάντος πολέμου τοιοῦτον ἀπέβη τὸ τέλος.

II. RES MACEDONIAE

3. Ὅτι Περσεὺς ἀνανεωσάμενος τὴν φιλίαν τὴν
πρὸς Ῥωμαίους εὐθέως ἑλληνοκοπεῖν ἐπεβάλετο,
(xxvi.5) κατακαλῶν εἰς τὴν Μακεδονίαν καὶ τοὺς τὰ χρέα φεύ-
γοντας καὶ τοὺς πρὸς καταδίκας ἐκπεπτωκότας καὶ
2 τοὺς ἐπὶ βασιλικοῖς ἐγκλήμασι παρακεχωρηκότας. καὶ
τούτων ἐξετίθει προγραφὰς εἴς τε Δῆλον καὶ Δελφοὺς
καὶ τὸ τῆς Ἰτωνίας Ἀθηνᾶς ἱερόν, διδοὺς οὐ μόνον τὴν
ἀσφάλειαν τοῖς καταπορευομένοις, ἀλλὰ καὶ τῶν
3 ὑπαρχόντων κομιδήν, ἀφ' ὧν ἕκαστος ἔφυγε. παρέλυσε δὲ καὶ τοὺς ἐν αὐτῇ τῇ Μακεδονίᾳ τῶν βασιλικῶν
ὀφειλημάτων, ἀφῆκε δὲ καὶ τοὺς ἐν ταῖς φυλακαῖς
4 ἐγκεκλεισμένους ἐπὶ βασιλικαῖς αἰτίαις. ταῦτα δὲ ποιήσας πολλοὺς ἐμετεώρισε, δοκῶν καλὰς ἐλπίδας ὑπο-
5 δεικνύναι πᾶσι τοῖς Ἕλλησιν ἐν αὐτῷ. ἐπέφαινε δὲ
καὶ κατὰ τὴν ἐν τῷ λοιπῷ βίῳ προστασίαν τὸ τῆς

---

11 A remarkably positive account of the king's beginnings. For
his first years see P. Meloni, *Perseo e la fine della monarchia*

bria, Chersonese, and Cyzicus. The last claim related to the number of hostages to be given by Pharnaces. Upon the arrival of the latter, the armies at once departed. Such was the end of the war between Eumenes and Ariarathes in alliance and Pharnaces.

II. AFFAIRS OF MACEDONIA

Opening of the Reign of Perseus

(Cp. Suda)

3. Perseus,[11] immediately after renewing his friendship with Rome, began to aim at popularity in Greece, calling back to Macedonia fugitive debtors and those who had been banished from the country either by sentence of the courts or for offenses against the king. He posted up lists of these men at Delos, Delphi, and the temple of Itonian Athena,[12] not only promising safety to such as returned, but the recovery of the property they had left behind. In Macedonia itself he relieved all who were in debt to the crown, and released those who had been imprisoned for offenses against the crown. By this action he aroused the expectation of many, as it seemed to show that for the whole of Greece much was to be hoped from him. He also showed in the rest of his behavior true royal dig-

179–178 B.C.

Macedone (Rome 1953), 61–129, and P. Derow, *CAH* (2nd ed.) 8 (1989), 303–304.   [12] Her temple, a federal sanctuary of the Thessalians, close to Karditsa, was identified and excavated by D. R. Theocharis, *AD* 19 (1964 [1966]), 246–255. He found a decree of the Thessalian League from the time of Perseus; see C. Habicht (18.7.6), 124–133 and 294.

6 βασιλείας ἀξίωμα. κατά τε γὰρ τὴν ἐπιφάνειαν ἦν
   ἱκανὸς καὶ πρὸς πᾶσαν σωματικὴν χρείαν τὴν διατεί-
   νουσαν εἰς τὸν πραγματικὸν τρόπον εὔθετος, κατά τε
   τὴν ἐπίφασιν εἶχεν ἐπισκύνιον καὶ τάξιν οὐκ ἀνοίκειον
7 τῆς ἡλικίας. ἐπεφεύγει δὲ καὶ τὴν πατρικὴν ἀσέλγειαν
   τήν τε περὶ τὰς γυναῖκας καὶ τὴν περὶ τοὺς πότους,
   καὶ οὐ μόνον αὐτὸς μέτριον ἔπινε δειπνῶν, ἀλλὰ καὶ
8 οἱ συνόντες αὐτῷ φίλοι. καὶ τὰ μὲν προοίμια τῆς Περσέως ἀρχῆς τοιαύτην εἶχε διάθεσιν.

9   Ὅτι Φίλιππος ὁ βασιλεύς, ὅτε μὲν ηὐξήθη καὶ τὴν
   κατὰ τῶν Ἑλλήνων ἐξουσίαν ἔλαβε, πάντων ἦν ἀπι-
   στότατος καὶ παρανομώτατος, ὅτε δὲ πάλιν τὰ τῆς
10 τύχης ἀντέπνευσε, πάντων μετριώτατος. ἐπεὶ δὲ τοῖς
   ὅλοις πράγμασιν ἔπταισε, πρὸς πᾶν τὸ μέλλον ἁρμοζόμενος ἐπειρᾶτο κατὰ πάντα τρόπον σωματοποιεῖν
   τὴν αὐτοῦ βασιλείαν.

III. RES ITALIAE

4. Ὅτι μετὰ τὴν ἀποστολὴν τῶν ὑπάτων Τεβερίου
(xxvi.7) καὶ Κλαυδίου τὴν πρὸς Ἴστρους καὶ Ἀγρίους ἡ σύγκλητος ἐχρημάτισε τοῖς παρὰ τῶν Λυκίων ἥκουσι
2 πρεσβευταῖς, ἤδη τῆς θερείας ληγούσης, οἵτινες παρ-

---

13 Philip, in contrast with his son (3.1–8), is bettered by misfortune and personal tragedy at the end of his reign.

nity. For in personal appearance he looked capable, and was expert in all kinds of bodily exercise which are of real service. In his demeanor too he had a gravity and composure not unsuited to his years. He also had kept clear of his father's incontinence in the matter of women and drink, and not only was he himself moderate in his potations at table, but so were the friends who dined with him. Such was the character of the reign of Perseus at its opening.

Philip V in Misfortune

At the time when King Philip[13] grew great and was powerful in Greece, no one had less regard for good faith and law, but when the wind of his good fortune veered, he was the most moderate of men. When finally he entirely came to grief, he attempted to adapt himself to all contingencies and by every means to build up his kingdom again.

III. AFFAIRS OF ITALY

Embassy from Lycia

(Cf. Livy 41.6.8)

4. After the dispatch of the consuls[14] Tiberius Sempronius Gracchus and Gaius Claudius Pulcher against the Istri[15] and Agrii, the Senate, when summer was approaching its end, gave audience to the envoys from Lycia who

178–177
B.C.

[14] Of 177; *MRR* 1.397–398.
[15] For the Istrian War see Livy's account in Book 41 and *RE* Histria 2111–2116, esp. 2115 (J. Weiss).

ἐγένοντο μὲν εἰς τὴν Ῥώμην ἤδη καταπεπολεμημένων
τῶν Λυκίων, ἐξαπεστάλησαν δὲ χρόνοις ἱκανοῖς ἀνώ-
3 τερον. οἱ γὰρ Ξάνθιοι, καθ᾽ ὃν καιρὸν ἔμελλον εἰς τὴν
πόλεμον ἐμβαίνειν, ἐξέπεμψαν πρεσβευτὰς εἴς τε τὴν
4 Ἀχαΐαν καὶ τὴν Ῥώμην τοὺς περὶ Νικόστρατον. οἳ
τότε παραγενηθέντες εἰς τὴν Ῥώμην πολλοὺς εἰς
ἔλεον ἐξεκαλέσαντο τῶν ἐν τῷ συνεδρίῳ, τιθέντες ὑπὸ
τὴν ὄψιν τήν τε Ῥοδίων βαρύτητα καὶ τὴν αὐτῶν
5 περίστασιν. καὶ τέλος εἰς τοῦτ᾽ ἤγαγον τὴν σύγκλητον, ὥστε πέμψαι πρεσβευτὰς εἰς τὴν Ῥόδον τοὺς διασαφήσοντας ὅτι, τῶν ὑπομνηματισμῶν ἀναληφθέντων
⟨ὧν⟩ οἱ δέκα πρέσβεις ἐποιήσαντο κατὰ τὴν Ἀσίαν,
ὅτε τὰ πρὸς Ἀντίοχον ἐχείριζον, εὕρηνται Λύκιοι δε-
δομένοι Ῥοδίοις οὐκ ἐν δωρεᾷ, τὸ δὲ πλεῖον ὡς φίλοι
6 καὶ σύμμαχοι. τοιαύτης δὲ γενομένης διαλύσεως, οὐδ᾽
7 ὅλως ἤρεσκε πολλοῖς τὸ γεγονός. ἐδόκουν γὰρ οἱ
Ῥωμαῖοι τὰ κατὰ τοὺς Ῥοδίους καὶ Λυκίους διαγω-
νοθετεῖν, θέλοντες ἐκδαπανᾶσθαι τὰς παραθέσεις τῶν
8 Ῥοδίων καὶ τοὺς θησαυρούς, ἀκηκοότες τήν τε νυμ-
φαγωγίαν τὴν νεωστὶ τῷ Περσεῖ γεγενημένην ὑπ᾽
αὐτῶν καὶ τὴν ἀνάπειραν τῶν πλοίων.

9   Συνέβαινε γὰρ βραχεῖ χρόνῳ πρότερον ἐπιφανῶς

---

16 Xanthus was the largest city in Lycia. Its impressive ruins
have yielded rich archaeological and epigraphical finds. *RE* Xan-
thos 1375–1408 (P. Demargne and H. Metzger). Nicostratus, "not
otherwise known" (WC 3.270), was perhaps a relative of the Xan-
thian Prasidas, son of Nicostratus, who is attested as municipal

reached Rome after Lycia had been entirely reduced, but had been dispatched a good deal earlier. For the Xanthians,[16] at the time they were about to embark on the war, had sent Nicostratus at the head of a mission to Achaea and Rome. He arrived at Rome only now, and appealed to the sentiments of many of the senators by bringing before their eyes the oppressiveness of the Rhodians and their own imminent danger. Finally they succeeded in persuading the senate to send legates to Rhodes, to inform that state that after referring to the reports that the ten commissioners had drawn up in Asia when they were arranging matters with Antiochus, they found that the Lycians had not been handed over to Rhodes as a gift,[17] but rather to be treated like friends and allies. The imposition of these terms by no means pleased many people in Rhodes. For it was thought that the Romans were stirring up conflict between Rhodes and Lycia with the object of exhausting the stores and treasure of the Rhodians, having heard of their recent home-bringing of the bride[18] of Perseus and of the refitting of their ships.

Indeed, a short while previously the Rhodians had held

priest of "the kings" (Antiochus III and his son and coregent Antiochus) in two decrees of the city from 196 (*SEG* 33.1184, lines 3–4, and 46.1721, lines 3–4).

[17] This is in stark contrast to 22.5.4. See H. H. Schmitt, *Rom und Rhodos* (Munich 1957), 113–126, esp. 122, and 129–150.

[18] In 178 the Seleucid princess Laodice was escorted to Macedonia by a Rhodian fleet, since the Seleucid fleet was prohibited to sail that far (21.43.14). A hoard of one hundred mint-fresh silver coins was connected with the event by H. Seyrig, *Trésors du Levant* (Paris 1973), 47–48.

καὶ μεγαλομερῶς ταῖς παρασκευαῖς ἀναπεπειρᾶσθαι
τοὺς Ῥοδίους ἅπασι τοῖς σκάφεσι τοῖς ὑπάρχουσιν
10 αὐτοῖς. καὶ γὰρ ξύλων πλῆθος εἰς ναυπηγίαν ἐδίδοτο
παρὰ τοῦ Περσέως τοῖς Ῥοδίοις, καὶ στελγίδα χρυσῆν
ἑκάστῳ τῶν ἀφρακτιτῶν ἐδεδώρητο τῶν νεωστὶ νε-
νυμφαγωγηκότων αὐτῷ τὴν᾽ Λαοδίκην.

IV. RES RHODIORUM

5. Ὅτι εἰς τὴν Ῥόδον παραγενομένων τῶν ἐκ τῆς
(xxvi.8) Ῥώμης πρεσβευτῶν καὶ διασαφούντων τὰ δεδογμένα
τῇ συγκλήτῳ, θόρυβος ἦν ἐν τῇ Ῥόδῳ καὶ πολλὴ
ταραχὴ περὶ τοὺς πολιτευομένους, ἀγανακτούντων ἐπὶ
τῷ μὴ φάσκειν ἐν δωρεᾷ δεδόσθαι τοὺς Λυκίους
2 αὐτοῖς, ἀλλὰ κατὰ συμμαχίαν. ἄρτι γὰρ δοκοῦντες
καλῶς τεθεῖσθαι τὰ κατὰ Λυκίους, αὖθις ἄλλην ἀρχὴν
3 ἑώρων φυομένην πραγμάτων· εὐθέως γὰρ οἱ Λύκιοι,
τῶν Ῥωμαίων παραγενομένων καὶ διασαφούντων
ταῦτο τοῖς Ῥοδίοις, πάλιν ἐστασίαζον καὶ πᾶν ὑπομένειν οἷοί τ᾽ ἦσαν ὑπὲρ τῆς αὐτονομίας καὶ τῆς
4 ἐλευθερίας. οὐ μὴν ἀλλ᾽ οἵ γε Ῥόδιοι ⟨δι⟩ακούσαντες
τῶν πρεσβευτῶν καὶ νομίσαντες ἐξηπατῆσθαι τοὺς
Ῥωμαίους ὑπὸ τῶν Λυκίων, παραχρῆμα κατέστησαν
τοὺς περὶ Λυκόφρονα πρεσβευτάς, διδάξοντας τὴν
5 σύγκλητον περὶ τῶν προειρημένων. καὶ ταῦτα μὲν ἐπὶ
τούτων ἦν, ὅσον οὔπω δοκούντων πάλιν ἐπαναστή-
σεσθαι τῶν Λυκίων.

naval maneuvers of all ships belonging to them with great splendor and elaborate equipment. For Perseus had presented them with a quantity of wood[19] for shipbuilding, and had given a golden tiara to each of the sailors in the galleys that had lately escorted his bride Laodice on her way to him.

IV. AFFAIRS OF RHODES

5. When the envoys from Rome arrived in Rhodes to announce the decision of the senate, there was a great commotion there, and much disturbance in political circles on account of their statement that the Lycians had not been given to them as a gift, but as allies. For they thought they had just put things in Lycia on a satisfactory footing, and now they saw the beginning of a further crop of troubles. For the Lycians, as soon as the Romans arrived at Rhodes and made this announcement, became again disaffected, and were ready to struggle hard for their autonomy and freedom. The Rhodians, however, when they had listened to their envoys, thinking that the Romans had been taken in by the Lycians, at once appointed Lycophron their envoy to enlighten the senate on the matter. Such then was the situation, the Lycians to all appearance being about to revolt again.[20]

177 B.C.

[19] Macedonian timber was particularly good for shipbuilding and much sought after. The Athenian fleet in the fourth century heavily depended on it: R. Meiggs, *Trees and Timber in the Mediterranean World* (Oxford 1982), 126, who also comments (p. 146) on this gift from Perseus to Rhodes.

[20] The Lycian's first revolt had just been suppressed (4.2).

V. RES ITALIAE

6. Ὅτι ἡ σύγκλητος, παραγενομένων τῶν ἐκ τῆς
(xxvi.9) Ῥόδου πρεσβευτῶν, διακούσασα τῶν λόγων ὑπερέθετο
τὴν ἀπόκρισιν.

2 Ἡκόντων δὲ τῶν Δαρδανίων καὶ περὶ τοῦ πλήθους
τῶν Βασταρνῶν καὶ περὶ τοῦ μεγέθους τῶν ἀνδρῶν
3 ⟨καὶ⟩ τῆς ἐν τοῖς κινδύνοις τόλμης ἐξηγουμένων, καὶ
διασαφούντων περὶ τῆς Περσέως κοινοπραγίας καὶ
τῶν Γαλατῶν καὶ φασκόντων τοῦτον ἀγωνιᾶν μᾶλλον
ἢ τοὺς Βαστάρνας καὶ διὰ ταῦτα δεομένων σφίσι
4 βοηθεῖν, παρόντων δὲ καὶ Θετταλῶν καὶ συνεπιμαρ-
τυρούντων τοῖς Δαρδανίοις καὶ παρακαλούντων καὶ
5 τούτων ἐπὶ τὴν βοήθειαν, ἔδοξε τῇ συγκλήτῳ πέμψαι
τινὰς τοὺς αὐτόπτας ἐσομένους τῶν προσαγγελλομέ-
6 νων. καὶ παραυτίκα καταστήσαντες Αὖλον Ποστόμιον
ἐξαπέστειλαν καὶ σὺν τούτῳ τινὰς τῶν νέων.

V. AFFAIRS OF ITALY

(Cp. Livy 41.19)

6. The senate on the arrival of the envoys from Rhodes heard their arguments and deferred their own answer.

A mission from the Dardanians[21] now arrived, telling of the Bastarnae,[22] their numbers, the huge size and the valor of their warriors, and also pointing to the common action of Perseus and the Galatians.[23] They said they were much more afraid of him than of the Bastarnae, and they begged for aid. Envoys from Thessaly also arrived confirming the statement of the Dardanians, and begging too for help. Upon this the senate decided to send some commissioners to inquire on the spot as to the veracity of these assertions, and at once appointed Aulus Postumius[24] and some younger men.

177–176 B.C.

[21] The archenemies of Macedonia, now threatened by the arrival of the Bastarnians and their alleged collusion with Perseus.

[22] Considered to be Celts by the Greeks of the time, but in fact a German tribe. See L. Schmidt, *Die Ostgermanen* (Munich 1933), 86–99, and for the events here mentioned 89–90. These are also recorded among the Roman accusations against Perseus, *RDGE* 40, line 10; see n. on 22.18.5. The "Galatians" in the decree of Olbia, *SIG* 495, 102, are in fact, the Bastarnae.

[23] P. is here identifying the Bastarnae with the Galatians.

[24] *MRR* 3.174, on A. Postumius Albinus, cos. 180.

FRAGMENTA LIBRI XXVI

I. RES ANTIOCHI

1a. Πολύβιος δ᾽ ἐν τῇ ἕκτῃ καὶ εἰκοστῇ τῶν Ἱστο-
(10) ριῶν καλεῖ αὐτὸν Ἐπιμανῆ καὶ οὐκ Ἐπιφανῆ διὰ τὰς
πράξεις. οὐ μόνον γὰρ μετὰ δημοτῶν ἀνθρώπων κατ-
έβαινεν εἰς ὁμιλίας, ἀλλὰ καὶ μετὰ τῶν παρεπιδημούν-
2 των ξένων καὶ τῶν εὐτελεστάτων συνέπινεν. εἰ δὲ καὶ
τῶν νεωτέρων, φησίν, αἴσθοιτο τινας συνευωχουμένους ὁπουδήποτε, παρῆν μετὰ κερατίου καὶ συμφωνίας, ὥστε τοὺς πολλοὺς διὰ τὸ παράδοξον ἀνιστα-
μένους φεύγειν. πολλάκις δὲ καὶ τὴν βασιλικὴν
ἐσθῆτα ἀποβαλὼν τήβενναν ἀναλαβὼν περιῄει τὴν
ἀγοράν.

---

[1] Book 26 was lost very early. Preserved are just two excerpts,
both from Athenaeus and both covering the same material, one
very brief, the other much fuller.

FRAGMENTS OF BOOK XXVI[1]

I. AFFAIRS OF ANTIOCHUS
EPIPHANES

(From Athenaeus 10.439a; cf. Livy 41.20)

174–172
B.C.

1a. Polybius in his twenty-sixth book calls him[2] Epimanes (the Madman) instead of Epiphanes owing to his conduct. For not only did he condescend to converse with common people, but even with the meanest of the foreigners who visited Antioch. And whenever he heard that any of the younger men were at an entertainment, no matter where, he would come in with a fife and other music so that most of the guests got up and ran off in astonishment. He would often, moreover, doff his royal robe and pick up a toga and so make the circuit of the marketplace.

---

[2] King Antiochus IV Epiphanes (175–164). See O. Mørkholm, *Antiochus IV of Syria* (Copenhagen 1966), P. F. Mittag, *Antiochos IV. Epiphanes. Eine politische Biographie* (Berlin 2006). Antiochus had been hostage at Rome after the peace of 188, but was released in 178 at the latest and dwelled henceforth in Athens (*Hesp.* 51 [1982] 60, no. 3), until he learned of the death of his brother, King Seleucus IV, in 175 and seized the throne with the assistance of Eumenes and his brothers, as the Athenian decree, *OGI* 248, vividly illustrates.

1. Ἀντίοχος ὁ Ἐπιφανὴς μὲν κληθείς, Ἐπιμανὴς δ᾽
(10 3) ἐκ τῶν πράξεων ὀνομασθείς ... περὶ οὗ φησι Πολύβιος τάδε, ὡς ἀποδιδράσκων ἐκ τῆς αὐλῆς ἐνίοτε τοὺς
θεραπεύοντας, οὗ τύχοι τῆς πόλεως, ἀλύων ἐφαίνετο
2 δεύτερος καὶ τρίτος. μάλιστα δὲ πρὸς τοῖς ἀργυρο-
κοπείοις εὑρίσκετο καὶ χρυσοχοείοις εὑρησιλογῶν
καὶ φιλοτεχνῶν πρὸς τοὺς τορευτὰς καὶ τοὺς ἄλλους
3 τεχνίτας. ἔπειτα καὶ μετὰ δημοτῶν ἀνθρώπων συγ-
καταβαίνων ὡμίλει, ᾧ τύχοι, καὶ μετὰ τῶν παρεπιδη-
4 μούντων συνέπινε τῶν εὐτελεστάτων. ὅτε δὲ τῶν νεωτέρων αἴσθοιτό τινας συνευωχουμένους, οὐδεμίαν
ἔμφασιν ποιήσας παρῆν ἐπικωμάζων μετὰ κερατίου
καὶ συμφωνίας, ὥστε τοὺς πολλοὺς διὰ τὸ παράδοξον
5 ἀφισταμένους φεύγειν. πολλάκις δὲ καὶ τὴν βασιλικὴν
ἀποθέμενος ἐσθῆτα τήβενναν ἀναλαβὼν περιῄει κατὰ
τὴν ἀγορὰν ἀρχαιρεσιάζων καὶ τοὺς μὲν δεξιούμενος,
τοὺς δὲ καὶ περιπτύσσων παρεκάλει φέρειν αὐτῷ τὴν
ψῆφον, ποτὲ μὲν ὡς ἀγορανόμος γένηται, ποτὲ δὲ καὶ
6 ὡς δήμαρχος. τυχὼν δὲ τῆς ἀρχῆς καὶ καθίσας ἐπὶ
τὸν ἐλεφάντινον δίφρον κατὰ τὸ παρὰ Ῥωμαίοις ἔθος
διήκουε τῶν κατὰ τὴν ἀγορὰν γινομένων συναλλαγ-
μάτων καὶ διέκρινε μετὰ πολλῆς σπουδῆς καὶ προθυ-
7 μίας. ἐξ ὧν εἰς ἀπορίαν ἦγε τῶν ἀνθρώπων τοὺς ἐπι-
εικεῖς· οἱ μὲν γὰρ ἀφελῆ τινα αὐτὸν εἶναι ὑπελάμβανον,

---

3 The value of the statements in this chapter is disputed; they
may have been nothing but gossip launched by the king's adversaries. His policy did not display symptoms of capriciousness or

(From Athenaeus 5.193d)

1. Antiochus[3] surnamed Epiphanes gained the name of Epimanes by his conduct. Polybius tells us of him that, escaping from his attendants at court, he would often be seen wandering about in all parts of the city with one or two companions. He was chiefly found at the silver-smiths' and goldsmiths' workshops, holding forth at length and discussing technical matters with the molders and other craftsmen. He also used to condescend to converse with any common people he met, and used to drink in the company of the meanest foreign visitors to Antioch. Whenever he heard that any of the young men were at an entertainment, he would come in quite unceremoniously with a fife and a procession of musicians, so that most of the guests got up and left in astonishment. He would fre-quently put off his royal robes, and, assuming a white toga, go round the marketplace like a candidate, and, taking some by the hand and embracing others, would beg them to give him their vote, sometimes for the office of aedile and sometimes for that of tribune. Upon being elected, he would sit upon the ivory curule chair, as is the Roman cus-tom, listening to the lawsuits tried there, and pronouncing judgment with great pains and display of interest. In con-sequence all respectable men were entirely puzzled about him, some looking upon him as a plain simple man and others as a madman. His conduct too was very similar as

insanity. His generosity to Greek cities and sanctuaries (1.10, where εὐεργεσίαις must be meant instead of θυσίαις) is well documented; see Mørkholm (1a.1), 55–63. There is much addi-tional bibliography on that subject in recent years. For Antiochus' gifts to Athens, see C. Habicht, *Chiron* 19 (1989), 18–20.

οἱ δὲ μαινόμενον. καὶ γὰρ περὶ τὰς δωρεὰς ἦν παρα-
8 πλήσιος· ἐδίδου γὰρ τοῖς μὲν ἀστραγάλους δορκαδεί-
9 ους, τοῖς δὲ φοινικοβαλάνους, ἄλλοις δὲ χρυσίον. καὶ
ἐξ ἀπαντήσεως δέ τισιν ἐντυγχάνων, οὓς μὴ ἑωράκει
10 ποτέ, ἐδίδου δωρεὰς ἀπροσδοκήτους. ἐν δὲ ταῖς πρὸς
τὰς πόλεις (εὐεργεσίαις) καὶ ταῖς πρὸς τοὺς θεοὺς
τιμαῖς πάντας ὑπερέβαλλε τοὺς βεβασιλευκότας.
11 τοῦτο δ᾽ ἄν τις τεκμήραιτο ἔκ τε τοῦ παρ᾽ Ἀθηναίοις
Ὀλυμπιείου καὶ τῶν περὶ τὸν ἐν Δήλῳ βωμὸν
12 ἀνδριάντων. ἐλούετο δὲ κἀν τοῖς δημοσίοις βαλανεί-
οις, ὅτε δημοτῶν ἦν τὰ βαλανεῖα πεπληρωμένα, κερα-
μίων εἰσφερομένων αὐτῷ μύρων τῶν πολυτελεστάτων.
13 ὅτε καί τινος εἰπόντος "μακάριοί ἐστε ὑμεῖς οἱ βασιλεῖς οἱ καὶ τούτοις χρώμενοι καὶ ὀδωδότες ἡδύ" [καὶ]
μηδὲν τὸν ἄνθρωπον προσειπών, ὅπου 'κεῖνος τῇ ἑξῆς
ἐλοῦτο, ἐπεισελθὼν ἐποίησεν αὐτοῦ καταχυθῆναι τῆς
κεφαλῆς μέγιστον κεράμιον πιλυτελεστάτου μύρου,
14 τῆς στακτῆς καλουμένης, ὡς πάντας ἀναστάντας κυ-
λίεσθαι ⟨τοὺς⟩ λουομένους τῷ μύρῳ καὶ διὰ τὴν γλι-
σχρότητα καταπίπτοντας γέλωτα παρέχειν, καθάπερ
καὶ αὐτὸν τὸν βασιλέα.

regards the presents he made. To some people he used to give gazelles' knucklebones, to others dates, and to others money. Occasionally he used to address people he had never seen before when he met them, and make them the most unexpected kind of presents. But in ‹benefactions›[4] to the cities and the honors he paid to the gods he far surpassed all his predecessors, as we can tell from the temple of Olympian Zeus at Athens and the statues round the altar at Delos. He also used to bathe in the public baths, when they were full of common people, having jars of the most precious ointments brought in for him; and on one occasion when some one said to him, "How lucky you are, you kings, to use such scents and smell so sweet!" he answered nothing at the time, but next day, when the man was having his bath, he came in after him and had a huge jar of most precious ointment called stacte poured over his head, so that all the bathers jumped up and rolled themselves in it, and by slipping in it created great amusement, as did the king himself.

[4] An obvious correction for the impossible θυσίαις (sacrifices).

FRAGMENTA LIBRI XXVII

I. BELLUM PERSICUM

1. Ὅτι ἐν τῷ καιρῷ τούτῳ παρεγένοντο πρέσβεις
παρὰ μὲν Θεσπιέων οἱ περὶ Λασῆν καὶ Καλλέαν,
2 παρὰ δὲ Νέωνος Ἰσμηνίας, οἱ μὲν περὶ Λασῆν ἐγχειρίζοντες τὴν ἑαυτῶν πατρίδα Ῥωμαίοις, ὁ δ' Ἰσμηνίας
κατὰ κοινὸν πάσας ⟨τὰς⟩ ἐν τῇ Βοιωτίᾳ πόλεις διδοὺς
3 εἰς τὴν τῶν πρεσβευτῶν πίστιν. ἦν δὲ τοῦτο μὲν
ἐναντιώτατον τοῖς περὶ τὸν Μάρκιον, τὸ δὲ κατὰ πόλιν
4 διελεῖν τοὺς Βοιωτοὺς οἰκειότατον. διὸ τοὺς μὲν περὶ
τὸν Λασῆν καὶ τοὺς Χαιρωνεῖς καὶ τοὺς Λεβαδεῖς καὶ
τοὺς ἄλλους, ὅσοι παρῆσαν ἀπὸ τῶν πόλεων, ἀσμένως
5 ἀπεδέχοντο καὶ κατέψων, τὸν δ' Ἰσμηνίαν παρεδει-
6 γμάτιζον, ἀποτριβόμενοι καὶ παρορῶντες. ὅτε καὶ
συνεπιθέμενοί τινες τῶν φυγάδων μικροῦ κατέλευσαν

---

1 Citizens of Thebes, both pro-Macedon. Ismenias (Kumanudes [18.1.2], no. 1009) was scion of one of the most illustrious families. Neon (K. no. 1402, stemma 308a) was the son of
Brachylles, for whom see n. on 18.1.2. For events in Boeotia on
the eve of the Third Macedonian War, see P. Roesch, *Études
Béotiennes* (Paris 1982), 372–377.   2 Quintus Marcius
Philippus head of a committee preparing the ground in Greece

FRAGMENTS OF BOOK XXVII

I. THE WAR WITH PERSEUS

Events in Boeotia

(Cf. Livy 42.43.4)

1. At this time Lases and Calleas came as envoys from Thespiae and Ismenias on the part of Neon,[1] the former to put their city in the hands of the Romans, and Ismenias to place all the cities of Boeotia together at the discretion of the legates. This was quite contrary to what Marcius[2] and the other legates wished, it suiting their purpose far better to divide up the Boeotians into separate cities. So that while they very gladly received Lases and made much of him, as well as of the envoys from Chaeronea and Lebadea, and all others present from separate cities, they exposed Ismenias to contempt, fighting shy of him and treating him with neglect. On one occasion some of the

–171 B.C.

for war against Perseus. "They went on to break up the Boeotian League, placing pro Roman parties in control and attaching the communities individually to Rome" (*MRR* 1.413). The League had recently, probably in 173, concluded an alliance with Perseus (Livy 42.12.6 and 42.43.9), of which two inscribed fragments have been found at Dium (*CRAI* 1998, 1194–1195). See also H.-U. Wiemer, *Hist.* 53 (2004), 22–37.

τὸν Ἰσμηνίαν, εἰ μὴ κατέφυγεν ὑπὸ τὰ δίθυρα τῶν

7 Ῥωμαίων. κατὰ δὲ τὸν καιρὸν τοῦτον ἐν ταῖς Θήβαις

8 συνέβαινε ταραχὰς εἶναι καὶ στάσεις. οἱ μὲν γὰρ
ἔφασαν δεῖν διδόναι τὴν πόλιν εἰς τὴν Ῥωμαίων πίστιν, οἱ δὲ Κορωνεῖς καὶ Ἁλιάρτιοι συνδεδραμηκότες
εἰς τὰς Θήβας ἀκμὴν ἀντεποιοῦντο τῶν πραγμάτων
καὶ μένειν ἔφασαν δεῖν ἐν τῇ πρὸς τὸν Περσέα συμ-

9 μαχίᾳ. καὶ μέχρι μέν τινος ἐφάμιλλος ἦν ἡ διάθεσις
τῶν στασιαζόντων. Ὀλυμπίχου δὲ τοῦ Κορωνέως
πρώτου μεταθεμένου καὶ φάσκοντος δεῖν ἀντέχεσθαι
Ῥωμαίων, ἐγένετό ‹τις› ὁλοσχερὴς ῥοπὴ καὶ μετά-

10 πτωσις τοῦ πλήθους, καὶ πρῶτον μὲν τὸν Δικέταν
ἠνάγκασαν πρεσβεύειν πρὸς τοὺς περὶ τὸν Μάρκιον,
ἀπολογησόμενον ὑπὲρ τῆς πρὸς τὸν Περσέα συμμα-

11 χίας. μετὰ δὲ ταῦτα τοὺς περὶ τὸν Νέωνα καὶ τὸν Ἱππίαν ἐξέβαλον, συντρέχοντες ἐπὶ τὰς οἰκίας αὐτῶν
καὶ κελεύοντες αὐτοὺς ὑπὲρ αὐτῶν ἀπολογεῖσθαι περὶ
τῶν διῳκονομημένων· οὗτοι γὰρ ἦσαν οἱ ‹τὰ› περὶ

12 τὴν συμμαχίαν οἰκονομήσαντες. τούτων δὲ παρα-
χωρησάντων, ἐξ αὐτῆς ἀθροισθέντες εἰς ἐκκλησίαν
πρῶτον μὲν τιμὰς ἐψηφίσαντο καὶ ‹δωρεὰς› τοῖς Ῥωμαίοις, εἶτ᾽ ἐνεργεῖν ἐπέταξαν τοῖς ἄρχουσι τὴν συμ-

13 μαχίαν, ἐπὶ δὲ πᾶσιν πρεσβευτὰς κατέστησαν τοὺς
ἐγχειριοῦντας τὴν πόλιν Ῥωμαίοις καὶ κατάξοντας
τοὺς παρ᾽ αὐτῶν φυγάδας.

2. Τούτων δὲ συντελουμένων ἐν ταῖς Θήβαις, οἱ
φυγάδες ἐν τῇ Χαλκίδι προστησάμενοι Πομπίδην
κατηγορίαν ἐποιοῦντο τῶν περὶ τὸν Ἰσμηνίαν καὶ Νέ-

exiles[3] attacked Ismenias, and came very near stoning him, but he took refuge under the porch of the Roman mission. At the same period there were quarrels and disturbances in Thebes, where one party maintained that they ought to surrender the city at discretion to the Romans; but the people of Coronea and Haliartus flocking to Thebes, still claimed a part in the direction of affairs, and said that they ought to remain faithful to their alliance with Perseus. For a time the rival views maintained an equilibrium; but upon Olympichus of Coronea being the first to change his attitude and to advise joining the Romans, the balance of popular opinion entirely shifted. They first of all compelled Dicetas[4] to go as their envoy to Marcius and offer his excuses for their having allied themselves with Perseus. In the next place they expelled Neon and Hippias,[5] going in a crowd to their houses and ordering them to go and defend their conduct of affairs, since it was they who had arranged the alliance. Upon Neon and Hippias giving way, they at once assembled in a formal meeting, and after in the first place voting honors to the Romans, ordered their magistrates to take steps to form the alliance; and, last of all, they appointed envoys to put the city in the hands of the Romans and bring back their own exiles.

2. While these proceedings were taking place in Thebes, the exiles in Chalcis appointed Pompides as their representative to accuse Ismenias, Neon, and Dicetas. As

---

[3] Boeotians favoring Rome and driven into exile by Ismenias.

[4] Theban citizen Kumanudes (1.2), no. 501.

[5] Another Theban, allied with Neon, Kumanudes (18.1.2), no. 979.

2 ωνα καὶ Δικέταν. προδήλου δὲ τῆς ἀγνοίας οὔσης τῶν
προειρημένων, καὶ τῶν Ῥωμαίων συνεπισχυόντων
3 τοῖς φυγάσιν, εἰς τὴν ἐσχάτην διάθεσιν ἧκον οἱ περὶ
τὸν Ἱππίαν, ὥστε καὶ τῷ βίῳ κινδυνεῦσαι παρ' αὐτὸν
τὸν καιρὸν ὑπὸ τῆς ὁρμῆς τοῦ πλήθους, ἕως οὗ βραχύ
τι τῆς ἀσφαλείας αὐτῶν προυνοήθησαν οἱ Ῥωμαῖοι,
4 παρακατασχόντες τὴν ἐπιφορὰν τῶν ὄχλων. τῶν δὲ
Θηβαίων παραγενομένων καὶ κομιζόντων τὰ προειρημένα δόγματα καὶ τὰς τιμάς, ταχεῖαν ἕκαστα τῶν
πραγμάτων ἐλάμβανε τὴν ἀνταπόδοσιν, ἅτε τῶν πόλεων παρακειμένων ἀλλήλαις ἐν πάνυ βραχεῖ δια-
5 στήματι. πλὴν ἀποδεξάμενοι τοὺς Θηβαίους οἱ περὶ
τὸν Μάρκιον τήν τε πόλιν ἐπήνεσαν καὶ τοὺς φυγά-
6 δας συνεβούλευσαν καταγαγεῖν εἰς τὴν οἰκείαν. εὐθύς
τε παρήγγειλαν πρεσβεύειν πᾶσι τοῖς ἀπὸ τῶν πόλεων εἰς τὴν Ῥώμην, διδόντας αὑτοὺς εἰς τὴν πίστιν
7 κατ' ἰδίαν ἑκάστους. πάντων δὲ κατὰ τὴν πρόθεσιν
αὐτοῖς χωρούντων—ταῦτα δ' ἦν τὸ διαλῦσαι τῶν
Βοιωτῶν τὸ ἔθνος καὶ λυμήνασθαι τὴν τῶν πολλῶν
8 εὔνοιαν πρὸς τὴν Μακεδόνων οἰκίαν—οὗτοι μὲν μετα-
πεμψάμενοι Σέρουιον ἐξ Ἄργους καὶ καταλιπόντες ἐπὶ
τῆς Χαλκίδος προῆγον ἐπὶ Πελοπόννησον, Νέων δὲ
9 μετά τινας ἡμέρας ἀνεχώρησεν εἰς Μακεδονίαν. οἱ δὲ
περὶ τὸν Ἰσμηνίαν καὶ Δικέταν τότε μὲν ἀπήχθησαν
εἰς φυλακήν, μετὰ δέ τινα χρόνον ἀπήλλαξαν αὑτοὺς
10 ἐκ τοῦ ζῆν. τὸ δὲ τῶν Βοιωτῶν ἔθνος ἐπὶ πολὺν χρόνον
συντετηρηκὸς τὴν κοινὴν συμπολιτείαν καὶ πολλοὺς
καὶ ποικίλους καιροὺς διαπεφευγὸς παραδόξως τότε

the offense of all three was clearly proved, and the Romans lent their support to the exiles, Hippias and his friends were in the last stage of distress, and their lives were even in danger from the violence of the populace, until the Romans took some slight thought for their safety, and put restraint on the hostility of the mob. When the Thebans appeared, bearers of the decrees I mentioned announcing the honors conferred, everything quickly moved in the opposite direction, the cities lying all quite close to each other. Marcius and his colleagues on receiving the Thebans thanked the city, and advised them to bring home the exiles, ordering all the representatives of the towns to repair at once to Rome and separately announce the submission of each several city. When all fell out as they desired—their object being to break up the Boeotian League and damage the popularity of the House of Macedon—the legates, sending for Servius Cornelius Lentulus[6] from Argos, left him in charge of Chalcis and went on to the Peloponnese, but after a few days Neon left for Macedonia. Ismenias and Dicetas were now led off to prison and shortly afterward took their own lives. Thus the Boeotian people after remaining for many years faithful to their League and after many marvelous escapes from various perils, now by rashly and inconsiderately espous-

[6] One of the members of Marcius' committee, as was also Atilius (2.11); *MRR* 1.413.

προπετῶς καὶ ἀλογίστως ἑλόμενον τὰ παρὰ Περσέως,
εἰκῇ καὶ παιδαριωδῶς πτοηθὲν κατελύθη καὶ διεσκορ-
πίσθη κατὰ πόλεις.

11   Οἱ δὲ περὶ τὸν Αὖλον καὶ Μάρκιον παραγενηθέντες
εἰς τὴν τῶν Ἀργείων πόλιν ἐχρημάτισαν ταῖς συναρ-
χίαις ταῖς τῶν Ἀχαιῶν καὶ παρεκάλεσαν Ἄρχωνα τὸν
στρατηγὸν χιλίους ἐκπέμψαι στρατιώτας εἰς Χαλκίδα, παραφυλάξοντας τὴν πόλιν μέχρι τῆς Ῥωμαίων
12   διαβάσεως. τοῦ δ' Ἄρχωνος ἑτοίμως συνυπακούσαν-
τος, οὗτοι μὲν ταῦτα διαπράξαντες ἐν τοῖς Ἕλλησι
κατὰ χειμῶνα καὶ τῷ Ποπλίῳ συμμίξαντες ἀπέπλεον
εἰς τὴν Ῥώμην.

3. Ὅτι οἱ περὶ τὸν Τεβέριον καὶ Ποστόμιον ‹καὶ
Ἰούνιον› κατὰ τοὺς αὐτοὺς καιροὺς ἐπιπορευόμενοι
τὰς νήσους καὶ τὰς κατὰ τὴν Ἀσίαν πόλεις . . .
2   πλεῖστον δ' ἐν τῇ Ῥόδῳ, καίπερ οὐ προσδεομένων τῶν
3   Ῥοδίων κατὰ τοὺς τότε χρόνους. Ἀγησίλοχος γάρ,
τότε πρυτανεύων, ἀνὴρ τῶν εὐδοκιμούντων, ὁ καὶ μετὰ
ταῦτα πρεσβεύσας εἰς τὴν Ῥώμην, ἔτι πρότερον ἅμα
τῷ φανερὸν γενέσθαι διότι μέλλουσι πολεμεῖν Ῥωμαῖοι τῷ Περσεῖ, τἆλλα τε παρακεκλήκει τοὺς πολλοὺς
ὑπὲρ τοῦ κοινωνεῖν τῶν αὐτῶν ἐλπίδων καὶ τετταράκοντα ναῦς συμβουλεύσας τοῖς Ῥοδίοις ὑποζωννύειν,
4   ἵν', ἐάν τις ἐκ τῶν καιρῶν γένηται χρεία, μὴ τότε

---

7 See n. on 22.10.8.   8 Also a member of Marcius' committee.   9 Head of another committee that moreover included
Spurius Postumius and Marcus Iunius (*MRR* 1.412–413).

ing the cause of Perseus, and giving way to insensate and childish excitement, were broken up and dispersed among their several cities.

Aulus Atilius and Quintus Marcius on arriving at Argos sat in council with the magistrates of the Achaean League. They asked Archon,[7] the strategus, to dispatch a thousand soldiers to Chalcis to guard the city until the crossing of the Romans, and on his readily complying, these legates, after making the above arrangements in Greece during the winter, joined Publius Cornelius Lentulus[8] and took ship for Rome.

The Rhodians Support Rome

(Cf. Livy 42.45)

3. At the same time the legates, Tiberius Claudius,[9] Spurius Postumius, and Marcus Junius, visited the islands and the Asiatic cities, exhorting the people to take the part of Rome. They spent a good part of their time at other places, but most of it at Rhodes, although the Rhodians at that period had no need of such exhortation. For Hagesilochus,[10] their prytanis, a man of much influence, who subsequently came as their envoy to Rome, had previously, when it became evident that the Romans were about to make war on Perseus, exhorted the people in general to make common cause with the Romans, and had advised the equipment of forty ships; so that, if circumstances required their help, they might not have to make prepara-

---

[10] H.-U. Wiemer (16.26.10), 301 (and the following pages); for *prytanis* see n. on 13.5.1.

παρασκευάζωνται πρὸς τὸ παρακαλούμενον, ἀλλ'
5 ἑτοίμως διακείμενοι πράττωσι τὸ κριθὲν ἐξ αὐτῆς. ἃ
τότε προφερόμενος τοῖς Ῥωμαίοις καὶ δεικνὺς ὑπὸ
τὴν ὄψιν τὰς παρασκευάς, εὐδοκουμένους τῇ πόλει
τοὺς πρεσβευτὰς ἐξαπέστειλεν. οἱ δὲ περὶ τὸν Τεβέριον ἀποδεδεγμένοι τὴν τῶν Ῥοδίων εὔνοιαν ἐκομί-
ζοντο εἰς τὴν Ῥώμην.—

4. Ὅτι Περσεὺς μετὰ τὸν σύλλογον τὸν πρὸς τοὺς
Ῥωμαίους, . . . τῶν Ἑλλήνων, πάντα τὰ δίκαια κατέ-
ταττεν εἰς τὴν ἐπιστολὴν καὶ τοὺς ὑφ' ἑκατέρων
2 ῥηθέντας λόγους, ἅμα μὲν ὑπολαμβάνων ὑπερδέξιος
φανήσεσθαι τοῖς δικαίοις, ἅμα δὲ βουλόμενος ἀπό-
3 πειραν λαμβάνειν τῆς ἑκάστων προαιρέσεως. πρὸς
μὲν οὖν τοὺς ἄλλους δι' αὐτῶν τῶν γραμματοφόρων
ἔπεμπε τὰς ἐπιστολάς, εἰς δὲ τὴν Ῥόδον καὶ πρε-
4 σβευτὰς συναπέστειλεν Ἀντήνορα καὶ Φίλιππον. οἳ
καὶ παραγενηθέντες τὰ γεγραμμένα τοῖς ἄρχουσιν
ἀπέδωκαν· καὶ μετά τινας ἡμέρας ἐπελθόντες ἐπὶ τὴν
βουλὴν παρεκάλουν τοὺς Ῥοδίους κατὰ μὲν τὸ παρὸν
5 ἡσυχίαν ἔχειν, ἀποθεωροῦντας τὸ γινόμενον· ἐὰν δὲ
Ῥωμαῖοι παρὰ τὰς συνθήκας ἐγχειρῶσι τὰς χεῖρας
6 ἐπιβάλλειν τῷ Περσεῖ καὶ Μακεδόσιν, πειρᾶσθαι δι-

---

11 The conference with Marcius at the Peneius River in Thessaly. Marcius encouraged the king to send envoys to Rome under a truce (although war was not yet declared), which he used to complete Roman preparations for the war (Livy 42.38.10–43.4, based on P.). For the lacuna see Livy 43.46.1: embassies to Rome (following Marcius' suggestion), to Byzantium, and to Rhodes.

tions to meet the demand of the Romans, but, being in
a state of readiness, might be able to act instantly in any
way they decided. He now, by informing the Romans of
this and actually exhibiting his preparations, sent them off
highly pleased with Rhodes. Having thus gratefully accepted the kind offices of Rhodes the envoys sailed back
to Rome.

Perseus and Rhodes

(Cp. Livy 42.46)

4. Perseus, after his conference[11] with the Romans[12]
. . . Greek states, in which he drew up a statement of all
questions of right, and quoted the arguments used on both
sides, with the double purpose of making it appear that in
point of right his position was superior, and of sounding
the intentions of the several states. To other peoples he
sent the letters in charge of the couriers alone; but to
Rhodes he sent also Antenor[13] and Philippus as envoys.
On arriving there they delivered the letter to the magistrates, and after a few days appeared before the Rhodian
senate and begged the Rhodians to remain for the present
quiet spectators of what would happen; but, should the
Romans attack Perseus and the Macedonians in violation

[12] The contents of the following lacuna can be gleaned from
Livy 42.46.1: Perseus sent some envoys to Rome, others to Byzantium and Rhodes, and letters to other Greek states.

[13] Probably Perseus' admiral (29.11.3), who surrendered the
fleet after the battle of Pydna. *RE* Antenor, *Suppl.* 4, 31–32 (P.
Schoch).

αλύειν τοῦτο γὰρ πᾶσι μὲν συμφέρειν, πρέπειν δὲ
7 μάλιστα Ῥοδίοις. ὅσῳ γὰρ πλεῖον ὀρέγονται τῆς ἰσηγορίας καὶ παρρησίας καὶ διατελοῦσι προστατοῦντες
οὐ μόνον τῆς αὐτῶν ἀλλὰ καὶ τῆς τῶν ἄλλων Ἑλλήνων
ἐλευθερίας, τοσούτῳ καὶ τὴν ἐναντίαν προαίρεσιν μάλιστα δεῖν αὐτοὺς προορᾶσθαι καὶ φυλάττεσθαι κατὰ
8 δύναμιν. ταῦτα καὶ τούτοις παραπλήσια διαλεχθέντων τῶν πρέσβεων, ἤρεσκε μὲν ἅπασι τὰ λεγόμενα·
9 προκατεχόμενοι δὲ τῇ πρὸς Ῥωμαίους εὐνοίᾳ, καὶ
νικῶντος αὐτοῖς τοῦ βελτίονος, τἄλλα μὲν ἀπεδέξαντο
φιλανθρώπως τοὺς πρεσβευτάς, ἠξίουν δὲ τὸν Περσέα
διὰ τῆς ἀποκρίσεως εἰς μηδὲν αὐτοὺς παρακαλεῖν
τοιοῦτον ἐξ οὗ φανήσονται πρὸς τὴν Ῥωμαίων ἀντι-
10 πράττοντες βούλησιν. οἱ δὲ περὶ τὸν Ἀντήνορα τὴν
μὲν ἀπόκρισιν οὐκ ἔλαβον . . ., τὴν δὲ λοιπὴν φιλαν-
θρωπίαν ἀποδεξάμενοι τὴν Ῥοδίων ἀπέπλευσαν εἰς
τὴν Μακεδονίαν.

5. Ὅτι Περσεὺς πυνθανόμενος ἔτι τινὰς τῶν ἐν τῇ
Βοιωτίᾳ πόλεις ἀντέχεσθαι τῆς πρὸς αὐτὸν εὐνοίας,
Ἀντίγονον ἐξαπέστειλε τὸν Ἀλεξάνδρου πρεσβευτήν.
2 ὃς καὶ παραγενόμενος εἰς Βοιωτοὺς τὰς μὲν ἄλλας
πόλεις παρῆκε διὰ τὸ μηδεμίαν ἀφορμὴν λαμβάνειν
3 ἐπιπλοκῆς, εἰς δὲ Κορώνειαν καὶ Θίσβας, ἔτι δ᾽ Ἁλί-
αρτον εἰσελθὼν παρεκάλεσε τοὺς ἀνθρώπους ἀντέχε-
4 σθαι τῆς πρὸς Μακεδόνας εὐνοίας. τῶν δὲ προθύμως

14 Not identified.   15 The city, together with Haliartus
(1.8) and Thisbe, remained faithful to Perseus.

of the treaty, they asked them to attempt to effect a reconciliation. This they said was in the interest of all; but the Rhodians were the most proper people to undertake the task. For the more they were the champions of equality and freedom of speech, and the constant protectors not only of their own liberty, but of that of the rest of Greece, the more they should do all in their power to view with apprehension and guard against the victory of principles contrary to these. When the envoys had spoken thus and further in the same sense, what they said pleased everybody; but, prepossessed as the people were by their friendly feeling for Rome, better counsel prevailed, and while they gave a kind reception to the envoys in other respects they begged Perseus in their answer to request them to do nothing which might seem to be in opposition to the wishes of the Romans. Antenor and Philippus did not therefore receive the answer they wished, but after thanking the Rhodians for their kindness in other respects sailed back to Macedonia.

Perseus and Boeotia

(Cf. Livy 42.46.7)

5. Perseus, on learning that some of the Boeotian cities were still favorably disposed to him, sent Antigonus,[14] the son of Alexander, on an embassy there. On arriving in Boeotia he left the other cities alone, as he found no pretext for making approaches; but visiting Coronea,[15] Thisbae, and Haliartus, he begged the citizens to attach themselves to the Macedonian cause. His advances were

ἀποδεχομένων τὰ λεγόμενα καὶ πρεσβευτὰς ψηφισα-
μένων πέμπειν εἰς Μακεδονίαν, οὗτος μὲν ἀπέπλευσε
καὶ συμμίξας τῷ βασιλεῖ διεσάφει τὰ κατὰ τὴν Βοι-
5 ωτίαν. παραγενομένων δὲ καὶ τῶν πρεσβευτῶν μετ᾽
ὀλίγον καὶ παρακαλούντων βοήθειαν ἐκπέμψαι ταῖς
6 πόλεσι ταῖς αἱρουμέναις τὰ Μακεδόνων· τοὺς γὰρ Θηβαίους βαρεῖς ὄντας ἐπικεῖσθαι καὶ παρενοχλεῖν αὐτοὺς διὰ τὸ μὴ βούλεσθαι συμφρονεῖν σφίσιν μηδ᾽
7 αἱρεῖσθαι τὰ Ῥωμαίων· ἅπερ ὁ Περσεὺς διακούσας
βοήθειαν μὲν οὐδαμῶς ἔφη δύνασθαι πέμπειν οὐδενὶ
8 διὰ τὰς ἀνοχάς, καθόλου δ᾽ αὐτοὺς παρακάλει Θηβαίους μὲν ἀμύνασθαι κατὰ δύναμιν, Ῥωμαίοις δὲ μὴ
πολεμεῖν, ἀλλὰ τὴν ἡσυχίαν ἔχειν.

6. Ὅτι οἱ Ῥωμαῖοι τῶν ἀπὸ τῆς Ἀσίας παραγεγο-
(7) νότων πρεσβευτῶν διακούσαντες τά τε κατὰ τὴν Ῥόδον καὶ τὰ κατὰ τὰς ἄλλας πόλεις προσεκαλέσαντο
2 τοὺς παρὰ τοῦ Περσέως πρεσβευτάς. οἱ δὲ περὶ τὸν
Σόλωνα καὶ τὸν Ἱππίαν ἐπειρῶντο μὲν καὶ περὶ τῶν
ὅλων λέγειν τι καὶ παραιτεῖσθαι τὴν σύγκλητον· τὸ
δὲ πλέον ἀπελογοῦντο περὶ τῆς ἐπιβουλῆς τῆς κατὰ
3 τὸν Εὐμένη. ληξάντων δὲ τῆς δικαιολογίας αὐτῶν, πάλαι προδιειληφότες ὑπὲρ τοῦ πολεμεῖν προσέταξαν
αὐτοῖς ἐκ μὲν τῆς Ῥώμης εὐθέως ἀπαλλάττεσθαι καὶ
τοῖς ἄλλοις ἅπασιν Μακεδόσιν, ὅσοι παρεπιδημοῦντες
ἔτυχον, ἐκ δὲ τῆς Ἰταλίας ἐν τριάκονθ᾽ ἡμέραις ἐκ-
4 χωρεῖν. μετὰ δὲ ταῦτα τοὺς ὑπάτους ἀνακαλεσάμενοι
παρώρμων ἔχεσθαι τοῦ καιροῦ καὶ μὴ καθυστερεῖν.

readily received, and they voted to send envoys to Macedonia; upon which the Macedonian envoy took ship, and when he met the king reported to him how things stood in Boeotia. Shortly afterward the envoys arrived, and begged the king to send help to the towns that had taken the side of Macedonia, as the Thebans were putting powerful pressure and inflicting annoyance on them, because they would not agree with them in supporting the Romans. Perseus, after listening to them, replied that it was quite impossible for him to send armed help to anyone owing to his truce with Rome, but he gave them the general advice to defend themselves against the Thebans as well as they could, but to remain quiet, rather than fight with the Romans.

6. The Romans, when their legates[16] returned from Asia, on hearing their report about Rhodes and the other towns, summoned the envoys of Perseus, Solon, and Hippias.[17] They made some attempt to discuss the general question and conciliate the Senate, but most of their speech was a defense of their conduct in the matter of the alleged plot[18] against Eumenes. When their attempted justification was over, the Senate, which had already decided on war, ordered them and all other Macedonian residents to quit Rome at once and Italy within the space of thirty days. After this they summoned the consuls, and urged them to take the matter in hand at once and not to lose time.

[16] 3.1.
[17] Solon: see Tataki (16.19.8), 430, no. 23. Hippias of Beroea, Tataki, 78–79, no. 28
[18] See n. on 22.18.5.

7. Ὅτι Γάιος ἔτι περὶ τὴν Κεφαλληνίαν ὁρμῶν
(6) ἐξέπεμψε τοῖς Ῥοδίοις γράμματα περὶ πλοίων ἐξαποστολῆς, συνθεὶς τὴν ἐπιστολὴν ἀλείπτῃ τινὶ Σωκρά-
2 τει. παραγενομένων δὲ τῶν γραμμάτων εἰς τὴν Ῥόδον,
Στρατοκλέους πρυτανεύοντος τὴν δευτέραν ἔκμηνον,
3 καὶ τοῦ διαβουλίου προτεθέντος, τοῖς μὲν περὶ τὸν
Ἀγαθάγητον καὶ Ῥοδοφῶντα καὶ Ἀστυμήδην καὶ ἑτέροις πλείοσιν ἐδόκει πέμπειν τὰς ναῦς καὶ συνάπτε-
σθαι τῆς ἀρχῆς εὐθέως τοῦ πολέμου, μηδεμίαν πρό-
4 φασιν ποιουμένους. οἱ δὲ περὶ τὸν Δείνωνα καὶ
Πολυάρατον δυσαρεστοῦντες μὲν καὶ τοῖς ἤδη γεγονόσι φιλανθρώποις πρὸς Ῥωμαίους, τότε δὲ προθέμενοι τὸ τοῦ βασιλέως Εὐμένους πρόσωπον ἤρξαντο
5 λυμαίνεσθαι τὴν τῶν πολλῶν προαίρεσιν. ὑπαρχούσης γὰρ τοῖς Ῥοδίοις ὑποψίας καὶ διαφορᾶς πρὸς τὸν
Εὐμένη, πάλαι μὲν ἐκ τοῦ πολέμου τοῦ πρὸς Φαρνάκην, ὅτε, τοῦ βασιλέως Εὐμένους ἐφορμοῦντος ἐπὶ τοῦ
κατὰ τὸν Ἑλλήσποντον στόματος χάριν τοῦ κωλύειν
τοὺς πλέοντας εἰς τὸν Πόντον, ἐπελάβοντο τῆς ὁρμῆς
6 αὐτοῦ καὶ διεκώλυσαν Ῥόδιοι, μικροῖς δ' ἀνώτερον
χρόνοις ἐκ τῶν Λυκιακῶν ἀναξαινομένης τῆς διαφορᾶς ἔκ τινων ἐρυμάτων καὶ χώρας, ἣν συνέβαινε κεῖσθαι μὲν ἐπὶ τῆς ἐσχατιᾶς τῆς τῶν Ῥοδίων Περαίας,
κακοποιεῖσθαι δὲ συνεχῶς διὰ τῶν ὑπ᾽ Εὐμένει ταττ-

---

[19] Gaius Lucretius Gallus, praetor in 171 and in charge of
the fleet (*MRR* 1.416).   [20] These men were pro Roman; as
for Astymedes, there are two possible candidates. The son of

Attitude of Rhodes

(Cf. Livy 42.48.8, 56.6)

7. Gaius Lucretius,[19] while still anchored off Cephallenia, wrote to the Rhodians asking them to dispatch ships, entrusting the letter to a certain Socrates, a gymnastic trainer. Upon the arrival of the letter in Rhodes at the time when Stratocles was prytanis for the second half-year, and when the debate was opened, Agathagetus, Rhodophon, and Astymedes,[20] and a good many others were in favor of sending the ships and at once taking part in the war from the very beginning without any hesitation. Now, however, Deinon and Polyaratus,[21] who were dissatisfied with the favor already shown to Rome, under shelter of a grievance against Eumenes in person, began to try to shake the resolve of the majority. For in the first place there had been at Rhodes a certain suspicion of Eumenes and hostility to him, ever since the war with Pharnaces when, Eumenes having stationed his fleet at the mouth of the Hellespont to prevent the entrance of vessels bound for the Euxine, the Rhodians checked the king's project, and prevented him; and a short time ago this sore had been reopened on the question of Lycia, owing to a dispute concerning certain forts and a strip of territory situated on the borders of the Rhodian Peraea, and subject to constant damage on the part of the lieutenants of Eumenes. All this made the

Theaedetus is probably meant here (*LGPN* 1, s.v., no. 20), rather than the son of Archocrates (ibid., no. 5). See also C. Habicht, *Rev. Ét. Anc.* 105 (2003), 552. N. Badoud, *ZPE* 172 (2010), 127. [21] The leaders of those Rhodians in favor of Macedon. As 7.10 shows, P. is prejudiced against them. He has much more on them in Books 28–30.

7 τομένων· ἐκ πάντων δὴ τούτων εὐηκόως διέκειντο
8 πρὸς πᾶν τὸ λεγόμενον κατὰ τοῦ βασιλέως. διὸ ταύτης ἐπιλαβόμενοι τῆς ἀφορμῆς οἱ περὶ τὸν Δείνωνα
διέσυρον τὴν ἐπιστολήν, φάσκοντες οὐ παρὰ Ῥωμαίων
αὐτὴν ἥκειν, ἀλλὰ παρ' Εὐμένους, θέλοντος αὐτοὺς
ἐκείνου κατὰ πάντα τρόπον ἐμβιβάζειν εἰς τὸν πόλεμον καὶ προσάπτειν τῷ δήμῳ δαπάνας καὶ κακο-
9 παθείας οὐκ ἀναγκαίας. καὶ μαρτύριον ἐποίουν τῆς
ἑαυτῶν ἀποφάσεως τὸ παραγεγονέναι φέροντα τὴν
ἐπιστολὴν [ἀλείπτην τινὰ καὶ] τοιοῦτον ἄνθρωπον,
οὐκ εἰωθότων τοῦτο ποιεῖν Ῥωμαίων, ἀλλὰ καὶ λίαν
μετὰ πολλῆς σπουδῆς καὶ προστασίας διαπεμπομέ-
10 νων ὑπὲρ τῶν τοιούτων. ἔλεγον δὲ ταῦτα, καλῶς μὲν
εἰδότες ὅτι συμβαίνει γεγράφθαι τὴν ἐπιστολὴν ὑπὸ
τοῦ Λοκρητίου, βουλόμενοι δὲ τοὺς πολλοὺς διδάσκειν
μηδὲν ἐξ ἑτοίμου ποιεῖν Ῥωμαίοις, ἀλλ' ἐν πᾶσι
δυσχρηστεῖν καὶ διδόναι προσκοπῆς καὶ δυσαρεστή-
11 σεως ἀφορμάς. ἦν γὰρ τὸ προκείμενον αὐτοῖς ἀπὸ μὲν
τῆς πρὸς Ῥωμαίους εὐνοίας ἀλλοτριοῦν τὸν δῆμον,
εἰς δὲ τὴν τοῦ Περσέως φιλίαν ἐμπλέκειν, καθ' ὅσον
12 οἷοί τ' ἦσαν. συνέβαινε δὲ τοὺς προειρημένους οἰκείους
ὑπάρχειν διὰ τὸ τὸν μὲν Πολυάρατον, ἀλαζονικώτερον
ὄντα καὶ κενόδοξον, ὑπόχρεων πεποιηκέναι τὴν οὐσίαν,
τὸν δὲ Δείνωνα, φιλάργυρον ὄντα καὶ θρασύν, ἐξ ἀρχῆς οἰκεῖον εἶναι τῆς ἐκ τῶν δυναστῶν καὶ βασιλέων
ἐπανορθώσεως. ἐφ' οἷς Στρατοκλῆς ὁ πρύτανις ἐπανα-
13 στὰς καὶ πολλὰ μὲν κατὰ τοῦ Περσέως εἰπών, πολλὰ
δὲ περὶ Ῥωμαίων ἐπ' ἀγαθῷ, παρώρμησε τοὺς πολλοὺς

Rhodians ready to lend an ear to anything that was said against the king; and now Deinon and the others, availing themselves of this prejudice, cast aspersions on the letter, saying that it did not come from the Romans but from Eumenes, who wished by any and every means to drag them into the war, and to impose unnecessary expense and suffering on the people. As a proof of their assertion they adduced the low station of the man who had arrived bearing the letter, the Romans not being in the habit of proceeding thus, but, as regards their communications on such matters, employing excessive care and ceremony. They said this, well knowing Lucretius to be the author of the letter, but for the purpose of persuading the people never to do things readily for the Romans, but always to make difficulties and give cause for offense and dissatisfaction. For their object was to alienate the people from their attachment to Rome, and, as far as was in their power, to induce them to contract friendship with Perseus. These men were adherents of Perseus owing to the fact that Polyaratus, who was a somewhat assuming and vain fellow, had burdened his property, while Deinon, who was avaricious and unscrupulous, had always been disposed to look to kings and princes for advancement. Upon this Stratocles the prytanis got up, and after saying many things against Perseus and in favor of the Romans, exhorted the

εἰς τὸ κυρῶσαι τὸ ψήφισμα τὸ περὶ τῆς ἐξαποστολῆς
14 τῶν πλοίων. καὶ παραυτίκα καταρτίσαντες τετρήρεις
ἕξ, πέντε μὲν ἐξαπέστειλαν ἐπὶ Χαλκίδος, ἡγεμόνα
συστήσαντες ἐπ᾽ αὐτῶν Τιμαγόραν, τὴν δὲ μίαν εἰς
15 Τένεδον, ἐφ᾽ ἧς ἄρχων ἐπέπλει Νικαγόρας. ὃς καὶ
καταλαβὼν ἐν Τενέδῳ Διοφάνην, ἀπεσταλμένον ὑπὸ
τοῦ Περσέως πρὸς Ἀντίοχον, αὐτοῦ μὲν οὐκ ἐγενήθη
16 κύριος, τοῦ δὲ πληρώματος. ὁ δὲ Λοκρήτιος πάντας
ἀποδεξάμενος φιλανθρώπως τοὺς κατὰ θάλατταν
παραγεγονότας συμμάχους ἀπέλυσε τῆς χρείας, φήσας οὐ προσδεῖσθαι τὰ πράγματα τῆς κατὰ θάλατταν βοηθείας.

8. Ὅτι μετὰ τὴν νίκην τῶν Μακεδόνων, συνεδρίου
παρὰ τῷ Περσεῖ συναχθέντος, ὑπέδειξάν τινες τῶν
φίλων διότι δεῖ πρεσβείαν πέμψαι τὸν βασιλέα πρὸς
2 τὸν στρατηγὸν τῶν Ῥωμαίων, ἐπιδεχόμενον ἔτι καὶ
νῦν ὅτι φόρους δώσει Ῥωμαίοις, ὅσους πρότερον ὑπέσχετο [ὁ] πατὴρ καταπολεμηθείς, καὶ τόπων ἐκχω-
3 ρήσει τῶν αὐτῶν. ἐὰν ⟨τε⟩ γὰρ δέξωνται τὰς διαλύσεις, καλὴν ἔφασαν ἔσεσθαι τῷ βασιλεῖ τὴν ἐξαγωγὴν
τοῦ πολέμου, πεπροτερηκότι διὰ τῶν ὑπαίθρων, καὶ
καθόλου πρὸς τὸ μέλλον εὐλαβεστέρους ὑπάρξειν
τοὺς Ῥωμαίους, πεῖραν εἰληφότας τῆς Μακεδόνων

---

22 Island with city of that name at the shore of the Troad. *RE*
Tenedos 494–498 (W. Fiehn).

23 The name is uncertain; the MSS give Timagoras, obviously
an error.

people to ratify the decree relating to the dispatch of the vessels. Having at once fitted out six quadriremes, they sent off five for Chalcis under the command of Timagoras, and one to Tenedos[22] commanded by Nicagoras.[23] The latter, finding in Tenedos Diophanes the envoy of Perseus to Antiochus, failed to capture him, but captured his crew. Lucretius, after giving a kind reception to all the allies who had arrived by sea, relieved them of their service, saying that as things were no naval assistance was required.

Perseus Applies for Peace

(Cf. Livy 42.58, 62)

8. After the victory of the Macedonians[24] Perseus held a council in which some of his friends suggested to him that he should send an embassy to the Roman general, consenting still to pay the same tribute to Rome that his father on his defeat engaged to pay, and to evacuate the same places. For, they said, if they accepted these terms, the result of the war would be in favor of the king after his success in the field; and the Romans after their experience of the bravery of the Macedonians, would be more cau-

[24] Over the army of Publius Licinius Crassus at Callicinus, in spring 171 (Livy 42.57–62). The location was close to Sycurium, *sub radicibus Ossae montis* (Livy), somewhere between Mikro Keserli and Marmariani (Stählin [18.3.12], 90, n. 3). The Romans suffered heavy losses and only the bravery of the Thessalians and Eumenes prevented a major disaster. In memory of the event, the Thessalian Confederacy held contests still attested two hundred years later (J. and L. Robert, *Bull. ép.* 1964, 227, pp. 176–182. *SEG* 53.550).

ἀνδρείας εἰς τὸ μηδὲν ἄδικον μηδὲ βαρὺ προστάττειν
4 Μακεδόσιν. ἐάν τε μὴ δέξωνται θυμομαχοῦντες ἐπὶ
τοῖς γεγονόσιν, ἐκείνοις μὲν δικαίως νεμεσήσειν τὸ
διαμόνιον, αὑτῷ δὲ διὰ τὴν μετριότητα συναγωνιστὰς
5 ὑπάρχειν τοὺς θεοὺς καὶ τοὺς ἀνθρώπους. ταῦτα μὲν
οὖν ἐδόκει τοῖς πλείοσι τῶν φίλων. συγκαταθεμένου
δὲ τοῦ Περσέως ἐπέμποντο παραχρῆμα πρεσβευταὶ
6 Πάνταυχος Βαλάκρου καὶ Μίδων Βεροιεύς. ὧν παραγενομένων πρὸς τὸν Λικίννιον εὐθέως ὁ στρατηγὸς
συνῆγε συνέδριον. τῶν δὲ πρέσβεων διασαφησάντων
τὰ κατὰ τὰς ἐντολάς, μεταστησάμενοι τοὺς περὶ τὸν
Πάνταυχον ἐβουλεύοντο περὶ τῶν προσπεπτωκότων.
7 ἔδοξεν οὖν αὐτοῖς ὁμοθυμαδὸν ὡς βαρυτάτην δοῦναι
8 τὴν ἀπόκρισιν. ἴδιον γὰρ τοῦτο πάντῃ παρὰ Ῥωμαίοις
ἔθος καὶ πάτριόν ἐστι τὸ κατὰ μὲν τὰς ἐλαττώσεις
αὐθαδεστάτους καὶ βαρυτάτους φαίνεσθαι, κατὰ δὲ
9 τὰς ἐπιτυχίας ὡς μετριωτάτους. τοῦτο δ᾽ ὅτι καλὸν
πᾶς ἄν τις ὁμολογήσειεν· εἰ δὲ καὶ δυνατὸν ἐν ἐνίοις
10 καιροῖς, εἰκότως ἄν τις ἐπαπορήσειεν. πλὴν τότε γε
τοιαύτην ἔδωκαν τὴν ἀπόκρισιν· ἐκέλευον γὰρ ἐπιτρέπειν τὸν Περσέα τὰ καθ᾽ αὑτόν, καὶ καθόλου διδόναι τῇ συγκλήτῳ τὴν ἐξουσίαν, ὡς ἂν αὐτῇ δοκῇ,
11 βουλεύεσθαι περὶ τῶν κατὰ τὴν Μακεδονίαν. οἱ δὲ
περὶ τὸν Πάνταυχον ταῦτ᾽ ἀκούσαντες ἐπανῆλθον καὶ
12 διεσάφουν τῷ Περσεῖ καὶ τοῖς φίλοις. ὧν τινες ἐκ-
πληττόμενοι τὴν ὑπερηφανίαν παρωξύνοντο καὶ συνεβούλευον τῷ Περσεῖ μήτε διαπρεσβεύεσθαι μηκέτι
13 μήτε διαπέμπεσθαι περὶ μηδενός. οὐ μὴν ὁ Περσεὺς

tious about making unjust and severe demands upon
Macedonia. But if they did not accept, out of vexation for
what had happened, they would incur the just wrath of
Heaven; while the king by his moderation would earn the
support of gods and men alike. Such was the opinion of
most of his friends; and, on Perseus agreeing, Pantauchus[25] the son of Balacrus and Midon[26] of Beroea were at
once dispatched as envoys. Upon their arrival at the camp
of Licinius, he at once called a council. When the envoys
had explained themselves according to their instructions,
the Romans requested Pantauchus and his colleague to
withdraw, and consulted about the message. It was unanimously decided to give as severe a reply as possible, it
being in all cases the traditional Roman custom to show
themselves most imperious and severe in the season of
defeat, and most lenient after success. That this is noble
conduct every one will confess, but perhaps it is open to
doubt if it is possible under certain circumstances. In the
present case, then, their answer was as follows. They ordered Perseus to submit absolutely, giving the senate authority to decide as they saw fit about the affairs of Macedonia. The envoys, on receiving this answer, returned and
reported it to Perseus and his friends, some of whom, astonished at the pride of the Romans, chafed at it, and
advised the king to send no further embassies or any other
communications about anything whatever. Perseus, how-

[25] One of Perseus "First friends." *RE* Pantauchos 694–695 (H.
Berve)

[26] Another of Perseus' "First friends." *RE* Medon (Suppl. 12),
840–842 (E. Olshausen).

τοιοῦτος ἦν, ἀλλὰ προστιθεὶς καὶ τὸ πλῆθος αὔξων
τῶν χρημάτων διεπέμπετο πλεονάκις πρὸς τὸν Λικίν-
14   νιον. προκόπτων δ' οὐδέν, ἀλλὰ καὶ τῷ πλείστων φίλων ἐπιτιμώντων αὐτῷ καὶ φασκόντων ὅτι νικῶν ποιεῖ
15   τὰ τοῦ λειπομένου καὶ τοῖς ὅλοις ἐπταικότος, οὕτως
ἠναγκάσθη τὰς διαπρεσβείας ἀπογνοὺς μεταστρατο-
πεδεῦσαι πάλιν ἐπὶ τὸ Συκύριον. καὶ ταῦτα μὲν ἐπὶ
τούτων ἦν.

9. Ὅτι τῆς κατὰ τὴν ἱππομαχίαν φήμης μετὰ τὴν
(7a)   νίκην τῶν Μακεδόνων εἰς τὴν Ἑλλάδα διαγγελθείσης
ἐξέλαμψε καθαπερεὶ πῦρ ἡ τῶν πολλῶν πρὸς τὸν
Περσέα διάθεσις, τὸν πρὸ τούτου χρόνον ἐπικρυπτο-
2   μένων τῶν πλείστων. ἦν δὲ περὶ αὐτοὺς τοιαύτη τις,
ἐμοὶ δοκεῖ, διάθεσις· παραπλήσιον ἦν τὸ γινόμενον
3   τῷ συμβαίνοντι περὶ τοὺς γυμνικοὺς ἀγῶνας. καὶ γὰρ
⟨ἐν⟩ἐκείνοις ὅταν πρὸς ἐπιφανῆ καὶ ἀήττητον ἀθλητὴν
εἶναι δοκοῦντα συγκαταστῇ ταπεινὸς καὶ πολὺ κατα-
δεέστερος ἀνταγωνιστής, εὐθέως ἀπομερίζει τὰ πλήθη
τὴν εὔνοιαν τῷ καταδεεστέρῳ καὶ θαρρεῖν παρακαλεῖ
4   καὶ συνεξανίσταται τούτῳ ταῖς ὁρμαῖς· ἐὰν δὲ καὶ
ψαύσῃ τοῦ προσώπου καὶ ποιήσῃ τι σημεῖον τῆς
πληγῆς, παραυτίκα πάλιν ἁπάντων ἀγὼν μικρὸς γί-
5   νεται· ποτὲ δὲ καὶ χλευάζειν ἐγχειροῦσι τὸν ἕτερον, οὐ
μισοῦντες οὐδὲ καταγινώσκοντες, ἀλλὰ παραδόξως τε
συμπαθεῖς γινόμενοι καὶ τῷ καταδεεστέρῳ φύσει
6   προσμερίζοντες τὴν ἑαυτῶν εὔνοιαν· οὓς ἐὰν ἐπιστήσῃ
τις ἐν καιρῷ, ταχέως μετατίθενται καὶ παρὰ πόδας

ever, was by no means so disposed, but sent several times to Licinius, always offering a larger sum. But as he made no progress, and most of his friends found fault with him and told him that now he was victorious, he was acting as if he were unsuccessful and indeed utterly defeated, he was obliged to give up these embassies, and to transfer his camp again to Sycyrium.[27] Such was the situation there.

Position of Perseus in Greece

(Cf. Livy 42.63.1)

9. When after the Macedonian victory the news of the cavalry engagement spread abroad in Greece, the attachment of the people to Perseus, which had been for the most part concealed, burst forth like fire. The state of their feelings was, I think, more or less as follows. The phenomenon was very like what happens in boxing contests at the games. For there, when a humble and much inferior combatant is matched against a celebrated and seemingly invincible athlete, the sympathy of the crowd is at once given to the inferior man. They cheer him on, and back him up enthusiastically; and if he manages to touch his opponent's face, and gets in a blow that leaves any mark, there is at once again a general struggle taking place in miniature. They sometimes go so far as to make fun of the other man, not out of any dislike for him or disapproval but from a curious sort of sympathy and a natural instinct to favor the weaker. If, however, one calls their attention at the right time to their error, they very soon change their

[27] See n. on 8.1.

7 ἐπιλαμβάνονται τῆς ἑαυτῶν ἀγνοίας. ὅ φασι ποιῆσαι
(7b) Κλειτόμαχον· ἐκείνου γὰρ ἀνυποστάτου δοκοῦντος εἶναι κατὰ τὴν ἄθλησιν, καὶ τῆς αὐτοῦ δόξης ἐπιπολαζούσης κατὰ πᾶσαν τὴν οἰκουμένην, Πτολεμαῖόν
φασι τὸν βασιλέα φιλοδοξήσαντα πρὸς τὸ καταλῦσαι
τὴν δόξαν αὐτοῦ, παρασκευάσαντα μετὰ πολλῆς φι-
λοτιμίας Ἀριστόνικον τὸν πύκτην ἐξαποστεῖλαι, δο-
κοῦντο φύσιν ἔχειν ὑπερέχουσαν ἐπὶ ταύτην τὴν
8 χρείαν· παραγενομένου δ᾽ εἰς τὴν Ἑλλάδα τοῦ προειρημένου καὶ συγκαταστάντος Ὀλυμπίασι πρὸς τὸν
Κλειτόμαχον, ἐξ αὐτῆς, ὡς ἔοικεν, ἀπένευσαν ⟨οἱ⟩
πολλοὶ πρὸς τὸν Ἀριστόνικον καὶ παρεκάλουν, χαίρο-
ντες ἐπὶ τῷ βραχύ τι τετολμηκέναι τινὰ συγκαταστῆναι
9 πρὸς τὸν Κλειτόμαχον· ὡς δέ γε προβαίνων ἐφάμιλλος
ἐφαίνετο κατὰ τὸν ἀγῶνα καί που καὶ τραῦμα καίριον
ἐποίησε, κρότος ἐγίνετο καὶ συνεξέπιπτον οἱ πολλοὶ
ταῖς ὁρμαῖς, θαρρεῖν παρακαλοῦντες τὸν Ἀριστόνικον.
10 ἐν ᾧ καιρῷ φασι τὸν Κλειτόμαχον ἀποστάντα καὶ
διαπνεύσαντα βραχὺν χρόνον, ἐπιστρέψαντα πρὸς τὰ
πλήθη πυνθάνεσθαι τί βουλόμενοι παρακαλοῦσι τὸν
Ἀριστόνικον καὶ συναγωνίζονται ᾽κείνῳ καθ᾽ ὅσον
11 εἰσὶ δυνατοί, πότερον οὐ συνοίδασιν αὐτῷ ποιοῦντι τὰ
δίκαια κατὰ τὴν ἄθλησιν ἢ τοῦτ᾽ ἀγνοοῦσι διότι
Κλειτόμαχος μὲν ἀγωνίζεται νῦν ὑπὲρ τῆς τῶν Ἑλλήνων δόξης, Ἀριστόνικος δὲ περὶ τῆς Πτολεμαίου τοῦ
12 βασιλέως. πότερον ἂν οὖν βουληθεῖεν τὸν Ὀλυμπίασι,
στέφανον Αἰγύπτιον ἀποφέρειν ἄνθρωπον νικήσαντα

minds and correct it. This was what Cleitomachus[28] did, as is told. He was considered to be a quite invincible boxer, and his fame had spread over the whole world, when Ptolemy, ambitious to destroy his reputation, trained with the greatest care and sent off the boxer Aristonicus, a man who seemed to have a remarkable natural gift for this sport. Upon this Aristonicus arriving in Greece and challenging Cleitomachus at Olympia, the crowd, it seems, at once took the part of the former and cheered him on, delighted to see that someone, once in a way at least, ventured to pit himself against Cleitomachus. And when, as the fight continued, he appeared to be his adversary's match, and once or twice landed a telling blow, there was great clapping of hands, and the crowd became delirious with excitement, cheering on Aristonicus. At this time they say that Cleitomachus, after withdrawing for a few moments to recover his breath, turned to the crowd and asked them what they meant by cheering on Aristonicus and backing him up all they could. Did they think he himself was not doing his best, or were they not aware that Cleitomachus was now fighting for the glory of Greece and Aristonicus for that of King Ptolemy? Would they prefer to see an Egyptian conquer the Greeks and win the Olym-

[28] Son of Hermocrates of Thebes, one of the most famous athletes of the time. Victor in numerous contests, including at Olympia in the *pankration* in 216 (Paus. 6.15.3–5), where an epigram by Alcaeus of Messene (see n. on 18.34.2) was inscribed on his statue, *AP* 9.588. L. Moretti, *Olympionikai, Atti Accad. naz. dei Lincei* 354 (1957), 141, no. 584. The king was Ptolemy IV Philopator; Cletomachus' opponent at the time is not otherwise known.

τοὺς Ἕλληνας, ἢ Θηβαῖον καὶ Βοιώτιον κηρύττεσθαι
13 νικῶντα τῇ πυγμῇ τοὺς ἄνδρας. ταῦτα δ' εἰπόντος τοῦ
Κλειτομάχου τηλικαύτην φασὶ γενέσθαι τὴν μετά-
πτωσιν τῶν πολλῶν ὥστε πάλιν ἐκ μεταβολῆς μᾶλλον
ὑπὸ τοῦ πλήθους ἢ τοῦ Κλειτομάχου καταγωνισθῆναι
τὸν Ἀριστόνικον.

(7c)   10. Τούτῳ δὲ παραπλήσιον ἦν καὶ τὸ κατὰ τὸν
2   Περσέα συμβαῖνον περὶ τοὺς ὄχλους· εἰ γάρ τις
ἐπιστήσας αὐτοὺς ἤρετο μετὰ παρρησίας εἰ βούλοιντ'
ἂν εἰς ἕνα πεσεῖν τὴν τηλικαύτην ὑπεροχὴν καὶ λαβεῖν μοναρχικῆς πεῖραν ἐξουσίας, ἀνυπευθύνου κατὰ
πάντα τρόπον, ταχέως ἂν αὐτοὺς ὑπολαμβάνω συν-
νοήσαντας παλινῳδίαν ποιῆσαι καὶ μεταπεσεῖν εἰς
3   τοὐναντίον· εἰ δὲ καὶ βραχέα τις ὑπέμνησε τῶν γεγονότων ἐκ μὲν τῆς Μακεδόνων οἰκίας δυσκόλων τοῖς
Ἕλλησιν, ἐκ δὲ τῆς Ῥωμαίων ἀρχῆς συμφερόντων,
καὶ λίαν ⟨ἂν⟩ παρὰ πόδας αὐτοὺς ὑπολαμβάνω μετα-
4   μεληθῆναι. πλὴν τότε γε κατὰ τὴν ἀνεπίστατον καὶ
πρώτην ὁρμὴν ἐκφανὴς ἦν ἡ τῶν πολλῶν εὐδόκησις
τοῖς προσαγγελλομένοις, ἀσμενιζόντων διὰ τὸ παράδοξον, εἰ καθόλου πέφηνέ τις ἱκανὸς ἀνταγωνιστὴς
5   Ῥωμαίοις. περὶ μὲν οὖν τούτων ἐπὶ τοσοῦτον προήχθην εἰπεῖν, ἵνα μή τις ἀκρίτως εἰς ἀχαριστίαν
ὀνειδίζῃ τοῖς Ἕλλησι τὴν τότε διάθεσιν, ἀγνοῶν τὰ
φύσει παρεπόμενα τοῖς ἀνθρώποις.

pian crown, or to hear a Theban and Boeotian proclaimed by the herald as victor in the men's boxing match? When Cleitomachus had spoken thus, they say there was such a change in the sentiment of the crowd that now all was reversed, and Aristonicus was beaten rather by the crowd than by Cleitomachus.

10. Very similar to this was the present feeling of the multitude toward Perseus. For if anyone had secured their attention, and asked them frankly if they really would wish to see the supreme power in so absolute a form fall into the hands of a single man and to experience the rule of an absolutely irresponsible monarch, I fancy they would very soon have come to their senses and, changing their tune, have undergone a complete revulsion of feeling. And if one had reminded them even briefly of all the hardships that the house of Macedon had inflicted on Greece, and of all the benefits[29] she had derived from Roman rule, I fancy the reaction would have been most sudden and complete. But now, when they gave way to their first unreflecting impulse, the delight of the people at the news was conspicuous, hailing, as they did, owing to the very strangeness of the fact, the appearance of someone at least who had proved himself a capable adversary of Rome. I have been led to speak of this matter at such length lest anyone, in ignorance of what is inherent in human nature, may unjustly reproach the Greeks with ingratitude for being in this state of mind at the time.

[29] P. is here and in 10.5 ("ingratitude") very partial to Rome, which is not always the case.

11. Κέστρος. ξένον ἦν τοῦτο τὸ εὕρημα κατὰ τὸν

(9) 2 Περσικὸν πόλεμον. τὸ δὲ βέλος τοιοῦτον· διπάλαιστον
ἦν, ἴσον ἔχον τὸν αὐλίσκον τῇ προβολῇ. τούτῳ ξύλον

3 ἐνήρμοστο τῷ μὲν μήκει σπιθαμιαῖον, τῷ δὲ πάχει

4 δακτυλιαίαν ἔχον τὴν διάμετρον. εἰς δὲ τούτου τὸ μέσον ἐσφήνωτο πτερύγια τρία ξύλινα, βραχέα παν-

5 τελῶς. τοῦτο, δυεῖν κώλων ἀνίσων ὑπαρχόντων τῆς
σφενδόνης, εἰς τὸ μέσον ἐνηγκυλίζετο τῶν κώλων εὐ-

6 λύτως. λοιπὸν ἐν μὲν τῇ περιαγωγῇ τεταμένων τούτων
ἔμενεν· ὅτε δὲ παραλυθείη θάτερον τῶν κώλων κατὰ
τὴν ἄφεσιν, ἐκπῖπτον ἐκ τῆς ἀγκύλης καθαπερεὶ

7 μολυβδὶς ἐκ τῆς σφενδόνης ἐφέρετο καὶ προσπῖπτον
μετὰ βιαίας πληγῆς κακῶς διετίθει τοὺς συγκυρήσαν-
τας.

12. Ὅτι ὁ Κότυς ἦν ἀνὴρ καὶ κατὰ τὴν ἐπιφάνειαν

(10) ἀξιόλογος καὶ πρὸς τὰς πολεμικὰς χρείας διαφέρων,

2 ἔτι δὲ κατὰ τὴν ψυχὴν πάντα μᾶλλον ἢ Θρᾷξ· καὶ
3 γὰρ νήπτης ὑπῆρχε καὶ πραότητα καὶ βάθος ὑπ-
έφαινεν ἐλευθέριον.

---

[30] A bolt hurled from a sling, used by the Macedonians to
great effect against the Romans: Livy 42.65.9–11.

[31] Son of Seuthes, king of the Thracian Odrysae. Livy
(42.51.10) has him join Perseus' army earlier in the year (WC
3.310, therefore thinks the correct place for this fragment to be
after 6.4). He was one of the commanders at Callicinus. P.'s praise
of him resembles his words about the Galatian Ortiagon in
22.21.1–4. See G. Chiranky, *Athenaeum* 60 (1982), 461–481.

The Cestrus or Cestrosphendone

(Suda; cf. Livy 42.65.9)

11. The so-called cestrus[30] was a novel invention at the time of the war with Perseus. The form of the missile was as follows. It was two palms long, the tube being of the same length as the point. Into the former was fitted a wooden shaft a span in length and a finger's breadth in thickness, and to the middle of this were firmly attached three quite short wing-shaped sticks. The thongs of the sling from which the missile was discharged were of unequal length, and it was so inserted into the loop between them that it was easily freed. There it remained fixed while the thongs were whirled round and taut, but when at the moment of discharge one of the thongs was loosened, it left the loop and was shot like a leaden bullet from the sling, and striking with great force inflicted severe injury on those who were hit by it.

Cotys, King of the Odrysae

(Suda; cf. Livy 42.51.10)

12. Cotys[31] was a man of striking appearance and remarkably skilled in warfare, and also in character he was not at all like a Thracian; for he was sober, and one noticed in him a certain gentleness and steadiness of character distinctive of a gentleman.

II. RES AEGYPTI

13. Ὅτι Πτολεμαῖος ὁ στρατηγὸς ὁ κατὰ Κύπρον
(12) οὐδαμῶς Αἰγυπτιακὸς γέγονεν, ἀλλὰ νουνεχὴς καὶ
2 πρακτικός. παραλαβὼν γὰρ τὴν νῆσον ἔτι νηπίου τοῦ
βασιλέως ὄντος ἐγίνετο μὲν ἐπιμελῶς περὶ συναγωγὴν
χρημάτων, ἐδίδου δ' ἁπλῶς οὐδὲν οὐδενί, καίπερ αἰ-
τούμενος πολλάκις ὑπὸ τῶν βασιλικῶν διοικητῶν καὶ
3 καταλαλούμενος πικρῶς ἐπὶ τῷ μηδὲν προΐεσθαι. τοῦ
δὲ βασιλέως εἰς ἡλικίαν παραγεγονότος, συνθεὶς
4 πλῆθος ἱκανὸν χρημάτων ἐξαπέστειλεν, ὥστε καὶ τὸν
Πτολεμαῖον αὐτὸν καὶ τοὺς περὶ τὴν αὐλὴν εὐδοκῆσαι
τῇ πρότερον αὐτοῦ συστολῇ καὶ τῷ μηδὲν προΐεσθαι.

II. BELLUM PERSICUM

14. Ὅτι κατὰ τὸν καιρὸν ἡνίκα Περσεὺς ἐκ τοῦ
(11) πολέμου τοῦ πρὸς Ῥωμαίους ἀπελύθη, Ἀντήνορος
παραγενομένου παρὰ τοῦ Περσέως περὶ ⟨τῆς⟩ τῶν
αἰχμαλώτων διαλυτρώσεως τῶν μετὰ Διοφάνους πλε-
όντων, ἐνέπεσε μεγάλη τοῖς πολιτευομένοις ἀπορία
2 περὶ τοῦ τί δέον εἴη ποιεῖν. τοῖς ιὲν γὰρ περὶ τὸν Φι-
λόφρονα καὶ Θεαίδητον οὐδαμῶς ἤρεσκε προσδέχεσθαι τὴν τοιαύτην ἐπιπλοκήν, τοῖς δὲ περὶ τὸν Δεί-

---

32 This is the Ptolemy called Macron, appointed by king
Ptolemy VI Philometor to be governor of Cyprus, but in 168
defecting to Antiochus IV. He took his own life under Antiochus

II. AFFAIRS OF EGYPT

13. Ptolemy,[32] the Egyptian commander in Cyprus, was not at all like an Egyptian, but gifted with good sense and capacity. For having taken charge of the island when the king was still an infant, he applied himself diligently to the collection of revenue, and never gave away a penny to anybody, although the royal finance officials[33] were frequent beggars, and he was bitterly abused for never opening his purse. Upon the king attaining his majority,[34] he put together a considerable sum of money, and sent it off, so that the king and the members of the court now approved of his former closefistedness and refusal to part with money.

II. THE WAR WITH PERSEUS

14. At the time when Perseus had retired from the war with Rome, Antenor,[35] the envoy sent by him to ransom the prisoners who were in the same ship with Diophanes,[36] reached Rhodes, and public men there were in great doubt as to what course to take, Philophron and Theaedetus[37] by no means wishing to involve themselves in such a

171–170
B.C.

V (164–162). From the voluminous bibliography see, e.g., L. Mooren (22.17.6), 187–188, no. 0350, and L. Boffo, *Iscrizioni greche e latine per lo studio della bibbia* (Brescia 1994), 87–90

[33] P. probably meant the central *dioecetes* at Alexandria, the plural perhaps indicating that its incumbent changed during Ptolemy's governorship of Cyprus.

[34] In 169.   [35] 4.4–10.

[36] See 7.14.   [37] See n. on 22.5.2 and see 22.5.7.

*νωνα καὶ Πολυάρατον ἤρεσκε. καὶ τέλος ἐποιήσαντο
διάταξιν πρὸς τὸν Περσέα περὶ τῆς τῶν αἰχμαλώτων
διαλυτρώσεως.*

15. Ὅτι Κέφαλος ἧκεν ἐξ Ἠπείρου, ἔχων μὲν καὶ
(13) πρότερον ἤδη σύστασιν πρὸς τὴν Μακεδόνων οἰκίαν,
τότε δὲ διὰ τῶν πραγμάτων ἠναγκασμένος αἱρεῖσθαι
τὰ τοῦ Περσέως. ἡ δ᾽ αἰτία τοῦ συμβαίνοντος ἐγένετο
2 τοιαύτη. Χάροψ ἦν Ἠπειρώτης, ἀνὴρ τἄλλα μὲν καλὸς
κἀγαθὸς καὶ φίλος Ῥωμαίων, ὃς Φιλίππου τὰ κατὰ
τὴν Ἤπειρον στενὰ κατασχόντος αἴτιος ἐγένετο τοῦ
Φίλιππον μὲν ἐκπεσεῖν ἐκ τῆς Ἠπείρου, Τίτον δὲ καὶ
3 τῆς Ἠπείρου κρατῆσαι καὶ τῶν Μακεδόνων. οὗτος
4 υἱὸν ἔσχε Μαχατᾶν, οὗ Χάροψ ἐγένετο. τοῦτον ἀντί-
παιδα κατὰ τὴν ἡλικίαν ὄντα τοῦ πατρὸς μεταλλάξαντος ὁ Χάροψ μετὰ τῆς καθηκούσης προστασίας εἰς
τὴν Ῥώμην ἀπέστειλε χάριν τοῦ καὶ τὴν διάλεκτον
5 καὶ τὰ γράμματα τὰ Ῥωμαϊκὰ μαθεῖν. τοῦτο τὸ μειράκιον πολλοῖς σύνηθες γεγονὸς ἐπανῆλθε μετά τινα
χρόνον εἰς τὴν οἰκείαν. ὁ μὲν οὖν πρεσβύτερος Χάροψ
6 μετήλλαξε τὸν βίον. τὸ δὲ μειράκιον μετέωρον ὂν τῇ
φύσει καὶ πάσης πονηρίας ἔμπλεων ἐκορωνία καὶ πα-
7 ρετρίβετο πρὸς τοὺς ἐπιφανεῖς ἄνδρας. τὰς μὲν οὖν
ἀρχὰς οὐδεὶς ἦν αὐτοῦ λόγος, ἀλλ᾽ οἱ προκατέχοντες
καὶ ταῖς ἡλικίαις καὶ ταῖς δόξαις, οἱ περὶ τὸν Ἀντίνουν,
8 ἐχείριζον τὰ κοινὰ κατὰ τὰς αὐτῶν γνώμας. τοῦ δὲ

negotiation, while Deinon and Polyaratus[38] were in favor of it. Finally they made an arrangement with Perseus about ransoming the prisoners.

Epirot Statesman to Perseus

15. Cephalus,[39] who now came from Epirus, had previously had relations with the royal house of Macedon, and was now forced by circumstances to take the part of Perseus. The reason for what happened was as follows. There was a certain Epirot called Charops,[40] a man well principled in general and a friend of the Romans. At the time when Philip held the passes to Epirus, it was by his agency that the king had to abandon Epirus, and that Flamininus became master of it and worsted the Macedonians. He had a son named Machatas who had a son also named Charops. Upon the death of his father this Charops, while still a boy, was sent to Rome by his grandfather Charops with a retinue that befitted his rank to learn to speak and write Latin. The boy made many acquaintances, and returned home after a certain time. The elder Charops soon departed this life; and the young man, who was naturally ambitious and full of all kinds of cunning, became presumptuous and began to clash with the leading men. At first no notice was taken of him, but Antinous and the others, his superiors in age and reputation, administered public affairs as they thought best. But when the war with

---

[38] See 7.4–12.   [39] A leading figure among the Molossians.
[40] See n. on 20.3.1. Father of Machatas, grandfather of the younger Charops (15.3). For other members of the family, see C. Habicht (18.7.6), 85–90 and 292.

πολέμου τοῦ Περσικοῦ συστάντος, εὐθέως διέβαλλε
τὸ μειράκιον τοὺς προειρημένους ἄνδρας πρὸς Ῥωμαίους, ἀφορμῇ μὲν χρώμενον τῇ προγεγενημένῃ συ-
9 στάσει τῶν ἀνδρῶν πρὸς τὴν Μακεδόνων οἰκίαν, κατὰ
δὲ τὸ παρὸν πάντα παρατηροῦν καὶ πᾶν τὸ λεγόμενον
ἢ πραττόμενον ὑπ’ αὐτῶν ἐπὶ τὸ χεῖρον ἐκδεχόμενον
καὶ τὰ μὲν ἀφαιροῦν τὰ δὲ προστιθὲν ἐλάμβανε πι-
10 θανότητας κατὰ τῶν ἀνθρώπων. ὁ δὲ Κέφαλος, τἄλλα
τε φρόνιμος καὶ στάσιμος ἄνθρωπος, καὶ κατὰ τοὺς
καιροὺς τούτους ἐπὶ τῆς ἀρίστης ὑπῆρχε γνώμης.
11 ἀρχόμενος γὰρ ηὔξατο τοῖς θεοῖς μὴ συστῆναι τὸν
12 πόλεμον μηδὲ κριθῆναι τὰ πράγματα· πραττομένου δὲ
τοῦ πολέμου τὰ κατὰ τὴν συμμαχίαν ἐβούλετο δίκαια
ποιεῖν Ῥωμαίοις, πέρα δὲ τούτου μήτε προστρέχειν
13 ἀγεννῶς μήθ’ ὑπηρετεῖν μηδὲν παρὰ τὸ δέον. τοῦ δὲ
Χάροπος ἐνεργῶς χρωμένου ταῖς κατ’ αὐτοῦ διαβολαῖς
καὶ πᾶν τὸ παρὰ τὴν Ῥωμαίων βούλησιν γινόμενον
εἰς ἐθελοκάκησιν ἄγοντος, τὸ μὲν πρῶτον οἱ προειρημένοι κατεφρόνουν, οὐδὲν αὐτοῖς συνειδότες ἀλλότριον
14 βουλευομένοις Ῥωμαίων. ὡς δὲ τοὺς περὶ τὸν Ἱππό-
λοχον καὶ Νίκανδρον καὶ Λόχαγον εἶδον τοὺς Αἰτωλοὺς ἀναγομένους εἰς τὴν Ῥώμην ἀπὸ τῆς ἱππομαχίας
ἀλόγως, καὶ τὰς διαβολὰς τὰς ἐκ τῶν περὶ Λυκίσκον
πεπιστευμένας κατ’ αὐτῶν, οἵτινες κατὰ τὴν Αἰτωλίαν
τὴν αὐτὴν αἵρεσιν ἦγον τῷ Χάροπι, τὸ τηνικάδε προ-

---

41 Nicander was the Aetolian strategus in 190/89 (n. on
20.10.16), Lochagus in 180/79.

Perseus broke out, the young man at once began to traduce these statesmen to the Romans, taking advantage of their former relations with the house of Macedon, and now by scrutinizing all their actions, and putting the worst interpretation on all they said or did, suppressing some things and adding others, he made out a plausible case against them. Cephalus, who was in general a wise and consistent man, now also at this crisis had adopted the very best attitude. For at first he had prayed to Heaven that there should be no war and no such decision of the issues; and now, during the course of the war, he desired to act justly by the Romans according to the terms of their alliance, but beyond this neither to court them in an ignoble manner, nor to be unduly subservient to them. When Charops continued to be active in his accusations against Cephalus, and represented everything that occurred contrary to the wish of the Romans as the result of his deliberate malice, Cephalus at first made light of it, as he was not conscious of having acted in any way in a manner inimical to Rome; but when he saw that Hippolochus, Nicander, and Lochagus[41] the Aetolians were arrested and carried to Rome after the cavalry action[42] for no valid reason, and that credence was given to the false accusations brought against them by Lyciscus,[43] who was pursuing in Aetolia the same course as Charops in Epirus; then foreseeing

[42] At Callicinus; these Aetolians were accused (unjustly according to P.) of having failed during that battle.

[43] Of Stratus, ardent supporter of the Romans like the Achaean Callicrates or the younger Charops of Epirus. He was Aetolian general in 172/1. Deininger (22.10.8), 168–176.

15 ἰδόμενοι τὸ μέλλον ἐβουλεύοντο περὶ αὑτῶν. ἔδοξεν
οὖν αὐτοῖς παντὸς πεῖραν λαμβάνειν ἐφ' ᾧ μὴ προέσθαι σφᾶς αὐτοὺς ἀκρίτως εἰς τὴν Ῥώμην ἐπανάγεσθαι
16 διὰ τὰς Χάροπος διαβολάς. οὕτω μὲν οὖν οἱ περὶ τὸν
Κέφαλον ἠναγκάσθησαν παρὰ τὰς αὑτῶν προαιρέσεις ἑλέσθαι τὰ τοῦ Περσέως.

16. Ὅτι οἱ περὶ Θεόδοτον καὶ Φιλόστρατον ἐποίησαν
(14) ἀσεβὲς πρᾶγμα καὶ παράσπονδον ὁμολογουμένως. πυ-
2 θόμενοι γὰρ τὸν ὕπατον τῶν Ῥωμαίων Αὖλον Ὁστί-
λιον παραγίνεσθαι κομιζόμενον εἰς Θετταλίαν ἐπὶ τὸ
στρατόπεδον καὶ νομίζοντες, εἰ παραδοῖεν τὸν Αὖλον
τῷ Περσεῖ, μεγίστην μὲν ⟨ἂν⟩ πίστιν προσενέγκασθαι, μέγιστα δ' ἂν βλάψαι κατὰ τὸ παρὸν Ῥωμαίους,
3 ἔγραφον τῷ Περσεῖ συνεχῶς ἐπισπεύδειν. ὁ δὲ βασιλεὺς ἐβούλετο μὲν ἐξ αὐτῆς προάγειν καὶ συνάπτειν,
τῶν δὲ Μολοττῶν κατὰ τὸν Ἀῷον ποταμὸν τὴν γέφυ-
ραν κατειληφότων ἐκωλύετο τῆς ὁρμῆς καὶ πρῶτον
4 ἠναγκάζετο διαμάχεσθαι πρὸς τούτους. συνέβη δὲ
τὸν Αὖλον εἰς τοὺς Φανοτεῖς παραγενόμενον καταλῦσαι παρὰ Νέστορι τῷ Κρωπίῳ καὶ παραδοῦναι καθ'
αὑτοῦ τοῖς ἐχθροῖς καιρὸν ὁμολογούμενον· ⟨ὃν⟩ εἰ μὴ
τύχη τις ἐβράβευσε πρὸς τὸ βέλτιον, οὐκ ἄν μοι δοκεῖ
5 διαφυγεῖν. νῦν δὲ δαιμονίως πως ὁ Νέστωρ τὸ μέλλον
ὀττευσάμενος ἐξ αὐτῆς ἠνάγκασε μετελθεῖν εἰς Γί-
6 τανα τῆς νυκτός. καὶ ἀπογνοὺς τὴν διὰ τῆς Ἠπείρου

---

44 Molossians.
45 Aulus Hostilius Mancinus, cos. 170. *MRR* 1.419–420.

what would happen, he took thought for his own safety. He resolved, in consequence, to take any measures rather than allow himself to be arrested and sent to Rome without trial, owing to the false accusations of Charops. This is why, against his conviction, Cephalus found himself compelled to side with Perseus.

Attempt to Seize the Consul

16. Theodotus and Philostratus[44] in the opinion of all were guilty of a wicked and treacherous action. For learning that Aulus Hostilius[45] the Roman consul was present in Epirus on his way to his army in Thessaly, and thinking that if they delivered him up to Perseus they would be giving the king a signal pledge of their fidelity and would inflict great present injury[46] on the Romans, they wrote repeatedly to Perseus to hasten his arrival. The king wished to advance at once and join them; but as the Molotti had occupied the bridge over the river Aoüs, his design was checked, and he was forced in the first place to fight with this tribe. Hostilius, as it happened, had reached Phanote,[47] and was staying there with Nestor the Cropian, which gave an evident opportunity to his enemies; and, had not a mere chance determined for the better, I do not think he could have escaped. But now, in some mysterious manner, Nestor divined what was brewing, and made him at once leave for Gitana[48] by night. Renouncing, hence-

---

[46] By driving Epirus firmly on Perseus' side.

[47] Fortified city of the Epirotic Chaones, modern Raveni. N. G. L. Hammond, *Epirus* (Oxford 1967), 676 and map 16.

[48] Thesprotian city, now Goumani. Hammond (previous note), 82, maps 4.16.18.

πορείαν ἀνήχθη καὶ πλεύσας εἰς Ἀντίκυραν ἐκεῖθεν
ἐποιήσατο τὴν ὁρμὴν εἰς Θετταλίαν.

III. RES ASIAE

17. Ὅτι Φαρνάκης πάντων τῶν πρὸ τοῦ βασιλέων
(15) ἐγένετο παρανομώτατος.

18. Ὅτι Ἄτταλος χειμάζων ἐν Ἐλατείᾳ καὶ σαφῶς
(15) εἰδὼς τὸν ἀδελφὸν Εὐμένη λυπούμενον ὡς ἔνι μάλιστα καὶ βαρυνόμενον ἐπὶ τῷ τὰς ἐπιφανεστάτας
αὐτοῦ τιμὰς ἠθετῆσθαι παρὰ τῶν ἐν Πελοποννήσῳ
διὰ κοινοῦ δόγματος, ἐπικρυπτόμενον δὲ πρὸς πάντας
2 τὴν περὶ αὐτὸν ὑπάρχουσαν διάθεσιν, ἐπεβάλετο διαπέμπεσθαι πρός τινας τῶν ἐν Ἀχαΐᾳ, σπουδάζων ἀποκατασταθῆναι τἀδελφῷ δι' αὐτοῦ μὴ μόνον τὰς
3 ἀναθηματικάς, ἀλλὰ καὶ τὰς ἐγγράπτους τιμάς. τοῦτο
δ' ἐποίει πεπεισμένος μεγίστην μὲν ἂν ἐκείνῳ ταύτην
⟨τὴν⟩ χάριν προσενέγκασθαι, μάλιστα δ' ἂν τὸ φιλά-
δελφον καὶ γενναῖον τῆς αὐτοῦ προαιρέσεως ἐναπο-
δείξασθαι τοῖς Ἕλλησι διὰ ταύτης τῆς πράξεως.

---

49 See n. on 9.39.2.

50 This is undoubtedly part of his obituary; see n. on 23.9.1.

51 In fact, the Achaean Confederacy, comprising at the time
the entire Peloponnese. The decree predates 172 (Livy 42.12.7).
The Achaeans had firmly rejected a generous, but somewhat in-
sensitive offer of Eumenes and at that occasion vented their anger
at his continued possession of Aegina (22.7.3–8.13). See further
28.7.1–15.

forth, his design of marching through Epirus, he took ship, and sailing to Anticyra[49] started from there for Thessaly.

III. AFFAIRS OF ASIA

Pharnaces, King of Pontus

17. Pharnaces surpassed all previous kings in his contempt for laws.[50]

Attalus and Eumenes

18. Attalus was wintering in Elatea, and well knowing that his brother Eumenes was exceedingly hurt by all the most brilliant distinctions conferred on him having been cancelled by a public decree of the Peloponnesians,[51] but that he concealed from every one the state of his feelings, decided on sending a message to certain Achaeans with the object of procuring by his own action the restoration not only of his brother's statues but of the inscriptions in his honor. This he did with the conviction that he would thus not only be conferring a very great favor on his brother, but would give the Greeks by this action a signal proof of his brotherly love[52] and nobility of sentiment.

[52] The dynasty was notorious for its family unity; Attalus was widely given the title *Philadelphus*.

THE HISTORIES OF POLYBIUS

19. Ὅτι Ἀντίοχος ὁρῶν ἐκφανῶς ἤδη τοὺς κατὰ τὴν
(17) Ἀλεξάνδρειαν παρασκευαζομένους εἰς τὸν περὶ Κοί-
λης Συρίας πόλεμον, εἰς μὲν τὴν Ῥώμην ἔπεμψε πρε-
2 σβευτὰς τοὺς περὶ Μελέαγρον, ἐντειλάμενος λέγειν τῇ
συγκλήτῳ καὶ διαμαρτύρασθαι διότι παρὰ πάντα τὰ
δίκαια Πτολεμαῖος αὐτῷ τὰς χεῖρας ἐπιβάλλει ⟨πρό-
τερος⟩ ...

(17) 20. Ἴσως μὲν οὖν ἐν πᾶσι τοῖς ἀνθρωπείοις τῷ
καιρῷ δεῖ μετρεῖν ἕκαστα τῶν ἐνεργουμένων· μεγίστην γὰρ οὗτος ἔχει δύναμιν· μάλιστα δ' ἐν τοῖς
2 πολεμικοῖς· ὀξύταται γὰρ περὶ τούτων εἰς ἑκάτερα τὰ
μέρη γίνονται ῥοπαί· τὸ δ' ἀστοχεῖν τούτων μέγιστόν
ἐστι τῶν ἁμαρτημάτων.

3 Ὅτι δοκοῦσι πολλοὶ μὲν τῶν ἀνθρώπων ἐπιθυμεῖν
τῶν καλῶν, ὀλίγοι δὲ τολμᾶν ἐγχειρεῖν αὐτοῖς, σπάνιοι δὲ τῶν ἐγχειρησάντων ἐπὶ τέλος ἀγαγεῖν τὰ πρὸς
τὸ καθῆκον ἐν ἑκάστοις ποιούμενα.

The War between Ptolemy and Antiochus

19. Antiochus, seeing that at Alexandria preparations were being made for the war[53] concerning Coele-Syria, sent Meleager[54] as his envoy to Rome with orders to inform the Senate and protest that Ptolemy was entirely unjust in attacking him.

20. Possibly in all human affairs we should regulate all our actions by the time factor, for this is more important than anything else; and this is especially true in war, for there it is that the balance shifts most abruptly from one side to the other. Not to avail oneself of this is the greatest of mistakes.

Many men, it would seem, are desirous of doing what is good, but few have the courage to attempt it, and very few indeed of these who do attempt it fully accomplish their duty in every respect.

[53] The Sixth Syrian War, beginning in fall 170 or early 169: *CAH* (2nd ed.) 8 (1989), 343–346 (C. Habicht).

[54] See for his mission 28.1.1–9 and for a second mission 28.22.2.

INDEX

595

INDEX

INDEX

INDEX

INDEX